The Collected Works of Thomas Tomkinson & John Saddington: The Muggletonian Disciples

Edited by Mike Pettit

Visit us online at www.muggletonianpress.com and
view our entire range of Muggletonian Literature

A Muggletonian Press Book

Copyright © Mike Pettit 2010

All rights reserved. No portion of this publication may be reproduced, stored in a retrieval system, or transmitted in any form or by any means, electronic, mechanical, photocopy, recording or otherwise, without prior written permission of the copyright owner. While many of the original texts which form the basis of this publication are to be found in the public domain the texts found herein have been typographically modernised and reformatted at great expense. Please respect the resulting copyright that such work has created.

ISBN 978-1-907466-08-3

Cover Image: plate 3 from Isaac Frost's "Two Systems of Astronomy" published in 1846, depicting Newtonian cosmology.

Published by:
Muggletonian Press
129 Hebdon Road
London SW17 7NL
England

I would like to make it clear that in editing and publishing this volume I am not seeking to advocate any element of *Muggletonian* theology. I fully subscribe to historic orthodox Christianity as expressed in the Reformed Confessions of Faith and would plead with all the readers of this work to consider the claims of the triune God.

From the Heidelberg Catechism

Question 20. Are all men then, as they perished in Adam, saved by Christ?

Answer: No; only those who are ingrafted into him, and, receive all his benefits, by a true faith.

Question 21. What is true faith?

Answer: True faith is not only a certain knowledge, whereby I hold for truth all that God has revealed to us in his word, but also an assured confidence, which the Holy Ghost works by the gospel in my heart; that not only to others, but to me also, remission of sin, everlasting righteousness and salvation, are freely given by God, merely of grace, only for the sake of Christ's merits.

Question 22. What is then necessary for a christian to believe?

Answer: All things promised us in the gospel, which the articles of our catholic undoubted christian faith briefly teach us.

Question 23. What are these articles?

Answer: I believe in God the Father, Almighty, Maker of heaven and earth: 2. And in Jesus Christ, his only begotten Son, our Lord: 3. Who was conceived by the Holy Ghost, born of the Virgin Mary: 4. Suffered under Pontius Pilate; was crucified, dead, and buried: He descended into hell: 5. The third day he rose again from the dead: 6. He ascended into heaven, and sitteth at the right hand of God the Father Almighty: 7. From thence he shall come to judge the quick and the dead: 8. I believe in the Holy Ghost: 9. I believe a holy catholic church: the communion of saints: 10. The forgiveness of sins: 11. The resurrection of the body: 12. And the life everlasting.

Mike Pettit

CONTENTS

	Page
Introduction	7

Thomas Tomkinson

Thomas Tomkinson DNB entry	11
The Muggletonian Principles Prevailing	13
Truth's Triumph	67
A System of Religion	449
The Harmony of the Three Commissions	499
A Practical discourse upon the Epistle by Jude	591

John Saddington

John Saddington DNB entry	667
A Prospective Glass for Saints & Sinners	669
The Articles of True Faith	731

INTRODUCTION

John Saddington was known as the "Eldest Son" of the Muggletonians, as he was one of the very first converts to the revelations of the Muggletonian prophets. A short time later Thomas Tomkinson also joined the church, as time passed it became clear that these two capable individuals would form the backbone of the movement. Not only were they unswerving in their orthodoxy (which proved crucial in defending Muggleton against the challenges to his authority by both Clarkson and the 1671 rebels) they were also able writers and theologians. In particular Thomas Tomkinson proved to have remarkable talents. For a self taught man his insights are amazing in their depth and complexity, and his output (although largely unpublished at the time) was prodigious.

This volume contains the published works of both Tomkinson and Saddington in their entirety, together with the Dictionary of National Biography entries in respect of both individuals.

The following texts are included in this volume:

Thomas Tomkinson

Thomas Tomkinson DNB entry

The entry in respect of Thomas Tomkinson that can be found in Volume 57, page 13 of "The Dictionary of National Biography" (published in 1899), written by The Rev. Alexander Gordon, the Muggletonian biographer and great confidant of the Muggletonian Church. It is this link between Gordon and the Church that makes his insights so valuable and unique; he had access to the oral history and traditions of the church, a history that has now been lost or obscured.

The Muggletonian Principles Prevailing

Originally published in 1695 (and republished in 1822) this work was written in response to John Williams "A true representation of the absurd and mischievous principles of the sect, commonly known by the name of Muggletonians", which has been republished by the Muggletonian Press in its volume "Early Muggletonian Polemics"

Truth's Triumph

This work was originally written in 1676, updated by the author in 1690 and first published in 1823.

A System of Religion

This work was unpublished in the authors lifetime, being first published in 1729 and reprinted in 1857. A strange feature of this work is that it does not mention either Muggleton or Reeve, the reason possibly being explained by the preface which proudly states that:

> "The resurrection answers all the purposes of the Christian religion, and therefore makes this scheme perfectly orthodox."

This work maintains all the vital aspects of Muggletonianism, seeking an acceptance of these views as being orthodox (in a protestant sense). The omission of any discussion of the commission of John Reeve and Lodowick Muggleton is consistent with the belief that such knowledge was not necessary for salvation, merely for the assurance of salvation.

I find the following quote to be quite beautiful:

> "For hope not to have pardon by lessening of sin and saying "I am sorry for what I have done and it was not myself, but the temptation of the devil, who crept into my will and understanding and seduced me". For it is evident, there is no other Satan but man's own lust and pride;"

The Harmony of the Three Commissions

This work was unpublished in the authors lifetime, being written in 1692 then being revised and abridged by the author. It was first published in 1757, and was reprinted in 1822.

A Practical discourse upon the Epistle by Jude

This work was unpublished in the authors lifetime, being written in 1704 and published in 1823.

John Saddington

John Saddington DNB entry

The entry in respect of John Saddington that can be found in Volume 50, pages 100 and 101 of "The Dictionary of National Biography" (published in 1897), written by The Rev. Alexander Gordon.

A Prospective Glass for Saints & Sinners

This work was unpublished in the authors lifetime, being written in 1704 and first published in 1673, being republished in 1823.

The Articles of True Faith

This work was written in 1675 and was unpublished in the authors lifetime, finally being published in 1830 and republished in 1880.

DICTIONARY OF NATIONAL BIOGRAPHY

TOMKINSON, THOMAS (1631-1710?), Muggletonian, son of Richard and Ann Tomkinson of Sladehouse, parish of Ilam, Staffordshire, was born there in 1631. He came of a substantial family of tenant-farmers long settled in the parishes of Ilam and Blore Ray. His mother was a zealous puritan. He had not much education, but was a great reader from his youth, and especially fond of church history. His namesake, Thomas Thomkinson (buried at Blore Ray on 25 Dec. 1640), was locally reckoned a great scholar; it was probably from his representatives that Tomkinson 'procured a library of presbyterian books.' Other theological works he borrowed from his landlord, Thomas Cromwell, earl of Ardglass, at Throwley Hall. On his mother's death his father made over his affairs to him, boarding with him as a lodger.

In 1661 he fell in with a tract written as a Muggletonian by Laurence Claxton or Clarkson [q. v.], probably his 'Look about you,' 1659. Just before his marriage he went up to London to see Lodowicke Muggleton [q. v.], arriving on May day 1662. His family did not favour his new views. Till 1674 he went occasionally to church 'to please an old father and a young wife,' but he made over twenty converts, who met at each other's houses. After 1674 he was harassed for recusancy, and at length excommunicated. By the good offices of Archdeacon Cook, who had heard him confute a quaker at the Dog Inn, Lichfield, he was absolved on payment of a fine, and thought it 'cheap enough to escape their hell and to gain their heaven for twenty shillings.' He made frequent visits to London, and finally settled there some time after 1680. He was the ablest of Muggleton's adherents and their best writer. Imperfect education shows itself in some extravagant literary blunders, and his orthography is a system by itself, yet he often writes with power. His 'no whither else will we go, if we perish, we perish' (Truth's Triumph, 1823, p. 76) anticipates a well-known phrase of John Stuart Mill. He seems to have brought under Muggleton's notice (in 1674) the 'Testaments of the Twelve Patriarchs,' which is one of the sacred books in the Muggletonian canon. He was living in 1704, and probably died about 1710. He had a son Thomas and a daughter Anne.

He published: 1. 'The Muggletonians Principles Prevailing,' 1695, 4to; reprinted, Deal 1822, 4to (by T.T., wrongly assigned to Thomas Taylor in Bodleian and British Museum Catalogues; in reply to ' True Representation of the ... Muggletonians,' 1694 4to, by John Williams (1634-1709) [q. v.], bishop of Chichester). Posthumous were: 2. 'Truth's Triumph . . . pt. viii.' 1721, 4to pt. vii. 1724, 4to; the whole (8 parts), 1823 4to (written 1676, revised 1690). 3. 'A System of Religion,' 1729, 8vo; reprinted 1857, 4to. 4. 'The Harmony of the Three

Commissions,' 1757, 8vo (written 1692). 5. 'A Practical Discourse upon . . . Jude,' 1823, 8vo (written 1704). Still in manuscript among the Muggletonian archives in New Street, Bishopsgate Street Without, are: 6. 'A Brief Concordance of . . . all the Writings of John Reeve and some of . . . Muggleton,' 1664-5 (copy by William Cheir). 7. 'Zion's Sonnes,' 1679 (autograph). 8. 'The Soul's Struggle,' 1681 (copy by Arden Bonell). 9. 'The Christian Convarte, or Christianytie Revived,' 1692 (copy by Arden Bonell; this is an unfinished autobiography). 10. 'The White Divel uncased' 1704 (autograph; two recensions). 11. 'Joyful Newes . . . the Jews are called' n.d. (in verse; copy by Arden Bonell).

[Tomkinson's works, printed and in the Muggletonian archives; Reeve and Muggleton's Volume of Spiritual Epistles, 1755 (letters from Muggleton to Tomkinson); Smith's Bibliotheca Antiquakeriana, 1873, pp. 322 seq. (bibliography revised by the present writer); Ancient and Modern Muggletonians, in Transactions of Liverpool Literary and Philosophical Soc. 1870.]

A. G.

THE

MUGGLETONIAN PRINCIPLES

PREVAILING:

BEING

AN ANSWER IN FULL TO A SCANDALOUS AND MALICIOUS
PAMPHLET, ENTITLED

A

True Representation

OF THE

Absurd and mischievous Principles of the sect called

MUGGLETONIANS;

WHEREIN

*The aforesaid Principles are vindicated and proved
to be infallibly true, and*

The author of that Lible, his scandalous title and subject proved as false to truth, as light is to darkness: and that he knows no more what the true God is, nor what the right devil is; nor any true principle or foundation of faith, for all his great learning he so much boasts of, than those Jews that put the Lord of life to death: for learned and taught reason is but natural, and so falls short of the glory of God: as will appear in the following; discourse.

THINGS THAT ARE DESPISED HATH GOD CHOSEN TO BRING
TO NOUGHT THINGS THAT ARE. I COR. I. XXVIII.

BY T. T.

Printed in the year of our Lord God 1695.

REPRINTED BY T. HAYWARD, BEACH STREET, DEAL

1822.

Epistle to the sober reader.

Courteous reader,

I have here, in this ensuing treatise, vindicated the principles of the people called Muggletonians from that aspersion and slander that envious reason hath cast upon it; I being a member of that body, and knowing those principles to be truth, having lived in the knowledge and practice of them above this thirty years.

And now that providence should bring thee in, to see this my answer, and shalt find some things very strange to thy understanding: and tho, perhaps thou canst not comprehend it at first view for truth, yet if thou canst preserve thyself from dispising it, thou dost well to thine own soul.

Therefore keep thyself from judging, if thou wilt live in peace, because that none can judge of spiritual things but spiritual men: and know this that the unjudging man is easy, and may afterwards come to believe, being in the time of a commission, and so with the five wise virgins bring oil in their lamps, before a the door be shut, or death approach.[1]

But to contend against truth held forth by a commission from heaven, is an evident sign of rejection, for it will prove a sin against the holy Ghost: therefore I advise thee but to take care of these two things; the one, not to break the law; the other not to despise prophesy, because they are both damnable: and more people are damned for breaking the law than any other sin, for the sin against the holy Ghost is not commited in every age, but only in the time of a commission; so that more people have commited that sin within this forty four years than hath commited it of thirteen hundred and fifty years before: so that these two things are to be shuned, the last most especially, because there is no sacrifice for that sin, but the other is pardonable in the time of a commission, by having faith in the doctrine thereof, and living free from the breach of the law after, as to the act This is the benefit of a true ministry, but no true ministry, no true conversion from the act of sin: but the elect are preserved from the act of sin, and kept in innocency of life, at such times, and in such places as truth is not known by their generated faith, which leads them to that threefold precept of the prophet Micah. 1, To do justice, 2, to love mercy, and 3, to walk humbly with God: this is the substance of pure and undefiled religion: stand fast here, and be happy.[2]

---

[1] I. Cor. 2. 15. Matt. 25. 4.
[2] Matt. 12, 13. Rom 6. ult. I. Cor. 6, 11. Ephe. 2. 1. Jer. 23, 32. Mich. 6, 8.

So that from what thou findest here written thou upon sight thereof must examine thine own heart, and see how it stands in this case; if thou canst prove thy election by faith in the true God, now he is made manifest, it is well for thee, and the benefit will be thine; but if thou canst not believe it, yet if thou despises it not, thou art not against us, nor against thine own soul, neither are we against thee, be of what religion or opinion thou wilt; but shall leave thee as the two seeds shall find thee at the last day.

And so wishing well to all sober men, but more especially, to such as are not offended with these plain truths touching the Lord Jesus Christ being that most high and mighty God, and everlasting father, so abundantly exalted through the Scriptures of truth, as is now explained and fully declared, by the third and last spiritual commission, which was to finish that sacred mystery of God becoming flesh; and now it is finished, if thou canst believe: and he that hath ears to hear, let him hear. —Farewell.

THE

MUGGLETONIAN

PRINCIPLES

PREVAILING.

CHAPTER I.

The Church of God was never without opposition; nor truth without hatred; for in that there are two Seeds, there must be a War introduced, because the Seeds are in opposition to each other being from two several Roots, Faith and Reason, Light and Darkness, God and Devil; so that the Seed of the Woman and the Seed of the Serpent will hold continually enmity.

Now you that have accused the *Mugnletonian Principles* for *impious* and *mischievous*, let us come to the *Trial* of it, with you and of you, and see how you durst be so bold, as to make so false a representation of the *Muggletonian Principles*; that you should intitle your *Diabolical Pamphlet* by the name of a *True representation* of the *absurd* and *mischievous Principles* of the *Sect* called *Muggletonians*.

If you the *Writer* thereof, had cast them Aspersions upon our Persons, and not upon our Principles, we would have borne it with silence, but in that you have judged our Faith to be blasphemous and mischievous, which we have received from the bounty and love of God; therefore in dispising and condemning it, you despise and condemn our God; so in this case we must resist you, and stand forth for the defence of our Faith.

And altho it should be where Satans seat is, yet we will not let go our Inheritance, for our Inheritance lies in the belief of our Principles, wherein we have the Charter of Heaven sealed to us; therefore we will not only vindicate those our Principles, which you so wickedly represent, but will also, through Grace, seal to them with our Blood, if your Law can do it, and we be called thereunto.

For we are able to maintain those Principles for Truth; therefore let us now come to the trial of Truth, and let us set our Principles each against the other; and them whose Faith and Wisdom is greatest, let them hold the other under in bondage for ever.

Sir, You are come forth to curse a quiet and still People, who meddle not with your affairs, nor Magistrates affairs: we lift not up our Hand, nor make use of a sword of steel to slay any man: we defraud no man, we wrong no man; neither are we for thrusting you out of your earthly Possessions; no, not out of your Pulpits or Parish-Livings; we will have none of them: but on the contrary we are obedient unto all the Civil Laws of the Land and give to every man the respect due unto him.

All therefore that we desire of you is, that we may pass peaceably through your Country towards our Inheritance, but you are not willing that we should, no more than *Edom* was with *Israel*;[1] but have presumed to stop our Course, by judging and condemning our faith: now if our faith be true, as we know it is, then you have given judgment against yourself; you were not aware of that caution of our Saviours saying, *Judge not, and thou shalt not be Judged*; now in that we know that our faith is of God, and is truth, therefore is it of power to reign over that which judgeth it.[2]

But if we might come to reason together, then I would demand of you, wherefore you did send out your judging Pamphlet against us, and would not subscribe your name to it? Were you afraid of holding a trial with us for fear you should be worsted by us, as others have been heretofore; and so were for working mischief privately, and yet lye *in Cognito*, thinking belike, that faith's power could not find you out, to give you an answer; otherwise how could you find a name to your Book, and a name to the People you wrote against, but have found never a name for yourself, but have left it to us to find a name for you, which according to holy Writ is *Elimas* a Corruptor, a sworn enemy to the truth, and the Accuser of the Brethren;[3] being of a worthy descent, successor to *Simon Magus*; being newly crept out of the College of Priests, which came out of the Mouth of the false Prophet; such a one as *Amaziah* the priest of *Bethel*, who could not abide a poor prophet; a herdsman, that he should once speak near the King's Chapel, because it was the King's Court, in which learned *Amaziah* was the Doctor and Chaplain.[4]

Thus have you dealt with these prophets of the Lord; and for fear that this poor prophets doctrine (which you, like *Amaziah*, call mischievous) should take any effect amongst the people: from hence yon have secretly spread this your Pamphlet into your brethren, the Priest's hands, all the nation over; and have endeavoured to make our Principles as contemptible and odious as possibly you could, in order

---

[1] Numb. 20.
[2] Matt. 7. 1.
[3] Acts 13, 10.
[4] Rev. 16, 13. Amos 7, 12.

to make them seem the more ridiculous; and this your book must be as a pattern for them to frame their Arguments by, and those their Arguments must be as Bulwarks of defence to them, and as Bullets shot against us.

Sir, You have acted in the very same way as *Haman* did against *Israel*, saying in this manner to the King, *There is a certain malicious and mischievous People scattered abroad amongst the People in all places and their Laws are differing from all People; neither keep they the King's* (Church-laws) *therefore it is not for the King's profit to suffer them; let them be destroyed, for their* Principles *are mischievous.*[1]

Now I being a member of this despised People, seeing your spite and malice against us (who have broke no Law) am from hence moved to return an answer, and this my reply shall not spare you, altho I am given to understand, that you are a Doctor of the National Church, for God and Faith is no respector of Persons in such a case; therefore this my reply shall pursue you until it overtake you, and when it hath overtaken you, it shall fasten a witness in your Conscience, that you have been a Fighter against God, his Prophets and People, and against the Sacred Scriptures; and a false Representer of the *Muggletonian* principles and I shall not be long in proving the same: for,

In the Preface of your Book you say, that *John Reeve* was, by profession, a Baker; which saying of yours is utterly false: so here you have forfeited your Title-page, which instead of a true representation is a false one.

But you bring him in as a Baker, to make him the more contemptible with the learned; but if he had, would that have made him more uncapable of being Gods last Messenger, I tro not, no more than it did *Amos*, who was but a Herdsman as aforesaid.

For this is evident that the Saints have found in all ages, that the learned have ever stood up as an enemy and judge of spiritual Truth; as will more appear in the sequel of my Discourse: but to proceed to

The Accusation against us.

In your Preface you call us, *poor deluded Souls, and by the name of a contemptible and pernicious Sect*; and blasphemously affirm, *that it is made up* of Impiety, Nonsense, *and* Absurdities; *and that we have not so much as the shadow of Reason to support us: from hence say you, we will not submit to the trial of it, being incapable of argument, and that you wrote not that your Treatise for our sakes, that have not reason & argument* (as you say) *to answer you; but for the sake and satisfaction of the World, and of the Learned, who are capable* (say you) *to hear reason and argument.*

---

[1] Esther 3, 8.

CHAPTER II.

ANSWER.

AS to them judging and condemning Censures against us shall be answered *Chap.* 15. And as to your reason and argument, you so much boast of, I am willing to allow it its Prerogative, and give it its due of having Government as to all terrestrial affairs.[1]

But wherefore should it enter upon God's Prerogative, so as to take upon us to judge divine things, that are eternal, by its unclean serpentine reason.[2]

But to such as are learned in faith's school doth know, that he that doth minister spiritual things, is to lay reason and argument by, as to the finding out of any heavenly secrets by the most piercing reason that is.[3]

For reason is not Heaven-born, and so is but natural; and it is the natural or moral Law that enlightns it; but faith being of another nature, which is spiritual, and so the law of faith serves to quicken and enlighten faith; and when it is enlightned, then she rules as mistress over reason.[4]

Therefore, though the Kingdoms of this World lye in reason, yet the Kingdom of Christ lies in faith, which ever appears simple, and yet it is this poor despised seed that receives the Gospel; it is the simple and the foolish that catch Heaven: the poor are filled with the substance of spiritual truth, whereas the rich in reason, notion, and argument, are sent empty away.[5]

Therefore away with your arguments where faith is sought, there the *Fisher*, the *Herds-man*, the *Tent-maker*, aye and he that you call the *Baker*, rather than the *Philosopher* are to be trusted.[6]

Do you teach the World by your reason and argument, as you say; this manifests that you and your brethren are the World's ministers, and the World hears you; and hence it is that you appeal to the World, for the World will love its own.[7]

Here now you appear to be a right Legalist, in imitation of the *Levites* of old; for that priesthood was to teach reason, the moral law

---

[1] Deut. 1, 13. Acts 26, 3. & 18. 14, 15.
[2] Luke 20, 14.
[3] Matt. 11, 25. James 3, 15.
[4] Psal. 19, 7. John 1, 4.
[5] John 18, 36. Luke 17, 21. 2 Cor. 1, 12. Luke 1, 53, & 6, 25.
[6] Matt. 4, 18. Amos 1, 1. Acts 18, 3. Coll. 2, 8.
[7] 1 John 4, 5. John 7, 7.

for its reasonable service, that it should not *Murder, commit Adultry, Steal, or bear false Witness,* which reason is subject to do.[1]

But all the prophets spiritual declarations belonged to the elect seed of Faith, and was spoken unto that innocent nature that cannot do evil, and that in order to a further degree of knowledge, love and obedience.[2]

Wherefore then, if by your teaching you can keep your disciples in sobriety and the bounds of reason, this is a virtue, and brings with it the temporal blessing promised that seed; but if so it be, that your reason will seek Lordship, and would be a judge and controller of faith, it is nothing less than a Devil, and will, be damned to eternity.[3]

And herein appears your blindness, notwithstanding your earthly wisdom, because by it you cannot distinguish betwixt the two seeds of faith and reason, or the law and the gospel. But to proceed, and come to the matter in question.[4]

Would you Priests have us to be tried by your arguments? Then you are like to have the cause, if you must be your own judges, like the *Jews* by our Saviour, his Prophets and Apostles.

But this we presume to tell you, that your reason, being but natural, therefore it cannot try spiritual truth, but our faith can try your arguments, and it can take up reason as a servant, to argue with you in the balance of your own reason, the Angle nature fallen; nevertheless we can no more agree than the prophet *Jeremiah* and those national false priests did in the like dispute.[5]

Because faith when it takes up reason, it takes it up, not to expound and open the sense of Scripture sayings, but as a servant, to illustrate that revealed Word by argument, for the further confounding of that unclean domineering reason that doth oppose its spiritual sense.

But on the contrary, when learned reason takes up words of faith, it expounds it by the imagination of reason, in respect its reason is Lord in its Soul, and so turns truth into a lie; and the elegancy of its speech must form the substance of the matter, and then war is proclaimed against the truth, and so truth must be trod under foot.[6]

Thus did the false Priests deal with *Jeremiah, Come say they, let us devise Devises against him, and let us destroy the Tree with its*

---

[1] Deut. 27. Judg. 17, 10, 11, 12, 13.
[2] Psal. 119, 199.
[3] Deut. 28. 2, 3, 4, 5, 6. John 19, 7. Matt. 18, 6.
[4] Ezek. 34, 17. Matt. 25, 33. I John 1, 17.
[5] I Cor. 2, 13. I John 4, 1. Rom. 2, 2. Acts 17, 2. & 24, 25.
[6] Rom. 1, 25. Rev. 3, 9. I Cor. 1, 20. Rev. 11, 2. Jer. 11, 19.

Fruit, and let us cut him off that his name may be no more remembered: that is, let us destroy his Prison, which is the Tree; and let us destroy its Fruit, that is, his Doctrine or Declarations, for he is in bringing in another Priesthood therefore report and we will report; let us frame our arguments against him, for he saith, *That they that handle the Law know not God*, when as it is written, *That the Law shall not perish from the Priests, nor Counsel from the Wise.*[1]

Misrepresenting Doctor, are not your arguments answerable to theirs, even to a Hair: therefore as true Wisdom was departed from them, so it is now from you, and from all those national pretended Gospel Ministers, tho you boast as they did; yet have you nothing but an empty title, not so much as a grain of spiritual sense appeareth; but as, it was their blindness, so it is yours, who understand not, that the spiritual law of faith will never depart from that spiritual Priest, the true Christian, but his lips shall ever preserve true knowledge: and this Priesthood will never terminate, but will be with them to the end of the world.[2]

For after faith is enlightened by a commission from heaven, then it needs no other teacher, but that unction which it hath received; for the spirit of faith is Christ's Vicar.[3]

But your outward visible worships that are taken up from former commissions, they are ended, and. the spirit of God is gone out of them; but this will bring a box upon my checks by your non commissioned minister, as your predecessor did to *Micaiah* the prophet, with a *Which way went the spirit of God from me to thee.*[4]

But the law of faith, which we have known and received, will never depart from us, so we heed not to your assumed counterfeit priesthood, but live by our own generated faith now awakened, or dominated, by the doctrine of this commission of the Spirit; for we have no new faith given, but the old awakened, as afore-said; for faith was but once given, and every commissioned prophet, messenger, or minister of God, adds a further light and knowledge to it.[5]

So that now through Grace, we have attained to a more principal degree of knowledge of the true God, and the right Devil; than others had before us; so that from hence, we are not wanting in wisdom to answer your strongest arguments your reason can devise.[6]

---

[1] Jer. 18, 18. & 20, 10. & 2, 8. Mal. 2, 7.
[2] Ezek. 7, 26. I Peter.
[3] I John 2, 27.
[4] I Kings 2, 24.
[5] Isa. 59, 21. Heb. 19, 38. Ephes. 5, 14. 2 Peter 3, 18.
[6] Isa. 41, 21.

Therefore muster up your army, raise all your forces, from all parts, and from all your Priests that you have distributed your books to; yet shall you never be able to disprove by your subtility, quell by your power, or subdue by your force, the *Muggletonian* Principles, because Salvation, and nothing less is their assured walls and bulwarks.[1]

But to your following arguments, I apply myself to answer by truth of Scripture.

The Accusation against us.

In Page the first, you make your Book to consist of two Queries. *First,* whether *John Reeve,* and *Lodowick Muggleton,* are sent of God. *Secondly,* whether they are the Witnesses spoken of in the 11th. of the Revelations.

To your *first Query;* you have largely repeated several of their sayings, which you say, they pretend to be true characters, and evidences of their commission. Now, after your ramble in Page the 4th. your first evidence is, that *John Reeve* saith, *That God spake to him three mornings together:* and say you, *Muggleton* saith, *That it is God's speaking plain words, to the hearing of the outward Ear, as well as the inward Soul, that doth make a man a Commissioner.*

This evidence, say you, *is of no value; because,* say *you I cannot tell whether it be a true voice, or an imaginary lying voice, such a one as* John Reeve *said was in* John Robins: *it is,* say you, *but their say so.* And then you conclude saying; *For let their voice be never so true, if it be alone, and without the visible evidence of working Miracles, it is of no value: as also,* you say, *it must be proved by Scripture;* without which you make it of no value, &c.

CHAPTER III.

ANSWER.

1. THIS your way is to overthrow all prophesy: you will tie God to work Miracles, or you will not believe him: either God must do as you will have him, or he must not be God.[2]

It is no wonder that you cannot distinguish between a true voice and a false; because God never chose you by voice nor never will. But how should you believe a vocal voice, when as your God has never a tongue: you have made it here plainly appear, that you are of the same spirit as those murdering *Jews* who bid Christ *come down from*

---

[1] Isa. 26, 1.
[2] Numb. 11, 29. 2 Pet. 1, 19. 1 Thes. 5, 20.

the Cross and they would believe in him. True doctrine without Miracles is to you most detestable.[1]

2. Again, was not all true prophets chosen by voice of words; nevertheless the seed of the Serpent could never believe them, neither could the Priests or Rulers ever abide them; and there was few of them but what was either persecuted or put to death, by the Magistrates and their national Priests: there were 450 false prophets mustered up against two or three true prophets, as *Elijah* and *Micaiah*; and one of them must strike *Micaiah* on the Cheek; as aforesaid, and this priest and *Ahab's* son flung him down to break his neck.[2]

But *Elijah* the representor of God's person, by word of power slew them all, as a type of the destruction of all false prophets, and false priests, at the end of the world: such a Miracle you want.[3]

When *Isaiah* prophesied of his God's becoming flesh, not one would believe him, neither priest nor people: therefore, saith he, *Lord, who hath believed our report*; and *Elijah* said, *That all were gone after* Baal. Nor regarded truth, for that was ever hated; *I hate him*, said *Ahab, for he never said good of me, but evil*; it's now as it was then, unless we could bring fire from Heaven, as *Elijah* did, there can be do belief; and it must be to destroy them; it might convince them, but it would never convert them.[4]

If Miracles were wrought now, what would it avail this bloody unbelieving World; they would but say as the *Jews* said of Christ, *That they wire done by the Devil,* But what said *Paul*, Tongues and Miracles are but for a sign, not to them that believe, but to them that believe not; but prophesy serveth for them that believe only; *John the Baptist*, a great: prophet, and yet did no Miracle.[5]

Thus you call in question the glorious truths of God, under pretence of *John Reeve*'s weakness, as to outward Miracles, that you might believe, when as his commission is all spiritual.

Now the seed of faith believes not, because of the Miracles wrought, by the Lord or his Prophets; but in that they were of the election, and fore-ordained to believe, for the saving, of the soul; and as the Christian Dove waits for a sign within him, or from behind reason, for a word saying, *This is the Way, walk in it*; even so, on the contrary, the carnal Serpent, he requires a natural sign before his

---

[1] Matt. 27, 42.
[2] Isa. 6, 8. & 54, 1. Jer. 15, 10. 1 Kings 18, 22.
[3] Zeph. 1, 4.
[4] Isa. 55, 1. 1 Kings 19. 1 Kings 22, 8. Psal. 78, 32.
[5] Matt. 12, 24. 1 Cor. 14, 22. John 10, 41.

reason, that may be seen with his outward eye, to make him believe spiritual truths; and therefore reason cries, saying, *Where are your Miracles, and where is your Scripture evidence to prove it:* prove by Scripture.[1]

Now if this Witness should write nothing but what is exactly set down in Scripture, then should they write nothing at all; but always true prophesy hath something new to deliver.[2]

Again, did the Prophets and Apostles, write by imitation, or study, or by inspiration only; they might allude sometimes to the prophets words for convincing of gainsayers.[3]

Furthermore, the Scriptures in themselves are words of pure truth, to all that spiritually discern them; and that is, such as have the life and power of them in their own souls; but they that have not the inner life and meaning thereof, they study the outward letter by their reason, to find the life and meaning thereof, and then, this their imagination, the child of study, trumpets, out it's own conceptions upon it.[4]

This is the work and way of all the seven anti Churches of Europe, every one of them endeavouring to prove their Ministry by the letter of the Scripture, or by the light within them; but never a one from the glorious voice of the everliving God without them: and from hence, though they judge and condemn each other for false whilst they are all false, yet can they agree to fight against God and his true prophets, by the letter of the Scripture.

And you keep these chests and boxes of precious things, but the jewels and treasure is quite gone, and is a stranger to you; you know it not but do despite unto it, and put your own imaginations into the letter, and so turn and wind it about like a nose of wax, and make it speak for your honour and riches. Oh! how profitable hath this letter of the Scriptures been to reprobate Preachers.[5]

Wherefore then, we who are called *Muggletonians*, in scorn do boldly affirm, that though you have got the letter of the Scriptures, and run away with it, as a Dog doth with a bone, yet none of its spiritual declarations were ever written for your instruction, but for the instruction of the seed of faith; for the Law only belongs to you, and it may make you wise, but not unto Salvation; that is the property of the Gospel to the seed of faith, the seed of the Lord's own body; for the man of God that is made wise unto Salvation; so that he must be

---

[1] Isa. 30, 27.
[2] Jer. 31, 22.
[3] Matt. 15, 32. 2 Pet. 1, 21.
[4] John 6, 63. Obed. 6, 8. John 7, 52.
[5] 2 Pet. 2, 18. verse 3. Jude 13, 16.

a man of God, and have faith in those Scriptures, before he can be wise unto Salvation, because they are given by the inspiration of the holy Spirit, and no man can know them but by the same Spirit, as those that had wrote them.[1]

These things considered, how is it possible that you should apply Scripture to purpose, when your wisdom is not inspiration, but education; what will your form do to you without the power: if you have the words of God, and not that word which is God, what good will your word do you.[2]

What commission have you to preach to the people; Christ tells you that you are but thieves and robbers, climbing up to Heaven by ordinances of your own, and your own stolen doctrine; for you steal the words from your neighbour, the seed of faith, and then cry, *Thus saith the Lord*.[3]

What do you bring as an Offering, but what you have stolen from others; do you deliver any thing but transcriptions and historical notions, the repetitions of the letter of the Scriptures, and the sentences of the ancient Fathers; there is the line you boast in, so that you do no more, in effect, but rob the dead to cloath the living: for have you so much as opened the meaning of one text of Scripture in all your blind Pamphlet; you have named the words, and then left them to answer for themselves, as I shall show hereafter.[4]

Again, you further object against their doctrine of infallibility, in that they say, *They write by an unerring* Spirit: now, say you, *an infallible Spirit implies the highest certainty: but,* say you, *his book is inconsistent with itself;* for Muggleton saith, *I am persuaded in my spirit, and I do rather believe that there were seven hundred thousands, than seven thousands, though the Revelation of* John *doth but express it seven thousands: now,* say you, *to be persuaded, and to believe a thing to be so, are inconsistant to infallibility; for that admits no less than I am sure of it,* say you.[5]

---

[1] Rom. 15, 4. Deut. 4, 6. Jer. 9, 13. 2 Tim. 3, 15.
[2] 1 Cor. 4, 20.
[3] John 10, 1.
[4] 2 Cor. 10, 16.
[5] Rev. 11, 13.

CHAPTER IV

ANSWER.

THE Prophets did both of them write, by an infallible and unerring spirit, the doctrine of them six Principles, the knowledge of which, Salvation doth depend upon; but as to some particular points that are besides the foundation, there is not that necessity to he so positive. But as to the essential points of faith, they were written by an unerring spirit, and are infallibly true; and against men and angels they affirm it, and we as truly believe it, to the great peace and satisfaction of our minds: for what is it that can satisfy the mind of man but truth, having the seal of life in it, as every true Minister of God hath,[1]

For every true Minister of God hath power to set life and death before men and can say, *Now is fulfilled such and such things*: also he that is sent of God, knoweth the things of God, and he that believeth in such a one, knoweth the things of God likewise.[2]

But how can you judge of infallibility; that, do not own yourself infallible, but fallible? What is fallible but a lie, and must a lie be the Judge of truth? He that knoweth the mind of the Lord, he may instruct from the Lord; but he that hath not the infallible Spirit; doth from his lying Spirit prescribe rules to God, and would be God's counsellor.[3]

Now must such ignorant, carnal, fleshly men as these judge infallibility, that have, nor own no other Spirit but what is fallible: but to come to the point and charge against *Lodowick Muggleton*.

For although the Prophets and Apostles were infallible as to all essential points of faith; yet as to other things that were circumstantial, and not so essential, in such things Prophets and Apostles may differ about them in their experience and judgment.

Thus *Paul* withstood *Peter*, and reproved him; and though *Paul* there gainsaid *Peter*, yet in some other thing *Paul* himself was not positive: as for instance, *Paul* treating on Marriage, he speaks as the prophet *Muggleton* doth here, and tells the believers *That it was his Judgment, that it were better for them not to marry*: and further adds *That he* [thinks,] *that this his Judgment is right, and. that it was from the Spirit of God.*[4]

---

[1] John 17, 3.
[2] Mat. 18, 18. 1 Cor. 2, 15.
[3] verse 16
[4] Gal. 2, 11. 1 Cor. 7, 6. verse 39, 40.

Now I presume, (by what you have said of these) that had you been living then, and had heard of *Paul's* talking of having the infallible Spirit of God, you would presently have judged him a false Apostle; notwithstanding the Miracles he had done; and that he had contradicted himself; and that his [thinking] was inconsistent to his infallibility, and so was not to be believed.

Again, if you had heard that *Paul* circumcised *Timothy*, and yet nevertheless told the *Galations, that if they were circumcised they could not be saved.*[1] I say, had you been in those days, would not you have said, That *Paul* had contradicted himself, and the Scriptures both? and would you not also have judged the four Evangelists to have contradicted one another in several places; for as you judge and condemn these, so you would have judged them, for these were sent by Jesus Christ, and Paul was sent by no other God.[2]

Again, in Page 9 you quote *John Reeve*, saying, that he saith, That he is indued with a divine Gift, to write a volume as large as the Bible; and as pure a language as that is without looking into any book, or having any real contradiction in it. Upon these words you make the reflection following.

Your Accusation runs thus, saying.

That if the purity of the language be a sign of truth then, say you, I am sure it is far from being either true or infallible. For, said you, they do not write true English, nor good sense; as likewise, it often fails in the propriety of words, in concord, and connection; being without method, purity or elegancy, &c.

CHAPTER V.

ANSWER.

SIR, in answer to this, the truly wise do know, that God's messengers never regard fineness of speech, but soundness of matter: not so much the original of words as the original of things, even such as they, are moved too by the Holy Ghost; and not such language as you are moved too by your educated spirit of reason, which is the Angle's nature fallen: but in that, you have no where contradicted our Principle, which shews what the person and nature of Angles are; therefore there is no occasion given here to dispute it; but to return to the matter aforesaid.

Spiritual truth, or Gospel life, was ever plain, and was never delivered with new coined or high flown words of man's wisdom. This

---

[1] Acts 16. 3, 12. Gal 5. 2.
[2] Matt. 28, 2. Luke 24, 2.

made an old learned philosophical Bishop judge so hard by the Revelation of John, not thinking it John's, because of the rudeness of the style: for, said he, I see his Greek not exactly uttered the dialect and phrase not observed I find him, said this Bishop using barbarous phrases.[1]

Dionisius

And Paul was called a clouter of skins, a cobler by the Philosophers, and a man of no breeding: and he acknowledged himself but rude in speech, though not in true wisdom; but he had taken some learning up at the foot of Gamaliel, but he laid it down there again, as soon as the Spirit of faith became his teacher: all his wisdom that he now valued, was the knowledge of Christ crucified, and risen again; which his former wisdom could not know, but on the contrary, was the persecutor of him.[2]

Again, spiritual truth, or faith, was ever brought in naked and simple, and in poor array: but falsehood doth ever endeavour to attire herself in all her bravery. These rascals, said the Pharisees, are accursed, they know not the Law: but said Paul, That learning of theirs will come to nought.[3]

But as for truth, that guides to Heaven; it needs no gloss to make it seem better than it is, for it hath light enough in itself, to shew it the way to Heaven.[4]

The Scriptures were written in as homely a style is Reeve's and Muggleton's were; only wise men in reason, have put them into a better form, and now boast of their literal accuteness, whilst they are out of all spiritual power; and it must be so, for he that hath learned nothing of truth, must teach by an eloquent tongue of empty words only.[5]

For Sophisters, who want substance of truth, must use their sophistry, to corrupt truth, and adulterate the true sense, and then cover their own errors with paint.

And thus have you done, in this Libel of yours; for in page 18 you affirm, That John Reeve doth say, (pretending to quote his words) That the substances of earth and water were from all elements: when as John Reeve's words were in that place, that the substance of earth and water was from all eternity

---

[1] 1 Cor. 2, 1.
[2] Acts 22, 3.
[3] 1 Cor. 12, 8.
[4] John 1, 4.
[5] 1 Cor. 13, 1.

Thus you turn their good sense into nonsense, and so belie them; for by this your way of clouding their words you would darken the sense, and make them appeal the more ridiculous; and to prevent a further dispute on that subject, Of the substance of earth and Water being made of nothing, which you were not able to maintain; and though you say, you would confute that principle, yet passed it by, und would say no more of it: and so you let it drop.

Now, as to your elegancy of speech; your tongues and languages you boast so much of (and you have need of it to paint your errors, as aforesaid) we will leave this all to you Bable builders, as acquired by your study and learning; it being your trade; which teacheth your reason to play upon the letter of the Scripture as upon a Harp, being very melodious to the outward ear: and by these means you (Arts-Masters) grow rich and honourable, according to your skilful merchandising of the letter of the Scripture, and ancient Fathers and Philosophers: these must be made to agree together, for the Scripture must either make good Philosophy, or else Philosophy must be brought to make good the Scripture; and in your wise handling of this, you grow rich; some hundreds some thousands a year, equalling the great men of the earth; and as to others of your brethren. though they be more inferior yet must they be called masters, although they be but servants; yet will they be well paid, for no Penny, no Paternoster.[1]

So having found you all in the way of Balaam, to bless and curse for money, which is your soul's chief delight, there I leave you to go on in your trade, and receive your wages of men here, and of God hereafter, whom you pretend to serve; then will you have full reward.[2]

A further accusation against this Witness you have, for affirming the power of sealing men up unto eternal life and death, as they receive or despise their Doctrine: this you deny, that any man ever had this power: saying, that it is quite contrary to the Scripture, and the temper of the Gospel, which is love; and then bid us prove it by Scripture.

CHAPTER VI.

ANSWER.

IT is confessed by us that the temper of the Gospel is love; but then that Gospel and eternal love is but to the seed of the Lords own body, and it must needs be so, because that Grace is written in faiths

---

[1] Rev. 18, 31. Rev. 18, 7.
[2] Matt. 23, 7. Mica 3, 11. John 10, 13. Jude 11. Phil. 3, 19. Matt. 6, 5. 7, 23.

nature;[1] and though that seed did fall in Adam, yet the Gospel came to seek and to save that which was lost and fell in Adam; for the Serpent's seed never fell in Adam, nor never knew themselves lost.[2] So the Gospel belongs not to them, but according to their obedience to their own Law, so they have the blessing of the Law, That the Rain may rain, and the Sun may shine, and the Earth bring forth her increase, with long life and health: and thus Christ, which is the Gospel, shewed his love to that seed, when he wept over Jerusalem: now as he was man he wept to see what temporal Judgements they would bring upon themselves.[3]

But then on the other hand, as he was God, he rejoiced at their eternal destruction; for upon their despising those declarations of his; he thereon pronounces upon eternal wrath; calling them Devils, Serpents, and a generation of Vipers, and that they should not escape the damnation of Hell: and John the Baptist pronounced the like sentence; and all the Apostles had the like power after they had received their commission.[4]

As for that saying of Christ's to them, to bless, and curse not; that was but when they were but private believers; as also, it taught that clemency, as not to resist temporal injuries: bet when they had received the Holy Ghost, then was the keys of Heaven and Hell committed to their charge; and they had power by them, to bind and to loose, to remit and to retain sin. What was that but blessing and cursing? for the blessing of a commissionated Prophet or Apostle, it opens the gate of Heaven; that is, it opens the heart in love, to that God that sent such a message of glad tidings of salvation: so on the contrary, the curse of a Prophet, it opens the gate of Hell; that is, it opens the heart in envy, malice, and revenge; and whose heart that spiritual key doth, open no. man can shut; and whose heart they shut no man can open.[5]

Therefore it was that Paul said, that they were the savour of life unto life, unto those that believed them, and the savour of death unto death unto those that denied them. Again, Paul and the rest of the Apostles, did declare, That whosoever denied the faith of Jesus, or despised prophesy, or turned apostate, that there could be no sacrifice

---

[1] Titus 2, 11. Ephes. 1, 3.
[2] John 10, 27. Mark 2, 17.
[3] Matt. 6, 45. Luke 6, 6. & 14, 14.
[4] Matt. 23, 23. John 6, 7. Matt. 3, 7. & 13, 11. & 12, 34. John 12, 40. Matt. 5, 44.
[5] Matt. 16, 19. Luke 10, 16. Luke 20, 23. Psal. 24, 7. Acts 7, 54.

for such sins, neither were such to be prayed for; but upon the contrary, to be sealed up unto eternal death.[1]

All the spiritual declarations of the Prophets reach to the eternal state of man, for they pointing at their God becoming flesh, and that upon his death and resurrection the eternal state of the two seeds of faith and reason takes being; for the resurrection of Christ gains power to raise the dead, and give each seed his reward.

And therefore the Gospel appropriates David's key to belong to it, which key lies in such and the like sayings,[2] The Lord takes pleasure in his people, he will beautify the meek with salvation; this is the key that opens Heaven: and as follows, Let the high praises of God be in their mouth, and a two edged sword in their hand; and then with the other key and sword, to execute vengeance upon the heathen and punishment upon the people; To bind their kings with chains, and their nobles with fetters of iron; To execute upon them the judgement written: and this is the key that opens and none can shut, and shuts and no man can open. This honour, saith David belongs to all living saints. For these keys and sword belongs to all saints; and David himself, in those and the like sayings, had flung into the fire all that despised his spirit of prophesy, of his God becoming flesh, and sealed them up in these words; saying, Divide their tongues, for I have seen violence in the city. Cast them down in thy anger, consume them in wrath, let them not come into thy righteousness, blot them out of the book of life, and let them not be written with the righteous; let burning coals fall upon them; let them be cast into the fire.[3]

The Prophet Jeremiah likewise, meeting with the seed of the Serpent, opposing his spiritual declarations, concerning God becoming flesh, and his sufferings by that seed, seals them up to death eternal; for they were devising devices against that doctrine of his; therefore he poureth forth these imprecations against them; saying, O Lord, forgive not their iniquity, neither blot out their sin from thy sight, &c. And then changing his words, he speaks in the person of God saying, They are all unto me as Sodom. So that we see that the Prophet's curse is God's curse: and further saith he, The saints shall call them reprobate silver.[4]

This is the Gospel power; the Law's curse penetrates down into the grave, the first death: but, the Gospel's power and curses raises it

---

[1] 1 Cor. 6, 2. Heb. 10, 29. Thess. 5, 20. 1 John 3, 8. & 5, 16. 2 Cor. 2, 16.
[2] Psal. 149, 4.
[3] Psal. 149, 9. Isa 54, 17. & 57, 4. Psal. 55, 9. Psal. 59, 13. Psal 140, 10.
[4] Jer. 18, 23. & 29, 22. Jer. 23, 14. Jer. 6, 30.

again from the first death into a second and eternal death; being a living death, and dying life.¹

And thus we see that every true Minister that power to set life and death before Men: and that ministry that hath not that power, is no true ministry. Now what a blind guide is this, that cannot see these plain Scriptures; but cries out, Prove this by Scripture. Woe to all such as are led by the blind guides! Oh, that all the elect were but delivered from their captivity and bondage under their formalities, and might come to hear of truth; that their joy and peace might abound, being the seal of eternal life.²

But it is a wonderful tiling, that such Preachers as those, who cannot believe that any Prophet hath power as aforesaid, and yet they themselves shall take upon them to judge man's faith, and condemn him for it, so is it not a wicked thing to deny the Prophet's and Apostle's power of the keys of Heaven and Hell, and yet presume to do that thing themselves, whilst they acknowledge themselves but fallible men: doth not this make you justly damned in yourselves? but it is no wondering at it, for what saith the Scripture, He hath blinded their eyes, they stumble at noon day, they have all the spirit of slumber.³

And now I shall return to answer this Misrepresentor's false reflections upon our main Principles; yea, such as the very Scriptures stand upon, and on which eternal life wholly depends.

In page 18th. you bring in John Reeve sciteing him thus; saying, God Is not a spirit, but hath a body: Your reflections are thus.

The Accusation.

The Scripture makes a body and spirit two opposite things, so that a body is not a spirit, nor a spirit a body Eccles. 12. 7. A spirit hath not flesh and bone, Luke 24. 37. The Scripture calls God a spirit, but never a body; God is not in the form of a man, but is invisible, and no man ever saw him or can.

CHAPTER VII.

ANSWER.

1. YOUR citation is false; for John Reeve's words are thus, That God is not a spirit without a body. By your false citation, you would have your worldly disciples to think, that he affirms, That God is a body without a spirit. But to come to the point; I must tell you, that the body and soul are not two contrary things; and if your Solomon,

---

[1] Ezek. 32, 24, 26, 27, 29.
[2] Mark 16, 16. John 3, 18.
[3] John 12, 40.

told you so with one breath, he tells you the quite contrary in another: but many times wise Solomons, do not know the meaning of their own sayings.[1]

Solomon was a wise man, but the wisdom which he craved, and that God gave him, was but natural; so that Solomon's writings are but the operations of his natural reason, and from some intricate sayings of his father David: so they are no Scripture for he was no prophetical man.[2]

Again, if the body and soul are two contrary things, (as you say) and in opposition to each other, then was the body and soul of Christ at variance with itself; and in opposition with each other, and so two opposite things: if so then Christ's body did not go to Heaven nor never would: and belike, you do not believe that Christ's body is in Heaven, any more than the Quakers; and I know not how you should believe it, because your God hath never a body: So Christ is none of your fatherly God if he have a body.

Can a spirit live and subsist without a body; where do the Scriptures say, that God is a spirit without a body: did you not learn your own catechism, or if you did, have you forgotten? doth it not teach (saying) to your pupils, That God is a spirit, or a spiritual substance, most holy, wise just and infinite.

Now if it be so, that God hath a substance, then he must on necessity have a body: and if he be holy wise, and just, he must have a person to possess his ravishing glory in, and yet to be of uncompounded purity. Is it not said, That God was a man of war; that shows that he is in the form of a man: also Christ told the Pharisees, That there was no man perfectly good but one, which was God.[3]

3. Moreover if your soul can be more wise, just, and holy without your body, then turn it out of the body, and see what holiness and justice it can act without its body.[4]

But the truth of Scripture is, that God had a body and person from all eternity; a spiritual body, brighter than the Sun, more clear than crystal, and that is the reason why mortality cannot behold him as he is in his full glory; if God was willing at any time that some of his servants, the Prophets should behold him, he was compelled to vail his glory, so as that their frail nature might be in a capacity to behold him.[5]

---

[1] Eccles. 3, 19. verse 29.
[2] 1 Kings 2, 12. & 10, 24. & 11, 4. Matt. 12, 42.
[3] Exod. 15, 3. Matt. 19, 17. Josh. 5, 1, 3.
[4] 1 Cor. 6, 19.
[5] Rev. 21, 23. & 1, 4. & 10, 1. Deut. 10, 6.

And this we further affirm, that we can sooner find in Scripture that our God hath and ever had a distinct body of himself, then you can find in Scripture a trinity of persons in one Godhead; for if you find three distinct persons, then you must find three bodies; and where then is your spirit God become.

4. Again, are not the Scriptures clear, that the fathers of old did see God, and ever beheld him in form and shape of a man: will you say that God assumed that shape, and yet had no shape of his own; this is to make God a conniver.[1]

It is no wonder, as I said before, that you despise John Reeve for saying that the Lord spake to him to the hearing of the ear; for you do not believe that God hath any tongue to speak at all: For, say you, a spirit hath no flesh, and hath no body: For, say you body and Spirit are two contrary things.

As the Scripture saith that God hath a body, so it attributes to this body, hands, eyes, face, nose, mouth, ears, arms, legs, breast, heart, back, &c, And yet must he have never a body, this is clearly to deny Scripture, for the Scripturian saith, That God hath a body; but the Antiscripturian saith, That God hath neither body, parts or shape, but yet is an infinite vast God, filling all things, and is in all places at one and the same time, and so can neither ascend nor descend, come nor go, but is every where at once; as your great Augustine saith.[2]

This is yours and the world's monstrous God: are those the men that are so capable of Argument; if we should be as ignorant in the Scriptures as you, it were no matter if our tongues should cleave to the roof of our mouths.

I wonder you are not ashamed to pretend to Scripture; do you believe the Scripture? certain I am, that there are many doctors of your church that do not believe them at all; for instance hereof, there is one of your doctors, namely Dr. More: this man in one of his books, called his Cabila, doth little less than give the Scripture the lie; for treating upon the creation of man by Moses, saith That the Scripture doth not always speak according to the exactness of truth, but according to their appearance in sense and the vulgar opinion; and he quotes Chrisostim, Bernard, and Aquinus, as holding the same things, and instances it as to the creating of Adam and Eve: saying thus, God hath no figure or shape, altho Moses saith he hath; he only permits the ignorant and vulgar people to believe so, it being his prudence and policy so to do.

---

[1] Gen. 17, 3. Exod. 24, 10. Isa. 6, 5. John 35, 5. Exod. 33, 23.
[2] Dan. 7, 9. Rev. 10, 1. & 1, 14. John 6, 6. Psal. 94, 9. Numb. 12, 8. Isaiah 65, 5.

Now is not this odious, for what prudence is it to flatter, dissemble and deceive the people; for must God's Prophets be but like politicians of State, pretending one thing and acting another.

Again, this man brings in Moses speaking thus; God took of the dust of the ground, wrought it with his hands into such a temper that it was fit to make the body of a man; which when framed, then comes near to it with his mouth, and breathed into his nostrils the breath of life.

And when God had made a woman of one of Adam's ribs, he takes her by the hand, and brought her to Adam; so when Adam was awaked he found his dream to be true, for he dreamed that God took a woman out of him, for God stood by him with a woman in his hand.[1]

Now it is true, says this doctor, Moses speaks in this manner to satisfy the rude multitude, who was ever ready to think that God was in form and shape as they were and thus Moses complied with their humour, and permitted them to believe so; yet saith he, it is a contradiction to the idea of God, to have figure and shape.

Now what say you to this, is not this giving Moses the lie? Moses, you see, would permit people to believe, that God was in the form of a man: now why will you not permit us to believe so? Moses did not count this doctrine a mischievous principle, as you do; but you with this man, set yourselves against Moses, and against the Scriptures; they are counted no other than a lie with you: Now it clear by this, that many of you doctors are stark blind Atheists.

Your Protestant Church is now grown as blind with age, almost as your fathers the Papists, and as atheistical as one of the Popes, who said, That that fable of Jesus Christ has brought their Church great riches: and one of that Church said to me, that the Scriptures were but balderdash stuff.

Now as to that saying of Christ to his disciples, That a spirit had not flesh and bone as he had; it was only to inform them that there was no such spirit as the world imagined, that could be seen, that had no body; for eyes of flesh must have a substance for its object: therefore said Christ, handle me and see, for I have a body, a substance of very flesh and bone; and they felt, and believed him to be their Lord and God.[2]

For Christ, from hence, would have them forever after to know that all spirits, whether of God, man, or angels, are always invisible; for it is the body that is visible, for the soul that is in it is always invisible,

---

[1] Gen. 27, 21.
[2] John 10, 27.

which spirit comprehends all visible things, yet cannot live, act. or operate without its body. And so much for that principle.

Again, page 19th. you Representor object against that most divine and mysterious principle, of God the Father becoming flesh; and call this a doctrine quite contrary to Scripture, and produce those Scriptures for proof against us; namely, that God sent his Son made of a woman, and the Word was made flesh; but, say you, there is not one word, that the Father was made flesh.

CHAPTER VIII.

ANSWER.

IT is confessed by us, that the Scripture, saith, That God sent his Son, as also, that Christ came of himself, and that he laid down his life of himself. Mow if he laid down his life of himself, then where was the Father but in himself; for it was his divine Spirit that was the Father, by which he could lay down his life by that self, and by that self could take it up again: for God transmuting his spiritual body into flesh so gained the Godhead and human nature together, and so hath a twofold self human and divine.[1]

Therefore, when he saith he hath power of himself to lay down his life, then he speaks as in reference to his Godhead; and when he saith, That he can of himself do nothing, and the like, then he speaks as in relation to his manhood: God then hiding himself compared in that manhood.[2]

Again, if it he granted, that Christ is God and man, then it must be acknowledged, that where Christ is, there the Father is; and Christ affirms it himself, saying, That he that had him had the Father and he that had seen him had seen the Father.[3]

Now from all this, doth it not plainly appear, that he was the Father himself, as well as the Son; and John saith, That in the beginning was the Word, and the Word was with God: and this Word was God; and that God, or Word became flesh: then surely that one God was Father as well as Son; unless you can prove there were two Gods, or with the Arians, that Christ was one with the Father in union, but not in essence; and if so, then every believer is as much God as Christ is: but you have your two Gods, one of which, you say, took flesh, the other did not; here you divide the substance.[4]

---

[1] Gal. 4, 4. John 5, 26. & 10, 18. Eph. 5, 2. Heb. 1, 3.
[2] Titus 2, 14. Isa. 45, 15, 21, 22, 23, compared.
[3] John 14, 1, 9. Gal. 1, 4. 1 Pet. 3, 24.
[4] John 1, 1. Verse 11. Matt. 1, 20.

What a monster do you here make of God; for you had before Christ's incarnation those two Gods in Heaven, a Father God and a Son God; and that Son you say, the Father begot before all Worlds, and then was begot again in this World; so your God the Son was twice begot, or twice made: is this good sense, is this your wisdom, is this good divinity; nay without all controversy, this is quite contrary to Scripture, and to sober reason also.[1]

For was there ever any more than one God, and did not the Prophet Isaiah say that God would not give his glory to another; and yet it is said, That all the angels of God should worship Christ, and that to him every knee should bow; and that not only in Earth, but in Heaven also: who then could share with him, for he was the Lord God of all the Prophets, testified by the angel unto John; which angel bid John worship God, even that God of the Prophets, which was no other but Jesus Christ; therefore it is said, I Jesus have sent my angel, and behold I come quickly, &c.[2]

There is no other God to come, no other Father, no other resurrection and life, no other name or power but Jesus Christ our Lord, tho men or angels should gainsay it; as I have abundantly shewed in a treatise entitled [None but Christ.].[3]

Moreover, to prosecute this principle a little further here, because it is our life and foundation principle, and it is impossible for any man to be saved that shall presumptuously dispise this doctrine of Jesus being the everlasting Father after so plain a discovery.[4]

I am now to enquire how you Trinitarians, Socinians, and Arians, bring Christ in for your Saviour: you say, That by the fall of Adam all men had incured damnation, and so were become God the Fathers debtors; and the Father standing upon justice would not be reconciled with them, without the full payment of that debt, as life for life. Now, say you, the Father was so far pleased as to send his Son, to pay the full debt: and say you, this Son came voluntarily and paid the debt; and by this means satisfied the wrath of his Father, and so purchased your life by his ransom.

Wherefore, if it be so as you teach, that the Father is distinct from that Son, then are you not beholding to the Father at all: for take this similitude for the illustration thereof; suppose, I owe a man a 1000 Pounds, or more, and I have not wherewith to pay him, and he will not forgive me any of the debt; or I must either pay it all or to prison;

---

[1] Zach. 14, 9. Deut. 6, 4. Isaiah 52, 8. & 48, 11. Psa.103, 20. Heb. 1, 6.
[2] Isaiah 45, 23. Phil. 2, 10. Rev. 22, 6. compared with Verse 14.
[3] 1 John 2, 23. & 5m 7, 2 John 9. Acts 4, 12.
[4] John 17, 3.

there to remain till I have paid the utmost Farthing; the son of this my Creditor sees the strait I am in, commiserates my case; steps in voluntarily, and pays the father the full debt and so sets me at liberty.

Now in this case, who am I most beholding to, the father, or the son; not to the father at all, for he was for justice, and I wanted mercy; the son therefore was my friend, and to him only am I bound, and him only am I to love, serve, and obey.

This is the very plain case; it is the Son Christ Jesus that all the elect seed of Adam are beholding to, and not to any Father that either is, or ever was distinct from him: but the Father of Christ was his own Godhead spirit, which through his eternal love to the seed of his own body, was moved to change his spiritual body, (which was his everlasting son) into flesh, to the end he might be capable to die, and shed his blood for their redemption; as also, that he might have power to raise the seed of the Serpent, to a second and eternal death, for their cruelly acted against him and his elect seed.[1]

Therefore his coming in flesh was foretold by *Isaiah*, and all the other Prophets; and that the Son that was to be born of a Virgin, should in time be called the mighty God, and everlasting Father: now at this time this Prophesy is fulfilled, and by this Commission of the Spirit, he is both called and known to be the high and mighty God, and everlasting Father: this Scripture is positive, and shall command all primative Scriptures to bow down to it.[2]

Thus the Scriptures are clear, to all that are appointed to salvation, that Christ Jesus is that one only, and alone true God, and everlasting Father: to this the holy Patriarchs agree, observe their testimony, which is consonant to Scripture, being grounded upon Enoch's prophesy.

Sim shall be glorified, when the great Lord God of Israel appeareth on the earth as a man to save Adam; for God taking a body upon him (namely of flesh and bone) and eating with men, shall save men.

Ye shall see God in the shape of a man (said Zebulun) he is the Saviour, he is the [Father] of nations; he that believeth in him shall certainly reign in heaven, saith Levi and Judah.

God shall appear and dwell amongst men upon earth, to save Israel; the Highest shall visit the earth, eating and drinking, as man with man; he shall save Israel: that is God hidden in man.

---

[1] Phil. 3, 8. Ephe. 6, 24. 1 Cor. 16, 22. 1 Tim. 6, 15. Rev. 5, 12. John 17, 5. 2 Cor. 5, 19. 2 John 9. John 8, 36. 1 Pet. 1, 19. & 2. Pet. 6. Heb. 2, 14.
[2] Isaiah 9, 6.

The Muggletonian Principles Prevailing 39

At the last day we shall rise, every one of us, to his own scepter saith Benjamin, worshiping the king of heaven, which appeared in the base shape of a man; and as man believed in him shall reign with him at that time: and all faithful men shall rise again, and the residue to shame, because they believed not in God that came in the flesh to deliver.

Thus it is made clear, that God the Father became flesh; but one evidence more from John, before I conclude this point: he, in admiration of his Lord's love cried out saying, O what love the Father hath bestowed upon us, but the world knoweth him not, but we know him.[1]

Now who was this Father of love, was it any other but the apostle's Jesus; his following words doth show it as clear as the light; saying thus, We who are his apostles do know him; and we further know, that when [he] doth appear we shall be like him for we shall see him as he is: that is, when comes to change our vile bodies, and make them like his own glorious body, then shall we see him as he is in himself, one personal God cloathed with flesh and bone, as a garment of eternal glory.[2]

This is the faith (saith John) that maketh pure, and he whose faith abides in Jesus Christ, that came by water and blood, hath the everlasting Father; and he that holdeth this faith sinneth not: that is he sinneth not to act; he may have the motion to sin, but it preserveth from the act; for that golden grace of faith crusheth that Cocatrice egg of the motion of sin, before it become a stinging Serpent, and so conquers and overcomes.

This is the doctrine of the Gospel, and he that embraceth it hath the Father and the Son, where and to whom the blessing and the salvation of God-speed is given: this is the true God, and the amen, and all other gods are idols.[3]

This is the Muggletonian principle, which the Anti-Scripturian calls a mischievous principle. Thus you curse the true God, and defy the holy one of Israel, choosing to yourself a God of your own lying imagination.

In page 19. you further object against that principle, how that the Godhead died. This, say you, is quite contrary to the Scripture, which saith, God is immortal, and that he hath immortality, 1 Tim. 1. 17. & 6. 16. Also, you say, That Muggleton teacheth, that the soul of man is mortal, and turns to dust: to this, say you, the Scripture tells us, that

---

[1] 1 John 3, 1.
[2] Psal. 3, 21.
[3] 2 John 10, 9. 1 John 5, 20. Rev. 3, 14.

the souls of men are alive after their death. Matt. 22. 32. And that God is said to be their God after they are dead, Matt. 10. 28. And that we are not to fear them that can kill the body and not the soul. And that Lazarus when he died, went to Heaven, and Dives to Hell, Luke 16. 22.

CHAPTER IX.

ANSWER.

The Scriptures, say that God purchased the Church with his blood: now the blood of Christ was no other but the blood of God, and when he poured forth that blood, then did he pour forth, his life; for life lay in that blood.[1]

Therefore it is said that, he poured forth his soul unto death, and that he offered up himself through the eternal Spirit: what is that, but that the eternal Spirit entered into death, or passed through death, in a moment, into eternal life; death being too weak to keep him under; so that whatever life was in Jesus did enter into death.[2]

Therefore he that was the Alpha and Omega, the first and the Last, was dead, but is now alive; and behold he now lives for ever more, and is that immortal only wise God, blessed forever; so that we do affirm, that God is immortal; and we also know that eternity did become time, for flesh was in time, and time did become eternity again.[3]

Now, in that you teach, that God cannot die; it is evident that you do not believe that Christ was any God at all; so that you Trinitarians, Arians and Socinians, you are all alike, and that you are no more Christians than they: for it will necessarily follow, that if it were nothing but human nature, or life in Christ, that died, then the death of any other man had been equivalent to Christ's sufferings, and as meritorious as his; and so your spirit God, without a body, might have saved you by shedding of any other man's blood.

But the true Christian doth know that no blood can make atonement for sin, but the most precious and invaluable blood of a God; to believe this, is to drink his blood: and to believe that that blessed body of his was no less than the very body of God, this is to eat his flesh; so that whosoever eats his flesh, and drinks his blood so, hath by so doing gained the full assurance of eternal life; this is a standing truth and shall prevail.[4]

---

[1] Acts 20, 28.
[2] Isa. 53, 2. Heb. 9, 14. Col. 2, 9. 1 Cor 15, 54.
[3] Rev. 1, 18. 1 Tim. 6, 16. 2 John 7. Rev. 1, 18.
[4] John 6, 54.

But how is it possible you should believe this, when as you cannot believe that any life dies at all; for say you, The soul of man is alive after death; here your ignorance appears very great for all your learning; where did you ever find by Scripture, That the soul of any man was ever alive without its body? The Scripture no where affirms it, if rightly understood; they are but old wife's fables, or Monks or Friar's forgeries, and heathenish principles from their own blind imaginations.

As for those sayings concerning Dives and Lazarus, it is but a Parable, and so must have a spiritual meaning; for souls without bodies have no tongues, nor eye, nor bosoms, as that Parable speaks of; but that Parable was only to set forth the two seeds here in mortality, which is largely opened by this commission of the Spirit.[1]

And as to Christ speaking of God being the God of the living, and not of the dead, it was spoken to the Sadducees, who denied the resurrection; therefore Christ shows that there was a necessity of a resurrection, seeing that Abraham, Isaac, and Jacob, and the rest of the prophets were dead, and their sepulchres are with us at this day; and if God do not raise them again to that glory their faith was pitched upon, then was he the God of the dead and not of the living; in that all died to him instead of living to him.[2]

And as to that, saying, Fear not them which can kill the body, &c. that is, fear not him that may kill both soul and body by a natural death, but rather fear him that hath an absolute power in himself to slay both soul and body with an eternal or second death.

Moreover when the Scripture saith the body die, doth not that include the soul, or natural life? what have you your natural learning for, but to understand the natural sense of words? do you not find, that that which our translation calls body, the Greek calleth souls? as Numb. 6. 6. there it is said, That he shall come at no dead body, in our Bible; but after the Greek, your own doctors read thus; ho shall come at no dead soul.[3]

Is it not said, That man was made a living soul? and was not the threatening charge given out, That that soul that sinned, that soul should die? and yet say you, the soul cannot die.[4]

Now that which the national ministry do make a ground of the immortality of the soul, is to all spiritual wise men, an evident proof of its mortality; as where it is said, so such a one died, and was gathered

---

[1] Luke 16.
[2] Acts 2, 31. & 13, 36.
[3] Gen. 2, 17.
[4] Ezek. 18, 4. verse 20.

to his people; now where is it, that they were gathered but into the grave? as for instance, see 2 Kings 22. 20.

If the soul can enjoy heaven without its body, what matter of a resurrection? but it is certain that the Scriptures affirm the contrary, and that there can be no salvation without a resurrection.[1]

When God shall raise the dead, he hath his Angels attending to gather the saints together, as God raiseth them; neither God nor his Angels doth not bring their souls from heaven to assume their dead bodies; but our God raiseth soul and, body together, out of the grave by speaking a word, as he did the body and soul of Lazarus.[2]

Again, on the other hand, must all the damned souls come from hell to fetch up their cursed bodies?[3] what hell do they come from, but out of the grave, soul and body out of the grave; and when the soul and body rises, then the Devil rises to his eternal punishment; and this earth will be the place of the Devil's torment, where he acted all his lies and cruelty; there shall he suffer eternally (after the elect men and angels are ascended with their God into eternal glory) the Plagues of Egypt were a type of this.[4]

These things will be so in their time: and so much in answer to this principle.

In page 20th you oppose John Reeve for saying, How that but one Angel fell from his created purity and glory.

The Accusation

This doctrine, say you, is quite contrary to Scripture; which tells us in Jude, that the Angels fell: and this, say you cannot be applied to Cain and his posterity: for they, say you, by your own words never fell: and as for Cain, say you, he never was from that fallen Angel, but was of *Adam's* begetting as well as Seth. And again you affirm also, that all Cain's offspring perished in the Flood.

CHAPTER X.

ANSWER.

IF that offspring of that Serpent-Angel that was cast from Heaven could know itself, then you might know that these Angels spoken of in Jude were the offspring of cursed Cain, the Serpent-Angel transmuted into flesh, and reserved in chains of unbelief, and the darkness of

---

[1] Col. 3, 4. 1 Thes. 4, 14.
[2] Matt. 13, 41. c. 24, 51. c. 25, 31. John 5, 38. c. 11, 43.
[3] Rev. 20, 13. Isa. 66, 24.
[4] Jer. 17, 13. Mich. 7, 71. Exod. 10, 21. Rev. 10, 10.

ignorance: for Jude spoke of no other Devils but what were clothed in flesh; and it was they that were the Devils ordained to condemnation.[1]

And therefore mind; for he brings in Sodom and Gomorrah, and the rebellious Jews against Moses, and those upstart hypocrites who denied the Lord to be the only and alone true God, and yet pretented his name: all these, saith he, were ordained to condemnation in that Serpent-Angel aforesaid, being reprobated in the seed; and Cain was that seed. And therefore Jude pronounces the woe unto them, as the offspring and seed of Cain, to whom eternal torment doth belong.[2]

Again, where it is said, that there was a war in heaven,[3] Michael and his Angels fighting against the Dragon and his Angels: that Michael was the spirit of the Lord Jesus in all his angelical believers; and the Dragon was the spirit of cursed Cain, in all his seed. This war was on Earth, though said to be in Heaven, because the original of both seeds came from heaven; for there never was any actual rebellion in Heaven, but that Angel-Serpent aforesaid being cast out, all his seed fell in him, and was cast out with him, and so actual rebellion took place: and therefore, said John, woe to the inhabitants of the earth for the Devil (not Devils) is come down amongst you. And if was this Devil that brought the woe, both to saint and serpent; in this warfare doth these two woes take place to them two seeds; one in this fight having his heel bruised, which is in persecution, loss of goods and death natural; the Other having his head bruised by the saint's weapons of war, which reacheth to a second death.[4]

And this Devil that was cast down, was the father of Cain,[5] from whence all wickedness and cruelty hath down; for Cain was the very first born of that Devil, and the fullness of that Serpent-Angels Godhead lived bodily in Cain; and such of his seed, that have in them a great share of that piercing reason, or God-head power, became potent Angels, lords and governors of this world, it being given to that seed; and they labour in thin their kingdom, to imitate the grandeur of that glory their father, the fallen Angel, had before his fall; and they come as near to it as possibly they can.

And here it is that the prophet Ezekiel compares Pharoah king of Egypt to the great red Dragon:[6] and the Assyrian monarch was said by the prophet, to be in dimity, power, glory and beauty, like unto his father the angel before his transmutation into flesh, when he walked

---

[1] Isa. 29, 10. John 12, 40. Rev. 11, 7.
[2] v. 11.
[3] Rev. 12, 7.
[4] verse 12, 17. Gen. 3, 15. Rev. 13, 7, 10.
[5] 1 John 3, 12.
[6] Ezek. 29, 3.

once in the garden of Eden, being greater than several other of his father's children:[1] the great kings of Babylon were said to be from Lucifer, and therefore were called by his name, Lucifer the son of the morning: and they are said by the prophet Isaiah, to be cast down from heaven; which could not be, if they had not proceeded from the fallen Angel.[2]

And as they were cast down from heaven in that Angel, even so they were for exalting their thrones above the stars, and to be like unto God; which doth show, that they were evil kings, and evil beasts, for good kings, and such as proceed not from Cain, they are not for exalting themselves so high, as to that heavenly throne of judging men's faith and conscience; neither will they tyrannize over their subjects, but do justice according to the law. But to the matter aforesaid.[3]

The great king of Tyrus, seems to out-top all the foregoing kings with angelical perfection; for he is said to be the very anointed Cherub himself; he having as great a share of that lost glory as his fallen nature could afford him; for that Angel that he proceeded from was a Cherub, which was the highest order of Angels; and this king was of the highest degree of wisdom, beauty, and glory:[4] and therefore his perfections were such as that he was said to be wiser than Daniel; by which wisdom he had gotten him riches of gold and silver in abundance; as also in his kingdom all sorts of cunning arts and sciences, and a great merchant, mighty in traffick: all this from his father the Angel.

Therefore, said the prophet to this prince, thou hast been in Eden, the garden of God; every precious stone was thy covering; yea, the tabret and the pipe was prepared in thee in the day that thou wast created: this was not Adam, but the Angel, &c.

Again, thou art the anointed Cherub that covereth and I have set thee so. (Again saith the prophet) thou wast in the holy mountain of God, and hast walked in the midst of stones of fire; thou wast perfect in thy ways from the day that thou wast created, till iniquity was found in thee: thou hast corrupted thy wisdom, by reason of thy brightness.[5]

Now can this prince of reason, so exalted, be derived from any other root, but that angelical reprobate, that was cast down from heaven for his pride, in those his great perfections: therefore his

---

[1] Chap. 33, 3.
[2] Isa. 14, 12.
[3] Ezek. 28, 3.
[4] Verse 31, 14.
[5] Verse. 15, 17.

wisdom is Matthew, said to excel Daniel's: and so it might be said to excel Adam's to.[1]

Therefore these princes are not related to Adam, but to that Angel, that corrupted his wisdom of pierceing reason; for had his wisdom flowed from faiths nature, it could not have corrupted itself; but the wisdom of reason is subject to sin: yea, reason itself (though so noble a nature and splendant, if not upheld by that power that created it) is sin itself; and here is the offspring and root of all fleshly glory: so that, that which is adored for a God is damned for a Devil. If this gives offence, I cannot help it: but to proceed.

Again, whereas you, (the opposer of the Muggletonian principles) say; first, that Cain was of Adam's begetting; and then secondly, that all Cain's offspring perished in the Flood: these are both absolutely false: for,

First, it is evident, that Adam never begot Cain, neither do the Scriptures affirm it, if rightly understood: for tho Moses saith, that Adam knew Eve his wife, and she conceived and bare Cain;[2] yet Moses doth not say, that she conceived Cain of Adam's seed: and therefore in the very next words after, Moses hath these words [And she again bare his brother Abel:] without mentioning a word of his knowing of her after;[3] and this was to keep the seeds of aspiring reason in the dark; for Eve had conceived Cain of the Serpent-Angel, before ever Adam knew her; and that was it that made her full of lust after her innocent husband.

Again, to clear this further, doth not the apostle John, say, that Cain was from that Serpent-Angel, which he calls by the name of wicked one. Now dare you say, that Adam was that wicked one, from whence (as John saith) the spirit of Cain sprung; surely no, for that were wickedness indeed to men that profess Scripture.[4]

Furthermore, Cain and Abel altho they are said to be brothers, yet their brotherhood comes but by the mother's side, even as it is apparent, that Heli and Jacob, the two attributed fathers of Joseph, the husband of Mary, were brothers by the mothers side.[5]

Now it is worth the minding here, that Joseph could not be the natural son of both these men; for observe in the genealogy of our Saviour, Matthew makes Mathan to be the father of Jacob, and Jacob

---

[1] Matthew.
[2] Gen. 4, 1.
[3] Verse 2.
[4] 1 John 3, 12.
[5] Matt. 1, 15.

the father of Joseph: but Luke makes Melchi the father of Heli, and Heli the father of *Joseph.*[1]

Now here is a different race, for Jacob the natural father of Joseph, he proceeded from Solomon, but Heli sprung from Nathan, and was Joseph's father by law or title, but not by nature.

Therefore, as Heli was the supposed father to Joseph, and Joseph the supposed father of Christ; even so was Adam no more than the supposed father of Cain nay he is no where called the father of Cain, not in all the Scriptures; but on the contrary, that Cain's father was called that wicked one, or Devil; for wicked one and Devil are both of one signification. See and compare, Matt. 13. 11. Luke 8. 12. Mark 4. 15.

Therefore it is without all controversy, that Adam is not that wicked one, Satan, or Devil, that begot Cain: nay your own doctor Ainser, upon Genesis saith, that Cain was from the Devil; and he quotes some of the Hebrew doctors for proof of the same: saying, that they teach how that Cain was born of the filth, and seed of the Serpent, which was conveyed into *Eve;* and that one Menacham, a Jewish Rabbi saith, that unto this world there cleaveth the secret filthiness of the Serpent, which came upon Eve; and because of that filthiness death is come upon Adam, &c. but no more of this here, having wrote largely upon it in a treatise entitled, Truth's Triumph, or the witness to the two witnesses, which may some time come to public view.

Secondly, as it is proved that Adam did not beget Cain; so it is false for you to say, that all Cain's offspring perished in the Flood. Now you that affirm this, will find it to the contrary; for if that had been so as you say, then there would be no damnation for any that have been born since.

But tho Cain was dead, and most of his offspring, yet his seed was alive in cursed Ham;[2] so that the compared, curse given to the Serpent-Angel in the womb of Eve run in a line, even from Cain to Ham, and so to Ishmael and Esau, and so on to the end of the world. For altho Ham was begot by Noah, a good man, and an elect vessel, yet was not Ham of that good seed; for Noah had in him two seeds, as all men else have, since the sons of God saw the daughters of men, and took them wives of such as were the seed of Cain: and so the seed of Adam and that seed of Cain, through copulation, did participate of each others seed; and which seed is uppermost in conception, that seed grows to be Lord over the other; and so a man comes to have his denomination according to the predominancy of his seed: and thus it

---

[1] Luke 3, 28.
[2] Gen. 9, 25. & 3, 14. compared. Isa. 1, 4. & 14, 20. Deut. 32, 5.

was with Ham, for Cain's seed was predominant in Ham's conception.¹

So it was with those Jews that boasted themselves to be of Abraham: and tho they might be Abraham's seed according to the flesh, yet Christ branded them for Devils, telling them, that the Devil was their father: which was no other than Cain, being the first liar and murderer.²

Now, from hence, all sober men may see, that a devil and a saint is all one to you; for you can find but one Scripture seed; for God and Devil, Heaven and Hell, Saint and Serpent, with you come all from one root.

Now, seeing it is so with you, I would advise you to leave off playing the hypocrite, and forbear telling your hearers, that any of them will be damned: for if there be but one seed, and that seed the seed of Adam, then all will be saved; so deal plainly to your people, and preach to them general redemption, and prove it from Paul's words, where he saith, that as in Adam all die, so in Christ shall all be made alive.³

But will yea, or nill yea, this we must tell you, that there is a seed, namely Cain and his offspring, that never fell in Adam, but in the Serpent-Angel, and so are incapable of ever being redeemed by Christ: for when on earth, he never prayed for them: for though he would have. all men saved, yet it is but all those that fell in Adam, that he had any spiritual salvation for.⁴

This is that which makes that seed fret themselves and call it a mischievous principle; and it will prove sad to that mischievous man that condemns true prophesy; and the true believers thereof: as likewise that justifieth the seed of the wicked to be the seed of Adam, who was the seed of God.⁵

Your further Accusation runs thus.

In page 20. you say, that there is a Devil distinct from man, and would seem to prove it from that Devil that tempted Christ; which you would have to be a bodily spirit; and you scoff at wicked imagination being the Devil: and from hence you query from that Scripture, Mark 5. 4. saying, doth imagination break chains &c. and that their

---

¹ Gen. 6, 2. Matt. 13, 37. Matt. 10, 37.
² John 8, 38. 36, 37, 44.
³ 1 Cor. 15, 22.
⁴ Rom. 9, 27. Matt. 9, 13. 2 Pet. 2, 12. John 17, 9. 1 Tim. 2, 4. Matt. 18, 11. & 10, 6. Rom. 11, 26.
⁵ Mal. 3, 15. Isa. 6, 20.

affirming, that Ely should be Christ's representative: this you call all fable.

CHAPTER XI.

ANSWER.

IE you will have a Devil without a body, you must go seek out a new found world, to find out your unknown Devil: the works of this Devil are manifest, and yet you cannot know him; for is there any wickedness in this world but what flows from that carnal spirit of men and women, who is a kingdom of wickedness in that Tophet or bodies of theirs; for it is the heart where the court is kept, and is the only nursery of all evil spirits conceived there by imagination.[1]

Oh! the depth of this imagination in this its bottomless Pit, and the uncleaness of the same: do but compare Scripture, and in it we may find a very pit-devil: all the imaginations of man's heart, (saith God) are evil, and continually evil: what is that but the Devil. And hath not this continual work its first formation in the heart, being it own work from its own seed; and its work is in this manner following.[2]

For this is to be minded, that as the spirit of faith in the heart of man, is the womb or mother, for the revelation of faith to beget a son out of the seed of faith.

So likewise the seed of reason is the womb or mother, for imagination to beget a son or familiar spirit, for all evil spirits are conceived in the heart:[3] if envy be conceived, then murder is brought forth; if lust be conceived, then adultry is brought forth; and if a familiar spirit is conceived, then it brings forth such a spirit as speaks forth motional voices;[4] and if by its transformation into angelical light, then as false prophets, it produces visions, revelations, and internal voices within them: now this familiar spirit is nothing else but a witch; so that when it motions forth spiritual or religious matters, then it becomes spiritual witchcraft, and when it motions forth upon a temporal account, then it becomes natural witchcraft: the one or other of these witchcrafts almost all the world lies under.[5]

Therefore it follows, that this familiar spirit that is begot by imagination, doth sometimes produce such a voice in itself, as if some spirit without them did appear to them without bodies, and reveal

---

[1] Rev. 18, 2. Matt. 15, 19. Gal. 6, 19.
[2] Gen. 6, 5. Jam.4, 5, 6. Isa. 32, 6. Jer. 17, 9.
[3] Jam. 1, 15. & 2, 15, 16. Jam. 4, 1.
[4] Jer. 23, 16. Isa. 8, 19. Deut. 18, 10.
[5] Eph. 6, 12.

things to them as it was by the witch of Endor, and as Samuel spoke in Saul's conscience.[1]

This hath been a common thing in all ages, and guilt of conscience can quickly coin an object, and produce a motional voice, thinking it is without the body, when as all is but from the familiar spirit.

And when this familiar spirit, or new begot wisdom is quickened in the evil heart, it grows from strength to strength, from one degree of knowledge, to a further degree of evil knowledge and evil wisdom, creating to itself such things as God never created; as an immortal soul, or spirit, without a body: and it hath made it so, as that it can appear in any shape, form, or likeness, whether it be God, man, devil, or angel: all these are made spirits without bodies.[2]

Also it hath created to itself, such a devil as can whip into man, and out of man, at his pleasure: and when sin is committed, then all the evil is charged upon that bodiless devil: and yet men must be hanged for murder, whenas, they say, it is a bodiless devil that is the murderer, or tempts to murder.

And more than this the devil must be chained in hell-fire; and yet a bodiless spirit, and in all places at one time, where he can tempt all the world to sin, and yet nobody can see him; and yet he is in hell-fire in chains, but may be called out at the pleasure of a witch: this is the world's bugbear devil, and the pitchey darkness all the world lies under.

Thus we what fruits the imagination of reason brings forth: and whereas you scoffingly ask, whether imagination breaks chains, pointing to that saying of the Gospel.[3]

Here you shew your ignorance, that cannot distinguish between devils in nature, and devils produced by accidents in natures nay, you know nothing at all, of neither one nor the other, and so make no difference of their actions.

For tho distempers in nature are devilish, yet not damned devils: for this we find, that Christ never called distracted or mad men devils; for these may come through some extraordinary fright, grief, or loss; and in some may increase to that strength, as to break iron chains: for having broke the brain, the seat of reason is quite out of order, and so makes them more strong, than when their reason was in order. And Christ never judged and, condemned these, but cast those fiery distempers, and devilish diseases out, and restored them to their right mind.

---

[1] 1 Sam. 28, 1.
[2] Exod. 1, 10. Jer. 4, 23.
[3] Mark 5, 4.

So that it is not the distracted or unreasonable that Christ condemned, but the learned, and sensible, and prudent man; even such as commit murder for conscience sake, and condemn true prophesy, from their conceited wisdom of high flown piercing reason: this is evident throughout all the Scriptures, especially in the learned Scribes and Pharisees, who held a council and reasoned in themselves how they might intrap Jesus in his words.[1]

And that devil that tempted Christ, he was one of them, and no such bodiless devil as your reason hath created to itself, that, should, carry Christ up to the pinnacle of that outward material Temple in Jerusalem, no, no: but against all your wisdom of reason, we affirm, that he was a man-devil, being a learned Scribe well read in Scripture, and could argue the same from this pinnacle of his subtile pate; but Christ repulsed his Scripture argument with Scripture again, saying, it is written, thou shalt not tempt the Lord thy God, but him only thou shalt serve.

Mow where was this Scripture written, was it not in Deut. 6. 13. 16? and was it not written to men indued with the wisdom of reason? it was not written to a bodiless devil; for bodiless devils do not commit murder, adultery, or tempt God, it is man that doth all this; and it was to man that the law was given, and so the law saith, thou shalt not tempt the Lord thy God, as your fathers tempted him; and again, you shall not corrupt yourselves.[2]

Now, from what is here said, it must needs follow, that if pride, envy, lust, coveteousness, and hypocrisy be the devils in men, are not men and women those devils that arc brought under the power of those evils when the apostle said, that the devil should cast some of them saints into prison; the saints were not cast into prison by devils that had no bodies.[3]

Therefore lay not your brats at other men's doors, but charge your own souls home with the evil you do, for as it is a man's own soul that sins, so it is his own soul that must suffer.[4]

This will prove true, and so will that of Moses and Elias, altho you call it all fable: for why will you tie God up to your imagination of cursed reason? is any thing too hard for God to do, when his divine wisdom moves him to it?[5] did not he swear by himself, to himself, what he proposed to do? and may he not, by the same rule, change his own glorious condition into flesh; and having humbled himself to

---

[1] Mark 2, 6. Luke 20, 20. Matt. 26, 3. Luke 20, 5.
[2] Exod. 20 & Deut. 4, 13, 15. Psal. 78, 18. & 41, 56.
[3] James 1, 14. & 4, 1, 2, 7. compared. Rev. 2, 10.
[4] John 6, 70. & 8, 44. Acts 13, 10. Isa. 3, 9.
[5] Gen. 22, 16.

himself, may he not cause his humanity to pray and cry unto his divinity within him, or to his spiritual charge, committed unto his angels, without him, for a further manifestation of his unsearchable power in shame and weakness, as well as in power and glory.[1]

Is it not written, how that his Angels had given them a charge to watch over him? and did not Moses and Elias do so from his birth to his ascension? also is it not written, that John the Baptist came in the spirit and power of Elias? which is plain that John the Baptist had his commission from Elias; for there was none greater in heaven than Elias was at that time, for God was then on earth, eating and drinking with man as man, as was before said. Thus much may serve to satisfy all sober men, who will not violently oppose plain Scripture.[2]

Again you further object against that saying of theirs, where they affirm, that no one ever did declare the knowledge of the true God, in his form and nature, as they have done.

Now, in answer to this, say you, there was Sabulus and Noetus held but one person in the Deity, called by different names: these you representor call broaches of our doctrine, which you judge so mischievous,

CHAPTER XII.

ANSWER.

IF these bishops of Sabulus and Noetus taught so they were in the right of it, and they might hint at truth, but they wanted a full revelation; for it was not revealed to them as it is now, and these two prophets never read any of their writings, neither do I think that there is any of them, that are truly theirs, in being: we have the prophet's and apostles writings through providence, to shew that Christ was the only God, altho they were very sparing in their proof how God became flesh, to what this commission doth, and wherefore; why, because the mystery of God was not to be finished (according to John) until the days of the voice of the seventh anti-angel's sounding of his trumpet, or ministry; namely the Quakers: and Sabulus and Noetus were before the sounding of the first anti-angel, the Papist with power.[3]

Sabulus the bishop being about two hundred years after Christ, and Noetus was contemporary with him; so that this being in the time of the ten Persecutions, there was truth then in the world, and a

---

[1] Psal. 8, 5. Phil. 2, 7, 8. John 17, 5, 19. Matt. 27, 46. & 28, 2. Luke 24, 4. Acts 1, 10. Rev. 22, 9.
[2] Luke 1, 17. Matt. 4, 5. Matt. 4, 5. Matt. 17, 12, 3.
[3] Rev. 10, 7.

trinity of persons in one Godhead had not got footing at that time during the ten Persecutions.

But after religion was set up by imperial power, then bishops were chosen out of learned and philosophical men, and Churches (as they called them) builded, and riches given for their support; then were Synods and Councils called to establish error and formal worship, and to suppress truth: that was ever without outward pomp and glory.

Thus was Noetus and Sabulus' doctrine judged heresy, both by Trinitarian and Arien; and tho they cursed, excommunicated, and condemned each other, by several Councils, as if hell was broke loose; and so it was for the thousand years time after Satan's binding was ended, as soon as the ten Persecutions were over, for then the devil went forth to deceive the world with false worship, as John declareth.[1]

The Arian, being but as a branch sprouted out of the Roman Catholic, altho in Constansius' days, and some time after a very great branch, insomuch that the Catholics could not then boast of number; for in the Council of Ariminum and Selencia there were, 560 bishops, the greatest convention that ever was known, and yet they decreed the Arian faith: so what will you Catholics say, that number is an argument of truth.

But whichsoever of them that got the emperor of their side gained power over the other; so that both of them altho they, persecuted each other with deadly hatred, as they got uppermost in power, nevertheless they could agree together, to kill Christ in his members, and to tread the holy City under foot, of innocent minded men and women, by their Penal laws, that could not bow down to their outward formalities and antichristian principles: these were as two thieves that Truth was crucified between.[2]

Now these Catholics prevailing, and they having not only the Scriptures ordered by the emperor Constantine to be translated into their tongue, but likewise their learned Councils collected and gathered into a heap, and all other writings of proceeding bishops; then must them books and traditional reports be viewed by the learned now made bishops', and what agreed and acquiesced with their principles were counted apostolical; and what did not agree, was rejected and counted heresy; or else they translated them falsely, placing down some things of their sayings, and leaving others out that made against them.[3]

And when any man was by these established bishops judged or accused for heresy, tho he lived before their days, then all his books

---

[1] Rev. 20.
[2] Rev. 11, 1. Matt. 27, 38.
[3] Rev. 2, 2.

must either be corrupted or burned; for they must be made to speak quite contrary to what they did in several things, on purpose to make those authors the more contempible: for it was ever so that all that are non-commissionated ministers of God, and such as head an anti-church, are for hiding truth from the people, as the Papists do the Scriptures, to the end they may keep up their fleshly honor; so that there is but little known and received in the world at this day, as will as heretofore, but the universal common opinion.

Therefore it is, that your national and traditional Churches doth so sound forth their own triumphs, raise heaps of authors of the first centuries, as agreeing with their catholic principles; crying antiquity, church visability, famous men are on our side, &c.

Whereas the truth of it is, all is but clamour and noise; for many of your authors are mere forgeries and lies.

For Instance

1. There be several books that have the name of such men's works, as were never their works; as Abdyus bishop of Babylon, is said by some of your catalogue makers to live in the days of Christ; others say that he knew their great church historian Egisipus, who lived near two hundred years after: now the one of these must be a lie; and they make the substance of this book to be of curious talk with bodiless or infernal devils, which is a mere Roman forgery.

2. There is also that which is called Saint James the apostle's liturgy, which hath a prayer in it for all that live in Monasteries, and yet there were none built for some hundreds of years after the apostle's days.

3. And that Egisipus, before spoken of, hath five books under his name: but it is said by some of your church writers, that Ambrose that Roman-church bishop (who lived in the year 380,) was not only the translator, but the author of them books; which is like enough, for he was not chosen bishop for his goodness, but for his greatness; even as one of the Dukes of Savoy was chosen Pope for his greatness sake, as your church history doth show.

4. These corruptions have been very common, and very ancient; for Dionisius bishop of Corinth, who lived about the year of Christ two hundred, complained sadly of his being abused in this nature: therefore said he, in one of his books (if that book was his) I wrote several epistles, but the messengers of Satan hath sown them with

Tares, pulling away some things and putting to other some, for whom (said he) condemnation is laid up.

And as there were these forgeries and corruptions aforesaid, so likewise there are many of your other great authors which you would make apostolical, and yet they do not agree with you in several things that you quote them for; nay some differences are so great between you, that I wonder you do not condemn them for heretics, as for example.

1. Turtulyon, who lived in the time of the ten Persecutions, being a great historian, and by your church counted famous, did not much contend for bishops, nor much valued ordination; but said that laymen were priests, and gave this reason for it; saying, that after faith is received, then man lives by his faith; and that faith, said he, becomes Christ's vicar; and from hence he concluded that three believers will make a Church.

He also denied children's baptism; and therefore, said he, why hasteneth this innocent age to the remission of sins, we are much more wary in worldly things; is it meet we should commit the sacrament of baptism which is a divine thing, unto them we would not commit the things of this earth: he also condemned second marriages, and much more persecution for conscience; all these things are quite contrary to you.

2. Irinius, bishop of Lyons, who it is said, knew Ignasius and Policarp, yet he held and taught, the soul's mortality.

3. And Justin, who lived in those days, you cannot deny but that he did both hold and teach, that God was in the form of a man from all eternity,

4. And further, there was never a one of all these aforesaid, that held a trinity of persons in one Godhead; no not Origen himself, whom your church doth so extol, altho he turned apostate, and denied the faith, and sacrificed to devils, to save his life; but what is he so cried up, both by Papist and Protestant for; is it not for his lofty style, and philosophical notions, and in that he would make his divinity to stoop unto his philosophy: for he held with Plato,

1. The soul's infusion, and taught that all souls were made together, and sent down from heaven to be imbodied.

2. He taught, that after we rise again, we shall have all need of baptism to purge us clean. 3 He in one place condemned second marriages, and in another contradicts it again. 4. He taught that devils were bodiless spirits; and also that all devils would be saved at last. This sure is it that pleases you at a hair.

But as to his doctrine concerning God that cannot please you so well, for the Arians challenge him to be for them, and therefore they say, that Origen denied that the Son was to be adored or prayed to; for he is, saith Origen, not the author, but procurer of the good things of God: so that we pray not to him, but to God for his sake. And Augustine your saint produceth this as Origen's opinion concerning God, And thus much as to your great apostolical Fathers, as you call them, who lived in the time of the ten Persecutions.

As to those other ancient Popes, Bishops Fathers, and Councils, that have been setup by the Roman imperial power and authority, I shall not treat on them here; for he that hath a grain of spiritual sense predominating in him, will easily see them no other but the mother of harlots, or mystery Babylon, that sits upon tongues, nations, and languages, as hath been unfolded in a treatise intitled, The white devil uncased; which may come to be extant in time.

This is the sum of your church history; so that what satisfaction can any man have by all your authors and apostolical Fathers, as you call them, as also your translators of their works, who were most of them corrupters, each one endeavouring to force the matter to suit with his own opinions, as Epephanius, Rufenus, and several others, who it is said corrupted several authers.

So that all their books are but troubled waters to drink, being not of that efficacy as to quench the thirst of sin; for their silver is become dross, their wine is mixed with water of a standing pool. This will not pass current with us, for no wine to us like the wine of the Spirit; no water to us but the water of life: no balm for us but what is in Gillead, in one personal God-man, Christ Jesus, blessed for ever, that will be accepted of with us, the only true christians in the world at this day.[1]

Therefore take you all your books and learning to yourselves; we have but three to read, to wit, the prophets, the apostles, and the witnesses of the Spirit: in these is fulness of perfection; for the light and life of their words, sinning in our hearts, is the rule, prop, stay, and guide of our faith; which is but one, and this one faith hath one God of a single person or substance for its object to pitch itself upon, and not a trinity of persons, or substance; but Father, Son and holy Ghost is one single substance, and no more; which cannot be denied, neither by Scripture, or sober reason; for,

First, was not the eternal Godhead Spirit the everlasting Father.

Secondly, was not that glorious body, wherein God the Father did eternally dwell, the eternal Son.

---

[1] Isa. 1, 22. John 4, 14.

Thirdly, and was not that powerful word, which proceeded from his Godhead Spirit through his glorious mouth the holy Ghost, or holy Spirit, by which he made the worlds, and governeth all things.

Is not this trinity in unity and unity in trinity, more agreeable to the Scripture of truth, than any other trinity, to all men that acknowledge but one eternal being and no more? now your trinity of persons, will neither be made to agree with Scripture, reason or sense; so that your striving to explain it doth but the more darken the sense about your airy God, and you are quite lost in your definition, and now of late more than ever; are you made a confounded Bable, and your clergy clash one against another, which doth make your hearers begin to stagger, as well it may: for,[1]

1. One party of your church doth hold and teach that God is [three distinct persons, and but one substance] which is a contradiction.

2. The other party of your church teacheth, that God hath not only [three distinct persons] but [three distinct substances likewise;] and from hence doth boldly charge the Homausion, or one substance, with the heresy of Sabilism, as they call it.

3. The contrary party makes their rejoinder again, and chargeth the other party with holding of a plurality of Gods: for, say they, if there be [three substances] then there are [three Gods,] which is true enough.

4. Again the adverse party replies, saying, that if there be [three persons] there must be [three substances] which is true enough too: and they give their reason why they are to hold three substances, as well as three persons; it being a forst-put, For, say they, there is now a greater necessity than ever there was, to hold and maintain three distinct substances, as well as three persons: otherwise, say they, we are in great danger to lose the catholic faith, by the revival of the heresy of Sabulus, which walks publicly abroad, tho under the disguise of a new name: and therefore if we do not allow the Godhead intirely to be (three distinct substances) as well as (three distinct persons) then comes in Sabalism: and there is an end then say they of the trinity.

5. To this, the other old dark light replies, saying, that if by retaining the old words of (three persons and one substance) there is danger of losing the catholic faith, it must be lost out of the catholic church: and the revolt by Sabalism (say they) must be both the most lasting, and the most general apostacy that ever was foretold, or feared, should happen to the christian world. But, say they, we hope we need not to be frighted out of our religion.

---

[1] Heb. 1, 3. John 1, 13. Eph. 4, 5. Isa. 45, 21, 22. Chap. 43, 10.

And thus, you see what a confusion is fallen upon you; your Babylon is now crying out, Alas, alas! did not the prophets and apostles speak of these things now is fulfilled that saying of David's to the full, divide their tongues, O Lord, for I have seen violence in the city.[1]

Doth not this your division tend to confusion, or is it not confusion itself in a superlative degree? for tho you be divided, yet our God is not divided, but is one, yesterday, to day, and for ever: for I demand,[2]

First, how can Christ be called the great, the high and mighty God, if he had two other Gods to share with him?[3]

Secondly, how can Christ be eternal in your creed, if he were begotten?

Thirdly, and how can that, which receives a being from another, ever be made equal with that which hath its being of itself alone.

Certainly, whatever you Trinitarians say to the contrary, yet it is evident that you make Christ no more than a titular God, the very same with John Biddle, that you so much disown in your Pamphlet: but I cannot see any great difference between you; I am sure you are as much out of the way of truth as he.

For, said John Biddle, Christ is our Lord and God: but how, why, said he, not really but appellatively, as magistrates are called Gods; and so he makes him God by deputation, as to title; being God, not in nature, but in name; and so is subordinate to God.

Now, do not you do so to; for you make the Son but to be begotten: and if you will make him God, yet he must be divided from the Father and holy Ghost. Now this is certain, that if there be a Father distinct from the blessed body of Christ, it must then be as John Biddle said; and therefore it is, that John Biddle, as well as Arius and Sosinus, make him but man; because they would have but one single God: but you if you make him God, yet you will divide him from the Father and from the holy Ghost; and so at the best, you make him but a third part God.

And whereas you are so bold, as to condemn Sabulus and Noetus, for worshiping one personal God, under the names of Father, Son, and holy Ghost; condemning and judging them for broachers of heresy, how will you free yourselves from this crime: as also those Councils of Arians and Trinitarians, as cursed them and their principles; together with those Councils and Synods, on both sides

---

[1] Rev. 18, 10. Psal. 55, 9.
[2] Isa. 11, 11, 15. 1 John 5, 7, 20.
[3] Heb. 13, 8. Titus 2, 13. 1 Tim. 1, 7. & 6, 12.

judging and condemning each other with deadly malice, as your church history doth show: what, were those the church of God? no.

But when God gathers up his Jewels, many of those that have been judged heretics will rise saints, and many of those that your churches have canonized for saints will rise devils: for no persecutors of conscience will escape the stroke. If any man object Paul's persecuting the church, they may know that Paul at that time acknowledged no Jesus at all; therefore when both sides acknowledge a Jesus, take heed how you persecute.[1]

I have been something larger than I intended, as to church history, and that because your church doth so much boast and glory upon antiquity, like the Papists; for there is no great difference between you nor the other churches, only in outward things; tor the essential points of faith are one and the same with you all; for you have all one God, and one devil, one heaven and one hell. So that if one of you be true, you are all true; and if one of you be false, ye are all false: therefore it were well, if your reason would be so moderate, as to bear with, and forbear one another: being you are all one, both in the root, and in the fruit, but that you will never do; but on the contrary, you will ever be exciting the magistrates to persecution and bloodshed: but happy is it for that nation in the temporal, and that nation or holy city in the spiritual, whose magistrates are so prudent as not to hearken to the priests instigations; but on the contrary, to stop the course of the violent by wholesome laws.[2]

These are those good beasts, or head magistrates, spoken of by the Scriptures, who are said to have eyes before and behind: the eye of faith before, which shows them that conscience belongs to God: and the eye of reason behind, to see that all affairs in the temporal be kept well, exercising justice and true judgment; preserving and defending the innocent who break not the civil law: and on the other hand, punishing the transgressors of any of the civil laws of the land, according to their demerit.[3]

These, and such like magistrates, are the truly nursing fathers, and shall prosper: this we leave to providence and proceed.

In the latter end of your Pamphlet you pretend a great many of contradictions committed by Lodowick Muggleton and John Reeve; but the answer before might serve for them all that are worth the answering; yet I shall answer to two or three things more that you charge against them.

---

[1] Mal. 3, 15, 16, 17, 18. Acts 24, 14.
[2] Rev. 17, 3. & 15, 6, 18. & 18, 24.
[3] Rev. 4, 6. Rom. 13, 3. Acts 5, 38.

In page 25 you say, that John Reeve doth affirm, that no man can foretel eclipses of the sun or moon, but by revelation: from whence, say you, the astrologers are much beholding to him, who tells them they write their Almanacks by revelation, if they therein foretel eclipses, as what astrologer doth not.

CHAPTER XIII.

ANSWER.

1. HERE you wrest their words, and frame a wrong sense of them; for the time when an eclipse falls out is one thing, and the time of the effects of working is another: of some of the eclipses, the astrologers say, the time of their effects last for so many months, others the time of so many years, before the effects will have done working,

Wherefore then it follows, that John Reeve doth not say, that none of the figurative merchants doth know when, or at what time an eclipse will fall, but their effects, and time of their effects, how long they will be in working: these things, said John Reeve, can no man know but by inspiration; which is positively true.

And thus you, church-doctor, raise slanders to blast their reputation; and so truth comes to be vilified as I showed before, for truth may be buried under falsehood for a time.

Again, page 25, you charge them with another error, saying that they affirm that the eclipse of the moon is never but when it is near the Sun. Whenas, say you, it is manifest that its eclipse is when it is opposite to the sun, and that the earth is between them, which doth occasion it by withholding its borrowed light. But to this I answer.

2. Here again you have abused John Reeve; and in plain terms belied him; which one would think a man of that seeming purity would not have done: for John Reeve doth not deny its eclipse when opposite to the sun; but saith (for these are his words) the eclipse of the moon is through her near conjunction with the natural light or ruler of the day, or a planetary fire, answerable to its nature that occasions the eclipse.

Now this we do affirm, and your astrologers do not deny it but that there are stars of a fiery nature, and experience shows it: for what is the reason that there is more heat when the sun is in Leo, than there is when it enters Cancer, when as the sun is nearest to us, when it enters that sign, but only that the heat is occasioned by the rising of some fiery stars, as that which they call the Dog star, and others of the like nature.

So likewise the occasion of the moon's eclipse, it is not by the sun not rendering its borrowed light, by reason of the earth interposing herself betwixt those luminaries; but it is through her being near to some of them fiery Stars, as those which the astrologers call the Dragons head, or Dragon's tail; one of which being always near to the moon when she suffers an eclipse.

We do likewise affirm that the moon borrows no light from the sun, but that it is a real created light of itself; for Moses saith, that God made two great lights; but your astrologers and you say, that God made but one: whether should we believe, Moses or you? for saith Moses, one of them is made to rule the day, and the other is made to rule the night.[1]

The sun and moon are of contrary natures, one is fiery hot, the other is cold and watery; therefore it is contrary to reason that the one should receive any light from the other, and therefore there can be no agreement betwixt them, for experience shows us that the moon is cold and watery, being made out of the water, and so is the lady of the water, and occasions the ebbing and flowing of the seas, and the running of all rivers, drawing the waters after her, as the loadstone doth iron.

But on the other hand the sun is hot and fiery, being the captain of all fire, and so draws combustible matter up to itself, which occasioneth thunder, which is a war betwixt fire and water; and thus they appear in their contrariety of natures, which we see further by experience, the clearer the sun doth shine, the hotter it is, but the clearer the moon doth shine the colder it is.

So that from what is said, may be seen who the astrologers are most beholding to, whether to you or John Reeve, let all men judge: for John Reeve, in this principle, is as contrary to the astrologers, as the sun and moon are contrary in nature.

Furthermore, you object against John Reeve, for saying that the sun, moon, and stars move all in one firmament: and for saying, that they are not much bigger than they appear to us. To this you say, that they are quite contrary, and that they move in several orbs, and that each orb at so much distance from each other, as the astrologers affirm.

---

[1] Gen. 1, 16.

CHAPTER XIV.

ANSWER.

1. IS it not as good sense, and better, to believe, that the sun, moon, and stars move all in one firmament, or heaven, as so many as nine several heavens, as your blind astrologers teach you: and yet our fleshly eyes can pierce through them all; nevertheless every one of these must be so many thousands of miles beyond each other; and this blind opinion must be ratified forsooth, because the planets and fixed stars have several motions; and therefore from hence you will have these several heavens, and these their differences in motion, must show their difference in height and substance.

Because Saturn moves so slowly, as to be near upon thirty years in finishing his coarse through the twelve signs, whereas the sun finishes his in one year: therefore, from hence, do you conclude, that he must be of necessity thirty times higher, and thirty times bigger than the sun, and thirty times further to go; nay, and the next orb above Saturn to move so slow, as to be forty thousand years in finishing his course: pray how many millions of miles is it to that heaven, or Primum Mobila? one of your mathematicians says it is one hundred and seventy millions, eight hundred and three miles.

Is this your wisdom, in which you say we are not capable to answer you in? I pray is this good pulpit doctrine? one of your ministers that I did know, whose name was Mountney, did mount so high, as to affirm, in the pulpit, to his parishioners, that it was so far to the primum Mobila, that if it were possible to fling a millstone down from thence, that it would be seven years before it would reach this earth: and yet in another doctrine he taught, that a departed soul would be in heaven in a moment, which is much higher than that primum Mobila.

And your reverend doctor More, before quoted, must be remembered here, for he taught, that a star of the first magnitude is twenty thousand times biger than this earth, and nine hundred thousand times biger than the moon.

These are your rare learned men, I wonder how they could get a line of that length to measure so far, and yet to stand upon this earth: but let them go on, for the time of their sophistry is almost at an end, But to conclude this point; as you upon oar principles of the sun, moon, and stars aforesaid, do call all men to for judges against us; so we, to retort your language do call all sober men to judge, whether your opinion of sun, moon, and stars be not an error of the greatest magnitude; and also, whether you have done us justice yea or nay. And so much in answer to your first query.

CHAPTER XV.

SIR, your second query, or latter part of your pamphlet, was to prove Lodowick Muggleton false from his interpretation of the 11th. chapter of the Revelation of John.

But your proof is but your denial, for you do not so much as show the meaning of one word in all that chapter: if they could but ascended up to heaven in a cloud, as they had showed how Moses and Jesus did, all had been well enough; even as the Jews, if they could but have seen Elias to have come in person as John Baptist, did, then they would have believed as they said.

So, if you could but have seen these prophets to ascend up in a cloud, then perhaps you would have said you, would have believed them: but soft (say you) they are not the two witnesses, for they cannot ascend to heaven, for John Reeve is dead: besides (say you) they must have been put to death by the hands of violence, and then to have risen again, and ascended to heaven, in the sight of all men.

This is all the interpretation you can give of them, which is none at all, and all the proof you have against them; and as to Lodowick Muggleton's interpretation of that chapter, you seem to be at a great loss about it, being astonished at his words: for, (say you) I cannot tell how to reconcile his words; and from hence you fling all off to others, faying, reconcile them as can, for I cannot.

And what is the difference and matter that cannot be reconciled: why, say you, he saith, that they two are the two witnesses; and yet they say, that the body of those two witnesses are the letter of the Scriptures, and that the witnesses, or letter was slain 1350 years before, and yet was slain in them again by the beast out of the bottomless pit. To this I answer.

1. Here you would have the letter to be slain, whenas it was the spirit and life of that letter that was slain; for the life being gone, therefore the letter of the Scripture remained as a dead body, in regard there was none living that could give a true interpretation of it.

Now this spirit and life was killed 1350 years ago; for the last of the persecutions did kill and root out all the true ordained bishops, or ministers of the gospel; so that there were none left to give the holy Ghost to others, by laying on of hands; so then there was no quickening power remaining until a new commission was given, which now is fulfilled at this day; for the same spirit that gave the other witnesses their commission, hath chose these to be witnesses.

3, So that they having received that same spirit of life from God, as the others had; therefore it is they only that can, and do interpret the letter of the Scripture; for the Scripture is put into their hands, as the priesthood was into the hands of Aaron, and they by their interpretation do put life into the Scriptures, making it to stand upon its feet in the consciences of men and women, with great power, both to the seed of faith, and to the seed of reason, to save and destroy; for words of truth have spirit and life.[1]

4. And as that spirit of reason did kill that spirit of life that did speak that letter so that now that spirit and life is come into them again, they will stand upon their feet, and kill the spirit of reason with a death eternal; for there is now both body and life in the Scriptures, and it is the body of the witnesses of the spirit, which is not a dead body, but a living body now, and so will remain to the end of the world.

5. Again, whereas you do affirm, that these witnesses do declare, that the spirit and life was killed in them, by the beast out of the bottomless pit, in their persecutors: that saying of yours is utterly false, and you did it maliciously, on purpose that his words might not be reconciled; for Lodowick Muggleton did say, that the beast out of the bottomless pit made war against them, and would have killed them, if their law could have done it. And that roaring lion Jefferies did say afterwards, that he was sorry that their laws were so unprovided, that they could not take away Muggleton's life.

To that it is apparent, that the spirit and life of these two witnesses is not killed; but after the two witnesses of the spirit are dead, the spirit and life will remain in vigour.

6. Wherefore as the other two witnesses of water and blood did last to the end of the appointed time of their commissions, even so likewise will the revelation of this commission last to the end of the world; for though the doctrine is declared as to the substance; yet in that doctrine will revelation arise, grow and increase, in such as hear and understand it, to their eternal happiness, joy and glory; and shall prevail and triumph over all forms and opinions in religion, that now totters more than ever through its own instability.

And now Sir, are you not either blind or malicious or both, that would forge contradictions where there are none; yea and to make lies, on purpose to make truth appear infamous? so that are you not a shifter of all shifters; and know not where to fix, or what to say, or how to disprove it, either by Scripture or sober reason? it is a poor shift to falsify the words of your opponent, because you have not any thing that seems plausible to answer.

Sir, is this your learning? pray do you believe that book of the Revelation by St. John, to be this revelation, and a part of holy Writ? if

---

[1] John 6, 68. & 15, 36.

you say you do, then why will you not give your own sentiments of so much as one verse, and tell the meaning thereof? and if this interpretation of theirs be not good sense, why do you not reprove them with better?

But finding your ignorance to be such, therefore it had been better for you to have let this book alone, and plainly to have said, that it was sealed, and you could not read it in its own sense. And it had been better for you to have let these two witnesses alone, and all the believers of it alone; but you were appointed to that end, that your lies and slanders against it may bring you to a full reward.

For this book of the Revelation by John was not written for your edification, but for the instruction of this last witness, and benefit of the weed of faith, to the end of the world, as a peculiar blessing scaled to them from heaven: and therefore by this blessing of faith and knowledge in the Scriptures of truth, which are now given unto us, we do from hence find, that you have no part of the blessing of this book of the Revelation of St John, as may appear by these seven particulars following.

As first, this commission of the spirit hath seen into the book of life, wherein they have found the names of the prophets, apostles, and the witnesses of the spirit recorded there, as true commissionated messengers of God; but your name was not found there as a minister of God: this is the first evidence of your exclusion.[1]

Secondly, these witnesses, and the believers thereof, have looked and seen those hundred forty and four thousand virgins that were redeemed from the earth, standing with the Lamb, their only God, on mount Sion, singing that new song of, all praise to the Lamb: but you not having learned that song of, all praise to the Lamb, were not found amongst them: but we looking about, have seen you in that great city, mystery Babylon, the mother of all harloting and blaspheming priests; who are said by the spirit, to have the curse of this book, for adding and taking away from it. For you add your own imaginations to it and so from thence will make your own confounded reason to be the judge of it; as I shewed before in chapter 2.[2]

Thirdly, as we have seen you add your own vain thoughts to it, so likewise have we seen you taking away from the words of this prophesy, and the two witnesses thereof; for you will not suffer those last true prophets to have any footing here, but would thrust them out of the book of life, and thrust yourself into it.[3]

---

[1] Chap. 20, 15.
[2] Chap. 14, 3. Chap. 17, 5. & 22, 18.
[3] Chap. 11, 2. Chap. 18, 7.

But this commission showeth us, that God will take away your part out of the book of life; not that you had any there, but that you thought you had and thought your name was there; but you are not in the book of life to be found, neither as a teacher, nor as a true believer, as those two witnesses are and the true believers thereof; we have found our names in this book of life of the Lamb, the only and alone wise God, to our eternal comfort, and his everlasting praise.[1]

Fourthly, again, you have further taken away from this book, in that you denied God to have any body, face or shape; so that as the blessing of this book is, that the saints shall see his face: so the curse of this book is, that such as have denied him, as aforesaid, shall never see his face to their comfort.[2]

Fifthly, you have likewise taken away from this book, in that you teach, that the Alpha and Omega. did not die; but this book doth declare that the Alpha and Omega, the first and the last did die, and shed his blood; by which he redeemed his elect seed; so what part can you have in this purchase, seeing you deny that God had any blood, or offered up any life by sheding of the same.[3]

Sixthly, you also further add, and take away from this book of John, in that you say, that there is a God distinct from Christ: and further say that Christ Jesus Lord is not the sole God: but this book of John owns no other God at all but Jesus Christ; giving him the titles of first and last, the Alpha and Omega, king of kings, God, very God, true God, great and almighty God, and the God of all prophets: where then should there be any other God besides Jesus Christ our Lord; for this divine apostle who lived and leaned in the bosom of this Lord, knew not any other God as is abundantly proved.[4]

Seventhly and lastly, this God the Lord Jesus, you have renounced, his prophets you have persecuted and belied, the true faith you have despised; for you have not only contradicted and despised the doctrine of the second commission, which was the commission of blood, but you have also, to aggravate your crime, called the doctrine of this third and last commission, which is the commission of the spirit (and which is one of them three great armies that in heaven will follow the Lamb upon white horses, which is the righteousness of faith in his blessed person: I say you have called this commission) blasphemy, delusion, deceit: and that it is (say you made up of impiety, nonsense, and absurdities: and in general, calls them

---

[1] Chap. 3, 5.
[2] Chap. 22, 4. & 2, 18. & 19, 12. & 1, 18.
[3] Chap. 1, 8, 18. & 2, 8.
[4] 1 John 5, 20. Rev. 19, 16. 17. & 15, 13. & 1, 8. & 22, 6, 16. & 18, 8. & 17, 14.

mischievous principles, confusion and contradiction; and that we are a pernicious and contemptible sect.[1]

So that, from hence, it doth plainly appear, that you have brought yourself under the judgement and censure of that book of John, and of this commission of the spirit, which doth so fully explain that prophesy being sent to finish the mystery of God: and now behold it is finished, and you have heard, and now you will find, that power belongeth unto this God, and to this his commission of the spirit.[2]

FINIS.

Hayward, Printer, Deal

---

[1] Chap. 19, 14.
[2] Chap. 19, 14. Chap 19, 15. 20. & 21, 22. Chap 10, 7. Psal. 62, 11.

TRUTH'S TRIUMPH:

OR,

A WITNESS TO THE TWO WITNESSES.

TRUTH'S TRIUMPH;

OR,

A Witness to the Two Witnesses;

FROM THAT UNFOLDED PARABLE

OF

Our Lord and Saviour, Jesus Christ, the High and Mighty God

MATTHEW, CHAP. 13, VERSE 30 TO 42,

WHEREIN

THE FUNDAMENTALS OF FAITH ARE CLEARLY DISCUSSED, OPENED AND EXAMINED;

Being drawn up into these Eight Heads following:

THAT IS TO SAY,

First	*Of the True God.*	Fifthly	*Of the Law's Nature.*
Secondly	*Of the Two Seeds.*	Sixthly	*Of the Soul's Mortality.*
Thirdly	*Of the Right Devil*	Seventhly	*Of the Devil's Torments.*
Fourthly	*Of Predestination.*	Eighthly	*Of the Saint's Joys.*

BY THOMAS TOMKINSON.

A Believer and true Lover of the Commission of the Spirit, being written for the benefit of himself and others, who are of the Seed of the Son of Man, the Lord Jesus Christ, the High and Mighty God, being both Father, Son, and Spirit, in one single Person, blessed for ever. Amen.

Be not forgetful to entertain Strangers, for by that means some have received Angels unawares, and have not known it. Heb. 13. 2.

WRITTEN IN THE YEAR OF OUR LORD GOD, 1676;

Transcribed by the Author, with some Alterations, 1690, and Printed by Subscription, 1823.

London:

PRINTED BY W. SMITH, KING STREET, LONG ACRE.

CONTENTS

Subscribers Names... 70
Dedication... 71
Preface to the Reader.. 72
Introduction 76
I.   Treating of Christ the True God 82
II.   Treating of the Two Seeds............................... 147
III.   Treating of the Right Devil 169
IV.   Proving the Doctrine of Predestination............. 255
V.   Of the Nature of the Law 294
VI.   Of the Soul's Mortality..................................... 331
VII.   Of the Devil's Torments 376
VIII. Of the Saints Joy's in Heaven.......................... 398

LIST OF SUBSCRIBERS, 1823.

Mr. and Mrs. Thomas Amor
Mrs. Rebecca Burton *
Miss Elizabeth Bilhald *
Mr. Thomas Barlow *
Mrs. Sarah Bush †
Miss Mary Buck
Mrs. Frances Brown §
Mr. Thomas Brown §
Miss Sarah Brown §
Mr. William Cates
Miss Elizabeth Clay *
Mr. and Mrs. T. Crundwell ‡
Mr. John Drummond
Mr. George Dickisson, jun.*
Mrs. Sarah Fever
Mr. and Mrs. Frost
Mr. and Mrs. James Frost
Mr. and Mrs, Joseph Frost
Mr. and Mrs. Isaac Frost
Mrs. Mary Flinders *
Mrs. Sarah Gandar
Mr. and Mrs. Joseph Gandar
Mr. Edward Gandar
Mr. and Mrs. Timothy Gandar
Mr. Elhanan Gascoyne
Mr. and Mrs. Wm. Graham ‡
Mr. and Mrs. Thomas Hewett
Mrs. Elizabeth Hewitt *

Mr. Benjamin Hall §
Mrs. Hannah Hunt §
Mr. and Mrs. George Hunt §
Mr. Samuel Hunt §
Miss Hannah Hunt §
Mrs. Theodosia Hogg §
Mr. Robert Hogg §
Mr. Edward Kitchin *
Mrs. Ann Law
Mr. James May ||
Miss M. A. Morrison*
Mr. Joseph Mason *
Mr. Charles Marsh ||
Miss Sarah Norledge †
Mr. and Mrs. G. Robinson
Mr. Richard Smith
Mr. James Pearce Smith
Mr. Thomas Spooner
Miss Ann Slates §
Mr. William Vincent
Mr. William Vincent, jun.
Mrs. Wilthew
Mr. James Windsor
Mr. Robert Wallis
Mr. and Mrs. John White §
Mr. William White ‡

---

* Nottingham, † Macclesfield. ‡ Maidstone. § Derbyshire. || Deal.

TO

HIS HONOURED FRIEND,

MR. LODOWICKE MUGGLETON.

GREAT SIR,

IN this Treatise is an account given of my faith, and an evidence to your evidence, grounded from an enlightened knowledge in the Scriptures of truth, from those sacred words of yours spoke into me, or begot in me, by the report thereof.

If I have done well, I reckon it to you; if not well, the fault is from myself; if I have done ill, I beg your pardon.

But if well, and that I have your acceptation of this Treatise of Truth's Triumph, then have I what I desire, and shall be filled with joy, in that by you, I shall be found worthy to witness to the truth of your witness in all your Six Principles, which to me is life, as your words have been light and life all along, which hath led me this path.

So shall presume to say no more, but subscribe myself,

Sir,

Your real friend in the eternal truth,

THOMAS TOMKINSON.

Sladehouse, August 7th, 1691.

THE PREFACE TO THE READER.

COURTEOUS READER,

1. THE life of a true Christian, is faith in the true Christ; Paul's life, was his faith in the Son of God; and our life under this last Commission, that we live, is by faith in that Son of God, as the one only true God.

2. Here is the fountain of all wisdom, the light of life, the spring of lasting peace, and the way to felicity, joy, and glory.

3. What saith that divine Scripture, John the 17th, and 3rd; is not this the sense which follows? to know Jesus Christ to be the true God, is eternal life.

4. Dear friends, hold fast here, for this Lord is your life, and for you hath he given his life, because you are the seed of his own body.

5. I through mercy, having had the faith of his own Glorious Person quickened in me, have thereupon been moved, to treat of that divine portion of Holy Writ, namely, of the two seed's-men of heaven and earth, being the quintescence of all Scripture record.

6. From the knowledge of these two seed's-men, in their forms and natures, depends the knowledge of the two seeds, wheat and tares, reason and faith, light and darkness, life and death, heaven and hell.

7. All which is opened and unfolded by this Commission of the Spirit, and this Treatise of mine is a building upon it, and a bearing witness to their witness, from variety of Scripture records, that do clearly agree with their doctrine of their Six Principles; first, of the True God, his Form and Nature; secondly, the Right Devil, his Form and Nature; thirdly, the Form and Nature of Angels; fourthly, the Place and Nature of Heaven; fifthly, the Place and Nature of Hell; sixthly, with the Mortality of the Soul.

8. This Treatise of mine upon this unfolded parable, doth illustrate all those doctrines, and shews that the Scriptures in their inner sense, are clear, for the proof thereof, to all that have the single eye of faith, and the hearing ear.

9. Now the reason that hath induced me so much to enlarge this Treatise, and put it into a method for the press against future times, as that the press shall be open, is because I had sent the three first parts of this Treatise of Truth's Triumph, up to London, as soon as it was written, to our dearly beloved brother, Mr. Alexander Delamaine, senior.

10. Now, he liking them so well, caused them to be transcribed into a book, in folio, by his son, leaving room for the rest, but he never obtaining them all, in that he died before they were fully perfected, so having them but in part, and in that our London friends did so approve of them, it encouraged me the more to go on with them, according to my promise to them.

11. Therefore, our dear and never-to-be-forgotten friend, Mr. Delamaine, writes thus to me, as to this Treatise, in his letter, bearing date, December the 18th, 1677: My dearest Brother, I salute you in the true faith, of a personal God, the only and alone true God, the Lord Jesus Christ, by which we shall enjoy eternal life, a testimony of the truth of this, abides in our souls, as a seal while in mortality; I received your consolatory lines, they are like apples of gold; I have drank of them cordials, and I have found them to revive my heart wonderfully, &c.

12. And in another place, saith he, my son is now wholly busied in transcribing your Truth's Triumph; and in another letter after, saith he, my son having finished your last volume you sent me, having transcribed it fairly in a large volume, in folio, hath left a sufficient room, if you are so pleased to insert the residue of your revelations, (for so he was pleased to call them.)

13. Also, Mr. Alexander Delamaine, junior, desired of me, in his letter, dated December 15th, 1678, to grant his father and him their request, in sending the rest belonging to that volume, &c.

14. So, that from the desire of these friends, and finding their well liking of them, and of several other friends, both in the city and country, I have gone on with this Treatise with more earnestness, and have perfected my promise in writing it, though not in sending it all up to London, having not perfected it before the death of those eminent friends of Mr. Delamaine's, both, and Mr. John Saddington, that famous believer, and true brother, and faithful friend; as, Mr. Futerall, Mr. Cooper, Mr. Burton, Mr. Cooke, Mr. Shelye, with several others, who are gone before me, leaving me and this Treatise behind them.

15. Moreover, I have been the more encouraged to perfect this work, in that I have had the surviving Prophet's approbation of it, as by the testimony of Mr. Alexander Delamaine, senior, in a letter of his to me, dated London, April 12th, 1679, writing thus:

16. Your last sweet writings I have received, and have read them over to the Prophet, who doth, with all that hear them, approve well of them, and they shall be transcribed with as much haste as can be: pray send me those twelve sheets you wrote to the Dissenter; I long to see them, if you have a copy of them, &c.

17. And now, having shewed to all that read this ensuing Treatise, the grounds of my proceeding to so large a Treatise, was, in that it was so approved of by such faithful and knowing Christians, whose wisdom is in Christ, as God, from eternity, in time and to eternity, that is, who knows him to be God yesterday, to-day, and for ever.

18. We, who are under this Commission of the Spirit, our learning is the learning of the Spirit, whose life is large, but its voice is still, yet works and will work, and who knows the extent thereof,

Doctrine

19. For salvation truths are comprised in a little room; the true spiritualist hath for his subject, as well as his object to learn by, this short doctrine, "Christ God over all, blessed for ever."

20. We have but two Prophets of truth in this age, one is not, and the other is yet in being, they have laid a foundation for faith to build upon, even as aforesaid.

Applied

21. Now faith works upon that, and by dwelling there, multiplies in wisdom, and from the true God knows the right devil, and the person and nature of angels, with the nature and place of heaven and of hell, and of the rise of the two seeds, with the soul's mortality, and much more besides.

22. Wherefore, from the knowledge of this, true spiritual worship comes to be known, and performed by seeing itself to be the seed of the Lord's own body, and to be in the book of life, for this assurance of life is begot, by faith's fastening its hold upon Christ its redeemer:

True Worship

23. Now this operating faith offers true worship unto the true God, the Lord Jesus, who creates in it raptures of joy, and from this joy doth spiritual praise flow, and so hath a return of acceptation which doubles the blessing.

24. But the worship of all Scripturian literalists, let them be of what church they will, hath not the like effect in it, because they know not the true God, nor of what seed they are of, which occasions that fearful darkness in them.

25. Yet we see that the world hath heaps of teachers; but what is the fruits? but more ignorance than if they had none; is it not a strange thing that reason should be so captivated, both in teacher and hearer, priest, and people?

26. A curse is upon the learned and unlearned of priest and people; are not the Scriptures to them a sealed book? their preaching is such they might never have seen them.

27. Therefore to convince the teachers, and stop the mouths of their hearers, I have here undertaken to prove, that all the Scriptures are clear against them, and do justify and give evidence to the faith of this Commission of the Spirit, as the only truth, therefore have I entitled it Truth's Triumph, or a Witness to the Two Witnesses.

28. And now I recommend this Treatise to the sober, as well as to the faithful Christian; therefore if thou be preserved from judging things that at first may seem difficult, who knows the worth and virtue thou mayest receive by reading hereof? if thou be of the elect, before death comes upon thee, thou wilt close with the doctrine thereof, to the assurance of eternal life, and this is a blessing.

29. And if Providence doth make this Treatise instrumental to the conversion of some, or many, it will add to my glory likewise, so I shall say no more as to this point, but leave it to Providence, whether it shall be born and live, or die in the birth, and never be public.

30. I myself am satisfied, life and salvation is sealed to me, by my faith in this Commission. I have believed, therefore I have written, and I have written what I have believed, and whoever believes what I have written, may have the like return as I have had, which is a certain peace in a seal of life, as aforesaid, to the glory of the true God, the Lord Jesus Christ, blessed for ever. Amen.

THOMAS TOMKINSON.

Sladehouse, May 6th, 1691.

TRUTH'S TRIUMPH;

OR,

A Witness to the Two Witnesses.

MATTHEW, CHAP. xiii. FROM VERSE 37 TO 42.

"He that soweth the good seed is the Son of Man, the field is the world, the good seed are the children of the kingdom, the tares are the children of the wicked one, the enemy that soweth them is the devil, the harvest is the end of the world, and the reapers are the Angels, as therefore the tares are gathered and burned in the fire, so shall it be in the end of the world, the Son of Man shall send forth his Angels, and they shall gather out of his kingdom all things that offend, and them which do iniquity, and shall cast them into a furnace of fire; there shall be wailing and gnashing of teeth, then shall the righteous shine forth as the Sun in the kingdom of their Father; he that hath ears to hear let him hear."

INTRODUCTION.

IN this Scripture is contained the whole counsel of God as to the knowledge of himself, the knowledge of the right devil, and rise of the two Seeds, the original of all mankind. In a word, Heaven and hell, God and devil, saint and serpent, the office and nature of Angels, the soul's mortality, the nature of the last judgment day at the end of the world, with the two seeds, with the eternal life and eternal death, fully manifest themselves in this portion of Holy Writ, to all those that have the inward ear of the soul, and are the seed of the Son of Man, the Lord Jesus Christ, that mighty God and everlasting Father, blessed to eternity.

2. This is that unfolded parable, the spirit and life of which becomes a foundation for the Scriptures to stand on; and he that hath the spirit and knowledge of the same in his heart, doth stand on such ground as that he can see into the highest heavens and lowest hell with one turn of his eye, and again upon a direct view can see through

the field of the world, and behold the two contrary seeds of Wheat and Tares, Elect and Reprobate, and knows the seedsmen of both.

3. But though this parable is unfolded, yet is it but to the seed of the Lord's own body, for it is those that have the eye salve, (a) and the hearing ear;[1] to others it is a mystery and a wonder, knowing not of what seed they are.

Doctrine 1

4. For since religion hath been painted upon banners by Gospel professors, and maintained by a sword in Princes hands, under the title of Lord of Hosts, the true Jesus or Seedsman of Heaven hath never been known, and if it had, it could never have been affected; for Jehovah in power became Jesus in poverty, reproach, and contempt; and what prince or potentate would submit to this? Not any: for prosperous and honourable errors were ever preferred before afflicted truths.

Applied

5. Therefore you poor despised seed of the Son of Man, a suffering Saviour, fear not to hold fast afflicted truths for the love of affected triumphs in the glorious kingdom of your Father the Lord Jesus Christ, which you shall have at the end of the world; for then shall the prosperous errors of your enemies be turned into terrors of a burning fiery furnace, according to this Scripture. But to the matter in hand, and to my text.

Text explained

6. He that soweth the good seed is the Son of Man, &c. This Son of Man was Christ Jesus, and he sowed this seed when he was in the state of the Father, which was before he became flesh. Now the seed which he sowed was Adam, for as it is written Adam was sowed a natural body, yet was Adam God's real seed,[2] because the breath of life breathed into that body of his, taken out of the dust, was of the divine nature,[3] and by virtue of this divine nature[4] Adam became the Son of God, as well as God, in the fulness of time, became Adam's Son, by clothing his Godhead-nature with pure human flesh, taking upon him even that same nature which before was given unto Adam.

---

[1] Revel. 3.
[2] 1 Cor. 15.
[3] Gen. 2. 7.
[4] 2 Pet. 1. 4. Opened.

7. Wherefore the Creator, the Lord Jesus, by his wisdom and power, out of one of Adam's ribs, makes a woman, and in them he places a law of generation in these words, be fruitful and multiply.[1]

Doctrine 1. Explication

8. In these last words you see, that our God did decree that his seed should generate and bring forth a people, appointed for glory; but before this seed could generate and bring forth, it must be tempted and stirred up to lust by another seed, for the nature of Adam and Eve being of a divine nature, even divine faith, the nature of which being full satisfaction in itself, therefore you that are his seed must know that there could be no motion of desire in the least to the act of generation, until it was cast into the mind by a subtile serpentine Language, and so it was by that wicked one that was cast out of Heaven.

Text Explained

9. Now that wicked one was the serpent that tempted Eve, and the tree of knowledge of good and evil, of which Eve was not to eat of, for there was but one serpent Angel cast out of Heaven. As it is written, Woe unto the inhabitants of the earth, for the devil is come down amongst you.[2]

Text opened

10. This Serpent Angel overpowering Eve by his subtlety, caused her to consent to him (she being left to her own strength), upon which condescension he entered her womb (through her secret parts), being capable so to do, being a spiritual body, and not of a gross substance.

11. Wherefore as soon as he had entered her womb, and being united to her soul and body, his serpentine nature dissolved itself into her pure seed and defiled her throughout, and so became essentially one with her, through which naturally she conceived a serpent dragon devil into a man child of flesh, blood and bone, and brought forth her first begotten son of the devil, yea the very devil, and called his name Cain, though ignorantly she said she had received him from the Lord.

1. Inference

12. This Cain is the father of all reprobates; this Cain is not of Adam's begetting, but he is the serpent angel transmuted into flesh, and so was of that wicked one, or wicked one himself; therefore it is

---

[1] Gen. 2.
[2] Rev. 12.

written, not as Cain who was of the wicked one, and slew his brother, &c.

13. Therefore this Scripture declaring the tares to be the children of the wicked one, and that the seedsman that sows them is the devil, relates both to the serpent angel and to Cain; for the serpent angel became seed through transmutation, but Cain produced seed through copulation.

Proved

14. And from hence it is that Cain becomes the father of all reprobates, because they all proceed through his loins; therefore it is that Christ and the Scriptures fathereth all wickedness upon Cain. See therefore what Christ saith by the Scribes that resisted him, You are of your father the devil, who was a liar and murderer from the beginning; which lying and murdering devil was Cain.

2. Inference

15. Even so on the contrary, Adam, he being the good seed of God, he was made father to all the Elect, they all proceeding through his loins, &c.

Both proved

16. Wherefore from hence now it is clear to the hearing ear, and to the eye of faith, that Election and Rejection have their originals from Adam and Cain, and that both seeds sprang from these two roots, they being made on purpose for the production of two generations of mankind, for the manifestation of these two great attributes of God, of justice in the condemnation of one seed, and mercy in the justification of the other, that the prerogative power and glory over the creature may be his, to the eternal damnation of the one, and everlasting glory to the other. And who shall dare to dispute against it? None will do it but the reprobate seed of the serpent.

17. Thus much by way of explication of the rise of the two seeds. Now follows the divine doctrines that are presented to us in open face, from this unfolded parable, being the very quintessence of all Scripture record.

Doctrine 1

18. First, in this my text it is clear, that this Son of Man, or Lord Jesus Christ, is the only true God, and though he is called by several titles, as Father, Son, and Spirit, yet is not, nor can he be proved to be any other than one personal Glory in the form of a man, in time, before time, and to all eternity.

Doctrine 2

19. Secondly, it is also evident, that there are two seeds or two generations of people in this world; the one are children of God, the other are children of the devil; the one seed be the posterity of Adam, the other seed are the offspring of Cain.

Doctrine 3

20. Thirdly, seeing there is mention made of two seeds and no more in this world that are appointed for eternal life and eternal death, hence it is undeniably evident, that there are no devils in this world or any other that is to be damned to eternity, but Cain and his offspring.

Doctrine 4

21. Fourthly, in that it is also said that the one seed are the children of the kingdom, and that the other seed are as tares for to be flung into the fire; from hence we gather, that the seed of Adam are predestinated unto eternal life, and that the seed of the serpent are from the foundation of the world appointed to damnation.

Doctrine 5

22. Fifthly, from these words [offend and do iniquity] and [the righteous shall shine] we find from hence that each seed hath a law given unto it; the one the law of Reason, the other the law of Faith; otherwise sin could not be imputed to the one seed, nor grace to the other, upon these two appellatives [offend and righteous].

Doctrine 6

23. Sixthly, seeing it is said that the two seeds are to receive their rewards at the end of the world, which is eternal life to the one, and eternal death to the other; hence it is clear that the soul of man is mortal and doth die, and so cannot be capable of either eternal joy or sorrow without the Resurrection and gathering together by Christ and his Angels at the end of the world.

Doctrine 7

24. Seventhly, in that it is said that at the end of the world the children of the wicked one shall be cast into a furnace of fire, where shall be weeping and wailing and gnashing of teeth; from hence we collect, that the nature of the reprobate's torment, is an eternal fiery vengeance both upon soul and body at the end of the world; then endeth the devil's kingdom of power and glory.

Doctrine 8

25. Eighthly, in that this divine oracle doth say, that at the end of the world the righteous shall shine as the sun in the kingdom of the Lord Jesus; from hence it follows, that all the seed of Adam, who are the seed of God's own body, shall have glorious bodies and possess a personal glory in the presence of their God and the holy Angels, with astonishing new joys continually springing from their own seed of faith in that kingdom above the stars of all soul ravishing delights.

Doctrine 9

26. Ninthly and lastly, in that the period of this unfolded parable ushers in these words, saying, he that hath ears let him hear; from hence it is clear that none but the seed of the Son of Man hath the hearing ear of Heavenly truth; but I shall forbear at this time the prosecuting of this, being that it would make my Treatise too large.

27. Wherefore, now in the handling of these eight distinct observations, or divine doctrines, there will variety of matter ensue; and first of the First Part.

THE FIRST PART,

TREATING OF

CHRIST THE TRUE GOD.

CHAP. I.

Contents—1. How God became Seed. 2. A great Mystery to understand Christ's Incarnation. 3. Jehovah became Jesus.

1. THAT the Son of Man should be the eternal God is a great mystery to know and to declare, yet the knowledge hereof is revealed to us, so far as to understand, that he who made man became man, and dwelt amongst us.

Doctrine : Text opened

2. He that was the Seedsman became Seed himself, therefore called the seed of the woman,[1] because he took seed of the virgin wife Mary, which seed as he took was the seed of Abraham, which was the seed of Adam, which was the seed of faith, which was the seed of God, and so he took upon him his own seed, but changed into a condition of mortality, by dying unto his own seed, that was made mortal, and so quickening in that mortal seed, he became this Son of Man as to the human nature, but as to the divine nature he was the Son of God, yea, very God, as well as very man.

A mystery yet revealed

3. Though this mystery be deep, yet the divinity is true; and although the surviving Prophet doth say in one place that he wanted words to set forth the mystery of God's becoming flesh, yet doth he know more concerning it, and hath declared more than ever either Prophet or Apostle did, or ever could do, and we who believe are made partakers of their knowledge, besides our own experience which we daily get, by reading the three Records of water, blood, and spirit.

4. And the benefit we receive is much, for it brings with it eternal life, according as it is written, saying, It is life eternal to know the true God, and Jesus Christ whom he hath sent.[2]

---

[1] Gen. 3.
[2] John 17,. 5.

5. These two particles [of, and he]¹ doth not divide the titles into two persons, no more than that other saying of Paul, where he saith, Now unto God and our Father be glory, &c.;² but it is expressed in reference to the twofold appearance of God.

Doctrine 2

6. Hence the meaning of these words is no more but to read it thus: to know that Jesus Christ is the true God is eternal life, and so that Scripture is unfolded, and joins and twists itself with that other Scripture, He that hath the Son hath life.— 1 John, 5. 12.

7. Now these two sayings joined together with a third become impregnable [he that hath the Son hath the Father also.]³

8. Here now is a rock and a sure foundation for to build upon;⁴ the gates of hell (though thousands more be up in arms there, than in the narrow gate of heaven) can never, I say, be able to destroy the faith that is builded here; therefore my faith in the God of a despised Christ, shall, by his grace, ascend so high as to demonstrate in some measure, what the true God was before he became flesh, and what he is now and will be to eternity, and of the inexpressible benefits that accrue to us by our knowledge of him who is blessed to all eternity.

CHAP. II.

1. God is without all beginning and knows no beginning of himself. No end to the two Seeds after their Resurrection. God himself alone, yet a Kingdom in himself. Of the Properties of Divine Faith in the Saints, and in their God and Father. Of the Creation.

Doctrine 1

1. YOU that are under the teachings of the Spirit may know that God was from eternity, that is, he was without all beginning, and before all time; therefore let none propose this question, to ask, what was before God, for nothing can be before or after eternity; neither let no man ask how God became to be God, for that which is known to be from eternity, is not capable itself to know its beginning.⁵

---

¹ Philip. 4, 20.
² 1 Thes. 1, 3. & 3. 11.
³ 1 John 5, 12. John 1, 36.
⁴ Matt. 7, 25. 1 Cor. 10, 4. Applied.
⁵ Psa. 41, 13. Isa 9, 6. & 63, 16. Deut. 33, 27.

Divine chap.

2. Therefore it is that the Creator himself doth not know how he came to be God; for as the Prophet saith, If he knew a beginning of himself, then would he know an end of himself: for this is certain, that where there is a beginning, there will be an ending, but that which hath no beginning, will have no ending.

Objection

3. But some men may say, if every thing that hath a beginning will have an ending, then the joys of the Saints and the torments of the reprobates will terminate and have an end, for they were both seeds created in time, and that which hath its beginning in time, will end in time; to this I answer,

Answer

4. Although the two seeds were created in time, yet the matter of which they were made of, was from eternity; for the serpent angel was produced and made, both spirit and body, out of the substance of water and earth, being an eternal chaos of senseless and confused matter, in the place where the person of the Creator was resident.

5. And as for Adam's body, it was made out of the dust of this earth, the substance of which was from eternity, and the Spirit that was breathed into Adam was of the divine nature.[1]

Text opened

6. So that we see, that the matter that both the seeds were made of were from eternity, and that brings them both into a capacity of eternal life and death.

Doctrine 2

7. But to the matter aforesaid, the Creator was himself alone before any sensible living creature appeared in his sight, and yet did he not want company to associate himself with, because he was a kingdom in himself.

8. For this we are to mind that our God is a kingdom himself, and a kingdom in himself, therefore in his mortal state he called himself the kingdom of God, and John calls him after his glorification, the New Jerusalem, and the City of God, and a foursquare City, having

---

[1] Gen. 3, 19. 2 Pet. 1, 4.

reference to his arms and his legs, when stretched forth upon the Cross, then was the Holy City seen to be four-square.[1]

Text amplified

9 And our Lord may most fitly be called a Kingdom and City, if we seriously ponder in our minds the variety of those divine qualifications that are inherent in his blessed person; for these glorious and heavenly properties operating in the person of God, do make him become a City in himself: for what necessity of much company without, when there is such society within, and in such harmony, and it must needs be so, in that it all proceeds from one divine voice, called Faith.

10. A taste of this is most lively felt in many of these children of the kingdom; for as their Lord is, so are they in their measure, for the divine nature in them are streams from the same fountain, which doth abundantly nourish them.

11. Now those that have these companions within, have many times more variety of pleasures, than if they had a hundred companions without, unless they be such, that in wisdom and nature answer to the spiritual companions within, which if they do, then there is a blessed union, and it adds to the glory and makes strong and victorious. 2 Cor. 1. 11.

12. Even thus it was with the glorious Creator, he having these divine properties infinitely dwelling in him, must needs possess full satisfaction in himself, and not only so, but from the increase of wisdom, &c. in his heavenly and blessed nature of unutterable infinites, he must on necessity abound with continual new joys and ravishing glories.

Doctrine 3.[2]

13. Wherefore from his divine revelation and increase of new wisdom, power and glory, the Creator did foresee that his unsearchable wisdom lay hid in the infinite power of his word speaking, and the knowledge of his mighty power, together with his royal will and pleasure, was the glorious wheel that moved him to form living creatures to appear in his sight.

14. Which, upon the counsel of his will, he did most abundantly, Angels and man being the chiefest beings made purposely for his spiritual society, and then did the Creator take pleasure in the work of his hands, because in the hand is power, but the Creator's work in

---

[1] Luke 10, 11. Revel. 21, 2 explicated.
[2] From 5 J. R. 3. 15. 19.

the creation of every thing was without any bodily labour; it lay in the virtue of his word speaking only.[1]

15. And now had the Most High God enlarged his kingdom, and got spiritual companions without him, Angels being chief, but Man the chiefest, he having the nearest fellowship, according to the saying of John, saying, You have fellowship with the Father and the Son, which Father and Son is one God, as shall further appear hereafter.[2]

CHAP. III.

Doctrines

The Creator a God of a glorious form from Eternity. What the form of his uncreated Person was. Of the darkness of those that deny God to be in a Form.

Doctrine 1

1. IT is already declared, that the Creator's most glorious Spirit, is infinitely full of all divine virtue. Now is it to be shewed, that these holy and divine properties, as faith, love, justice, righteousness, goodness, truth and wisdom, with all other virtues, cannot be sensible of its divine excellences, or be a perfect blessedness, unless he hath a distinct body suitable to his glorious and eternal Spirit, to enjoy his divine pleasures to himself, and at his pleasure to distribute by measure into the spirits of elect men and Angels, the inshining glimpses of his incomprehensible glory.

Illustrated

2. For if it were as Reason hath imagined, in the prudent of the world, that the Creator were an infinite Spirit without any body or form, and that his formless Spirit infused itself into the whole creation, then could there be no God at all, unless the creature were God, it all participating of his spirit, in that its life were God's life and spirit, and then there would be as many Gods as living creatures, and then would the ox and the ass be more noble than an Angel, for the life and nature of Angels is different from the life and nature of God.

3. But such as are the seed of the Lord's own body they are enlightened from above, by this his last commission, to know, and may comprehend in the verge of their understandings, that as the

---

[1] 5 J. R. 3.
[2] 1 John 1, 3.

Most High God was a most substantial personal glory from all eternity.

Doctrine 2

4. Wherefore from hence, then, you the quickened seed of faith must know,[1] that it was of absolute necessity that he should continue and remain in his own divine centre, and so for ever be a distinct glorious being, that as in time he gave being to every creature, so there should still be and remain an everlasting distinction between the changeable creature, and the unchangeable Creator.

Explicated

5. And now to prevent an objection, this know, that though the Creator did in time change his Godhead glory into flesh, yet the purity of his nature neither was, nor could be changed, but only his infiniteness laid down in flesh for a season.

6. That he might for an everlasting astonishment unto men and Angels, clothe his God-head spirit with pure human flesh.[2]

Inference from text

7. Again, you are to know, that the form of the uncreated Majesty, before he became flesh, did not consist of any elementary matter, but it was a bright shining glory of uncompounded purities of so unutterable a nature in virtue, as that it was swifter than thought, clearer than chrystal, sweeter than roses, more purer than the purest gold, yea, and infinitely more glorious than the sun.[3]

2. Inference

8. Behold, you Saints, and wonder that this infinite Spirit should change itself into flesh; yea, be wrapt up in rags of flesh, and remains now in a body of flesh and bone; but this body being now glorified is as glorious, yea, this his body of flesh and bone is more glorious than it was before, when it was a spiritual body;[4] for a very glimpse of this his new spiritual body of flesh and bone glorified, struck Paul blind, and so it would have dazzled John's eyes too,[5] if his eyes had not been strengthened above nature, or the person of Jesus presented unto him with a veiling a part of his glory.

---

[1] 5 J. R. 20. 24.
[2] 5 J. R. 18. 16.
[3] Verse 24, 1.
[4] Acts 9, 8.
[5] Revel. 1, 17.

3. Inference

9. Moreover, although the body of the uncreated Majesty was of so pure, thin, light, soft and sweet nature, yet was it absolutely from the crown of his glorious head, to the soles of his divine feet, like unto the first man, Adam, not, the visibility of their persons that differed, but the glory of them only.[1]

A use of reproof

10. Now the learned professors resist this doctrine of God's being in the form of a man, and what is the reason? Is it not through some guilt of fleshly lust, which is in their natures, thinking the same thing should be in the person of God as they find in themselves, were he in the form of man; but I will not exhort the wise of the world to change their judgment, for they can but believe from the bare letter and the dictates of their own reason, which they have derived from their father the fallen angel, in the spirit of Cain:

A use of consolation[2]

11. But it is the seed of the Son of Man, that in time of a commission when true prophets are sent to enlighten that seed; they, I say, can trace the footsteps of the prophets till they come to the paths of God, and so find him out and know him, when their faith beholds him.

Text applied to both seeds.

12. Thus doth the seed of faith,[3] and the seed of reason, each of them run forwards in their several channels, until they come to their fountains, and there they drink; the one seed comes to God and believes that he is one personal glory, the other seed is flung out of Heaven, and hath lost its knowledge.

13. Therefore, said Christ to his own seed, to you it is given to know the mystery of the kingdom;[4] but to them, that is, to the seed of the wicked one, it is not given to know the kingdom, to know the true God; for the true God is that kingdom, and to the seed of Cain that kingdom is a mystery.

15. Therefore, am I now resolved to address myself to a free and full dispute with the sons of Solomon for their further convincement, for it is at hand now to be proved against all gainsayers, that the

---

[1] 5 J. R. 18.
[2] I L. M. Ep.
[3] Heb. 11,6.
[4] Matt. 13, 11.

Creator he is a God of a glorious form, and was, and ever will be, in the form of the first man, Adam.

CHAP. IV.

Doctrine 1. God is in the Form of a Man. Doctrine 2. No Nature without a Form.

1. O, ALL you wise Rationalists and Scripturian merchants, do you not find it written that Christ is not only equal with the Father, but in the very form of God; then must God be in the very form of man, if Christ was in the form of a man.[1]

2. Again, doth not the Scriptures abundantly prove this. What is the meaning of Moses, when he said, that God created man in his own image and in his own likeness?[2] Had not these words relation to Adam's body as well as his spirit? Surely it had, although it be written that we are created after the image of God in righteousness and holiness, as Paul saith.[3]

3. Can righteousness and holiness act forth itself without a body? Or do you ever read that righteousness and holiness was ever acted forth in, or by any other form, but the form of a man? When God said, be you holy as I am holy,[4] what, must their souls run out of their bodies to be like him? If they did, they would be nothing. Where would mercy, justness, meekness, and humility be? Why there could be no such virtue in being did not that nature centre in a body. It is said we are created in Christ Jesus unto good works: can good works be done by the soul without its body?

Cleared

4. Again, every living being was created with a body; why then should not the Creator have a body, and if a body and form, why not the form of a man, seeing no creature was made after his image but man? But more of this in Chapter V.

---

[1] Phil. 2, 6, 7.
[2] Gen. 2.
[3] Ephe. 4, 29.
[4] Matt. 6. Lev. 11, 44.

CHAP. V.

The World's doctrine

How that the principle of God's being a Spirit without a Body, is derived from Cains Seed.

Heathen Doctrine: Doctrine 1

1. THIS principle of God's being a Spirit without a body, is derived from the offspring of Cain; for none of that seed would ever own the God of the Children of Adam to be the true God, but did ever create to themselves a God of their own imagination.

How proved

2. For all the Heathen philosophers do teach that God is a Spirit without a body, and is diffused through the whole universe, every creature participating of his nature. This is the doctrine of Pliny, Plato, Pithagoras, and others.

3. And when any man had attained to some high pitch of reason, then they presently concluded that God was come into them, or a great part of God at leastways; for their Spirit God was of such a bulk, as that he could diffuse himself into all, and he that had a great measure of wisdom, was honoured as a God.

The antiquity of this principle proved

4. This principle took its ground in Nimrod, that great monarch and first establisher of idolatry, and the first grand persecutor of God in his select seed, therefore called the mighty hunter before the Lord. Some of the Jews[1] say that he persecuted Abraham for acknowledging one God in the form of a man, and cast him into the fire, saying, let the God whom thou worshippest come and free thee by his right hand.[2]

5. This Nimrod, having the fulness of the Angels nature in him, made him exceeding proud, thinking himself equal with God, for he was owned as a God; and hence it was that those princes and potentates that came after had their statues erected, giving forth a law to do adoration to them, conceiting their Spirit God to be in them after they were set up, as one Arnobos confessed before his

---

[1] Josephus, lib. 1. c. 3.
[2] Rchama, Jew Rabie.

conversion, saying, I did speak unto it and flatter it, as though some present virtue was in it.

National church, its doctrine the same

6. Now, doth not the Scripturian letteralist receive this doctrine of a formless God, and not only so, but glory in it as the fountain of life? Do they not shew themselves the children of Belial, for Belial is derived from Bel the son of Nimrod? One would think that Scripture professors should have a light surpassing Heathens concerning God, and yet they are as dark in their minds as the blind Heathen; for though they have eyes, yet can they not see, &c.

Proved

7. Otherwise that great learned Augustine could not but have acknowledged that God was a glorious substance, and his form the form of a man; yet he joins with the Heathen, and praises Plato for holding that God hath no body: therefore he argues thus, saying, if God were a body, he should have substance and form, and be subscribed to place; but saith, God is every where present, he is in all places at once.

8. Yet no place includes him, for he can be present, and unconceived, and depart away again unremoved (said this doctor). Now is not here a great wonderment of an infinite nothing, and yet is every thing, that is every where, and yet no where? Oh! palpable darkness. Oh! blind ignorance and sottish senselessness, what confusion and contradiction is here?

9. And Cresostom and Gregory are as dark as he, for they say that God is a spirit without a body, even as Plato, Thales, Democritus, and the Stoicks held; furthermore, Cresostom and Gregory say, that not only man, but the Angels nor the Archangels neither can or do see God, and their children in these days do say the same thing, which shews that the same error is entailed upon them; therefore said one of the learned priests of this age, that it was a great question whether we shall immediately see the essence of God in heaven, or only see him in the glorified Redeemer.— Again he saith, that he is uncertain whether seeing face to face, be an immediate intuition of the essence of God.

10. To this purpose writes several others, which would be too tedious to relate. I shall only recite the sayings of learned Carill,[1] who, on the 9th of Job, and verse 12th, saith, that neither Moses, Job, nor any Saint in Heaven did, or ever can see God; and Baxter[2] questioneth

---

[1] Carill on Job.
[2] Baxter.

whether ever any Saint or Angel in Heaven can see the essence of God or no.

Applied

11. Behold, what darkness is here, even Heathen like. Now you seed of the Son of Man, give glory unto your God in honouring his prophets, for they have taken you by the hand and led you into the paths of God, the Scriptures, and unlocked it to you; so that by faith quickened, you see your God, and do know that he is a personal God, and at the Resurrection shall see him face to face, as I shall make it abundantly appear in the eighth part of this Treatise. Have patience till then, and rejoice withal.

12. For this we may know, that these mens' disciples and hearers, can have small comfort in their hearts, when as they are taught that they must neither see God in this life by faith, nor in the life to come by spiritual sense, and so they must never see him at all; in these dark spirits is that Scripture fulfilled. 2 Tim. 3. 7.

13. Again, saith Carill, though Isaiah said he did see God,[1] yet he was judged by the Jews to come to the pitch of high blasphemy for so saying, making God corporeal, and for that the Jews put him to death, together for calling the Jews the rulers of Sodom, &c.

14. In answer to this, I shall not deny but that the rulers of the Jews might put the prophet to death for his doctrine of a personal God; but this I say, if they did, they will never see the face of God, but shall be kept out of his kingdom, as all will do that despise and speak evil of a personal God.

Carill

15. And Carill himself hath come short of the glory of God; for saith he with them Jews that were rulers of devils, Isaiah did not see God; he saw, said he, but a manifestation of God. Now what was that manifestation, if it were a shadow? Then it were not God, but the dark reason of Carill put a shadow upon God, and so it would not be God as Isaiah saw, but the dark side of God, as the Ranter said.

Error is old

16. Therefore this doctor gains nothing by alleging that the prophet Isaiah was put to death, for affirming God to be visible and to have a body; for though this principle of the Jews be as old as Isaiah, yet it is a lie: for let no one boast of tradition, conceiting it to be ever the truer, because the custom and practice hath been so long, for

---

[1] Isa. 5.

error and false principles have been ever since Cain; therefore in matter of religion, it is no pleading for custom, antiquity, or tradition; for Antichrist in Cain was before Christ in Abel.

CHAP. VI.

Doctrines

1. How that those that Worship a personal God are the Seed of Faith. 2. Why this principle hath not been public. How God, being without Form, is the Language of the Sons of Cain; being in Form, is the Language of the Sons of Adam.

Doctrine 1

1. ALTHOUGH Augustine doth say, that they may be ashamed that say God hath a body, yet none of Adam's seed, being truly enlightened, were ever ashamed of it; for it is certain that there hath been a remnant in all ages that have not bowed in their souls to Baal, but no age was there so many as believed in a personal God, as when the Apostles' Commission was extant in the world, as in the time of the Ten Persecutions.

2. All that time there was many that believed and taught that God was in form of a man, and how that Christ Jesus was that God, and that his Godhead Spirit was the everlasting Father, and his powerful Spirit was the Holy Ghost, and

3. These people that professed this faith were called Sabilians, from one Sabilis, their teacher, and were afterwards called by the name of Athrapamorphets, which name signifies the adorers of a God that hath all parts of a man.

Why truth cannot be public, proved by two Reasons

4. But the reason why this principle hath not been public, you that are skilful in truth may know, was for these two causes; first, in that the mystery of God, as to his form and nature, were not to be fully published until the commission of the Spirit came forth, and therefore it was but sparingly delivered of by the Apostles, because their work was to worship God in the name of a Son, as well as in the name of a Father, because of his twofold appearance; and therefore in their doctrine they preached the faith of a personal God, but in that they clothed it with the appellation of several titles, it appeared more intricate and mysterious; but yet there was enough declared by them to prove one personal Majesty and no more, to every discerning eye.

Reason 2

5. But then, secondly, this principle of Christ the only God, the cause why it hath not been public was, in that it never could be countenanced by earthly authority, but ever hath been suppressed through laws that have been made for that purpose by angelical devils.

Amplified, Revel. 11. opened

6. For as soon as Reason in the Gentile power had got the outward Court of the Scriptures into their hand, then did they subvert and suppress all men, and made them bow down to their way, telling them that they were the men that must interpret Scripture, and so they sat in the Apostles' Chair, even as the Scribes, Lawyers, and learned Rulers of the Jews sat in Moses' chair,[1] teaching for doctrines the traditions of men of Canaanitish offspring.

7. And this was one of the doctrines of the Jewish Babies, to wit, that God consists of no form; very many of them did teach, saying, neither composition, nor division, nor place, nor measure, nor going up, nor coming down, nor right hand, nor left hand, nor face, nor back parts, nor sitting, nor standing; and where it is said, he that sitteth in the heavens, doth laugh, &c.; these wise men of all such places have said that the Law speaketh after the language of the Sons of Adam.

Error discovered

8. But sure it is these wise men speak a language according to the language of the sons of Cain, and they conceit that their Law speaks so too; for they will have the Law to speak as they speak, for in that the Law doth not declare to them the form and nature of the true God; therefore by their interpretation they force the Law to affirm what they imagine of God, or else to say that the Law speaks after the manner of their own manners, speaking one thing, but doing another.

---

[1] Matt. 23.

CHAP. VII.

1. The Doctrine of a personal God the Language of the Seed of Adam, and will continue for ever. 2. How Jacob could wrestle with God, and how the Angels appeared and did eat and drink. 3. How Moses could see God. 4. And how Moses and David did teach that God was in the very form of Man.

Doctrine 1

1. BUT in that Moses and the prophets are the children of Adam, they in their Law do declare that God hath a glorious body, and that body in the form of a man, and this is the proper language of the Sons of Adam that hath been for ever amongst Adam's seed, and will continue for ever; first, because it is the true lip or language of heaven; secondly, because it is the soul-doctrine of all the true prophets and apostles; and, thirdly, in that it is engraven in the tables of the heart by the pen of a divine diamond.

Proved

2. Oh! you knowing seed of Adam, you may behold it written, and read the record both within and without, according to Moses's testimony, that God created man in his own image, likeness, and similitude; also Moses hath said God talked with Adam, talked with Abraham, and walked with Enoch; and Abraham, Isaac, and Jacob, they talked with God, and it was God that wrestled with Jacob; but some may say how could Jacob wrestle with God, seeing that God was a spiritual body, and not of a gross substance as Jacob was;[1] unto this I answer,

Exod. 29 opened

3. The most glorious Creator, as he did at that time lay aside his heavenly robe of divine glory, even so did he appear in a solid body as a type and figure to Abraham of what he should have as from his loins, not that his body was changed from its nature, but only veiled with a solid semblance.

Angel's nature opened & explicated

4 Much like as the Angels did when they appeared to our forefathers; they then as it were divested themselves of their glory,

---

[1] Gen. 2. cha. 3. 9. 11. 13. ch. 12, ver. 1. 7. cha. 5, ver. 24. cha. 32, 29.

and appeared as mortalized for a season, and so did eat and drink with man as if they had been as mortal men, when as it is certain that they remained spiritual at that time, only they veiled their glory, and the meat they ate did not pass through them and return into the draught as it doth with man, but was dissolved or swallowed up into their own nature; for their internal fiery glory did convert it into its own substance, as we find that the nature of fire doth diminish the substance of that which it takes into itself. Even thus when the great Jehovah hath appeared unto man, he hath either veiled himself or veiled the eyes of his servants, that his glory might appear, but as their spirits might be capable to behold; for no mortal eye is capable to behold God as to the glory of his essence.

5. Therefore when the glorious God, upon the request of Moses, would manifest unto him his personal presence in his form and glory, yet nevertheless was he constrained to cover the eyes of Moses, whilst his face and fiery flaming eyes were towards him, to the end that Moses might have power in the organ of his external eye to behold the glory of his back parts.[1]

Doctrine sound

6. Whence, therefore, the Lord having left Moses in the cleft of a rock, laid his hand upon Moses's face as he passed by, to hide Moses until he had turned his face by, that so he might see his back parts, because his face was too glorious for Moses to behold.

7. Again, Moses saith that God looked down from heaven, that God came down from heaven, that God went up to heaven, that God heard, that God saw, that God had eyes, ears, hands, and a mouth whereby he spake the Ten Words of the Law, and not only so, but that he wrote it with his own fingers.[2]

8. Moreover, doth not David attribute hands, ears, mouth, and tongue unto his God; and in the 94th Psalm, he proveth undeniably that God hath all these parts of body. In that Psalm, David was troubled to see wickedness so much abound, and he shews the cause wherefore it was that the hearts of wicked men were fully set in them to do evil, and it was because they did think that God was some infinite formless Spirit that could neither hear nor understand.[3]

---

[1] Exod. 24. 10. Cha. 33. 1. Ver. 20. 22. Proved.
[2] Deut. 26. 15. Gen 11, 5 & 7, 12. & 17, 22. Exo. 19. 20. & ch. 20. 1. Gen. 1. 10. 31. & cha. 3. 10. Num. 14. 28. Exo. 31. 18.
[3] Psa. 119. 73. & 34. 15. & 33. 16. 18. Psa. 2. 5. & 85. 8.

Cleared

9. But for this their wicked imagination, David calls them fools and brutish people, and convinces them of their ignorance, telling them that he that made the eye should he not see, and he that planted the ear should he not hear, and he that teacheth man knowledge shall he not have a heart of his own to understand, &c.

Abraham to Father's eye

10. Behold now, my friends, is it not evidently declared that the true God is in the form of a man; what need be more said: if there did, there were more variety of proof at hand, but time would fail to divulge one half of what hath been said by true commissionated prophets and messengers of the Lord's own sending, and yet, notwithstanding all this, the Scripturian Merchants count it a shame to acknowledge such a God; but those that be filthy, let them be filthy still.[1]

---

[1] Rev. 22. 11.

CHAP. VIII.

Doctrines

1. Shewing how that the Principle of God's being a Spirit without a Body, is the inducement to Atheism. 2. The Learned English Scripturian Doctor contradicts himself and condemns the Scripture, charging it with untruth in its Declaration of a personal Majesty.

Preface: Similitude

1. LIKE as that man that goeth into his garden more for the love of the colour and beauty of an herb or flower, than for its virtue or goodness; being thereunto enslaved either from his own fancy, or because of an ancient praise to that colour, is not to be reputed wise.

2. Even so, likewise, that man is not to be counted truly religious or spiritually wise, that walks into the garden of the Scriptures, not for the flower of truth, but for the colour of ancient received opinion, minding nothing more but as it agrees with ancient received opinion, or imagination of such as have been counted wise.

Doctrine 1

3. For in the nature of Reason, that depends on custom, there is not so much or great love to the truth of a thing, as there is a desire for the maintaining of its own opinion; hence it is that learned Reason loves or honors Scripture truth no further or otherwise than they can force it to acquiesce with their own imagination.

Doctrine 2

4. Also, again, learned Reason that seeks for honor, makes not truth the ground of its faith, but it claspeth either upon long custom, or man's counsels, or the authority of princes, or on great multitudes of people, or else on outward glittering shews of holiness, &c.

Doctrine 3

5. Wherefore if the truth of the Scripture, yea, the very literal record itself might be the ground of belief, then would the principle of God's being a Spirit without a body, fall to the ground, and there vanish away like smoke; then would there not be so many Atheists as now there is, for most certain it is that this heathenish principle hath made most professors mere Atheists; for that the Scripturian and Anti-Scripturian differ nothing but in name.

Proved

6. These things do I clearly apprehend, by viewing their writings and hearing their reasons; for by their words and by their works are their spirits made known to me; an instance of which I shall here give for a further information to such as willingly would not be deceived.

Doctrine 4

7. In my perusing a Treatise of one Doctor More's, called his "Natural Cabala," upon his expounding the three first Chapters of Genesis, I find these words of his verbatim,[1]

8. When God came to the greater masterpiece, man, he encourageth himself, saying, go to, let us now make man, and I will make him after the same image and shape as I bear myself, &c. So God created man in his own shape and figure, with an upright stature, with legs, hands and arms, with a face and a mouth to speak, and as God himself hath. Again, saith he,

9. God, taking of the dust of the ground, wrought it with his hands in such a temper, that it was matter fit to make the body of a man, which, when he had but framed, was as yet but like a senseless stature, till coming near unto it, with his mouth he breathed into the nostrils thereof the breath of life.

Note: it was Revelation

10. Again, when God had made a woman of one of Adam's ribs, he took her by the hand and brought her unto Adam; for when Adam was awaked, he found his dream to be true (for he dreamed that he took a woman out of him), for God stood by him with a woman in his hand which he had brought.

The doctrine above contradicted

11. Lo! hear you, Church of England, what doctrine your learned doctor hath preached; hath not he here declared God to be the very express image of Adam, but doth this doctor believe as he saith; no: he doth but dissemble; for in his defence (or forced violence) of his literal Cabala, he doth utterly destroy or condemn his former doctrine of a personal God; he speaks the faith, but believes it not, but contradicts it, saying, that it was the opinion of the Athrapamorphets that God had all the parts of man; this opinion he calls vain and ridiculous, saying, again, that it is contrary to the idea of God to have figure and parts, as his great grandfather Austin had said before.

---

[1] Dr. More's "Natural Cabala".

The doctor's blasphemy

12. But why then did he say before that God had figure and shape, and that God himself did declare the same; why he did not declare it, he said, because it was truth; neither saith he is it truth, although the Scriptures declares it; for, saith he, it is manifest that Scripture speaks not according to the exact curiosity of truth, describing things according to the very nature and essence of them, but according to their appearance in sense and the vulgar opinion.

13. Now you seed of the Son of Man, do you not see where these literal-mongers are? Do they not manifest themselves to be Atheists? It is not Dr. More alone, but thousands; for the Doctor saith it is not his judgment alone, but the judgment of Cresostom, Bernerd, Aquinus, and Augustin also.

His further blasphemy

14. But if you would know wherefore it is that the Scriptures hold forth such things, and yet are not truth, why this doctor's answer is, that God and his prophets doth permit the ignorant and vulgar sort of people to conceit of God as having shape and figure, because, saith he, the rude multitude conceive it a great advantage to think of God as some all-powerful person, that can personally appear to them, and chide them and rebuke them.

15. This, saith he, takes more with them than Omnipotency placed in an immaterial being, so that it was requisite to the ignorant to have some finite and figurative apprehensions of God, and there was nothing so fit as the shape of a man, and this dissembling, this doctor counts true prudence and pious policy.

Application

16. That dissimulation and deceit, is the fruit of worldly wisdom, it is most certain; but this doctor would have it to be the effect of heavenly wisdom.

17. Now what is this but counting the Scriptures a lie, and an offering violence to the fundamental law of heaven? Oh! that the Lord God of heaven would be pleased to cause this his commission of the Spirit to be made known to all whom he will save, that they may be delivered from such sophisters, and may know him, as he is declared by his prophets, for an everlasting consolation of their souls.

CHAP. IX.

Doctrines divine

1. Of God's becoming a Child. 2. Some ancient Prophecies recited, 3. How Enoch was the Priest of God, with the Manner of his Teaching.

Doctrine 1

1. NOW, having proved to both seeds, how that the true God hath a true, perfect, substantial body, distinct to himself for everlasting, and that it was in the form of the first man, Adam, now it remains for me to declare how that eternal personal God humbled himself and became a child, by clothing his pure Godhead Spirit with pure human flesh, dwelling amongst us hereon earth a matter of thirty-three years, and did eat and drink with man, and by man-devils, the seed of the wicked one, was he crucified and put to death in that body of his flesh, but quickening again by virtue of his Godhead Spirit, in that it was too potent for death to keep under, and rose and ascended to his kingdom of glory, and there doth he in his blessed body of flesh and bone glorified, shine as the sun, and is God over all, blessed for ever; Amen.

Prologue

2. This my epistle now is not communicable to any but the seed of faith, being too sublime for the children of the world to comprehend. Now, therefore, hearken to this all you, the seed of the Son of Man, for it is your life and your glory to know your Redeemer; for, for your sake and in your seed are revelations written.

3. That your Creator was a spiritual body, in form of a man, hath been declared to you already: now shall my faith endeavour to unfold his wisdom and power in his transmutation into a body of flesh and bone, which was an action of a wonderful humiliation, to the astonishment of men and angels.

The doctrine proved

4. Wherefore, in the fulness of time, his eternal Spirit moved him to descend from his throne (immediately (after the forewarning of Mary the Virgin by his angel of his incoming), even as swift as thought, insomuch that the eternal God was in the womb of the Virgin before

she was aware of him, only by a wonderful change in her soul she felt him converting his Godhead glory into flesh.

Illustrated

5. This was that wonderful mystery of God the everlasting Father, manifesting himself in a body of flesh, at which most men and women stumble and perish; for who can believe this report? none of the wise of the world, for a God of a non-omnipotency, the immaterial being, will take the best with them.

6. But you my brethren in faith and truth, behold your Redeemer, who (as one said) came skipping upon the mountains, bringing glad tidings of peace, skipping from heaven to earth, from the throne to the cradle, from the cradle to the cross, and from the cross to the crown again.

Amplified: Doctrine 2

7. Oh, you Saints, be astonished with admiration at the wonderful love, meekness, and humility in your good God and gracious Redeemer, who was the very brightness of heaven, the paradise of Angels, the redeemer of men, the death of death, the king of saints, and yet should be so poor as not to have a house to put his head in, nor a penny to pay tribute till he had received it of a fish. Oh, you Angels, look down (said one) and you may see the Almighty at the feet of man.

8 Lanctansius had some ancient prophesies of Christ from one of the Sibels. His words are as followeth:

Doctrine 3

9. Thy God, thy good, thou brainless, senseless dust, not know who past and played in mortal words and works below.

Doctrine 4

10. Afterward it follows: he shall be taken with the ungodly, and they shall lay hold on God with wicked hands, and spit their venomous spittle in his face; he shall yield his holy back to their strokes, and take their blows with silence, lest they should know that he is the word, or whence he came to speak to mortals: thou foolish nation knowest not thou thy God.

Doctrine 5

11. Ovid had these words from one of the prophets; God takes a view on earth in human shape,

12. I have caused, by my order, these verses following to be in legible and capital letters by the painter, to be set up in my house for every one that comes in to read, which were by me collected from an old author, being thus, verbatim:

Doctrine 6

13. I, who at first did make all things alone,
Am vainly asked my number, being one;
Three did not the work, it was only I
That in these three made this great Zizogie;
I know no three persons, I am the God-man alone,
In one single substance clothed with flesh and bone,

All the foregoing doctrines powerfully and clearly

14. But, my endeared brethren, above all that ever I read, next unto the Scriptures, that doth bear testimony to the truth of God's becoming flesh, is contained in the twelve Patriarchs blessings of their children, and I question not but that these writings are infallibly true, and did undoubtedly proceed from the sons of Jacob, whose prophecies shall be recited in the next chapter.

Proved: a preface to the proof from Enoch

15. Yet, mistake me not; for it did not so proceed from them as that all their speech and blessing was from their own inspired wisdom, but these divine prophesies of their God's becoming flesh, did most of them flow from Enoch; for many prophesies of God's incarnation were published by Enoch and other prophets but came to be lost.

Doctrine 1

16. Nevertheless, I will not positively affirm that Enoch did write down his own prophesies, for there was little writing or none in those days; but this I am confident, that the prophesies of Enoch were well known unto all the families of the faithful, being the ground of their faith at that time, and it is evident that there were very many families in his days, they all depending upon the teachings of Enoch.

Proved

17. For as Enoch was the seventh from Adam, so all the heads of the six families or generations were alive in the days of his prophesies; for Enoch was born about the six hundred and twenty-second year of the world, and Adam lived nine hundred and thirty years, so that Adam lived till about the three hundred and eighth year of Enoch's

life; so that Adam received much benefit and comfort in the latter end of his days by the prophesies of Enoch, the sixth from him, being his own seed and nature.

18. So that all these six heads, being all sons of God, honoured Enoch as the priest of God, and all their offspring that took of their seed and nature, were educated up in the faith of Enoch's prophesies, and this benefit was to the fathers before him.

Illustrated

19. And for the generations following Enoch, they taught it traditionally, from father to son, &c; Now this was as much authentic, and every way as much effectual, as if it had been recorded in books; for the table of the heart is the only place for spiritual epistles to be written in, because the writing there can never be corrupted, defaced, or changed; in that it is written by the finger of faith, and folded up in the chamber of the soul, the ark of the testimony.

Amplified

20. Especially, considering the long lives of the fathers before the flood, for their lives outlasted books of parchment, the ancient manuscript could hardly be found to last the life of Methusalem's age. Now this Methusalem was Enoch's son, and he lived through many generations, even till the end of the old world, for he died but about the year before the flood, so that Methusalem's declarations of his father's prophesies became a book in which all the faithful seed learned, and being under Enoch's teaching, they were thereupon carried on successively, and taught traditionally, from father to son, from Enoch till Noah, from Noah till Abraham, and from thence till Moses; and then came forth the Law moral to Reason, written in tables of stone, that the outward light might discover the inward nature of blind Reason.

Applied

21. Now if we had had but all the prophesies of Enoch, it would much have heightened our joy, because they were so full and so clear concerning God's becoming flesh; but Enoch's declarations were so heavenly, that the world was not able to bear it, and it must needs be so, because he was so conversant with God, for God had abundance of love for Enoch, therefore he vouchsafed him his company here on earth; for God came down from heaven, and walked, and talked with Enoch, and Enoch with him.

1. Inference

22. Now, if God had not had a body, Enoch could not have walked with him; but Enoch knew that God had a body, that made his sayings so full, and so sweet, declaring that his spiritual body would become a pure natural body.

2. Inference

23. Moreover, the Lord had such love for Enoch, that he took him to himself, to walk with him and to reign with him in the kingdom of eternal glory, as he did Moses and Elias afterwards; and as Moses and Elias were made the protectors of their God, when he had made himself a child, and clothed his Godhead with mortal nature, even so it is my faith, that Enoch was made the protector of the Angels, and was sole governor of heaven, whilst Moses and Elias were ministering comfort to their Lord and Saviour here on earth.

CHAP. X.

Divine doctrine

1. Christ prophesied of by the Twelve Patriarchs, and declared by them to be the true God.

Reuben's testimony: doctrine 1

1. GOD (saith Reuben) hath chosen Judah to be the king of all people, wherefore worship you his seed; for he shall die for you in battles, both visible and invisible, and shall reign over you world without end.

Simeon's testimony: doctrine 2

2. In the fulness of time (saith Simeon) all Adam's seed in the twelve tribes shall be glorified, when the great Lord God of heaven and earth appeareth, as a man, to save Adam in him, then shall I arise again in joy, and bless the highest in his wonderful works, for God, taking a body upon him, and eating with men, shall save men; for the Lord shall set up Levi, the Prince of Priests, and of Judah, the King of Kings, God and Man; so shall he save all the Gentiles, &c.

Testimony of Levi: doctrine 3

3. Levi, he prophesieth thus, saying, Now therefore my son understand, that the Lord will execute judgment upon the children of men, because that men continue in unbelief, even when the stone shall cleave asunder, the sun be darkened, and all creatures troubled

at the fainting of the invisible Spirit, and the spoiling of hell in the passion of the highest.

Testimony of Judah, doctrine 4

4. My kingdom (saith Judah) shall be knit up in strangers till the Saviour of Israel come; even until the coming of the God of Righteousness, he shall maintain my kingdom in peace for ever.

Testimony of Issachar, doctrine 5

5. Levi and Judah (saith Issachar) are glorified of the Lord among the children of Jacob, for God hath planted himself in them, giving to one the priesthood, to the other the kingdom.

Testimony of Zebulun, doctrine 6

6. God shall of himself raise up unto you the light of righteousness (saith Zebulon); he shall redeem all men from the bondage of Belial, and all the spirits of error shall be trod down, and he shall turn nations to the following of him, and you shall see God in the shape of man.

Testimony of Dan, doctrine 7

7. The Lord (saith Dan) shall be conversant among men, and the Holy One of Israel shall reign over you, in lowliness and poverty, and he that believeth in him shall certainly reign in heaven; for the Saints shall rest in him, &c.

Testimony of Nepthelem & Assher, doctrine 8

8. Nepthelem and Asher hath the prophesy following: By Judah shall help and welfare spring up unto Israel, and in him shall Jacob be blessed; for by his sceptre shall God appear, and dwell among men upon earth, to save the flock of Israel.

Testimony of Gad, doctrine 9

9. Honour Levi (saith Gad), for out of them shall the Lord make the Saviour of Israel to come.

Testimony of Assher, doctrine 10

10. You, my children (saith Asher), shall be dispersed into all parts, by reason of your sin, and so shall be despised as unprofitable water, until the Highest doth visit the earth, eating and drinking as a man with men, and breaking the serpent's head in pieces without

noise; he shall save Israel, and all the heathen by water, being God hidden in man.

Testimony of Joseph, doctrine 11

11. And Joseph (of whose son Ephraim I came) saith thus: I saw that out of Judah was a Virgin born, having a white silken robe, and of her came forth an immaculate Lamb, and on the left hand of the said Lamb was as it were a lion, and all beasts made against him, and the Lamb overcame them, and trod them under his feet, and in him joyed the Angels, the men and all the earth; these things shall come to pass in their time.

Testimony of Benjamin, doctrine 12

12. The Lord (saith Benjamin) shall take the kingdom upon him, &c.; he shall be despised and lifted upon high, to a piece of timber; he shall ascend out of his grave to heaven; he shall remember how base he hath been on earth, and how glorious he is in heaven. Worship the King of Heaven, which appeared on earth in the base shape of man, as many as believe in him shall rejoice with him at the latter time, and all these shall rise again to glory, and the other to shame.

Doctrine cleared

13. And thus you have the testimonies of all the Twelve Patriarchs, and do by them clearly see (you that are the offspring of Adam), that their faith was grounded in God's becoming flesh.

14. Moreover, for a further confirmation of this truth there is another evidence at hand, from an ancient prophesy that was found long since in Saint George's Church, in Venice, cited by Mr. Fox, in his "Book of Martyrs" and I am persuaded it was one of Enoch's prophesies. The words are these, verbatim: [1]

Doctrine 1

15. In the latter age God shall be humbled, and the divine offspring shall be abased, and Deity shall be joined with humanity; the Lamb shall lay in hay, and God and Man shall be bred up under a maiden's attendance; signs and wonders shall go before among the circumcised.

Twelve Apostles. Judas. Doctrine 2

16. Again, he shall choose himself out of fishers the number of twelve, and one devil, not with sword, nor with battle, in dejection and

---

[1] Fox's "Book of Martyrs," page 707.

poverty he shall conquer riches, and shall tread down pride, with his own death; in the night he shall rise up, and be changed; he shall live and reign; at last he shall judge both good and evil.

Doctrine 3

17. In the latter end of this prophesy, is a stretching forth and declaration of future times, following God's incarnation, touching God's third and last commission, in the judging of antichrist and the end of all things immediately following. The words are these:

The third commission, or last witness prophesied of

18. In the latter days two bright stars shall arise, raising up men lying dead in their sins, which shall resist the Beast and the waters of the Dragon, testifying or preaching the law of the Lamb, the destruction of the abomination, or antichrist, and judgment, and shall diminish his waters; but they shall be weakened in the bread of affliction and they shall rise again in stronger force,

Doctrine 4

19. Again, after the abomination, then truth shall be revealed, and the Lamb shall be known, to whom regions and countries shall submit their necks, and all earthly men shall agree together in one, to come into one fold, and to be ruled under one discipline, and after this shall be but a short time, &c.

Conclusion

20. Behold here all you worshippers of the Lord Jesus the one only God, have comfort and courage in your worship, for truth is on our side, sing a triumph over hell and darkness, for we are strong, for Prophets, Apostles, and the Witnesses of the Spirit, we all meet here in the faith of the person of Jesus.

21. These things being so, how can there be a trinity of persons, as the anti-churches of Europe do teach? from the seven Spirits to the seven true churches, I will use seven arguments, to confound the seven anti-churches in their doctrine of a three-headed God, as now doth follow.

CHAP. XI.

Divine doctrines

1. What a person in the Trinity is. 2. God is but one single person clearly proved.

First argument

1. FIRST, if God be three persons then there are three Gods, for what do you Churches call a person? or how do you define a person in the Trinity? do not you say it is a substance subsisting of itself? One of your Doctors defining a person in the Trinity, saith, that it is a living and understanding nature, subsisting of itself,

2. In this sense, saith he, a beast is not a person, because having life, yet they want understanding, now further saith he every person must subsist, that is, be some one particular thing, as John, James, Peter.

Proved

3. Now you seed of reason, by this definition, is it not plain that you have three Gods? for if a person be a distinct living being, as aforesaid, and there be three persons, each of them distinct understanding beings, as John, James, and Peter are distinct, then on necessity you have three Gods, and so you have divided the substances, and of one God made three, one in one place, a second in another, and the third distinct from the other two.

Proof 2

4. Now you formal Churches, you are so much the more in darkness and blindness and wilful ignorance, by how much the more you glory in your trinity of Gods, and yet you are to be pitied as children and fools, for saying and teaching that you believe that there is but one God in these three persons.

Proof 3

5. If James, John, and Peter, cannot be one distinct man, in one substance, how shall Father, Son, and Spirit, if they be in three distinct persons, be one God in substance?

Proof 4

6. Again, can they be one in substance, when distinct in place by their persons, or can James be in Heaven and in Earth at one and the

same time? if part of him be in one place and part in another, then is his life destroyed, and he ceases from being a person.

Argument 5, or Proof

Moreover, as aforesaid, can one of the three persons of the Trinity be in Heaven and a second in Earth, and yet these two persons to be but one in substance and undivided? no: this is impossible; and yet it is taught to the dark, blind, ignorant people, as one of their doctors saith, Christ (saith he) is every where called Jehovah, as by Old and New Testament doth appear, whereof (saith he) I lay before you this ground as most certain and infallible, that whensoever the true God Jehovah is said to have appeared in the likeness of an Angel or Man, this was the person not of the Father, nor of the Holy Spirit, but of the Son, who appeared to the fathers as a man, to note out the mystery of his incarnation, so that all these scriptures that speak of Jehovah appearing, do mean the Son, the second person, and neither of the other two, as Mal. 3, 1. Gen. 18, 13, 15, 17, 10. Hosea3 12, 5. Esa. 1. John, 12, 41, &c.

He confounded the substance

8. All these Scriptures, saith this Doctor are referred to the Son, and was the Son, but not the Father, nor the Holy Ghost; but where the Father and the Holy Ghost were then, he doth not tell, belike he means they were both in Heaven, whilst the God-son was on Earth.

Inquired into

9. Now I beseech you that are sober and moderate men, tell me how this doctrine can stand, either with reason, sense, or faith, if they would stand to it that they are three Gods, seeing they will hold three persons, they had some ground for their reason, as the heathen that held forth a multitude of Gods, or as others who held forth two Gods, a good God and a bad God.

The falsity of three persons discovered by a

10. But in that they teach that these three make but one God in substance, and yet are distinct each from other, as far as between Heaven and Earth; certainly if the God-father be in Heaven, whilst the God-son is on Earth, and yet notwithstanding be but one in substance, then must he be more monstrous and giant-like than the poets feign Hercules to be, who bears up the Heavens with his shoulders; but God, if he be as the world imagines, he must have his feet on Earth, his shoulders under the Heavens, and his head above.

6th Argument

11. Otherwise their God cannot be one substance, that can be both in Heaven and Earth at one and the same time, but how can they for shame say that their God is but one in substance; when, as they say that the two persons of Father and Holy Ghost have neither of them a body? yet they say the God-son had a body before his incarnation, and that he hath a body of flesh and bone for ever after.

12. But those that say that the Son, the second person, appeared to the fathers in the form of a man, yet notwithstanding they count it vain and ridiculous to believe that he had a body, for most of you Trinitarians say, that he had not a body, but only assumed a shape; and this is much what as true as to say witches may transform themselves into other shapes, or that men and women may be inchanted into a horse, a dog, a bull, or a bear, or any other animal; and is not this making of God a conjuror or enchanter, to change himself into shapes, and yet to say he hath no shape.

The 7th proof or argument

13. But to let these fooleries pass, let me insist a little more upon their doctrine of a divided God; you all acknowledge that Christ had a real body after his incarnation, and doth now for ever possess one to all eternity.

Proof 8

14. Now I reason thus with you, how can you make your God either co-equal or co-substantial; is there any equality between a man that hath a body, and a God that hath none, or what communion or concord can there be?

Proof 9

15. Besides, and how are they co-substantial? can that which hath no body, be one in substance? is there no difference between having a body and having none? can a shadow make a man? to be without a body, form or shape is to be nothing.

Proof 10

16. But reason, or rather the irrational doth say, that understanding and life doth make a person, and is a real substance; to this I say, understanding and life doth make a person, because it lives in a person, that is, it is one essence with its body, for understanding and life cannot subsist without a body, either spiritual or natural; can there be any understanding without a head, or any life

without a mouth and nose, to breathe forth itself by, and is not the egress and regress thereof the life in continuance.

Cleared

17. Now from hence doth it not clearly appear that the generality of professors of Christianity, do worship a divided God, but I shall further discover their error by several more powerful reasons.

CHAP. XII.

Doctrines

1. Christ being begot by a Father makes him non-eternal. 2. Of Trinitarians holding forth Christ as twice begotten. 3. Their Foolishness discovered.

Proposition

1. SECONDLY, it further follows, that seeing that Athanasion's creed doth say, that the Father is of himself unbegotten and uncreated, the Son is begotten by the Father that was uncreated; now you that are sober (though at present are under the discipline of this doctrine) may know, that that which is begotten by another, must be inferior to that which gave it its being.

Doctrine 1, proved by 3 reasons

2. Now how, or which way, God should beget a Son, none of them can declare, therefore, some do say he was begotten, not made, others say that he was not begotten of the Father's own substance, as fathers do their children, but that he did, by his mighty power, frame and fashion him after a wonderful manner.

Reason 2

3. Now from this I say, if the Son was from eternity, how could he be begot? and if the Holy Ghost were from eternity, how could he proceed and take his original from Father and Son? if the three persons were each of them eternal, that is, without all beginning, then they could not give being one to another.

Reason 3

4. Again, if the Son was begotten by the Father from all eternity, and begot again when he was incarnate of the Virgin Mary in a body of flesh and bone, then it appears by blind reason, that the Son was a double Son, and twice begot or made by the Father; and yet your blind reason will make this Son to be equal with the Father, although you confess that in his latter birth he was made lower than Angels.

Applied

5. O the darkness that lies upon the learned, had you known the Scriptures, then might you have known that the Son was but once begot or made, and that was through God's begetting himself into a Son, according as it is written, God became flesh; it is not said, you

blind guides, that God sent a Son to become flesh, that was begot by him before.

6. But the meaning of these words is no other but that God sent forth himself to be made of a woman, to redeem us from the curse of the Law, according as it is written, I lay down my life of myself.[1]

Text opened

7. Now where Christ saith that of himself he can do no thing, and that he bears not witness of himself, and that he came not of himself, and the like; that self as he speaks of is but his human nature, and that makes him but man, or our mortal weak nature.

Explicated

8. But then Christ's nature, which is divine, is that self that can do all things, and that is equal with, yea, and is the very Father, and hath power to do all things, having glorified himself in his new spiritual body of flesh and bone, which was conceived of the Virgin's seed, by his Almighty power, that could live and die, and live again; and now, behold, he lives for evermore, being one personal Majesty, distinct from heavens, earth, angels, men, and all things for everlasting.

Augmented

9. These things being so, is not your reason blind, to say that God sent forth any Son but himself? Is it not said that he gave himself for us? What do you think by that place, where it is said, I have sworn by myself, that unto me every knee shall bow? Now who was this that sware so by himself? Paul saith it was Christ, and he sware by himself, because there was none greater than himself. Heb 6. 13.

Cleared

10. Now, therefore, where was there a Father but in that Son, and a Son but in that Father, one God and Father in one person, all one; the spiritual and glorious body wherewith the divine God-head (which was the everlasting Father) was clothed withal, was his dearly beloved Son, in whom his soul or God-head Spirit eternally delighted in.

---

[1] John 10, 18.

CHAP. XIII.

Shewing how Father, Son, and Spirit, are proved to be one Essence. How the Father makes himself of no Value by undeifying Himself, to give his Son full Sovereignty.

REASONS ANNEXED.

Doctrine 1, Reason 1

1. THIRDLY, is not the soul, body, and spirit of man united and knit together, all making one essence or substance, individual and distinct to itself? And is not Father, Son, and Spirit as truly joined together? The Scriptures and all true prophets do affirm it positively; who then are they that do gainsay it? Are they not imprudent?

2. May they not as well say, that man doth consist of three persons, because Paul prayed that the Soul, Body, and Spirit might be kept blameless? How can God, who is one in himself, be divided into three persons?

Reason 2

3. If the Creator be one eternal Being, distinct from all other Beings, is it not necessary that he should so continue in his own divine centre? Infiniteness hath power to change its glory into flesh, but not to create other deities out of himself, because that would be against his glory.

Reason 3

4. And the most wise Creator can make nothing against his glory, but for his glory only; otherwise it would turn to his ruin: for if he should make out of himself other two Gods, as Son and Holy Ghost, and they both being; distinct from him, would on necessity require Sovereignty; for God cannot be God without Sovereignty.

Reason 4

5. Where, then, would his prerogative be? There can be but one prerogative; for if there be three, the kingdom is divided and cannot stand.

Reason 5

6. But this kingdom of one God will stand, because there is but one sole King, and he hath said that he will not give his glory to

another; yet all glory was given unto Christ, because he was the sole God; for men and angels, principalities and powers; yea, all things in heaven and earth, did, and for ever shall, bow to him and no other. This is my witness to the two witnesses, and the two witnesses do witness unto this God.

Reason 6

7. Again, if Father, Son, and Holy Ghost were not one individual substantial personal God, but that the Son and Holy Ghost were distinct from the Father, then, I pray you, what kind of a God would the Father be, seeing he both invested the Son with all power in heaven above, and in the earth beneath, and hath made the Holy Ghost co-operator with the Son, in order to the sanctification and government of the Church, the Son being made Head of it, and of all things else as aforesaid?

Reason 7

8. I say what a kind of a God would you make of the Father? Nay, do you make any God of him at all? Do you not make him useless, seeing he hath nothing to govern, nothing to do? Surely you think that one of your Gods growed weary with governing, as Pharoah, King of Egypt did, who made Joseph sole governor of his kingdom, and he himself did nothing, or else you think he is old, and so is willing to be at rest; and, therefore, having made a Son out of himself, and a Holy Ghost that he hath begot out of the Son and himself, doth therefore dispose of the government to them, not in tanto, but in toto, wholly and absolutely.

9. This is a necessary inference from your doctrine. What else can lie so incumbent upon it? Many more absurdities doth lie couched under your doctrine of a trinity of persons, but I have not time to mention all, only a few more according to promise.

CHAP. XIV.

Divine doctrine

1. Forcible Arguments to Disprove a Trinity of Persons in one God-head. 2. Of the Chief Good, and in whom it doth consist. Riches a chokepear to the Covetous.

Doctrine 1, Reason 1

1. FOURTHLY, if the Son be begot by the Father, and the Holy Ghost proceeds from both, and are so severed as that they are distinct each from other, then can neither Son nor Holy Ghost be God, because they receive perfection one from another.

2. Now where one gives perfection to the other, the other is not God, because he had not his perfection from himself; for if all had of themselves, none should give to other.

Reason 2

3. Therefore, if there be a Son and Holy Ghost distinct from a Father, then they can be no more than creatures, because they receive their perfection from the Creator, and not from themselves.

4. Moral philosophy teacheth, that there is but one chief good; whence therefore have you, Trinitarians, found out to the contrary: sure I am you cannot find out three Summum Bonums', neither by reason nor Scripture.

Text opened

5. The Scripture saith that all good comes from one good; even from the Father of Light, saith James. Now, whom is this Father of Light? Why, it is he you call the second person; for Christ is the word, and the word was the original of all light, and is the only chief good, and from him doth all perfection and goodness come; for he having all power, doth (since his Ascension) dispose of all gifts at his pleasure.

6. As when one called him good master, he replied, saying, why callest thou me good, there is none good but one, even God.

1. Inference

7. Here you may behold two things; first, that there is but one chief good, and that is God; secondly, that Jesus Christ was that one chief good, which is plain by these his words to the young man, in

saying, give that thou hast to the poor and follow me, and thou shalt have treasure in heaven; here did the one chief good promise the chief good.

8. Which might have been accomplished had Christ been received as that one good Master, or Lord, by him, who being the only God, had power to dispose of eternal felicity, joy, and glory.

Reason 3, 2. Inference

9. Observe, if Christ had not been that one good God, he would never have called the young man to the obedience of him for eternal life; but it is clear that he was himself that one good God, otherwise he might have bid him to have sought to a God distinct from him for the gift of eternal life.

10. But Christ knowing his heart, and that it was not according to his word, takes at his word's saying, why callest thou me good Master, or good Lord, as if he should say,

3. Inference

11. It is vain for thee to call me good, unless thou didst believe that I were he from whence all goodness comes: there is but one that is infinitely good, and the fountain of all goodness, and that is God; if thou canst believe me to be that good God, sell all that thou hast, &c., and cast thyself upon me, and though I here am poor, being out of my own kingdom, yet am I rich; for Heaven is mine, and Earth is your's: part with all the superfluities of it; if thou canst part with that part, go along with me, and thou shalt have given thee, by [me] the riches of Heaven, which is eternal life, joy, and glory.

4. Inference

12. But the man goes away sorrowful, because he was choaked with this world's riches, and so could not drink down the assurance of eternal life; for this world and his own fleshly devil was his chief good, and his soul's delight only; he could have been content to have, held fast his riches here, and to have had eternal life in Heaven hereafter, which is the religion of all the rich seed of reason, &c.

CHAP. XV.

Divine doctrine.

1. Of the dissimilitude there is in the Three Persons. 2. How Union is destroyed thereby. 3. Two great Furors in believing God to be a Spirit without a Body necessarily follows. 4. Of the Virtue of a Word from God.

Doctrine 1. With Reasons and proof abundantly

1. FIFTHLY, how can there be any similitude between the Father and the Son, or how can all the Three Persons be co-equal, when as you say that the Father and Holy Ghost have neither of them a body, and yet you say the Son or Second Person hath a body?

Reason 1

2. Shall the Son have a body, and the Father none? How then comes he to be the EXPRESS IMAGE of his Father's person?

Reason 2

3. Again, how can the Father have any person if he have no body, seeing a person is a substance subsisting of itself? Now, if he have no body, he cannot tell where to find himself; neither can the Son find such a Father. How then can blind reason find him?

Reason 3

4. Furthermore, how can there be any affinity or essentialoneness betwixt a spirit without a body, and a spirit with a body? Or how can the Son, that is a person and hath a person, be said to be in the Father, if the Father hath no body, shape, nor form.

Reason 4

5. Again, how can the Father be said to be in the Son? Surely he cannot for these two reasons, according to the article of the Five Antichurches, seeing they say that, first, he is a person distinct from the Son; and secondly, that he hath no body, but is a Spirit, and so is every where at one and the same time.

6. These two principles are as contrary as fire and water, or as light and darkness; nay more, for they are as contrary as something is to nothing, for there is a something of the one, but a nothing of the

other, but air, or an empty name, a cypher that stands for nothing, as mind the explication.

Reason 5

7. Observe, if the Father be a person distinct from Christ the Son, how should he be in the Son? For if he be in the Son, then he must cease from being a person of himself; for two persons cannot unite in one single substance, and yet be distinct from each other; neither can they unite as two qualities may, as wine with water.

Reason 6

8. Secondly, if he have no body, but is a spirit, and that this Spirit-God is every where at one and the same time, then he is incapable of being wholly in Christ; for being every where present at once, he can be but a part in Christ, for he must be parted into every thing, and every place, a part in Heaven, a part on earth, and a part in hell, a part in angels, a part in men, and a part in devils.

Cleared

9. Oh, the blindness of reason in the things of God, that cannot see that when the Scripture speaks of God's being in every place, and of living, moving, and having our being in him, and of his being in all, and such like; all which places are to be understood, of his unalterable Law, placed in every man's conscience, to be in the room of God, to tell God what is done, as a watchman, and to speak a voice in the conscience, to tell conscience likewise what it hath done; the nature of which Law shall be discoursed of in the Fifth Part of this Treatise; so no more of it here.

CHAP. XVI.

Divine doctrine.

1. Several more Arguments proving the Absurdity of Three Persons in one Substance 2. Of the Form of a Trinitarians Prayer. 3. Shewing thereby that they Worship a divided God.

Doctrine 1. Reason 1

1. SIXTHLY, again you say that the Holy Ghost is a person proceeding from the Father and the Son, and yet you hold that he is co-equal and co-eternal with the Father and the Son. Now this cannot

possibly be; for can that which receives its being from another, be made equal with that which hath its being of itself.

Reason 2

2. Can time be made equal with eternity: if the Holy Ghost proceeded from a father and son, then is he but a God of Time, and not a God of Eternity; and such a God will end in time. It is true eternity did become time, and time did become eternity again; but it did not create two Deities out of itself.

Reason 3

3. Again, if the Holy Ghost had not its being of itself, but proceeded from another, then is he no more but a creature, and being a creature, he must learn obedience.

Reason 4

4. Moreover, if the Holy Ghost proceeded as aforesaid, and was made distinct from Father and Son, into a person of his own, then must his God-head die, in his birth, or leave it behind him, otherwise he would have robbed God; for God will not give his glory to another, and if he parts with his God-head, he parts with his glory.

5. Certainly there is no such procession as the letteralists dream of, for God is one in three, and three in one; he is not one in three persons, but is one God in three titles: we worship a God in one person, called Father, Son, and Spirit; it is a self-begotten God, and not a God begotten by another that we worship.

Reason 5

6. Therefore, as Paul doth say, all that are of Israel are not Israel; so all that call themselves Christians are not Christians; some are semi-Christians, and the Trinitarians are but a third part Christians; for Christ is but a third part of their God.

7. From hence you may see, that the Five Anti-Churches of Europe do worship a divided God, a three-headed God, which is a monster, instead of the one true God.

A Trinitarian's Prayer

8. Therefore when they pray, they divide their prayers into parts, as they divide their God, and so they appropriate to each God a particular prayer, and their prayers are as follows:

9. Oh! Lord God Creator, give me grace to serve thee, and in order thereunto, give unto me thy Spirit, &c., that I may magnify thee, not

only for my creation, but also for thy continual preservation of me, for which I praise thee for ever. Amen.

10. Oh! Lord Jesus Christ, Son of the Father, I beseech thee to make reconciliation for me to thy

Father: Oh, stand thou in the gap between him and me, and pacify him, by shewing him thy wounds which thou didst suffer for me; pray thou unto him, for thou art his beloved Son, whom he will hear, and I will praise thee for ever and ever; Amen.

11. Oh! Holy Spirit, proceeding from Father and Son, sanctify me with thy grace, purge out my sins, and purify me from all filthiness, for the glory of thy names sake; Amen.

Application

12. Behold, now all that are sober, is not this a divided God that is worshipped in this manner? Oh, how are they lost in this their grand principle; they are in worse condition than the simple woman, that halted betwixt the Papist and the Protestant, for she not knowing whether to be right, but hoping that the one was, therefore in her devotion she prayed first a Papist prayer, and then a Protestant prayer, and when she had done, she cried, Blend, Lord, blend; and whether thou likest better, take too.

13. Even so, when these treble worshippers of these treble Gods, have made their orisons to all three persons, they should say, with the woman, Blend, Lord, blend; and which is the best accept of it, if thou thinkest that one may be above another; but if thou think they are co-equal, then must thou measure out to every one an equal share as aforesaid.

14. But it is certain they do not, for they are partial in their faith; for they give more glory to the Father than to the Son, belike it is because the Son hath a body, for they love a bodiless God the best, for the Jews are more honoured by them than we, because [though they deny the Son, yet] they own the Father, and the Father is such a one as they own, to wit, a Spirit without a body, and yet the Jews own no such thing as a person, but a God that is a paternal fire, a fiery spirit without a form, body, or person.

15. But I will contend with the treble worshippers in one Scripture argument more, and then I will leave them, and return into the channel where the water of life doth run. and into the garden of Eden, where the tree of life appears, and there we will feed of its fruit that we may live for ever.

CHAP. XVII.

Divine doctrine.

1. Of the one God and the one Faith; the 4th of the Ephesians Opened. 2. The Holy Ghost, and the Gift of the Holy Ghost distinguished: 3. Who it was that gave John the Baptist his Commission:

Doctrine 1. With Reasons proving

1. SEVENTHLY, and lastly, as there is but one faith, so there is but one God, as to be the object of that faith: this is evident as Ephes. 4th, compared with 1 Cor. 8, 4: In the first it is said, that there is one Lord, one God and Father of all, who is above all, and through all, and in you all.

Reason 1

2. Now, if there were many Gods, then must there be many faiths, one believing in this God, and another in that; but saith the Apostle in that other place, restraining the words to a particular select seed, [unto us there is but one God] the Father of whom are all things, and we in him, and one Lord Jesus Christ, by whom are all things, and we by him.

Scripture explicated

3. Lo! here is the union of Father and Son, in one personal existence, for what the one doth, the other doth, because they are one God and Father above all, through all, and in all; above all by his work of Creation, through all by virtue of Redemption, in us all by sanctification and belief of the truth, as the truth is in Jesus, he being; all in all.

Proved

4. For though the titles of God are many, yet faith finds but one single person in those double and treble names to pitch itself upon for eternal life; therefore what power soever is attributed to the Father, the like is given to Jesus, therefore said Jesus, you believe in God, believe also in me.

Inference

5. Christ did not here intend that they should have a double object for their faith, but that their faith should now be fixed upon him; as if he should say, you are a little wavering in your minds, because you

see me in a mortal state, thinking my Father to be God, whom you think to be distinct from me, but have faith in me, and then you believe in God; for in seeing me, you; see the true God: for I am the way, the truth, and the life; therefore believe in me and you shall have life, for I am now to leave you, and to return to my former God-head glory, or Father's throne again, &c.

Reason 2. 2. Inference

6. Again, as our faith is one, so our faith Jays hold but upon one; for there is but one God, one faith, one baptism; from hence have we peace, for now is the one spiritual baptism of fire and of the Holy Ghost made good and accomplished; when we have put on Christ, this baptism is said to be of fire, because of that spark of flaming forth in love and ardent zeal, which is of nature, to burn up the evil, and to purify.

3. Inference

7. Also this baptism is said to be by the Holy Ghost, because of that holiness and godliness that is in its nature, and because of the variety of the gifts and graces in order to sanctification of life, and true unity one with another.

4. Inference

8. Therefore it is that Paul saith, there is one body and one spirit, that is, there is one Spirit to animate that one body, and this is the spirit of faith, which is a spirit of union, which doth lead to none but Christ, because it came from no other God but Christ, as it follows in the next verse.

9. And thus the Saints come to be one mystical body, relatively so called, from the operations of the Spirit, which is the Spirit of Faith, which is the Spirit of God, and this Spirit of God is the Holy Ghost, which he promised to send to his disciples, as Acts 2, 4.

5. Inference, explicated

10. It is said there, that the Apostles were filled with the Holy Ghost, that is (saith my faith) with the gifts of the Holy Ghost; for we are to distinguish betwixt the Holy Ghost and the gifts of the Holy Ghost, as we are of those sayings of Christ being in us, and his light, grace, or faith to be in us. Now you may observe, that this saying of Paul, Ephes. 4, 8., doth expound that of the Acts, who saith that when Christ ascended he gave gifts to men, and what those gifts were, he shows in the following verse.

Scripture opened

11. Therefore you may understand that the Apostles had not the Holy Ghost essentially in them, but virtually, as it is in another place opened, to wit, Verse 38., so Acts 10, 45. Heb. 2, 4.

Opened

12. These sayings open that other saying of the Holy Ghost descending from Heaven in the likeness of a dove; this was but the gift of the Holy Ghost, that should rest upon Christ, of whom the heavenly dove was a type, or sign unto John, that he was the Christ that the dove should light on.

Opened

13. Now the Holy Ghost that came upon Jesus was given in these words: this is my beloved Son, &c. These words, though they came from on high, yet from no other than Elias and Moses, who being his representatives, had the gift of comforting left in their hands, to minister unto him at certain times whilst he went that sore journey in flesh:

Opened

14. John the Baptist had the knowledge of this, in that he had his commission from Elias, therefore said to come in the spirit and power of Elias; and it was Elias that did not only make him the messenger or forerunner of Christ, but also gave him a sign to know him, for the establishing him and better confirming him in the faith, because that certain knowledge gives strong assurance.

Amplified

15. Therefore saith John, he that sent me to baptize with water, the same said unto me, upon whom thou shalt see the spirit descending, the same is he which baptizeth with the Holy Ghost.

16. Now the voice that John heard from Heaven, proceeded from Elias, and from no other God; therefore it was that at several times Moses and Elias, either one or both, appeared to him and to his friends; as one time they were the instruments of making the face of Jesus to shine.

Cleared undeniably

17. Also, when Christ was upon the Cross, in the time of his agony, he cried with a loud voice to Elias; and it was Moses and Elias that were the

Angels that attended the sepulchre of the Lord, and that acquainted his disciples that their Lord was risen; and the two men in white that spake to the disciples at their Lord's Ascension, was the same Moses and Elias.

18. Thus all you that are appointed to know the truth, may see how and what is the meaning of those sayings, that speak of the Holy Ghost being given, for the gift of the Holy Ghost is one thing, and the Holy Ghost is another; for Christ is the Holy Ghost himself, as well as Father and Son.

19. Therefore you may read that Mary was with child of the Holy Ghost: what was that but the Holy God? And hence it is that he is called the Holy One, the Holy Thing, the Holy Child Jesus, the Holy Jerusalem.,

20. What then is all this but Holy Spirit, and Holy Ghost? See for proof hereof, Ps. 16, 10. and 71, 22. Isa. 43, 15. Acts 3, 14. 1 John 2, 20. Dan: 4, 13,

CHAP. XVIII.

1. An Advertisement to the sober Professors to ponder well the precedent Arguments. 2. From whence Strife and Division comes.

Applied

1. NOW for a conclusion as to these Seven Arguments. Let all sober men poise in their minds these reasons aforesaid that are exhibited, and see and examine whether there can be any solid ground in them, either from Scripture, sense, or reason, found to convince me of error.

2. Oh! vain heads of the Churches of England and Rome, cannot you agree in your worship; seeing you agree in your Gods, you might see the fruits of your religion (if you were not stone-blind) to be nothing else but divisions and strife, war and bloodshed.

3. And from whence doth this flow? Is it not from your worshipping of a false God? Your dividing and mangling God into parts and pieces, is the cause of your divisions and strifes as a judgment upon you.

4. Whereas if you worshipped one God, in the person of Jesus, then would that faith, life, grace or spirit that was given to worship withal, knit you into unity, and make you one body, to fit you to that one Head, and then could there be no discomposure, but you would be all one in the graces above said.

5. But this doctrine of yours', as it is the inlet to envy, so it is the road to Atheism; many thousands of the Romish Prelates have been mere Atheists, but for the glory and riches they have got, by their Ministry of the Trinity, they have concealed it.

6. Yet, nevertheless, one Pope Alexander VI., in the year 1492, brake forth into these words, saying, This fable of Jesus Christ hath gotten to us great riches.

7. But I shall leave all Atheists and false worshippers to their broken cisterns, and return now to the fountain of life, the Lord Jesus Christ our God, and prove by ten Scripture arguments, from positive sayings in Holy Writ, that Christ is the

one only wise and alone true God, being Father, Son, and Spirit, or Lord Jesus Christ, in one single person, blessed for ever; Amen.

CHAP. XIX.

Divine doctrine

1. No Redemption but by God's becoming Flesh. 2. Of the Virtue of Christ's Blood. None but Christ.

FIRST ARGUMENT.

Doctrine 1

1. THAT substantial sensible light and life, which was in form from eternity, was God; but Christ Jesus was that substantial sensible light and life, which was in form, and was from eternity to eternity; therefore Christ Jesus is the alone true God.

The minor proved clearly

2. As for the proposition of the argument, it is acknowledged of all that God was from eternity; now the proof of the consequent part is at hand, and clear enough. In the 64th of Isa, it is thus written, Oh! Lord, thou art our Father, our Redeemer, thy name is from everlasting; so Ps. 93, 2.

Inference opened

3. Here you, that can discern truth, may see that Christ and the Father is but one eternal being; for the Prophet says that God was a coming in flesh, therefore calls him a Redeemer: Now God was not a Redeemer actively, until such time as he was come, and taken a body

of flesh, and had trod the wine press of his own wrath against sin, which he did when he shed his precious blood.

Doctrine 2 Proved

4. It may well be called precious blood, upon a double account; for first it was the blood of God, for the God-head life was in it and suffered with it; secondly, it was precious blood indeed, for it washed away the sins of all the seed of Adam, and by this means he became our Redeemer, for his blood was our purchase.[1]

Doctrine 3 Proved

5. Again, it is said that Christ's throne was for ever and ever; to this Scripture Paul alludes to when he calls Christ the Creator: see and compare in the margin.[2]

6. Moreover, Paul salutes Jesus Christ thus, calling him King Eternal, Immortal and the only wise God; so that we see that Christ is the only wise God, both by the testimony of Paul and Isa.[3]

7. David's testimony may also come in, who saith he is from everlasting; and Christ said that he was before Abraham, &c. See and compare Psa. 90, 2. and 103, 17. and Psa. 106, 48. and 93, 2.[4]

Doctrine 4: John 27 opened

Christ tells of a glory before the world was, that he had and in his prayer (to his God-head Spirit within him, which was the everlasting Father), he said glorify me with the same glory I had.

Inference & 2. Inference

Now you that are quick may know, I say if you be quick in spiritual comprehension, you may know that this glory was not a distinct glory from his Father; therefore he said, glorify me with thyself. Did not Christ know here that he once did enjoy a Father's throne or glory, though now it seemed as lost, because mortality became an eclipse to his God-head spirit, insomuch that at some ebbs he scarcely knew whether the God-head spirit was within him, or without him.

---

[1] Acts, 20, 28. Ephe. 1, 5. Revel. 5, 7. Reb, 9, 14.
[2] Psa. 45, 6. Heb. 1, 8. Revel. 3, 21.
[3] 1 Tim. 1, 17. & ch. 6, 15. Rev. 17, 14. Proved.
[4] Psa. 41, 13. Isa. 9, 6. John 8, 58.

3. Inference

Nevertheless, revelation arose at certain times so high in him, that by the strength thereof he told the Jews, saying, unless you believe that I am he, you shall die in your sins.[1]

John 3, 18 Amplified

As if he should say, unless you believe that I am that God that the Prophets did say should become flesh, you shall die a second and eternal death: according as Isa, my Prophet, told your fathers, chap. 43, 10., If you would know who I am, search the Scriptures; they tell you there is but one God, and they all bear witness of me; therefore unless you believe that I am he, the Alpha and Omega, the first and the last, and that I came from the Father, and am with the Father, and one eternal bosom; unless you believe this, you shall die in your sins, and be damned to eternity.

Cleared

Thus all whose eyes are opened, may see that there is none but Christ, no other God but the Man Christ Jesus, though men or angels should gainsay it.

CHAP. XX.

1. Christ the sole Creator. 2. How we are created in Christ. 3. And how by Christ. Of God with us how understood, and of his Wisdom and Power.

SECOND ARGUMENT.

1. SECONDLY, he that is the Creator of the world, and all things therein, must needs be God; but Christ is the Creator of the worlds', and all things therein; therefore Christ must needs be God.

Proved

2. The major part is undeniable by all that own Scripture, the minor follows to be proved; in the 43d chapter of Isa, it is thus written, Thus saith the Lord, who created thee, O Jacob, and that formed thee, O Israel, fear not, for I have redeemed thee. So chapter 44, 24, Thus saith the Lord thy Redeemer, and he that formed thee from the womb, I am the Lord that maketh all things by myself, &c.

---

[1] John 8, 24. Ch. 13, 19. & 14, 1.

3. Behold here is it not clear that one personal Majesty made all things, seeing the order of speech runs thus, in the singular number [I myself] [by myself] [alone have I done it]. Now that Jesus Christ is this one only and alone true God, we have a positive proof at hand, and that he is the sole Creator, in John the 1st, verse the 8th, it is by him said that all things were made by Christ.[1]

4. Now compare this last cited verse with Ephesians, the 2d and 10th, and it will help to open that verse which saith, we are his workmanship created in Christ Jesus unto good works.

Ephes. 4, 6 Opened with Inferences

5. Here we are said to be created in Christ; in John, we are said to be created by him: now in him and by him is no great difference, it is but as he is Creator, and as he is Redeemer; and so it is expressed in another place [in him] [through him] and, [by him], are all things. This through him, and in him, brings the new creation, and so makes new creatures, and we are created for him that we may glory in his purchase.

6. Again, we are not only in him by our new birth, but he is in us by his spiritual seed of living faith, and thus is he a God with us, according to his divine nature, and not with reprobates, as one Philipes, a Priest of the Church of England, did say in his book.

The Priest's blasphemy

7. This Clerk, preaching upon Matt. 1, 23. on the significant name Imanuel, which is God with us, saith that Christ is not only God with us in nature, but in person; for, saith he, the reprobates are of the same nature with him, and he with them; yet is not he God with them, but against them.

If this Doctor's doctrine be not palpable darkness and horrible blasphemy, then am I mistaken; but let sober men judge.

Second proof

But to keep close to my subject, you may see that whatsoever God hath done, it hath been done in and by, through and for our Lord Jesus Christ; God hath created all things by Christ, said Paul, Eph. 3, 9.; and that this Christ was God, and this God Christ, is plain by Paul, also when he saith that all things that were made, were made by Christ, both things in Heaven and things in earth, and that in him every thing doth consist.

---

[1] Isa. 45, 23. John 1, 8.

John saith that he was in the world, and the world was made by him, yet the world knew him not,[1] but gazed upon him and said, what man is this that makes himself equal with God; we know not who thou art, or from whence thou comest; others said, is not he the carpenter's son, his father and mother we know are poor people of no account; if they had, they would have gotten some lodging at an inn at the time of his birth, who was born but in an ox stall, and had but a manger for his cradle.

Another proof

But although these Jews could not believe he was the Messiah, yet, notwithstanding his poverty, he was that God that created the world, and destroyed pride by humility, though his glory was wrapt up in rags of flesh; [2]although this be a strange truth, yet it is a sound truth, that he that made man became man.

Here is a mystery; God became a little child, he that made the Angels, became lower than the Angels; Heaven descended into earth, that earth might be capable to ascend into Heaven.[3]

A note of admiration

Behold a pattern of humility, that the great God should divest himself of his glory, so far as that he should not only become a Son, but a servant, and confine himself in the womb of a Virgin, to the miseries of a sinner, to a state of poverty, and to the death of a malefactor.

Isa. 53, 3. Opened

What calamities were ever so great as his were? Therefore the titles of Great and Mighty God, Jehovah, Lord of Host, were turned into this appellation [a Man of Sorrows], that is, a God made man, and this God-man made up of sorrows. Thus do we behold the humiliation of God, who was in this world, and this world was made by him; but the world knew him not;[4] but we, the seed of his own body, do know him to be God blessed for ever; Amen.

---

[1] John 1
[2] 1 Tim. 3, 16.
[3] Heb. 2.
[4] John 1.

CHAP. XXI.

1. Christ a God of all Power. 2. Two Objections opened. 3. Two Natures in Christ.

THIRD ARGUMENT.

Doctrine 1

1. HE that hath all power in Heaven and Earth is God, but Christ hath all power both in Heaven and Earth, therefore Christ is God.

Proved

2. Now for the proof of the aforesaid assertion, peruse these scriptures in Zach. 14, it is written, the Lord shall be King over all the Earth, in that day shall there be one Lord, and his name shall be one.

3. This scripture is a prophecy of Christ, as we may gather from these words [in that day] which intimated he was not then come in flesh, but when he should come, be should be King over all the Earth; and he should be known by his own seed, to be one Lord, and his name one personal Jesus, King of Kings.

4. Now after he was come, and after his death, resurrection, and ascension,[1] he gained that name of King of Kings; and the apostles might well give him that honor, for the Lord Jesus himself said after his resurrection from death, that all power was given unto him, both in Heaven and Earth; also, he laid down his life by his own power, and by his own power he took it up again, which shews that he was God Almighty.

Rom. 8, 11. Opened

Here may we see how this scripture opens that other scripture, where it is said that God raised up Christ from the dead; now observe, if Christ had power to lay down his life and take it up again, as he said he had, then there was no other God that raised him from the dead but himself.

Explicated

6. And if that place be objected, that saith I can of my own self do nothing, the answer is, that this is spoken in reference to Christ's human nature, it being weak, because our mortal nature, but divine Godhead nature being united to it would increase in power, to

---

[1] Mat. 28, 18. John 10, 18.

overpower death, and to do all things as was decreed and fore-promised, and so is Christ the mighty God.

7. That self, of divine nature or heavenly spark, is powerful influentially, but more powerful essentially in its own person, according as it is written, by myself have I sworn, by myself have I done it, of my own self have I power to lay down my life and to take it again.[1]

Texts Opened

8. So that this Godhead self can do all things, and in Christ was this Godhead, and never in any other, for the Godhead is not communicable to any but God, and it centres in a body, and that body was Christ, therefore said that the Godhead lived bodily in him, Col. 2. 9.

2 Peter 1, 4. Opened

9. And although it be said that the Saints participate of the divine nature, that is not as that they should have the Godhead in them, but only the virtue or fruit thereof influentially, and not essentially, as aforesaid: and that Christ Jesus was the God of all power, as aforesaid, hath been sufficiently showed, and will in the following arguments be made more apparent, and for this place see and compare these scriptures, John 10, 18. Mat. 28,18. Luke 9, 45, 43, and 10, 19, Ephes. 1, 19, 21. Jude 25, 1 Peter 3, 22. John 3, 35.

CHAP. XXII.

Divine doctrine

How that the Prophets God was our Jesus. All Adams Seed centre and settle in Jesus.

FOURTH ARGUMENT.

Doctrine 1

1. HE that was the Lord God of the Holy Prophets was the true God; but Christ Jesus was the Lord God of the Holy Prophets; therefore Christ Jesus was the true God.

2. Wherefore for proof hereof, turn your eye to Revel, chap. 22, verse 6, and you will find it thus written, And he said unto me, these sayings are faithful and true, and the Lord God of the Holy Prophets

---

[1] Gen. 22, 16. Isa. 45, 23. John 5, 26.

sent his Angel to shew unto his servants things which must shortly be done.

Proved

3. Now that this Lord God is no other but Christ, see verse 16, being thus written, I, Jesus, have sent my Angels to testify unto you these things in the Churches, &c.

Scripture revived

4. Observe that he that in the 6th verse was called; the Lord God of the Holy Prophets, is in the 16th Verse called I, Jesus; so that if there were no other proofs to be collected, this were sufficient, to prove Jesus all-sufficient.

Scripture enlightened

5. But we have more cords to twist, and many more positive proofs at hand, and worthy witnesses. Do but read Psa. 73, 25. and you may plainly see who are enlightened from above, that the prophet David's God was no other but Jesus Christ; therefore said he, whom have I in Heaven but thee, and whom do I desire on earth besides thee.

And illustrated

6 Behold here, was not David's faith fixed upon God in a body of flesh, working redemption for him in that body; this made David so long for his coming.

7. Oh, saith he, that thou would'st bow the heavens and come down, that thou would'st conquer hell by thy death and resurrection, and so lead captivity captive, and give gifts unto men. Oh, Lord, delay not thy coming; for thou art the God that will do wonders, and thy strength will be known by working salvation in the midst of the earth, for his throne is for ever and ever.; worship him, be still, and know that Christ is God; but after his exaltation, declare it, then shout for joy, for thy king cometh and reigneth; God is gone up with a shout.[1]

Cleared

8. Thus, if we trace the footsteps of David, he will bring us to a full view of Christ, and to no other God; all the rest of the Prophets pointed here, they all fixed here, and they and we do meet here: for brevity's sake, see and compare Jer. 31, 23. & 23, 5, 6. & 33, 15. Psa.

---

[1] Psa. 74, 12. Psa. 77, 14. Psa 46, 10. Psa. 45. Psa. 64. Psa 47, 5. Zeph. 3, 14.

130, 5. Isa. 8, 17. & 28, 16. & 64. 4. & 63, 1. Zach. 9, 9. Isa. 12, 6 & 51, 5.

CHAP. XXIII.

Doctrines

1. Of one God to be Worshipped. 2. Christ a Lawgiver. 3. Of the Natare of that Law.

FIFTH ARGUMENT.

Doctrine 1

1. DIVINE worship is due to none but God, but divine worship is due to Christ Jesus our Lord; therefore Christ Jesus is the only true God.

Major proved

2. The Scriptures do declare that God only is to be worshipped, and the extent of it is with all the soul, and with all the heart, Deut. 11, 13. 1 Sam. 7, 3.

3. So as God is to be worshipped, so there is but one God to be worshipped; and therefore it is said that God will not give his glory to another, Isa. 42, 8.

Minor proved

4. Wherefore, then, in the second record, it is apparent that all glory was given to Jesus, both by elect men and angels: who then is Jesus but the everlasting God?

David declares this, and saith that the saints should worship Christ and praise him for ever;[1] see Psa. 66, 4. & 6, 7. 7. & 72, 11. By Isa, it is written thus, Sanctify the Lord God of Host, and let him be your fear, and he shall be for a sanctuary, but for a stone of stumbling, and for a rock of offence to the carnal Israel:

Note inference

6. Now this Lord of Host was no other but Jesus; see Isa. 45, 22, 23. Zach. 12, 10. Compare this to Paul's words, Phil. 2, 10. and you may see this Lord God was no other than Jesus; for saith Paul, at the name of Jesus every knee shall bow, every tongue shall sware; see the

---

[1] Psa. 45. Isa. 8, 13.

same doctrine in Romans the 14th, ver. 9, 10, only he changeth the name Jesus for God, the ground of which is because in this place of the Romans he speaks of him as a Judge, and so calls him God, but in Philippians, he treats of him as a Redeemer, and so calls him Jesus.

Doctrine 2 Proved

7. Again, as Jesus Christ is only to be worshipped, even so he is the Saints only Law-giver;[1] see Isa: 42. & chap. 51, verse 4 Jer. 31, 33. This Law that doth give grace, and forgive iniquity, proceedeth from Jesus.

Note

8. Moreover, it is said by the Prophet Joel, 2, 32, that the time should come that whosoever shall call upon the name of the Lord shall be saved: now this God is no other but Jesus, for Paul applieth it to Jesus only; see Romans, 10, 11. and so did Stephen, Acts 7.

Note

9. Furthermore, Paul tells the Jews, that that which they called heresy, so worshipped he the God of his fathers, which God was Jesus, and Paul's Jesus was this God;[2] to this God Paul bowed his knee, and declared that every thing both in Heaven and Earth did so likewise; see Ephes. 5, 14. Isa. 45, 23. Philip. 2, 10. Rev. 4, 10. & 7, 11. & 14, 3, 4.

Applied: note Faith's power

10. And we the believers of the Commission of the Spirit, or Third Witness, do bow the knee of our soul to no other God but to Paul's God, which is Jesus; and if this God be not able to save us, then are we willing to perish, for no whither else will we go; if we perish, we perish. Therefore we conclude with Jude, saying to the only wise God our Saviour, be glory, majesty, dominion, and power, now and ever; Amen.

---

[1] Isa. 33, 22.
[2] Heb. 1, 6.

CHAP. XXIV.

Divine doctrine

1. Pardon of Sin comes in by Christ. 2. Of Sins Weight, and Death's Power; both overpowered by the Death of the Eternal Spirit. 3. How God did Die. 4. And the Despisers of the Doctrine thereof will perish.

SIXTH ARGUMENT.

Proposition. Doctrine 1

1. HE that can pardon and take away sin by his own power, is the true God; but Christ Jesus hath that power in himself to pardon and take away sin; therefore Christ Jesus is the true God,

Proved

2. In the First of Matthew, it is written, And she shall bring forth a Son, and they shall call his name Jesus, and he shall save his people from their sins; here we see that the name Jesus signifies a Saviour.

Note Opened

3. Mind and observe this, that all the Prophets preached the Promise, but the Priests and Levites only preached the Law, and could go no further but to the words of the Law, do this and live; but the Prophets point out an arm of faith, and not an arm of flesh.

4. Therefore Isa encourageth the select seed not to fear, because their God would come; even Christ, who was the Promise, and he should save his flock.[1]

Doctrine 2. Doctrine 3. Doctrine 4. All the doctrines proved.

5. Moreover, when God was come in flesh, then all those that were weary and heavy laden with sin, came unto Christ, and he eased them by pardoning the same; they had no whither else to go but to him, for he was that fountain that was set open for them; he was that Lamb of God that took away the sins of the elect world if his blood was of that value, as that it washed away all sin in those that believed it to be the blood of God, Revel. 1. 5.

---

[1] Isa. 40, 1. & 41, 3. 10. 15. 25. & 45, 5. & 48, 11.

Heb 9, 7. & 14, 26 Opened

6. And for this very end, Christ came into the world to put away sin, by the sacrifice of himself; as Paul saith, from hence you will find that he puts away sin by himself; it is by the offering up himself, there is not another God to offer him up, though it be said God gave his Son, for he gave himself, and he came of himself, and offers up himself unto death, as being the only sacrifice to expiate sin, because it is done through the eternal Spirit, his God-head Spirit, which was the everlasting Father, and was himself.

Doctrine 5 Proved. Note: Spirit infinite, Sin infinite

7. For this Spirit which he gave for the life of his elect, was an eternal Spirit, for had it not been divine and eternal, it could not have been able to satisfy the cry of the guilt of mens' souls, because that sin was against an infinite majesty, and it in itself was infinite in weight and measure, and would have pressed all men down into death, and kept them there eternally.

Note: a deep doctrine but a divine doctrine

Nay, and not only so, but it was so infinite in weight, that it made the eternal Spirit in Jesus to bow so far as to taste death, and so did hold down all life in God for a moment; but the eternal life being too strong for death, break through death, hell, and the grave, and through all the sins of the elect, it being impossible for death to keep him under, though it was possible for death to enter upon the life of God, for God did know that although he submitted unto death for the redemption of his seed, that his eternal Spirit had power of quickening into life again, and that his word of faith spoken unto Moses and Elias before, was of power sufficient to raise him.

9. Oh, the depth of the riches of the wisdom of God: these are great mysteries; I want words to set it forth, but although it is life, joy, and glory in all the elect to understand and believe this doctrine of the nature of redemption from sin and wrath, yet it is so high and glorious, that none of the contrary seed can receive it, they having not the hearing ear; wherefore say they, how can your God be eternal, and yet was dead; to which I answer, but as a paradox to that seed, whose eyes are veiled, and ears unbored.

Doctrine 6. Note: A Mystery revelated

10. Oh, you children of error and unbelief, rest where you are, and where no rest is, whilst we are made to know, and believe that our God, the Lord Jesus Christ, was dead, and is alive, and behold he lives for evermore; nay further, and that our God was dead and alive

at one and the same time; for the virtue of his everlasting word was existent, and stood as God, whilst his God-head passed through death more swift than thought.

Proved

11. Is any thing impossible for God to do when: his holy Spirit, or divine wisdom, moves him unto it? Doth not the Scripture say that he is the Alpha and Omega, and that he was dead, but is alive, and that he poured out his soul unto death, and that God purchased the Church with his blood, and offered up himself through the eternal Spirit?

Note: Certainly true

12. Oh, my friends, behold here the work and power of redemption: Do we not see, and is it not certainly so, that he that looketh not upon Christ as upon God Omnipotent and all-sufficient, will never be saved? He that goes about to take away his divine power or God-head glory, shall never partake of his saving power; he that will not allow him his Crown Royal, shall drink deep out of the wrath of his phial; they that will not receive the Lamb, shall surely feel the wrath of the Lamb.[1]

Much more might be said in proof of this argument, but it is enough; only peruse the margin.

CHAP. XXV.

Divine doctrines

1. Christ gives all Grace, Faith being the Root. 2. Of the Virtue of Faith. 3. And of the production of Divine Wisdom. 4. How Grace doth Multiply.

SEVENTH ARGUMENT.

Proposition Doctrine 1

1. HE that is the giver of all grace, must needs be God, but Christ Jesus is the giver of all grace; therefore Christ Jesus is the true God.

---

[1] 1 Tim. 1, 15. John 1, 20. 1 Cor. 15, 3. Isa. 53, 4. Heb. 7, 25. & 9, 15. 14, 28. Luke 7, 47. 48. John 8, 44. Mark 2, 7. 1 John 1, 9.

Proved

2. That all grace is given by Jesus is clear, John 1, 14. There is no grace that flows from the Law; it springs from the Promise; unto every one of the Apostles was given grace, but it was measured out from Christ; when Christ ascended, he gave gifts to men, and he ascended above all heavens, that he might fill all things.[1]

3. Now how could he have given gifts to men, and to have filled men and angels with revelations of new wisdom, had not he ascended above all heavenly power, from whence he did fill all his chosen ones with grace, and this grace is divers; therefore Peter calleth it the manifold graces of God.[2]

4. Now faith is the root of all grace; all virtues are fruits of faith; its the only primum mobile; it sets all to motion: therefore the grace of salvation entering the heart, gives life there, which life is faith: that kindled spark stands still and beholds the salvation of God, in which salvation seal it works; for fire is operative, ever sending forth heat and light, the heat of love, the light of wisdom, the perfume of peace, and the pearl of patience.[3]

5. For where there is strong faith, there will be powerful love, excellent wisdom, sincere obedience, paradisical peace, and an undaunted spirit; all these graces have their original from Jesus, the fountain of felicity; for,

Doctrine 2

6. First, faith; it proceeds from Jesus, see Ephes. 4, 7, 8. compared with Rom. 12, 3, 6. 1 Tim. 1, 14. & 3, 15. And Paul, in Heb. 12, 1,2. saith that Christ is the author of our faith; it is faith that closeth with Christ; and saith as Abraham said, I will not let thee go until thou bless me; mind these Scriptures, Ephes. 2, 8. Rom. 3, 22, 28. Col. 2, 16. 1 John 5, 4.

Doctrine 3

7. Christ doth not give this grace of faith to all; see Luke 8, 12, 13, & 22, 67. John 5, 44, & 12, 39. It is given only to the elect, and how, see Rom. 10, 14. 1 Cor. 15, 11. 2 Cor. 4, 13. 1 Cor. 1, 18.

---

[1] Psa. 68, 18. Ephe. 4, 8.
[2] 1 Pet. 1, 10.
[3] Luke 7, 50. Exo. 1. 4. 13. 2 Pet. 1, 5. Rom. 5, 1.

Doctrine 4

8. Secondly, as faith is given only by Jesus Christ, so is wisdom; the workings of faith is the well-spring of wisdom; when faith's eye is upon Jesus, then the heart stands open as the marigold before the sun, that the stream of love and wisdom may come flowing in; then is Jesus known, and pointing him out, saying, yonder is he upon his glorious throne in Heaven, the Angels, with Moses and Elias, attending on him and beholding his glory.

9. Oh, what work this grace of faith makes in the soul, when it is quickened there; then it multiplies grace, as Peter saith, grace and peace is multiplied through the knowledge of Jesus.[1]

Doctrine 5 Applied

10. Thirdly, peace is given by Jesus Christ, and it comes as a river to water the garden; this peace passeth all understanding of reason, but not of faith; for faith comprehends it: Oh, the well-spring of faith, Oh, the river of peace, how sweet are your streams; Oh, what is that fountain, then, from whence they came? Is it not the Lord Jesus Christ, the author of all our felicity, joy, and glory? Here we fix; our faith is the bucket drawing water out of the wells of salvation; our fountain is open, our hearts is open; let us take the cup of salvation, and call on the name of the Lord, seeing we are Christians.

---

[1] 2 Pet. 1. 2. 7. 8. 9. Col. 2, 3.

CHAP. XXVI.

1. Whence Eternal Life springs. 2. Jesus our Joy. 3. His Nature discovered.

EIGHTH ARGUMENT.

Doctrine 1

1. HE that gives eternal life, must needs be the true God, but Christ Jesus is the giver of eternal life; therefore Christ Jesus our Lord is the true God.

Proved

2. Look about you all you that desire eternal life, and see from whence it comes, that so you may glorify him that is the author thereof; why, you that have the new birth wrought in you, do really know that it comes from the Lord Jesus Christ, for he which gives grace, gives glory; the one is the seed of the other, for grace is sown that glory may spring up.

Text Opened, Amplified

3. He that hath the Son, hath life (saith John);[1] and why so? because there was no other God that could give eternal life but Christ; it is as much as if the Apostle had said, pitch your faith upon Jesus Christ, if you look for eternal life, and be not wavering in your mind, as if you could have life from a father or God distinct from Christ, for Christ is God, and Father, and Creator of the worlds, therefore stick to him and you have the Father; for whoever hath the Son as his Lord and Saviour, he hath the Father, for Father and Son makes but one personal glory.

Cleared

4. This doctrine is so clear that eternal life comes in by Jesus, and the Scriptures so numerous in the proof thereof, that it is needless to take up more time about it; it is enough to the wise, and so I pass to the next.

---

[1] John 1, 7. 9. & 17, 3.

CHAP. XXVII.

Doctrines

1. Christ is the Searcher of the Heart, and knows what is in Man. 2. All things open before Him.

NINTH SCRIPTURE ARGUMENT.

Doctrine 1

1. HE that knoweth the thoughts of the heart, must be God, but Christ Jesus knows the thoughts of the heart; therefore Christ must needs be God.

Proved

2. To know the heart must needs be the work of God, that makes the heart; and therefore it is written that God only knows the heart: Now the Apostle Paul saith, that all things are naked and open before the Lord Jesus; see Heb. 7, 12, and compare it with Revel, chapter 19. verse 12, 13, and chapters, 23. Here we see that Jesus is that God as knows the heart.[1]

3. Moreover, when Christ was in the state of mortality, he could see into the heart of man; in Luke the 16th, Christ told the Pharisees that God knew their hearts; now this God that knew their hearts was himself and no other, as appears in Matt. 9. 4 Christ there curing a man of the palsy, said that his sins were forgiven him, upon which the Scribes and Pharisees said within themselves, this man blasphemeth, and Jesus knowing their thoughts said, wherefore think you evil in your hearts.

4. So likewise Acts 15, 8, there the Apostle declares that God only knows the heart, meaning Jesus Christ, for say they he gave us the Holy Ghost, and purified our hearts by faith, which things were only done by Jesus Christ.

5. Finally, in John 2, 23, Christ Jesus said that he would not commit himself to the Jews, and the reason was, because he knew all men, and needed not that any should testify of man, for he knew what was in man.

6. Now did the Lord Jesus know these things in the state of mortality, how much more now then, being in the estate of immortality and glory, seeing his eyes are now as a flame of fire, that

---

[1] Jer. 17, 19. Amos 4, 13. Psa. 94, 9. Jer. 1, 4.

seeth through heavens, earth, angels, and men, and beholdeth all things and places in a moment, without charging his spiritual memory in the least; so that known unto the Lord Jesus Christ is all his works, to whom be praise and glory, for ever and ever; Amen.

CHAP. XXVIII.

Of Christ's Miracles.

TENTH SCRIPTURE ARGUMENT.

Doctrine 1

1. HE that could cast out devils or devilish diseases, that could give light to the blind, cure the lame, raise the dead, with many more miracles in his own name, and by his own power, must needs be the true God; but Jesus Christ our Lord did do all this in his own name, and by his own power; therefore Christ Jesus our Saviour must needs be the true God.

2. Now, though many of the Prophets and Apostles could do miracles, yet it was not by their own power; therefore said Peter, when he had done that great miracle of healing the lame man, we have not done this by our own power, but by the power of Jesus Christ, in the name of Jesus Christ.

3. For as Peter had no other God whereby he could be saved, so no other name or God whereby he could do such miracles, but in Jesus Christ the Lord only.

Proved

4. But Christ's miracles were all wrought by his own power, as is seen by that great miracle of raising of Lazarus by the word of his mouth; to this Christ doth, as it were, call in all the power of his God-head, and with his voice, being the voice of God, spoken unto a dead soul in these words, Lazarus come forth, and Lazarus came forth, from the efficacy, virtue, and power of these words, they being the words of God; and then was his words to Martha made good [said I not unto thee, that if thou would'st believe, thou shalt see the glory of God]; here he manifested himself to be God.

5. Now this great miracle was not wrought from any other God but what was in the blessed body of Jesus; for in the preparation of the miracle Jesus groaned in himself; after which forthwith he said, I thank thee, O Father, &c.; which shewed clearly that the God-head, which was the everlasting Father, was in him, and his revelation from that Godhead-Spirit gave him infallibly to know his power to raise the

dead, as God of all power, blessed for ever, manifest in these words as aforesaid, Lazarus come forth.

CHAP. XXIX.

How that the Incarnation of Christ was a Miracle of all Miracles.

Arguments to prove the Doctrine

1. I HAVING now performed my promise of the Ten Scripture Arguments, might insert several more, as his being the Judge both of quick and dead, with several others, but it will be touched hereafter, when I come to treat of the Saints' joys, and the Reprobates' torments; only here a little consider of the great miracle of Christ's Incarnation; and then to end this point.

2. The manner and nature of Christ's Incarnation, doth evidently declare that Christ is God; for what is the Incarnation of Christ but the very Incarnation of God; for was not Christ born of a Virgin, and this Virgin remained a Virgin still after all?

3. If the Virgin-wife Mary conceived with-child without knowing of man, then it must be by knowing of God, and it was so, for the Holy Ghost overshadowed her, that is, God overshadowed her with his own spiritual person; for if he had not a person, he could not have overshadowed her, and she was forewarned of it beforehand by the Angel, what God would do.

4. Therefore after his descending into the womb and dissolving himself into her seed, and had quickened into life, she certainly knew that God was become a babe in her womb; for observe the speech of Mary the mother of God, from a revelation of that Christ within her, flings forth, saying, My soul doth magnify the Lord, and my spirit doth rejoice in God my Saviour, he having that name given him when he was in her womb by the Angel.

5. And Elizabeth, at the same time at the voice of the salutation of Mary the mother of Jesus, her babe leap in her womb for joy, as being quickened by the babe Jesus, by virtue of his word spoken before, she being thereby filled with the Holy Ghost, or spirit of revelation, from which she worships that babe Jesus, crying out with a loud voice, saying, Blessed art thou amongst women, and blessed is the fruit of thy womb; and whence is this to me that the mother of my Lord should come to me.

Applied. Quakers reproved

6. Lo! here now whether Elizabeth and Mary did not own this babe, though as yet in the womb, to be their God and Saviour, even in his lowest humiliation; if the Quakers' people could carry God in them as Mary did, then I should not blame them for worshipping a God within them.

But the Quakers' God is a Spirit-God without a body, but the true God is not so; for if God had been a spirit without a substance, and been in her spirit, then could there have been no distinction between her and God, but she would have been God, and so that people are all Gods by their own account, but I pass them by.

Now to draw to a conclusion, I appeal to all sober men in reason that own Scripture, and have read this Treatise, whether I have not made it clearly to appear by Scripture, that Christ Jesus is the only true God.

Hold fast this faith and be sanctified, for this is the truth and the rock on which we build;— this is the life of our Religion, and though we are but few, yet we shall stand, grow, and increase.

Although all the Anti-Churches are against us, even from the old dark Arian to the new light Quaker, for the Arian denies the Divinity of Christ, and the Quaker his humanity; the one his Godhead, the other his Manhood: this is the whole Antichrist that denies the whole Christ; the first Anti-Christ and the last Anti-Christ meet here, being now to be destroyed and to be judged by the spirit of his mouth of his last chosen Prophets; this testimony of mine, being a Witness to that Witness, from that spirit of faith quickened in me by the doctrine of their mouths, which distilleth as the dew, and their record will stand, being the record of the Spirit, which answers that Witness in Heaven in the finishing of the mystery of God manifested in flesh, in one single person of his own, called the everlasting Father, the high and mighty God, the Lord Jesus Christ, blessed to all eternity; Amen.

THE SECOND PART:

TREATING OF

THE TWO SEEDS.

CHAP. I.

1. One Seed cannot produce two contrary Fruits. 2. Of the Signification of Woman. 3. And of the Serpent's Downfall.

Doctrine 1

1. THIS Second Part is to prove that there are two Seeds, and this will be made clear by Scripture that there is a good and a bad; now being contrary in nature, they must needs proceed from contrary causes, and experience shews us that there is diversity of natures in man, being all comprised under these two terms of good and evil.

Proved

2. Now from what fountain, or from whence, or rather from what fountains these contrary natures flow, is our business now to declare; for as the Scripture saith, one fountain cannot bring forth a sweet water and bitter; even so one nature cannot bring forth both sin and sanctity, but must proceed from two several roots or causes.[1]

3. Therefore, let every Saint know, that the original of sin came by the fallen Angel's transmuting himself into flesh in the womb of Eve, she being called woman, in respect of her bringing forth that seed which brought woe to man, woe to the saints, and woe to the serpents; being according as it is written, Woe unto the inhabitants of the earth, for the devil is come down among you.[2]

Texts opened

4. This was the Serpent-Angel, or Tree of Knowledge of good and evil, that Eve was not to eat of with her teeth; for eating with the teeth would not have contracted an evil hereditably.

---

[1] James 3, 11.
[2] Rev. 8, 13. & 11, 14.

5. Again, when Eve had eaten of this devilish apple, to wit, when she had taken his evil nature into her pure seed, then had she gained the knowledge of the good she had lost, and of the evil she had procured, and now was she woman indeed, for she had not only brought sorrow upon herself, but a guilt upon all her issue; although when her first-born son Cain was born, she conceited he might have been of her husband's begetting, therefore she unknowingly said she had received him from the Lord.

6. But she seeing his actions, as soon as he was growed up, then she was convinced that he was that evil seed of that evil tree, as is apparently manifested by her words upon Seth's birth; then said she God hath granted me another seed instead of Abel, whom Cain slew.[1]

Text opened

7. As if she should have said, I had received one good seed before, even Abel, on which my hopes were fixed, but Cain slew him, yet now have I another good seed in his stead given unto me, of whom shall proceed a seed that shall bruise the head of that evil seed that beguiled me; then shall the slayer be slain, then shall the blood of Abel, and the blood of

all my seed of Seth that shall be spilled as Abel's was, be required, and vengeance shall be poured out upon that seed by a seed from heaven, which blessed seed of this Seth's seed will pardon me and all my husband's seed, and give us glory everlasting, through his eternal free love, according as he hath promised, saying, that the seed of the woman shall break the serpent's head, &c.

CHAP. II.

Divine doctrine

1. Shewing how Cain was not of Adam's begetting. 2. The Serpent-Angel proved to be Cains Father. 3. Scriptures order not so exact as Reason judges it, only to confound Reason and to keep it in Darkness.

1. BY what I have said, you may see that Cain was the seed of the serpent, and so was none of Adam's begetting, though it be said that Adam knew Eve his wife, and she conceived and bare Cain, yet it doth not follow that Cain was begotten of him, for if it were, then it would follow that Adam was that wicked one.[2]

---

[1] Gen. 4, 25.
[2] 3 John 3, 12.

Doctrine 1. Proved

2. Now you know it is written that Cain was of the wicked one; if so, then he was not of Adam: now several learned men in reason, and reason's kingdom, have been compelled by the force of their historical faith, and their adhering to the literal record of the Scripture, to acknowledge that Cain was of the serpent; so writes one Ainesworth, a Priest of the Church of England; and some of the Hebrew Doctors say that Cain was born of the filth and seed that the serpent had conveyed into Eve; and one Menicham, a Jewish Rabbi, Saith that unto this world there closeth the secret filthiness of the serpent which came upon Eve, and because of that filthiness, death is come upon Adam.[1]

Further proof

3. Again, for further proof, you the seed of the son of man may, or do know, that the Scriptures calls things that are not as though they were, and sets that first which should be last, and last which should be first; to the end that Reason should never find out the meaning of God in the Scriptures.

Explicated

4. As in this place where it is said, and Adam knew Eve his wife, and she conceived and bare Cain, now her conception had relation to Cain from the serpent-angel, though Adam be first mentioned in this verse; but the angel's knowing of her is in a secret hidden saying set down before.

5. And as for Abel's begetting, it hath reference to Adam's knowing of Eve; for it is not said that Adam knew Eve again, but it is said she again bare his brother Abel, without any more mentioning of his knowing of her.

1. Inference

6. But when Seth was begot, it is said that Adam knew his wife again; from whence we are to understand, that when it is said that Adam knew Eve his wife, and she conceived and bare Cain, his knowing of her had relation to the begetting of Abel, though Cain be first mentioned, and the begetting of Cain was by the serpent-angel in the manner aforesaid.

Note: 2. Inference

7. For further proof, in Genesis, ch. 25, ver. 20., we find that Moses setteth down the death of Abraham and Ishmaell before he

---

[1] Rom. 4, 17.

describes the birth of Jacob, which was fifteen years before the death of Abraham, and sixty-three years before Ishmaell died; for Abraham lived 175, and were Isaac younger than Abraham by a hundred years, and Ishmaell by fourteen, they are found so long to live after the birth of these twins.

Doctrine proved

8. Thus we see that sometimes that is set down first which is done last; and why might not Moses do so in this place of Cain and Abel's begetting? Who shall dispute against this doctrine of Cain being begot of the serpent's seed, and Abel of Adam's? None but reprobates, after so clear a discovery.

3. Inference

9. Moreover, sometimes the Scripture speaks of one person, but implies another, as Psalms 89, verse 20, compared with verse 27., and Ezekiel, 34, 23.

4. Inference

10. From hence you may collect that the Prophets of God do sometimes put one person for another, and attribute that to one which belongs to another, as observe Psalm 89, verse 29., in that place is a prophesy of Christ, the words are these; His seed will I also make to endure for ever, and his throne as the days of heaven.

5. Inference or doctrine

11. Now observe the next verse, and you will find a change in person, though a close connexion in words with the verse before, being ushered in in these words, [if] His children forsake my law, &c.; now this particle [if] seems to make a connexion with the verse and person before, but these words have relation to Solomon, the other to Christ.

Proved

12. Even so, it is the very same thing concerning Cain and Abel, in the doctrine discoursed of; for Moses hath been as close in his description of. the rise and original of Cain and Abel, as David was of Solomon and Christ.

13. But who can understand and believe but the Seed of the Son of Man, to whom the knowledge of truth and promise of eternal life belongs?

CHAP III.

1. Of the Signification of Satan, Devil, and Wicked one. 2. Of the Genealogy of Cain. 3. Two Seeds in every Man. 4. No boasting of fleshly kindred, and of the vanity thereof

Doctrine 1

AGAIN, the scripture calls Adam the Son of God, whose son then should Cain be but the son of the devil, or the very devil clothed in flesh, and so became the father of all devils.

Doctrine 2

2. Moreover you that are quick in comprehension may know that wicked one, satan and devil be all one sense, for that which is called satan in one translation, is called devil in another, and that which the Hebrews call satan the Greeks call devil, or wicked, or wicked one, or wicked person, or wicked thing, see Mat. 13, 19, compared with Luke 8, 12, and Mark 4, 15.

Doctrine 3

3. Furthermore as the genealogy of the good seed do spring from Adam, so the genealogy of all evil doers ariseth from Cain, all those Jews that resisted Christ sprang from Cain.[1]

Objection

4. But here it may be said, how could those Jews come from Cain, seeing as they said, they proceeded from Abraham; to this I answer, they might proceed from Abraham's loins, as Ishmaell did, but not from Abraham's loins as Isaac did, for as they came from Abraham's loins as Ishmaell did, so they came from Cain, for that seed or nature that took in Ishmaell's conception was Cain's own spirit, it being uppermost in his conception, and that seed or nature that took in Isaac was faith, and was uppermost in his conception, which made him acceptable.

---

[1] John 8, 44.

Doctrine 5

5. For in Abraham was two seeds, faith and reason, or flesh and spirit, and so there is in every man and hath been ever since the Sons of God, namely, the sons of Seth took them wives of the daughters of men, that is the daughters of wicked men, the sons of Cain,

Proved

6. Thus these two seeds were brought in conjunction in one soul by the Sons of God going into the daughters of men,[1] and so the two seeds came to be mixed in one person in the moment of his conception, and according to the force and predominancy of each seed in the time of conception so will its growth be.

7. Therefore look what seed was uppermost in time of conception, that seed will grow up above the other, (or at leastways in time get mastery, by being capable to receive a word of faith to the raising of it up) and so became Lord, as for example, Abraham's good seed which was the seed of faith, was predominant in Isaac's conception, but this bad seed, which was the seed of reason, which in scripture is called flesh, was uppermost in Ishmaell's conception.

8. Therefore those Jews that Christ branded to be from Cain, were but of Abraham according to that flesh, although something of Adam's seed each one might have, yet the evil seed becoming governor or Lord, keeps the other seed down, as a conqueror keeps his captive under him.

Applied

9. From what is said, you see that it is no boasting of fleshly kindred, no, nor a spiritual stock, unless we be slips from that stock, or tree receiving the pure sap and vertue from the same life, and not by works of unrighteousness and infidelity, as the fleshly seed of Abraham prove themselves to be of the wild olive tree, though called by many rare titles, as sun of the morning, queen of heaven, prince of the earth, merchants of the world, and trees of Eden, and men of renown. Isa. 14, 12. Jer. 7, 18. Revel. 18,7. John 14,30. Ephes. 2, 2. Revel. 18, 3, 11. Gen. 7, 4. Acts 4, 26.

---

[1] Gen. 6, 2.

CHAP. IV.

Divine doctrine

1, No Evil from Adam's created Nature. 2. What is meant by Eternity. 3. Of the Extent of the Serpent's Enmity, 4. Forcible Arguments to prove Two Seeds.

Proposition prosecuted

1. TO proceed, if Adam did beget Cain, then there could have been but one seed, and if but one seed, and that seed the seed of Adam, and Adam the seed of God, then there could not have been neither strife nor enmity in this World, for the seed of Adam being the seed of faith, and the operation of that faith is perfect peace, full satisfaction, and pure love.[1]

Doctrine 1 opened

2. Wherefore then from this nature cannot proceed the evil of enmity, for pure love thinketh no evil, but this enmity lying in the two seeds, according as it is written, I will put enmity between the seed of the woman and the seed of the serpent; now observe, it is not said, I will put a difference, but I will put an enmity, that is, an absolute hatred or perpetual war, and not a strife or debate, for that may be reconcileable.[2]

Doctrine 2 Proved

3. Again, seeing it is written that there is an emnity put between the two seeds, this shews clearly that there are two seeds, and it was most apparently made manifest when Christ suffered death by the hands of wicked men, then was the seed of the woman put to death by the seed of the serpent.

Objection

4. But here it may be objected, is it not said that the seed of the woman should break the serpent's head, which seed was Christ; how then did that seed break the head of the serpent, seeing the serpent appeared to have the greater power, in that its power extended so far as to put Christ the Lord to death,[3] answer,

---

[1] Rom. 13.
[2] Gen. 3, 15.
[3] Mat. 23, 33.

The serpent's seed putting Christ to death, was but bruising of his heel, because it was natural death, but Christ that seed of the woman broke the head of the seed of the serpent in all his persecutors, by sealing them up to the second or eternal death, and this he did when he called them vipers, serpents, devils, blind guides, and the like, and pronounced those woes against them.[1]

Moreover, if all the world sprang from one root, then the doctrine of election and rejection were vain, and of no value, for either all must be saved or all must be damned, if a good seed, then saved, if an evil, then damned, for as is the tree, so is its root; a good tree cannot bring forth evil fruit, nor a corrupt tree good fruit.

Two seeds proved

But it is evident that there are two seeds by the opposition and contrariety of natures, if you were of the world, (said Christ) the world would love its own, &c. as if the Lord should have said, you are my peculiar people, I have chosen you and set my love upon you, I have brought you out of the world from amongst the children of the wicked, you were polluted but I have purged you and made you clean by my word, in bidden you or bringing you out of that wicked generation.[2]

Therefore it is that they hate you for the nature of the world is to hate those that are not of their own nature, therefore look for no peace but what you have in me, for there is no agreement betwixt me and Belial.[3]

Cleared

Wherefore from hence it is clear that there are two seeds, and that Cain sprang from the serpent angel, and was not of Adam's begetting, now there are many of opinion that Cain and Abel were both born at a time, as Calvin and others, and of the Jewish Rabbi's, as Perkins and Eleser do hold that they were twins, but this opinion is not true, I only shew what reason doth hold or can say, &c.

---

[1] Mat. 7, 17.
[2] Mat. 2, 18. Isa. 43, 20. Psa, 132, 13. John 13, 18 and 15, 16. 1 Pet. 2, 4.
[3] John 14, 27, and 16, 33. John 8, 23. Mat. 10, 22. And 24, 13.

CHAP. V.

Doctrines ingrossed

1. How Men are called by the Name of Trees. 2. How that Nature in Man that is uppermost, gives the denomination to Man. 3. From whence Evil is derived. 4. How the Elect are saved between Commissions.

Doctrine 1

1. HERE I shall shew that the tree of knowledge was not a natural tree; if it had, it could not have operated such venom in all mankind: the Scripture, we know, calls men by the name of trees; there is mention made of the good olive tree, and the wild olive tree, the wild olive is the state in nature,[1] or Reason the devil, which is wild by nature, and the good olive tree is the person of Christ.

This good olive tree is called by the name of the tree of life, the wild olive is called by the tree of knowledge, &c. Also the Son of Man he is called a vine tree, and his seed are called vines, because they participate of his nature,[2] and although the seed of the fallen angel are called vines, yet are they but strange vines; even as adulterate gold shew one thing but are another.

The two seeds distinguished

Therefore their fruits discover them, the good vine brings forth sweet and tender grapes, which makes delicate wine, called the pure blood of the grape, which is of such virtue, as that it makes glad the heart of man.

But the strange vine, its grapes are called sour grapes, and wild grapes, as in Isa, chapter 5, Jeremiah complains of the House of Israel, saying (in the person of God), I had planted them a noble vine, holy an upright seed: how then art thou turned into a degenerate plant of a strange vine unto me.[3]

This House of Judah and Israel degenerated, that is, their evil seed growed stronger and stronger, until it had captivated the good seed, and brought it under.

---

[1] Rom. 11.
[2] Rev. 22, 2. John 15, 1. Isa. 5. Jer. 2.
[3] Deut. 32, 22. Ezek. 18, 2.

So that every one comes to have his denomination according to the operation of his seed; if the good seed be prevalent as in Abraham, Isaac, Jacob, then it is a noble vine; but if the evil seed be prevalent as in Sham, Ishmaell, Esau, and the like, whose fruits are covetousness, oppression, envy, malice, &c., then it is a wild olive; and so are trees that bear wormwood and gall, and as Moses saith, their wine is the wine of dragons.[1]

Doctrine 2 Explicated

Mind here and observe, and you will find it clear, that this evil tree is described to be from the dragon, which dragon is the serpent-angel, which serpent-angel was the tree of knowledge of good and evil, and through his becoming flesh, in that flesh was the poison and venom of the dragon-devil, and so streamed through the loins of Cain and his offspring, and this became poison in the pot, as 2 Kings, 4, 39, 40., that is in the bodies of men and women, and in all the sons of Adam, but is purged out through belief and obedience to the Lords Prophets, their faith being quickened by a true ministry, are again brought into the true vine, Christ Jesus.

For Christ, the tree of life, is merciful to his own seed, and will save it to his elect, who live not under a true ministry, he there preserving their generated faith even from the womb, causing the innocent seed to keep uppermost, and to such innocency of life, serves for their way, and is acceptable without further knowledge, especially if any have but so much light, either from the hearing of the letter of the Scripture or without it, as to understand that there is a God without them, whose grace they long to know, that they might be saved by it

Doctrine 3

But as for the elect that live under a true ministry and have broke the Law, this ministry quickeneth them (for there is no quickening power but in a Commission), and brings them from under the power and dominion of sin, of whom before they were led captive; to these having much forgiven and much given, there is much required, and such become lovers of God, through the knowledge of free-grace in the pardon of sin.[2]

---

[1] Deut. 2, 9. Lam. 3, 19. Deut. 32, 33.
[2] Ephe. 2, 1. Rom. 6, 14. 2 Tim. 2, 16. Luke 7, 47.

CHAP. VI.

1. How that Wicked Men are called Trees, the King of Assyria had his original from the Tree of Knowledge in the Garden of Eden, with many other Princes, proved clearly. 2. Of a Prelates Doctrine of the Tree of Knowledge.

AGAIN, for a further consideration, that all wicked men are called trees, let it be considered what the Prophet Ezekiel writeth concerning Pharoah, and of the Kings of Assyria, with other Princes and Potentates of the Earth.[1]

Doctrine 1

The Assyrian (saith the Prophet) was a cedar in Lebanan, with his branches, and with a shadowing shroud, and of a high stature, &c. The waters made him great, and his rivers running round about, he plants, and sent out his little rivers unto all the trees of the field.

Therefore his height was exalted above all the trees of the field, for under his shadow dwelt all great nations; thus was he fair in his greatness, in the length of his branches, for his root was by great waters.

The cedars in the garden of God could not hide him; the fir trees were not like his boughs, and the chesnut trees were not like his branches, nor any trees in the garden of God.

Behold here the state of Reasons glory, in the seed of the tree of knowledge of good and evil. Do you not see that it was such a tree in its spiritual state, that it would not only make one wise that eat thereof, but he should be great and powerful also.

Inference

Here this great King of Assyria, having the fulness of the Angel's nature in him bodily, is said to be a cedar tree; yea, a tree higher than all the trees of the field; no tree in the garden of Eden was so high, though they were of the same nature with him: yet was he so high as to overtop them all, and to overshadow all nations; no tree in the garden of God comparable to him, no prince or potentate that were in those countries that could out-top him for beauty, height, strength, and compass; and the ground of his greatness was, first, because he was a tree of large stature, and of lovely beauty, and of great power;

---

[1] Ezek. 31, 3. 4. 5. 6.

secondly, in that he was a tree placed by the rivers of waters, and all his subjects were as plants about him; thirdly, because the Lord had not blowed upon this tall cedar, but was pleased to let him have all the glory of this world to serve himself in, and all his adherents, especially such as are ripe in his nature.

Inference

For these trees receiving of the dews of the natural heavens, and being rooted in this earth, and the earth being made fruitful by virtue of the waters, it became as rivers of waters in their souls, or as a Heaven in their hearts, especially considering their dominion and power in conquering kingdoms and taking of spoils. This made them grow high as cedars in arrogancy and pride, looking upon themselves to be as gods of this world, and so they were, and were honoured accordingly by the branches, which were great nations.

Thus you may see, whose eyes are opened, what glory is given to the trees of Eden, the spirit and seed of reason, the king in man.

There was none of this glory to the tree of life, when he was in mortality; for though he was Lord of all, yet was he servant to all.[1]

Inference

Again, it is said that this reprobate tree was so great, that all the trees of the garden of Eden envied him: now these trees were of the same nature with this great tree, therefore called trees of Eden also, and they were so called, because they proceeded from that tree of the knowledge of good and evil, that was in the garden of Eden.

4. Inference

Also this great King Sancherub, with other Kings of Assyria, Egypt, Edom, and other countries, were trees of Eden and sprang from the Angelical tree, only Sancherub at that time was the greatest tree, and out-topped them all, yet they were all of the same nature and of the same descent; yet did they fight one against another, being ambitious of Godlike authority, that seed never delighting in equality or inferiority, that being abominable to that proud angelical seed.

Inference

For all those trees in the garden that envied Sancherub, were princes and kings of the earth, that were to be heirs of heaven here, and hell hereafter, and eternal wrath after all, as appears by the Prophets' words.

---

[1] Ezek. 5, 3. Phil. 2, 7.

Proved

Therefore saith the Prophet, chap. 31, 32., that all those trees of Eden, with their branches, go all down into the pit, the grave, and hell, where all the uncircumcised seed are; they are gone down to hell with their weapons of war, and they have laid their swords under their heads, but their iniquity shall be upon their bones, although they were terrible in the land of the living.

Illustrated

As if the Prophet should say, although these great trees of the fallen Angel's seed did think to have been rule for ever, yet their decreed time is over, and they are gone down in the grave which is hell, and their bones shall bear their iniquity, for the resurrection-day will come that the earth shall no more hide her slain, but shall cast her out, and those bones that were so strong here to cause suffering, shall then receive the fruit of its iniquity, which shall be a living death and dying life.

Applied

Thus have I made it evident, that wicked men are called trees, and not only so, but that the great men of the earth are called trees of Eden, because they spring from that angelical tree, and had the fulness of that rational nature or God-head spirit living in them bodily.

Cleared

Now doth it not appear from hence, how blind the land of this seed are, even in such as go under the notion of spiritual guides, though notwithstanding they have the letter of the Scripture to be their guide.

I speak to sober men, are not those blind who teach that the tree of knowledge of good and evil, was a natural tree, bearing apples, and such like natural fruit, that Adam did eat with his teeth, and that damnation was procured thereby?

This brings me in mind of the story following:—

There was a prelate in France once very tragically insisted upon this point of the eating of the forbidden fruit, but it seems a certain blacksmith in the Church, when he had heard from this venerable Doctor that universal mankind were irrecoverably relapsed into eternal damnation, save a small handful of Christians, by Adam's eating of an apple:

Now the smith, having no satisfaction in his doctrine in that literal sense, took the boldness to argue the matter with him; but the smith finding the priest still go no further, brake out, saying, what a great deal ado has here been about the eating of an apple, which word was presently got into the Court, and became a parable.

Now what a lamentable foundation was here, and how ridiculous it is for people to believe that mankind came to be damned to eternity for eating of an apple, plucked from a wooden tree, and as simple and wild a principle it is to teach that it was a natural serpent that tempted the woman to eat thereof, and as groundless a conceit it is for some to fancy that the serpent at that time went upright, and was beautiful, but through his temptations, being the devil's instrument, was changed into an ugly serpent, creeping and crawling on the ground; but some men will believe any thing, though never so contrary to reason, and yet would be counted for wise men, but greater is their darkness.

CHAP. VII.

Doctrines

1. Two Seeds proved. 2. Of Ishmaell's Blessing. 3. A great privilege to be Children of good Parents. 4. Of Christ's lineal descent.

Preface

1. IT will be necessary, if I draw on the thread of my speech a little further, in proof of the two Scripture seeds, because it is the key of the Scripture, for if you would have the door of the word opened to you, then open your ear to the doctrine of the rise of the two seeds.

Doctrine 1

2. It is written by Moses, that when Rebecca was with-child, that there were two nations in her womb; this is a proof that there are two seeds, seeing they were not said they were two persons, but two sorts of people.

1. Inference

Again, had there not been two seeds, why should it have been said that in Isaac should the seed be called, rather than in Ishmaell or in Esau; but those that have faith may see that Esau and Ishmaell were not of that seed to whom the promise was made, but on the contrary, they were of the seed of the serpent, and so were under the curse.

2. Inference

4. But if it be objected, how can they be under the curse, seeing they received great blessings? Now those blessings they received, were but such as that great tree Sancherub, Pharoah, and others had as aforesaid, for the Kings of Edom proceeded from Esau; and Herod, the King that put John the Baptist to death, proceeded from Ishmaell, as Joseph saith, and this was the blessing that Esau and Ishmaell had.

3. Inference

5. And Ishmaell's blessing is great at this day among the Turks, for most of them are of his seed, and it is like that Mahomet, the Prophet of the Turks, was from him, because he granteth him such honour, as in his 19th chapter of his Alcoran, he saith that Ishmaell was a Prophet and an Apostle of the Lord, and preached purity, and was pleasing to the Lord.

6. But we will leave Mahomet and Ishmaell to their Lord, and Esau to their blessings, got here by their swords bathing in blood, until the time that the curse comes forth that shall cast them down into an eternal living death, and dying life.

Doctrine 2

7. But to the matter in hand. Jacob and Esau were, without doubt, of two contrary seeds, and that made the Prophet Malachi say, that the Lord loved Jacob, and hated Esau, before they had done either good or evil, and why so? Why was it not because the Lord knew them in the womb as he did Jeremiah?

Proved

8. Now when these two brothers were born, and came into the world, and grown up into maturity of years, then they manifested themselves to be of two different seeds by their actions, as you may read.

1. Inference

9. Wherefore as they did act forth themselves, so did their posterity in the general, each participating of the nature and spirit of the vessel it was first seasoned with, or the sap of that tree from which it was taken.

Application

10. From hence, then, we make this application, that it is a great privilege to be a child of a good parent, especially when the parents of both sides have been upright and godly for several generations.

Amplified

11. For although we see here that a good parent may have a bad child, and also that a bad parent may have a good child, as Saul had, the cause why that is, I have shewed to be through predominancy of seed, but though this is so, yet the rule is not general, but the privilege appears; for the seed of godly parents, being united lawfully, doth for the general part produce a good seed, even a seed that is of their own image and likeness, as Seth was said to be of Adam's own image and likeness.

Doctrine 3 Opened

12. Now this own image and likeness, is not only in respect of the virtues of the mind, neither altogether of the form of the person, but also in feature and complexion (as Christ was like Adam), as these three properties usually concur to make a child of the parents' own image and likeness.

Doctrine 4

13. For this is a principle worthy of belief, that the outward composition of the body shews the inward inclination of the mind, and the one follows the other, the invisible life is seen by the eye, it being the glass of the mind.

Proved

14. Therefore, when a child looks with a countenance, like, his father, and is of the like feature and proportion of body, we say this child is the very image and likeness of his father, and for the generality, his works and ways are much like unto his father.

Examined

15. This is a rule that we may judge of a child when he is young, but if he be not like his parent, but his parents' parent, or mother, or mothers' mother, or kindred, then will he be the like in nature to those he doth resemble.

Applied to both seeds

16. Therefore it will be a blessed thing to be a child of an upright stock, and not only so, but of a faithful and holy parentage, for it is true for the general part that the issue of the upright are blessed, for this we may observe, that that nature that is most active, doth most take, and we find that the good seed in good men and good women, is for the general part the most active.

17. Even so on the contrary the seed of wicked parents, being united together, doth produce a wicked brood, for do we not find by experience that a bastard begets a bastard, and wherefore is it, is it not because that commonly your bastards are got in the fiery heat of hellish lust?

Proved

18. Therefore it is written, Zach. 9, 6, that a bastard shall dwell in Ashdod, the Philistines (who came of Ham) being given to filthy lusts, through the pollution of their seed, it shall reign among them successively from father to son, and so forth.

A use of exhortation

19. Therefore let every one that knows the truth and loves it keep his vessel in sanctification and honor, and not to deal treacherously with the wife of his youth to the end that he may seek a goodly seed.[1]

20. This Rebecca had a special care of when Isaac and her gave Jacob a charge to take a wife of their kindred, saying thou shalt not take a wife of the daughters of Canaan, for they knew very well that the Canaanites were a cursed seed, and if their son should sow his seed in that soil it would spoil his crop, for instead of wheat, he would have tares, and then where would the blessed seed have been, in which all the seed of faith in the world should be saved.

21. Therefore this might well make both Isaac and Rebecca so desirous of Jacob's matching in a good seed, and the love of truth was so precious in Rebecca and so strong in Jacob, that it produced in her both fear and anguish, for extraordinary love to any begets a fear, lest the thing so longed for should by any means miscarry.

22. Therefore Rebecca through a mixture of love and fear cries out, saying, I am weary of my life because of the daughters of Heth; if Jacob take a wife of the daughters of Heth, such as these be that are the daughters of the land, what good will my life do me?

---

[1] 1 Thes. 4, 4. Malachi.

Doctrine 5

23. As if she should say it were better for me to die than to live to see my son join issues with the serpent's seed, for be sure Rebecca knew well that the Nethites and Canaanites were a wicked seed, and how that, that wickedness run in a line of death eternal.

Inference

24. Therefore she knew very well that the current of Jacob's pure seed would be devoured in that evil seed, if he had mixed it therewith, for nature takes that into itself which is suitable and agreeing, and evacuates the rest.

25. But here it may be queried, what if Jacob had taken a wife of the wicked seed? would it have prevented Christ's line or pedigree from Jacob, seeing it is said that he proceeded from some that were wicked, &c.; to this I answer,

Inference 2

26. If Jacob had matched in a wicked seed it had hindered Christ's lineal descent that way, for Christ descended not or passed through the loins of any wicked person, but he proceeded from the line of the light of life eternal, and not from a wicked or reprobate person.

3. Inference

27. Those men do err exceedingly that say that some that Christ proceeded from were wicked, and their error is through the misunderstanding of Matthew, who brings Christ's pedigree from Solomon.

4. Inference

28. But certain it is that Christ came not by Solomon, for I suppose that the difference of the recital of Christ's pedigree by Matthew and Luke lay here, that Matthew shewed his regal line, as that to be rightly interested in the kingdom, for to stop the mouths of the Jews, who railed against him, as a poor carpenter and a carpenter's son.

5. Inference

29. But Luke sets down his natural line, and brings him from David to Nathan, and this my assertion will further appear if we consider that the light of Solomon was extinguished in Jeconias; the rest that succeeded were not the natural posterity of Solomon, and where it is said that Jeconias begat Salathiall, that Salathiall was not

the natural son, but only succeeded him in the kingdom by legal succession, as next heir, for Jeconias had no sons, but the house of Solomon ended in him, as appears, Jer. 22, 30. Ezekiel, 21, 26, 27; this shews that Solomon's line must cease, 2 Kings 20, 8.

6. Inference

30. Furthermore, it is clear and evident that though some persons that Christ proceeded from, had many and great failings, yet were they every one of the elect seed, and Christ took his flesh from that good seed, it being in everyone predominant, though reason sometimes scouted or rallied forth or sallied out, yet by the good seed which was Lord, it was bid to come behind again and to couch down as a slave.

Application

31. Now if this doctrine would but sink into the heart of every one of the true profession, it would give great light into the scriptures and a pure lovely life to themselves, by purifying the good seed, and will also see how that seed run as a river in itself, and if it keeps itself from being polluted and unequally yoked, it will by its union and conjunction in a lawful way by a virtuous woman, bring forth a seed for heaven, being of its own image and likeness.

32. And from hence it was that godly virgins so much desired marriage of old that they might become mothers of a blessed seed, it was not for lust of concupiscence, but for love of a loyal and faithful posterity.

CHAP. VIII.

Divine doctrines

The Two Seeds Opened, Proved, and Distinguished by Scripture abundantly, to the Confounding of all Gainsayers.

Prologue

1. NOW that it hath been made clear that there are two seeds, none that are sober can deny, and as for those that have the eye of faith, they see it clearly; and for a further confirmation of this truth, I shall give you the scripture's distinction of their names and nature, and how that there are two seeds to which all the prophets, Christ,

and his apostles give witness to, behold a cloud of witnesses, believe and be happy; wonder in unbelief and perish.

Doctrine 1. Doctrine 2. Doctrine 3. Doctrine 4

1. First, Moses calls one seed an evil generation and a people in whom is no faith, and David he calls them a stubborn and rebellious generation, also Moses in another place calls them a perverse and crooked generation, and Christ calls them a generation of vipers, and a wicked generation, proceeding from Cain.

Doctrine 5. Doctrine 6

2. On the contrary, Moses calls the good seed the Lord's own portion, and the lot of his inheritance, and Zachariah calls them the apple of the Lord's eye, and David, Jeremiah, and other prophets give them the like names, and Malachi calls them precious jewels.

Doctrine 7. Doctrine 8

3. Again, Moses and Stephen calls the seed of the serpent a stiff-necked people, and the prophet Jeremiah calls them a haughty people, and Paul calls them haughty proud boasters, and Ezekiel calls them an impudent and stiff-necked people.

Doctrine 9. Doctrine 10

4. On the contrary, Moses calls the seed of Adam, the Lord's own people, so doth David, Zachariah, and Paul, also they are called the saved of the Lord and the redeemed of the Lord by his prophets.

Doctrine 11. Doctrine 12. Doctrine 13

5. Furthermore, Moses calls the other seed corrupters of themselves, saying that their spot and mark is not the mark of God's children, and a people void of counsel, and Isaiah calls them a seed of evil doers, and David calls them a wicked seed, and Zephaniah calls them a filthy and polluted people, and Malachi calls them a cursed people, and so doth Christ Jesus the Lord.

Doctrine 14. Doctrine 15. &c.

6. Moreover Moses calls the other seed the beloved of the Lord, and the blessed of the Lord, and a purchased people, so doth Isaiah, Paul, Peter; Isaiah calls them the holy seed and the seed of the blessed of the Lord, so doth Daniel, and David calls them a blessed seed.

Doctrine 16. Doctrine 17. Doctrine 18, &c.

7. On the contrary, Moses calls the evil seed children in whom is no faith, and Samuel calls them children of wickedness, and my text calls them children of the wicked one; Isaiah calls them rebellious children and lying children, and children of transgression; Hosea calls them children of whoredoms, and children of iniquity, and Christ calls them children of this world, and Paul calls them children of disobedience, and Peter calls them coveteous and cursed children, and the Lord Jesus and his beloved apostles calls them children of the devil.

Doctrine 19 &c. Doctrine 20 &c.

8. Again, as that evil seed are called children of the devil and sons of Belial, even so on the contrary the other seed are called children of promise, children of the kingdom, children of the highest, children of light, children of God, children of the resurrection, sons of God, sons of the Living God, dear children of God, his chosen people; David calls them an upright generation, and Peter calls them a chosen generation, a royal priesthood, and a peculiar people; and Moses calls them a holy people, Job calls them the island of the innocent, and my text calls them the seed of the son of man, and the commission of the spirit calls them the seed of the Lord's own body.

9. What should I say more, for the time would fail me to speak of all the titles, names and natures of those two seeds, but it is enough to the sober, and for others that have kindled a fire of their own, let them walk in the light thereof, they that are of this elect seed, and the seed of the son of man, will be satisfied.

OF

THE RIGHT DEVIL.

A Preface to the Third Part ensuing.

1. ACCORDING to Scripture order, we find there are but two seeds, no mention of any third sort, only these two saints and serpents, as now shall more abundantly appear in this following Discourse, so that now shall I demonstrate what, who, and where the devil is.

2. And now, you seed of the wicked one, be not angry with me for shewing you the devil; for the sight of him will not fear you, the false report makes you afraid, but your imbrued dark devil that is born with you, is the cause of your fear; because the sentence of death is born in the seed, and as the one grows, the other grows, for fear grows out of guilt, and guilt out of the breach of the Law.

3. Therefore look into yourselves, and you may behold the devil, for evil doing is devil doing, and you will suffer for your own sin; this is for your conviction, from your pleading and lessening sin by saying, I have done wickedly, but hope to have pardon for two causes; first, because I am sorry for what I have done; and secondly, in that it was not wholly from myself, but by the temptation of the devil, who crept into my will and understanding, seducing the one as its choice, and the other as to its judgment.

4. And now I shall come to the point in hand, to give you a clear description what the right Devil is, and though it be for your condemnation, yet will be for the consolation to all the seed of the Son of Man, the Lord Jesus Christ, for whose satisfaction I write it; for to them belongs the knowledge of truth.

THE THIRD PART:

TREATING OF

THE RIGHT DEVIL.

CHAP. I.

Doctrines

1. Of the great Red Dragon, and of his Three Evil Properties. 2. Of the War in Heaven, and of the Devil's Downfall. 3. And of his Angels.

Introduction, with the text

1. IN Revelations the 12th, there is mention made of a great Red Dragon, and of another Dragon and his Angels. Now this great Red Dragon was Herod the King, that sought to slay Jesus; and he is said to be a dragon; first, because he proceeded from that serpent dragon devil, that was cast down from heaven; and secondly, he hath this title of great dragon, because of the fulness of the dragon's nature that was in him.

Explicated

2. Now that fulness consisted of these three things—pride, presumption, and cruelty; from cruelty and murder, had he that crimson red attributed to him, being called a great red dragon.

3. Wherefore, because the greatest wickedness of reason, the devil, lies in murder and bloodshed for conscience sake; therefore it is called red, and he that hath power in his wrath of reason to oppress, persecute, or murder, is a right cavalier, and mounted on horseback, not upon a white horse (for that is the righteousness of faith), but upon a red horse, which is the unrighteousness of reason, which carries forward to battle and war with the Saints.

Doctrine 1 Opened

4. According as it is in the Scripture before cited, where it is said that there was a war in heaven, Michael and his angels fought with the dragon and his angels; this battle is said to be fought in heaven, because the original of those two great armies came from heaven; for this we may be sure, that there never was any actual rebellion in heaven; the first verse of this chapter clears this, where it is said a

wonder appeared in heaven, which was this, a woman clothed with the sun, &c.

5. Now that woman was the Virgin Mary, and she was not in heaven when she was clothed with the sun, or the eternal God within her.

Opened

6. Again, as for the war it is said that Michael and his angels fought with the dragon and his angels; now that Michael is the Spirit of the Lord Jesus in his angelical believers, whose weapons are faith, love, and patience, unto the death, as it is in the 11th verse, where it is said, and they overcame him in the blood of the Lamb, and loved not their lives unto the death, &c.

7. So on the contrary, the dragon and his angels are cursed, Cain and all his bloody offspring, whose cruel weapons are guns and swords, and all kind of murdering weapons, flowing from cursed covetousness and vain-glorious envy; and this was in Herod, in seeking to slay the holy and blessed babe Christ Jesus, being the head of all his angelical believers.

8. And because he could not come at him, therefore his spirit sought to destroy his seed by cruel persecution; and this is the war that is said to be in heaven, and this war hath been ever since Cain and Abel, and will continue to the end of the world.

Doctrine 2

9. Again, it is said that the dragon was cast out into this earth; that old serpent, called the devil and satan, and his angels, were cast out with him;

Explicated

10. I shewed before how that the war might be said to be in heaven, because the heads of the two armies came from heaven; now this dragon that was cast down relates both to Cain and the serpent-angel, being both one, just as Christ and the Father are both one.

11. Therefore it being said the dragon was cast out into this earth, it is the same as to say Cain was cast out; for Cain was the serpent dragon devil transmuted into flesh, and all his offspring were his angels; they being of his own seed and spirit, were cast out with him.

12. That is, they were all cast out of the kingdom of glory, so as that they shall never have any after redemption, nor never be admitted into the kingdom of heaven more, but shall be out of the favour of God eternally, and in this earth they shall weave the web of

their own woe, and spin the thread of their own thraldrom, as in the 7th Part of this Book shall be declared.

Doctrine 3 Proved

13. Thus you see that there was but one dragon-devil that was cast out of heaven, and that dragon transmuting himself into flesh, became the father of all devils in flesh.

14. This opens that saying of Christ, by Matthew, Depart from me, ye cursed, into everlasting fire prepared for the devil and his angels.

15. Now, let all sober men poise well in their minds these things that are written, and see whether they can have any tolerable conceit against it from the Scripture.

16. For if you seriously consider, then without doubt you cannot but be convinced, that there was but one serpent-angel cast down from heaven to this earth, and not millions.

17. Wherefore to him that so conceiteth, if there were millions of devils cast down, I ask what are become of them, or where are they, or in what form and nature do they appear? Hath ever any learned man in reason described where they are, or what they are, to the satisfaction of any man's spirit? Certainly they have not; for reason doth ever fall short both of the glory of God, and of their own peace, as to things of a spiritual and eternal nature.

Therefore that you, who are either of sober spirits or enlightened souls in the faith of this Commission of the Spirit, may see how weak and unsatisfactory the opinions of the learned are concerning the descriptions of devils, and of their downfall, I shall relate unto you their doctrine concerning the same.

CHAP. II.

1. Various Opinions amongst the Learned what the Devil should be. 2. Of two sorts of Devils. 3. Several Errors discovered.

Angelical doctrine

1. THE old learned Romish Priests and Fathers of Protestants have taught, that upon the war which they say was fought in heaven, that God cast them down from heaven innumerably, and they ceased not until God bid them stay, upon which words, say they, they stopped at that very moment in the place of their fall; some being in the air, some in the fire, some in the water; and look what place each devil is in; there they will keep their stations to the end of the world.

An aerial devil

2. Now, although these Clerks doth say, that these angels did all become devils, yet are they at strange disputes what their nature should be, and whether they have bodies; these disputes began to be very brief in the first forming of the Imperial Romish Church, in Augustine's time, and the question was, what the devil should be, and whether he had a body or no? some affirmed the one, and some the other.

3. But those that held them to have bodies, did teach that their bodies were but of air, as one Apilus defines it, saying, the devils are in the air, and in the midway between heaven and earth, and that their bodies are aerial; and Purphery held, that wicked men's souls, when they died, became devils,

4. Augustine said, he could not tell whether they had bodies or not; but, said he, according to Apilus, if they have, it is but of condensive air, even such as we feel in a wind; these disputes Were ripe after the Council of Nice.

5. But to leave these old doctors, and come to the new, we shall not find the matter much mended; for one of the doctors of the Church of England saith, that the devils have bodies of air, and he goes about to prove it.

6. Now you learned children of the prince of this airy devil, how do you think he proves it, or by what arguments? Why just thus: this is one reason, saith he, to prove they are of air, is because their bodies are cold; but how doth this doctor know they are cold? Why, saith he, there was one Burgatus confessed that when the devil gave him his hand, it felt cold; this is brave university learning, a tale of jack pudding; these cold devils might do well to get into hell fire to warm them; this doctrine is contrary to the Turks, and yet they are both contrary to the truth, for the Turks' great Prophet Mahomet did teach them that the devils were made of fire without smoke.

7. Again, this English doctor doth further say, that the angels have bodies of air also; but whether they handle cold or not, he doth not declare; also he saith that the souls of wicked men, when they depart from their bodies, they have bodies of air, and are in the air, and do in their aerial bodies tempt men to vice and uncleanness, according as they frequented themselves in this life, and so they are near akin to the devils.

Invisible devils

8. Furthermore the learned do all teach, that the devil is invisible, yet notwithstanding they some time fancy them to appear in shape, as

I read of one who said he saw a troop of devils going to battle, and that they told him they were going to battle against the King of Berma, that so they might receive the souls of the slaughtered, and one Blance tells a story (a French papist) of a maid being frequented by one of these bodyless devils, or airy devils, and that he had two children by her, but saith Blance, seeing spirits are incapable of generation, we cannot tell how such things should be.

9. Yet there where many professors in the primitive times, that were of opinion, that angels formerly had carnal copulation with women, and from thence came giants, but then those that taught so, did conceive that the angels were corporeal.

10. There are two kinds of devils, said Lanctansius,[1] for saith he, the angels were allured by their daily conversation with women, to have carnal action with them, and so sinning, were kept out of heaven, and these the devil took up to be agents and officers, but those whom they begot, who being neither pure angels nor pure men, but were between both, and thus became there to be two kinds of devils, one celestial and another terrestrial, and these are the authors of all mischief.

11. Thus did Lanctansius write, and Ewesebius teacheth the like in his Fifth Book (if it be truly translated,)[2] also, Oregon was of the same opinion, who lived two-hundred years after Christ, the like held Bassill, and Augustin is partly of the same judgment, and the ground of this their simple opinion was from that scripture in Genesis, concerning that saying of the Sons of God, seeing the daughters of men that they were fair, took them wives of them.

12. Behold what darkness there is spread upon the hearts of almost all the world, now can we experimentally say with the apostle, and apply it to ourselves, that we are of God, and the whole world lieth in wickedness, or in the devil, and yet they know it not, because they know not what the devil is, nor whom he is.

13. But I shall leave them to their foolish fancies, and by the light of saving faith, and sanctified knowledge shall discover to you my friends the mystery of iniquity, from the Spirit of Reason in man, that works wickedness, and so man and his own spirit is the devil.

14. And this take notice of, that it is not only the ignorant soul and spirit that is low in comprehensions of reason, that is the devil in man, but it is the learned soul or spirit of prudence of praise and policy, the greater knowledge the more pride possesses the spirit, and hence it is that the learned devil is most majestical, and will rule;

---

[1] Lanctansuis, Book 2, chap. 15.
[2] I question this of Lanctansius to be rightly his.

these things shall be declared in their place, but first I shall show the ground of magic conjuration, witchcraft, and the like, and how they are wrought, &c.

CHAP. III.

1. All Apparitions are Two-fold. 2. How produced Imaginary Apparitions is the Plague of Plagues. 4. Of the Blindness and Darkness of Men in their Judgment of Apparitions. 5. How Fear coins an Object. 6. The Believers of this Commission freed from the World's Bugbear.

1. IT is objected by the dark reason in religious men, because of the manifold apparitions and spirits appearing in variety of shapes, together with that diabolical power that is acted in and by magicians, sorcerers, conjurors, and witches, which they cannot do as they imagine, by art, wit, or by strength of their own spirits, but must be helped on or abetted from suggestions of a bodyless devil without them; to these I shall answer distinctly.

Doctrine 1

2. Now all the apparitions that ever did appear doth not nor cannot prove that there are any living spirits without bodies, neither can any devil change its shape, but is compelled to continue in its own centre of creaturely being, &c.

Explained

3. Therefore you may observe and mind it well, that all apparitions are two-fold, either outwardly or inward; that is, they are either seen with the external eye, or the internal, which is the eye of the mind,

Doctrine 2 in three branches

4. Now an apparition is produced either as proceeding by virtue of the first word, speaking of the Creator, in his creation of all terrestrial things, or else by fancy, conceit, and strong imagination of the spirit of reason in man, or from some extraordinary cause of nature in the universe.

Branch 1

5. From these three causes doth all apparitions take their original; as for the first, we experimentally find that upon their appearance some grand judgment follows, for these outward visions are

forerunners of some ensuing plague, and they become threatenings to kingdoms or nations before their overthrow.

6. Jerusalem had many signs before its total destruction, as may be read in Josephus, in his wars of the Jews; also, in this land before the last war, there were strange things seen, and sad events followed them, so that still they may be termed natural things, because they are signs to the rulers of the earth, that they may rule well, or else be destroyed by war or some other judgment as a punishment due for their pride, oppression, or other the like sins.

7. These dreadful apparitions were by the Prophets threatened to the rulers of the earth, to wit, that their houses should be full of doleful creatures, and owls should dance there, and saters should appear there, and that the wild beasts of the desserts should meet with the wild beasts of the islands, and this became a double plague, being both external and internal.[1]

Clearly. The second branch prosecuted

8. For visible shapes of horrible doleful visions should be presented to the eye and ear and the imagination of dark frased reason in wicked men, which is the wild beast in the dessert, through fear and horror should coin to itself strange and doleful apparitions within, and that is worse and a greater plague to the spirit when it is produced by imagination of terrified thoughts within its own body, which is its hell.

9. I say and declare it boldly, that it is a worse plague than that external vision, (be it never so dreadful) that is but presented to the outward eye, as shall be declared hereafter.

10. For although these apparitions that are visible to the external eye do very much amaze and trouble the seed of reason within, yet nothing in comparison to these apparitions which the imagination of reason doth dictate to itself in its state of bondage, ever gendering to fear.

11. This is the plague of the heart, or the plague of plagues which the law threateneth the transgressors with, as may be seen, Leviticus the 26th, where it is said unto reason, if you despise my statutes or if your soul abhor my judgments, &c., then will I appoint over you terror, consumption, and the burning ague, &c.

12. Again it follows, and if you will not yet amend, I will bring seven more plagues upon you, which are reckoned up verse 19 and 20, and if that doth not do, there are seven more plagues numbered

---

[1] Isa. 13, and 34, 14. Jer. Zeph. Opened.

up, ver. 24, 25, and if they yet would not be reformed to an external holiness, then should the plagues be again multiplied by sevens.

13. And thus would God multiply his plagues until it came to that plague of creating plagues in its heart, from its own seed, in its imaginary faculty which should coin to itself the plague of most prodigious and frightful apparitions, and internal commotions, as in the 36th verse, being declared in this wise.

14. And upon them that are left alive of you, I will send a fainting into their hearts in the lands of their enemies, and the noise of a shaken leaf shall chase them, and they shall fly as flying from the sword, when none pursueth.

Text explained

15. Thus it was with the whole army of the Assyrians that came against Samaria;[1] they were struck with a terror in themselves, that is, God had given them to their evil imagination of meditating terror, trouble, and faintness, as above said, insomuch as that it presently begot a motional sound, voice, or noise of the horses and chariots of Israel coming fiercely against them, which made them say one to another, Lo! the Kings of Israel have hired the Hitites and the Egyptians also against us, upon which they arose and fled as for their lives.

Further opened

16. Lo! here what a plague it is to be given up to internal commotions, and evil suggestions, that imaginary reason doth dictate to the mind, especially when the law doth lash into the conscience upon the anvil of the heart, and this produceth fear, and the imagination working in the fear begetteth voices and visions, storms and tempests, thunder and lightnings, with variety of shapes and sounds, and the prodigious shapes of strange forms, and that by the conscience making an echo to the hammer of the law, which strikes upon the conscience as aforesaid.

Applied

17. Hence it is that the generality of men in all ages (especially when Popery and ignorance hath borne sway), have been so blinded in their understandings, that they have either believed that spirits may and do appear in strange shapes and haunt houses, and yet without bodies, or else have seen such things themselves as they say. The world is full of lies in this nature.

---

[1] 2 Kings 7.

18. From hence it comes to pass that many have cried out, saying, they see the devil stand by them ready to devour them; telling the people with hideous cries, saying, Lo! where he stands; do you not see him in such a form, and such a shape? Yet nobody else can see any thing at all which shews that it is not the outward eye that sees, for if it were, then would one see as well as another any outward object.

19. However, it is not denied by me but that at some times it hath been so that one man amongst others having formed an apparition, sound, or voice in himself, through fear and guilt crying out suddenly, he sees a spirit, and describing to the rest in what form (they now being as dark as he in their own spirits), conceiting the truth of what he relates, their spirits upon such an amazement may, through fear, beget in their imagination the like, by which they may think they see the thing without them, when as it is nothing but a motional voice or vision within, begot by imagination, the father, as it was by Saul, and the witch of Endor, and the Assyrians as aforesaid; and also as the Egyptians in that three days darkness that was upon them, did with the eye of the mind, see prodigious shapes of wild beasts, which was greater terror to them than the darkness itself abundantly, &c.

Doctrine proved

20. Again, in the prosecuting this point a little further, let us see what history further saith. Plutarch, writing of Brutus's life, saith that he was one of the murderers of the Emperor Julius Caesar; this Brutus saith be had this vision following:

21. One night late as he was in his tent with a little light, thinking of weighty matters, being the night before he was to engage battle with the nephew of him whom he had murdered, he thought he heard one come into him, and casting his eye towards the door of his tent, that he saw a wonderful shape, horrible to behold, coming towards him, and said never a word; so Brutus boldly asked what he was, a god or a man?

22. The spirit answered him, I am thy evil spirit, Brutus, and thou shalt see me to-morrow: well, said Brutus, then I shall see thee; the spirit presently vanished away, and Brutus called his man to him, who told him he heard no noise, nor saw any thing at all. But he went to Cassius in the morning to tell him what vision he had over-night; now Cassius reasoning thereon with Brutus, spake to him touching the vision thus:

Proved

23. In our sect (Brutus) we have an opinion that we do not always feel or see that which we suppose we see or feet, but that our senses

being credulous, and therefore easily abused, are induced to imagine they see that which in truth they do not, for our mind is quick and cunning to work (without either cause or matter) any thing in the imagination whatsoever, and therefore the imagination is resembled to clay, and the mind to the potter, who without any other cause than his fancy and pleasure, changeth it into what fashion and form he will, and this doth our diversity of dreams show unto us; for imagination doth grow from conceit to conceit, altering both into passions and forms of things imagined; yet there is a further cause of this in you, for you being by nature given to melancholy, and of late continually occupied, your wits and senses having been overlaboured, do easily yield to such imaginations. And these words of Cassius did a little comfort Brutus; yet afterwards, the next day after, Brutus losing the battle, killed himself.

Cleared

24. Thus we see how reason genders to fear, after the breach of the law, and what terrible visions it forms in itself, whilst the knowing seed of faith enjoy true peace, and nothing doth make them afraid, being by their faith freed from all such bugbears, as Psalms

CHAP. IV.

1. How that all Beings are restored to their Originals. 2. Of the Power of Nature, and how from it Apparitions are begot.

Doctrine 1 divided into three branches

1. ALL beings are resolved into three originals, and so are either the workmanship of God, or of nature, or of art; whatever appears hath its fountain, from one of these three.

Explained

2. Now this I would have you to mind, that in that word nature, I comprise the imaginary faculty of reason, as well as in the word God, I comprehend the divine influential faculty of faith in the seed of Adam.

Nature distinguished

3. And yet this is to be minded, that nature in the imagination of reason is to be distinguished from nature in the universe, it being small in itself, yet is of greater variety in its operation, than any other creatures' nature abundantly; and yet let us behold the power of

nature in the universe, and we shall see wonderful things produced from the life thereof.

Branch 2

4. Wherefore, it is to be observed, that ever since the Creator brought life out of death, and light out of darkness, as at the Creation, by a powerful word speaking, there hath been, and is, and will be a wonderful operation in nature, according to course of times, and properties in nature concurring for producing of strange things, and apparitions of amazement.

Insisted on

5. Hence we see, that nature produces life as a God; this occasions so many atheists in the world, that looks upon the cause, but seeth not the cause of causes.

Proved

6. Wherefore, if nature have such a power in insensible life, as to beget a sensible life in substance and form, why may it not as well beget vapours of bodies, moving on the earth, or in the air, as it doth, that we call going fires, tumbling up and down like a wisp upon the earth?

7. Therefore, it is possible for nature to produce the resemblances of men and horses, or other kind of forms on the earth or in the air; now if it be produced from imagination within the mind of man, then the apparition is internal, but if as abovesaid, then the vision is external, and may be seen with the outward eye.

8. Therefore, when any have related that they have seen their deceased friends, and talked with them, as Pope John did, and as the Icelanders, by report; yet the productions of these apparitions of the Icelanders, for the most part, are little else but the reke and vapour of those bodies that are dead, which will fall into the like stature and shape of the man it comes from.

Further proof

9. Especially, considering the strength of its fancy, for imagination of reason at such a time helps forward nature in the universe, and so by potent fancy, it converts the thick vaporous air into complete shape of their absent and deceased acquaintance.

10, When, as it is nothing else but an airy image, produced by the power of lying fancy or imagination, from the rugged rudiments of those thick flying vapours, even as men fancy shapes in the broken clouds: now. the night is the time for these apparitions, because the air then is more clammy and thick, and so is apter for representation.

Third proof

11. As for armies, that have been seen fighting in the air, is, as one Zaesar Vaninus saith, nothing but the vapours of mens' bodies, which are carried up into the air, and fall into a certain proportionable posture of parts, and so imitate the figures of them aloft, among the clouds.

12. Now these fightings in the air, (saith he) are the reflections of some real battle on the earth, but the greater part of apparitions, are produced by imagination and fancy, which is a modification of his own brain.

Tried

13. The latter part of the rationalist's words are true, but the former are but true in part, for though nature may produce a resemblance of men and horses, in such a case as aforesaid, yet it would fall short of forming instruments of war, because there is not the like sympathy between them.

The first branch

14 But I am apt to believe, that when such apparitions are visibly seen by the external eye, that they are either immediately from heaven, or else they proceed by virtue of the first word, speaking of the Creator, as, when the shepherds saw a host of angels in the heavens, and heard their voices; this now was an immediate act from the invisible heaven, and so comes not under the notion of nature; no more did that hand-writing upon the wall, as Belshazzar saw, and the sun's going back in Joshuas time, Chesachia's time, and the eclipse of it at Christ's death, being then at the full moon; this miracle astonished the wise, which made Diontius the Philosopher, seeing it, cry out, saying, that either the God of nature suffered, or the world was at an end, which saying of his was true.

15. So that these things being the works of a divinity, are miracles, but all other occurrences being the operations of nature and art, be they never so strange or admirable, yet they are but wonders, &c.

CHAP. V.

Doctrines of nature's workings

1. Of Conjuration and how it is Wrought. 2. And of the Extent of its Power. 3. Of Witchcraft, and how Produced. 4. Who are Preserved from being harmed by Witches.

The third branch of the doctrine insisted on

1. I come now to treat of those things which may be reserved to art, as the operations of reason; and first for magic and conjuration; know therefore this, that it is all cunningly done by art and figure; your astrologers know this very well, for that is the ground they go by, therefore it is that they have their figure to show how every thing is known, as John Hidon hath showed in one of his books, and Lellye, with several others; now those that can skill of them, may tell many things, and do some, to the wonder and amazement of dark reason, but it causeth many of the students of it to turn atheists, because they see how far nature and art can go, therefore are they ready to ascribe all honour to their wisdom and to nature, and much more the people that are blinded by them.

2. As John Hidon beforesaid, was so presumptuously proud to say, that those miracles that were done by Moses, the prophets, and apostles, were done by art in nature, but if he had said that those, seeming miracles done by the magicians of Egypt before Pharoah, in imitation of those real miracles, done by Moses, were all done by art, he had said truth.

3. For if you seriously mind, there was a great deal of difference betwixt those things the magicians did and those which Moses did, for those frogs, grasshoppers, and lice, that Moses brought up in the sight of Pharoah, were real living substances, but those that the magicians produced, were nothing but shadows, which did no harm, but quickly vanished away, even as soon as their witchcraft power was over.

Note

4. Now to say that a conjuror can raise a devil in form and substance, is false, for he can raise nothing but a mere shadow like those magicians aforesaid, and that not always; neither, unless it be to such spirits as are ignorant and subjected to him in fear, for fear and belief in a magician's art helps forward his power in order to their beholding some apparitions to the amazement of their blinded fancy.

5. And as for those ignorant and hard favoured women, which are witches, their witchcraft lies in their desired nature, which nature is as foul as their form; for as the philosopher saith, the composition, of the body shows the disposition of the mind, therefore it is rare to find virtue under a foul cover, but an ugly countenance hath a vicious nature for the most part.

6. Now, these ignorant women, their witchcraft lies in their desiring nature, and it takes effect upon the ignorant and upon such as are afraid of them; these ignorant women give themselves up to believe that there is no God at all, but nature only.

7. And so by that strong faith that they have in nature, they have power over them whose understandings are of a lower capacity than themselves, and so people being ignorant and fearful of them, doth many times from hence disturb their blood with the extremity of fear, which they have of one which is suspected for a witch.

8. And so by their own fear they come to be bewitched, as a man comes to be overcharged with extreme grief, or being prevented of one that he loves he goes distracted, or runs mad, which is no other but his being bewitched.

Proved by Doctor Willett, upon Genesis

9. There is hardly any sober person but they own this to be true, therefore, one of the doctors of the national church, upon this subject, writes thus, the fantasm and affection is very strong to work upon its own body, sometimes upon another's; children have been bewitched by the malevolent sight of those that have intended them hurt; some by immoderate joy have presently died, hence it is that the very sight of that which goeth against the stomach causeth vomit, some by seeing others bleed have swooned; others by looking down a steep place have tumbled down, the imagination of the mind doth do and conceive strong things; so much for this English church doctor.

10. As for children or cattle that are bewitched, it is by other sorcery which they do use with herbs and plants, and some other things of nature, together with their having some small knowledge of that sympathy and influence that the stars have over those bodies and herbs, and so they mix their faith and experience together, pretending to do good, but intendeth nothing but evil.

11. But as for both children or cattle, or any thing that belongs to knowing or believing parents, they are preserved from the malevolent power or influence of their witchcraft, and wherefore? why?

12. Because, first, that faith in God is too sublime for faith in nature.

13. Secondly, because that faith in the true God is that armour of proof which keeps back the darts of the devil.

14. Well, then you see from hence that witches and conjurors have not power from devils without them, but all the devil that is, is their own dark reason, and that spirit that doth bewitch any creature it doth arise out of their own imagination, as abundantly beforesaid.

CHAP. VI.

Doctrines

1. Showing what the Devil was that Tempted Christ. 2. An Objection answered concerning of God's Tempting of Abraham. 3. Of Temptations in general 4. Shewing what the Devil is, and what he is not. 5. And how he enters into Man.

Doctrine 1

1. NOW I come to a more clear manifestation and the description of the right devil; and therefore mind this, in the first place (all that are not willing to deceive and be deceived) that as there ever was a diabolical power reigning in this world from the days of Cain, even so this diabolical power was never acted forth against God or his saints by any invisible spirit or devil, but man devil only.

Proved, and that Scripture opened

2. For proof hereof I begin with that devil that tempted Christ Jesus, the Lord of Life, Matt. 4. that devil was a man devil, and a Scribe of one of the most piercing reason, and the end of his temptation was, that he and the rest of the rulers of Israel might be lords of the whole earth, for as reason, the devil hath this earth given him for a possession, so they would have the rule and dominion of it only to themselves.

3. Therefore, if Christ would but have submitted to become a temporal king, all the rulers of the Jews would have gloried in it, for they saw his power so great, that if they could have prevailed with him to have submitted, which they called worshipping, they knew they should be able to conquer the whole world.

4. And that this was a man devil none of the seed of faith need to doubt, when or whilst they mind those words of Christ, where he

saith, upon the repulse of that devil, get thee behind me, it is written, thou shalt not tempt the Lord thy God, and him only thou shalt serve.

5. Now where is it written that invisible bodyless devils should worship God as their Lord? why not any where in the scripture; but it is written, Deuter. the 4th, that the people of the Jews, to whom the law was given, that they should worship the Lord their God, and him only they should serve.

Doctrine 2

6. Therefore, from hence it is clear that it must needs be the spirit of reason in its fallen state that the law was given to, and that spirit and seed of reason must needs be the devil, in that it tempts to evil, for it is the reason of man that tempts man to sin or evil, and why doth it tempt to evil, but because it is evil; for nothing can tempt to sin or evil but that which is evil.

7. But here it may be said, did not God tempt Abraham to offer up his son Isaac? and that he moved David to number the people? how will these things stand with God's purity? to this I answer,

Proved

8. God's temptation is but probation, for as James saith, God tempts no man to evil; the evil of action is from the evil nature, God doth but rouse up or awaken that nature, or present an object, as for instance;

9. The sun that shineth upon filthy carcases maketh the savour, yet is no cause of any stink, for out of sweet flowers comes a pleasant odour, as it was in Abraham's case in offering of Isaac, there was God's moving upon the spirit of faith to bring forth purity.

1. Inference

10. When God moves upon reason it brings forth sin, but how? not by infusing of evil, but by stirring up evil, as it is said by David, God moved David to number the people, that is, God left David to his own reason's meditation, upon which came forth a powerful motion of numbering the people, for God turneth the heart of man which way he pleaseth, and maketh one sin many times the punishment of another.

2. Inference

11. Now these motions and imaginations that arose in David's spirit of reason, was that Satan that tempted him to it, for it is said

that Satan stood up against Israel, and provoked David to number the people.[1]

3. Inference

12. This Satan's standing up was nothing else but; David's reason being got into a full resolution to number the people, even as where it was said of Judas, that after the sop the devil entered into him, which was no other thing but that he then entered into a full resolution to betray his Lord and Master.

4. Inference

13. Judas, he took the bread of God, but not that bread which was God, and this outward elementary bread quickened into life, for meat doth give life by death, and from that life in a moment of time sprang out a motion of coveteousness and treachery, resolving to betray his Lord and Master.

5. Inference

14. This was the Satan that entered into him, for the conception of sin is the entrance of Satan, this is undeniable; behold therefore for proof hereof and compare, Psa. 7, 14. Acts 5, 4. James 1, 5.[2]

6. Inference

15. The devil is not a flying spirit in the air, but a lying and lustful spirit in, the heart; he comes not flying in at the man's mouth, as a bird in its nest, but he springs up out of his own seed in the heart, as the thorn and the thistle out of its corrupted mother, the earth.

Doctrines proved, and all the inferences the life of the doctrine

16. This is taught by our Saviour and believed by his seed; the word of faith doth seem to scatter itself into the seed of reason (at sometimes) called thorny ground, but in comes several devils and repulses it; now from whence doth these devils come? and what are they? why they are called cares of this world; riches, deceit, and lusts of other things, as murder, adultery, ambition, honour, and renown, &c.[3]

17 These are the devils that enter into man, and defile him; they do not come from without, for that which goeth into a man doth not defile a man, but that which cometh out of man, and is bred and born

---

[1] Chron.
[2] Isa. 59, 4.
[3] Mark 4, 19 Opened.

with man, being of his own seed and nature, as the scriptures doth abundantly declare.

CHAP. VII.

Doctrines

1. Showing how that there was no invisible Spirit or Devil distinct from David Peter or Judas, that caused them to Sin. 2. Whence Obedience comes.

1. O ye seed of the son of man, is it not now clear to your understandings what that Satan was that entered into Judas; but for a further confirmation to the saints, and condemnation to the serpents, I intend to proceed a little further in this particular.

2. You know that David might as well be called Satan for his numbering of the people, as well as Peter was called Satan, through his reason getting that head as to dissuade Christ from suffering death.

Doctrine 1 in two branches

3. From hence then you may comprehend these two things, first, that there was no invisible spirit, Satan or devil, distinct from David, Peter, or Judas, that caused them to sin, or secondly, it was not God that either could, or did tempt them to the evil of sin.

Proved

4. For this we may be assured in, that the most that the Creator doth in matter of temptation to reason, is but these two things, first, he withholds from them all good motions, and secondly, (at sometimes and to some particular persons) he chuseth them a delusion, for in so much (that through the absence of his good spirit,) their reason cannot cease from conceiving some sin, therefore he directs it its course, and so pleasures them according to their desire.

Proved

5. And when it hath an object presented to its fancy, then doth it make all speed to hasten the work of their wilful wickedness, thus it was with David, though at other times a man after God's own heart, yet now he was left to himself, and from this self he rushed into folly, and could not be stopt by all the advice of Nathan.

6. But after the thing was done, David's heart smote him, (observe this well) by that which he sinned, by that he was punished; David doth not charge any Satan, devil, or evil spirit, with the sin he had done, that was without or distinct from him; but he chargeth his own soul with the evil committed.

Proved

7. For it was his seed of reason, the angel's nature fallen, that was the Satan that stood up in his heart, and tempted him to number the people, for this reason in David looked upon its own strength, thinking that victory was got by number, not minding at that time, that God had promised obedient reason in the law, that he would fight for them, and that one man should drive a thousand.

Applied by two inferences

8. By what is said, we may see these two things; first, that reason can never be truly obedient to its Creator's law, until that faith, which is of divine nature, be supreme head in the soul; for it needs no other temper to provoke it to evil, its own seed and nature is of sufficient potency to do it.

9. Secondly, it is evident that there is not any other Satan or invisible devil, that doth, or can suggest an evil motion, but man's spirit only, and that shall further be cleared by scripture, against all opposers in the world, if God permit.

CHAP. VIII.

Deep but divine doctrine

1. When Sin came. 2. Of the Angel's fall. 3. How Sin runs in a line, and how it comes to act. 4. No Devil but Man. Of the Lying Spirit in the four-hundred False Prophets, and how it came.

1. YOU that are grounded in the faith and knowledge of the Commission of the Spirit, may know, that the original of all sin or evil, issued from the fallen angels nature.

Doctrine 1

2. Wherefore then it must needs follow, that seeing that that angel dissolved himself into seed (as aforesaid,) that all the evil that is in this world, must needs be derived from the offspring of Cain.

3. Wherefore, then were not those devils, that said upon the crucifying of Christ, his blood be upon us and our children, and those that bid God depart from them, for they desired not the knowledge of his ways.

Proved

4. Again, and what devils were those that afflicted the Israelites in Moses' time, and persecuted the Christians in the primitive time, were they not devils, was not Pharoah a man, Sancherub a man, was not Herod a man, although John calls him a great red dragon, and was not Nero a man, although Paul called him a lion, and the Scribes and Pharisees men, although Christ called them serpents, and was not Judas a man, although Christ called him a devil, were not all these men devils, being a substance of flesh, blood, and bone, and not invisible spirit devils, without form and substance?

Proved by these 1. Inference

5. What was it that put to action in Pharoah, was it not Pharoah's own spirit, as is clear from these words, (I have stirred thee up saith God) (thee up) not another to tempt thee, but thee only, thy own spirit, thy own seed, and to that end have I hardened thy heart.

2. Inference

6. That is as much as to say, I have withheld good motions from it, and have left it to take counsel at its own wicked heart, when a motion of rebellion is presented, and from hence Pharoah begins to resist God, saying, who is the Lord that I should obey his voice, I know not the Lord, neither will I let Israel go?

7. Lo, what a proud devil this Pharoah was, had his mind not been blinded, and his heart not been hardened extraordinarily, he could not have been so wickedly obstinate, seeing so many wonderful miracles wrought by Moses to confirm his message, when, as king Darius, by one miracle of Daniel's being delivered from the lions, could acknowledge Daniel's God, to be the true God.

8. But Israel's God had designed this Egypt's Belzebub to an eternal fiery vengeance, for and above all others in that age, therefore said, for this same purpose have I stirred thee up, that I might show my wrath upon thee.

2. Inference

9. Observe it is not said, I have stirred up a devil, and commanded him to come and enter into thee, but I have stirred thee up, the spirit of reason, the devil in thee, which was bred and born with thee, for

this same purpose have I stirred thee up, that I might show my wrath on thee, wrath waites upon sin, and proportioned itself according to the strength of sin, so much sin, so much sorrow, see Rev. chap.

Cleared

10. Here we see that man's spirit exalts itself, it needs not another, its own seed will do it, neither is there any spirit that comes into man's spirit to persuade him to evil, but his own spirit doth it only as abundantly aforesaid.

11. But doth not that saying of the Prophet Mica, in 1 Kings, 22, intimate that an evil spirit was sent forth from the Lord to be a lying spirit in the mouths of all the four hundred false prophets against Ahab, it being thus written,

12. And there came forth a lying spirit, and stood before the Lord, and said, I will persuade him, and the Lord said unto him where with, and he said, I will go forth, and I will be a lying spirit in the mouth of all his spirits' prophets; and he said thou shalt persuade him and shalt prevail, go forth and do so.

Doctrine 2 Explained

13. This place, if rightly understood, contradicts not what I have said; for that host of heaven that stood at the right hand and left hand of God, did intimate the elect and reprobate; that is, those on the right hand were the Lord's true prophets, and those on the left hand were the false prophets. These were they who Matthew calls sheep and goats; but here the left hand host are called by the name spirit, because of reason's vision and lying imagination.

14. But more particularly this host on the left hand of God, were all those 400 false prophets (as the revelation of my faith tells me), who were prying and searching into their own reason to find a revelation from thence, concerning the King of Israel gaining victory over the King of Assyria, to the end they might gain credit and honour of the King.

Explained

15. And where it is said that some said in this manner, and on that the meaning is (as I take it), they were a little various in their judgments concerning the King; but in as much as their spirits were desirous to speak pleasing things to content the King.

1. Inference

16. From hence it was that their imagination of reason begot in them a vision or revelation of the King's conquest, all of them agreeing and concurring, and the more in that God put it into their minds to fulfil his will, that is he found them and the King Egelbert, and he flung them that bone to choak them withal, that is, he led their reason into the way of their ruin, because they chose to sin.

2. Inference

17. And in that they found not only powerfully carried forth with a persuasion of the truth of their lying vision, but also in that each one of them had one and the same revelation, and so agreeing all in one, they were very confident that it was the very revelation of God, whom they believed to be an infinite spirit without any body, and so they growed confident and resolute that it would be really so as they told the King.

Proved

18. And this was the one spirit that prevailed and became a lying spirit in the mouths of them all; so that this great host of 400 false prophets prevailed with the King, whilst the little host at the Lords right hand of Elijah, Mica, and other true prophets, were disregarded by the King, being appointed to be fed with the water of affliction, and the bread of adversity.

CHAP. IX.

Doctrines

1. Shewing who meets with Extraordinary Delusions. 2. God enforceth not Evil, hut only presenteth an Object to their fancy. 3. Of Temptations to Evil.

Doctrine 1 preceding. Inference

1. HERE is one inference to be drawn from the doctrine aforesaid, and it may be applied to the seed of reason, and that is this, that you may from hence collect that when your reason provokes you forwards to become messengers and ministers of God, to the end you may gain honour and renown here, you will ever be subject to meet with more than an ordinary delusion.

Inference

2. Hence it is that many false prophets and false priests have been so confident in their way, that they have suffered death for their opinion, and hundreds have been burned at a stake; and yet, notwithstanding, must burn in hell hereafter eternally, for running of themselves, being never sent of the Lord Jesus Christ, the High and Mighty God.

Doctrine 2

3. Therefore, this is an assured event, that when a man begins to choose his own ways, then God begins to choose his; and his chief dowry is their chief darling, for he fits them and pleasures them with an election suitable to their carnal desires.

Proved

4. This is confirmed by the Prophet Isa., chap 66, being there thus written; yea, they have chosen their own ways, and their souls delighteth in their abominations; I also will chuse their delusions, because they chuse that in which I delight not.

Inference

5. So we see here, that when truth is not loved, then is way made for a delusion. God punisheth sin by sin, the devil adds stripes to himself, and brings a scourge to his own back; mind the Apostle Paul's words, where he saith God will send them strong delusions

(this is their honey), that they might believe a lie and be damned (this turns all into gall).

Inference

6. By this we see that God helps forward sin in the soul of the sinner; but how? not by infusion of evil, but by presenting an object to its blinded fancy, which is no more but as if a man should point the finger and say, lo! there.

Proved

7. Thus it was with Jehosaphat, King of Judath, and the army that fought against him, and the King of Israel; for though he went with Ahab against Ramoth Gilead to battle, contrary to the Prophet's advice, yet he was a man that feared the Lord.

8. Therefore, when he was in battle, and beset about by the Captains of the King of Syria, he finding himself in a straight, cried unto the Lord of Heaven for help, and the Lord helped him; but how? why by moving them to depart from him.

Inference

9. Thus it is clear that God hath sovereign power over man's heart, and turneth it which way he will: when Solomon had displeased him as David had done, then were enemies stirred up against him, even God himself stirred them up, not invisible, formless spirits, but men, no other adversary, Satan or devil, but man Satan, man devil, as see 1 Kings 11, 14, 23.

Cleared

10. In all these temptations, we see that God infuseth no evil into them, but only puts a thought into their mind (being engendered from their own seed) to fulfil his will, and so is not produced from without them, but from within, being before hid in itself, as fire is in the flint, and brought to life by striking upon it.

11. And now do I purpose to proceed and declare to you, that a man's own lust that arises from his own seed of reason, is the devil that tempts men and women to all unrighteousness.

12. And furthermore, that it is most certain that it moves itself to evil by its own cogitation that naturally arises out of its bottomless pit of impure imagination, without God's immediate taking notice of it; for God doth that but upon some particular people when he hath some great work to do for the manifestation of his prerogative power over the two seeds of faith and reason.

CHAP. X.

Doctrines

1. Showing how that the Birth of Sin is from the Motion of Lust. 2. Pride, Envy, and Lust are the Devils to be resisted. 3. He that shuns Naughtiness, kills the Devil. Every Sin is an evil Spirit. 5. Every Grace is a good Spirit.

Doctrine 1

1. THE Apostle James doth clear this doctrine that I assert, If there be but ears to hear; his words are these: Man is tempted when he is drawn away with his own lusts and enticed.

Opened

2. Here it now appears that man's own lust is the devil in the seed; therefore saith James, lust, when it hath conceived, bringeth forth sin; and sin when finished, bringeth forth death.

Proved

3. Lo! now whether the birth of sin is not from the motion of lust; lust gives life, the heart nurses it, that life, growing up, acts forth itself; its action is sin, and its wages is death.

Proved

4. If sin takes conception from its own seed, and is enticed from its own lusts, then is its own lusts the devil that tempts to evil.

Scripture Opened

5. Again, James puts forth a query, saying, from whence comes wars? and answers by way of query, saying, come they not from hence, even from Just, that war in your members; as if he should say,

1. Inference

6. I would fain know from whence they come, if they come not from your own lusts, from your own life, from your own seed, is there any other? no; there is no other devil or evil spirits that provokes you to exalted thoughts of pride and envy, but your own spirits; therefore charge your own souls with it, and accuse no other spirit, for it comes from your own lusts; all fightings and brawlings, contentions and

strife have their original from within you, and the war is from within you, even from every member before you wage war without.

7. Here the Apostle lays the axe to the root of the tree of proud knowledge in the diabolical power of reason, he reasons the case with reason; and would have every thing stand upon its own basis, and so shows them the devil in their own faces.

Scripture Opened. 2. Inference

8. Therefore, said the Apostle in another place, do you think the Scripture speaketh in vain, the spirit that dwelleth in us lusteth to envy; as if the Apostles should say, do you think in yourselves that the Scriptures speaketh any thing in vain, or that the Scriptures is not truth? if you do, it is from this your spirit that dwelleth in you, that as it lusteth to hatred, pride, envy, and malice, even so likewise it persuadeth you to believe a lie, as that your own spirit is the spirit of God, and so cannot be evil; but if any evil be done, you are ready to charge another spirit with it, as being tempted and inticed from some invisible bodiless spirit or devil, distinct from your own spirits.

9. Now the Apostle, by this his doctrine, having convinced some of the Jews that it was their own souls that sent forth or begot pride, lust, envy, and all other wickedness, and that it was no other spirit but their own that wrought all evil, this doctrine pressed their spirits with fear that they should be damned, seeing that all their sin was from their own spirits that dwell in them as a master in his own house.

Doctrine 2

10. The Apostle perceiving such thoughts of fear arising in some of his auditors' hearts comforteth them in these words, saying, that God giveth grace to the humble, submit yourselves therefore unto God, resist the devil, and he will fly from you; as if the Apostle should further say, there is grace and favour held forth to you, if you can but condemn yourselves for your sin, that is to say,

Opened

11. If you can but humble yourselves for your iniquities, and receive the grace of faith and love which is preached unto you, whereby you may gain power and strength to resist the devil, which is the lust of envy, and then God will not reject you, for he resisteth the proud and envious devil, but he giveth grace to the humble and penitent soul that resisteth pride and envy, by beating down those motions when they arise in the soul.

Further explained

12. So that when any evil motion is conceived in your heart, then mind your grace of faith which is given you, and if that faith be in you, it will be stirred up by minding of it and meditating in it, and those good motions arising from your grace of faith will be of power, sufficient to expel the other before it become a stinging serpent, and then have you not only resisted the devil, but he will fly from you as the mist doth from the sun, as not being able to bear its heat and light

Proved

13. Behold here how the Apostle hath handled the point, powerfully declaring that the spirit of man is a spirit that lusteth to envy, and that that lustful proud spirit is the devil; so that then it must needs follow, that men and women are those devils that are brought under the power of those devils.

Exhortation to the elect

14. Therefore you Seed of the Son of Man, shun naughtiness and kill the devil in your good works, know the Angels of the Lord from the angels of satan, for if you cleave to wicked spirits, your souls shall be tormented of the wicked spirit whom you serve in wicked lusts and works; but if you acquaint yourselves with the Angel of love and peace, they shall comfort you, said a servant of the Lord.

15. Moreover, let me ask how can any man resist and fight his enemy, when he neither knows who his enemy is, nor where his great strength lies? therefore watch him, and look not for him without, examine your hearts, and see whether pride, lust, and other like spirits be not in you, if they be, down with them with all speed, or they will down with you, and then would you be tormented with them for ever.

Doctrine 3. Proved 3

16. Know therefore further that every reigning sin is a raging spirit, therefore so many kinds or sorts of sin, so many sorts of foul spirits, every evil motion and action makes a wicked spirit.

17. There is the spirit of jealousy, the spirit of treachery, the spirit of slumber, the spirit of whoredom, the spirit of giddiness, the spirit of divination, the spirit of sorcery, the spirit of bondage, the spirit of fear, and the spirit of the world, &c. Acts 16, 16. Romans 8, 15. 2 Tim. 1, 7. 1 Cor. 2, 12.[1]

---

[1] Numb. 5. Judg. 9, 23. Isa. 29, 10. Rom. 11, 8. Hose. 4, 12. Zach. 13, 2. Mark 9, 25.

Opened

18. Now all these spirits are but man's own spirit, Ezek. 13, 13; and this spirit is the spirit of the devil and when several of these are together in man, then is that man called a cage of unclean birds, or a hold of foul spirits, and a habitation of devils.

Sin mortified Doctrine 4

19. Thus you see, that lust is an evil spirit, and a devil that is to be resisted, and all other actions of corrupt nature are evil spirits, and must be fought withal, and mortified by spirits of contrary nature, which are as followeth:—[1]

20. The spirit of wisdom, judgment, and knowledge, these are good spirits; see Deut. 34, 9. Ephe. 1, 17. Isa. 28, 6. 1 Peter 4, 14. Isa. 4, 4.

21. The spirit of praise, the spirit of comfort, the spirit of joy, the spirit of humility; see Isa. 61, 1, 2, 3, and 66, 2. Mat. 5, 3. 1 Cor. 4, 21. Gal. 6, 1. 1 Pet. 3, 4.

22. The spirit of love, charity, and holiness, &c. Zach. 12, 10. Eph. 6, 18. Rom. 7, 4. 2 Thes. 2, 13. Eph. 5, 9. 1 Tim. 4, 12, and 3, 16. Rom. 12, 41. Acts. 2, 17. Rev. 19, 10. Gal. 5, 5.

23. The spirit of truth or true faith, John. 14, 17. 2 Cor. 4, 13. 1 John. 4, 2, 3; this truth, or faith is the glory of all because it compriseth all virtue, and so it hath the single name of the good spirit of God.

24. As reason in the unregenerate compriseth all vice, and so as from its operating seed and nature, it bears the name of (wicked one) (devil) or (evil spirit.)

A use of information

25. Thus you see how the spirit of faith and the spirit of reason do branch forth themselves, and what their weapons are on each side, and also you may see what soldiers there are raised out of these two men or two natures, all is up in arms till one is subdued, therefore if you will live in peace by faith, gain to yourselves those good spirits, and you will easily overcome all your domestic enemies.

---

[1] Isa. 28, 6

CHAP. XI.

Doctrines

1. The Servants of Lust are the Worshippers of the Devil. 2. Every Man of himself is a Devil, clearly proved.

Doctrine 1

1. BECAUSE the devil placeth his kingdom in lust, give me leave to proceed; for his lust is his life, and his own will is his own way, for as the love of truth is the life of a Saint, so the love of lust in error is the life of a sinner.

Exod. 15, 9. Opened, with several doctrines and inferences from thence

2. Moses, writing of the nature of lust as James hath done, and he attributeth it to Pharoah and all his host, the enemy said, I will pursue, I will overtake, I will divide the spoil; my lusts shall be satisfied upon them.

3. Behold the fury of these Egyptian devils, and their confidence from their cursed cruelty they had of conquering; here you see how powerfully their lust went on, there being nothing within to stop its course, but it swells higher, and ascends upwards in pride by degrees, speaking in the authority of their lying god of reason in this wise saying.

The devil's host

4. First, I will go on and pursue them; secondly, upon this pursuit I will overtake them; and thirdly, when I have overtaken them, I will divide the spoil; and fourthly, my lust shall be satisfied upon them, which shall be in killing of them, for I will draw my sword, my hand shall destroy them.

1. Inference

5. Observe what power the devil man attributes to himself; I will do this, I will do that, I will pursue, I will overtake, I will divide the spoil; my lustful devil shall be satisfied in the destruction of the seed of Jacob; for who is their Lord that we should obey him, we know him not; our God of reason and strength is in us, and will give us the victory, therefore our swords shall be bathed in their blood, and our hand shall do it.

2. Inference. Proved devils

6. Here is the devil unmasked a right devil; yea, a troop of evil spirits and incarnate devils, a whole multitude of fleshly, carnal, lying, murdering devils, and every devil had a body, and every body a hand, and every hand had a sword to murder the saints, and they sung the devil's song of triumph over Israel before the victory, so that they proved themselves lying devils of their father Cain, as well as murdering devils from their lusts of envy.

Proved

7. Thus you see that whosoever serves lust, serves the devil; and when a man is given up to his own heart's lust, he is given up to the devil, for God gives no one up to any other devil.

Cleared

8. Therefore Peter, speaking of the most wicked people that are or should be in the latter ages, gives then this epithet, of walking after their own lusts, lusts of the flesh, wanton lusts, 2 Peter 2, 18. & 3, 3.

9. This lust is a grand devil, or the father of all evil; for Peter saith that the corruption of the world comes in by it, 1 Peter 1, 4. Wherefore when it is said that man is tempted to evil, you may know it is meant of his being delivered to himself, for every man of himself is a devil.

10. Therefore it is said that God gave the murmuring Israelites up to their own hearts' lust.

11. Mind this well; it is not said that God gave them up to lusts, but to their (own) hearts' lust, to shew that sin or evil was from man's own seed, and so Paul preaches the same doctrine, saying,

12. The original of false worship springs from man's own lusts, 2 Tim. 4, 3. See further and compare Mark 4, 19. John 8, 44.

CHAP. XII.

1. Shewing what it is that gives being to Sin. 2. Of Reason and its Nature. 3. Reason ranked into three Heads.

Doctrine 1

1. THERE are two great luminaries in this little world, man, and that is faith and reason. This reason, though it be one of the eyes of the soul, yet it is but dark and ever erring, unless it have either the law of faith to captivate it, or the moral law to enlighten it and to guide it; if neither, then it grows not only dark, but unreasonable and brutish.

Opened

2. But if it make the law of nature or moral law its touchstone to try truth by, or make it its rule to walk by, then doth it do things by reason, and to the end that there may appear to be of prudence and pious policy; therefore they consult with each other's reason, and take advice, and hold a council of the most wise and judicious, grave and learned Rabbies, concerning their civil and religious government.

Opened

3. And if any thing that is good be done, it is but natural good, for spiritual good it cannot do, and the natural good that is done is not from the region of reason.

Reason's nature opened

4. For reason is but desire, so desire is bounded in reason to desire nothing but what is according to reason; it desires learning, that is according to reason; it desires glory and headship, honour, glory, and renown, together with health and long life; all this is according to reason.

The Law speak to Reason

5. Now the Law speaking to Reason, saith thus; Do justice, refrain oppression, adultery, false witness, and the like, and. thou shalt enjoy all these things thou desirest; and if thou wilt worship the Lord thy God with all thy heart, and keep his Sabbath and all his statutes, then shalt thou have glory, and thy seed after thee, for ever.

And Reason speak to the Law

6. Learned or sober reason approves of this, yet this reason is but flesh, and so falls short of the glory of obedience; for from the works of the law no flesh shall be justified, because there is an inability to do what it requires, and although reason may have a great light, wisdom, or knowledge by adhering to the law, from which it is puffed up to think that its light is the true light, notwithstanding it be void and without the motions of faith to teach it what belongs to God and his divine will; for let there be never so much light of the law of reason, yet if it enjoy nothing of the angelical light of saving truth, it cannot chuse as from itself, but in all violence make resistance to God's divine wisdom, and more especially if it be of a piercing wit, because the declarations of divine truth are not only contrary to reason, but above its reach, and that makes wise men and diviners mad.[1]

Proposition. Doctrine 2

7. Wherefore then it follows, that that which resists the Creator's divine will, is a devil; but there is nothing that opposeth God's statutes, or fights against him or his saints, but the wisdom of reason in man, therefore the wisdom of reason is the devil.

8. This may seem strange to many, but certain I am that wickedness proceeds from wisdom. O! how many gliding shining sins are there in the world, and from whence spring they but from a god-like wisdom?

Proved. Reason's wisdom branched into three heads

9. As John doth rank all reason's love into three heads, as lusts of the flesh, lusts of the eyes, and pride of life; even so, in like manner, Saint James he doth branch forth reason's wisdom into three several orders, or rather disorders, which he calls earthly, sensual, devilish. The wisdom that is from below (saith he) is earthly, sensual, devilish, &c.

1.

10. First, earthly, in that it looks upon this earth, and the riches thereof, as the kingdom of heaven.

2.

11. Secondly, it is sensual, in that it indulges itself in those lustful pleasures which its eye beholds, and therefore it sets its wisdom to

---

[1] Reason of itself is without true light and makes them wicked and wise men mad.

work and contrive ways for the bringing about its desires, which chiefly consists in voluptuousness, which begets effeminate embraces, chambering, and wantonness.

3.

12. Thirdly, it is devilish, in that it looks for lordship and dominion, and in order thereunto, it puts wisdom and policy before it to pry, search, and find out methods, wiles, and ways for the better establishing of them in their desired kingdom.

Doctrine proved

13. Now from hence it follows, that learned reason finding its wisdom great, it is presently puffed up with pride, for wisdom blows the bladder, and being full, it then takes counsel at its own reason, which is as its God, how or which way he may overcome all those that oppose him, and likewise how he may subdue all people that either stand in his way to his dignity, or that will not submit to his demands.

14. Therefore all reason's resistance, whether it be against God or his saints, yet it is looked upon by him to be good wisdom, and that he hath good reason to do as he doth, and that it is just and right, and ought to be done. Of this doctrine, will I in the ensuing Chapter, give example and proof, to the confounding of the wise and prudent of this world, that no flesh shall glory in itself; for man of himself is a devil.

CHAP. XIII.

Doctrines

Shewing how Wickedness proceeds from Wisdom.

Doctrine preceding proved: Jonah

1. DID not Esau think he had good reason to kill Jacob, that had cheated him of his birth-right and blessing? Now what reason could blame this reason, and Esau he consulted with reason, and reason told him that his brother had utterly undone him through fraud and guile, and was not this cause enough to be angry (as Jonah could plead he had reason to be angry).

Proved

2. Now is it not reason to retaliate injuries, and doth not the Law require it, eye for eye, and tooth for tooth; wherefore might not Esau reason thus from the wisdom of his reason; as also further he might say,

3. What I shall I be so abused with such a one, even a brother, and a younger brother? flesh and blood cannot endure such injuries. Doth he not show himself to be in nature, according to his name, a supplanter and a deceiver? Well! but I will be even with him, for I will be his death, and then will his birth-right and blessing return to me, to whom it is clue by sovereign authority; thus the wisdom of his reason became devilish.

Obadiah opened

4. But what saith the Prophet Obadiah? Why, said he, I will destroy the wise men of Edom and understanding out of the mount (or head) of Esau, for thy violence to thy brother Jacob.

5. Here you, my brethren, being of the seed of the Son of Man, may clearly see that violence proceeded from the wisdom of reason; for this wisdom led them forth to fight against Israel, when they came forth of Egypt, as their father Esau from his mount or head of reason resolved to kill his brother Jacob, for stealing away his blessing.

A further proof

6. The like was it with Pharoah. Come, saith Pharoah to his nobles and counsellors, let us deal wisely with them, lest this people of Israel multiply; and it comes to pass that when there falls out any war, that they join with our enemies, and so fight against us; and so get them out of the land, let us afflict them.

Examined

7. Behold here how wickedness proceeded from their wisdom, yet all their cunning, wise, sage counsels became foolish, and those princes of Nob became fools, for this wisdom of reason becomes a snare to the wicked oppressor; therefore it is said that God catch the wise in their own craftiness. Now if God did not some time ensnare them, there would be no dealing with them by the simple seed of faith.

Augmented

8. For faith is plain and simple, single-hearted, and thinketh no evil; but reason is quick and apprehensive in prudence and policy, being full of stratagems to circumvent, and hath exercises of discipline to deceive and overcome, by agility and seeming affability, sometimes as well as by rigour and force; for it can frown as well as smile, where its baits and allurements are not prevalent. In a word, reason is various and large in contrivance for the effecting its desire, and accomplishing its end.

To the point in hand: Scripture opened

9. But to return to that proud devil, Pharoah. Come, saith he, let us deal wisely: here reason is put upon consultation what to do with Israel, and the result of their counsel was to afflict them; thus violence sprang out of their reason, and was a property thereof, and yet was it reasoned out with a great deal of wisdom, as thus;

Dilated and wisely reasoned

10. It is not for our safety, profit, or commodity, to let these people alone, for these four reasons; as first, if we let them alone they will increase and become a great people; secondly, when they are multiplied, they will be of power to join with our enemies, and so worst us.

11. Thirdly, and when they have done this, they may have opportunity to get forth of our land; fourthly, which if they should, it would be much to our loss with parting with so many slaves, which may do all our drudgery, and we may live as lords in our own land.

CHAP. XIV.

Doctrines

1. An Objection of Sin from unreasonableness Answered. 2. How Knowledge perverts the Soul of a two-fold Wisdom. 3. And of the Glory of Angelical Wisdom, and how the Tabrit and Pipe were prepared for Angelical Devils, And how Reason became Unreasonable.

1. BUT to answer that great objection that is made by all the wise men in reason, is necessary to be done before I go any further, which is this: Doth not sin proceed from unreasonableness? Sure to have the greatest reason, is to have the greatest virtue. To both these sentences I shall answer, and first for the first.

Argument

2. If all sin have its production from unreasonableness, and not from reason, then would ideots and fools that are void of the use of reason, be the greatest offenders above and beyond those barbarian unreasonable people that live without law; and the most wise and prudent in reason, would be most holy and innocent.

Doctrine 1

3. Would not this be contrary to the Scriptures that imputes the greatest sins to the wisest rationalists? For wisdom and knowledge doth pervert the soul; the fool is satisfied with what he hath, but the wise in reason doth covet riches, as the Prophet saith, Ezek. 28, 1.

Ezek. 28, 1. Commented on, with inferences drawn, in order to proof.

4. The Prophet there speaketh concerning the Prince of Tyrus, his height of reason, and he doth applaud him for wisdom and understanding marvellously; for he saith he is wiser than Daniel; he brings him in with a note of admiration, Behold! thou art wiser than Daniel; there is no secret that they can hide from thee; as verse 3.

Inference 1

5. But in the fourth verse, the Prophet shews in what nature his wisdom was above Daniel's; for Daniel's wisdom was the wisdom of faith that gave him the knowledge of secrets, although he had the

wisdom of reason very large too; for he was learned in all the learning of the Chaldanese,[1] but his wisdom of reason did not offend him, but befriend him, because it was made handmaid to its dame of divine faith.

Inference 2

6. But this Prince of Tyrus, his wisdom was but the wisdom of reason, and it was large, in that be was filled full; for the whole Godhead of the Cherub, the fallen angel, was in him; therefore he is said to have been in Eden, the garden, because of his being from that tree of knowledge, and from the greatness of that wisdom, he lifted up his heart into the throne of God, and set himself in the seat of God, as to be honoured by all the world.

Inference 3

7. Wherefore as this wisdom was great, its effects were great also; for as in the 4th verse, it is said, With thy wisdom, and with thy understanding, thou hast gotten thee riches, and hast gotten thee gold; by thy great wisdom, thou hast increased thy treasure.

Inference 4

8. Again, this wisdom of reason in this great king, or Son of the Morning, was no ordinary wisdom; for it was made bright not only from himself, but he took into his court the most knowing headpieces, the wisest critics, that were next with him to the cherub's deity in the perfection of wisdom.

Inference 5

9. And all these, by their great wisdom from the tree of knowledge, did find out all arts and sciences, insomuch, that in the 13th verse it is said, that every precious stone was the king's covering, as the pearl, the onyx, the diamond and jasper, gold, and the sapphire, as

10. Also the tabrit and the pipes, with their workmanship.

11. Now observe, the prophet saith, that all these were prepared in this king, in the day of his creation, how is this to be understood?

Inference 6

12. Truly my friends, according to my faith, I do conceive that the prophet's words are not straightened in this chapter, but are of large extension, for he speaks of the king as in the person of his father, the

---

[1] Dan. 1.

fallen angel, because they are one as to their spirit and nature, and from hence also under the denomination of this prince is comprised all princes, potentates, and people, that are of the fallen angels seed, and have the fullness of that nature of Godlike wisdom in them.

Inference 7

13. And now for the prophet's words, saying, the workmanship of thy tabrits and thy pipes was prepared in thee in the day that thou wast created.

Inference 7

14. Observe, it is as if the Lord by his prophet should say, O! thou proud cherub, or Son of the Morning, wherefore is thy heart so lifted up; is it because of thy glory, thy beauty, and thy wisdom? it is true, thou wast glorious in thy beauty, and in thy wisdom, as also in that thou wast in my presence, and walkest up and down in my mountain, and thou was perfect in the day of thy creation:

Inference 8

15. O thou cherub thou art not God, for I created thee, what hast thou therefore that thou hast not received? all the wisdom that thou hast was created in thee, as the tabrit and the pipe, the workmanship of them in refulgent gold, and the cloathing of thyself with all manner of precious stones; all this was prepared in thee in thy creation, and all this wisdom was good so long as I upheld it, for it was not good of itself, because it could not stand of itself, but whilst thy desiring nature was supplied with the overflowings of my wisdom, it was preserved as with salt.

Inference 9

16. But thy beauty and thy perfection continued not, for I withholding the divine motions of my spirit from thy spirit, to try what thy spirit would do, and behold iniquity was found in thine own spirit.

Inference 10

17. And now therefore it is that thy reason and thy wisdom, thy God and thy guide is become thy devil, and hath perverted thee; and thus much from the prophet Ezekiel's doctrine of the king of Tyrus.

Preceding doctrine proved

18. Now from all that is said, we may see, that evil is neither done, nor knows how to be done without wisdom's instructions; the prophet Isaiah tells reason, that it is wise to do evil.

Doctrine 2. Doctrine 3. Doctrine 4

19. From hence take this observation, that there is no deceit or dissimulation but in learned reason, neither is there no growing rich or honourable, but by prudent reason; there is no resisting of God, or fighting against man, or persecuting of the ungodly, but by the wisdom of reason.

20. Reason is the king that governs the world, and that makes laws, and breaks laws, yet when it opposes morality, it contends with its own reason, and so becomes unreasonable, because it is beyond the bounds of reason's law; yet mistake me not, for although the action is unreasonable, yet the motion is from reason: but of this further in the Fourth Part.

CHAP. XV.

1. Shewing no Pure Reason in Man. 2. Who they be that have their Reason Innocent. 3. Whilst Reason reigns, Sin never Dies. 4. How Reason is variously carried on. 5. Reason cannot endure to be bound. 6. But would bind and be Judge.

Doctrine 1

1. SOME may object and say, although carnal reason be sin, yet pure reason is not, but is free from sin; and is not some men's reason innocent? To both these queries, I answer,

2. First, there is no pure reason in man; pure reason is peculiar to the angels, by virtue of the pure spirit of faith that preserves them; now all the reason in man is impure, and being impure, it must needs be sin.

3. Some men's reason is somewhat more enlightened than others, and some seem more pure than others, yet as the bright shining moon hath her dark spots within her, even so the purest reason hath its pernitions; in a word, reason is impure altogether.

Proved

4. It must needs be impure, when it hath not power to think a good thought; Paul said, that in his flesh dwelt no good thing; and Moses said, that every imagination of the heart was evil, and nothing but evil; and what is that learning that is acquired by study, but a work of the imagination of reason.

Doctrine 2

5. Secondly, no reason in man is innocent, in children it is; therefore every child that dies before it be capable of the breach of the law will be saved, and raised up into the rational glory from whence its father fell if it were of that seed by conception.

Doctrine 3

6. Again, let reason (being of age) in its refined irreligion wrestle or fight never so hard with sin, yet as long as reason lives, sin never dies; Oh! therefore take faith, and kill reason in its dominion, but Jet him live if he will be servant, and then shall sin loose it strength, and die out of hand.

7. Let this doctrine contend with Pharasaical purity, in external holiness, in high places where spiritual wickednesses, which are shining sins, take place, in the soul, instead of that which is carnal.

8. It is confessed that reason is variously moved forth, therefore called a bottomless pit, because its imaginations are boundless, endless, but although reason is fruitful to evil motions, yet one Just may suppress another.

Doctrine 4

9. All sin reigns not in one man, though the seed of innumerable sins are in each, if the mind settle upon one thing, then the soul eagerly pursues that, or is pursued by that till it come into action, or brought into birth.

10. Some men's reason motions forth into covetousness, then that sin contends with prodigality.

Reason distinguished

11. Again, some men's reason roams at religion, this reason is angelical, and aims at its first purity, this is the reason or nature that is wise and learned and is as a king, and so would rule in Church and State.

12. Now this reason being learned in the law of nature, and the law of nations, if it would content itself in the sole practice thereof, doing and commanding justice according to that known law, not meddling with the conscience of any man, as to spiritual worship, then were his reason unreproveable, and would bring the blessing of the law, which what it is; see Deut.

Doctrine 5

13. But learned reason cannot content itself unless it may sit as judge in both the courts of heaven and earth, for it must bear rule in the ecclesiastic as well as in the state politic, if it be zealous reason, and then its reason leads it forth to persecution.

14. So that then doth spiritual wickedness take place in such a person, and will stand up in the conscience and be as a God, for that religious reason will be judge of the scriptures and the judge of men's faith, and will boast of its religion, being possessed of spiritual pride, because it cleanseth itself from some polutions of the flesh, that it may sport itself in the glowworm light of legal righteousness, as the proud Pharisee did.

15. This reason rides upon the magistrate, and the magistrate rides upon a red horse, when he is excited by religious reason to make strict laws against such men as bow not to their Baal, and by this means they make themselves greater sinners by their shining shews of holiness, than those that are in bondage to their fleshly wickedness.

CHAP. XVI.

Doctrines

Reason's Cheat discovered in its Light of Nature. 2. Natural Learning Wars with Divine Faith 3, Reason's Fountain fully opened, 4. No Holiness in Reason.

The proof of the aforesaid doctrine

1. BUT to proceed, and show the cheat of learned reason, for because it is wise and prudent in things natural, far and beyond the plain and simple seed of faith; therefore from hence its wisdom mounts higher, and arrogates to itself, the knowledge of spiritual mysteries, applying it to its wisdom of reason.

2. Therefore, every naturalist that attains to a high pitch of reason, glories in it, as if it were the divine nature of God, and those whose reason is lower, admire at the gifts and graces of learned reason in the higher powers, in their dispensation thereof, by their rhetorical disputations and sugared eloquence, in their long orations and logical phrases.

3. All non-commissionated preachers of the letter of the Scriptures, who are chosen by men without, and their reason within to preach up the light of nature; O, if they be zealous, and carry an eloquent tongue and a fair outside, how they dazzle the eyes of all by

their learned arguments, and yet all is but patching up their old garments with new cloth.

Scripture opened

4. However, their devised arguments doth much take, both with the wise in reason and the foolish, see and compare Jer. 2, 8. and chap 4. Isa. 29. The fear of this people, saith Isaiah, is taught by the precepts of men.

5. Now the saying of the prophets, did gall the consciences of the false priests and lying prophets;, wherefore, being vexed, they apposed the wisdom of God; come, say they, let us smite Jeremiah with the tongue, that is, with our arguments and reasons drawn from God's law; and in order hereunto, let us ground on these two assertions, first, the law shall not perish from the priests, and secondly, neither shall counsel ever perish from the wise, as if they should say,

Reason gliding, showing sins discoveted

6. God hath given us not only the law, but also wisdom to understand the law, also he hath appointed levites and priests to officiate for ever, and hath confined wisdom to the lips of the priests, so that all are to seek wisdom at his mouth, and he is to be their guide for ever.

7. Therefore, we will not believe the report of these men, that say, that the wisdom of the wise shall perish, and that the law shall perish from the priests, Jer. 49, 7. Ezek. 7, 26. Obed.

8. The very like, dealt the rulers of Israel in the days of Christ, search, say they, and look, for out of Gallilee comes no prophet; what, a carpenter, a prophet?

Inference

9. This man destroys the worship of our law, and sets up a worship clean contrary, but we from, the Scripture can prove it false, as first, all the offerings and oblations of the law, were to continue for ever.

10. And circumcision is to continue throughout all generations for ever, and every ordinance and statute commanded by Moses, is to continue for ever.

11. Now some of the Jews, being almost persuaded to believe in Christ, these Pharisees, in their learned reason cheeked them by these words, saying, have any of the rulers of the people believed in Him, but this people that knows not the law, are cursed, as if reason the devil should say,

Inference 2

12. Why do you give ear to that deceiver? have ye not wise and learned men to advise withal? is there any but ignorant unlearned fools that believe in him; you see that none of our rulers do, and they are sage, wise, prudent, knowing men; you are to hearken to what they say, for they are read and learned in the law, they are Moses successors, and sit in his chair and have the interpretation of the Jaw, you must adhere to them and their counsels, or you are cursed, for cursed is the people that knows not the law.

13. Now, what was this wisdom, or from whence did it proceed, if not from reason? was it not wisdom that was guided by a law, and the Mosaical law? and what is it that that law is given to but reason? and what is this reason that strives against God, but the devil?

Inference 3

4. For this reason though it had the law, yet could it not find by its interpretation of the law, but that Christ was a false prophet, even as the learned in our time, cannot by their interpretation of the two Testaments, that Christ is the true God and everlasting Father, because he was called a Son.

15. Moreover the Jews as aforesaid, could not find that Christ was a true prophet, but that he ought to die, therefore said they, we have a law and by our law he ought to die; now to this end they consulted with one-anothers reason, first, how they might outwit him and entangle him in his talk, and then how they might put him to death,

Inference 4

16. Therefore, (say they) in their hearts, if we could but catch him in his words, it will help us to witness against him, and here lay one of the hidden things of dishonesty, for they came unto Christ in a pretence of belief and obedience to him, saying,

17. Master, we know that thou art true, and teachest the way of God truly, and so forth.

Doctrine is clearly proved

18. Behold here the wiles of the old serpent, the devil, becomes a preacher of Christ, but it is but in that they may be persecuters of Christ, and therefore these hypocritical devils consulted how they might put him to death, and it was by their reason that he was put to death, for the Scriptures saith, they reasoned in their hearts, and their reason judged him worthy to die, Mark 2, 6. Luke 20, 5,14.

Reasons of proof to confound reason. First reason

19. Now from henceforth let no sober man say, that there is any holiness in reason or any divine righteousness, moreover can there be any purity in that reason, that opposed God in heaven, and put him to death here on earth.

A second reason

20. Or can there be any other devil but the spirit of reason, that in pride opposed God in heaven in a spiritual body, and put him to death here in an earthly body, through envy and malice.

A third reason. A fourth reason

21. Again, can the spirit of reason excuse itself, that it is not guilty of murder; from what nature should sin come from, if not from man's? and have not I shewed from Scripture, that it is from the highest wisdom of man's, and doth not that high wisdom proceed from reason?

22. But from what I have said, I begin to perceive that learned reason doth begin to exclaim against me, and are all about my ears for alledging that reason is the devil, when as they teach that reason is God's divine nature.

23. But lest they should say, I write through ignorance, not knowing what wise men in reason have written and taught in several ages concerning reason, how it is divine and holy;

The Author shews reason their opinion of reason

24. Therefore to the end they shall have nothing of that nature to boast against me, I shall set down, first, the opinions of their greatest rationalists to pleasure them all, and shall shew what descriptions they give of reason; and then, secondly, I shall shew that reason is not of the divine nature, and when I have so done, let all sober men judge betwixt us, and spare not.

CHAP. XVII.

Doctrines handled

1. The Opinion of the Learned concerning Reason. 2. Their Madness discovered. 3. A wise Saying of Aristotle and Scalinger. 4. A Prelate contradicts Himself, and how; and of his Devilish Zeal.

Philosophical notions of reason

1. Hermes

1. HERMES, the Heathen philosopher, calls reason a divine gift and the God's nature; Philo calls reason an unshaken law, an eternal spirit, written or engraven in the heart with the point of a diamond.

2. Plato. 3. Alexander

2. Again, Plato saith (who lived in the Prophet Jeremiah's time), that there is. no way to happiness but by the footsteps of reason, and calls it the nature of God; and the like doth Alexander the Great call it.

4. Augustine

3. Augustine, the pillar of the Romish Church, about the year of our Lord 400, goes no further in this than those Heathens, and therefore he doth approve of Plato's judgment, and all the rest of the Heathen philosophers, in their holding that God's nature was reason; and in one place Augustine saith, that God made us in his image Reason, whereby we know him.

Platonists

4. Moreover the Platonists and Augustine doth hold, that all reasonable creatures are three-fold, and that is Gods, Men, and Devils; the first residing in heaven, the second in the air, and the third on earth.

Platonists

5. Again the Platonists say, that the devils have reason but not virtue, and that they yield to unreasonable passions. To this Augustine agrees, and thousands more with him, both Scripturianists and Anti-Scripturianists. Now in answer to this, I say,

An argument of conviction

6. Now if God's divine nature be pure reason, and that devils participate of that nature, what should hinder them but that they would be holy as God is holy; for nature distributing itself into several beings, makes all these beings correspondent with itself, and in harmony one with another.

A second argument of conviction

7. Furthermore it is apparent, that every creature acts forth itself freely from its own nature. Now if the devil's nature be reason, then the devil must needs act forth itself from that nature of reason; and if that nature of reason be the divine nature of God, then must the devil do the very work of God, unless he be compelled to act contrary to his nature.

Proved folly

8. Thus is discovered the wisdom of the world, and it doth appear to be foolishness. But to, proceed,

Aristotle and Socrates's opinions

9. Aristotle saith, that that law that is most filled by reason, must needs be most victorious and triumphant; and it is in vain, said Socrates, to trust any thing but that which reason tells us hath the seal of God upon it.

Scalinger enlighted. Aristotle.

10. Howbeit, Aristotle was something dampled in his judgment by reading Julius Scalinger, who said, that the beginning of reason was not reason; Aristotle admiring of this sentence, said, certainly there is something before and better than reason, wherein reason itself had its rise.

11. Behold! now was not here a light above ordinary? These came near to the truth, and gave it a single salute once in their lives; they saw by a glimpse that there was a want in reason, and where there is a want of something there can be no satisfaction or true felicity.

A third argument

12. Therefore if God's nature were reason, and reason want, and want desire, then God could not be God; this Doctor Featly could see; for saith he, upon Ezekiel 18, 23., there can be no desire in God, because desire is of something we want, but God wanteth nothing; when God is said to desire any thing, the speech is borrowed; see

Doctor Feately; the like may be said of that place of the prophet, come let us reason together.

Constantine

13. Again, Constantine the Emperor, did adore reason, saying, the perfect comprehension of sound reason is the true and perfect virtue.

Dr. More's doctrine of Reason

14. Doctor More, one of the modern national church divines, writes thus, saying, surely that spirit of illumination which resides in the souls of the faithful, is a principle of the purest reason, and what this spirit has, it has from Christ, who is the wisdom and reason of God.

15. Here this knowing doctor calls Christ the reason of God, a title that never was given him by any true prophet or apostle.

Calverwell

16. Again, another clerk saith, that true or right reason never opposed any thing of the word of God, but it is distorted reason that doth it. But to this I have answered before.

W. Thorpe. Hiram

17. Moreover William Thorpe, in King Henry the Fourth's time, who was one that began to sound the second Anti-Angel's ministry, in his examination before that devil, Thomas Arundell, Bishop of Canterbury, cites Hiram to prove the Gospel the root of reason.

Calverwell's doctrine of Reason

18. Furthermore one Calverwell, a preacher in those times, speaking of reason, calls it an immortal breath, flowing from the nature of God. O! get up and be doing (saith he), the more you exercise reason, the more you resemble God.

19. Again, this Son of Solomon goes further in his praises of the Son of the Morning, and first-born of corporeal beings; for his zeal being such, as that he anathematizes all men that join not with him in sacrifice to this God of reason, saying,

Curse of all that is not of his opinion

20. Let him be condemned to a perpetual night, to a fatal disconsolatory grave, that is not enamoured with thy brightness,

21. Thus you, who have the celestial light, may see by this that the zeal of reason, the devil, will curse all to eternal torment that will not bow down to reason, the devil.

A former doctrine confirmed

22. This makes my former sayings true, that the more zeal that learned reason hath, the more devilish it is; as but mind a little further, and you will find this angelical artist contradicting himself when he sneaks of faith, as thus,

Reason's doctrine at strife in itself

23. Revealed truths (saith he) shine with their own beams; they do not borrow their primitive original lustre from reason, but from a pure light (observe); they are not sparks of reason's striking, but they are flaming darts of heavens shooting, that both open and enamour the soul.

Note

24 Behold here, you seed of reason, and be amazed; and lo! here you seed of faith, and rejoice; for Lucifer hath lost himself in the labyrinth of his lore. But then in his following words he saith thus: Though I so speak in the praise of faith, yet (saith he) is faith derived out of reason's root.

25. Here now hath he unsaid all again. What a notable dissembler is this, that shall one while say, and another while unsay; which is as much as to say, tongue thou liest.

26. But we whose eyes are opened, or have heaven opened unto us, may see what confusion and distraction there is in the sons of Solomon, about things of eternity, and the knowledge of themselves. He that hath ears to hear, let him hear; but he that is filthy, let him be filthy still; time sleepeth on: But I shall proceed.

CHAP. XVIII.

Doctrines

1. Shewing how that Reason is none of the Divine Nature. 2. How Eternal Truths are known. 3. Natural Learning comprehends not Divine. 4. Of its Weakness.

Reason reasoned with all

1. COME near, you Sons of Solomon, let us reason together, whether or no is not reason natural; if; it be, as I know it is, and you cannot deny, then it is not that nature that Adam was created in; for will any man say that Adam fell from natural reason, or that he was created in reason, and that reason was debrained.

Argument

2. Now if natural reason was debrained, then natural learning will heal that, and so then there is no need of Christ, no need of faith; for reason can work out its salvation by its own weapons. But,

3. Reason objects, saying, if we were not created rational creatures, then what are we better than brutes. To this I answer,

4. You seed of reason were created rational creatures, but not in Adam, but in the Angel, and that nature is a nature above and beyond the brutes; if you will follow the footsteps thereof, and be guided by that law written in your seed, which if you do, yet will you never by it attain to the wisdom of God's nature of faith, which was Adam's nature; therefore beat not your brain about the secrets that are locked up in Adam's seed, for they will never be discovered unto you; for your eye is but the eye of reason.

5. Therefore if you would know eternal truths, you must get the Saint's eye of faith, and then if you would see (by that eye of faith), you must shut the eye of reason, or else pluck it out and cast it from you.[1]

Doctrine

6. Do but peruse Ephes. 4, 18. and Rom. 1, 21. and Ephes. 2, 3., and compare them together, and you may see that the will of the flesh, and the reasoning part, are joined together as both corrupt and nought. Knowledge in reason without faith (said one), is but a

---
[1] Matt. 5.

spiritual evil, for it hath no existence in divine love; such knowledge begets pride.

7. It was a good saying of one in the primitive times. We ought (saith he), before all things, to understand the deception of the old serpent, when as through wisdom hath deceived you, as by certain reason creeping into your senses, and beginning at the head, doth slide into the interior parts, &c., said Clemand, in his 5th Book to James, the brother of the Lord; if that were his.

8. Grace or faith (saith another author) transcends reason as much as reason does sense; for in reason tallying of injuries is but justice; and again it is not reason, but religion, that is divine and supernatural, which returneth good for evil; this puts a philosopher by his reason. Rom. 5, 3. James 3, 1, 4.

Proof

9. Again, if natural reason were the divine nature, then the Heathen philosophers, as Aristotle, Plato, Pythagoras, Socrates, Pliny, Plutarch, and others, wise critics, would be the only holiest people and the most beloved of God of any, and their peace and satisfaction would be answerable to their wisdom, and so surpass other mens', whose wisdom is weaker and divine gifts less.

Proof

10. But to all discerning men, it is clear that the greatest of their wisdom was nothing of the nature of God; for their wisdom neither made them truly, holy, nor gave them satisfaction; therefore it was that Cato cut his own throat, and Aristotle drowned himself: and yet a wise rationalist, speaking of Cato, said that he was more wise than fortunate; for, said he, his reason was ever sound and perfect.

11. And Seneca commends Cato for killing himself, and saith further, that he had thoughts at certain times to do the like, but for the love that he had to an indulgent father for grieving of him, that his spirit might have rested with the Gods, or have been wholly annihilated into nothing, &c.

Applied with the effects and defects of reason

12. Wherefore as to all these wise head-pieces, their study is but strife, their gorgeous garments are but made of fig-leaves, and their fine-spun language is as burned thread to sew these leaves together; only their moral virtues are shining glasses, soon broken to pieces, or as a blazing comet, giving a splendent light in the night, whilst the matter thereof lasteth.

Clearly opened

13. In brief, their revelations from their own reason, is but a fire of their own kindling, being hammered out by the stroke of study, as iron striking upon a flint, brings forth fire, and in this self-begotten fire they warm themselves, and take pleasure whilst it is measurable; but because its sweet odours is reason's incense, and strange fire upon the altar of its own angelical nature, therefore it pleases not the true God.

14. Neither doth it please themselves any longer, but whilst its zealous fire is fed with that sweet odour as aforesaid; but if the revelation fail, and the spark go out, or is quenched as to that, and kindles upon some fuel of an interior malignity, then is light turned into darkness, and joy into sorrow; and that which before was as life, now is it converted into death, and carries all into death, as in Cato, Aristotle, Achitaphell, and others as aforesaid.

Exemplified

15. Furthermore, let the revelations of reason, and all that legal light or natural learning can attract to itself by all its studies, be never so great, yet can it not procure to itself neither full satisfaction, nor continued peace or true tranquillity: witness Pereander, one of the seven wise men of Greece, who was admirable for these two things, wisdom and cruelty; who flung his mother down a pair of stairs, and afterwards stamped upon her with his feet.

Applied to reason doctrinely

16. Wherefore then, seeing these things are so, let me reason with reason, and say, Oh! man of the highest reason in mortal flesh, what hast thou to glory in, if thou knowest thyself? O! man of mould, thou could'st not live and rejoice, for thou hast nothing but earth to root in, the troublesome seas to sail on, and the pinnacle of thy studious brain to ride on; thy wisdom is thy woe, thy riches are thy ruin; and whilst thy reason is thy ruler, thy glory is thy shame; for as to pure religion thy reason is vain, and acquired learning, by study, is ineffectual.

17. And though thy soul delights in learning, and thy learning adds to thy lustre, whilst it keeps in the path of the law, yet is it soon satiated and glutted, because it is eaten with sour herbs and grapes of gall, which is in the fear of death, or fear in death, and want of peace and assurance of everlasting life.

Illustrated

18. Moreover, all the wisdom of Solomon was but natural wisdom, which gave him neither power of purity, nor perfect peace, for the greater has light was, the greater his lust was; for who ever had more wives and concubines than he, and these drew away his heart, and blinded his soul, in his eye of reason, to worship false Gods in the latter end of his days.

19. And as his reason, from its imaginary part, roamed at every thing, yet found it rest in nothing, for every thing was vanity; yea, all his great wisdom was vanity, which shews that his wisdom was not the wisdom celestial.[1] Therefore, saith he, in his Book of Retractions, I gave my heart to know wisdom and folly, and I had more wisdom than any man, yet was it all but vexation of spirit, for in much wisdom is much grief, and he that increaseth knowledge, increaseth sorrow.

1. Observation

20. Now had this wisdom been divine, it would have been as James saith, both pure and peaceable; but as it was but from below, it was impure and unpeaceable, and full of sorrow and vexation, when the stream of it was stopped, or the emptiness of it appeared by a reflection upon the conscience, with a spiritual echo of fear and horror, through its disobedience to so great a light.

2. Observation

21. Thus you, who have ears to hear, may know that man of himself and from himself, never hath one day of perfect rest or heavenly peace to himself, but either something molests him, or nothing satisfies him, or his very fulness swells him; his joys in his studies are but as a blaze of thorns, extinguished quickly; although it be sweet in the mouth, yet is it bitter in the belly, and cold in the maw.

Objection

22. But my next business must be to prevent an objection in that the seed of the serpent are ever opposing truth. Of what value is reason, saith angelical carnal reason; if it be so, it is but a fool, seeing it is the father of folly, and natural learning of no gracefulness; then to what end and purpose do they serve? Must the saints banish and pack out of their souls all reason? Then will they brutify themselves, and not live like men; neither can they fulfil the Apostle's advice as to give a reason of the hope that is in them.

---

[1] Eccles. 1.

23. Now to all these things I shall give answer, and because the subject seems intricate and hard, therefore the more words are requirable, especially considering we contend with that noble nature of reason, Son of the Morning, that is so universally applauded with all the wise men of the world.

CHAP. XIX.

Doctrines

1. Shewing how Reason is useful in several respects. 2. A Light given to open that Scripture that saith, be able to give a Reason of the Hope that is in you.

1. IF reason would be ruled by the law in its seed,
And keep itself pure in word and in deed,
Then might it have praise, but its nature is such,
That evil springs from itself, little or much.

Doctrine 1

2. But to proceed, reason and learning have their virtue, and serve in their place; but if the servant dismounts the master, and gets up into the saddle himself, as this is presumption and abominable pride in him, so it is high time to take him down.

3. Even so, this is the very case with reason, if it will not content itself to serve faith, and act with submission thereunto, but will be Lord, this lofty spirit will lead itself into error, and when its own wisdom and natural learning is made its guide, then faith or the seed of promise shall be scoffed at, as Ishmael did unto Isaac.

Doctrine proved by three circumstances

4. But where faith gains power to be Lord, and doth pare reason's nails, then is it serviceable, and natural learning becomes beneficial when it is curbed by the law, and washed by the prophets' soap, then it becomes the handmaid to its dame of divine faith, and is serviceable in several cases; as,

1. 2.

5. First, it serves faith in its wisdom as to all arts and sciences that are lawful. Secondly, it assisteth faith in its inlight into the nature of the civil law for the defence of faith from unbridled reason, and acts as far in that case as faith gives liberty; and

3.

6. Thirdly, it is serviceable for the illustration of the things of God, to the weak comprehensions of men, by way of argument and eloquence, finely drawn put and framed.

Illustrated

7. For although that spiritual truth needs no gloss from reason to make it seem better than it is, because it hath light enough in itself to shew it the way that is good; yet the truths of God delivered in the balance of reason, are not only powerful to convince reason, but also are graceful and pleasing too, and are very much taking with sober reason, as being so congruous and correspondent to reason.

Exemplified

8. Hence it was that Paul took up arguments from the Scriptures, and by them reasoned it out to the Jews that Jesus was the Christ, so likewise his reasoning of righteousness, temperance, and judgment to come, made Felix tremble thereat; and thus, according to Peter, he gave a reason of the hope that was in him.

To give a reason of the hope of faith opened

9. Now you must understand how that faith that is taken up by reason, is buried in reason, and so becomes ineffectual, but that reason that is taken up by faith is ever beneficial, because of its being well qualified, and though natural learning be a work of the flesh, yet it ceaseth serving the flesh when it is taken up by faith and is obedient to the spirit.

The doctrine further proved, and the right way opened

10. Again, as fire and water are bad masters, but good and needful servants, even so, reason and reason's learning are bad masters, but very needful and necessary servants, and good hand-maids. Thus is good brought out of evil, and light out of darkness; and so, according to Sampson's riddle, there is meat in the eater, and out of the bitter comes sweet.

11. But man must learn to go the right way to work; for as he that seeks to find out the knowledge of God by the strength of natural reason, doth but seek the living amongst the dead: therefore the highest preferment of natural arts is only to be hand-maids, as to use the reasons of reason to confound Lord Esau, Lord Reason.

12. Wherefore, from what is said, you must know that reason and natural learning are blind in spiritual things that are eternal, but wise and famous in natural and terrestrial things.

Illustrated

13. Therefore when faith is fraught with height of reason and reason's learning, and hath dominion over it, then having an occasion,

it lays before it a subject of divine doctrine and bids it work; then doth earthly knowledge illustrate heavenly, and so the tongue being touched with a live coal of faith, as mistress and director, becomes admirable, having a language like the Angels; yet this angelical tongue is nothing but as sounding brass, without faith, as chief commandress.

14. From hence you may see, that whilst faith goes before reason and learning, and that reason doth nothing without faith's license, she is not only unreprovable, but also serviceable; but if she will not be governed, but will govern and rule as a queen, then out of the doors with her; for Hagar the bond-woman must not rule over her mistress, Sarah, the free-woman, &c.

15. But to leave reason here as subdued to faith and natural learning likewise, I come now again as to speak of reason, as lord of the world; because it rules the world and hath it given into its hands. Therefore shall I set forth the largeness of its comprehension, and the variety of its wisdom.

CHAP. XX.

Doctrines

1. Of Faith's Simplicity in Earthly Things. 2. And Reason's quickness and piercing Wisdom in all Arts and Sciences. 3. Of the three rare Properties in Music: 4. Of the World's Fame in Juball, Tuball, and Naamath,

Doctrine 1. Doctrine 2.

1. NOW faith can claim no property of this world's goods but what it hath given it, or what it purchases from reason; for reason is the elder brother and the inheritance is his, and he will hold it by the law martial if interrupted, and reason the best deserves it, because he better knows how to govern it; for faith is simple in earthly wisdom, yea, so simple, as that it could not tell how to get meat and drink for itself without reason's direction.

Doctrine 1 proved

2. Much less can it comprehend any thing of those arts, trades, and sciences, that reason is expert in; for in such things reason is admirable. O! how it digs about the earth for metals and minerals, and gains an art to refine them. Silver and gold, iron, brass, tin, and lead, are by the wisdom of reason refined out of stone by fire and art;

so that out of the dusky stone, they can produce refulgent gold, which is the basis of their kingdom and the glory thereof.

Doctrine 2 proved from all arts and music

3. Behold, what sciences and arts hath risen, and by its invention procured; what varieties of buildings hath man found out, and what attires, husbandry, navigation; what perfections hath he shewn in the shows of theatres; what millions of inventions hath he against others, and for himself, in poisons, arms, engines, guns, stratagems, and such like politics.

4. Furthermore, what rare musical inventions hath reason found out; what variety of instruments have they made, and do play harmoniously upon, to the ravishing of the spirit of reason, with astonishing joy at the celestial-like sound of these musical instruments.

Music's excellency in three properties described

5. This is such an invention as will raise joy, allay passion, and quiet the devil by charming him to merriness of heart.

6. David's reason having a knowledge in this art, made him very acceptable with Saul; therefore Saul would have David stand before him and play, especially when the evil spirit came upon him, as it is written 1 Sam. 16, 23. The words are as followeth:

7. And it came to pass, when the evil spirit from God came upon Saul, that David took a harp and played with his hand; so Saul was refreshed, and was well, and the evil spirit departed from him.[1]

1. Inference

8. Here you, that are of the seed of reason may see, how that that evil spirit that came upon Saul was Saul's own spirit, otherwise he could not have been refreshed and made well by the music of the harp; for that evil spirit was a spirit of frenzy and madness, having envy and murder in it, and a contempt of God and goodness, as may be seen by these Scriptures: chap. 18, 10, 11. chap. 19, 9, 10. chap. 22, 15. to the 18th, &c.

9. Now his passion was pacified by the pastime of the harp, and his fear and horror of heart was abated, charmed, and lulled asleep for a moment, even as wine will do the like.

---

[1] 1 Sam. 16, 23.

2. Inference

10. Therefore it is the practice amongst the seed of reason, that when they have got a wounded spirit by breaking the law, then have they no way to ease their spirits but by wine and music, and that puts the evil day far off, and sends the soul dancing to death, as the fly doth about the candle.

The original of music

11. But to return to the discourse aforesaid. It was a most exquisite wit in reason to invent the art of music, and he that was the first inventor thereof was Tuball, one of Cain's progeny, and it sprang from Cain, and was of the serpent angel's nature, being prepared in him in the day of his creation for his temporal heaven, as I shewed before out of Ezek. c. 28, verse 13, 14.

Doctrine proved

12. Furthermore, this Jubell had a brother by his mother's side, whose name was Tuball Cain; he was the father of all artificers in brass and iron, and these two brothers had a sister whose name was Naamath; these three were the crown and glory of reason's kingdom.

Illustrated

13. And now at this time did reason's kingdom begin to be famous; and as revelations of powerful faith did abound in Enoch the seventh from Adam, that blessed seed, even so likewise did revelations of politic reason, together with exquisite wit and beauty effeminate, were got admirable great in Jubell, Tuball, and Naamath, the seventh from Cain, the cursed seed.

14 Again, this Tuball Cain, being a master of smith's work and instruments of war, was therefore from hence honoured as a God, and Jubell, being the master of the muses, had the like honour, and Naamath was the mother of the goddesses, and was herself honoured accordingly.

15. This Naamath was the mirror of the world for beauty and wit; the Jewish Rabbis' say, that at this Naamath all the world wandered in love after; even the sons of God (which were the sons of Adam), many of them doated on her, and gazed at her beauty.

16. And from hence it was that through their carnal knowledge of her (for she was a whore) and others of the same lineage with her, faith and reason, good and evil, came to be in conjunction in one womb, and from that union arose several natures in one person, each

nature acting as it gained strength, according to the seed it sprang from.

Music's nature in itself not hurtful

17. And from hence, also, it was that David was excellent in the harp, in that he had participated of Jubell's nature, by mixture of seeds, in persons preceding him as aforesaid.

18. But then we are to mind, that the music of his did not nourish any carnal delight, because the mistress of faith had the government, and so prevented it from becoming detrimental to him.

Music occasions evil to the evil

19. But as to the seed of reason, this science being a branch and part thereof, it can do no less but become a cause, instrument, or motive to indulge them with carnal pleasures, and so cause them to make this present and self-created joy their only felicity, not looking forwards for any other pleasures but what its own dictates of reason in this life can afford them, as aforesaid.

Music occasions good to the good, exemplified in several particulars

20. But on the contrary, in the knowing seed of Adam, it became a means through faith to put them in mind of the glorious quire of Angels, and of their melodious songs and tunes upon the harps of their tongues in praise to their Creator.

21. Also faith made this reason to see the glory of the Angels, and gave it liberty to act forth itself in a resemblance of their innocent joy for its own consolation, as a reward to its being sober.

22. And not only so, but it by virtue of the law, was made a part of God's worship, and so it became a reasonable service, serving as types and figures, and to that end the priests had the rational of understanding put upon them, and it was by this that David danced before the ark, and here now lay both his reasonable service and divine, for he saw through that type the anti-type God, coming in a body of flesh, which was his ark, which caused his joy. But to proceed.

CHAP. XXI.

Doctrines

1. Of the contrariety of Faith and Reason. 2. Of their Regency. 3. Disobedient Reason will be damned. 4. No Devil but Mankind. 5. Augustine's Definition of Devils detected. 6. Truth's Triumph.

Doctrine 1

1. NOW reason in the general is an enemy to faith, and faith an enemy to it, and there is a battle fought betwixt these two; now where faith prevails, there is no free quarter given to the enemy that stands out, but submittive reason lives, and the other dies, according as it is written, mortify the deeds of the flesh, flesh may live if the deeds be mortified, and it leaves its savour.

Opened

2. Only understand the extent of that life of submissive reason, it being the devil's nature, and having broke the law, therefore the highest of its glory is for ever to be a servant under faith, so long as mortal life continues, and then it dies with all the life that is in the body, and it never rises again; but faith rises to glory, and leaves it in the grave, having served its time, as the beast of the field, utterly annihilated to itself.

3. But on the contrary, that reason that rules, and submits not, dies with faith in the body, and as faith was kept under, so that faith dies (being as good as dead whilst living), and never hath resurrection, even as captivated reason, as aforesaid; but as for that reason as reigned as lord, it must rise again and suffer a second and eternal death: now woe, woe to this rebellious reason and disobedient, for this is the devil that must be damned to eternity.

Doctrine 2

4. Wherefore look about you, for what is lord in time, will be raised lord to reap the fruit of its doing after time is no more; therefore you that do evil, if you could look beyond the first death, you might see the second; look what I shall say again, for I shall now set him forth, I say I shall now set the devil forth as to his sensuality and satanical serpentine properties.

Proposition. Doctrine 3

5. That which motioneth forth evil, naturally of itself is a devil; but man of himself and from his own seed doth motion forth the evil of disobedience, therefore man must needs be a devil that is under the power thereof.

Proved

6. In order to the proof of the proposition, you may find that it is written, that all the sins that are committed, do arise freely from man's unconstrained will; they are so prone to sin, as that they cannot cease from sin; the Scripture saith, that every transgression is a work of the flesh.

7. Wherefore then, is there any fleshless devil, seeing that evil is from the flesh? Paul recites a catalogue of evil deeds, and calls them all works of the flesh, and every one of these deeds is a devil; see Gal. 5.

8. Oh, how fruitful the flesh is; how it multiplies in man until it come to a body of sin, every sin being a particular member, and every member a part of the flesh, and every part a devil in particular.

Opened

9. Therefore it is said that seven devils were cast out of Mary Magdalen, that is seven several works of the flesh.

Augustine's doctrine

10: Augustine, that great doctor of the Romish Church, writing upon Gal. 5. concerning the works of the flesh, saith that all the sins of an evil life are not to be laid upon the flesh.

Proved false

11. This doctrine is contrary to the text, and to the whole current of Scripture, and so is but at the best devilish doctrine; but what is his reason? Why, said he, because if we should grant that all sins were from the flesh, then should we make the devil sinless, which hath no flesh.

12. This doctor will not have man's spirit to be the devil, because it centres in flesh; yet he makes them to be one in nature; for, saith he, contention, wrath, and envy, are the works of the flesh: to all this, saith he, pride gives being, and so likewise doth it to his fleshly devil.

Reason reasoned with, and its wisdom detected

13. Behold, now if things were thus, wherefore should there be any variance between his spirit-devil and man's fleshly lusts, seeing they differ nothing in nature? What the one hates, the other hates; and what the one loves, the other loves; and what the one doth, the other doth: methinks they should sweetly unite, seeing every thing centres in likeness.

14. Oh, the darkness that is in the learned of the world, this palpable ignorance cannot chuse but produce much slavish fear, doubtful thoughts, and dreadful delusions in the followers of these false prophets.

Faith's joy, and truth's triumph

15. Therefore, let every true believer of this Commission of the Spirit, sound forth truths triumph over all fleshly voluptuousness that totters through its instability, being moved and shaken by the mighty power of faith, as also over all the doctrines of men by the wisdom given from above, which makes them all naked and bare, vain and fruitless to our joy and glory, who are more than conquerors.

CHAP. XXI.

Divine doctrines treated on

1. No Creature sins but Man. 2. What Sin is. 3. And when it came into Man. 4. The place of Sins conception, Exod. 29. Verse 13th, opened. 5. Why Sin is most in the Heart. 6. Wisdom and Policy serviceable to a Saint, and when.

Doctrine 1

1. YOU, my brethren, who are possessed with the spirit of the Scripture, do clearly find in them that there is no creature that opposeth the Creator but man, or that is defiled with sin but man, or that doth defile, delude, deceive, or do any wickedness but mankind only.

Sin opened

2. This is so clear a doctrine, that one would think no man could for shame deny it, that owns Scripture to be truth; but reason is blind, because it is sin, for sin knoweth not itself, if it did, it might know the devil; for one being asked what sin was, said it was not easily defined, and if any take upon them to tell what sin is, they but

repeat the Apostles' words, saying, Sin is the transgression of the law, but tell not what it is that doth transgress the law.

Well said

3. One clerk defines sin darkly thus, saying, sin is the Apolon, the destroyer that is gone out, and we hug the poison, and twist willingly with the vipers, till they bring us to the region of irrecoverable sorrow.

Better said

4. Another makes a better definition, saying, if any man be drawn after the thoughts of his heart, he will search after idolatry, and this he was compelled to speak, in that he hit upon Numb, chapter 15, verse 39.

Best of all said

5. Another, by his viewing of these Scriptures following, was compelled to say that all that riseth up in us is evil, and man's wisdom is earthly and devilish. Gen. 6, 5. 2 Cor. 3, 5. 1 Peter 4, 3. 1 Cor. 2,14. James 3, 15.

6. But in reading of books, I found a Jewish Rabbi, one Menacham, to give a wise answer from whom sin was upon, Numb. 19, 16. saith that the cause of the uncleanness of the dead, is by means of the angel of death, the devil, that brought poison into man, and so (saith he) there is no creature that sins, but man.

Doctrine argued. Doctrine 1 proved

7. From hence I argue thus, if there be no creature that sins but man, then there is no devil but man, for where there is no sin, there is no Satan.

Again proved

8. Again, the aforesaid Rabbi, treating upon pollution by the dead, on Levit. chapter 11, verse 21. saith, that there is no kind of living creature that is defiled whilst it is alive, or that defileth while it is alive, but man only.

Proved further

9. One being asked a question at what time sin entered into the world, made answer, saying, at the very hour of formation; this saying was true, all men are conceived in sin; it was therefore that circumcision did shew and shadow forth sin's entrance into the world.

10. Now to shew the place of the conception of sin, it is to be known, that as the heart is placed in the middle of the body, so is sin seated in the middle of the heart, which is called the inmost part, as David saith, the inward part is very wickedness.

Doctrine 2 opened

11. The Apostle Paul calleth it the mind, but Jeremiah calleth it the inward parts;[1] thus the heart is called the inward, because it is in the middle of the little world, man, but although the heart is the most inward part of the body, yet the kidnies, or reins, or liver, may be called the inwards also, and are comprised in the word heart, mind, or entrails.

Explained

12. For the kidnies or reins, which are the instruments of seed for generation, are in Scripture used for the inward affections and desires, and are joined with the heart; these are to be mortified and put to death in the Saints, as Paul exhorts, Col. 3, 5.

Exod. 29, 13 opened

13. Moreover, in Exod. 29, 13., we read there that Moses commanded the people of Israel to offer up a burnt offering for the atonement of sin, and their offering was as followeth: when (saith he) you have killed a bullock, then shall you take all the fat that covereth the inwards, and the caul that is above the liver, and the two kidnies and the fat that is upon them, and burn them upon the altar.

Opened

14. Now the fat upon the inwards signified the corruption of the heart; this made David say, that the heart of the wicked were as fat as grease, Psa. 119. Now this must be burned or mortified in the time of this life, or else as David saith, in another place, they will be fed up for the day of wrath.

The life of the doctrines. Inference 1

15. Therefore know that it is of necessity that this fat, lustful, wanton, fleshly devil, that covereth the inwards, must either be burned here by the fire of faith, or it must burn eternally in its own fire of envy, kindled in it by the law of sin, to its everlasting sorrow and suffering of its whole man, because its lustful devil was governor.

---

[1] Heb. 8, 16. Jer. 31, 33.

Inference 2

16. Again, the kidnies and the fat that is upon the inwards, and the caul that covereth the liver, were burned unto God, to make atonement for the sin of man, which proceedeth out of the thoughts of the reins and lusts of the liver, and fatness of the heart; for these all conceive first, and then consent in sin, and so become a body of sin in the middle of the body of flesh.

Inference 3

17. But to shew why sin is most in the heart, it is because the heart is the principal seat of life, and sin is life when quickened in the seed; for sin lies in the seed, and seed is life, and the life is reason, and that reason is a fiery spark, which is the light, life, heat, or motion of the soul that both speaks, walks, and works.

Inference 4

18. So that that fire kindles life and strength throughout the whole body, only the principal part as to understanding of this natural fire liveth in the head of man, because that is the glory of man, yet the vital spirits flowing from the heart, do foster and cherish it; but if the course thereof be obstructed, then doth bad humours, proceeding from corrupted blood, ascend up into the brain, and so darkens the spirits, and spoils the glory.

Inference 5

19. But then as for all these parts that are to be mortified, lies or arises in the heart or inwards, for that is the seat of sensuality, and from thence doth all wickedness flow as from its fountain; the head would not do harm, if the heart were not hurtful.

A caution. Inference 6

20. Therefore, let every one look into his heart, and see what blossoms and blooms there; if his tree be the tree of knowledge, his fruit will be sin, and now have we found the fountain and head-spring of sin, and see where it is formed, framed, and fashioned.

Exhortation and caution worthy of acceptation

21. Therefore give over looking for a devil (O, you sons of men) without you, but look into your heart, for that is the place of its conception, and behold the motions and imaginations to evil as they move in the heart, for that is the cockatrice egg of the devil, which crush him in time (by a motion of faith), before he become a stinging serpent, &c.

22. Now that all sin issues from man's seed, and is hatched in the heart, and from the heart, and that all evil that is done is the work of the heart of man, or from no other spirit or devil is now to be plainly shewed, and that from every Prophet and Apostle, from the beginning of Genesis to the end of the Revelations, as mind their divine sayings, all you that are upright in heart.

CHAP. XXIII.

Doctrines divine

1. Shewing how Evil is from Mans own Spirit. 2. Being all hatched in the Heart. Being consented to by all Prophets and Apostles.

1. MOSES being the first writer of Holy Writ, is not to be accounted a small Prophet, but the greatest Prophet of the Law, in that he gave forth the Law; therefore he best knows the Law, and the nature of reason in which the Law is written.

2. And he, in Genesis, views the heart of natural man, and in it he finds the original of all evil, even the stream of strife, the silk of sin, the seed of the serpent, and the fountain of fury.

Doctrine 1 opened

3. Therefore, saith he, every imagination of the heart is evil, and continually evil; he speaks it with an emphasis, and adds this aggravation, evil, and continually evil, as if he should say, there is more evil in man than man is aware of; he is not good and bad by turns, but continually, for the seed of the serpent abides in all the children of Cain, which sends forth evil thoughts, and lust in the seed becomes evil in the deed.

Doctrine 2 proved

4. Again, saith Moses, they have corrupted their ways so, that they were the authors of their evil imaginations; also, saith Moses, it was Pharoah's hardness of heart as would not let the children of Israel go, and their reason was, because their hearts worked wrath; it was not any other devil that tempted them to evil, but it was their own hearts' life that worked wrath.[1]

Joshua

---

[1] Exod. Levit. 19, 17. Deut. 8, 14. & 9, 4. & 15, 19. & 17, 20. & 24, 15. & 29, 19.

5. Furthermore, Moses tells us that hatred, whoredom, adultery, pride, and idolatry, and all wicked imaginations, are from the heart; and Joshua, in his 14th chapter, doth prove the heart to be deceitful as in the spies, for they differed in their hearts.

Judges. Ruth

6. And in Judges, Barak saith, that all thoughts proceed from the heart, and that in it are many searchings, and that love, grief, sorrow, anger, are from the heart, &c. See Judges 10, 16. & 16, 16. and chap. 5, verse 15,16. And Ruth saith, that joy and mirth are from the heart, 3, 7.

1 Sam. 2 Sam

7. Samuel saith, that all naughtiness is from the heart, as well as joy and sorrow, truth and trouble. 1 Sam. 4, 13. & 12, 24. & 17, 28. & 24, 5. & 25, 36, 37, & 2 Sam. 24,10.

1 Kings

8. Again, in Book of Kings, that imaginations and pride are in the heart, and from the heart, 1 Kings 12, 33.

1 Chron. 2 Chron

9. And in Chronicles, Samuel saith, that pride, hypocrisy, dissimulation, is the work of the heart, and hatched in the heart; see 1 Chron. 12,33, 38. 2 Chron. 25, 2. & 32, 26'. compared with Isaiah 59. 4, 5.

Ezra, Nehemiah, Esther

10. Ezra, Nehemiah, and Esther doth say, that every thing that is done is from the heart, as disobedience, dissimulation, pride, &c. See Ezra 6, 22. & 7, 10, 27. Nehemiah 6, 8. Esther 5, 9. & 7, 5.

Psal.

11. David, in the Psalms, speaking of the wicked, saith, that all filthy lusts, all mischiefs, hypocrisy, and wickedness, is the work of the heart, and is from the seed of its own soul; see and compare Psa. 9, 16. & 10, 2, 3. & 35, 20. & 36, 4. & 41, 6. & 58, 2. & 104, 2. & 81, 12.

Isa.

12. And Isaiah saith, that iniquity is the work of the heart, and that all sin hath its rise there. Chap. 32, 6. & 14, 13. & 4, 7, 8,10. & 59,4, 13.

Jeremiah

13. The Prophet Jeremiah declares the same doctrine, and saith, that pride, deceit, rebellion, and all evil that is done, is the work of the heart; see and compare chap. 4, 14. & 5, 23. & 14, 14. & 17, 9. & 23, 26. & 48, 29. & 49, 16. Lamentations 5, 13.

Ezekiel

14. The Prophet Ezekiel speaks the like, and shews plainly that whoredoms, despite, covetousness, and all sin, is from the heart and soul of the wicked; see and compare chap. 14, 3, 4, 7. & ch. 20, 16. & 25, 15. & 28, 2, 5, 17. ch. 31, 10. & 33, 31.

Daniel, Hosea, Joel, Amos

15. And Daniel saith, that pride, haughtiness, and all evil is from the heart, and all the twelve small prophets do concur hereunto; see Hosea 4, 8. & 7, 14. & 10, 2. & 13, 6. See Joel and compare with Amos; Joel 2, 12, 13. compare with Amos 1, 9. & 8, 5. & 2, 7. & 3, 10.

Obadiah, Jonah

16. For the Prophet Obadiah saith, that pride and deceit were the works of the heart, and Jonah saith, that upon the fainting of the heart, a motion of remembrance sprang up in his heart to pray unto the Lord. Ch. 2, 7.

Micha, Nahum, Habakuk, Zeph.

17. and Micha shews, that the heart of man hath its devices to do evil from its own seed; therefore doth he pronounce a woe upon it, being an evil spirit of covetousness, oppression, lies, and falsehood. Ch. 2, 1, 2, 11. compared with Nahum 1, 9, 11. & 2, 10., and with Habakuk 1, 5. & 2, 4., and with Zeph. 1, 12. & 2, 15.

Hagia.

18. And Hagia shews, that there cannot be any good work done, unless the heart be good; therefore he exhorts Israel to consider their ways, which according to some translations, it is, set your heart upon your ways.

Zach.

19. And Zachariah saith, that imagination of hatred is from the heart, and that disobedience comes by hardness of heart. Ch. 7. 10, 12.

Mal.

20. And Malacchi declares, that treachery is from an evil heart, as love is from a good heart. Ch. 2, 15. the last and last.

Matt. Mark

21. Thus have I gone over all the Prophets' doctrine of the first Commission or Testament; and now you shall see that Christ and all his Apostles do set their seals to this doctrine, or rather open it, and make it more plain; therefore saith Christ, murder, fornication, theft, blasphemy, false witness, evil thoughts, yea, all sin is all from the heart, as the evil treasury of the same.

Luke. John

22. And that they were all conceived there from man's own seed, and came not into him by any invisible spirit, but arose from his own seed, as see Matt. 5, 28. & 12, 34, 35. & 13, 15. & 15, 19. Mark 7, 21. Luke 21, 24.

23. Nothing that comes into man, defiles man (said Christ), but what comes from him, that grows up out of him from himself, from his own seed.

John opened

24. Lo! here now whether this doctrine is not positive proof clear enough to open those other places which speak of Satan's entering the heart, of filling the heart; for those evil thoughts, or evil and wicked devices afore-mentioned, are the devils the Scriptures speak of, and they are said to enter upon the conception of lust, through imagination, when corporated into a settled resolution.

25. This is undeniably true, unto which all the Apostles bare witness. But for brevity's sake, I will only recite the proofs; therefore at your leisure peruse these Scriptures, and compare; as,

26. John 12, 40. & 3, 2. & 16, 15. Acts 5, 3. & 8, 21, 22. & 28, 17. Acts 7.39. Rom. 1, 21. & 25. & 12.4, 2 Cor. 3, 15. & 5, 12. Gal. 4, 6. Eph. 5, 6. Phil. 1, 7. &4, 7. Col. 2, 2. & 3, 15, 16. 1 Thes. 2, 4. & 3, 13. 2 Thes. 2, 17. & 3, 5. 1 Tim 1, 5. 2 Tim. 2, 22. Heb. 3, 10 James 3,14. 2 Peter 2, 14. 1 John 3, 20. Rev. 17, 17. & 18, 7. & 22, 3. &c.[1]

Proved abundantly

27. To conclude, there is no creature that sins, or tempts to sin, but mankind only, and that from his own seed all evil is done; see further Exod. 23, 33. 1 Kings 12, 30. & 14, 16. & 35, 26. 2 Kings 14, 16. Nehe. 6, 26. Lam. 4, 13.

CHAP. XXIV.

Divine doctrines

1. Man's Nature admired at. 2. The greatest Evil to Man, is Man himself 3. Man's Defilement from himself. 4. No damned Devil to be found but in Man. 5. Sin charged wholly upon Man-

Doctrine 1

1. IT hath made many naturalists wonder and admire, above all other creatures, to see it so far drenched and drowned in evils, and in nature as changeable as the moon, never delighting in one condition long.

2. For if it have peace and plenty, that but pampers it up to pride and luxury, and that becomes the harbinger of war, and that ushers in poverty, and the effect of that is envy, whose fruits are stealth and murder.

Proved

3. Therefore (said one) formerly men accompanied themselves together, and builded towns, to save them from wild beasts; but now, on the contrary, for their best security, they are compelled to fly all company, and to live in woods and wildernesses, safer there among wild beasts, as bears and tigers, than in any towns among tame officers.

---

[1] Acts Romans 1 Cor. 2 Cor. Gala. Ephe., Philip., Col. Thes. Tim. Heb. James. Pet. John. Revel.

Proved

4. This made Hermes the philosopher say, and to cry out, saying, O! man, thou art more cruel than wild beasts; all things hate thee, because thou art the destroyer of all things, and may he not from hence be called a devil, for the word devil signifies a destroyer.

Truth is truth let who will speak it

5, The chiefest cause of all evils that happen to man, is man himself (said Socrates) man hath not a more mortal enemy or foe than man himself; could one Blanch, a French Papist say, and yet he would have a bodyless devil too.

Quickened faith makes the Scriptures speak and become fountains

6. But to the spirit of the Scripture where life is found, where truth is shewn, where light doth shine, to discover things that hath been veiled, to open things that have been hid, will I again have recourse, and by the knowledge of the true God, give you a further proof of the right devil in this world-man.

An argument forcible. Doctrine 2

7. Wherefore if it be so, that man doth defile himself, then is he the author of his own evil, and man doth defile himself from himself, this is the truth of Scripture record, for nothing doth defile man but man, one man defiles another, and every man defiles himself.

Proved

8. Defilement of sin is peculiar to man, if any other creature be counted unclean, is not the original cause from man? wherefore then it follows, that sin is hereditary to Cain and his seed for ever, for that being bred and born with man doth evermore defile man.

Ground of proof

9. Wherefore then as the heart is the place where sin is wrought, so the matter is there of which it is made; for proof hereof, the Lord being angry with Israel, according to the flesh, fathers them upon Moses, and saith, get thee down (for thy people) have corrupted themselves, and as the Lord said, so Moses was confident that their corruption and defilement was from themselves, see Deut. 4, 16, 17.

Note

10. The like he writeth, chap. 31, ver. 29. saying I know that after my decease you will utterly corrupt yourselves, and turn aside from the way that I command you, and (by this means) evil will befall you in the latter days, because you will do evil, through the work of your hands.

The marrow of divinity

11. Lo here and behold how closely sin is laid upon man's own spirit; for first, they corrupt themselves, there is no other spirit that doth defile them; secondly, they turn themselves aside, they are not turned by any other; for these two things, a judgement follows, evil will befall you (saith the prophet) that is the punishment of evil, evil for evil, because they do evil, and that through the work of their own hands.

The doctrines proved clearly

12. Here now is evil, and evil upon evil, and all from man's own seed, what is this, but the devil? where now can a devil be found but in man; man doth corrupt himself, man doth turn aside of himself, man doth receive the evil of punishment, because he doth commit the evil of sin by himself alone, through the work of his own hands.

Second proof. Deut. 32, 5 opened

13. Again, Moses in Deut. 32, 5, gives other proofs correspondent to this, he there, speaking of a wicked seed, saith thus, (they) have corrupted themselves, (their spot) is not the spot of God's children, (they are a perverse and crooked generation.)

Proved

14. See here now how the effect of this their defect of corrupting themselves, for by this means they had got a spot or mark which did constitute them the children of Cain, their father the devil, for he was the first devil in flesh that corrupted himself, and turned aside into the ways of murder and lies.

Proved

15. Moreover in Judges it is said, that they corrupted themselves more and more, and ceased not from their own doings, chap. 2, 19. see Hosea 9, 9.

Proved. Note proved abundantly

16. And let the Prophet Ezekiel be harkened to, he tells the people that they had both defiled themselves, and the land by their own evil doings, there-fore to the end he might make it more evident that their sin was from their own seed, and for their further convincement, he, in chapter 36, from verse 17 to 34, doth charge their sin upon their own souls, a matter of eighteen times, which was enough to die the soul into a scarlet red, especially if we consider some of his other sayings.

Doctrine cleared

17. Therefore saith he, chapter 22, thy city shedeth blood, and maketh idols against herself to defile herself, thou hast shed blood and defiled (thyself) (their own way will I recompence upon their (own) head.)

18. In chapter 16, verse 6, 22, the prophet saith, that they were polluted in their own blood, what was that but their own seed and their own nature?

CHAP. XXV.

Divine doctrines

1. No persecuting Devils, but Men Devils only. 2. No Devil entered Judas, but the Devil that was his own Seed, proved by three Reasons.

Doctrine 1

1. AGAIN, hath not persecution and hatred its rise from carnal flesh, or fleshly devils, and not from fleshless? and these hate the good and love the evil, as Mica 3, 2, and Gal. 4; hence it was that Christ said of his apostles, that they should be hated of all men, that is, by all wicked men.

Psalms

2. It is evident there is no worser devil than haters of God and good men, and in all the book of God I do not find any other devils that hate God and his saints, but men and women devils; what devils were those that bid God depart from them, for they desired not the knowledge of his ways.

Proved

3. In Luke the 4th, Christ treating upon a prophecy of Isaiah and applying it to that present time, it is said, that all that were in the synagogue were thereupon filled with wrath; now whence came that wrath? why not from without, but it boiled up out of the heart from their invisible fire of hellish fury.

Proved

4. Therefore this fulness of wrath forced them to rise up and thrust him out of the city, and would have flung him down a rock headlong if they could.

Hipocritical devil

5. And as devilish as these were, yet they pretended piety, they came to Christ, to the synagogue, to the church, but Christ did not come to them with his healing ministry, but on the contrary his words were the savour of death unto death to them, and condemned them through their unbelief, and this kindled the fire in them of wrath and malice, which made them as wrest less as wretched, so that they could not forbear to murder him.

Doctrine 2

6. From hence we see that this implacable malice and wrath is the most destructive devil, and all this centres in man and is from man, as see 1 Sam. 17, 45. Numb. 11, 20. Isa. 53, 3.

Proved

7. Also they despise his grace and condemn his person and call him a devil to his face, what a wicked brood was this; in the history of his passion we see how they mocked, scoffed, and scorned the Lord of Life, as Luke 23, 35, and they valued a Barabas, a rogue, a murderer, before the Lord Jesus, so that they would have the devil to live, and God to die, which thing they did effect, for with wicked hands they murdered the Lord of Life.

Cleared

8. Now you that are sober in reason whether do you think there could be worse devils than these aforesaid, nay is there any mention in all the history of Christ's death of any other devils that were instrumental to this murder.

Doctrine 3

9. Certainly let all the cursed seed of Cain say what they will, yet without all Controversy, no other devil can be found but what is in man's nature only; neither will that place disprove what I have said, concerning that saying of Judas, that upon his taking the sop the devil entered into him.

Reason 1. Reason 2. Reason 3

10. But let none say that an evil spirit that was distinct from his spirit, entered into him, for these three reasons; first, if that had been so, then Christ would not have called him a devil; secondly, neither would he have imputed or charged sin wholly upon his own spirit; thirdly, neither would Judas have taken the sin willingly upon himself, but would have had a partner to have borne part of his sorrows.

Doctrine proved

11. Now you cannot choose, but know that it was Judas' own soul that sinned, in that it was his own soul that smote him for it, laying his sin to the door of his conscience, saying, I have sinned in betraying of innocent blood;[1] even now as before his soul had wrought sin, so now the law worked wrath, and burned so violently, as he hanged himself for ease.

Proved by the devil himself as well as by the elect

12. Every wicked devil in flesh, at the lash of the law, are forced to acknowledge that their sin is from themselves: I have sinned, said Judas, I have sinned, Said Pharoah,[2] then they laid their brats on their own backs, which before they laid at other devils' doors; it is no telling a devil of his sin till the law break in; if an elect vessel have broke the law he is sure to meet with hell, before he recover heaven, and to feel the lash of the law there.

13. This made David cry out against himself for his sin,[3] and Peter likewise; the one is said to water his couch with his tears every day till the pardon came, and the other had such a current of tears continually trickling down his cheeks, that as ancient history relate, made dents in his cheeks.

---

[1] Matt. 27, 4.
[2] Exod. 10, 16
[3] Psa. 6, 6. & 39, 12.

Rom. 7. Gal proved

14. This made Paul exclaim against himself, when his former evil actions of persecutions of the Saints reflected upon him, crying out in these words, O! wretched man that I am, &c.; I am the chief of sinners, I was mad against the Saints.

Doctrine 4

15. Thus we see that neither Saint nor serpent doth deny, but acknowledge, that sin doth issue from their own seed; for where doth the Scripture charge sin upon any other creature.[1] Everyman shall suffer for his own sin, said Moses; shall die for his own sin, said Ezekiel. Chap. 18.

Note Chap 16, 6 abundantly proved

16. You that would not willingly be deceived, observe well the doctrine of the Prophet Ezekiel, together with Jeremiah; see and compare Ezek. 2, 6. & 6, 9. & 11, 21. & 13, 17. & 15, 6, 9, 15, 20. & 16, 47, 48, 49. & 18, 20 & 20, 43, compared with 36. 29, 31. & 37, 10.; see also the Prophet Jer. 2, 19, & 3, 17. & 4, 14, 18. & 7, 24. & 9, 5. & 23, 16, 26. & 32, 30, 35.

What other devils needs there to compel man to sin, whilst man's own soul runs mad with sin, and is so eager of it, as that it will lose its life before it will lose its lust.[2] Is it not said that their hearts do run after their covetousness, and after all excess of riot? Yea, they are said to rush into sin as a horse rushes into battle; and to neigh after their neighbours' wives; and that their feet are swift to shed blood.[3]

The doctrine cleared as the sun in its strength

18. Now they must needs run that the devil drives; but what devil is that? why their lustful devil, in the dungeon of a dark heart, being bred and born of the will of the flesh, the angels' nature fallen.

---

[1] Psa 94, 23. Jer 2, 19.
[2] Is this not a divine saying?
[3] Ezek. 33, 31. Jer. 8, 6. Isa. 59, 7. & ch. 1, 15. Rom. 3, 15.

CHAP. XXVI.

Doctrines

The Tenth Psalm commented on, shewing a proud Devil, and his Downfall.

Psal. 10

1. AGAIN, for further proof, give me leave to paraphrase upon the 10th Psalm, for there is the devil-man elegantly described by David: he that hath ears to hear, let him hear; and he that is wicked, let him be wicked still.

2. In Psalms 10th, verse 1st, David calls upon God, being troubled at the works of the wicked, and complains against them in the second verse, saying, that the wicked in his pride doth persecute the poor; pride, we see, is the inlet to oppression; pride is from man's spirit, therefore called his pride.

Verse 3 opened

3. In verse the 3rd, he is said to boast himself of his heart's desire; here now we may note three things.

1. Observation

4. First, that sin is the desire of a man's own heart; he acts forth evil freely with heart and good will.

2. Observation

5. Secondly, no spirit is co-partner with wicked men in sin, but it is their own heart, their own desire, and their (own) choice in their (own) and from their (own soul).

3. Observation

6. Thirdly, pride and boasting are inseparable;— when the devil is puffed up, then he pulls down and plunges all that oppose, resist, or any way hinders his glory.

The cause of boasting

7. Now one cause of this devil's boasting was, in that he had power to persecute and oppress the Saints, and in that he had the desire of his mind accomplished. Therefore from hence he begins to extol the covetous whom God abhorreth, and in so much that the love of this world's goods are precious to his eyes, sweet to his taste, and

delightful to his heart; therefore his affections are wholly set upon riches, got by oppression.

Verse 4 opened. Doctrine 3

8. Now he having power to get riches by oppression, and finds no present judgment, therefore he sacrificeth unto his net, and burneth incense unto his drag, and so it becomes his God. Verse 4th.

Verse 5 opened

9. Moreover, he being so possessed with riches and honour, and finding himself to prosper, his heart begins to be further puffed up with a conceit that he shall conquer all his enemies, he not minding to know the judgments of God, because they are too sublime for proud spirits.

Verse 6 opened

10. Therefore he looks upon himself as a rock immovable, and that his riches (though got by oppression) shall continue for ever, and with such conceits he flatters his own heart; as Verse 6th.

Verse 7 opened. Five grand devils

11. Wherefore he having attained to so great riches and power over the poor, he from hence begins to be filled with wickedness, even so full of filthiness, that it flowed over; for out of his mouth, from under his tongue, came forth such a spawn, as quickened into five grand devils, as cursing, deceit, fraud, mischief, and vanity.

12. Thus comes this devil to be furnished with furniture from hell; now having so enlarged his kingdom, he begins to keep his court with his several courtiers: for he is like to the Centurian, bidding one go, and he goes; and another run, and he runs.

1. Inference

13. Now here comes to bean habitation of devils, and a hold for foul spirits, and a cage for five unclean birds; yet mind here that all these foul spirits were all from this one devil's own soul or seed, against David in the history, and that dragon, Herod, with his seven heads and ten horns, against Christ and his Saints in the mystery.

Verse 9 opened

14. Again, this dragon-devil aspires higher in his wickedness; for now he begins to contrive which way he may murder the poor in spirit, and slay the innocent, and he acts forth himself cunningly from

his fraud, for he puts himself into a three-fold posture, in order to his slaying the innocent.

15. First, he sits in the lurking places; and secondly, he lieth in wait; and thirdly, he croucheth and humbleth himself.

Verse 10 opened

16. Behold, how diligent this devil is, how politic and subtle; he gets himself into a secret place, and there he sits down, and his eye is watching the innocent to murder him, even as the fowler doth the bird, &c.

Verse 9 opened. 2. Inference

17. Secondly, he doth not only sit, but finding more difficulty to overcome some than others, therefore he lieth in wait, as a lion in his den, to catch the poor; and where this taketh not effect, he hath another curious compliment of discourtesy, for he croucheth and boweth himself, as if it were with hat in hand, even as if there were no harm or guile in him, saying as Jael to Sisera, come in, my lord, fear not; and he thinking no evil, came in, and upon his repose, she struck a nail into his head. Judges 4, 21.

3. Inference

18. Thus this devil by his cringing effects, his cruelty, his hostility, is painted with humility; he also goes crouching like a spaniel, when he is near his game, giving notice to the fowler to fling over his net.

Verse 11 opened

19. And now having accomplished his design, he begins to say in his heart, God hath forgotten, he hideth himself, he regardeth not; therefore if he can but hide himself from man, he fears not God, for he thinks that God hath not made man to punish him, though he murder his fellow-creature; as Verse 11.

20. So far now hath David, and all good hearts with him, lamented at the flourishing state of this devil; we come now to see and to dance at his downfall. Selath.

Verse 12, Verse 13, Verse 14, Verse 15 opened

21. David leaving this devil glorying in his wickedness, and addresses himself unto God, as the way to pluck him down, saying, Arise, O Lord God! lift up thy hand, forget not the humble; for though proud man saith thou seest not, yet thou seest, and beholdest mischief and spite; and although the wicked say thou wilt not requite

it, yet requite it by breaking the arm of the (wicked man), of the (proud man), of the (evil man), of the (man of the earth).

22. Not a bodiless, fleshless devil, but a bodily, fleshly devil, that hath an arm, even the wicked man, the proud man, the evil or devil man, and man of the earth.

23. Oh, break his arm, take away his power, and destroy his strength. Oh, seek out this evil man, this devil man, and make a final end of him, that the man of the earth may no more oppress.

Verse 16 opened

24. Lo! this was the Prophet's prayer, the end of which was the beginning of the Lord's vengeance against this devil-man; for faith and fruition, desire and deliverance, prayer and power, do all meet together in the words and prayer of a Prophet.

Verse 17 opened

25. Therefore, no sooner had David made an end of his prayer, but a triumph was sounded over the enemy in these words; the Lord is King for ever, the Heathen are perished out of his land; Lord, thou hast heard the desire of the humble, to judge the fatherless, and the oppressed, that the man of the earth may no more oppress; for upon the wicked he shall rain snares, fire, and brimstone, and an horrible tempest; this shall be the portion of their cup for ever.

26. Which, what that cup and portion is, shall be shewed in the Seventh Part of this Treatise, if my God permit.

Verse 18 opened

27. Wherefore, upon the paraphrase of this Psalm, it is made plain, that wicked men are the only devils, and in that the latter part of the Psalm doth shew God's enmity against them; therefore will it be an occasion further to declare, that both God's enmity, and the Saints prayers, are wholly against proud men, as the only oppressing and persecuting devils that are upon earth.

CHAP. XXVII.

Doctrines

1. Shewing God's Enmity against no Devils, but what are in Man. 2. No Devils trouble the Saints, but Man without and their own Nature (abstracted from the Angels' Seed) within. 3. Of those Devils that afflicted Christ and the Saints. 4. Man of himself is a Devil.

Doctrine 1

1. IT hath been declared, that there is no other devils that hate God and persecute the Saints but mankind, now shall you hear from the Scriptures, that God returns their hatred upon their own head, or as David saith,[1] upon their own hairy scalp, and therefore saith he, God shall wound the head of the enemy.

Opened

2 This enemy that God should wound the head of, is but man; God hath no enmity to any other creature, hence it is that the children of Cain are called the people of God's wrath, yea vessels of wrath prepared for destruction, and in my text called by the Lord Jesus Christ [workers of iniquity.][2]

Doctrine proved

3. So that we see, that all other spirits are excluded from an eternal wrath, and that, because there are no other creatures that are said to be heirs of eternal wrath but man only, therefore called children of wrath, Ephes. 2, 3. and 5, 6. Col. 3, 6.

Doctrine 2. Proved

4. When God punisheth the devil, he punisheth him in man, and man feels it as being his own seed and nature, and one in person without division, see these Scriptures if your eye be single, Psa. 5, 3. Ezek. 21, 31. and 22, 31. Zeph. 1, 14. Ezek. 38, 19. to these may be applied that of James, the devil believes and trembles, Felix being one of them devils that trembled at Paul's sermon of judgment.

---

[1] Psa. 68, 21.
[2] Psa. 2. 5. 12. And Psa. 95, 11. Esa. 10, 6. Jer 7, 20. Ephes. 2, 3. and 5, 6.

Secondly proved.

5. The Scripture further declares, that God poureth out his fury upon man, beast, trees, fruits of the ground, and upon the earth, seas, rivers, the sun, moon, and upon the heathen, and finally, upon the seat of the beast, but where is wrath poured out upon a bodyless devil.

Thirdly

6. If wrath be poured out upon any thing but man, is it not for the sin of man?

Fourthly

7. Furthermore, you must note that the saints in all times and ages, have made their prayers against no other devils but wicked men without them, and their own corrupt hearts within them, which doth imply that there were no other devils, as it was said of Israel, that God gave them up to their own hearts' lust, &c.

Fifthly

8. Well then it follows, that the saints of old and the prophets, are all against wicked men without them, and their own bad nature within them.

9. O Lord (said Jeremiah) give them sorrow of heart, thy curse unto them and destroy them in anger. O Lord, let me see thy vengeance on them, Lam. 3, 64, 65, 66. chap 11, 20. Jer. 12, 20.

Sixthly

10. God makes devilish man his rod, to scourge his people for their sins, or for their trial of faith, and when God sees his own time, that is, when the saints' afflictions are at the highest, and their hearts the lowest; as also, when their persecutors are in heart the highest, and made ripe by pride and cruelty, then, even then, doth God step in upon the prayer of his saints, and takes up his rod and casts it into the fire.

Seventhly

11. Again, David in one place prays thus, Arise, O Lord, and deliver me from the men of the earth, whose portion is in this life; again, my soul is among lions, even the sons of men, whose teeth are

spears; O save me from bloody men, who make a noise like a dog, behold they belch out with their mouth; consume them in wrath, &c.[1]

Eighthly

12. Again, David proceeds in prayer, O save me from the wicked that oppress me, from the deadly enemy that compass (me, my Christ,) for these words have relation to Christ as well as David. Save me, O Lord, by thy name, because of the voice of the enemy, because of the oppression of the wicked, for they cast iniquity upon me, and in wrath they hate me.

Ninthly

13. Destroy, O Lord, and divide their tongue, hide me from the secret counsel of the wicked, deliver me from the cruel man, O deliver not the soul of thy turtle dove into the multitude of the wicked.[2]

The tenth proof

14. Furthermore, you that have never so little of the light of heavenly truth in you, so that it be rooted, may certainly know, that Christ Jesus the Lord of life, was afflicted with no other devils but wicked men, and it was into their hands he was delivered.

The doctrine cleared

15. The Son of Man (said Christ, meaning himself,) shall be delivered into the hands of men, see Luke 9, 44. and 24, 7. and Peter saith, that by wicked hands he was slain, Acts 2.

---

[1] Psa. 17. Psa. 57. Psa 59. Psa 17. Psa 53.
[2] Psa. 65. Psa 74.

CHAP. XXVIII.

Doctrines

Shewing there can be no worse Devils than Mankind.

Doctrine 1. Doctrine 2. Doctrine 3. Doctrine 4. Doctrine 5

The first doctrine insisted on

1. BEHOLD now, from what I have said, is it possible there could be worse devils than wicked men? Are not the haters of the workmanship of God, devils? And are not the murderers of mankind, great devils? But they are greater devils that murder the Saints; but the murderers of God are the greatest dragon-devils of all. Woe to such, and to men this woe belongs; woe to man that killeth man; but woe, woe, woe to man that killed or consented to the death of Christ, the eternal God, and Creator of all men.

2. Thus now it is clear that all sin is from man, all evil in man, and all evil of punishment on man: there is no wickedness but from wicked man; for as David saith, wickedness proceedeth from the wicked.[1]

3. I could bring abundantly more proofs from Scripture to prove this doctrine; yea, thousands of places, for the whole current of the Scriptures proves it; yea, a great part of the Scripture stands upon it, for the Scripture stands upon these two foundations, namely, the true God, and the right devil; and yet the devil cannot know himself.

4. And as the Scriptures doth clearly shew to the seed of the Son of Man, who have the hearing ear, that the devil is clothed with flesh, so experience by the sight of the works and actions of wicked man, may be evidence sufficient to sober reason, that there is not a worse devil than a wicked man, who is in power and authority.

5. I could prove this abundantly, if I would trace the footsteps of the great Monarchs and Rulers of the world, whose actions have been such, as have startled and amazed the very devils themselves, much more the sober in reason, whose quiet and still devil did not hurry them to such wickedness.

---

[1] This doctrine hath been proved, and may be proved abundantly further, as shall be done in some instances, and so conclude.

Doctrine 1

6. I shall give some instances, and conclude this point. Was there a worse devil than Nero, that ripped open his mother's belly, that he might see the place he lay in? that put Seneca, his tutor, to death? and hundreds more that had done him no evil; and hundreds of Saints that had done least of all.

Proved

7. Was there a worse devil than Julian, the apostate, who flung his blood up towards heaven in despite of Christ, saving, thou hast overcome me, thou Galilean?

Secondly

8. Was there a greater devil than the Emperor Galerius and Askelepiades, who cried out against Rominon's, the Christian, saying, scourge him with whips, with knobs of lead at the ends; truss him up, draw out his bowels, lance his sides with knives until the bones appear white? Doth the rogue say, that Christ is God, and his God? O villain, thy God is a yesterday God, but the Gentile's God was a God for ever; thou trustest to a hanged God; scourge the rogue, lance him, whip him, plague him, punish him, &c.

Thirdly

9. Again, was there a worse devil than Valerius the Emperor, in the year of our Lord 1259, and yet appeared as a Saint, before or at his first coming in to the Empire, when Larance, before the Emperor, was called, to demand of him where the treasure of their Church was (for it was told that he had great treasure which the Christians had intrusted him with for the poor).

Of the Saints Love

10: Larance answered, pointing at the poor, these (saith he) are the precious treasure of the church; these are the treasure indeed, in whom the faith of Christ reigneth, in whom Jesus Christ hath his mansion place.

Of the Devil's wrath

11. Upon this no tongue was able to express the fury and madness of the tyrant's heart; now he stamped, he stared, he ramped, he foamed as one out of his wits; his eyes like fire glowed, his mouth like a boar foamed, his teeth like a hell-hound grinned.

A roaring lion

12. Now, saith he, kindle the fire of wood, make no spare; hath this villain deluded the emperor; away with him; whip him with scourges, jerk him with rods, buffet him with fists, brain him with clubs, jesteth the traitor with the emperor, pinch him with fire tongs, gird him with burning plates, bring out the fire-fork, and the grated bed of iron; on the fire with it.

No worse devil can be found

13. Bind the rebel hand and foot, and when the bed is fire hot, on with him; roast him, broil him, toss him, turn him, on pain of our high displeasure: do every man his office; the word was no sooner spoken, but all was done.

The doctrine clearly proved

14. Was not this a devil in grain? Therefore, without all controversy, there is no greater devils than man; nay, no devils to be damned to eternity, but men and women devils only.

15. Therefore let no man flatter himself; for of himself he is a devil; and without grace, a damned devil.

The conclusion applied to reason

16. So to conclude this Part, let man for ever after charge his own soul with the evil he doth, and lay his brats no more at other men's doors. For, O man, I tell thee, thou spinnest the thread out of thy own web, and they are hatched from thy own heart, begot by thy own invention, and are acted by thine own will; so that thou, and all men that sin, do thereby weave the web of their own woe, and spin the thread of their own thraldrom.

THE FOURTH PART:

PROVING THE

Doctrine of Predestination.

THE TEXT SAITH,

That the one Seed are the Children of the Kingdom, and the other Seed are the Tares for to be flung into the Fire. Matt. 13.

FROM HENCE THE OBSERVATION IS,

That the Seed of Adam are predestinated unto Doctrine, eternal life, and that the Seed of the Serpent are from the foundation of the world, appointed to damnation.

CHAP. I.

Doctrines

1. Of the Grounds of Election and Rejection. 2. How Doctrines. Justice and Mercy in God are known. 3. Shewing who can preach Predestination. 4. Of the Nature of Conversion.

1. ALTHOUGH every man naturally loves himself, so as that he flatters himself with a conceit of goodness, will, and power to do the commands of the Creator, from which nature, pride, and presumption spring up in all Cain's seed and offspring, and offers violence against the prerogative power of the Creator.

Doctrine 2

2. But let God be true and all men of this seed of reason be liars, for the power of the Creator is omnipotent, therefore all those that will have him to rule over them, are his elect, but all the rest are reprobates, by these fruits are they known.

Proved

3. Now that election and rejection to eternal life and eternal death, is grounded upon the prerogative power, will, and pleasure of the

Creator, and not upon the foresight of good or evil, that is in the creature is now to be declared by me, according to my measure.

Secondly

4. It was shewed before, how God had formed two vessels, the one to honour, the other to dishonour, and it is clear that these two vessels were Adam and the serpent angel, and insomuch that the one was capable to dissolve into seed, and the other to beget a seed; and these two seeds having a law of generation in them, therefore it must follow, that as it befel the root, so it would the branches; for as the roots of these two seeds, were the one appointed to eternal life, and the other to eternal death, so would for ever their branches.

Thirdly

5. Therefore how can it choose to be otherwise, but that there are two seeds, the one pre-ordained to eternal life, and the other reprobated to eternal death, to the end that God's purpose may stand according to election and rejection, and not to be founded in creaturely strength.

Fourthly

6. This doctrine being of divine power, bow down unto it, and receive consolation, all you the seed of the son of man, for this is to be minded, that if God had not made two seeds, according to his eternal will, and leave them both to their creaturely strength, and to withhold from them both that divine power by which they stood, to the end they might unite themselves unlawfully together, for the producing of two several generations of people of this earth, for the manifestation of his inestimable glory for one, and for the demonstration of his divine justice in the other.

Fifthly

7. Would not all his wonderful wisdom or divine power have been hid or concealed from men and angels, and so they would have failed in their comprehension of the mighty, wonderful, and various wisdom, power and glory of the Creator, blessed for ever, and honoured by them, being chosen for his eternal pleasure and for their everlasting joy and felicity.

Sixthly

8. Again it is written, that the Creator made all things for his own glory, and the wicked for the day of wrath; now God can make nothing

against his glory, because his nature is nothing but variety of heavenly perfections.

Seventhly

9. Therefore his forming of wicked men for wrath is for promoting of his glory, by making known that great attribute of his justice.

Eighthly

10. Therefore let no man (in pain of damnation) offer to interrupt our God by opposing his prerogative royal, for he with his two feet of justice and mercy, walk in his ways, for all his paths are mercy and truth;[1] salvation and damnation, justice and clemency, is mercy and truth; and both stands up on God's prerogative, and not on man's power.

Ninthly

11. Therefore said the Lord by Moses to Pharoah, the king, for this same purpose have I stirred thee up, that I might shew my power on thee.

Tenthly

12. Again it is written, whom he hath prepared for destruction—prepared for glory—ordained for destruction.

13. Here it is clear, that eternal torment, as it is the portion of the wicked, even so they are made on purpose for it, being prepared for the devil and his angels, which is Cain and his offspring.

Eleventhly

14. Therefore when the serpent angel was cursed all his seed was cursed with him.

Twelfthly

15. So on the contrary, Jacob is said to bless Joseph, when as Joseph's children had the blessing,[2] which shews that blessings and cursings, whether temporal or eternal, do run in a line.

Thirteenthly

16. This is made clear by that saying, cast out the bond-woman and her son, what is that but the law, and the seed that the law is

---

[1] Psalm.
[2] Gen. 48, 15. 16.

written in, for they both gender to bondage, for as the law works nothing in that seed, but fear and horror, because of its non-election, even so likewise, as woeful companions, they are to be cast out of God's presence; the seed of reason, the son, to remain with his mother, the law, in thraldom for ever.

Fourteenthly

17. Whilst the seed of faith, as Isaac, the son of Sarah, the free-woman, shall on the contrary, as sweet companions gender to love, peace, and assurance of eternal life; for that Sarah, the free-woman, signifies the law of faith, and Isaac, the son, signifies the seed of faith, in which that heavenly healthful, happy, and holy law is written.

Doctrine 2

18. Now this seed of faith is it which is clear, to whom the heavenly inheritance is given, which in this life is sealed to it by that law of faith, written in its seed, and this seed that hath this gospel golden law engraven in it, doth clearly read its own election in that book of life, and in the time of a commission doth behold its inheritance with open face.

Note Doctrine 3. The ground of the doctrine

19. Lo here, for at such a time, this is the minister that can preach predestination, election, and rejection, and is acquainted with the decrees of God, for when the spirit of faith hath made itself conspicuous in the soul, then can the light of that soul enlighten another soul, by words of truth, for words of truth are light and life.

Explained

20. But then this is to be understood, that words of truth is of efficacy in that heart, in which there is a seed of heaven, for though that seed should be dead, yet in regard of nature, the virtue of the word will enter the spirit, and by its spiritual voice will awaken it, when Epapriais pronounced the work is done.

21. But to the matter aforesaid, let no man think that he can preach God's decrees or councils without, until he can read his own election within, and as he sees his Creator's free love to the one seed, so he will see his just anger to the other.

22. But here reason keeps a great clamour, and saith, doth God make man to damn him? to this, and several other objections, I shall now return my answer in the chapters following.

CHAP. II.

Doctrines

1. An Objection answered. 2. Foresight of Works no cause of Salvation. 3. Wherefore God loved Jacob, and hated Esau.

By 14 several proofs

1. HOW that there are two Seeds, and the one appointed for wrath, that is clearly proved by Scripture records; therefore how will cavilling reason deliver itself, if you, free-willers' say, that if this doctrine be true, then God is unjust, that will make man on purpose to damn him.

Reasons argued with, as first from his prerogative

2, But how will you prove God to be unjust? Will you make obligations for the eternal Creator, and bind God by a law, as if you were greater than he?

Secondly, from the potter, Rom. 9

3. Do you not know, that he that made man, may do with man what he please? Doth not the Apostle tell you so, that an earthly potter hath power over the clay?

4. Now, if an earthly potter hath such power, how much more power hath the great potter of heaven and earth, to make two seeds or vessels, as Paul calls them? And when he hath so done, to shew mercy unto one by making it a vessel of honor, and to dash the other in pieces like a potter's vessel.

5 And who shall dare to charge God with injustice, as to say, why didst thou make me so? for there is no law to bind an infinite Majesty to protect his creature, and to keep it in its first created purity?

6. For if God make a seed to suffer eternal sorrow, who shall gainsay it; and he hath done so? therefore he calls the seed of Esau the borders of wickedness, and the people in whom he hath indignation for ever; and why did he set his anger against Esau, whilst to Isaac and his seed he made an everlasting covenant of peace?[1]

---

[1] Mal. 1, 4.

Fourthly

7. Why should any that own Scripture say that it was their good works and evil that occasioned his love and anger, when as the Apostle affirms to the contrary, saying that God loved Jacob and hated Esau, before they had done either good or evil.[1]

8. But to this, reason in the free-will mongers, hath a seeming plausible answer, saying that that was spoke in relation to Gods foreknowledge, he foreseeing them to be in men's estate, and so in their own persons, acting good or evil, which works, say they, were the cause of his love and anger.

The Apostle's doctrine opened

9. But this answer is but a leg made of clay, and cannot stand; for the Apostle Paul, and the Prophet Malacchi, are clear in their doctrine for eternal election and rejection, without any foresight of either good or evil; therefore the Apostle shews the cause of election and rejection in these words, that the purpose of God might stand or remain according to election.

10. The Apostle, you see, prevents all pleading for works; for if it be by purpose or decree, then it is the grace of election; and if it be by election or free choice, then not of works or merit, for merit confounds mercy, but with us mercy is the only merit.

The Prophet's doctrine opened

11. Again, Malacchi saith, was not Esau Jacob's brother, yet he brings in God, saying, I loved Jacob and hated Esau; now this hatred and love was not in the temporal, for then Esau could not have been and his seed the people of his indignation for ever; neither could Jacob have been the object of his eternal love.

A reason given to reason. Note

12. But you, seed of unbelief, if you would have a reason why God loved the one, and hated the other, take this for one; for though God hated Esau before he was born, yet was his indignation just, because God saw him to be the seed of that serpent-angel which abhorred to be guided by his Creator, after he had withheld from him his creaturely purity.

---

[1] Rom. 9.

An answer to the ground of Election and Rejection

13. For the Creator, upon the conception of Esau and Jacob in the womb of Rebecca, did by his infinite wisdom, discern the roots they both sprang from, as Esau from the seed of the serpent, through the loins of Cain, and Jacob from the seed of God, through the loins of Adam; and here is the objects of love and anger, and the ground of blessing and cursing, life and death, salvation and damnation.

CHAP. III.

Doctrines

No free Will in Man to good from his own Nature, proved by Three Reasons. Who is the most proud?

Doctrine 1

1. AGAIN, for a further convincement of all free-will mongers, I shall shew that, according to the Scripture, it is not in him that willeth, or him that runneth, but in God that sheweth mercy.

Scripture

2. It is written that the gift and calling of God are without repentance. Again, it is written, when you were in your blood, I said unto you, live. Again, it is written, I was found of him that sought me not.[1]

Opened and cleared

3. Here we see that eternal election and rejection depends on God's will and pleasure, and not on man's; it is not in him that willeth, or him that runneth. But the free willers' would have that place meant, that seeketh his own will, or runneth in his own way, but not in him that runneth in God's way. But to this I answer,

4. Until the Lord hath presented an immortal crown of glory, there can be no walking in God's way, as David saith, when thou hast enlarged my heart,[2] then will I run the ways of thy commandments; for the Lord cannot truly be known, till his name and nature be written in the heart, which when so done, then the soul that was backward to all goodness, is now by virtue of that divine light, made willing to chuse the better part, and not before.

---

[1] Rom. 11, 29. Ezek. 16, 16. Isa. 65, 1.
[2] Psa. 119, 32.

5. For until the Lord hath wrought our righteousness, we can work nothing but unrighteousness from our own blind born spirits; for in their natural state they would sooner chuse death than life.[1]

6. And wherefore are they so averse to goodness? Why, because that which should act forth divine goodness or righteousness, is asleep or dead, till a virtue from a divine word spoken quicken it, for natural reason will never chuse spiritual faith, for these three reasons:

Reason blind

7. First, because it knows not the nature of faith, and so is a stranger to it; secondly, in that it grounds upon its own strength; and thirdly, and lastly, in that its wisdom is so great and of such efficacy, as that it appropriates to itself a knowledge and capacity to merit eternal life, from those places of God's commanding them to works of righteousness, and promising blessings upon condition.

Note

8. But to the matter aforesaid; if eternal election and rejection depends upon the acceptation of man's will, then no man will be saved, for heaven is not heaven to a natural man; the purest of man's will, what would it strive for? Is it not for pre-eminence in Church and State?

9. And pray, what are the fruits of such desires? Is it any thing but spiritual pride and natural pomp? and there is none more proud than the spiritual conceited perfectionist; he is ever ready to say, stand further off, for I am more holy than thou.

CHAP. IV.

Doctrines

1. Of Repentance, and how it doth not merit Pardon. The Way to Life, and the Cause of Life distinguished. 3. Of a two-fold Repentance.

Doctrine 1

1. IT is not in him that willeth, let his natural light be never so great, his will never so pure, or his zeal never so strong, though he continually preach and pray, read or hear, though he thunder in the skies, with pathetical cries, with Lord, Lord, open to me.

---

[1] Note. Psa.119, 40. Isa. 45, 24. & 54, 17. Philip. 3, 9.

2. Yet this, and all that ever can be done by man, although he should shed rivers of tears, will not, nor cannot move the eternal God to set the seal of divine love upon any, until he is graciously pleased of himself, from his own free and unconstrained love.

Doctrine proved

3. For if the gift and calling of God be without repentance, then doth not repentance purchase the gifts and calling of God; if it did, then Judas would have found mercy, as well as Peter; for he is said to have repented for his betraying his Lord, as Peter did, for his denying of him; yet the one found mercy in his repentance, the other wrath, notwithstanding his repentance.

Illustrated

4. Therefore let sin or seeming sanctity be what it will in man or angel, yet the prerogative power, will, or pleasure in the Creator is all. Changing the state and condition of things already created, from their present conditions, when how and which way he pleases, without having any respect to outward appearances, for the manifestation of his infinite power of eternal condemnation, or salvation; as for instance,

Note. Exemplified

5. Did not the Lord transmute the most glorious angel in heaven, and made him become the most great and most chief devil in hell, or flesh, and to convert one of the greatest devils by nature on earth, to become one of the most glorious saints in heaven? Let Cain and Mary Magdalen bear witness to this.

Reason met with all, and spoke to

6. Thus may you, my friends, see as I have learned, that it is not man's will or work, but God's gracious will, that works our salvation. Man would be his own saviour, if his own will had power to good; then might proud man, as he ever doth, ascribe all to his own net, to his own will, to his own power, in his spirit of pride.

7. But art not thou vain, O, proud man, to rob God of his prerogative royal, by making eternal life depend upon thy way? when, as the Scripture saith, that the way of man is not in himself, and that it is not in man to direct his steps.[1]

---

[1] Jer. 10, 23.

Objection

8. But finding reason full of cavils, I must answer some of their greatest objections: if repentance doth not merit pardon, then, say they, wherefore doth the Scriptures require repentance, as the way to eternal life? To this I answer,

Answer. Doctrine 2

9. There is a great deal of difference between being the way to life, and the cause of life; for repentance, love, and good works, are the way to life, and the electing love of God is the cause.

10. But then mind this, that though repentance, love, and good works, are the way to life, yet reason knows not that way in reality, for it hath but the law's shadow of it; but faith's way being in the path of the new covenant of peace and power,

Cleared and proved

11. Therefore its work is not with reason in the law of works to seek for life, but to repent through life, and then to love and work in that life; therefore from hence it is called repentance unto life.

Illustrated

12. And what is it now through you that leads the way to that repentance, but only spiritual faith, therefore called a fruit, worthy, meet, or fit for repentance to life.

13. And wherefore is faith a fruit of that worth, but because it is life, and leads to life; being the calling and gift of God without repentance.

Repentance not the cause but the effect

14. Repentance being but the effect of that gift, for as the cause goes before the effect, so the call and gift of faith makes way for Godly sorrow, working repentance, never to be repented of.

2 Cor. 7, 10 opened

15. But then as faith's repentance worketh life, even so on the contrary, reason's repentance works death; therefore, saith the Apostle, the sorrow of the world worketh death; and why so? but because it wants the call and gift of God in Christ, the way in which all spiritual gifts do come.

Reason's repentance. Rom. 7

16. But the call of the law that reason sometimes (when convinced of sin) hearkeneth to, and reason runs thither for refuge, but finds no rest; for finding itself bitten, with the fiery serpent of sin, it runs to the righteousness of the law, to be cured of its deadly wounds, of aspiring thoughts, words, and actions against the Creator, or his heavenly ways, and the law doth but inflame their wounds.

17. But that the gift of eternal life depends not upon man's will and power, way or wisdom, is evident by that which is recorded of Esau. Give me leave to present unto you the recital thereof more at large.

CHAP. V.

Doctrines

1. Godliness not to be measured by Mans will. 2. An Objection about the Day of Grace answered. 3. What is meant by Selling of the Birth-right.

Doctrine 1

1. WHO could ever have thought to the contrary, but that Esau himself should have found mercy to eternal life, if we must measure godliness by man's will.

Gen. 27 opened

2. For observe, do you not find him striving for the blessing, as with all his power; O how tractable was he to his father, and had a belief that his father was a prophet, and his carriage was such to his father, as that is father was greatly deceived in him.

3. For Isaac thought that Esau, his eldest son had been the chosen of God, therefore he had intended to have given him the spiritual blessing, but that the policy of Rebecca prevented it, through her revelation and practice, which gave knowledge and assurance to Isaac, that Jacob was God's chosen vessel.

4. But now behold Esau's diligence to serve his father, for he forthwith upon demand, obeyed his father, and his care also of his father's blessing was very great; and when he heard that Jacob his younger brother had got the blessing by stealth, he was grieved at heart, and cried out to his father, (when his father had told him, that he had blessed Jacob and he should be blessed.)

5. Then, I say Esau cried out with an exceeding great and bitter cry, saying, bless me, even me also, O my father.

Verse 36

6. Again, and after all this, Esau yet replied by way of query, saying, hast thou not reserved a blessing for me?

Verse 38

7. But Isaac still putting off Esau, which makes Esau still come on with a third request, saying, hast thou but one blessing, O my father? bless me, even me also, O my father; and Esau lift up his eyes and wept.

Doctrine illustrated

8. Behold, here now you Oracle-grace-merchants, do you not see what virtue there is in the will of man? where now is your power of free-will? indeed, here is will, but where is power? here is desire, but where is strength?

Prosecuted

9. Here is praying and entreating, here is crying and craving, with tears trickling down the cheeks, and yet no heavenly blessing, but the birthright and blessing are both lost, and will not be gained notwithstanding all this struggle.

Amplified

10. This Esau is one of those that the gospel speaks of, that shall cry, Lord, Lord, open to us, open, O we pray, open to us thy gates of mercy, is it not in thy law? why then if not, where shall we find it?

Applied

11. O, wilt thou not give entrance 10 them that strive, that so struggle, that so pray with sighs and sobs, that fast, that give alms, that preach and teach thy name among the people, is not this the way? yea the door, why then will it not open? and we travel so sore, and knock so hard, and take such pains, O open the door, and let us enjoy thy blessing.

Established

12. But their impulse will be to this purpose, who; are ye that knock? I know ye not, I approve not of your doings, for you are none of my children, my special gifts and graces belong not to you, your

inheritance as it is by the law, so keep to you to the law, and then that blessing shall be yours, so that you shall have riches, honour, wealth, and long life; this shall be your portion, and this is the one blessing that is for you.

Isaac's blessing and Jacob's

13. But as for the other blessing that is entailed and fastened to Jacob and his seed, which is the seed of faith; doth this current of life run, and so is the object of grace and the subject of mercy, to everlasting life, bliss, and glory.

Objection

14. But here reason is ready to object and say, that the cause that Esau found not mercy was, in that his day of grace was past; once (say they) he might have been happy if he would, grace had been offered to him, but he refused it, he sold his birthright, and was willing to part with heaven.

15. And now repentance being withheld, (say they) there could be no repentance, as Pharoah said, come let us deal wisely, then, even then, did he give sentence, that repentance should be hid from him, as a Jewish Rabby expounds it for the freewillers.

The objection answered

16. Now, that Esau might have been happy if he would, or that spiritual grace was ever offered to him, is contrary to Scripture, for when he was in the womb of his mother, he is said to be in nature contrary to Jacob, and Malacchi saith, that God hateth Esau, and Paul saith, that this hatred was before he had done any evil.

Cleared

17. Wherefore, certainly God will never offer eternal life to that person which he hates; and whereas it is said, that Esau sold his birth-right, yet we are not to conceive (although the spiritual birthright be meant,) that Esau had any inheritance in the heavenly inheritance.

Opened

18. But it was only to show, that he (before his sensibleness of his rejection) valued not any thing but this world and his belly, for an inheritance in heaven that was out of his sight, and so there was no such desire of it, as was a mess of pottage, the portion of Cain's people.

Illustrated

19. And in regard of the prevalency of the love of a belly full of corruptible meat, more than for that which is spiritual and incorruptible, therefore it may be called a selling, according as the Scripture saith, that a carnal man is sold under sin, that is, he parts with all for sin, or sells himself wholly as a servant to sin

Explained

20. For when a man parts from the semblance of grace willingly, it may be said that he hath sold it, according as it is said, he that hath shall be given, but he that hath not shall be taken away,[1] that which he seemed to have; seeming grace is no grace, but only a shadow of grace.

Proved

21. Thus it was with Esau; he seemed to have an interest in heaven, and that which he seemed to have, was taken from him by sale, and the substance of that, which that seeming virtue did shadow, was given unto Jacob.

The ground of election

Not for any works of righteousness that he had done or should do, but because he was the seed of Adam, which was the seed of faith, which was the seed of God, the service from which seed is acceptable with God.

Cleared

But as mercy from similitude, was the cause of favour to Jacob, so the promise was only Jacob's staff of strength, because he was the son of promise; here then lies the offer of life, here now lies the gift of life; how could Esau have the offer of spiritual grace, when as he was not the son of the promise of grace.

---

[1] Mat. 25, 39.

CHAP. VI.

Doctrines

1. No Prayer available to eternal Lift for a Reprobate. 2. Something praiseworthy in a Reprobate. 3. How a Reprobate is known. 4. Of perfection of Faith. 5. Of God's having a two-fold Will answered.

Doctrine 1

1. AS Esau could not find any place for repentance to life, because he was not the Son of the Promise, and so of the reprobate seed, even so likewise none of that seed, be he never so wise or seemingly holy, can ever, by whatever by them may be done, cause God to set the seal of his love upon them.

Doctrine 2

2. Nay, and not only so, but if all the prophets and holy men of God should pray for their conversion, yet all in vain, for they should do no more but deliver their own souls out of the camp of Cain and his progeny.

Proved

3. Though this be a hard saying, yet it is a true saying; for this is to be known, that man is to live by his own faith.

Secondly

4. Now if a man have not the faith of God's elect, how can the elect help him by their prayers or tears, or any thing they can do?

Thirdly

5 If this could have been, then certainly Samuel would have helped Saul, for he loved the king greatly. And also Isaac, he would have helped Esau, for he loved him above Jacob; as also old Ely, how much over indulgent was he to his ungracious sons; and what would Paul have suffered for his brethren in the flesh for to have saved them, his love was such as that he would have borne all the curses of this, life; but all would not serve.

Fourthly

6. And indeed this is certain, that many a Saint hath more love to some that are of the reprobate seed, than to some of those that he knows to be of the elect seed; and the cause is, because that the one hath such good natural parts, and the other hath such bad and corrupt natures hanging upon them, that are even hateful to the devil himself, that is moderated and educated up into civility, morality, and manners.

Fifthly

7. And yet, notwithstanding, God will love the corrupt natured person because of his faith, and reject the well natured person for want of his faith.

8. Only this, the good moral nature will have a blessing in this life, and the corrupt nature hath a curse in this life, as poverty, contempt, non-assurance, &c.; but this follows but to the grave's mouth.[1]

Sixthly

9. Again, you know that Christ the eternal God, healed many by virtue of their faith; but where there was not faith, Christ could not heal (although he was God), as you read.

Seventhly

10. It is said by John,[2] that if any man see his brother sin a sin, which is not unto death, he shall ask and shall have life by that means given to him.; but then it is pre-supposed that this brother hath faith, and so the faith of the one, and the prayer and faith of the other, concur together for the producing the effect.

Eighthly

11, But in the following words, the Apostle tells of another sin that was unto death, and forbids the praying for that, and that is the palpable sin of despising truth. Now a reprobate doth not discover himself to be a reprobate until the despising of true prophesy.

Ninthly

12. For though election and rejection lies in the seed, yet can we not give a final judgment of an eternal state by some single operation from each seed; for when we see a man wallowing in sin and

---

[1] Matt. 13, 58. Mark 6, 6.
[2] 1 John.

uncleanness, like the swine in the mire, we may say that he acts from the seed of the serpent, and so is in the state of damnation.

Tenthly

13. But whether he will be damned or no, it is not known but that he may be a vessel of honour, and called in time, unless his sin do grow so high as to despise and judge things he knows not, and then he manifests himself to be the seed of the serpent, and appointed for wrath; or that he do forsake truth as Demus did;

Reason's progress

14. And as to the profession of faith, a hypocrite may go far in a seeming purity; yet know this, that he hath not the seed of that faith he professes in his heart savingly.

15. Therefore, though eternal life in its seed may seem to scatter itself into several sorts of ground, yet is there but one ground possessed with the grace of salvation; therefore it is written, that salvation is far from the wicked, and that to them there is no peace.

Doctrine 3. Scripture perfection

16. But where salvation faith arises to that perfection, as that salvation is knowingly abiding in it, no doubts or distrustful fears can in that soul enter, but it stands immovable in its measure, even as God doth, and knows itself to be freed from an eternal wrath. This is one fruit of Predestination, and one degree of perfection the Scripture speaks of.

17. But to the matter in hand. If a man sin unto death by despising truth, there remains no more sacrifice for that sin, neither is any Prophet or Saint to pray for such a one, but on the contrary, to lay the curse of eternal damnation close to their consciences; as Jeremiah, where he prays that God would give them sorrow of heart, and to give them the curse, &c.

18. From hence, now you the seed of faith, may clearly see, that it is not only the secret will of God to damn to eternity a people of his wrath, but likewise he hath revealed unto his own seed, in every Commission (though to none so much as to this), that it is the pleasure of his prerogative power to damn as well as save; according as it is written, I will have mercy on whom I will have mercy,[1] and whom I will I harden; for this same purpose have I stirred thee up, &c.

---

[1] Rom. 9.

Applied

19. From hence now appears not only the darkness of the free-will mongers, but also the ignorance of the Scripturian, Presbyterian, Independant professors, that though they teach Predestination, yet it is of such weak grounds, as will not stand; and how should it, seeing they have but one seed, and not two, and so want a foundation? for although they do maintain that doctrine in one respect, yet do they destroy it in another; for say some of them,

The legal professor of Predestination

20. God hath a two-fold will, a revealed will, and a secret will. Now as to his revealed will (say they), God would have all men saved, but as to his secret will, he will have some to be damned.

Convicted

21. Now, what ignorance is here and presumption; what have they to do with God's secret will? for what is not revealed, is unknown. But they might have seen, had they had but the spirit of the Scripture, that it was revealed clear enough by the Apostle's Commission.

Second conviction

22. Again, if God, by his secret will, would have some to perish, and by his revealed will, would have all to be saved, then must God be at variance with himself, and something must impugn and resist his will; but let me ask, with the Apostle, who hath resisted his will?

Third conviction

23. It had been sounder doctrine for them to hold forth a two-fold salvation rather than a two-fold will; for where it is said that God would not have the death of a sinner, but would have all men saved.[1]

Text opened

24. This having all men saved, is not to be understood with an eternal salvation, but a temporal one suited to their obedience to the Law, which reason hath made promise to perform; and the Apostle doth clear the matter as to a two-fold salvation as common and special; would have all to be saved, especially they that are of the household of faith, and believe.

25,. Here it is clear that God hath a special salvation for his elect; but as to the seed of reason, he hath but a temporal: for all the

---

[1] 1 Tim. 2, 4. Rom. 11, 26.

promises of the Law extend no further than the comforts of this life; therefore if reason be obedient to the Law, it is to have the blessings of the Law, as you may read in the margin.[1]

CHAP. VII.

Doctrines

1. Of the Will of Man further in its striving in the Law, and how it works for Life. 2. But Faith works from Life.

Query

1. IT is of great importance to know, how the will of man and the will of God acquiesce together, seeing God's will commands man's will, and exhorts it to chuse the good and refuse the evil, which if so done, then God's will is, that it shall have the blessing. Hath man, therefore, will and power to do so, or no? To this I answer,

Answer. Doctrine 1

2. Reason hath not power to act either spiritual or natural good of itself, or to resist spiritual or natural evil; it may have a will operated in it by the Law, but power it hath none, for the Law giveth no power, only some will or desire to good it may beget, as Paul said (speaking as to the unregenerate estate), to will is present with me, but how to perform that which is good, I know not.[2]

Opened

3 Here was a looking-glass for reason to see his face in, and to shew him what was good, and reason, willing to be saved, had a desire to do good; in order thereunto, there was will and desire, prayers and promises, but no performance for want of power in the inner man.

4. For the Law begets a will, and an outward formality in reason, and the Gospel begets a will and an internal power of obedience in faith;[3] therefore it is said that none but the elect are strengthened by the power of Christ's might, as the fruit of redemption from the fountain of grace.

---

[1] Jer. 31, 18. 19. Deut. 7, 12. Chap. 14 & chap. 28. Ezek. 18, 32. Chap. 33, 11.
[2] Rom. 7
[3] Note: Ephe. 3, 16. Col. 11, 11. Rom. 5, 6.

Inference 1

5. If there be any seeming purity in reason, or virtuous actions from the same, it springs not from man's nature, for man as from his own nature is a devil, and cannot think a good thought.

Inference 2

6. Therefore, when any naturalist does any thing that is good or virtuous, understand that it is by adhering to the Law, which may remove some pollutions of the flesh.

Inference 3

7. Furthermore, by virtue of the Law's influence, it may convince a man of evil, and that conviction begets fear, and that fear begets a will to worship, and worship begets hopes.

Inference 4

8. Again, from this connection (through fear), it may cause a man to confess the truth, and several times to wish that he could love it or obey it, or that he might die the death of the righteous, as Balaam did.[1]

Inference 5

9. Moreover by the virtue of this Law, or convincing light thereof, and by the study and practice of the same, it may have many goodly and heavenly words, insomuch as that it may have a language so high, as to curiosity of style, and so garnished with eloquence, not only as to a terrestrial discourse, but also as to a celestial.

Inference 6

10. Furthermore, it may also have such a shew of holiness, that by its pathetical cries, and weeping eyes, so far as would even deceive the elect if it were possible.

Solomon, Periander

11. But let this legal light be never so high or great, yet gives it no power of purity that is spiritual, and seldom it gives natural purity; witness Solomon, and Periander, one of the seven sages of the world, who lived in the time of the Jews' captivity, his motto was this, Love, and not arms, guard him that must rule.

---

[1] Numb.24.

12. But as he could give good counsel, yet he himself sought nothing less, for he was a most cruel tyrant, who flung his wife down a pair of stairs, and stamped upon her with his feet until she was dead, and would have slain all his sons for mourning for her, but was prevented as history relates.

13. Thus we see how reason falls short of the glory of God, or of natural purity; yet moderated reason by the law may cause God to remove from them some temporal plagues upon reason's repentance, through the stroke or threats of the law, as it did by Manasseth, Nebuchadnezzar, Rehaboam, Ahab, and others, and grant them temporal blessings.

14. And hence it is that God would have reason to look upon his law, to read it often, in order to the preparation of the heart, for the turning of its mind to the obedience thereof, as to be displeased with itself for sin, and to desire to do his commands.

15. And then will God withhold his anger, and in the room thereof will he manifest his love to them; not his special love, for that belongs to his elect, but it is a temporary love.

16. As it was with the young man in the Gospel, that from a convincing light came unto Christ, with a good Master, what shall I do that I may gain eternal life? Jesus said unto him, keep the commandments, &c.[1]

Opened

17. The young man answered and said, I have done all from my youth; upon this his answer it is said that Jesus loved him, and yet notwithstanding he was short of gaining heaven by this his obedience to the law, for the law only maketh ears for earth, for no reason that hath broke the law, is ever to enter into heaven; for Christ came not to redeem reason, the Angels' nature fallen; and hence it was that he prayed not for the world, but for those that were given him out of the world,[2] namely, the seed of faith.

Illustrated

18. Again, Christ told the young man that he wanted one thing, and the parting with his earthly treasure and laying it up in the bowels of the poor, that followed Jesus; and that he did follow him likewise through reproach and scorn, for the enjoyment of an everlasting treasure in heaven.

---

[1] Matt. 19, 16. 17.
[2] John 17.

19. But this he could not do, because his righteousness was from a rational nature, which loves a present glory.

Disputed

20. Now God tells reason that if it perfectly obey the law, it shall be saved, and reason thinks it hath power to do all that is commanded, and so looks for no salvation no other way, because it wants the spiritual light of saving faith, and so it keeps to the law working there to gain life.

Unfolded. Cleared

21. So that here is this difference in the worship of the evangelical believer, and legal professor, for the one works from life, and the other works to gain life.

CHAP. VIII

1, The Darkness of the Free-will Mongers discovered. 2. What it is that purges from Sin. 3. The knowledge of God's free Love begets many Divine Properties. 4. Will-worship leads to Blasphemy.

1. NOW from what I have said, we see how dark those men are that say that all rational men hath so much true light in them, that will lead them to eternal life if they will.

2. Now if this doctrine were true, then would there be none that would be children of wrath by nature; neither would there be any need of a new birth, for man's spirit would be his own saviour; he needs but look to the law to get a will, and then he needs not come to Christ for power, to be insured of everlasting life.

Doctrinal

3. For if the law can purge from sin, it can purchase sanctity; but it can do neither (as will be shewn in the Fifth Part). Wherefore then it must follow, that it is not in the power of any man's will, at its own pleasure, to obey or disobey the light that is in him, but it is in the power of God's will only, by his blessed Spirit, to persuade man's spirit to be willing to yield obedience to the light which he hath freely given him.

Inference, as with David

4. Furthermore, sometimes the Lord may leave a Saint to his own strength; then may he rebel against the light that is in him, to the

wounding of his own soul, as it was with David, to the intent that he may learn to know that the power, by virtue of which he is preserved from eternal ruin, is not in himself, but in the living God that made him, who freely giveth the light of eternal life to whom it pleaseth him.

Inference 2

5. Therefore from hence it is, that all well-grounded believers give all power, glory, and praise to Christ, for the gifts of his free grace, and in that the Lord hath as much power to withhold spiritual motions, as to give them. Therefore it is that a Saint doth walk in low lines and humility, because he is afraid of quenching the spirit, and so he works out his salvation with [fear and trembling], not a slavish fear, but a fear to offend through law.[1]

Inference 3

6. Also it maketh a Saint to be full of compassion towards his brother, that is overtaken in a fault, and doth commiserate his condition, especially if he himself have ever been under desertion by a slip or fall.

Applied

7. How contrary now doth this spirit appear from the spirit of the free-will mongers; for when his rational soul is now salted by the law, insomuch that it is so preserved thereby from some outward pollutions, as nature was not very prone to, as the young man in the Gospel, as aforesaid.

Pride's rise

8. Pride in that soul springs up, and saith, I am not like such a man, &c. This man glories in himself, because he goes by thinking, that he stands, which is the certain token of a fall,[2] and the common road of all the seven anti-churches of Europe.

9. But to return to the matter aforesaid. That soul that is truly enlightened from above, it puts no confidence in its own works, though its works be the works of faith; but its confidence is in the Author of that work, who having given power to begin that good work, doubts not but that he will give power to finish it also to eternal life.[3]

---

[1] Philip. 2, 12. 1 Thess. 5, 19.
[2] 1 Cor. 10, 12. View.
[3] Psa. 115, 1. Titus 3, 5. Philip. 2, 13. Ephe.1, 14. 19. & ch. 6, 10. Jude 25. 1.

10. For praise and glory is not to be given to the fruit, as it is to the tree that bears the fruit.

Agreement with hell

11. These things considered, O the darkness then that is in those Papists, and Pelagons, and Scripturian perfectionists, that do not only look to merit salvation by Gospel works, but also teach, that an unregenerate man, well using the gifts of nature, may merit at God's hands the grace of justification; and so in effect they teach that grace doth little more than bring forth that power that is in nature to act, or to heal the wound a little that sin hath made.[1]

The doctrine of the free-willers

12. And so all that they ascribe to grace is but the assistance of nature, that is, it is but a strengthening of reason, the devil; and so God and devil must associate themselves together, and faith and reason must walk hand in hand, and nature and grace go cheek by joul together.

13. And when their grace hath strengthened their reason, then they judge that he works that are done by grace and nature will merit eternal life, or else they judge God not to be just.

Reason at a loss

14. Certainly, say they, we cannot believe that ever God would give a law which no man is able to keep, and promise life under an impossible condition. Were it not tyranny (say they) to damn for breach of that law, which possibly could not be kept by man.

15. For we can believe no other ways (say they) but that there was given unto man sufficient strength at his creation to perform those duties enjoined by law, and we are not to think that the moral law was first given at the publishment in Sinea, but that the very same law, for substance, was given to Adam in innocency. But I shall answer this cavil in my Treatise of the Law, being the Fifth Part.

16. This is the plea of rational wise men and-free-willed, and oracle grace merchants. Either they must have power from their wisdom in natural reason, and their will in that wisdom must have sufficiency in itself, or else they will judge God to be not only unjust, but also no better than a tyrant.

17. All free-willers' in heart, speak what Mark Auralus, once Emperor of Rome, said with his tongue; of troth (said he), if the gods

---

[1] Isa. 28, 15.

have commanded my flesh to be hidden in the sepulchre, and to be as mortal, yet if they be just and do well, they will make my renown to be immortal, because I have lived well.

18. Thus doth reason challenge to itself immortal glory, due from its will-worship; or else it charges God with injustice. But I shall in the following chapter reason with reason about the matter in hand.

CHAP. IX.

1. An Expostulation of the Author with the Blaspheming Free-willer, shewing the Manifestation of God's Justice against all Opposers of his Prerogative Royal.

Reason argued with

1. OH! ye seed of the fallen angel, because God made you, is he bound to save you? Art thou greater than he, then command him and he must obey; but if thou be his creature, how then darest thou call thy Creator to the bar to plead with thee? Darest thou say unto him, why hast thou made me for the day of wrath?

2. Again, what can'st thou expect but damnation, that darest be so bold as to challenge thy Creator with injustice? What injustice is it for any artist to cut or grave any picture or image, in either wood, iron, stone, or brass, and when he hath done, upon dislike of it, shall with his hammer dash it all to pieces?

3. But thou wilt say, it matters not what is done by inconceivable creatures; but man is a noble living creature; but I should be loth to do so by either dog or toad, or the vilest of living creatures, much less by man.

4. To this I say, there is no cause that thou should'st, because they are thy fellow creatures; though thou be lord of them, yet is it but by donation. Thou art not the creator of that life; if thou wast, then mightest thou have sole power over them to put them to what use thou pleasest, without any injustice, even as the Creator hath over thee.

5. Again, because God hath given thee a law which is impossible for thee of thyself to keep, therefore thou said'st that he is no better than a tyrant for doing so; why, if thou can'st not perform it, how comes thy disability? Hath God taken any thing from thee that was thy own? If he have, blame him; if not, why findest thou fault?

6. Thou hast all thy strength that ever thy creaturely nature could afford thee. Now what if God did (after the creating of thee) give thee a power of obedience once for a moment, and then withheld himself from supplying thy nature with sufficient power to stand, he but left thee as he had made thee at first, which though a brave, glorious creature, yet could not stand of thyself without him, and there was no law could be made by a finite creature to bind an infinite God?

7. For God is a great God, and Omnipotent; he is also a just God; and justice on such as thee shall be manifested to thy condemnation, that shall presume to charge God with injustice. If he gives thee a law of obedience, and withholds from thee the power of obedience, go and learn what that Scripture means, if thou can'st, that saith, Make the heart of this people fat, and their ears heavy, and their eyes blind, lest they should hear with their ears, and see with their eyes, and understand with their hearts, and be converted, and I should heal them.[1]

8. But for the comfort of the elect, let me now set forth the spirit of the humble; for it is for such to have power to yield obedience to the prerogative power of God; and as for those that cannot yield obedience to the prerogative power of God, are manifested to be reprobates, and so appointed to damnation.

CHAP. X.

1. Of the Nature of Humility. 2. Reason will have Heaven by beating the Air. 3. Of the Language of an Elect Vessel. 4. Of the Authors submitting to a Prerogative before he knew Truth. 5. Of Reason's displacing God out of his Judicatory.

1. YOU that are sober, and of a meek spirit, though as yet have not the ingrafted word of truth planted in your heart, I advise you to have a care (and if you be elect, you will have a care) of standing out against the prerogative power of God.

2. Therefore you may know, that it is his prerogative will and pleasure to save who he will; and it is a sign of an elect vessel to humble himself unto his prerogative power, even so far as to yield himself to be damned.

3. Now who is there amongst the sons of Solomon that knows this, or what reason can submit to this?, it loves itself so well, and it hath

---

[1] Mat. 13, 15.

so much pride in that love; for pride in self-love is the hangman to humility.

Reason's plea

4. For reason will have heaven, by beating the air in its strength of natural abilities; it neither will nor dares trust God in nakedness without arms; it dares not fall down at his feet, and say, do with me what thou wilt.

Doctrine 1: a prayer

5. But the humble soul, from a yielding heart, pours out such sayings as, Lord, do with me what thou wilt; if thou wilt save me, then shall I glory in thee, and sing forth thy praise; but if thou dost not, yet I submit, and will never speak ill of thy name; yea, if thou kill me, yet will I trust in thee: I will not resist thy will, but that it may be done on earth as it is done in heaven; if I perish, I perish; for to thee be all power, praise, and glory, for ever. Amen.

6. Here now is the language of an elect vessel; this is the humility that flows from election, and the evidence of a gracious heart, in that person that is not as yet certain of the knowledge of truth, and as yet is kept captive under the discipline of a false Ministry.

7. I speak this experimentally, for thus it was with me before I knew the truth; for though I had procured a library of Presbyterian books, of having a love to those people, yet as my faith was not altogether fixed to their sole doctrine, even so, also, was not my love wholly estranged from the ministry of the other churches.

8. For as I was not satisfied fully of the infallibility in truth in what I joined with, even so was I preserved from condemning or censuring the other Ministrys', which I then refused, for some doubts in the one made me carry a fair correspondence with the other.

A prayer

9. Therefore, I having drawn up a table-book, containing the principal heads of all the rest, I in the conclusion of my table-book, made my prayer thus unto God (though I knew him not), saying,

10. O! Lord God of heaven, I beseech thee grant, that whatsoever there is in these books that is agreeable to thy holy word, fasten it, I pray thee, in my heart, as a nail in a sure place; and that which is in them books, which is not truth, let it not infect me, but give me a discerning spirit, &c.

11. Here you, my friends, may see that I had a little stay, but no rest, no certain knowledge of truth; but as I was innocently ignorant,

so was thereby made the more fit to receive truth, and to be kept from tumult and noise, and the strivings of the people.

12. Therefore it was that my innocence and charity persuaded me to act forth itself in all simplicity and lowliness, without fully uniting myself to any form, seeing I could not find rest in any, so in a short time after I had collected all the heads of their doctrines in my table-book, I grew weary of all, because I found that it could not reach to give life, peace, joy, and satisfaction.

13. Therefore it was that I left off all, and resolved to innocency of life, and submitted myself unto the unknown God, being content to let him do what he pleased with me, either save me or damn me, according to his pleasure.

14. Now by this my humility and submission, I got to myself fruition. In a short time after, the Lord made himself known to me by his Commission of the Spirit, and knowing of him. I came to know and understand his divine secrets; for now that which was lost, was found, and that which was undone, was made happy.

15. And now do I see that this is the way that God doth walk in; it is not a great road, or the broad way of the will of man, but he makes his way in the wilderness, and there he finds his lost sheep. All the seed of Adam were lost, a lost people in the world, but pilgrims and strangers at the best.[1]

16. When Christ came into the world, he came to seek and to save the lost. Now none of you, free-willers', were ever lost, and so are incapable of being found. Now you say you see (said Christ), therefore your sin remains; the whole need not the physician, but the sick; I came not to call the righteous, but sinners to repentance.[2]

17. Thus as you see the way of our God, so you may see the way of his select seed. Those that as yet know him not, first they cry to every one, saying, see you not where our beloved feedeth his sheep; but when they have tried many a counterfeit, they lie down in humility of soul, saying, I will wait until he comes, I will look for him no more in the way of these guides.

18. Nevertheless, my soul shall yet submit to his prerogative-royal, let him do with me what he will; but when they meet with the messenger of the Most High, as Agar did with the Angel, and as Tobias did with Assureias, then comforts come in, and the soul sings, saying, unto thee, O Lord, be all glory, &c.[3]

---

[1] Isa. 43, 19 and 51, 3. Jer. 50, 6. Matt. 10, 6. Ch. 18, 11. Luke 15, 6.
[2] John 9. Matt. 9, 12. 13.
[3] Psa. 115, 1.

19. But this is the way of faith; reason hath none of this humility, as to submit to a prerogative, and yet thou art compelled to confess that an earthly king hath power to put to death whom he pleases, upon the breach of the law.

20. But to reason with thee: wherefore, then, would'st thou grant this prerogative to man, and deny it to God? Is it not for one or both those reasons?

Reason reasoned withal

21. First, thou would'st not let God rule in his seat of justice, because thou art conscious of thy own guilt; therefore thou wilt displace him out of his court of judicatory, and think it is enough for him to be always on his mercy seat, granting out absolutions to whom thou thinkest meet.

22. Secondly, doth not this pernicious principle proceed from self-love? for there is no creature so evil but it loves itself, and hates that which is against itself, and surely the devil loves himself too well to submit himself to be damned, for his work of iniquity.

23. Therefore, free will and power of obedience from reason, must be reason's plea, and none must resist it; no, not God himself: if he do, then they charge him with injustice.

Penn, the Quaker's blasphemy against prerogative power

24. As William Penn, the Quaker, calls this doctrine a cruel doctrine. O! barbarous cruelty (saith he), and most aggravated injustice; warn men of damnation, prophesying no delight in the death of a sinner, but that they should be saved, and for fear they should believe and be saved, determine by an irrevocable decree that they should be damned.

O! vile, hideous, and blasphemous doctrine (saith he;) for God desires not the death of a sinner; all men may be saved, if they will; they have a stock of grace given them sufficient for eternal life, and if they will sin it away, they may; God may chuse whether he will give them more.

Thus we see the doctrine of the free-will mongers; and observe them well, and you will find that their bottom is without bottom, or else one bottom serves for God and devil, saint and serpent; for they have but one seed, but one root, but one plant, but one stock, but one foundation, for light and darkness, for heaven and hell, for good and evil, and God and devil.

CHAP. XI.

Doctrines

1. Wherefore God made Man for Eternal Suffering. 2. When the Seed of Immortal Praise began in the Angels. 3. When it began in Man. 4. Justice and Mercy in God made famous. 5. How God is said to be Love. 6. And how Love in the Elect is kindled.

Doctrine 1

1. NOW, if any be inquisitive to know wherefore it was that God made any creature for eternal suffering, my answer is, that it was for the manifestation of his divine justice, otherwise that great and dreadful attribute or virtue could never have been known, and so one of his greatest properties would have been hid or concealed from the knowledge of elect men and angels.

2. And then where had all that praise, power, and virtue have been from elect men and angels, unto their Creator, for his free electing love towards them?

3. For this we are to know, that the angels themselves had no certain knowledge of abiding in their created purity, until the Lord assured it unto them to all eternity, upon his casting down that angelical reprobate.

4. Then, even then, were their mouths filled with variety of spiritual praises, unto their good God, for his free electing love, where as they saw that if he had pleased, he might have done the like to them for everlasting; but his mercy was eternally made over to them, and his excellencies in his prerogative royal did shine forth with an incomprehensible splendour.

5. And now began the seeds of immortal praise to spring in heaven in the angels, and his electing love produced this appellation [gracious and merciful].

6. But now no sooner had they with acclamation of joy given due praise unto their Creator, but in an ensuing revelation they were stricken into admiration when they saw that the reprobate angel had taken possession of the garden of God.

7. But in process of time, when they saw their God leaving his throne (according as to Gabriel it was revealed), and come down into the lowest parts of the earth into the virgin's womb, and there transmuted his glory into flesh, this produced a silence in heaven; but

at their Lord's incarnation, they rose up with Moses and Elias, and in all speed, through their commission, came down from on high, and over the place where their Lord was born, they to the visible sight of elect men were seen innumerable, and were heard to sing praises unto their God, with astonishing admiration of his infinite wisdom, power, and glory.

8. But of the Angels love to man, of their celebrating their happiness, I shall speak more of in the Eighth Part of the Saints Joys in Heaven.

Doctrine 2

9. Again, as justice in God could not have been known but in and by this his electing love, so neither could mercy have been known to have been mercy, had there not been such a thing in God as wrath and displeasure.

10. For although God may be said to be not only love, but all love, yet is that to be appropriated to his own seed, because that they are saved through his eternal, free, and unconstrained love.

11. Therefore it is that the redeemed of the Lord give all glory to him, and the virtue of his eternal free love creates or renews love in his saints, for the grace of faith in divine wisdom, given in Adam, and quickened in his seed by the sound of a true ministry, kindles love which ascendeth up, and fasteneth itself upon the God of love.

12. For knowledge of eternal life, freely given, must needs kindle love, and this love will make to that which is the author of its bliss, and having the tongue touched by that coal, it will ascribe all love, power, and glory unto its Redeemer, the Lord Jesus Christ, blessed for ever.

CHAP. XII.

1. Of the Nature of Anger in God, and when it first took place. 2. Of the Nature of Sin. 3. A further Discourse of Anger.

1. SEEING I have begun to speak of anger and love, give me leave to prosecute this point, and that the more because some teach that there is no anger in God.

2. Now if there be not, nor hath been, no anger in God, then there can be neither hell, death, nor damnation to any creature, but all things that were created to life, were created to pleasure.

3. But it may be objected, that there can be no anger in God, because that in one place it is written, that fury is not in God;[1] but in answer to this, we are to know, that that sentence was spoken in relation to the elect seed of Adam, as to their eternal estate.

Doctrine 1

4. The following words of the Prophet shews who fury belongs to, when he saith, who will set the briars and the thorns against me; I will consume them, I will burn them up.

Opened

5. The reprobate seed are compared to briars and thorns, for sin or devil is as a thorn in the side of a man; it pricks and hurts the good seed, and destroys the fruit of the tree of life inasmuch as it can, and it begets hatred, and its opposing nature is such, that the Divine Majesty itself hath an eternal enmity against it.

6. And well it may, seeing through pride it would have been above God in heaven, and through its cruelty in that pride, did smite at the eternal God here on earth, and put him to death, in that he was made mortal.

7. Now, might not this very well kindle anger, and was it not meet that the Creator should be even with such a rebellious creature, by making it the object of his eternal wrath?

Doctrine 2

8. Again, this we are to know, that though the Creator hath an eternal enmity to that seed, yet doth not the perturbation of anger continually keep hold in his divine breast, for that would diminish glory in perpetual joy, which properly is inherent in his most glorious person.

Explicated

9. But thus much we may understand, that so much time as serves for the expression of God's anger, is sufficient to hold a creature in misery, either for a time or for eternity.

---

[1] Isa. 27, 4.

Cleared

10. For the Creator's nature being all powerful faith, therefore his word in that power fulfils his pleasure, and becomes his prerogative royal; therefore the manifestation of his anger, and the demonstration of his pleasure in that anger, becomes a perpetual law in that creature to whom it is given.

11. Therefore it was that the Lord engraved the moral law in the seed of reason, the devil, in those and the like words, Thou shalt do no murder, thou shalt not commit adultery, &c.; upon the transgression hereof, death and eternal torment doth ensue.

12. Thus you see how the Creator is disburdened of his anger, and yet his anger to burn eternally, not in his own breast, but the breast of his disobedient creature eternally; for where it is said that God is angry with the wicked every day, and the like, we are to know that his anger boils not up in his breast every day, but it is in those same wicked that adds to their wickedness every day.[1]

Proved, and a sound saying

13. For what the law doth, it maybe said that God doth, because his anger is in that law, and that law is as God to punish.

14. Here I might take occasion to shew, how that God doth not take notice of every particular thing that is evil and that is done; but that it is the law that takes notice, and this law stands instead of God, &c. But I may treat something of this when I come to the Fifth Part of the Law's Nature, &c. if there be occasion.

Query

15. But now some may ask, whether this divine quality of anger that is in God, hath been as apparently known to him from eternity, as any other divine virtue he was possessed with? to this I say, that,

Answer. Doctrine 3

16. Before the glorious Creator formed any creature to live in his sight, anger was not known to him; but yet, notwithstanding, he did foresee before he formed any living creature to live in his sight, that in the great globe of earth and water, there would be something, if formed and brought to life, and left to itself in its own creaturely strength, would be in antipathy to his blessed nature.

17. Yet, nevertheless, (according to my faith), he perfectly knew that his prerogative was such, as could order and govern every thing

---

[1] Psa. 7, 11 opened.

by him created, though in nature never so much opposite to him, by obligation, so as whether obedient or disobedient, yet to be for his glory.

18. Now, by the way, let me dictate to the sober this secret, that seeing that nature that was the most high, or of the purest lump, that lay hid in the eternal substance, of dark and dead earth and water, was (when brought into a sensible form), in contrariety of nature to the Creator thereof.

Definition of God hinted at

19. Hence, therefore, it appears that the Creator, neither as to his form or nature, did partake or consist of any elementary matter, but was from eternity a distinct being from that matter of earth, air, fire, or water.

Foregoing doctrine proved. Doctrine 4. Anger took place

20. Now to the matter in hand. In the creation of Angels, the Creator bringing forth, by the power of his word, the purest life and light the dark earth could afford, it being in his power to bring light out of darkness, and good out of evil; and having so done, he leaves one of those Angels to himself, to see what he would do, who finding him to grow into cursed pride and rebellion against his divine person, who was his Creator, upon which the anger of the Lord did arise against him, and cast him down from the highest heaven to the lowest earth.

Proved

21. Here, now, did anger begin, and quickened at that very moment; for opposition is the ground of anger, and this anger in God was holy anger, for God is not bound to preserve every thing he makes.

22. Now, in that the spirit of the mighty Angels were not of the nature of God, they might have been changed from good to evil, as the reprobate angel was, for as the Creator had power to create light out of darkness, so likewise had he power to change it again as from a sensible good into a sensible evil; and who is he that shall dare to dispute against this his glorious prerogative power over the creature he hath made?

Saith the third record

23. But this, let me further add, that if the glorious Creator could possibly have known any other way for the making known his divine

excellency unto men and angels, certainly he would never have created any thing on purpose for eternal suffering.

Further calculated

24. Neither would he ever have suffered any creatures' natures to have become rebellious against himself, for occasioning such wonderful transactions in the world, and suffering both of God, angel, and man, if he could have possessed his infinite glory in the creating of every thing unto eternal pleasure.

Application

25. Therefore, opposition hath now taken place; heaven and hell, God and devil, light and darkness, saint and serpent, are now at variance, and the nature of the one, makes the nature of the other more conspicuous. Now is God known to be God indeed; things are best known by their contrarieties; health is known by sickness; liberty by bondage; light by darkness; mercy by justice; truth by error; love by envy; and riches by poverty, &c.

CHAP. XIII.

Doctrines

1. How Vocation and Election go together. 2. How the Elect are said to be under Wrath. 3. A Simple Saying of Calvin. 4. Few of a False Ministry saved.

Query

1. BEFORE I end this point, I must answer reason, who says, if election and rejection depends not upon man's will, it makes no matter what I do; if I do never so well, &c. yet if God had predestinated me to damnation, I cannot be saved. To this I answer,

Two daughters to election

2. All those that are enlightened in the knowledge of spiritual truth do know, that God's purpose to life and the means of life go both together, and are inseparable. There is two daughters belongs to election, and these are faith and holiness, these are fruits of election, and belongs to it after vocation, which vocation gives confirmation to election.

Doctrine 1

3. This is according to the Apostle Peter's words, saying, elect according to the fore-knowledge of God, through sanctification of holiness, and belief of the truth, see 2 Thess. 2, 13, there, saith Paul, God hath from the beginning chosen you to salvation, through sanctification of the spirit and belief of the truth.

Opened

4. Not that sanctification, &c. were the cause of election, as the Baptists teach, but it was the fruit of it, and so became the only infallible evidence of eternal life, this is the calling that makes the election sure.

5. For though our election is sure as to God's eternal purpose and fore-knowledge, yet is not the benefit ours till it be sealed, and made sure to us, through the obedience of faith; for what comfort can any man have to believe that God is sure that there is a certain number of elect, until he have an assurance in himself, that he is one of those that are elect, and shall assuredly be saved.

2 Peter 1, 10 opened

6. Therefore though election goes before vocation, yet can there not be the knowledge without vocation, although Peter exhorts the saints to make their calling and election sure; now let them make but their calling sure, and they need not fear their election, for then are they sure as God is sure, for election being God's gift, and vocation the seal, which seal makes the inheritance certain.

Proved

7. Good motions are the blossoms of election, and good actions are the fruits; election produceth much grace, as faith is the mother-grace, so election is the mother of all grace.

Cleared

8. Every virtue knows itself to be the daughter of election, therefore it is written, that whom God predestinated, them he called, and whom he called, them he justified, and glorified those that he justified.

1 Sam 24, 13 opened

9. So on the contrary, reprobation and the works of darkness and unbelief are unseparable, wickedness proceedeth from the wicked, and as belief in truth is the fruit of election, so infidelity and disobedience is the mark of reprobation.

Ephes. 2, 3 opened

10. Not but that an elect vessel may be filthily polluted and may look like reprobate silver until conversion, and whereas it is said, that by nature the elect are the children of wrath as well as others, it means; not that the elect seed are under the same wrath as the seed of reason are, but it is the nature of the seed of unclean reason that captivates the spirit of faith that is under wrath.

Cleared

11. How God's wrath is upon their sin to destroy it, and finding that there was a seed of election buried under it, his mercy was upon that seed to quicken it, so that his wrath went into the evil seed, but his mercy into the good, so that he had come to them in his anger, according as it is written, when thou wast in thy blood I pitied thee.[1]

---

[1] Isa.

Applied

12. How dark now do those men appear who would have all men alike, both as to root and branch until conversion come, and that God chuses and refuses, as Christ his substitute shall affect or disaffect, as Calvin the Anti-angel of the Presbyterian ministry soundeth his trumpet, saying after the manner following:—

Calvin's institutions

13. The ground and cause of man's election, (saith he) sprang through the election of Christ, for God chose Christ and gave him honour that afterwards he might make some others partakers of his gifts, for therein the whole seed of Adam God saw nothing or found nothing worthy of his election; therefore he turned his eyes unto his Christ to chuse, as it were, members out of his body.

Calvin confuted

14. O! what darkness you see is here in this learned Calvin, his election, you see, is grounded upon two Gods, God must look on Christ, and Christ must look on man and take one of Adam's children and reject another, and yet they be all alike, and all of one father; now, if Calvin's doctrine stands good, then in those that were rejected there was judgment without justice, if they were of the same seed with the other.

15. Thus you see the darkness of Calvin in his doctrine of predestination, but here is one word above, that may be counted a hard saying of Calvin's, being an anti-angel, and so of the fallen angel's lineage, but bear with me you that are sober, and you may know that every false ministry is set up by the serpent angel's nature, neither will any elect vessel run into the ministry without a commission from God, to teach or preach unto the people as a messenger of God, and give ordnances of worship.

16. Many of the hearers of a false ministry may be saved, but few of a false ministry will be saved, because it is written, without are liars and workers of iniquity;[1] as also,

17. A man that takes upon him to be a minister, he becomes impudent and rash in judging divine things he knows not, and by the letter fights against the spirit.

18. But I pass by Calvin, and all false ministry, and shall return to the point in hand, and conclude this point, in a few words, concerning the ground of election.

---

[1] As in my text.

Election where founded

19. Election was founded or established in Adam, he being the first object of mercy; therefore take notice of this, that none are to look no higher for election, but to Adam; for though Peter saith elect before the foundation of the world,[1] yet that is meant only as to God's purpose and decree in making a seed to eternal life; now Adam being made, the decree was perfected, and so election was established and seated in Adam's seed.

20. Therefore he who looks higher than Adam to find his election, will never find it, for there's the ground as aforesaid, and therefore this election was to run in a line through procreation, insomuch as that Adam and all his offspring are but as one man in God or Christ, that is, they are children of one father.

21. Now if Adam had not been of God's seed, and if God himself had not become seed, then could it not be said that we are chosen in Christ, therefore it is certain, that the seed of Adam, when it is grown up to the hearing of Christ, it forthwith, through a union in nature, embraces him as its life, if it be or when it is revived and not hindered by that potent enemy of impure reason, being innured in its nature.

22. Thus we see that all Adam's seed will be saved, because election lies in that seed, and the blessing runs in a line, even the line of the light of life eternal.

And so much as to this point or doctrine of predestination.

---

[1] 1 Peter.

THE FIFTH PART:

OF

The Nature of the Law;

FROM

MATTHEW, CHAP. xiii. VERSES 41 AND 43.

Offend and do Iniquity, and the Righteous shall shine.

THE DOCTRINE FROM HENCE IS,

How that each Seed hath a law given unto it, the one the law of Reason, the other the Law of Faith, &c.

CHAP. I.

Doctrines

1. Whether the Devil was Created or no? 2. What Sin is. 3. Of the Law that was Written in the Angel's Nature.

1. WHAT the devil is, I have showed before; it remains now, that I unfold the nature of the law of which he is under, (so far as I have learned by faith in this commission,) for he was not created in a lawless condition, for there is no creature, but it is under a law; for creature implies a creator, and a creator implies an authority and command of obedience.

Query. Answer. Doctrine

2. But here it may be said, did God create or make the devil? to this I say, God did not make the devil, nor any thing that is evil; God created the angels, and the work was good, so long as God upheld it; but the matter being mutable of which it was made, therefore being not upheld would become changeable, as it was with one of his angels which he left to himself, and therefore from himself he fell.

Sin unfolded

3. Now there could not have been any thing that could have been called a fall, had there not been a law engraved in their nature, that obedience was due to God, for sin is a declining from a rule given by a superior, or a missing the mark, &c.

4. Now all the evil in the world, is caused by the angel's fall, and though the angel, by dissolving himself into seed, became mortal, and by generation doth multiply its kind; yet was there not a dissolution of the law, by means of transmutation into mortal flesh, blood, and bone.

5. But this law kept in the angel's nature, and as the angel's body was spiritual, but upon transmutation, became earthly, even so the law became earthly, and was to wait upon the nature in mortal state.

6. For now was reason subject to many sins that were gross and filthy, which could not be done in that region above, as murder, adultery, theft, and the like.

7. Wherefore this law, as it appeared in that mortal fleshly nature, became as a judge, to acquit and condemn, according to the works of the flesh, whether good or bad; also it was as a candle in the soul, to lighten him in the way and show him this work, saying, this shall be done, and that shall not be done; for instance,

Text opened

8. As soon as Cain was grown up,[1] some glimmering of that law remained in his mind, from the dictates thereof, he began to worship God, and from his reason, could offer sacrifices unto God as well as Abel; but it was not acceptable unto God, as to eternal life as Abel's was, because it was offered up in reason, whereas Abel's was offered up in faith, and so would as it were have challenged life, from the bare outward action of worship.

Cleared

9. For the law in his nature, showed Cain's reason, that obedience was due to the Creator, and that he was bound to worship him, on pain of damnation.

Applied

10. Hence observe, that there is no man that is a rational man, but he is forced to acknowledge that there is a God, and that he ought to be worshipped.

---

[1] Gen. 4. Ver. 3. 4.

James 2 opened

11. Therefore, those Atheistical Epicurion people that denies the Godhead, are brutish and unreasonable devils, for a rational devil will own a God, and that makes them many times, as James saith, believe and tremble.

12 And Felix was one of these rational devils, for he had faith in his reason, that Paul's words were true, but he had not faith above his reason, to make him obedient to these words.

Cleared

13. Although some are so dull as not to comprehend this law in the verge of their understanding, yet the generality of Cain's seed, did ever acknowledge a Deity, and did devise how to pacify him, when they had done evil.

14. But because the light of nature was so dim in the seed of the serpent, God to show his prerogative, was pleased to give unto some of the seed of reason, of the Jew's nature, an outward law to enlighten that within, as a glass of the mind.

Illustrated by these reasons

15. Now he gave not this outward law to all the seed of Cain, although the substance of that law did belong to all, and the reason of this may be for several causes, as

First

16. First, negatively, because the Creator is not bound to do alike unto all his creatures,

Secondly

17. Secondly, his prerogative would be infringed, if he had not the power to chuse and refuse, to enlighten or let it alone, as to be covered in their own darkness.

Thirdly

18. Thirdly, God gave an outward law to the outward Jewish nature, because their reason or person was something more esteemed, through its coming through the loins of Abraham, having thereby a temporal sanctification.

Fourthly

19. Fourthly, the Creator gave the outward law, moral and judicial, to the Jews, to the end that they might be the more inexcusable, who desire and have such a law, according to their desire to enlighten them, and yet not walk accordingly.

Applied

20. Therefore, whoever they are, that have the benefit of enjoying the oracles of God, for the guide of their reason, and are disobedient thereunto, will receive a greater condemnation,

Rom. 2

21. For they will be judged by that outward Jaw, when as the gentiles that had not that outward law given to them, they will be judged by that dark law, that is written in the seed, they being a law unto themselves, and seeing that law was dark, it doth not require that exactness of obedience, as it doth in those that have greater means of knowledge.

22. For as the Scripture saith, he that doth not his master's will, shall be beaten with stripes, but to him that knoweth his master's will, and doth it not, shall be beaten with many stripes.

CHAP. II.

Doctrines

1. What Devil that was that tempted Christ. 2. The Law a double Glass to Reason. 3. Reason knows not the true God by the Law.

Doctrine 1. Mat. 4 opened

1. THAT the devil is under the law, it is evident, and that law that was given by Moses, was given only to the devil; therefore in Matthew 4th, it is written, that Christ was tempted of the devil, and the Lord repulsed him by his law, saying, it is written, thou shalt not tempt the Lord thy God, but him only shalt thou serve.

Examined

2. Now from hence we observe these two things, first, that there is a law that belongs to the devil, and, secondly, that that law is a written law; it is evident that this written law belongs to a mortal devil

in flesh, for no written law belongs to bodyless devils, but some may say, where is it written? my answer is,

Deut. 6

3. In Deut. 6th, it is written, thou shalt not tempt the Lord thy God, but him only thou shalt serve.

Opened

4. Here now he that hath faith, may see, that that devil that tempted Christ, was a man-devil, and by faith I know, that he was a subtle Scribe well learned in the law, yet knew not himself to be a devil, neither did he believe, that the moral law was given to the devil, although he found it written in his nature.

5. For he thought, that his learned reason in the law, by which he tempted God, to be the only wisdom of God; but Christ's words being a greater God, had an influence into his spirit, and wounded him thereby.

Verse

6 From these words it is written, thou shalt not do so, and so when truth sets upon falsehood, it striketh to the quick; reason that hath but the letter of the Scripture fights, but as it were with the sheath against him that hath a two-edged sword in his hand.

Verse opened, proved

7. Get thee behind me Satan, (said Christ) it is written, &c. the devil where well if such a thing were not written, neither within nor without, but being written, and the door of the conscience opened to see sin, then is he whipped and scourged by his own law, for the law is the tyeband of the devil, it is the chain that binds him, and a rod to scourge him, for the devil breaking the law, wants a whip, and there is nothing better to scourge him than his own law.

Illustrated and distinguished

8. Now the substance of the law that is given to the devils is contained in ten commandments; these are the two tables or books of the law; this law is a double glass; in the one book they are to see their Creator's face, and the other, their own faces.

9. But the organ of their right eye being weak, hath not strength enough to take in the external light of the law into their internal sense, to give them a full sight, either of God's face or their own.

Reason weak

10. And yet if it were so, that they did take in the whole law, yet nevertheless could they not know the form and nature of God; because the law expresses it not as to that part, as is written in reason's nature, the substance being the second table of the law.

11. Moreover, though in the writings of Moses and the rest of the prophets, there are proofs clear enough to the seed of faith what the form and nature of God is, yet nevertheless reason, the devil, is ignorant of that; for nothing belongs to reason, the devil, but the moral part of the law, and a shadow of holiness in the ceremonial part.

12. Again, though reason, the devil, studies the first book of the law with great industry, yet can it not know the true God, because their part of the law discovers it not; it something shews the manner of worship as to the first table, to wit, that they shall have but one God, and that should be that God that Moses told them of, and that brought them out of the land of Egypt, and that they should love him with ail their heart, and observe his Sabbath, worship, &c.

Applied

13. Now reason judged this very fit and reasonable, and therefore set to practise, thinking that they can do all that is commanded; and as for the second table and book of the law, their whole work consists in sinning and praying, and then to their sinning again.

14. And then some external sacrifice for their sins again, as for sins of omission, sins of commission, sins of ignorance, and wilful sins; so that upon a little sin, they take a little of the holy water of their law and wash it away again; like the devils of our time, who cry, God damn us, and then wash it away again with the holy water of England and Rome, with a God forgive us for so saying.

Hypocrisy

15. Furthermore the Jews, to whom the law was given, had a great esteem to the worship of their law, yea, and not only so, but they would over-do the plain precepts of God's commands, and hereupon they used to have their phylactores upon their forehead, and on their left arm, near their heart, were these Scriptures, Exod. chap. 13. verse 2, to the end of the 10th verse, and from the 11th verse to the 16th verse; and Deut. chap. 6. verse 4th to the 9th verse; and chap. 11. verse 13th, to the end of the 21st verse; in all there were 30 verses, and they were all written in parchment, folded up, covered with leather: they were tied with strings upon the head, from the crown forward.

16. They used these religiously, blessing God always for the commanding these things. Always, when they put them on in the daytime, especially when they went to read the law, and to pray; and they superstitiously taught, saying, that all the while a man had the phylactores upon his head or arm, he was meek, and fearing God, not conceiving any evil thought, but turning his heart towards truth and justice.

17. The like rites they used for their fringes, and this was the manner of the worship of reason, the devil, otherwise it would have pleased God, but Christ, the eternal God, regarded it not; as Matt, chap. 23. verse 5.

18. For this is to be minded, that let the devil worship God which way he will, yet will his worship never please God, so as to give him eternal life; because that eternal life comes not in by legal or moral righteousness, much less by ceremonies, for the law begets no children unto God, because it is not of faith, and without faith, it is impossible to please God.

19. Only this, if the devil learn sobriety by the law, he may obtain the favour of God, as appertaining to temporal blessings; as it is said by the young man, who telling Christ that he had kept all the commandments of his law, upon which saying, it is said, that Jesus loved him, although that his righteousness fell short of eternal life.

20. Wherefore this shews, that if the devil would be something civilized, and made conformable to his law, he would find most civil and significant favours from his Creator, but never as to eternity, his righteousness being too weak to accomplish that.

CHAP. III.

1. Of the Office of the Law; the Law both pleasing and displeasing to Reason. 2. Of the God-head becoming a Law to his Creatures. 3. When Death entered.

1. THE law of nature willeth that God should be obeyed, and the outward precepts of the law given, doth much acquiesce with that light within, and strengthens it to a further insight, which is very grateful and pleasant unto its reason, because it looks for life by it through its obedience.

Doctrine 1

2. But through reason's disobedience, the law that was expected to give life, works death, and brings with it a fire of envy, which it stirs

up out of disobedient reason, and then it finds the law a quite contrary thing than what it judged it to be; for it thought that it would have given it life, but it was too weak to do it, by reason of the flesh, for the flesh, or spirit of reason, became its law to command iniquity.[1]

Rom. 7. The Law's office

3. Here, then, doth the law of sin and death meet, a cross couple; but the law that commands righteousness gets uppermost, and over that commanding seed, and worker of iniquity, and doth pour forth wrath upon the life thereof.

And how it becomes a scourge to reason

4. For the law doth not acquit sin, but the office of the law is not neither to acquit sin, nor cleanse from sin, but to condemn for it, and to justify righteous deeds, so that perfect righteousness meets with perfect justification, otherwise not.

5. From hence then we understand, that the uncreated God-head itself is unto the created beings of angels or man, either a law of perfect faith, and pure burning love in them unto God and man, unto life eternal, or else a fiery law of unbelieving burning envy in them against God, elect men, and angels, unto death eternal.

6. Thus it was with the serpent-angel, upon God's withholding from him the inspirations of his blessed spirit of faith, which was all love and perfect purity; then the law became a fire of envy, because there was not a power to stand, and that which was before as life, now became death.

7. Although death could not enter until his spiritual body became a mortal body, which when so done, then did that law become earthly, and death entered; for though the Jaw of death was written in the serpent-angel's nature, yet could not be brought forth until the angel's spirit and his spiritual body did become natural and mortal, and then came death into the world, being the first-born of the law.

8. For although the serpent-angel did oppose the Creator, yet sin was not imputed to him whilst in his spiritual body, but he was to leave the punishment of that sin in his mortal body, that the law might lay hold upon his actions in flesh, which was born with him.

9. And death and sin was to be revived by that law for eternal punishment, in that his dark spiritual body, which he shall have at the resurrection thereof at the last day.

---

[1] Rom 8.

10. The seal of this death was visible in Cain, when the mark of reprobation was made, and as his sin first lay at the door, so after the action of sin, the door of his conscience was opened, and the fire broke forth, being kindled in hell, with this seal upon it, My punishment is greater than I can bear.

11. Therefore let now reason, the devil, look to his actions, who thinks there is life in the law, before sin revived, and before he hears the voice of the law thunder in his conscience, upon some breach thereof, and then will he, with Cain, find work enough with that fiery law, and severe judge.

12 But no more of this here touching punishment for sin; for the Seventh Part of this Treatise shews the nature of the devil's torment.

13. But I shall go on and shew further the ground wherefore the law was given to the devils, and of the law's pursuit and arraignment of disobedient reason.

CHAP. IV.

1. Shewing how the Heathen have a feeling of the Law. 2. And how the Law pursues Man, and finds him out.[1]

Doctrine 1

1. WHETHER it be the written Law of Moses, or the law that is written in the seed, it matters not; for each shall be judged by the law that he hath and doth profess.

2. Now the law was given to the end it might serve for the conviction of sin; for sin would not have appeared to have been sin, had not the law of their mind said, Thou shalt not murder, kill, steal, or do so and so.

Observe the Law's working

3. Now not only the outward letter of the law, but the law in the seed of reason in the Gentiles, who bad not the outward law given to them, yet did that natural spark give them to understand the substance of the written law, as is seen by the writings of the Gentiles and Heathen philosophers, as Plato, Aristotle, Hermes, Pythagoras, Menander, Pericles, Tully, Socrates, Lycurgus, Cato, Zeno, the stoick, and Seneca, of the same sect, with divers others.

---

[1] Rom. 1.

4. Likewise we read in profane history, of many amongst the Gentiles, as Turks and barbarians, who have many times been tormented in conscience, for doing things contrary to the same, and have thereupon made supplication to their gods for pardon.

5. Again, some have whipped themselves, yea, and some have killed themselves, and others of the Turks have gone to Mecca, (as the Papists do to Jerusalem), to make satisfaction, and some have offered all their means to their idol temples, and others pined away with voluntary hunger, as may be read.

Application

6. Therefore let the devil seek never so much to hide his sins, as Achan did the gold, yet the law will find him out, and cut through the thickness and darkness which several devils crowd themselves in.

7. Sometimes there may be a space of time between reason and wrath, sin and suffering, the law lying dormant, and not working, torment, whilst it falls out thus, then the spirit of wicked men is fully set to do evil, and that because judgment is not speedily executed.

8, But forbearance proves no quitance, but brings with it a flood of fiery vengeance; the stroke is so much the greater, by how much it is longer in fetching its blood.

9. If the law have leaden heels to some, yet hath it iron hands, it pays home when it comes, for it strikes with a vengeance, as it did in Cain and Judas.

10. But the stroke in Judas was the greater, for it struck and would not cease striking, which became so insufferable as forced him with such violence as to hang himself for ease.

CHAP. V.

Doctrines

1. Of the Law's being a Rule to Reason. 2 How the Law and the Gospel differ. 3. Diversity of Nature in Reason.

Query

1. BUT seeing reason knows no other law but what is born with him, I know he will knash upon me with his teeth, and say, what? am not I under the law as well as he, &c.? To this I answer,

Answered by the two witnesses

2. The moral and civil law is a rule to reason, but not to faith, for the law of faith is a rule that the saints walk by, and though the moral and civil law are good in itself, and was added for transgressions.

Doctrine 1. Divine looking glass, chap. 14, 3

3. But whosoever hath the divine light of faith in him, that man hath no need of man's Jaw to be his rule, but he is a law unto himself, and lives above all laws of mortal men, and yet is obedient to all laws.

4. For the spirit of faith is a law of equity, of justice, mercy, and charity, with joy, peace, and assurance of everlasting life.

1 Tim. 1, 4

5. But as to the moral or civil law, it is only given to the wicked, as Paul said, the Jaw was not given to a righteous man, but for the lawless, and sinners, &c.

Inference 1

6. Thus we see that the law is given to curb the devil, and to keep him in awe, or at the least, to condemn him for breach thereof, and seeing sin is found no where but in man, (as I have showed in the Third Part) therefore man must needs be that devil, to whom the law is given.

Inference 2

7. Again, it must needs be that the law was made for the devil, because the Apostle saith, it is not of faith, and so genders to bondage, and so becomes a law of sin and death, because reason is sin, and death the law's wages; for the law discovering sin, lays death upon sin, even the second death, which what that death is will be showed in the Seventh Part, if God permit.

Difference of the two Testaments

8. Now the devil is mistaken to think there is no difference between the law of Moses and the gospel of Jesus, for if there had been no difference between them, then the beloved Apostle John would not have said, that the law came by Moses, but grace and faith by Jesus Christ.[1]

---

[1] John 1.

Opened

9. Here we see that the Apostle opposes grace to the law, as contrary to each other, not that the law is evil, but that it reacheth not to justify, because of the want of obedience.

Proved

10. For reason not obeying, sets the law again-saying, and so fights against reason, in whose nature it dwells.

Proof 2

11. Again, that the law of Moses and gospel of Jesus are contrary, appears by their distinct operations, for grace gives power to deny all ungodliness.

12. But the law and sin are a cross couple, and a sad society, in that they gender to bondage, whilst faith in the free-woman genders to peace.

Law's use

13. Again, although the law is not only made for sin, but written in sin's seed, saying to it, sin not, yet seeing reason is sin; therefore it can no more cease to sin, than cease to be of its own nature, if lust provoke.

Faith's use

14. But the law of faith, if the voice of it say sin not, sin ceases immediately from its first motion and conception, saying shall I do this wickedness and sin against God?[1]

Faith's virtue. Law's weakness.

15. And all this is because faith is of promise, but the laws forbidding sin is of no efficacy, because it is but bare precept without promise.

Sin has variety in it

16. Moreover although all Cain's offspring do partake of his seed, yet is there variety of natures in that seed, and are carried out variously, for every operation doth not take in all, for Gain had fleshly love as well as carnal envy, and so hath his offspring, as for instance:

---

[1] Gen. 39, 9.

Proved

17. Some persons are naturally loving and charitable, and naturally chaste, temperate, sober, grave, and courteous, and yet are the seed of the serpent, and all these virtues aforesaid, are nothing thankworthy in a strict sense, for two causes, first, because their natures were not prone to the contrary voices, and secondly, because they rest themselves upon that righteousness, as upon a rock, and do by it grow proud, coveting the praises of men, whilst they resist the teachings of faith.

Spiritual pride the worst evil

18. Spiritual pride is the worst of wickedness, being gliding like an angel, and so is a cheating devil, and the more especially when it is carried forth with the blind zeal of persecution.

19. Now although such as these have a seeming god-like purity when they settle to religion, and are not prone to gross sin, yet notwithstanding their zeal, if their natures once move in them to lust it will be done, if it provoke they cannot forego; this have I known in some great zealots.

Hypocritical

20. Again, some endeavour to keep from some sin not, because it is evil, but because it is held disgraceful to moral men, for moderate reason hath some care and decorum in sinning, and holds it dishonourable, as it was said of Scipio (one of the Roman Emperor's Generals) when a beautiful strumpet was tendered him, to abuse himself withall, I would willingly, (said he) where it not for the great place I am in.

CHAP. VI.

Shewing whether the Moral Law doth Purge from Sin. 2. And what Law it is that doth Convert.

Query

1. SOME may say is there no virtue in the law? doth it not purge from sin? is it not said that the Jaw of the Lord converts the soul, &c.? to this I answer;

Answer. Doctrine 1.

2. It is not the office of the law to purge from sin neither moral nor ceremonial.

3. As for the ceremonial law, all the offerings and worship of the law could never take away sin,[1] the outward washing with water could not reach the conscience, nor the outward circumcision did not touch the heart, neither was it the blood of bulls, or goats, &c. all fall short of the glory of God.[2]

4. And though the seed of faith, in the Jewish Church, were under those elements in schools, as children under age, yet were they not justified by it, but by their faith, which those shadows did tipify.

Doctrine 2. Proved

5. And as for that law of the Lord, that was perfect, converting the soul, as David speaks of, is not the moral law, but it is the law that comes forth from the Lord, even the law of the spirit of life which came from Jesus, and not the law of death which came from Moses to meet with sin.[3]

6. Therefore it is written, a law shall go forth from me, and again, hearken my people, in whose hearts is my law; seal the law among my disciples, I will write my law in their hearts, &c.[4]

Opened

7. This is the law that converts the soul, and this was the law that converted David, that made him so much praise the law, as Psa. 119.

8. This law of life, this quickening law, was his law of love, and was more sweeter to him than honey, or the honey-comb; therefore it was this law that made him the sweet singer of Israel, chaunting it out in such words:—

9.[5] Within my heart and secret thoughts
  Thy law I have hid still,
  That I may not at any time,
  Offend thy godly will.

10.[6] O Lord how sweet unto my taste,
  Find I thy law allway,
  Doubtless no honey in my mouth,
  Feels half so sweet I may,

---

[1] Heb. 9.
[2] Rom. 2, 29.
[3] Rom. 8, 2.
[4] Isa. 51, 4. 7. Chap. 8, 16. Jer. 31, 33. Psa. 19. 7.
[5] Psa. 117, 11.
[6] Psa. 119, 103.

11. For by it thou hast quickened me,
    Now, Lord, its my delight,
    To give the glory unto thee,
    For by thee comes my might.[1]

Secondly

12. The law of liberty is the law of life, for faith sets at liberty, and hath the true spiritual praise and a divine love growing in it.

Thirdly

13. This love begot by this law is perfect, because it hath respect unto all the commandments of spiritual faith, as also the old commandments of works, and hath a love to all purity, whether natural or spiritual.

14. But the love that is to the moral righteousness from the nature of reason, is not perfect, though a man from such a love may give himself to be burned.

15. For it is the spiritual love, from or in the divine law that makes perfect, that gives peace, that gives joy, praise, and the assurance of eternal life, which is the white stone, and the new name written.

CHAP. VII.

Doctrines

1. Shewing the Benefit of the Moral Law to Reason 2. How the Law of Man to some is more effectual than the Law of God. 3. How the heart of a Hypocrite comes to be garnished. 4. How that seeming Purity is better than Professed Wickedness. 5. Of the Way of the Rude Multitude.

Doctrine 1

1. BUT this I would have the sober to know, viz. that although the law of Moses doth not convert from sin, yet it is useful several ways, and that both to saint and sinner; I speak both as to the moral law and the law of nations, which is the law of nature.

---

[1] Though religious reason hath turned these spirits into verse, yet the matter is divine but those spirits reach it not.

Proving civil and the moral law useful four several ways

2. For this understand, that the civil law is grounded upon reason, for nothing can govern the world but reason, only some laws are more piercing than others, as the civil laws of England surpass all the law in the world for equity and justice, as that called Magna Charta.

1.

3. First, the moral law is useful to the devils, in this particular, in that it many times puts a stop to reason, the devil, who many times rush into sin without fear.

4. But when a wickedness is intended, if the law do then present itself, it may stay the hand of wickedness in this wise saying, take heed what thou do'st, for if thou do'st so and so, thou wilt be damned, this fears the devil, and becomes a flaming sword.

5. Yet take notice of this, that though the law may sometimes hinder a sin, yet it can never root out sin, and though it hindereth the hands, yet it changeth not the heart, if it sometimes stops the fruit of evil, yet doth it not eat up the root of evil.

2.

6. Secondly, likewise the civil law, it puts a stop to sin, for when he hath thoughts to murder, commit adultery, or steal, the law, if then it comes into his mind, it saith, if thou do'st thou will be hanged.

7. So this law sometimes is more effectual than the law of God, for the restraining of sin, for some had rather venture to be damned than hanged, they regarding nothing but the punishment in this life; those are such whose conscience are seared; those are unreasonable devils.

3.

8. Thirdly, when the law prevents the action of sin, it produces this benefit also, for it causeth those torments under the second death to be less, for torment is proportioned according to the measure of sin. Revel.

4.

9. Fourthly, the law doth help to garnish the house, it trims it up with an outside holiness, or formality, for prudent reason, all men exercising themselves in exterial purity makes them to become full of manners, free in compliment, and courteous in behaviour, and so the house or heart is famously garnished with hypocrisy.

10. And though hypocrisy is evil, yet the pretence of holiness, and a command, for it in rulers is a great and strong curb or bridle to restrain the people from gross sin, for this is certain, that pretended holiness is better than professed wickedness.

11. And this we may generally see, that the great men have ever their eyes upon their kings and rulers, walking by example more than precept.

12. Therefore as they see men live, that are in authority, they endeavour to live so too, making themselves conformable to the fashions, both as to religion and flesh pollution.

13. For look what religion the Kings and Rulers is? and the generality of men will be so too, if it were to kill and slay all before them.

14. So that if they regard any precept or law, it is the precept of their kings or rulers; therefore they have no other reason for what they do, but this; viz. doth not the king say so, or is it not the king's law:

No matter what the King of Heaven hath said,
It is the kings on earth must be obeyed.

CHAP. VIII.

Doctrines

1. Shewing that the Law to Reason is a Flaming Sword. 2. Whence Persecution Springs.

Doctrine 1

1. I come now to show, that the giving of the law, was chiefly and principally for the benefit of the saints, for the saints could not possibly have lived in reason's kingdom; had it not been for reason's law, both moral and civil; but first let me speak of the law moral.

Proved

2. First, God hath made the moral law to reason, as a flaming sword to keep the way of the tree of life;[1] therefore, when reason, the devil, would kill and slay any of the seed of faith, this flaming sword presents itself betwixt the devil and the saint, and so keeps the devil back.

---

[1] Gen. 3, 24.

Opened

3. As it did by Laban and Esau, O Lord, (said Jacob) deliver me I pray thee, from the hands of my brother, for I fear him; Jacob was sensible, that there was wickedness of murder in the heart of his brother, if the Lord by his law did not restrain him from it.

4. But the law wrought in Esau, and the Jaw qualified Laban to keep them off from the tree of life, the seed of the son of man.

5. Also, the law wrought upon Pilot, which made him desirous to acquit the Mesiah,[1] but that the Lord had determined it, in his secret decree.

Applied

6. Now it is a great benefit to the saints, when the devil is captivated to his own law; especially when the law is so quick as to give warning before hand, for then it so terrifies reason, as that it cools the motion of sin, so far as that it puts a stop to the action.

7. And it is a great mercy to the saints, when God by his law, doth come into the mind of the sinner, before the sin be done against the saint, for then it gives warning to reason to consider his ways, and this tempers reason that it does not rush forward, for fear of being damned.

Further illustrated

8. But generally the law lies dormant till sin be cemented; sin going before and the law following after, clapping reason upon the back, before reason knew well what it had done, then is reason startled at the stroke, and cries out, saying, hast thou found me, O my enemy?

Sins fruits dictated on

9. Then springs up fears and torments, for the law works wrath as soon as reason hath wrought sin.

10. Now if the law had been as visible to Cain and his fury, before the murder of his brother, as it was to him after the fact was done, surely he could not have done it; but that could not be, for sin is not known to be sin till it be cemented.

---

[1] Mat. 27.

Laws usefulness

11 Moreover, the benefit of the law appears in this, in that it puts a stop to persecution, for though reason may ground its, persecution from the law, upon the law, yet the law bears it not, but its dark interpretation upon the law that bears it.

12. As when zealous reason set upon the Lord of life to put him to death, they judged him worthy to die by their law.

13. And though religious reason, through a blind fiery zeal, doth persecute, yet it must be by the standard of the law, and reason must be put on both sides, and the law must be the rule of judgment.

14. And the trial must be by a legal way, and if they cause persecution by misinterpretation, yet it is better than if unreasonable and lawless persons, should make their implacable wrath and malice the ground of their actions; rushing upon men like roaring lions, without law or restraint, like those men that bound themselves with an oath, that they would neither eat nor drink, till they had killed Paul.[1]

15. Or like unto those devils, upon one slanderer's word, against the christians, by the Emperor Nero, did forthwith, without either law or justice, fall upon them, and murdered all they could find in Rome, and put them to most exquisite torment, without either proof or examination.

16. Hence then we see, that if it were not for the law, the rude multitude would be like bulls of Basian upon the least offence so that it is a blessed thing to the saints, that the devils have a law to curb and bridle them.

Persecution stopped by the law

17. And though persecution attends upon the power that is in being, yet if the kings or chief magistrates be well learned in the law and sober withall, the saints liberty undoubtedly will be the larger, and that, because that with the law, they (European magistrates) take in the profession of Jesus, in whom the saints faith principally stands, and this doth abundantly help and stop persecution.

18. For this is to be minded, that whosoever professes to be saved by Jesus Christ, and yet, notwithstanding doth persecute others who profess faith in Jesus Christ, though differs in opinion about his person and worship; I say, whosoever doth this is not only sure to be damned, but also his persecution is the seal to him of his damnation.

---

[1] Acts.

Favor expected, and the reason of it showed

19. So that it is expected in this age of the world, and in these parts of the world, who have received more light than their predecessors formerly, that religious reason will be fearful of going on to persecution, because the letter of the gospel doth not only depart from it, but also threaten damnation to all unmerciful minded men and women.

Cleared

20. Besides the manifold differences of professions in christianity, will, without doubt, enlarge liberty, it being now the safest way for a king to grant toleration, in reference to the multitude of dissenters to one party.

Considered

21. For this take notice of, that if one party should appropriate to themselves a power to suppress all others, as to their liberty, it would cause all the other anti-churches to join together against that power.

CHAP. IX.

Doctrines

1. Shewing how that Sin knows itself by the Law. 2. Of the Usefulness of the Civil Law. 3. What Properties are requirable in a Magistrate.

Doctrine 1

1. AGAIN, had there not been a law given to the devils, then sin would not have appeared to have been sinful; for sin could not have been imputed, were there not a law to forbid and command, so that now by virtue of the law, sin comes to know itself to be sin.

Observation

2. Therefore as they came to know sin by the law, even so they came to know that punishment is due to sin by the law.

Humiliation

3. This brings humiliation, repentance, and tears, but not absolution, and so is a repentance ever to be repented of; for the Law of Moses gives no life, let the repentance of reason be what it will as to an eternal life; but as to a temporal it doth, as it did to Maneseth and the Nenivites.

Amplified

4. The Scripture is full of reciting the repentance of reason, through the lash of the law, as I shewed in Esau, Balaam, Achan, and Solomon; all confessed they had sinned. Now, who told them so?— Was it not the law? Though Achan hid his gold, yet the law will not hide his sin.

Law's force

5. O! what power hath the law to discover sin; it matters not whether any body see the secret sin of the close sinner, so long as the law sees it; for the law will be a worse enemy than any other enemy, and will many times reveal the evil to the death of its own soul, when it is stirred up either by itself, or by another.

Cleared

6. Doth not many a murderer, or thief, when had up, on a suspicion before a magistrate, presently confess the action, although there is no witness to prove it? yet the law in the conscience cannot be silent, but becomes a witness against itself.

7. And now let me treat a little of the civil law, and consider the use and benefit thereof to the seed of faith.

Observation, with powerful proof

8; The civil law keepeth every thing in order and reason; there would be nothing but disorder and confusion, were it not for law; it is the law that creates *meum tuum*, mine and thine, and decides all controversies in that kind.

9. Again, it is the law that gives propriety. A man could call nothing his own, if it were not for the law. The desperate destructive devils would cut one another's throats; they would not, with the unmerciful devil spoken of in the Gospel, take their fellow by the throat, saying, pay me what thou owest me; but give me what thou hast, or I will be thy death.

Further prosecuted

10. Moreover, there would be no distinction of men, or arts and sciences, and so would be neither rule nor manners; but the world would be a wilderness of wild beasts, every small creature would be worried by the greater; there could not be a sober man left upon the earth.

11. The most devilish would be the most lord, till they had left none but themselves, and then they would, as Bandages, worry one another, and the world would soon come to an end.

Application

12. So that there is a necessity of law, and need of magistrates, to keep one another in awe. The generality of Cain's seed run into riot and all manner of filthiness; it is but few, in comparison of the multitude, that are enlightened by the law, and endeavour to conform themselves accordingly.

13. Therefore it is requisite that the magistrates be wise and learned in the law, to the end that they may examine causes, hear complaints, and give righteous judgment, without bribery, favour, or affection.

Doctrinally

14. For every magistrate is to abound in these two properties, wisdom and justice; for the first he is to know the law; and then, secondly, he is to minister justice truly according to the tenor of the law.

Applied

15. Which if he do, then he is a good magistrate, and will have the blessing of the law, which blessing will extend to eternal life, if there be added hereunto faith in Jesus, so far as to persecute none for conscience-sake, but leave that to the Judge of all Judges.

CHAP. X.

1. Shewing how far a Saint doth owe Obedience to the Civil Law. 2. Of the Usefulness or Unusefulness of Oaths.

1. BEFORE I treat of the further privileges of the civil law to the saints, give me leave to shew how far the saints do owe obedience thereunto.

Doctrine 1

2. First, the saints do owe obedience in general to all civil laws that relate betwixt man and man.

Doctrine 2

3. Also a magistrate is to be obeyed as to civil government, whether he be just or unjust, because in his place he represents the person of God; so that a saint is to honour him with all the honourable titles and appellations that are conferred upon him by his own seed, or that hath by precept or custom been given to him.

4. As to a king or emperor, no saint is not to think scorn to fall down before him on his knees, with those or the like titles, If it please your Majesty; if it like your Grace; your Excellency, or the like; and to other persons of honour, honour may be given.

Honour restrained

5. But as for such as serve not the office of magistracy, but are private men, though they be never so rich, or honourable to the world, yet do they not deserve that honour, because they do not judge as gods, having not the power of the law invested on them.

Observation

6. But to speak more particularly of the saints' obedience to the civil law, first, although they are to be obedient to the civil law, yet can they not well serve any office for two causes; first, in that its kingdom is not of this world; and secondly, because of some injunctions that relate to divine authority, which some magistrates have mixed with their law; as also engagements to be performed, which are above the power of nature to do.

Explication

7. To explain this, every officer of state, from the king to the petty constable, you know, comes to his authority by oath. The king he is sworn to maintain all rights, and customs, and privileges of law established, as well ecclesiastic as civil.

8. And as the king is to maintain that form of religion, as well as all former rights, privileges, and customs of the law then in use and being;

9. So likewise every officer under him, as much as to the under constable, is by oath bound to that form of mixed government.

10. Therefore the constable is by oath at every quarter sessions, to give in the names of such persons as came not to the public worship, and so by this means they become instruments of persecution, whilst this oath is given and taken.

11. Having touched on this point of oaths, let us see now how far tender consciences may go in this way, as I understand all oaths are not forbidden; for any one may declare the truth, according to his knowledge, before a magistrate by oath, upon any case betwixt man and man, for deciding of controversies; for an oath of confirmation is an end of all strife.

Civil Law, its force & use

12. But although every one is bound to declare the truth, according to their knowledge, yet none is bound to accuse himself, nor no man hath authority, by the civil Jaw, to give any man an oath to swear against himself for his own hurt, according to Magna Charta, or the great Charter of England.

Oath of Supremacy

13. Again, there are several oaths used in the civil Jaw of England, that cannot be submitted to by the knowing seed of faith: first, as to the Oath of Supremacy.

14. None can take this oath but the national church of England, for the king to them is the supreme head of their church; but to no other sect of people.

15. Those that are minded to pin their faith upon their king's sleeve, may do it, but wise and knowing men are not so taught. But the Protestant hath raised his church, or profession, by this means, by giving the king this power.

16. But we are satisfied that a king ought not to appropriate supreme authority over others in spirituals, but such as are commissioned of God, by voice of words from his own glorious mouth, to the hearing of the ear; such a one is a prophet, and may challenge the title of spiritual supremacy, as Peter, who was supreme over all the rest of the Apostles. But no more of this here.

Oath of Allegiance

17. Now, as for the Oath of Allegiance, there are many tender consciences cannot submit to this likewise, because it requires more (in my judgment) than man is able to perform, who hath not power of himself to think a good thought.

A good saying

18. It was a good saying of one that was required to take this oath: how should I (said he) swear to defend another, when as I am not able to defend myself?

19. In a word, I am not free to any oath, but what is according to knowledge of things done, that I have heard, seen, or known; I could swear for things that are past, but not for things that are to come.

20. Indeed, if the Oath of Allegiance be no more but to submit ourselves to the present power established, so far as not to resist him, but yield him obedience in all righteous things whatsoever, in that sense I suppose an oath or promise may be made.

21. For whoever understands truth, will never oppose a head magistrate in any thing that is of civil government, unless it be in case of conscience; and if it be so, he may oppose not against, but not to do, as not resist in force, but suffer in patience; for none ought to take up a sword, not only as against the government, but likewise not as to defend himself.

22. Therefore if the Oath of Allegiance be to defend the king's person by a sword of steel, if there be occasion, then are we not to take that oath, whose religion teacheth us to suffer all things, rather than to fight with a sword of steel, but to leave that to the world to whom it doth belong; for the saints' kingdom is not of this world.

Double blasphemy

23. But no more of this here. Now shall be shewed the duty of the magistrate, and shall leave oaths, covenants, and engagements, seeing most of them are beyond the compass of the civil law, and so are absolute bonds of iniquity. Even like that of the priests in Scotland, who say, cursed is he that saith faith is without sin, and let all the people say amen.

24. Or like the Scotch covenant and oath that the English Presbytery swear to. These things are so blind, and without law, though acted by men that would seem to be spiritually wise, that it is out of the compass (as to this subject) for me to treat of; seeing I am to discourse of the moral and civil law.

CHAP. XI.

Doctrines

1. Shewing the Magistrates' Duty. 2. Of unreasonable Magistrates. 3. What is the Destruction of Reason. 4. And who are the most unreasonable Men. 5. Of Persecution for Conscience.

Doctrine of the third testament

1. THE duty of the Magistrate is to be skilful and knowing in the civil laws of the land, so that if they find any man to wrong another, contrary to those laws, then impartially ought they to execute justice between man and man, and this is the extent of their authority.

Inference

2, Now, if they take into their commission and authority, a power to inquire into the hearts of men about their faith to God's words, then do they pry into secret things which belong not to them; for they must content themselves with the law of reason, and not by it usurp the law of faith into their authority; and wherefore why?

A reason given

3. Because the law of reason is utterly ignorant of the law of faith; the one being natural, the other spiritual.

Cleared

4. Therefore seeing that the civil Jaw is grounded upon reason, and reason being natural, therefore the magistrates who are to be the judges thereof, are to have an eye to natural and moral purity, and cherish it where ever virtue is found, as also to take notice of fleshly and carnal actions, and punish it according to the demerit of the law.

A use of reproof

5. Wherefore, then is not that magistrate most unreasonable, that finding a man acting in virtue, in a laudable manner, doing justice, loving truth, hating falsehood, detecting vice, embracing temperance, eschew prodigality, and in all thing obedient to the civil law, and yet, notwithstanding, shall bring him in as guilty of the law, and thereupon imprison or punish him with death, and all because he worships his God, otherways than the earthly powers doth.

Unreasonable and wicked

6. And then again on the other hand, although a man swear, lie, cozen, cheat, whore, or the like, which are all branches of the civil Jaw, yet shall he find more favour if he go to the public worship and bow to Rimon, (with corrupt magistrates and their fawning priests and flattering doeges,) than the conscientious man, that absents from thence, although he worship God in spirit.

First reproof to Unjust magistrates

7. Now in such magistrates where is their reason? they know they ought to judge according to reason, and yet do nothing less; certainly their usurping an authority over the consciences of men, becomes a canker, and eats up their reason.

8. For in that, they cannot content themselves with their earthly authority, but would aspire further, even into God's chair, to rob him of his glory of being Judge of Quick and Dead, and by this aspiration, robbed of their reason.

Doctrine 2

9. To stretch reason beyond its bounds, is the distraction of reason, seeing reason hath no other object but the moral law, it ought to go no farther then the law of nature directs.

Proved

10. Why was Pithagorus, Plato, Aristotle, Hermes, Socretes, and other rationalists, above and beyond all other rationalists in those our days? was it not because they confined reason to its own orb, and therefore kept it learning in its own line, in its own systum, in its own elements?

Exhortation

11. O ye powers on earth and judges in the civil law, stretch not your reason beyond its bounds, keep you in your seat, and let God and Faith sit in theirs, let God and his prophets dispense spiritual Jaws, and do you dispense natural.

12. Let the visible law of reason be your guide as to temporals, and meddle no further by the sword, if you will not bear it in vain and punish none without reason.

Doctrine 3

13. Therefore those magistrates that arrogate to themselves authority over men's faith, they are always the worst of men, being

Exemplified and proved

14. Let Plutarch and Seneca, (two rational heathen men) be judges hereof, who were schoolmasters to emperors.

Rational men

15. Yet though they were no christians, yet did they abhor cruelty and persecution for conscience sake, even so did Pleny Secundus, who would have none to be prosecuted for their worship:

16. And when the Emperor Tragenes sent to him to punish the Christians, he afterwards wrote to the Emperor, certifying to him, that he had examined and tried them every way, but found no evil in them, save only they worship one Jesus, whom they say is their God, but no evil actions are found in them.[1]

Further proved

17. Again, amongst the Turks, very many sober men there are that hold that it is fit there should be liberty of conscience to every one, as to divine worship, and the ground of their judgment is, because their reason tells them, that every one shall participate of eternal happiness, that live a holy and innocent life, what religion soever they profess.

And this, one Busbequis and Ruston Basa affirms, cited by one Burton. Although Mahomet was sent, as he said, to enforce all by a sword of steel, to follow him, as in his Alcoran.

Application of reproof

18. Now, are not those men who profess the Scripture, and yet will persecute for religion, worse than Turks and Heathens? Let the Spanish inquisition, and the several massacres in France, with Queen Mary's doings, be witnesses hereof:

19. And let Bernard and Augustine be ranked with them, though they go under the name of Saints; for Bernard would have club law, fire, and sword for heretics, as he called dissenters from his formalities.[2]

20. And Augustine, when the poor Manaches and others were persecuted, and came to him to entreat for them to the Emperor

---

[1] See his 10th book, epistle 317.
[2] See his 190th Epistle.

Theodosius, he, instead of helping them to liberty, helped them to bondage, and derided them in their misery, to augment their affliction.

Imperial Law for persecution

21. For this Theodosius, who came after Constantine, made a law, saying, Let all heresy, forbidden by the law of God [and Imperial sanction], keep silence forever. And again,

22. Let all heretics understand, that all places of meeting, as well churches as private houses, are to be taken away from them; let them be debarred from all service day and night: the lord deputy to be fined one hundred pounds if he permits such a thing.

23. Again, we persecute the Manaches and all others with all deserved severity; and first, we determine this heresy shall be held a public crime.

24. We punish them with confiscating their goods; we debar them from buying and selling, bequeathing of goods, or enjoying their fathers' inheritances; and let all be liable to such penalties that harbour such in their houses, &c.

25. By this citation of the Emperor's decree, and by Augustine's justifying of it, were those cruelties and unreasonableness of their doings; but though they plead the law of God, yet their own blind will and ignorant zeal was their law; for the Emperors decree for persecution is joined the Imperial law with the law of God, calling it an Imperial sanction.

Doctrine 4

26. But all sober men were ever against this tyrannical way. But Lanctansius, who lived in the latter end of the Ten Persecutions, was of another mind. Who is so proud (said he) to forbid me to lift up my eyes to heaven, or would impose a necessity upon me to worship that which I will not. It is against religion to enforce religion, and to constrain men to dissemble with God.

Illustrated and distinguished and proved

27. Again, saith he, it is force that makes hypocrites; he followeth Christ that is persecuted; he followeth anti-christ that persecuteth.

28. We compel none by force (said Lanctansius, in his Divine Institutions), for he is unprofitable unto God which hath neither faith nor devotion; and yet none departeth from us, because the truth holdeth them.

29. There is great difference between cruelty and pity; and truth cannot be joined with force, or righteousness with cruelty.

Inference 1

30. Religion ought to be defended, but how? not in putting to death, but in suffering themselves to be killed. To kill and exercise cruelty is wickedness.

Inference 2

31. That which a man doth by compulsion, is no sacrifice; for as much as if it be not done voluntarily, and with the heart, it is most execrable and accursed. And further, saith Lanctansius, in his 5th Book,

Inference 3

32. They are worthy to be detected of men by whom sacrifice is made with tears and sighing.

33. But we on the contrary require not that any will, or nill, shall adore and worship our God; nor we are not angry if they do not worship him.

34. This is a divine saying of Lanctansius, and worthy of all acceptation. Had all his doctrine been like this, he had been eminent; however, truth is truth, let who will speak it.

35. So to conclude this point, I shall conclude with Helery (though in other things dark enough), who writing upon those words [Let both grow together], saith, if heretics should be imprisoned or put to death without alliance of peace, war should then be without truce, a thing contrary to all sober reason that is sober.

CHAP. XII.

1. Shewing how that all Men that compel to Worship, are irrational. 2. Whether the Law of Nature will bear Persecution, answered. 3. The Meaning of these Precepts of Stoning to Death false Prophets opposed.

Doctrine 1

1. ALL that savour either truth, natural or spiritual, may discern that all men that compel to worship, are irrational; and let no man repair to the Old or New Testament for proofs to contradict this doctrine.

2. For though there are several examples and precepts in the Old Testament for putting to death false prophets, yet the moral law bears it not, for the ten words of the law in neither table commands it.

Inference

3. It is said thou shalt have no other God but me, and that thou shalt make no graven image; but it is not said thou shalt imprison or put to death all that have any other gods, or that make to themselves any graven image.[1]

4. For if these words had been part of the moral law, then would the Jews have persecuted the Gentiles for their idolatry.

Secondly

5. Again, it would have been perpetual, and Christ would never have repealed it, had it been of moral institution; for he came not to destroy the law, but fulfil it.

6. But Christ did destroy the very principle of persecution, saying, let both grow together till the harvest; with other proofs abundantly.

7. And as for that saying of compelling the guests to come in to the wedding, that compulsion was no other but by persuasion and entreatance.

Deut. 13 opened

8. Now as to those precepts of stoning to death all false prophets, and the people that fell to idolatry, it was only given to reason, in the Jew's nature, to shew unto it that all those Jews that forsake that

---

[1] Exod. 20.

God, that by his mighty hand had brought them out of the land of Egypt, should suffer death for it here, and eternal damnation in the world to come. For this and the prophets destroying the four hundred false prophets of Baal was a type hereof.

Cleared

9. And that this was a precept given only as to the revolting Jews that were of the serpent's nature, for none of the prophets of the Lord did either execute this law, or require it to be done by the people, saving Elijah, who did it once in the authority of a god by fire from heaven, only to be a type and figure of all false prophets' damnation at the end of the world.

10. And though this law-judicial was given to the carnal Jew to put to death false prophets, and all that entered to idolatry, yet they on the contrary did establish false prophets, and put to death the true, that they justly may be damned at the day of the great God.

Doctrine 3

11. But as for the Lord's true prophets, they were altogether for reproving falsehood, but not for persecuting any, and not only so, but pitying the condition of the elect, who were deluded by false prophets to commit idolatry and worship false gods.

12. It would be too tedious for me to relate the prophets' doctrines as concerning this; besides it would swell this volume too much, but observing brevity, at leisure peruse those Scriptures, and consider them well, whether they will bear the persecution aforesaid, or no. See Jer. chap. 2, verses 19, 30. chap. 3, ver. 1.

Proved

13. Jeremiah told Henath, the false prophet, that he should die; now he was not put to death, but died a natural death in the seventh month, as may be read.

Doctrine 4

14. The true prophets denounced judgments against false prophets, but laid no hands an them, nor commanded others so to do; but false prophets ever laid their hands upon the true, or incited others to do it.

15. So that those that are sober, may see that truth did never persecute, but was ever persecuted by men of a blind fiery zeal.

Inference 1

16. That religion that persecutes, hath in it the power of the sword, but not the power of godliness. True religion puts on no other armour but faith and patience, and fights with no sword but the sword of the spirit.

Inference 2

17. Those that pretend religion, and yet persecute by laws of restraint, is a synagogue of Satan, a church with a sting in her tail.

Applied

18. A sad thing that men should be under such a government, as that they must either have no conscience, or else must be imprisoned or hanged for having a conscience, not conformable or after the court fashion.

19, What dotage is this to think, that those harmless souls that endeavour to keep the faith, and serve God, have wicked hearts, and that the tyrants and hangmen have good ones.[1]

CHAP. XIII.

Doctrines

1. Shewing whether Saints may go to Law. 2. Whose Natures are averse to Law, and whose not. 3. Shewing that the Saints may challenge a propriety in the Civil Law, if Justice be not gone out of it.

Saints' simplicity

1. SOME of the Seed of the Son of Man are so weak in judgment, so timorous and afraid of offending, that they had rather lose all, than go to law to maintain their lawful interests and propriety, thinking that because the world's glory thereof is given to the devil, therefore they may take what they have without resistance.

2. But they do not well; yet will I not blame them, for they cannot help it, only some who through timorousness of offending, by reason of weak judgment, may learn to defend themselves, being enlightened hereby.

---

[1] Said Lanctansius.

A harmless nature

3. But as for others, their very natures are averse to law; for the Moabitish nature would lose all, before it would go to law, not because they judge it evil, but through fear as aforesaid, which is a kind of cowardliness.

Judath's nature

4. But the Jewish nature is excellent, especially that of Judath, Levi, and Dan; it is of a bold, wise, judicious carriage, and will rule and hold, and hold its own, and not suffer every envious devil to wrong or domineer over it.

5. So that by reason of variety of natures, the saints may seem different in several things; some will go to law, some will not go to law, some hold it lawful, but love it not; some love it not, because they understand it not; others love it not, because it is so much managed with the serpent's nature.[1]

Doctrine 1. Matt. 10, 16 commented on

6. But others love it well, because they understand it, and in that they understand it, they have the serpent's wisdom, and may use it, provided they do nothing but what is just according to the civil law; it is to those natures that the Scripture saith, be as wise as serpents, and as innocent as doves.

7. This nature will not let every envious devil trample upon it, but will lash it soundly with the rod of its own law; and this nature, joined with innocence, hath power to prevail with men that are in authority, to do him justice against the evil doer.

8. Such a man fears none, nor will be governed by none, but by such as are in authority, and such he honours, and gives him his due respect according to law.

Inference 1

9. This wisdom of reason is made faith's handmaid, else it would offend; but when faith hath mastered it, then it permits us the use of it, for the defending of ourselves from the evil of that serpent's wisdom that is separated from innocence.

---

[1] Matt. 10, 16.

Inference 2

10. No man is bound to offer himself, and that which he hath, into the hands of wicked men, when otherwise we need not; neither is any man compelled to offer his throat to an unjust stroke.

Inference 3

11. Meekness of spirit often draws on injuries; the crow (as one said) will often stand upon the sheep's back, plucking of wool, but dare not for his life stand upon the dog's.

Inference 4

12. The wickedness of evil people do most commonly seek out those who not deserve worst, but who will bear most.

Inference 5

13. He that will make himself a sheep, may be destroyed by foxes, or eaten of wolves; forbearance proves dangerous, for it provoketh our enemies to boldness, and so becomes an impulse to draw on more injuries, bear one wrong, and invite many. To suffer a little wrong many times invites a greater.

Inference 6. A use of information

14. Evil natures grow presumptious by forbearance. Mercy had need to be guided by wisdom, discretion, and judgment, lest it grows cruel to itself; it may be a virtue sometimes for angry reason to take the rod out of the hands of wrath; anger is not always evil, but becomes a virtue when it acts but in justice.

Doctrine 2

15. Well then, seeing faith permits reason to act as aforesaid, for its better security for a temporal freedom, as also that it gives power of obedience to the civil law, so likewise may it challenge an interest and propriety in the law, as for our defence in the temporal, against cruel men, who would wrong us contrary to the law.

Proved by practice

16. It was the practice of the saints, in the primitive times, to challenge a propriety in the law, therefore the persecuted christians complained against their adversaries to the Emperor,[1] desiring justice,

---

[1] Julian.

he replied to them, saying, it is your master's commandment to bear all kinds of injuries with patience; they answered,

17. It is true he commands us to bear all kind of injuries patiently, but not in all cases; besides, say they, we may bear them patiently, yet crave the magistrates' aid for deliverance, to rescue, or prevent what is like to ensue.

18. I have read in Mr. Fox's Book of Martyrs, a relation of one Julia, who lived in the time of the last persecution, and came to her martyrdom upon the occasion following:—

19. A certain greedy person of great authority, violently took from this Julia, all her goods, lands, and cattle, contrary to all equity and right of law.

20. Whereupon she made her pitiful complaint to the Judges; a day was appointed when the cause must be heard; the spoiled woman, and the spoiling extortioner, stood forth together.

21. Now when she had proved that of good right the goods were her own, this unlawful cruel tyrant affirmed her action to be of no force, for that she was an outlaw, in not observing the Emperor's gods, unless her Christian faith had been first abjured.

22. Now his allegation was allowed as good and reasonable, whereupon incense and fire was prepared for her to worship the gods, which unless she would do, neither law, judgment, nor life should she enjoy in the commonweal. When she heard those words, she said,

23. Farewell life! welcome death! farewell riches! welcome poverty! All that I have, if it were a thousand times more, would I rather lose, than to speak one wicked word against God, my Creator. Further she said,

24. I am the servant of Christ, and after some other words of advice to stick and hold fast to Christ, embraced the flame, and sweetly slept in the Lord.

Application

25. Here we see that this poor saint, upon the unjust taking of her goods, thought to have found refuge in the law, but justice was gone out of it, and all equity and right was disannulled by a devilish edict against the Christian faith.

1. Exhortation to the godly

26. Now at such a time, and under such a government, it is better to let all go, than to seek redress by the law; for where a law is introduced of confiscation and taking away life, for non-conformity, therein non-conformity deprives itself of the benefit of the civil law, or rather the wicked deprive them of it, through their devilish laws being made on purpose to ensnare the innocent, and to destroy the godly.

2. Exhortation to the Magistrates

27. But O! you Magistrates (if I may be so bold to tell you), if you mind your own peace, be sober and take heed you intrench not on God's sovereignty, which is the only King of men's consciences, as King Charles the First could say (after conviction by the law in his conscience) to his parliament,

Of conviction

28. I see now (saith the King), it is a bad exchange to wound a man's conscience, to salve state sores, to calm the storms of popular discontents, by stirring up a tempest in a man's own bosom.

29. This lamentation King Charles the First made, upon his being overcome by his parliament, to sign the Bill of Attainder of the Lord Strafford, Deputy of Ireland, against his conscience.

30. Again, said the King, I had rather be condemned to the woe [ve soly] than to that of [ve vobis] hypocrite, by seeming to pray what I do not approve. See Bakers Chronology.

31. Offensive wars for religion, King James I. was of an opinion, was never just, not to force the conscience which guides the soul, with the power of the sword.

And one Sanderson saith, writing upon the Life of King Charles the First, that King James was [Defenser fide], if opugned, yet was he not authorised to quarrel with another man's belief.[1]

---

[1] Sanderson, page 9.

THE SIXTH PART:

OF

THE SOUL's MORTALITY.

CHAP. I.

1. Shewing whence the Doctrine of the Soul's Immortality proceded. 2. The Darkness of Oregan discovered, &c. 3. How Reason slays the Spirit.

Error taught by Philosophers

1. THE common opinion of the world is, that all men's souls are immortal, and can not, nor do not die, but slip out of their bodies as out of a prison, into some other world, either of pleasure or misery; that of pleasure is by the Greeks called the Elysian fields.

2. The heathen philosophers were the first preachers of that doctrine. Thales, Democritus, the Stoics, and Plato, taught, that as God was a Spirit without a body, so souls must leave their bodies entirely, before they can be joined with God.

Doctrine of Hermes

3. And Hermes saith, that the soul is immortal, therefore saith he to me, thy grandfather Æsculapius, the first inventor of physic, hath a temple on Mount Lobia, there lieth his worldly man, his body, but his residence, his soul, is gone up to heaven, helping all sick persons by his deity, as he did before by his physic.

Plato

4, The soul only is man, (say the Platonites) the body is but the case or cover to it, and Plato, with the Chaldean philosophers do all so teach, that all souls were made together, and afterwards were sent into bodies, as into so many dark lanterns.

Oregan

5. Oregan, a philosopher of Christianity, in the time of the Ten Persecutions, was much taken with this platonical notion, therefore, saith he, according to the carriage of these naked spirits before they were embodied, there were prepared answerable mansions for them.

6. That such a soul that had walked with God acceptably was put into a fine prison, and was clothed with an elegant and amiable body, but that soul that had provoked and displeased its creator, was put into a darker dungeon, into a more obscure and uncomely body.

7. This Oregan is as dark in this doctrine, as the heathen, and if any scripturian professor produce this Oregan, as a good witness for them of the soul's immortality, let them be answered thus, that Oregan by me is not owned as any true minister, for he was a philosopher first, a scripture professor, and a christian by profession in the second, and an apostate in the third, for he could not suffer, for his faith, but offered incense to the Emperor's gods, abjuring the faith of Jesus, and though it is said he repented afterwards, yet I own not that repentance of any efficacy. But to the matter in hand.

8. I find all professors in a manner, in as great darkness as was Oregan above said, for they will have the soul to be immortal, as well as he, and that every man's soul is made in heaven.

9. But whether they be made altogether, or some at one time and some at another, as bodies are got by carnal copulation, so souls are made and fitted for those bodies, and infused into them from above. I say it matters not for the one or other of those two points, they all of them teach yea all the churches of Europe.

10. So from hence I find there is as pitchy a darkness spread over the hearts of professors of scripture as ever there was upon the heathen philosophers, nay, their darkness is greater and their sin is heavier, for though they own the letter by their reason, yet their reason condemns the spirit of it all ways, and sometimes the letter itself, when it crosses a principle of their dull philosophy.

Blasphemy

11, This I know to be true, for I heard a priest of the nation, once blasphemously say, speaking of 1 John chap. 3, verse 9th, that that scripture, as to the literal sense, was a lie.

12. Angelical reason is lofty and proud, and though the law was given to be a rule to reason, and the letter its guide, yet reason will rule it, by making its own blind born reason the standard of truth; so then the spirit of reason slays the spirit of the scriptures and makes the scripture fruitless yea, a nose of wax to turn it into the doctrines of men, grounded on natural wisdom.

13. Nevertheless many of these doctrines and principles that are held forth by reason are contrary to reason, and the soul's immortality is one, and this is a general error, as will more appear in the following discourse.

CHAP. II.

1. Shewing the Cause of the Irrationality of the Soul's Immortality. What the Principles of the Magistrates Religion is. The Doctrine of Martial Men. What it is:

The cause of this opinion

1. IT were worth the knowing what should be the original cause of this general recorded opinion amongst the wise and learned of this irrationality of the soul's immortality; the resolutions being needful, therefore give me leave to unfold it.

The founders of this opinion

2. The gods of the earth have raised up this principle in order to raise themselves, it first took beginning from Mars, the god of war; prowess, courage, strength, and valour, flowing from ambitious pride, must have some lively object to fix on for the encouragement of valour, and nothing could be found out fitter for the raising of monarchy or imperial power, than the principle of the soul's immortality.

Their power

3. Therefore angelical reason being lifted up to authority through his wisdom and policy, he having a martial spirit, a Jupiter's dignity, and a Mercurian tongue, he can make his oration admirable, so that he is presently judged to have the spirit of the gods, and all are ready to proffer their service to him, as one ordained from heaven to make them happy.

And effect

4. Now when angelical reason hath got power, then he plots how he might conquer others, and become sole lord himself; therefore having raised an army he governs them as a god, and by his wise counsellors, and chief learned men, he preaches to them a double happiness, the first is, they shall be all gentlemen soldiers, and shall never want silver.

A two-fold doctrine of martial men

5. And till they come to battle, they mind no other doctrine than this,

Neither faith nor conscience common soldiers carry,
Best pay is right, their hands are mercenary.

6. But when they come to battle, then the general must, to encourage them to fight, preach the other doctrine of the soul's immortality.

7. And this was ever the practice as well as doctrine of bloody martial men, as history doth abundantly relate:

Inference 1

8. Josephus, (in his book of the Wars of the Jews) reports that one city of the Jews being besieged by the Romans, and being not able to hold out any longer, the chief governor, and a zealot of the law advised them all rather than to fall into the hands of the uncircumscised Gentiles, to lay violent hands upon themselves, and to become their own executioners.

9. And in order here too he made an elegant oration of the soul's immortality, and shewed them in that the soul could not die, but would, upon the death of the body, go immediately to heaven.

The fruits of false doctrine

10. This doctrine or flesh pleasing principle had such an influence into their ignorant spirits that they all committed that bloody tragedy of killing themselves, each soldier run himself through with his own sword; the masters first killed their servants, then their children, then their wives, and lastly themselves.

11. In fine, there was none left alive, ave two, who had hid themselves, as Josephus hath related.

Evidenced

12. Several men hath made death fearless through a belief of this doctrine, one hearing an oration of the soul's immortality, threw himself down a rock, that he might kill death and run to the Elysian fields.

13. The Turks uphold their war with this principle, and so is all other wars upheld thereby, for as money is their pay here, so immortal glory, without death, must be their reward. But to proceed.

CHAP. III.

1. Shewing the Opinion of the Heathen what the Soul of Man is. 2. The Opinion of the Professors of Christianity also opened, examined, and detected. 3. The Author's Description of the Soul

The two string music

1. I HAVING here touched the string of the heathen doctrine of the immortality of the soul, let me come to touch the other strings of their opinion, what the soul of man is, and see what music it makes, and let who will dance after that pipe.

Reason's doctrine of the soul, proved by

2. The soul, (said a magic, or sorcerer of the Chaldee philosophy) hath not its being from seed, neither conceives of corporeal mixtures, but as a spark from the paternal fire.

1. Pythagorian

3. The Pythagorian and Platonist philosophers do hold forth a three-fold soul, whereof the one or two are wholly separated from matter or form. The first they call super-celestial intelligence, which is rationally pure, and that is God's; the second soul hath a substance subsisting, but not of itself, and is capable of dissolution, by reason of its nature being subject to mutation, and so it perisheth; and this, they say, is in all irrational creatures.

2. Doctor More

4. The third soul, and that which they place in man, they call an immaterial and incorporeal fire, being exempt from all compounds, say some; others say, that it hath an aerial body, so subtle, that can neither be felt nor seen; but both opinions conclude, that it is a ray or beam of the Deity, and is immortal; but by what other more significant names to give it, they know not, being distracted in their definition of it.

3. Democritus

5. Democritus saith, it is of the nature of fire, dispersing itself into sparks and fiery atoms; so say some of the stoics, as Zeno, and others.

Diogenes

6. Others have thought the soul to be nothing but air, as Diogenes; others make it a spirit mixed of fire and air; others say it is made up of all the four elements, but most exclude earth and water, because they are solid substances.

Seneca, Cicero

7. Others there are that having no satisfaction what the soul should be, do therefore conclude, that no man can tell what the soul of man is. Seneca, treating upon it, was in amaze, whilst he said, what other thing can I think it to be, but a God dwelling in the body of man. Again, saith he, no man can tell what the soul is; the like said Cicero.

Dryer

8. And the literal Scripturianists is in as great a stand, and that made a priest of these times cry out, most pathetically, saying, Oh! let man study, invent, yea search, the very inward of obscured nature, yet shall he never know what the soul is. O! saith he, this inexplicable wonder of that ray in thee, this emanation of the Deity.

9. I having shewed the opinion of the most eminent naturalists, I come now to view the doctrine of the Scripture professors in the several churches of Europe, and I find them all agreeing in the same principle, to wit, that the soul is a semi-god, being a part of his essence, as they say.

Augustine

10. Therefore, say they, God is a spirit, and his nature is reason, and the soul of man is a spirit, and its nature is reason; so God made no difference betwixt them but this, that man's soul is clothed with a body, but God is pure spirit, without body.

11. Their spirits twist together, and are in union, and when the soul leaves the body, it turns into God again.

12. This is Quaker and Ranter like.

Applied

13. O! foolish men, how can you once be so sottish as think that your soul is soul without a body; you would describe a thing that is not, nor never was; you may well be in the dark, and cry out with your brother, being required to define the soul, saith,

Reason unsatisfied

14. O! yea men, why do you require me to unfold that, I know not? Can a man dissect an atom? Can he grasp a flame, or hold the wind in his hand?

15. Sure I am (said a Minister of the Church of England) I have a soul, but what it is I know not.

Their doctrine confuted

16. Is this a man fit to preach life to another that knows not what his own life is, nor of what matter he is made of himself? Man would turn his soul out of his body to know it, when he cannot know it whilst within. He must go to school to a dead soul, that will not learn of a living body.

17. Nevertheless, though these men do confess that they know not what the soul is, yet some of them pretend to know what God is, and for others that acknowledge they are at a loss to find out what the spirit of God is, yet are they so proud as that they will not admit any other man to know what God is. because they do not know him themselves.

18. But you, chosen ones, who have been educated up in the faith of this Commission of the Spirit, do know, that as the souls of the men of the world naturally are a fiery spark of reason, whereby they desire to pry into the height and depth of all things;

A divine doctrine

19. So likewise the souls of the seed of Adam are a fiery divine spark of faith, whereby they discern the glory of God, both as to his form and nature.

Doctrine 2

20. Again, though the souls of the select seed are made up of the divine nature, yet are they not wholly divine; but that divine life hath mixed itself, or been mixed with a nature taken out of the dust, and this makes still but one soul, although distinguished by its several properties, earthly and heavenly, human and divine.

Examined

21. And although this earthly in the divine life hath contracted to its nature the spirit of reason, by adhering to a suggestion and making trial of a glorious pretended show of excellence, yet hath it

still but one soul, though of contrary voices, and the soul is either good or bad as the voice carries it.

22 Therefore man's soul hath its denomination from the ruling voice, or predominate property.

Proved

23. For that nature, seed, or spirit that is under government, is not accounted lord; for a house is not called by the name of the servant, but by the name of the master.

Illustrated

24. Now by the government of this divine spark, man comes to be called the image of God, the seed of God, &c., which could not be in case they had not sprung from the divine nature, and participated of the breath of the divine and immortal life.

Unfolded

25. Yet though the divine part of the soul be of the immortal seed, yet nevertheless it cannot be immortal, because it is made one essence with a body taken out of the dust.

26. Therefore it must either change to mortality, or change mortality to it; for mortality and immortality cannot dwell together. But of this bye-and-by.

CHAP. IV.

1. Of the Soul's traduction. 2. The Foolishness, if not Blasphemy, of those that assert the Soul's infusion. 3. How Sin hath its original from the Will.

1. THE most of the learned do hold the soul's infusion, yet hath there been here and there one that have gainsayed it, and maintained the soul's traduction; as Augustine for one (though wonderful dark in other things), yet chides with Hiram for his peremptoriness against the soul's traduction.

2. For this Hiram, through devilish zeal, pronounced a present curse to all such as hold the soul's traduction.

3. But Augustine knew not how to deal with the Pelagons, who denied original sin, had he not held to the traduction of the soul; yet Gregory the Great held it to be a question that cannot be determined in this life; but then Tertullian doth hold for the souls traduction, yet denies the soul's mortality. But most of those that held the soul's traduction, hold the soul's mortality.

4. But the other principles being in fame with the great men of the earth, not one who looked for honour would own the soul's traduction, but especially its mortality; for such would have eternal life, without death. But to proceed,

Their doctrine confuted by

5. All or most of the learned as aforesaid, do hold the soul's infusion. Now give me leave to be so bold as to argue with you thus: you say man gets the body, but God gives the soul.

1. Argument

6. Now do you think that God hath nothing to do but to watch man's carnal actions, and join himself with every one when in the fleshly act of copulation?

2. Argument

7. Must he help to beget every child to life, and as soon as a man hath parted with his sperme, then God must part with his spirit into that sperme; and worse than this still, for God must be co-partner with every lustful devil at or in the begetting of a bastard, for he must come in and join issue, or there would be no bastard?

3. Argument

8. O! you wretched world, what would you make of your God, who is of purer eyes than to behold iniquity? Would you have him to give you a soul to work iniquity?

4. Argument

9. Again, if God infuse into the babe a spirit or soul, then whether is it by breathing it into the babe, or massy flesh, as he did to Adam's body of dust, or by making the soul before, and at that interim sending it down (I know not how) to enliven and animate that body?

5. Argument

10. Moreover, whether is that a good soul or a bad? If it be a good soul as Adam's was, how comes it to sin? If you say by Adam's fall, that cannot be; for if Adam had not power to generate the soul, as well as the body, then is there not one soul related to Adam, for they came from heaven, as well as Adam's, and so was perfect in their formation as well as Adam's; and if they had not of Adam's spirit, then could they not fall in Adam.

6. Argument

11. Furthermore, if this were so, God would never finish the work of creation; the world would have God to be restless, after his six days work; they will not grant him an everlasting Sabbath of rest from the work of this world's creation, but every time a child is born, the question is, what hath God sent? What, hath he made a boy or a girl?

12. Hence comes this principle in their babe's catechism, from the question, who made you? The answer is, God made me, as if they were made a part from Adam, when as all the children of God were undoubtedly made in Adam, and so do proceed through his loins, by course, through generation, and not by creation.

7. Argument

13. Again, if you blind guides say, that sin only come in by the body, then must I tell you, that that cannot be; for what can a lifeless body do? Can a man breath that hath no soul? And can a body sin, that hath no life? What is sin but life, and a fiery life too, drawing upon itself the body of death?

8. Argument

14. As the soul cannot live without the body, so the body cannot sin without the soul; nay, it is the soul that is the man; it is the soul

that sins, yet the soul could not sin without the body, because it is inseparably united to the body.

9. Argument

15. Wherefore by reason of this near union, what the body doth, the soul doth; and what the soul willeth, the body doth, the soul being of power to turn about its body, and the act of the body is the soul's will, and to be counted the soul's act, when nothing doth resist the will.

10. Argument

16. But if a bodily action be done, whether it be good or evil, and in the doing had not consent of the innermost will of the soul, then the action is forced, and so not reckoned or counted the action of the soul; as for example,

17. If a virgin be deflowered by a man, and be forced by strong hands, against the will of the soul and power of her body to preserve herself, this is not to be accounted a sin, because it had not the soul's consent, &c.

11. Argument

18. Again, as aforesaid, the soul is the life of every action, for nothing acts but life and soul; it is the soul that walks, that talks, that eats and drinks, that sleeps, that wakes, that lives, and dies; and it is universal in every part of the body of a perfect man; so that a man cannot be touched with the point of a pin in any place, but his soul feels it.

12. Argument

19. Furthermore, if the soul come into the body immediately from heaven, how comes it to be capable of sin? Will you say, as some do, that it is by imitation? then prove this; and lock up a child in a room, and withhold him from the sight and hearing of evil, and see whether time will not cause the seed of evil to bud. Now from whence doth that spring?

20. If you know not, then, you simple prelates, go and learn of the Jewish Rabbi; who, being asked when wicked imagination entered into man, answered, at the very hour of formation.

21. And have you not read, or have you forgotten what David said, that in sin had his mother conceived him?

CHAP. V.

1. Shewing that no Souls are made without Bodies.
2. Of the Creation of Adam and the Angels.

Preface

1. I COME now to shew the nature and original of the soul; this doctrine is the cognoserey ebsom, know thyself, which all the wise philosophers were at a stand at, as I have shewn.

Doctrine

2. Now you, who are enlightened in truth, do know that the Creator never made souls without bodies, neither in heaven above, nor earth beneath; but they were always made one individual essence, that so it might appear a distinct living creature, for God and man to behold; for the nature of a spirit is invisible, and therefore it must have a body, otherwise it could have no sensible being.

Proved

3. Therefore when God made Adam, he formed his body of dust, then breathed upon it, with a powerful word, and immediately Adam quickened into a living soul.

4. Now by faith in Scripture we find, that Adam's soul was never sensible of itself, until it was completed in its body; and though it was the breath of immortal life, yet was it capable to become mortal, because it was now one essence with a body taken out of the dust.

5. Now this dust that Adam's body was of, had in it the life of the four elements.

Doctrine 2: Use of humiliation

6. Again, through Adam's fall, all his seed have contracted a third nature into their spirit, which is the angels' rational of understanding, but they had better to have been without it, for by it we learn to do evil; as also from the earthly nature, man becomes corrupt, and full of putrefying sores, both within and without.

Doctrine 3

7. Again, when God created the Angels above, he gave life to them by words of faith, but breathed no faith into them; for all the Angels were made by one word speaking, and they were not made spirits without bodies, but bodies and spirits together.

CHAP. VI.

1. Of the Law that Adam was created under. 2. Of Sin and Death, and when they entered.

1. IT is written, In the day that thou eatest thereof, thou shalt die; now this Scripture shews that death entered upon sin. It is as much as if the Lord had said,

Doctrine 1

2. If thou eatest of this forbidden fruit, death shall enter into thy nature, thy whole nature, thy divine part, because it is polluted; so that thou shalt become a poor mortal creature, loaded with the infirmities of sickness, hunger, cold, pain, grief, and sadnesses, with many other frailties, as the fruits of death, and the forerunners thereof.

3. Now when Adam had broke this precept, immediately death entered into his whole man, with its seal of shame and horror, fear and trouble, which made him run to hide himself.

Doctrine 2

4. But the glorious Creator, through his mercy to his own seed, put a stop to Adam's fear by a gracious promise, that the seed of the woman should bruise the serpent's head; which was as much as if the Lord should say,

Inference 1

5. Fear not, Adam, I will have mercy on thee, though thou hast broke my law, and incurred death; yet shall it be but death natural, with sickness, sores, hard and painful labour, with persecution for thy faith's sake, which I will ensure to thee and to thy seed.

Inference 2

6. Therefore to that end, I will become seed myself in mortal weed, that I may deliver thee from thy mortal frailties, and from thy sin committed.

Inference 3

7. And I will be even with the serpent for deceiving of thee, and defiling of thee and thy seed; and though he persecute thee even to death, yet is it but the death of the body, that is, but a natural death, and death natural thou art to undergo.

Inference 4

8. But as for the serpent and his seed, I will inflict upon them an eternal death; this shall be the bruising of their heads, when as thy death is but the bruising of the heel, because it is but temporal.

Application

9. Thus you that are my friends, by faith in the Scriptures, may see, that the seed of Adam are to undergo but one death; but the seed of the serpent do undergo two.

10. For as Adam and his seed do pass through a natural death into eternal life, so on the contrary the serpent and his seed do and will pass through the first death into the second death, which what it is, will be shewn in the Seventh Part of this Treatise.

11. I having now shewn that death entered through sin, upon soul and body, I come now to declare how that they are both but one living and dying essence, and that the one cannot be without the other; but life to one, life to both; death to one, death to both.

CHAP. VII.

1. Several Arguments to prove that Man begets the Soul, as well as the Body. 2. Two great Scripture Objections answered.

Preface

1. IT is one of the simplest opinions in the world now to believe, that when a child is conceived in the womb, through mixture of seeds, that the parent only gets the body, and God only infuseth the soul.

2. How blind is the learning of reason in the knowledge of itself; if men did but understand the Scriptures, and had faith to believe them, they would find, that the body and soul of man is but one living and dying essence, proceeding from man's nature, by virtue of the word of the Lord, in the creation of Adam and Eve.

Gen. 1, 28 opened

3. Therefore it is written, Be fruitful and multiply, and replenish the earth. Now, if Adam had but begot the body, and not the soul, how could he have replenished the earth with people, or what fruitfulness had been from his loins?

Inference 1

4. Now if nothing but massy flesh, or some stupid senseless matter, wherein was neither life nor motion, or any thing as would produce or quicken into life, issued from it.

5. Had this been so, then Adam had been no better, if so good as a picture drawer, filling and replenishing the world with images of man and woman, but no life or breath through the nose; then might it be said as it was to a picture, very artificially drawn, O what a scull is here, but no brains within,

6. But mind the Scripture, it is written, and Abraham took Sarah his wife, and Lot his brother's son, and the souls that they had gotten in Haran, and went for to go into the land of Canaan, see Exodus 1, 5. and Acts 7, 14.

Inference

7. Again it is written, that all the souls that came with Jacob into Egypt, which came out of his loins, were in the whole sixty-six:[1] here we see that souls came out of their loins as well as their bodies.

Answer 1

8. But to this, reason replies, saying, souls are there put for persons; O blind reason would you have persons without souls? what is a person but a substance? and what is a substance without a soul; is it any thing but a lump of senseless matter?

Answer 2

9. Again, what is reason but an acuteness and quickness of conceiving? whether words bear a good sound or signification or not, and from your reason, then consider thus much, to wit, that that which our translation calls body, the Greeks, (as the learned in that tongue say) calls soul.

10. As Numbers, chap. 6, verse 6, there it is said, he shall come at no dead body; so Levet. 19, 28, and in Judges, chap. 8, it is said, that Gideon had seventy sons of his body begotten, that is, of his whole man body and soul, for a dead body cannot get a living body or soul, as Job saith, chap. 19, verse 17.

11. Wherefore then the body and soul being but one essence, it must needs follow, that what is attributed to the one, belongs to the other, as when it is said, mortify the deeds of the flesh, or deeds of the body.

---

[1] Gen. 46.

Doctrine 1. Inference

12. Again, it is said, that by virtue of Christ's resurrection many dead bodies arose out of their graves; did therefore their bodies arise without their souls, I trow not?

Objection

13. But reason will still come rushing in with that Scripture of, fear not him that kills the body, but fear him that kills the soul, &c. But to this I answer.

Doctrine 1

14. Now the meaning of this place, as to my faith, is no more than this, viz. fear not him that can do no more but kill or put to death this natural life, or mortal body, for as Paul saith, there is a natural body, and there is a spiritual body, and their glory differs, &c.

Proved. Heb. 12, 9 opened

15. This doctrine also opens that other objection, and brings it to this sense, namely, Heb. 12, 9. we, said Paul, have had fathers of our flesh, which corrected us, and we gave them reverence; shall we not much more be subject to the Father of Spirit and Life?

16. Now is not the meaning here of thus, namely, that our natural life and rational being is from the fathers of our flesh, or natural life, and this reason and flesh of ours which was their own seed, they did correct by stripes, for their pleasure, but the father of our spiritual, or new begotten life, corrected us for our profit.

Doctrine 2

17. As if the Apostle should further say, let us submit to correction from the father of our new created or renewed light, life, and spirit, for he doth it in love to ourselves, he will not let us lie dead in tresspasses and sins, and had rather preserve us in brine, then let us rot in honey.

Proved

18. For as fire refines gold, so affliction purifies the heart, and makes faith to shine; therefore murmur not at affliction, it is but the purging out the old learned lust of worldly honour, which your fathers of your flesh never corrected you for, but rather bred you up in it, together with morality and manners.

Proved

19. Now, therefore, you were willing to submit to your fathers of your natural life, by which nature you were but the children of wrath as others, for that spirit of divine faith in you died in Adam, and it wanted a quickening ministry to make it capable of life.

Proved

20. And now, even now, hath this quickening ministry sounded in your ears, and awaked you from death, so that now you have found God to be your father, yea, the father of your spiritual life, by my ministry.

Proved

21. Therefore by how much more this spiritual life is better than your old carnal life; by so much more are you bound to submit to his fatherly correction, it being done for your eternal good.

Conclusion

22. Now having shewed that man begets the soul. I shall now proceed to show how that man's soul is mortal, in a mortal body, and must die this first death as aforesaid.

CHAP. VIII.

1. Shewing that no Man's Soul can escape Death. That the very God-head Life in Christ did die. Clear Evidence of the Soul's Mortality.

1. THAT there is no man living that can preserve his soul from a natural death is certainly true; for if the Lord of Life himself did die, or pour forth his soul unto death, then how is it possible that the sinful soul of man shall escape death?

Doctrine 1

2. Now the Scripture is clear that Christ's soul did die, and it is certain that redemption to eternal life could not be had without the death of the God-head spirit.

Proved

3. Because the offering and atonement that was made for the sin of the elect, must on necessity reach so far as to be answerable to the offence, else pardon could not be had, therefore an eternal offence required an eternal remedy.

4. For the sin was against an eternal majesty, therefore there was no way to expiate sin, or to satisfy the cry of the guilt in men's consciences, but by the death of the eternal God.

5. Therefore God made himself capable to die, by uniting his Godhead spirit with pure human flesh.

6. But no more of this here, for blind reason can not endure to hear that the soul should die, much less that the Lord of Life should, but the seed of faith are satisfied in it.

Doctrine 2

7. But for proof that the soul of man doth die, the souls of Abraham, Isaac, and Jacob, yea, and of Adam and Eve are dead, yea David is dead, the Apostles are dead, and in the dust of the earth.

Inference 1

8. It is said of those, they died and gave up the ghost, and were gathered unto their people; it is not said that they went to heaven.

Inference 2

9. It is said of David, that he slept with his fathers, and was buried in his city; it is not said that he went to heaven, but on the contrary, the apostle said, that David was not ascended into heaven; Christ's soul was ascended, but David's remained in the grave; Christ was but three days in the grave, and saw no corruption, but David did see corruption.

Doctrine 3

10. Moreover David himself was well instructed in the souls mortality; therefore, saith he, Psa. 90, thou, O Lord, turnest man to destruction, and sayest, return yea children of men, for a thousand years in thy sight are but as yesterday.

Proved

11. Again, Psa. 30, David desires that his days may be continued, to the end that he might praise God, knowing that he could not praise God in the grave; therefore said, that he would praise God whilst he had a being, for when I go down to the pit, shall the dust praise thee.

Further explained

12. As if he should say, Lord let me live, that I may worship thee, for death cannot celebrate thee; I must die, and if I remain in the grave a thousand years, yet it is but to thee as yesterday, nor unto me

in death will appear more than the watch of a night, although while I am living the time doth seem long.

13. O therefore let me live, that I may praise thee, because in the grave there is no remembrance of thee, the dead cannot praise thee.

14. The very same faith is manifested by good King Hezekiah upon this occasion, the Lord sending his prophet to him, to tell him he should die and not live; upon which message the king turneth him unto the Lord, and prayed, saying, remember me, O Lord, how I have walked before thee with an upright heart, &c.

15. Now when the King was recovered, he saith thus, I said in the cutting of my days I shall go to the gates of the grave, but the Lord hath spoken to me, and done it; O Lord, by these things doth men live, and in all these things is the life of my spirit.

Doctrine 4

16. For thou hast in love to my soul delivered it from death, the grave cannot praise thee, death cannot celebrate thee; they that go down into the pit cannot pray or hope for thy truth, the living praise thee, as I do this day.

Inference

17. Thus we see that these two kings were of the faith of the soul's mortality; see for further proof, Psa 42, 2, and 17, 15, and 89th, and 48th verse, David in this verse asketh a question, saying, what man is he that liveth and shall not see death?

17. David answereth to this question, saying, by way of query, shall he deliver his soul from the hand of the grave, shall not his soul sleep in the grave, as if he should say, answer me to this.

Applied

18. You that are of opinion that the soul never dies; is not this your opinion vain and ridiculous? for every soul is mortal and must taste death; there is not one that can deliver his soul from the power of death, or the grave, but must if it be tainted with sin, it must see corruption.

Doctrine 5

19. I myself must die and see corruption, but my Redeemer shall see no corruption, for by faith I see him go up with a shout, having overcome death, his life being too strong for it; death could not hold him under, but he hath led captivity captive, and will give gifts to men, which will assure us that he will raise us from the sleep of

death, and give unto us eternal life, joy, and glory, in his appointed time. Therefore shall our souls rest in this hope.

Cleared

20. Thus we see that David was acquainted of the doctrine of the soul's mortality, yea all the Scriptures are full of proof hereof, and it being so full, to prove it therefore will I the more dilate upon it, and give it you my spiritual friends, as I have learned it, in twelve evidences, strong and powerful, drawn from the Scriptures of truth.

CHAP. IX.

1. Shewing how Death attends on Sin. 2. That Scripture opened, that saith, that every Sin is not unto Death.

EVIDENCE THE FIRST.

Doctrine 1

1. EVERY soul that sins shall die, saith the Scripture, sin is the author of death and gives strength to death to annihilate life; obedience to sin brings obstruction to life, by death riding upon all life, in that all have sinned; he that can clear himself from all sin, may free himself from all death; but who can do this? not one from the dark Papist, to the light Quaker.

Illustrated

2. It is written, that Adam was made a living soul, but Christ was made a quickening spirit of that soul.

3. Now there is a two-fold quickening of the elect, as I conceive, the one is a quickening it from the death of sin, and the other is the quickening it from the death of nature.

4. These are the two resurrections the Scripture speaks of, and blessed is he that hath part in the first, of such a one, the second death hath no power.

5. Now where the Scripture saith, that every sin is not unto death, that is meant the second death.

Doctrine 2. Explained

6. The same meaning hath that Scripture, that saith, he that believeth in me shall never die, that is, he shall never die a second

and eternal death; the same meaning hath that place, that saith, he that eateth of the bread of life shall never die.

Cleared

7. Now compare this with John 11, where it is said of Lazarus, that though he were dead, yet should he live, and of that Scripture that speaks of eternal life abiding in them, and it will be made clear that assurance of eternal life is looked upon as eternal life itself, because it knew nothing could prevent it.

Proved

8. Therefore it is that some Scriptures intimate an immediate glory after death, because faith lives in eternity, and so links time and eternity together, because there is no time to the dead, but the next thing after death is judgment.

9. Therefore though a soul should lie in the grave five thousand years, or more, yet at its resurrection it is not sensible of any time it hath lain there, it will appear to it but the minute of an hour; in life there is reckoning of time, but in death there is no remembrance.

CHAP. X.

1. Shewing that Christ's Soul did die. 2. The brute Beasts wiser than Man, for they fear and decline Death. 3; Innocent Nature doth naturally fear Death in the Saints.

EVIDENCE THE SECOND.

2. Argument proved

1. SECONDLY, if the soul of Christ did die, ours' must needs die; but Christ's soul did die, 'tis proved Isa, 53, 10. There it is said, prophesying of Christ, that he should make his soul an offering for sin; and the Apostle Paul affirms the same, saying, that he was offered up unto death through the eternal spirit; and Christ said as much, when he said, he had power to lay down his life, and power to take it again.

Proved

2. This life that was laid down was his God-head life, and therefore it is said, that God purchased his Church with his blood; and when he was near his sufferings, it is said, that his soul was heavy unto death.

Inference 1

3. Now, then, if his soul could not have died, why should it be heavy unto death? It is not said that his body, but his soul, was heavy unto death, although the Lord Christ's death, proved death's death, yet was it a dreadful cup to innocent nature.

Inference 2

4. There is no pleasure in wrestling with death; if death did not take away life, there needed no care of life, nor fear of death, and this is the way to be desperate; for the devil will fight and kill, and be killed, and yet his soul shall not die; there is pleasure in fighting and killing, without losing of life. This is a mad principle, none mader in bedlam:

5. But to the matter aforesaid. Every thing naturally declines death, as destructive to life; the ox, the cow, the ass, and the mule are all sensible of pain, and so consequently afraid of death, and fly from it.

Inference 3. From false opinion

6. But now there is a people of reason, and yet nothing more unreasonable in this; for amongst the multitude, there is a multitude that bids defiance to death.

Inference 4. Of false opinion

7. The blind, fleshly, carnal man, that wears a sword of steel, stoutly struts about with it, and counts that man a bastard, and a dastard, that will not murder and be killed without fear of death.

Inference 5. Of false opinion

8. And the spiritual zealots, or angelical devil, bids defiance to death likewise; therefore if death will not come to him, he will run to death, he will to prison, to fire, and faggot, when he needs not, into dungeon or death, because death will not kill him; it will but do as the stroke of the steel upon a flint, fetch out the fire; it will but by one stroke upon his body, fetch out his soul, and carry it straight to the Elysian fields, to heaven, into Lazarus's bosom, as he imagines.

Inference 6. Of true opinion

9. But a saint that hath his understanding enlightened to know the nature of life and death, he fears and declines death as much as in him lies, because it is the annihilating of all life; therefore shuns it when it can with a good conscience, and that is when for its

profession of faith it comes to this point, as that money or innocence will deliver it.

10. But if it will not, then must it arm itself with patience, and comfort itself by looking upon the recompence of reward, and as faith took away the fear of eternal death before, even so this its patience and suffering, and the recompence of reward hoped for, will help to exterminate fear of this temporal death in some good measure.

Inference 7

11. Again, if innocent nature did not naturally fear death or persecution for its faith, then would not the Lord have given so many exhortations to his children not to fear, as fear not, thou warm Jacob; fear not, my little flock, it is your father's pleasure to give you the kingdom.

Doctrine 2. Inference 1

12. Moreover, to prove further that Christ's soul did die, and that it was his whole life, both divine and human; now if it was but the human life in Christ that died, then comes redemption in by man.

Inference 2

13. Can a finite life or a man's human soul be able to bear upon his shoulder the infinite weight of all the sin of the elect, the iniquity of all was laid upon Christ; therefore he must needs be God as well as man. Every sin is as a talent of lead, yet the Lion of the tribe of Judah had the strength and power to unburden us thereof, being the Alpha and Omega, blessed for ever; Amen.

CHAP. XI.

1. Shewing that the Reward of well-doing is not given till the Resurrection-day. 2. Of the Book of Life. 3. How that Christ and the Crown came both together.

EVIDENCE THE THIRD.

Doctrine 1.

1. THIRDLY, that the souls of the saints do not go to heaven until the Resurrection, it is evident, because the Scripture saith, that the reward of welldoing is not given until the great day.

2. Now the great day is not when a man dies, but it is at the day when all shall arise from death, and this is at the end of the world. Then comes the Lord Jesus Christ, the saints' God, to give reward unto his servants.

Proved

3. Therefore it is written, Revel. 22, 12. Behold I come quickly, and my reward is with me, &c. Here we see every man will have his reward given him when Christ comes, and this is according to that saying concerning the talents given, that after a long time the Lord cometh, and reckoneth with them.

4. This long time was until the end of the world, and the reckoning day the Resurrection day. Then will he reckon for the one talent of reason, by the law in its seed.

5. And with the other that had his talents of grace. and will crown his own gifts with a Come, ye blessed of my Father, or God-head Spirit, inherit the kingdom prepared for you.

6. Now, can any man that hath but sober reason, believe that those were in heaven before in their souls? and now their bodies were to come and inherit, seeing he speaks of their works of mercy, and now gives rewards for it.

Proved

7. Again, what reward soever the saints have promised them after death, yet the Scripture doth not say that any is given until the end of the world; according as it is written, Be thou faithful unto the end, and I will give thee a crown of life.

8. Now this crown of life is given at the coming of Jesus; therefore, saith Paul, we shall reign in life by Jesus; death shall be swallowed through life. Rom. 5, 17. 2 Cor. 5, 4. 1 Cor. 15.

Col. 3 opened

9. Again, said Paul, our life is hid with Christ, and when Christ shall appear, then shall we appear with him in glory. Our life is hid, saith the Apostle.

10. This is a comfort to the saints, that though their lives will be dead in themselves, yet they are alive in Christ's breast, and hid there; all their life, crown, and glory lays hid in Christ:

Proved

11. Here is the Book of Life, where the saints' names are written; from hence it may be said, that the elect are dead and alive at one and the same time, being dead whilst in the grave, not in tanto,[1] but in toto, although alive in the memory of Christ, which is the Book of Life, and the white-stone, and their new name written in it, makes them to see their names in the Book of Life, and so through death, see eternal life.

Illustrated

12. This doctrine is a standing truth, however it be slighted through the whole world, for the world will not have patience, but would run to heaven, each and by himself, whether Christ came and call or no.

13. They will not stay for Christ; they will go another way; they will not enter in by the door, but they will climb up like thieves and robbers, and steal into the house whilst the master is asleep, or at least whilst his select are asleep.

False doctrine discovered

14. Reason is in haste; it must have heaven not in the Lord's time, but in its own; at a beck, its soul would be in heaven before its bones be cold; for when its body can live no longer, then the soul takes wings and flies away like a bird, and gets into heaven in a moment, and gets into heaven before it is aware it knows not how it came there.

15. Yet, notwithstanding, could hit the way when it was dead, but knows not the way when it was alive, so that it can, as it imagines, do

---

[1] Largely.

miracles when it is dead; no sooner dead, but it will have the crown of life, and yet it hath no life.

16. But the faith of the elect, and the truth of the Scripture teach otherwise, as is before declared, and as hereafter follows:

2 Tim. 4, 8 explained

17. Paul waited for a crown, for he said there was one laid up for him, yet did he not expect to wear this crown until the day of the Lord's appearance; so Peter saith, that when the Chief Shepherd should appear, then the believers of him should receive a crown of life, but not before.

18. Wherefore, then, from hence we learn, that Christ, and the Christian man's crown, comes both together; for when he comes, then doth he give reward to his servants, both small and great: then they that have lost their lives, shall find them; and they that have suffered with him, shall reign with him.

19. Behold, all shall be made happy together; they that died a thousand years since, shall not be made perfect without us, who live under this Commission of the Spirit.

20. So that the saints must have patience awhile, and wait for the coming of their Lord, and when their Lord cometh, then their crown of life and glory cometh; so come, Lord Jesus, for our souls waiteth for thee; Amen.

CHAP. XII.

1. Shewing when all Reprobates receive their Rewards. 2. A Reason given why Soul and Body must enter both into Torment.

EVIDENCE THE FOURTH.

Doctrine 1

1. FOURTHLY, as the souls of the saints do not go to heaven till the time beforesaid, even so the reprobate seed do not receive their reward until the end of the world.

Proved. Doctrine 2

2. Their souls do not go to torment tilt their bodies go with them; for as they sinned together, so they must suffer together, and

therefore it is that the sentence is passed against them at the latter day in these words, Depart from me, ye cursed, into everlasting fire.

Inference 1

3. Mind here, and you will find, that whenever the wicked are bid to depart into everlasting fire, doubtless they are there to remain to eternity, and so made incapable of ever coming forth again. Their souls do not come forth to fetch their bodies thither; after they are there, there is no coming forth.

Inference 2

4. Therefore, as long as the wicked do live, they are treasuring up wrath against that day of wrath; now this wrath is in treasuring up as long as the world remains, and at the end thereof, the phial of God's wrath will be full, and in one day will it be poured out, and then will it hold pouring to eternity, as will be shewn in Part the Seventh.

Inference 3

5. At the end of the world, the soul and body enter together into eternal torment; they entered into death and the grave together, and they will be raised together, and eternally suffer together, with weeping and wailing, and gnashing of teeth.

Inference 4

6. The measure and nature of torment is not measured forth till that day, and then is it proportioned according to the strength of sin; as it is written, Revel. 4.

7. When the Lord descends from heaven, then with flaming fire, he will render vengeance, and not till then; for that is called the great day of his wrath, and it is called a great day, because it is the day of recompence and reward.

Conclusion

8. This is the great day of his wrath to the one seed, and the great day of his love and mercy to the other. This is the all-saints day, and the all-souls day; this great day is not to be found in the Roman Calendar; that is but the mock day, but this is the marriage day to the one seed, and the mourning day to the other.

CHAP. XIII.

1. Shewing that there is no Separation of the two Seeds till the End of the World. 2. Of the Manner of the Separation. 3. The Saying of the Apostle of Soul, Body, and Spirit, opened.

EVIDENCE THE FIFTH.

Doctrine 1

1. FIFTHLY, a further evidence of the soul's mortality is this, because the Scripture saith, that the elect and reprobate are not severed one from another, until the Lord and his Angels come, which will not be till the end of the world.

Proved by several Arguments

2. This earth is like Peter's net—it holds both good and bad in it till the Resurrection-day, and then the separation is made betwixt the goats and the sheep, the wheat and the tares; let both grow together till then, saith the Seedsman of Heaven, and Great Shepherd of his sheep.

3. Pluck not up the tares (saith he), lest you pluck up the wheat (saith the Great Gardener unto his Apostles), whom he made gardeners also, and dressers of his vineyard.

The doctrine illustrated and continued

4. As if the Lord should say, this world is like the husbandman's fields, having in it two several seeds, and as the husbandman doth weed out the tares from his wheat, and burn them (they being fit for no other use), and the wheat, when ripe, he carefully gathers into his barn; even thus shall it be with the two grand seeds of faith and reason, in its season, which will be at the end of the world.

5. Now you, my friends and servants, your office is not to reap, but to sow and to plant; but you are to be reaped yourselves, and your plants, which you have nourished, when I and my Angels do come; you are now assigned by me to dress, to water, to cherish my plants, and settle my vineyard, until such time as it is completed into full number, and so made ripe.

6. Moreover, you are to cut down the tares that are in the way, making opposition to your labour; you have my sword, with two edges, the one of them edges serves for that use, but you are not to gather all in bundles, so far as to cast them personally into hell-fire; for you

cannot discover them all, but some of the tares may seem to be corn while in the blade, and also for a time after, till the sun come and discover it.

Powerfully proved

7. Besides, all the wheat cannot be discovered by you; you cannot sound every man's work or heart to the bottom; also, you cannot raise yourselves from death, for there will be no gathering of the wheat nor tares till they be cut down; therefore both must grow together until the harvest be ripe, and fall together, and lie and be mingled together in the dust.

Isa. 53. Opened

8. I myself must make my bed with the wicked, and so must you; but I shall not there stay to see corruption;[1] I shall arise from my death in three days, and ascend to my glory, to prepare places of glory for you; but you must have patience awhile, and as David did, see corruption; but at my appointed time I will come again, and bring my Angels, who are my reapers? then shall the separation be made. Have patience awhile; I have told you all things—have patience—let both grow together till the harvest be ripe.

9. Thus we see, first, who separates the sheep from the goats; secondly, when the day of separation is; and lastly, the place where it is. Now observe it is said, he will at that day gather the elect from the four parts of the earth.

Doctrine 3. Inference 1

10. Now, how could this be, unless they were found in the world? If their souls had been in heaven, they needed no gathering; neither could there have been any separation then, but the separation must have been before; neither can it be meant that bodies now should be separated, and souls separated before.

Inference 2

11. For can any sober man imagine, that the Angels were to gather nothing but dead corpses without souls? [Can dust be elect that is not completed into a body of spirit and life?]

12. Is not the soul elect, or the principal part of election? As it is written by Peter, Elect (saith he) through sanctification of the spirit, and belief of the truth. Now what is that which can believe truth but the soul?

---

[1] Isa. 53, 9.

13. Election lies in the seed, and the seed completes itself into form, through its invisible life, making both soul, body, and spirit into one living and dying essence.

Doctrine 4

14. Therefore it is that the Apostle prays, that the soul, body, and spirit may be kept blameless unto the coming of the Lord. Here observe two things,

Explained

15. First, that the soul, body, and spirit are in one essence, and so but one man and one elect, as Father, Son, and Spirit is but one single essence, being God-man, blessed for ever.

Proved

16. Secondly, we see likewise, that this soul, body, and spirit is to remain here in or upon this earth until the coming of the Lord, as aforesaid; for mind, if so that the soul could have gone to heaven without its body, why should the Apostle have prayed for its being kept blameless till the coming of the Lord?

Inference 1

17. If so as it went to heaven, it needed no praying for any longer than the death of the body, for it cannot be, that a soul should be faulty after it is immortalized in heaven.

Doctrine 5

18. Moreover, the Lord comforted the Apostles by telling them, that after he had prepared thrones for them in heaven, and made all things ready, he would come again to fetch them to him as aforesaid.

Inference 1

19. Mind here, Christ doth not comfort them by telling them that their souls should presently follow him, but ordered them to wait for his coming, and abide his leisure: Lie down and rest in peace, for both must grow together till the harvest were ripe.

Application

30. Thus we see no going to heaven till Christ come again to gather his elect; the saint and sinner remain in or on this earth till then; there is no purgatory or third place, but when dead, saint and sinner lie quietly in the grave together.

21. Because their spirits are quenched, or gone out, death making all equal; there being no preeminence in the grave, although elect and reject are crowded together, yet all is but inconceivable dust, and makes one heap until the Lord come.

22. Then that powerful God can tell how to separate them, notwithstanding their close union; yet though each seed, in its matter, be no bigger than a pin-head, yet shall quicken and come to life; the Lord knows how to do it; believe now and be happy then; but have patience, for both must grow together, and lodge together, till the Lord and his Angels from heaven come, as abundantly beforesaid.

CHAP. XIV.

1. No Soul capable of either Joy or Sorrow without a Body. 2. Several forcible Arguments to prove the aforesaid Doctrine.

EVIDENCE THE SIXTH.

Doctrine 1

1. ANOTHER evidence of the soul's mortality is this, because that no soul is or can be capable of either joy or sorrow, unless it be covered or completed in a body.

Proved

2. Is not the body the soul's tabernacle, or house for it to work in? Nature cannot work without form, nay, there is no actuating life without form. Is there breath without a body? Is there soul without substance?

Proved

3. How can it be said, such a man is a wise man, just, or holy man, unless there be seen some act of his wisdom, justice, or holiness? Can any such act be done without a body?

Cleared

4. Doth not all happiness that a saint shall enjoy in heaven, spring or arise from a seed of faith and law, that was acted in a mortal body? And shall it not solace itself in its spiritual body on the other side death, as it was refreshed in a mortal, natural body on this side death.

Doctrine 2

5. Again, if the soul cannot worship God without a body, then can it not receive any happiness without a body; if a man have neither house nor harbour to put his head in, he cannot subsist, no more can the soul; therefore it is that the Apostle desires to be clothed with a house from heaven. 2 Cor. 5.

Proved by Three Arguments

6. By this we see very well, that the Apostle knew that he could attain to no eternal happiness in the heavens above, after this life, without a body.

7. Therefore, said Paul, verse 1. we know that if our earthly house of this tabernacle were dissolved, we have a building of God, a house not made with hands, eternal in the heavens; and in the 4th verse, he saith, we being in this tabernacle, do groan, being burdened, not for that we would be unclothed, but clothed upon that mortality, might be swallowed up of life.

8. In these words, we may observe these three things;

9. First, that though the soul be clothed in a body, yet cannot the soul and body subsist without a further clothing, whilst in a mortal state; therefore it must have a house builded with hands, for its earthly harbour.

10. Secondly, although the body be the house of the soul, yet is it but burdensome, because of the afflictions incident to nature, or outward man; and therefore the renewed soul would willingly change its state.

11. Thirdly, the Apostle would not have the soul be without a body, but only would have it changed, and therefore desired that it might be freed from its earthly body, and be made a spiritual body, and that for those five reasons following:

Proved by Five Arguments

12. First, because they would be delivered from affliction; for a new spiritual body, springing out of the life of faith, is freed from all pain.

13. Secondly, because a spiritual body is light and fiery, and can ascend or descend at its pleasure, and so could easily and speedily ascend, and be with Christ, for there is no time to the dead, but after death or change, the judgment, as verse 8, 10.

14. Thirdly, the Apostle would willingly be clothed with his house from heaven, with his spiritual body, because he nor the saints after

should ever be pinched with hunger, cold, or nakedness; for that new spiritual body would be freed from all those things.

15. Fourthly, because it would in its spiritual body be made capable to behold, with open face, their glorious God, and gracious Redeemer.

16. Fifthly and lastly, the Apostle desired the change, that the believing saints might have the eternal life in full possession, of which their faith was the seal of assurance, &c.

CHAP. XV.

Shewing that Job was of the Faith of the Soul's Mortality.

EVIDENCE THE SEVENTH.

Seventh Argument

1. ANOTHER evidence of the soul's mortality is this; whenever it is that man dies, it is said that he is dead or resteth from its labours, or gone into the dust, or fallen asleep; but it is no where said that his soul is ascended into any sensible joy, light, or glory, or descended into any sensible pain, darkness, or shame, whilst his body is in the grave.

2. No sober man ever taught, that the soul was immortal in a mortal body. We have heard of the patience of Job; if any be as willing to hear of his faith, they may find his doctrine of the soul's mortality was plainly delivered in his book.

3. And though his book is not of equal authority with the books in the Holy Scripture, yet do I own it to be a true history, and that there was such a man before Moses's time, and he was a holy man, and one that feared God. And now for his doctrine.

Doctrine

4. In chapter 21, Job saith, that the wicked do spend their days in wealth; but then, saith he, they suddenly go down to the grave: one dieth in his full strength, another dieth in the bitterness of his soul, and never eateth in pleasure as the other did; but then what follows? why, saith he, they shall both sleep in the dust, and the worms shall cover them.

Inference

5. Mind here, Job doth not say that their souls shall not go into eternal torment, and their bodies to the grave, but that they both must sleep in the dust, and be kept there for a time.

6. Therefore, saith he, verse 30, the wicked is kept till the day of destruction, and that they are to be brought forth at the day of wrath, but until then, they are to be brought to the grave, and remain in the heap.

7. Again, in chap: 14, he saith, are not man's days determined, as also there is hope of a tree; if it be cut clown, and the stalk thereof dead in the ground, yet by the scent of water it will bud, and bring forth leaves like a plant.

8. But man is sick, and dieth, and perisheth, and where is he? Man sleepeth, and awakeneth not from his sleep till the heavens be no more.

Inference 2

9. Again, Job prayeth that God would take away his life, and hide him in the grave, until his wrath was passed, and then to bring him out again. Here it is clear, that Job knew not of the soul's going to heaven whilst the body was in the grave; for there is no wrath upon the body, whilst the soul is in rest.

10. Furthermore, in verse 14, Job propoundeth a question, saying, if a man die, shall he live again? To this Job makes answer, and that affirmatively, concluding, that he shall, saying, that he will wait till his change shall come; therefore, saith Job, the Lord shall call me, and I shall answer him, though now he number my steps, and scourgeth me for my sin.

11. Job's faith was strong in the Resurrection; his hope was there, and love was great to his Redeemer. Therefore, said he, I know that my Redeemer liveth, and though I die, and go to the grave, and worms destroy my body, yet I shall see him at the last day. Chap. 19.

Inference 3

12. Job doth not expect eternal happiness till the last day, nor to see his Redeemer till the last day of this world; but that after death the grave must retain him until then, and his troubles makes him wish for death, as for hid treasure; because death is insensible of pain, and is to the just as a sweet sleep, as aforesaid and as hereafter follows.

CHAP, XVI.

The Soul's Mortality abundantly proved by Lazarus's Death, and Paul's Doctrine.

EVIDENCE THE EIGHTH,

Doctrine 1

1. AGAIN, another evidence of the soul's mortality is this, is that when any do depart this life, it is said they die or fall asleep; it doth not say their souls go to heaven; it is said that Abraham, Isaac, and Jacob are dead, and fallen asleep; it is said that Stephen fell asleep; there is not a word of their souls going to heaven.

Proved

2. When Lazarus died, it is said he fell asleep, and that he was dead; therefore when Christ came to raise him to life, he looked down into the grave, and with a loud voice, said, Lazarus come forth.

Inference 1

3. Observe this well, you that are enlightened by this Commission of the Spirit, and you may see, that the Lord called him not from heaven, but from the grave.

Inference 2 opened

4. So likewise, when Christ was risen from the dead, it is said that many of the saints, which slept in the grave, arose also, and appeared unto many.

5. It is not said that their souls came from heaven, but that they arose from the grave, which was done by virtue of Christ's Resurrection; it having an influence upon them, did cause them to rise as a taste of his mighty power.

Examined

6. Now those that arose were saints newly dead: we do not read that they did eat or drink, or make any long stay. But some may say, what became of them? why they laid themselves down in their graves again, and fell asleep, and so will remain till their Lord come.

Doctrine 2

7. Again, Paul reproves the believing Thessalonians for their immoderate mourning for the death of their friends in the faith, telling

them, that they must not mourn as men without hope; for, saith Paul, those your friends that sleep in Jesus, will God bring with him when he cometh, for they are in his book, and their tears in his bottle; they are but fallen asleep in the faith of Jesus; their faith is lodged in Jesus's breast—he cannot forget them—comfort yourselves.

Inference 1

8. Now the Apostle doth not comfort them by telling them that their souls were gone to heaven, but he comforteth them in the doctrine of a Resurrection.

9. In the first Corinthians, chap. 15, Paul preacheth the resurrection of saints to life at the last day, and proves it by the Resurrection of Christ from the dead, by undeniable evidence; as

Doctrine. Inference

10. First, by Peter, then of the Twelve, and by himself, with five hundred of his brethren besides, of whom (saith Paul) the greater part remain to this present, but some are fallen asleep. Paul doth not say they were gone to heaven, or their souls were in heaven, but they were fallen asleep, just as the believing Thessalonians were as aforesaid.

11. And we may be certain, that Paul knew very well that they were not in heaven; for mind well his words, verse 12, there Paul reproveth them that deny the Resurrection, and saith, that if there be no Resurrection of the dead, then Christ is not risen, and if Christ be not risen, then is our preaching vain, and you are yet in your sins; and then it follows, that those that are fallen asleep in Jesus, are perished.

Cleared

12. Behold here, is it not plain, that Paul did teach that their souls were perished, as well as their bodies, otherwise their faith would not have been in vain? For where faith is vain, there they die in their sin, and if the soul die in sin, it never can be capable of happiness, neither of any resurrection; therefore, saith Paul, in the next verse, if in this life only we have hope, we are of all men most miserable.[1]

Doctrine

13. And are worse than Atheists, for they speak boldly, even as they think, and do, saying, let us eat and drink, and be merry, for tomorrow we shall die, and there's an end.

---

[1] 1 Cor. 15, 13.

14. Whilst the saints, through their faith of the resurrection of soul and body, do deny themselves of worldly pleasure, and do willingly suffer the reproach of the world; so that if there should not be a resurrection, they were of all men most miserable.

Inference 1

15. Moreover, if Paul had spoken only of the resurrection of the body, and not of the soul, why should he have said, that if there should be no resurrection, their faith and holiness was vain, and their sufferings vain, and their baptism was vain, and all their worship was vain, and of no effect, and without virtue, if the dead rise not at all?

Inference 2

16. Undoubtedly, if the souls of those saints had been in heaven, then could not their faith, nor the Apostle's preaching, have been vain; for what great matter were it if their bodies did lie and rot in the grave, so that their souls could be happy?

Inference 3

17. Paul knew well there could be no happiness without a resurrection, and this was Daniel's knowledge and faith likewise; therefore, saith he, chap, 12, many of them which sleep in the dust of the earth, shall awake, some to everlasting life, and some to shame and perpetual contempt.

18. Their souls were neither in happiness nor misery, but with their bodies in the dust, and at the resurrection the just should awake, and should shine as the stars.

19. Therefore it was that Daniel was bid to go his way also into the dust until the end, for till then he should not appear, but then he, with the rest, should arise and stand in his lot with the just to receive the reward of eternal life.

Cleared

20. And thus it is clear to all such as are by lot appointed to eternal life, that the soul and body lie down together in death, and not that one goes to heaven, and the other to the grave, bidding adieu to each other till the last day.

CHAP. XVII.

1. Shewing how the Saints do wait for the Coming of the Lord. 2. Of the Virtue of Faith. 3. Heb. Chap. 9, Verse 4, Opened and Applied.

EVIDENCE THE NINTH.

Doctrine 1

1. AGAIN, it is farther evident that the soul doth not partake of eternal happiness until the coming of Christ, in regard they are bid to be in a waiting and watching posture, until the very time of his coming, and be like unto the five wise virgins.

Inference 1

2. There is but two things that the saints have waited earnestly for, and that was, first, for their God's becoming flesh; and then, secondly, for his coming in glory. We that live now near the end of the world, and have known of his coming in flesh, and of the virtues thereof, our waiting is altogether for his second coming, because our happiness as to eternal glory comes not until our Lord come, to fetch us according to his promise, and our faith.

Inference 2. A use of reproof

3. We, who are of the true church, do with the church wait for the personal appearing of the Most High and Mighty God, the Lord Jesus in Heaven, in order to our eternal felicity, joy, and glory, and not with the Milenarys', or Quakers, expect him to reign here, and be with him in glory here.

Error reproved

4. Those that wait for a God and glory here upon this bloody earth, any other way than in the virtue, fruits, and effect of a personal Jesus, seated on a Throne of eternal ravishing glory, in the heavens above, before the end of the world.

5. I say, whoever looks for a God to come before the end of the world, or look for a God without a body or person, will never find him by that search, or have any lasting comforts by its hopes in the event.

6. Because such a one is out of the way of truth, as much as the Mosaical Jew, who as yet is gazing for his first coming in flesh. Such as these possess not the inshining virtues of a personal Jesus, given by a true ministry as the guide to godliness, and as the evidence of a

personal glory at the personal appearing of its Lord, which it truly knows.

7. This is it that makes it so long for its Lord, because of that personal glory and final deliverance from all maladies, afflictions, or persecutions whatsoever.

Doctrine

8. Therefore it was that the Apostle said, that the saints did wait for the Lord from heaven. 1 Thess. 1, 10. Phil. 3, 20.

9. And in Heb. 10, 36. the Apostle exhorts the saints to patience, and tells them, that they shall enjoy the promise after they have done the will of God; for, saith he, wait a little while, and the promise comes; wait a little while, and he that will come, will come, and will not tarry.

Explained

10. As if the Apostle should say, have you not faith? if you have, live by it, and let the life of it cause you to wait and watch for your Lord with patience.

Proved

11. For his promise of coming is sure. Apply it to yourselves, therefore, and by virtue thereof, possess yourselves with patience, waiting for your Lord Jesus Christ from heaven, who will come presently, in a little time, and then will he deliver you from all your troubles, and give you felicity, joy, and glory with himself, for everlasting.

12. Thus we see how faith waits for the appearing of its God. The Scriptures are full of exhortations hereunto,[1] and hence it is that the very last words in the Bible, of the second record, hath this petition of the saints put up unto their God, saying,

Cleared

13. Come, Lord Jesus, come quickly, and all, because the afflicted saints did know that they could never be avenged on their persecutors, not attain to an eternal personal happiness, until the coming of their God, the Lord Jesus Christ, blessed forever; Amen.

---

[1] Luke12, 36. 1 Cor. 17. 2 Thess. 3, 5. Heb. 9.

CHAP. XVIII.

1. The Resurrection Day the Saints' Rejoicing Day. 2. An Objection answered concerning Paradise. 3. Of the Triumphant Day of all Saints. 4. And of the All-Saints' Song.

EVIDENCE THE TENTH.

Doctrine 1

1. AGAIN, another evidence of the soul's mortality is this, because that eternal joy, felicity, and glory is not by the Scriptures attributed to the saints at the day of their death, but at the resurrection day.

Doctrine proved

2. When the saints bodies are changed from corruption to incorruption, from mortality to immortality, then comes the rejoicing day.

3. The soul cannot rejoice with the body in the grave, because the soul is in the grave with it. The Scriptures do not say that the soul can go to heaven, and rejoice there, and leave its body behind it to rot and stink in the grave, nor there is no such a thing; but life to one, life to both; death to one, death to both.

4. The soul, you must know, cannot be sensible of itself, if it center not in a body; the saints resurrection day is their experimental day of joy; then do they clap hands, and shout for joy.

5. Did ever any man read from either Prophet or Apostle, that the soul should have any particular joy at the end of its life, under the death of its body, and then a further joy at its resurrection at the end of the world; surely no.

6. That saying of Christ to the believing thief upon the cross, if it be alleged, proves nothing to contradict this doctrine; for his being that day with Christ in Paradise, was in the assurance of life before his death.

Paradise explained

7. So that this Paradise, in which both Christ and the converted thief were in, was the peace of their mind in their assurance of life, through faith, in that moment of time of that day, before that silent natural death did seize upon them.

8. This is clear; for Christ himself did not ascend from the grave for three days, nor to heaven for fifty days after, as the Scriptures do testify.

Doctrine

9. And now since his Ascension, he is upon his Throne; there with Moses, Elias, Enoch, and the Angels, preparing mansions for his Prophets, Apostles, and for his Witnesses of the Spirit, against the day of their ascension, and their children, whom they have begotten to the faith of that kingdom, and there is Christ to remain till the end of the world, till the restitution of all things, according to the Scriptures, Acts 1.

10. Then when the Lord comes, then will be the great rejoicing day of triumph over death, hell, and the grave. Here we conquer and die, there we conquer and live, and sing, O! death, where is thy sting; O! grave, where is thy victory, and devil where is thy power?

Proved

11. There is no entering into our Lord's joy until the resurrection of the body, so no immortal joy till that day; the day of conversion is a joyful resurrection day, because it is the seal of the other;—but the other is consummation, in making it immortal.

12. Therefore it is written, according to Paul, we are your rejoicing, even as you are Ours', in the day of the Lord Jesus.

Inference

13. Again, Paul encourageth the Saints to stand fast to their faith, and that for two causes; first, in that his labour might not be in vain; and secondly, that he might rejoice in the day of the Lord Jesus.[1] Paul doth not speak here of any joy that he should have at the coming of death, but at the coming of Jesus.

14. Again, the same Apostle saith, that the believers will be their hope, joy, and crown; but yet it is but in the day of the Lord Jesus, and not before.[2]

Peter

15. The saints' salutation, joy, do not come in at the coming of death, but at the coming of Jesus;— therefore, saith Peter, rejoice,

---

[1] Phil. 2, 16.
[2] 1 Thess. 2, 19.

inasmuch as you are partakers of Christ's sufferings, that when his glory shall be revealed, you may be glad also with exceeding joy.

Cleared

16. Thus we see that joy and Jesus come together; Christ and the crown come both together. When the saints die, they are said to rest in their graves for a while, Revel. 6, 11. there to remain till the harvest be ripe.

17. So that the saints joys must not be made perfect, until all be made perfect; one must not go to heaven this year, and another the next, but all will be made happy together.

18. The day of glory is at the glorious appearance of the great God, and this is the all-saints' day; this is the day in which the Lord hath made, or will make, in order to all saints' glory; this is the day of gaol delivery.

19. Then is the song of songs sung, and the all-saints' song, which makes a sound as of many waters.

20. This song will not be sung by now one, and then one, unto the Lamb, but by all together at the coming of the Lamb. But of this further, when I come to the Eighth Part, treating of the Saints' Joys in Heaven.

CHAP. XIX.

Christ, when he comes to Judgment, raises both Soul and Body.

EVIDENCE THE ELEVENTH.

Doctrine 1

1. AGAIN, it is written, that when Christ comes to judgment, that all that are in the grave shall hear his voice, and shall come forth; those that have done good to the resurrection of life, and they that have done evil to the resurrection of condemnation, John 3. 28, 29.

Inference

2. Observe this well, and you will find, that the souls of men go not to either sensible joy or sorrow at their death, but into the grave, and there Christ finds them; and from the earth and sea he raiseth them.

Inference 2

3. What should God bring millions of souls from heaven with him, and assume their bodies in the grave, and cause to be brought by whom or from whence they know not; all reprobate souls to assume their bodies likewise.

Inference 3

4. Doth this blind reason think, that God creates, makes, or forms again that old tophet, their old bodies, and then bid the damned soul go into it, and animate it again.

5. Again, it is written, Revel. 20. that the sea gave up the dead which were in it, and death and hell, or the grave delivered up the dead which were in them, and they were judged, every man according to their works, and death and hell were cast into the lake of fire; this is the second death.

Doctrine

6. See also 1 Cor. 15, 52. and 1 Thess. 4, 16. There, saith Paul, the trumpet shall sound, the Lord shall descend with a shout with the voice of the Archangels, and with the trump of God.

Inference

7. This trump of God will be the great voice of God to raise the dead; therefore it is said, that the sea and earth shall cast forth their dead at the command of Jesus, where then or from whence doth their souls come, but with their bodies; for,

Inference 2

8. Observe, that after their resurrection, they have their everlasting doom given to them, according to their works.

Inference 3

9. The reward of works being then given, and not before, see 2 Cor. 5, 10. So that it is clear, that the body and soul are raised together, and have their everlasting sentence given them together; the one as, Come, ye blessed; the other as, Go, ye cursed; and this from the mouth of the Lord Jesus, being the trump of God that now is expected every day by his elect when it will sound,

Application

10. There are seven trumpets sounding now, but none of them can give the dead so much as their first resurrection; yet the beginning of the sounding of the seventh trumpet made way for another trumpet

that should finish the mystery of God, as a forerunner of his coming, who is to judge both quick and dead.

CHAP. XX.

1. Shewing that false Prophets and false Priests do not plead their Ministry till the End of the World. 2. What is meant by agreeing with thy Adversary quickly. 3. The Conclusion.

EVIDENCE THE TWELFTH.

Doctrine 1

1. LASTLY, another evidence of the soul's mortality is this, in that the false priests shall not plead their ministry with God at the day of their death, each one apart, but at the day of their resurrection.

Inference 1

2. If their souls did not die when their bodies did, then surely they would plead for mercy at that instant, and that before they went into torment.

Inference 2

3. But there is no pleading with God by that seed before the resurrection, nor then neither, but what is in their own conscience; for God will say then to them no more, but Go, ye cursed; but their own consciences pleading, and the law will hold the contest.

4. The manner of the pleading and contest may be disputed on in the Seventh Part.

Inference 3

5. But as for the seed of the Son of Man, they may be confident that the Lord doth never bid the false prophets depart into everlasting fire, but thereupon they and their adherents are to remain to eternity, otherwise it could not be an everlasting fire.

This text opened

6. Therefore it is said, agree with thine adversary quickly, lest the adversary deliver thee to the judge, and the judge deliver thee to the gaoler, and thou be cast into prison, and so shall not come out till thou hast paid the uttermost farthing.

7. Now this uttermost farthing will never be paid, if it be not paid before death, by agreeing with the Lords true prophets, who are adversaries to sin and infidelity.

Inference 1

8. It is contrary to Scripture, sense, and sober reason, to believe that false prophets and priests should twice stand before God to be judged after death. Where do we find that God doth bid the soul depart from him, and its body, till the last day, and then come both to him again?

The application

9. Now from henceforth, let no sober man oppose this doctrine of the soul's mortality, seeing the Scriptures doth so abundantly demonstrate the same; but let them give glory to the Lord God Almighty, that can and will give every dead soul his life again.

A divine hymn

10. Then look what life at death ache dies,
    When Christ shall come, that life shall rise;
    When faith did die, whilst faith was king,
    That faithful body Christ will bring.

12. Saying, come thou, blessed one, to me,
    Thou did'st believe, and thou shalt see
    That I'm thy God, that once was dead,
    And I have thee from death raised.

13. Thou did'st believe me, and therefore
    Come live with me for evermore;
    Whilst the rejected of Cains seed,
    Who thought to live, and not to have died.

14. But die they do, and die they must,
    A second death to them is just;
    Which, what it is, the time is near,
    I shall declare, if they will hear.

THE SEVENTH PART:

OF

THE DEVIL's TORMENT.

CHAP. I.

1. Various Opinions concerning the Nature of the Devil's Torment; their Opinions all detected. 2. Why the Author wrote of this Subject.

Matt. 13 Text

1. I AM now to treat of a sad subject to the seed of the serpent. According to my text, which saith, that all that do iniquity and offend, shall be cast into a furnace of fire, where shall be weeping and gnashing of teeth.

2. But if that seed can make shift to disbelieve it, they may have the more ease and time to fit them for their everlasting burning, by making their bodies and spirits like a dry thorny hedge, to receive the fury of that fire; for they are sure to have it.

3. What the devil is, I have shewn before; I am now to speak of his torment, and to shew him his dowry, according to my faith and knowledge, operated in me by the Witnesses of the Spirit.

4. But before I enter into discourse of the nature of their punishment, I judge it requisite to inquire and shew where the place of their punishment shall be, and of the hell that reprobates shall be tormented in, with the place of their resurrection.

5. These things are copious, and all wits have handled them in the shadow, but the substance of it hath not been by them comprehended. Let us, therefore, see their opinions; in the first place,

6. The Heathen poets and philosophers did hold, that the soul after death should be tormented; but some of them would not have it be tormented to eternity, but after a long time it was to be purged and set at liberty, and the manner of its purging was thus, as Virgil describes it:

Virgil's doctrine of the soul

    7. For when the soul does leave, the body's dead,
       Their miseries are yet not finished;
       Nor all their times of torment yet complete,
       Many small crimes must needs make one that's great;

    8. Pain, therefore, purgeth them and maketh them fair
       From their old stains; some hang in dusky air;
       Some in the deep do pay the debt of sin,
       And fire is chosen to purge others in.

9. Here we see that they hold that the air, water, and fire, was the place of their tormented spirits, and that in time the air would serve to purge an serial and unbodied spirit.

10. And professors of Christianity did not much differ from those blind Heathens; for in Augustine's time, about the year 400, they were in diversity among themselves, whether devils had bodies or no, or whether their torments were mental or corporeal; but if corporeal, yet but of condensed air as the seed, and so could suffer in the air.

Jacob Beamon's hell

11. In this air, is also Jacob Beamon's hell, in which wicked souls do suffer, as he saith. Upon this question, how far is heaven and hell from one another? Answereth thus; as far as day and night, something and nothing.

12. What an answer is this? Is it not nonsensical? Yes. For his following words shews, which saith, that heaven and hell is in one another, and that they go both through and in the whole world, the visible world having both heaven and hell in it.

13. And several of our modern University scholars and doctors are of the same opinion, saying, that this air is full of wicked spirits, or demons, but being bodiless, they are invisible, and cannot be seen with us.

14. Also, they say, that heaven and all good spirits are in the air, but being that the one is light, and the other dark; therefore they comprehend not one another, but the one follows, or is distinct from each other, as the night follows the day.

15. But of late there is made a new discovery of another world placed in the moon, and is habitable as this is; but where hell is, they know not, unless in the air as aforesaid.

16. All the Quakers have their judgment not much differing from Beamon; for they have heaven and hell, God and devil, all within them.

17. Thus we see, that all professions have been ignorant, of the nature of the reprobate's torment of soul and body, as in the world to come.

18. Yea, many of the elect have been kept dark, ever since the Apostles' Commission was extirpated out of the world by the Ten Persecutions, there being no true ministry to enlighten them, until now in this age that the Commission of the Spirit being come, and broke open the prison doors, and set the captive free, and hath opened their understandings to the knowledge of the true God, the right devil, with the place and nature of heaven, and the place and nature of hell, and of the reprobates' torment to eternity.

19. These things are manifested to us now in this age; he that hath ears to hear, let him hear.

20. And you, my spiritual enemies, who have reproached and belied me, saying, that I do neither believe in God, nor own any devil, or heaven or hell, because I own no other God but Jesus, nor no other devil but the spirit of unclean reason in man and woman.

21. Therefore now am I resolved to make the devil to know by conviction, that I do hold forth a torment so extreme, as that he shall not for ever after need to say but that it is intolerably great, and yet must be suffered.

CHAP. II.

1. Where the Place of Hell is. 2. And what it is, largely Opened.

Doctrine 1

1. AS this world is the field in which the tares, being the children of the wicked one, are sown, so likewise is this world the place in which they are to be burned in, and on this earth will they receive their execution.

2. The Scripture saith, they shall be cast into hell, and they shall be cast into the pit; and my text saith, they shall be cast into a furnace of fire; they shall be cast down from heaven, cast down to the earth, cast down to the nether part of the earth.[1]

---

[1] Ezek. 22, 16. 2 Pet. 2, 4. Isa. 28, 2. Lam. 2, 1. Ezek. 31, 14. 16. 18.

Doctrine proved

3. The earth is the centre, of the serpent and his seed; for as it was their kingdom of heaven, so it will be their kingdom of hell; they can precipitate or descend no lower than into the nethermost earth.

4. What the Prophet Ezekiel threatened and sentenced the Ammonites withall, will certainly fall upon all the seed of the serpent, when the day is come that iniquity shall have an end. Then, saith the prophet, I will judge thee in the place where thou wast created, in the land of thy nativity. Chapter 21, verse 30.

5. Now, though this prophesy may mean a temporal judgment, yet the eternal is included and couched in those words; for the wrath blows upon them both ways, both for a temporal cutting off, and an eternal; the temporal judgment enters first, in those and the like words; the sword is drawn, deliver thee into the hands of brutish men.[1]

Doctrine proved and Illustrated

6. The eternal in those words; when iniquity hath an end, then will I blow upon thee in my wrath; then shalt thou be for fuel to the fire; thy blood and cruelty shall be in the midst of thy land; and there shalt thou be judged.

7. This earth we here see is the prison, this nethermost part of the earth; it hath opened its mouth, and received into it those Ammonites, and all the wicked of former ages, and they lie there in chains, reserved for the judgment of the great day.

8. When the Scriptures of the first records doth make mention of the cutting off with death, wicked men, it doth but in the wrath of the Almighty, precipitate them into the nethermost earth, into the grave and pit, there to fetter them till the great day.

9. When the destruction of the Assyrians, Egyptians, and Babylonians (who were a type of the destruction of all the reprobate seed), were foretold of by the prophets, they are all denounced to the judgment that follows. Ezek. 31. 14.

10. They are all delivered unto death, to the nether part of the earth, in the midst the children of men with them, that go down to the pit, down to the grave, down to hell. Ver. 16, 17, 15.

11. Cast down Egypt and her daughters unto the nether part of the earth, with the uncircumcised that go down to the pit.[2]

---

[1] Ezek. Ch. 21. Ver. 28. 29. 30. 31.
[2] Ezek. 32, 18.

Explained

12. Observe here, now, for this hell, grave, pit, and nethermost parts of the earth, are all one thing; there it is that the prophet placeth them, and there they are to remain for a time; they are there to abide that are dead, and thither to go that are alive; for, saith the prophet further, chap. 32, verse 22.,

13. Ashar is there, and all her company; his graves are about him; there is Elam, and all her multitude round about her graves; all of them slain by the sword, fallen by the sword, which are gone down un-circumcised into the nether parts of the earth, which caused their terror in the land of the living.

14. There is Mesech, Tuball, and all her multitude; their graves are round about him, all of them uncircumcised: they shall not lie with the mighty that are fallen of the uncircumcised, which are gone down to hell, with their weapons of war, and they have laid their swords under their heads; but their iniquity shall be upon their bones.

Proved

15. Lo, here, whether this hell be any other than the grave, the dark grave; for it is said that their iniquity, or punishment of their iniquity, should be upon their bones that were gone down into hell.

Inference 1

16. Whither, then, is it that the soul goes, when the body dies? Why it falls no further than that body, nor that body falls no further than their swords, or weapons of war, and that is but into the grave, and there they lie until their bodies be quickened, and when they are quickened, then iniquity shall be quickened, and the spirit of its fiery reason that had war in it, shall be quickened, and shall be felt in its quickened bones, being the sword under the head, in the midst of the conscience to torment it withall; then to all eternity upon that earth, being raised no higher.

Inference 2. The doctrine applied

17. Now, if it were not for this sentence of iniquity, being upon their bones, and of this quickening bones, there were no great ill news to the wicked, it having but cast him down into the nethermost parts of the earth. But O, thou that diest in thine iniquity, I am now to tell thee, I mean this Commission doth tell thee, they that I witness unto doth tell thee, thou shalt not lie long there, but the earth shall cast thee out again.

CHAP. III.

1. Of the Manner of the Reprobate's Resurrection. 2. This Earth the Place of their Torment.

Doctrine 1

1. THIS nethermost part of the earth is a deep and large hell; it is the deepest place the devil can descend into; but it is on higher ground on which his torment must be.

2. When the wicked are raised, then will his hell be changed; for instead of having the heart of the earth for his hell, he shall have the heart of a dark spiritual body for his hell.

3. Although the fleshly devil, when he hath fulfilled the number of his days, and his press as full as it can hold, doth then sink down into the pit in a slumber of death, as if he should for ever so continue.

Proved

4. Yet in a moment, even at the day of the Lord Jesus Christ appearing, will he be cast out again, and raised up on a cursed earth, to a dying life and living death.

5. Therefore it is written, that the earth shall disclose her dead, and their slain shall be cast out; again, it is written, that the earth and the sea shall give up their dead, and they shall be judged, &c.[1]

6. Those grand devils that in their life time shaked kingdoms, and made the earth to tremble, by cursing in the land of the living, shall now be made to tremble themselves; when they are raked out of their holes, or the earth hath spued them out, and by a powerful word or voice are awakened out of their slumber, to the damnation that slumbereth not.

Doctrine 2

7. No sooner are they cast out of their graves, but fear and horror comes forth with them, at an unexpected sight of Christ and his mighty angels.

8. Then shall they cry to the flying rocks to cover them from the presence of God, whose breath is to them a consuming fire.

---

[1] Isa. 26. Rev. 20.

Explained

9. But the rocks and mountains will not favour them, but with a roaring noise they will move forward and sink downwards into a dissolution of dust, into their former confused chaos, never more possessing life and virtue.

10. Now at this great day are all the wicked summoned to appear to judgment, and their gaoler brings them out of prison, for the graves are their prison, and they shall come out of their holes as worms, as one prophet hath it.

Isa. 24 opened

11. Then will that saying of the Prophet Isaiah be fulfilled, and they shall be gathered together, as prisoners are gathered together to the pit, and shall be shut in prison, and after many days shall they be visited.

Proved

12. This is according to Peter and Jude, who saith, that the graves are their prison, there to be reserved to the judgment of the great day.

Doctrine 3. Proved

13. And upon this earth is the place of their torment, according as it is written by Isaiah, saying, at that day, the Lord shall punish the host of the high ones, and the kings of the earth, upon the earth.

Inference 1

14. Here by faith we see where the devil and his angels are to be punished, even upon this earth, no lower can they go, because the firmamental heaven bounds it.

15. This firmamental heaven in which the sun, moon, and stars are fixed, shall melt with the heat of the fire of the sun, which shall be showered down upon the earth, to burn up all the beauty and glory thereof.

Inference 2

16. And the wicked shall be raised to see this flood of fire, yet that fire shall not devour their spiritual dark bodies now in a short time that fire will burn out itself, but will not be so favourable to burn the reprobate, he being reserved for a far greater fire.

Inference 3

17. Now the sun, moon, and the stars will go out like the snuff of a candle, never giving light more, for their decreed time is over.

Inference 4

18. But if any ask where the elect are at this time, my answer in the Eighth Part will be that they will rise first; and the reprobate will see them ascend with the Lord, for as soon as the Lord hath given the wicked his doom in those words, go, ye cursed, he with elect men and angels will ascend, and the flood of fire follows, as by the command of the Lord, in their ascension above the sun.

Cleared in the Eighth Part

19. So that the host of heaven is above the fire when it falls, and the elect of the Lord shall see the word of their God executed in the flood of fire descending upon the reprobate world before their ascension into the heaven of heavens, as will further be showed in the next Part, if God permit.

CHAP. IV.

1. The Darkness of this World after its Dissolution.
2. The Bodies of the Reprobate proved Black and Dark.
3. How Temporal Plagues tipify Eternal, Isaiah 5, 30.
3. Opened, the Condition of the Damned.

Doctrine 1

1. THE seed of the serpent in the time of their natural life, although they were dark in their spirit of reason, yet were they light, some without, but here in this their eternal suffering, they have gathered blackness, both within and without.

Proved

2. According to the saying of the Prophet Neamiah, chap. 2, verse 10, there it is thus written, she is empty and void, and waste, and the heart melteth, and the knees smite together, and much pain is in all the loins, and the faces of them all gather blackness.[1]

3. Here is terror and amazement, to that seed all that day, a dark devil, both in its body and spirit, and a dark earth a land to be scourged in; behold the Scripture testimony.

---

[1] Joel 2, 6.

4. Behold, (saith the Prophet Isaiah,) the darkness shall cover the earth, and gross darkness the people.

5. Again, it is written, all the bright lights of heaven will I make dark over thee, and will set darkness upon thy land.[1]

6. Again, it is written, through the wrath of the Lord the land is darkened. Again, it is written, if one look into the land, behold darkness and sorrow, and the light is darkened in the heavens thereof.[2]

Objection

7. But some may say, this place doth but signify some temporal judgment and calamity upon sinners; for who can see those dark bodies of the damned in so dark a dungeon, having neither sun, moon, nor stars to shine upon it. To this I answer,

Answer

8. Many places of Scripture that denounce plagues and judgments upon sinners, though it point to the temporal, yet hath it relation to the eternal, the one being the type of the other; for the mystery lies hidden in the history; the eternal plague in the temporal, and faith sees into it.

9. Therefore, when the prophets denounced temporal judgments upon Egypt and Babylon for their cruelty to God's people, those their temporal judgments had sealed in them their eternal.

10. Only the temporal extended no further than the casting them down into the nethermost parts of the earth, but the eternal lay in them; for their first death was the entering into the second.

11. Therefore, when the Apostle John declares the downfall of the reprobate seed, he alludes to the Prophets' words, where he saith, Babylon is fallen, is fallen; that twice fallen had relation both to the temporal and eternal destruction.

12. Moreover, he in his declaring the manner and nature of the spiritual Babylons' eternal torment, brings in the relation of the great plague of darkness that was in the land of Egypt for three days and three nights, as a type of the eternal darkness that shall be on all the earth at the latter day.

---

[1] Ezek. 32, 8.
[2] Isa. 5, 20. Chap. 9, 19.

Cleared

13. And where the prophet Isaiah, chap. 5, speaks of looking into the land to behold that darkness, he means not that they shall look with a bodily or outward eye, but with the eye of the mind.

Applied

14. Now reason, the devil, though in his flourishing state of nature, yet he wants this eye, and that makes him that he knows not where hell is, or what it is, or where the devil is, or what he is.

15. But it is by the eye of faith that we see into the heights and depths of all things, and of the mystery of the Scriptures.

16. It is light that discovers darkness; darkness cannot judge of darkness. If the light of nature be but darkness, what will the darkness of death be, and the death of that death, which is the second death?

17. When darkness descends into utter darkness, and death into death, in a place of darkness suitable for a living death and a dying life, then, O thou fallen Angel, which was once as the Sun of the Morning, now will thy state, and the state of thy seed be changed.

18. Then will that Scripture be fulfilled, Babylon is fallen, is fallen, from the first death to the second; and now follows the nature of the second.

CHAP. V.

1. How the Reprobate Seed will be raised. 2. Of the grievousness of their Torment. 3. Their Bodies heavy Bodies.

Doctrine

1. THE state and posture of this dark spiritual body will be such, as will still enlarge its torment; as first, they will arise and remain as naked as ever they were born, not having any thing to cover those cursed bodies.

2. Unless it be that which is worse than without, being the covering of confusion and stinking blackness, gathered upon them as the effects of their suffering sins, issuing out from a fiery frying vengeance.

Proved

3. According as it is written, Isaiah, chap. 3, instead of sweet smells, a stink; and instead of a girdle, a rent; and instead of well set hair, baldness; see chap. 34, verse 3. Their stink shall come up out of their carcases.

Doctrine 2

4. Secondly, for a further degree of their misery, they shall never see bright day more; they were quick of sight outwardly in their former natural life, but now they shall neither inwardly nor outwardly behold any object at all.

Doctrine 3

5: Thirdly, they shall never see the face of God, elect men, or angels to eternity; for as they could not believe in the time of their natural life, that God had any face, so shall they be debarred from the sight of it to eternity.

Doctrine 3

6 Fourthly, they shall never see the faces of one another, although they shall hear the shrieks and cries of one another; and they shall howl and yell one to another like dogs; and they shall be as wild beasts of the desert; yet shall they never see one another's dreadful faces, nor their own faces, and yet they shall have faces, gathered full of blackness and ugly deformedness, according to the Scripture of truth, if rightly understood.

Doctrine 3

7. Fifthly; again, although their bodies be but small to what they were here, yet shall they be heavy bodies, weighing them down as lead; for they will never be able to move hand or foot to stir from the place of their resurrection to eternity, even as if they had mill-stones about their necks.

8. So that they shall bow down as if their bodies were lead; according as it is said by the Egyptians (in their great destruction, it being a type hereof). They sunk like lead (said Moses) in the waters; then will that other Scripture be fulfilled, which saith, [Bell boweth down] and [Nobo stoopeth].

Application

9. O! you seed of the fallen angel, who have so slandered and belied my faith, saying, that I own neither heaven nor hell, what think

you? Can you endure all that hath been said? Will it not be hell enough? If not, you may hear of more by-and-bye, if you come to read or hear this Treatise. But,

10. First, consider how lamentably miserable it would be for thee, that blasphemeth against the Lord Jesus, if this thy natural body was but constrained to be bound down, though in a soft bed, for twenty years together, would not thy misery be great? But,

11. Secondly, if thou wast laid and fastened upon thorns in a dark dungeon, for twenty years; if it were possible for thee to hold out in life, and but in life, would it not be more miserable? But,

12. Thirdly, and lastly; Oh, then, how miserable and intolerable it will be to lie in utter darkness ten hundred thousand millions of years, and more, never stirring hand nor foot, but lying naked as ever thou wast born; is not this intolerable?

13. But this is not all, it is but the verge and outside of hell; it but as it were toucheth the skin, the other reacheth the bone's marrow and internal part, as follows.

CHAP. VI.

1. Of the Fire of Hell, what it is, and where it is. 2. Where Hell is. 3. Of three things working in order to the Reprobates' Eternal Torment.

Doctrine 1

1. FIRST, the place where this tormenting fire doth burn, in which the wicked are cast at the latter day, I declare as from my faith in Holy Writ, that it is in their own bodies, for that's the reprobates' hell. That, and in that is the fiery furnace in which their brimstone souls do burn. But of this in the Eighth Chapter.

2. So that if any now inquire where hell is, they may here know, that it is in the dark damned bodies of men and women; and if any would further know what and who that devil is that is appointed to burn eternally in hell, they may be assured that it is the disobedient spirit, or soul of man and woman.

3. Who are in this their immortal miserable state, shut up close prisoners within that tophet, or cursed bodies of theirs; who will become pillars of burning brimstone, having the fire kindled within, and so spreading itself into every part, both within and without, but consumeth not. But more of this hereafter.

4. Now there are three things continually working, in order to this their fiery torment; the first kindleth the fire, the second supplies it with fuel, and the third is continually blowing the kindled coal up into a flame.[1]

5. The first is the motion of sin that gives being to the fire.

6. The second is the action of sin, and it becomes as fuel to increase new sorrows, so that the remembrance of the action of sin, in its mortal body, becomes as dry wood for an everlasting burning.

7. The third thing, which is continually blowing the coal, is the moral law, and its office is to put in execution, and so it becomes as a pair of bellows, which doth blow up both the motions and actions into a flame; according as Paul said, he had not known sin, had not the law said, thou shalt not lust, or covet.

8 So that the law makes sin to appear sinful, by blowing upon it, this fire, broke out in Cain; and it broke out in Judas, as a seal to this, so that Judas, upon his betraying his Lord and Master, the law blowed up the remembrance of the action, and executed wrath,

---

[1] Proved by Three Arguments in the next Chapter.

insomuch as to rid himself from that invisible fire in his conscience, he hanged himself, as many other devils have hanged themselves, to ease their pain, and drowned themselves to quench that fire.

9. But to proceed, I shall show those three things following:

10. First, what the nature of that fire is.

12. Secondly, of the fiery furnace, what it is; and

13. Thirdly, the extent of that fiery wrath.

CHAP. VII.

1. Shewing what ariseth out of this Fire of Hell, and what tormenting Fury it begets. 2. And how the Seeds of it, or rather Sparks, are seen to arise in the natural Bodies of some as an earnest of that.

Doctrine

1. FIRST, this fire is not like unto a material visible fire, for a natural fire giveth light, but this fire is a dark fire, and of an envious and malicious nature; for envy and implacable wrath ariseth out of this black dark tormenting fire.

2. Therefore it is written, that the smoke of her pit shall ascend up for ever; this smoke is the envy, malice, wrath, and blasphemy, or the effects of it.

Explained

3. This smoke from this their envious fire, hath in it also a continual stink, arising out of the matter of that of which the fire doth burn, which is the fleshly seed of disobedient reason; according as it is written by the Prophet Isaiah, ch. 34. Their stink (saith he) shall come up out of their carcases.

4. Then will sin cease to be savory, being turned into wormwood and gall.

Applied

5. This stink must needs be great, for it is the poison of asps, disgorged, for there are several vents for it to issue out; for it shall fry out of the mouth in hideous cries, and shall stream out at the nose, eyes, ears, and at the fundament, fire, smoke, and horrible stinks.

Inference 2

6. Again, this fire being of such an injurious nature, therefore is it that their mouths will be filled with cursings and blasphemies against God, elect men, and angels to eternity.

7. Something of the nature of this fire, is seen in some of that seed in their mortal state here, for how hath the declarations of truth occasioned this fire to break forth into wrath.

Proved by experience

8. For by experience it is known, and though experience is inferior to revelation, yet is there good and sure doctrine raised from experience, as also experience serves to confirm revelation, by witnessing to it.

9. Now from experience have I seen the light of life to dance in some, whilst the spiritual pipe hath been played upon by others.

10. So on the contrary, I have seen the darkness of death arise in wrath against divine revelation, and the person of him that declared it, and the fire of envy was so hot, that they would destroy the men, if they could, for their declaration of the same.

11. I have seen some start up out of their seats on a sudden, staring as if their eyes were ready to leap out of their head, and so mad, that they have frothed at the mouth, like a wild boar, their hands have been held up, as if they would have struck with the same; others I have seen, their hands shake like an aspin leaf, and the knees knock one against another, and all the body to quake and tremble, and the tongue all the while belch forth blasphemy.

12. Others have stamped the foot, and wheted the teeth, as if they would eat the man, being tormented the more, as the others were not tormented as they would have them.

Applied to the workers of iniquity

13. Is not this now the beginning of that fire that will never go out in the world to come? and as it kindles in wrath, so it will burn in wrath, and envy, to all eternity.

14. For all the evil that was in the natural body, will quicken in that new dark spiritual body, that it shall have at the resurrection to condemnation, and then will its fiery torment be perfected, sitting upon that fiery brimstone soul.

CHAP. VIII.

1. Of the Fiery Furnace, and what it is. 2. What that Breath of the Lord is that Blows the Fire. 3. Of Tophet, and what it is.

Doctrine explained

1. SECONDLY, it is said, they shall be cast into a fiery furnace; now this furnace is no other but the reprobate's own body, for when the spirit is bound up close prisoner within the body, from motioning forth any peace or comfort, then is the body become a furnace for the spirit of envy to burn in.

Psa. 21 proved

2. Then will that Scripture be fulfilled, which saith, thou shalt make them as a fiery oven, and the fire shall feed upon them, and burn in them, and never be quenched; as also that other Scripture, that saith, I will gather you in my anger, and cast you into the furnace as dross, and there will I blow upon you in my wrath.

3. Here we see what it is that blows the fire into aflame, and it is the law, as I showed before, for that is called the breath of the Lord, and this makes the fire greater.

Text opened

4. Therefore it is written, tophet is ordained of old, for the king, and so forth.

5. This tophet is the body of man, and the king is the spirit of reason, that works, and rules, and governs in that body, that reigned in that body as a lord in its castle, and that sinned against his Maker, and controulled the saints, in this its body, which was its heaven.

6. But now this body in which it prided itself, as if it were its heaven, must become its spirit's prison, and fiery furnace, and hell, in which its lordship must burn and fry in to all eternity.

7. And this brings me up to shew the extent of the reprobate's torment.

CHAP. IX.

1. Shewing how the Reprobate's Heaven becomes their Hell. 2. And their God their Devil.

Doctrine 1

1. AGAIN, another aggravation of the damned's misery, is this, to wit, that which before was to them as God, will then become their devil; and that which before was their kingdom of heaven, will then become their kingdom of hell.

2. Now the thoughts of the imagination of reason seems pleasant, having egress and regress, but this spring will be dried up, for the spirits will be shut up in the furnace, or prison of that dark body, from ever motioning forth so much as one thought of comfort, for everlasting.

Inference 1

3. Then where will be all your learned disputes, and your seeming holy rationalists, that would have your light within you to be your God, and that your spirit of reason was his own divine nature, now that light becomes darkness, and that god a devil.

Inference 1

4. Then will your thoughts be changed, and you will cry out saying, did we ever think that this spirit of ours we so gloried in, would become our shame, sorrow, and suffering, and that this body, which Hooked upon to be the temple of God, I find it now to be a habitation of devils, that torment me; woe to me that ever I was born,

Inference 1

5. Then will the high and lofty spirit be brought low, and will find that their bodies are habitations of devils, and cages of unclean birds, and doleful creatures; every evil motion, thought, or desire that was in the natural body, will all be turned into unclean hateful birds, in that cursed dark body, and every evil action that was committed in the former body, shall turn all into fiery devils, foul spirits, and doleful creatures.

CHAP. X.

1. Shewing how that the Memory of the Damned shall add to their Torments. 2. Of the Three Offices of the Law, Conscience, and Memory, and what Woes they bring.

Doctrine 1

1. AGAIN, another exquisite torment that follows, is this, namely, that his memory shall set all his sins in order before him.

2. In the time of his natural life it was as his darling, now it will become his devil, and his eternal accomptant.

3. There will not be one sin, nor one evil thought that will be forgotten, for every evil action will arise afresh in the mind, and then will it kindle into a fire, and the law will kindle with it, for the fiery law shall sit upon the fiery soul, and the memory presents the action that the law sits in judgment of.

4. Thus the memory becomes the witness, the law the judge, and the conscience the hangman; so that mans own spirit, is man's own tormenter, and as the memory is a witness, so the law written in that memory is witness too, as well as judge, and so can never err in judgment.

5. Now if they had had no memory, it had been better for them, but woe to this their memory, for it lays the sin open to the conscience, and the conscience open to the sin, that they may lash one into another.

Proved

6. Moreover as the memory of a sin arises in the damned, the law hereupon gives wages to that sin, and as often as it is presented, so often is it punished with diversity of plagues, and every one heightened; for as here we see that as wood being laid to the fire, and taken away again before it be all burned, makes it more combustible afterwards, when laid to the fire again.

7. Even so it is with the damned, for as its sin kindles itself a fire to its own woe, upon the law and memories reviving of it.

8. Now whilst their memory lasteth, the fiery burning punishment for that sin lasteth; and when that sin and sorrow hath had its course, the memory in a moment presents another out of the record of the law and conscience, for there is no stand, but the wheel of

memory is ever moving, and when the cup is presented it must be drank off.

CHAP. XI.
No Cessation of Pain to the Damned.

Doctrine 1

1. AGAIN, there will never be any intermission of pain, for as soon as one phial of wrath is drank off, another is presented without stop or stay, coming rolling one upon another, like the waves of the sea.

Proved by four plagues

2. It is written, fill to her double; one Apostle tells of four plagues falling upon them in one day, which are death and mourning, famine and burning with fire:

Explained

3. These are four cups of vengeance which must be drank, and when drank, then they must be filled up with new plagues and drank again.

Plague 1 explained

4. Now this plague of famine is not a famine of sorrow and mourning, for that they will have enough; but the famine they are to undergo is in that they are everlastingly kept, from ever having one motion of peace or hope of deliverance out of its torment.

Plague 2 explained

5. Again, that other plague of death, is the second death, which they shall ever lye under, and this must needs cause mourning, because it is a living death, and dying life, ever dying, but never dead.

Plague 3 explained

6. For the law rising with them, will walk in their souls to eternity, to keep the worm of conscience that it never dies, and to blow the fire that it never goes out;

Doctrine. Causes mourning

7. Again, for a further aggravation to the torment, is in that it will grow and encrease, this is that which makes hell to be hell indeed, seeing their miseries are everlastingly encreasing.

Illustrated

8. For this the seed of the serpent shall find, that new pangs of sorrow shall lay hold upon them, and this their new plagues will be so great, as that it will beget new blasphemies, and new curses, both against God, elect men, and angels, to all eternity.

Applied to grand devils

9. Here will that cursed devil receive his pay, who in this age had found a new wickedness, as to bid God damn them at every word; now is God come with the commission of his spirit, to show those devils their damned state.

10. And you, Sir, that told Judge Bernard, upon the bench, that this our faith in this commission of the spirit, was made up of all manner of heresies, you will find it otherways when you enter into this second death.

11. Also, will not the persecuting devil receive his pay to the full, that drank the blood of the saint? now shall he drink his own blood in a flood of fiery vengeance.

12. And as his reason did invent and dictate to him new plagues and punishments against the saints, even so shall the wrath of God go forth in that soul, even to the horse bridles, &c.

CHAP. XII.

Shewing how that the Torments of the Damned are without End.

Doctrine. 1

1. THE grievousness of the torments of the damned are seen by their long lasting, which is everlasting; the life of the damned is to die without end.

2. The fire doth so consume, as yet notwithstanding it ever reserves, for so long as the remembrance of sin continues, the fire will never want fuel, as is aforesaid.

3. O! eternity, without all bounds, being not measured by any space of time, this is that which makes the fire of hell burn more hot, and makes the torment more violent.

4. What was it, to live a matter of thirty or forty years here, in pleasure, and sports, and to lie in thy soft bed? will it then be of any value, when thou hast lain thirty or forty thousand years in that lake of fire and brimstone aforesaid, grovelling upon this earth in utter darkness, and as naked as thou wast born? and when those years, and ten thousand times as many more are past, yet is it with thee, but the beginning of sorrow.

5. Oh! grievous is the torments of the damned, because of the sharpness of their torments; but it is still the more grievous in respect of the diversity of their torments, but still it is more grievous because of the encrease of new sorrows, but the most grievous of all is, for the eternity of their torments, for there shall be a death, without death, and an end, without end.

6. O! eternity, eternity; this word eternity is that which revives their sorrows; this will come to pass however slighted by that seed now.

7. But I must stop my hand and write no further, for I have written more, I suppose, than that seed can have patience to read; however, let them choose, for the workers of iniquity must have this for their portion.

8. And now do I intend to address myself to speak of the kingdom of the Son of Man, the Most High and Wise God, and of the glory that the children of the kingdom shall enjoy.

9. He that hath ears to hear let him hear.

THE EIGHTH PART:

OF

THE SAINTS's JOYS IN HEAVEN.

THE PREFACE.

1. I AM now to treat of the most great and weighty part of my subject, this is the delicate dish that my soul would be feeding of.

2. It is for the children of the kingdom to know their celestial kingdom, or country.

3. The life of faith is wrought in us by a heavenly ministry, to show us the way and to give knowledge of the invisible things of eternity.

4. Now will I leave this dark world, and the mantle of Elijah, and with the wings of an eagle will I swiftly ascend to the region of light, seeing the kingdom of heaven is opened to us by the Lord's last prophets.

5. And the golden sceptre is held forth, we all are freely admitted to come to see within the veil, and are bid to come and to drink abundantly, even as much as our vessels can hold, at the river that makes glad the city of God.

6. Come, therefore, and walk with me my beloved fraternity, into the garden of spices, for I am now to enter myself into a pleasant labyrinth; come, go into Nebre, let us view well the country that is given to us.

But qualify yourselves well before you enter into the divine contemplation hereof, for it is a kingdom of peace, joy, and concord.

Peace and love is the evidence of heaven's enjoyment, therefore follow after it and pursue it, and then will a flood of peace follow you in that kingdom, if you love it here, it is laid up for you there, for this know, there is no other righteousness available but that which is sowed in peace and love, this is the seed of heaven; sow here, and reap there.

True religion is grounded in peace and love, silence and secrecy, as it is written, enter into your chamber and be Still—be still and know that I am God; a still and low voice; and God was in that voice.

The true church, as it relates to Jerusalem, which signifies a vision of peace, even so it is kept from the strivings of the people of a formal and carnal worship.

Mind, therefore, the operations of that peaceful spirit, and it will lead into raptures of joy when it shows you that joyful country

And although you meet with troubles in the outward man in your way, yet what of that, seeing the peace of God and the assurance of eternal life is the charter you hold by? therefore, hold fast your earnest penny, for the possession of heaven is yours.

This is your city, and you must live with the new Jerusalem; heaven is your country, and there have you a city, which hath bars and gates to it, so that none of the troublers of Israel shall come in; and in

that country all the borders thereof are peace, or peace is the borders thereof, yea, and the bounds of the city.

Now if peace of mind be the great felicity (as Democritus could say,) what felicity then will that be when there is nothing but peace, neither within nor without, with the saints in this quiet country?

Come, therefore, go with me you peaceful and well qualified saints, and ascend by faith into the region of happiness, and behold your country given to you by the Lord Jesus Christ, blessed for ever. Amen.

THE EIGHTH PART:

OF

The Saint's Joys in Heaven.

CHAP. I.

Of the Mighty Power of Christ Raising the Dead.

Doctrine 1

1. IT is written in the text I have chosen for my theme, then shall the righteous shine forth as the sun in the kingdom of their Father; also, it is written, that when our Lord comes he will change our vile bodies, and make them like unto his own glorious body, and that he will give to every seed his own body.

Proved

2. This will be done by a word speaking, for his spirit of faith being all powerful, will by a word speaking, cause the saint's spirits of faith to take light and life again.

3. For as weak power in mortal nature can effect something in order to the recovering of light and life, as the breath of man, when the blaze of the candle is gone out, will recover it again by a blast, whilst the spark is remaining.

4. But then the breath of the mouth of the Lord Jesus Christ, the High and Mighty God, can go so much further, as to bring life out of absolute death, and light out of total darkness.

5. Wherefore although the spark be out, as well as the blaze, light shall come forth out of that matter, which was light before, though extinct with death, and mouldered to dust, by the breath of an Almighty God in his word speaking.

Doctrine

6. Thus it will be with the seed of the Lord's own body, when our Lord comes, he will speak a powerful word to our dead souls though mouldered into dust, saying, arise my beloved that lie in the grave, come forth with bodies all glorious like unto myself, and enter with me, and my mighty angels into my everlasting kingdom.

Proved. Amplified

7. Upon these very words speaking will there be a mighty shaking of the earth, in the raising of this seed, for each seed shall have its own body, that is, every spirit will bring forth its body, not the same body it lived in, for that was roted in the grave, (besides there was something of sin in that body), yet shall it bring forth a new body out of that body.

Illustrated

8. For as the Apostle saith, the wheat corn being sowed in the earth dies, and brings forth another body, not the same it was sowed in, for a new life arises out of the old, for the invisible life of the wheat corn quickens out of the old, and brings forth a new body, living the old body behind it.

Explained

9. Even thus it is with man, the same body that was laid down riseth no more, but a new body out of the invisible life of that body, so that when God raiseth the dead, he speaks to the invisible life that lies buried in dead dust, as fire lies hid in the flint.

Inference 1

10. Again, though that body that is corrupted in the grave, does not arise again, yet in that the invisible life did live in that body and died in that body; therefore, it will have its existance again out of its former body, though mouldered to dust.

Inference 2

11. Therefore though that dust be scattered into several places, and the parts of man's body severed from each other, into several lands, seas, and countries, yet shall all the principal parts thereof come together, that the spirit and life may, in a moment, spring or arise out of the whole, with a body suitable to its nature and looks, where the principal part of the saint lies, there will be the place of his resurrection.

Proved

12. Therefore it was that Joseph commanded that his bones should be carried out of Egypt, and buried in the land of Canaan, because he would have his resurrection amongst the chief saints in the land of promise, and the prophets of old and all true believers of their doctrine desired to have their burial places together, to the end they might rise together.

CHAP. II.

1. The Angels' Office in gathering together the Saints. 2. And of the Time they will be in gathering of them together. 3. And of the Nature of those Spiritual Bodies. 4. With the Manner of the Sentence to both Seeds at that Day.

Doctrine 1

1. AT this great day, which by faith we see is drawing near, the Lord Jesus will descend from heaven, with thousands of Angels surrounding his person, whose office is to gather the Saints.

Proved

2. Therefore after the Lord Jesus, the Most Mighty God (for no other God there will appear but he), hath spoke forth that powerful word of raising the dead, then are the Angels ready to go forth and spread themselves into all the four parts of the world, who in a moment (their motion being as swift as thought), they take up the Saints, and convey them towards the Lord, in the old Land of Promise, over the city of Old Jerusalem.

Cleared

3. For there will it be said by the Lord, [Come, ye blessed] and there will it be said, [Go, ye cursed] not that all the reprobate seed will be gathered thither; although it is said that in the valley of Jehosaphat he will plead with them, for that seed shall not be gathered, for they will be but raked out of their holes, never stirring from the places of their resurrection.

4. Nevertheless, wherever they are, they shall be capable to hear his voice, saying, Go, ye cursed.

Inference 1

5. All the grand devils that persecuted Christ, shall see the sign of the Son of Man over their heads Cain and Judas, Pilate and Herod, and those persecuting devils, that put Christ to death, shall be placed with all in the valley of Jehosaphat, for over their heads will the great God appear, and thither will all Saints be gathered, and from that place will the Ascension be.

6. The time the Angels will be in gathering the elect, will not be long; if any be inquisitive to know, my faith tells me there will be but twelve hours betwixt the Resurrection and Ascension; for the Angels

persons being in motion as swift as thought, they will soon gather together the elect.

7. And the Saints will have bodies of such a light, fiery nature, as that they will be of agility to keep company with the Angels; so that there will be no let on their parts, to hinder the work, but that a day or twelve hours may be sufficient, considering that the judgment of the reprobates will lie all in one sentence, even as aforesaid, [Go, ye cursed].

8. This is all that God hath to do with that seed, at that day, only leaving his law in that seed, to be their judge, accuser, and executioner, to eternity, as I have shown in the Seventh Part.

Inference 2

9. Moreover, then will all Saints be filled with admiration at the sun-shining splendour of their persons, that their God shall put upon them, at that instant of time, when he shall say, Come, ye blessed.

Inference 3

10. And it is believed by some (and I cannot gainsay it), that there will be a difference in the nature of the persons, of those whose bodies were corrupted in the grave, and those persons that are alive at the coming of Jesus, or but newly fallen asleep, their bodies being uncorrupt.

Inference 4

11. Which difference tends to this, namely, that those Saints whose bodies were corrupt, shall at their resurrection have spiritual bodies, of a bright, burning, fiery nature, like unto the body of the Creator, before he took to himself a body of flesh.

Inference 1

12. But those Saints that are alive at Christ's coming, or those that are newly dead, they shall be all changed from corruption to incorruption, yet so as that they shall retain to themselves bodies of very flesh and bone, even as Moses, Enoch, and Eli as are, and as the glorious body of the Lord Jesus Christ is the High and Mighty God.

A use of consolation

13. So that the most wise God and everlasting Father, the Lord Jesus Christ, He will look upon his Saints, and glory in them; and as he once had a spiritual body, therefore will he look upon those his

Saints that have spiritual bodies, and love them as his own spiritual body.

14. And as he is now clothed with a body of flesh and "bone, as a garment of eternal glory, therefore will he look upon those his Saints, that have bodies of flesh and bone, and love them, as if they were his own blessed body of flesh and bone glorified.

CHAP. III.

1. Of All-Saints Day. 2. A Day of New Songs. 3. The Angels congratulate the Saints Arrival, &c.

1. NO sooner will the Lord raise them by a word of faith, and the Angels gather them by a powerful expedition, but they will with their Lord ascend to heaven in their light, fiery, glorious bodies, so glorious that the cursed Canaanites are not able to behold them.

2. And now doth the Saints' glory begin to come in, seeing their bodies are made immortal and glorious, like unto their God, being suitable to that region of light.

Doctrine 1

3. For when the Saints' bodies are immortalized, they will shine as the stars, so that this world will not be a fit habitation for Saints to reside in, for some of the Saints will there shine as the sun.

Of the measure of their glory

4. For according as their strength of faith and life of love in that faith was, so will their glory be, and though that faith did die in that former body, yet will it quicken again, and its lustre will be as its life was before, a powerful life of faith, producing an exceeding weight of glory.

Amplified by Singing praises

5. The Saints being thus changed and immortalized, will ascend with Christ, in a song of triumph, over death, hell, the devil, and the grave, and the Angels will wonderfully congratulate their deliverance, and they will be ravished with joy of the Saints' society; the occasion of that love will be shewn hereafter.

6. And now upon their ascension and entrance into the Holy Land, will be a great shout for the marriage day of the Lamb, and the feast of fat things is made ready, and every Angel a new revelation given, that they may also sing the praises of the Lamb, as afterwards will more fully be declared.

7. Likewise, every living creature in that creation, will also be filled with love; every one as it were, according to its kind, will do homage to the Saints, in regard they are made like unto their God, for in that kingdom is nothing but love.

8. Then will be the great day of joy, and the day of new songs, from new revelations; then will every one sound his harp, and blow with the trumpet; that is, every one of their tongues will be as a harp, to sound forth the praise of the Lord God Almighty.

9. In the first of Samuel, chap. 4, it is said, that when the ark of the covenant of the Lord was come into the camp of Israel, then all Israel shouted with a great shout, so that the earth rung again:

10. Now was there such a shout at the shadow of God's presence? What a shout, then, will that be, when all shall arrive into the kingdom of eternal glory?

11. Again, was there not a great shout by the people of Israel, when they had built them up a material temple, and decked it with gold and silver, as a place to worship God in? O! what a shout will there then be, when every Saint's body is made a glorious temple, more brighter than gold, and is brought into the presence of God, to worship him there to all eternity.

12. Then will the Forty-seventh Psalm be put into both Saints' and Angels' mouths; for then will they clap their hands, and shout unto God, in the voice of triumph, and shall sing praises unto God, sing praises, sing praises, unto their King, sing praises.

13. When all the Princes of Israel, and the people of them, are gathered together, even the people of the God of Abraham, what exultation, what joy, what triumph, and what shouting will there be by all the seed of Adam? Will it not make that new heaven and new earth to ring, at the melodious strains of Saints and Angels;

14. O! my friends, are you by faith wrapt up into this third heaven? Be ravished at the vision or contemplation of this day of new songs; for thus it will be. Let your faith be strong, and walk with me still on, and behold more.

CHAP. IV.

1. Of the Three Armies in Heaven. 2. And of the Captain of those Armies. 3. And of the Mansions prepared.

Doctrine 1

1. UPON this All-Saints' day, the Lord Jesus, the Mighty God, he goes before, and all his prophets follow after, and the believers of those prophets' doctrines, with glorious new songs; every one according to his order and place, for every thing is done in order, for our God is the God of Order.

The doctrine roved

2. In the Revelations, it is written, that the armies in heaven followed the Lamb; again, by the same divine, it is written, that there are Three Commissions that bear record to God. Now these Three Commissions make the three armies that follow the Lamb in heaven, at that day of the glorious Ascension.

1. Army. 2. Army

3. Moses, the prophets, and the believers of their doctrine, make one great army; the Apostles, and their ordained bishops, with all the true believers of their doctrine, makes the second great army.

3. Army

4. The Witnesses of the Spirit, being the third record, and the true believers of their doctrine, make the third great army in heaven, and greater than either of the other, and these are the armies that follow the Lamb which way soever he goeth.

5. Now to clear it, that the Witnesses of the Spirit, and the believers of their doctrine in substance (though not all professors), do become the greatest army, we are to know, that alt those Saints that lived since the Apostles' Commission ended, will all be raised, and ranked under the third record.

6. Now the Apostles' Commission lasted but three hundred years; but this Commission of the Spirit, whom we are under, will last to the end of the world.

7. Moreover, that saying of our Saviour, that the true worshippers should worship the Father in spirit and truth, did introduce the third record; for the visible worship did last but for a moment, only serving

the infant church, which began to wear out, even in the Apostles' days, as where Paul said, I thank God, I baptised none at all, &c.

8. And although that outward worship was in force during that Commission, and the true spiritual worship lay in it, yet when all the true ministers were extirpated out of the world, as in the Ten Persecutions, then the Commission ceased, and there being no true ordained ministers left, the world steps into that outward form, namely, the Gentile power, and as the spirit of the world came in, so the spirit of the Lord went out.

9. Therefore all Saints since (or at leastways, elect, for there were no Saints till the third record came to be, for it is a true Commission or Ministry that makes Saints), I say all the elect since, have been taught by the inspirations of the Spirit, and so have worshipped the Lord in spirit, giving the glory to him due to his name, not regarding the formal worshippers' distinction of three Gods, or Trinity of Persons; these, I say, will all be raised under the Witnesses of the Spirit, and will make up that third great army in heaven, following the Lamb at this their coronation day.

10. Now as an earthly king doth, when he goes his progress, take his lords of his council and nobility with him, and the chief of his court, to attend his person, and that with all magnificence imaginable, to the great promotion of his glory;

11. Even thus will the King of Heaven do, at this day of Ascension of All-Saints; he will take all his Prophets and chosen messengers, which were of his privy council, and those his messengers will take along with them, all those their children, whom they or their doctrine begot to the faith, they being their captains, and fighting under their banners in their warfare for the immortal crown, shall now with them reign in glory, and go with them when they follow the Lamb, who is the Captain of Captains.

12. I say from my seed spring, begot by a prophet's blessing or doctrine, at this day the Lord Jesus Christ, in this day of the Saints' triumph, goes on his progress, with all those great armies, through his celestial kingdom, showing unto them infinite ravishing glories.

13. But the glory of all glory, is when he hath arrived to the throne of thrones, and to the several distinct mansions there prepared for his Prophets, Apostles, and Witnesses of the Spirit.

14. Then will the great God, the Lord Jesus Christ, for there is no other, we know not any; this God will bid them welcome into his court and kingdom, saying to his messengers, who shall all of them surround his person, in this wise following:

15. Come ye, my servants, partake of my joy, that I have prepared for you; you believed my promise, you grounded upon it, and forsook all for it; here are the mansions prepared for you; here now they are; behold they are here, the mansions reserved for you; they are yours', possess ye them, to all eternity.

16. Moreover, as all Prophets, Apostles, and Witnesses of the Spirit, have their distinct mansions here, even so the believers under each Commission hath their mansions and degrees of glory also.

17. Therefore, those that have been eminent in faith and holiness, and have suffered much for their faith, and love of Jesus, shall shine there, very gloriously, and be placed near unto the prophet they were under.

18. Therefore, all you that love the truth, press forward in that known truth; for your faith and holiness will be abundantly rewarded. But give me leave to hasten to further enlargements of particular excellences that each Saint shall partake of.

CHAP. V.

1. Shewing how that the Saints shall in their new glorified Bodies, he capable to see their God face to face.

Doctrine 1

1. MY brethren you may know, that when the Saints are immortalized, then shall they be made able to look upon their God, and be strengthened to see him. This will be a crown to us indeed; that we shall see him, that we have longed for to see the face of him that created us, and to behold the person of him, that died for us, and redeemed us by his own precious blood; this will add to our glory.

2. Then shall not Zaccheus need to get up to the top of a tree to see his Lord, but shall be admitted into his presence, and be made able to behold him in his bright, burning glory.

3. When the stock of all our sorrows are gone, then shall we rest like infants in our Lord's arms; there shall we see and behold our God, and our heart shall rejoice; then shall we sing forth and say, many a time have we heard of our God, by the hearing of the ear, but now our eyes behold him.

4. And for a further heightening of our glory, our God will come and take us by the hand, and embrace us as the dearly beloved of his soul, saying, Come to me, I am your Lord, I am he that hath wiped away all tears from your eyes, and done away all fears.

5. Every tear that you shed, I kept in my remembrance, to the end I might reward you with crowns of glory.

6. Then will that Scripture be fulfilled, And they shall see my face, and my name shall be in their forehead, and they shall behold my glory, and sing of my praise.[1]

Texts proved

7 Then shall we see God, and in seeing him, shall love him, and in loving him, we shall praise him. This is the joy of Angels and the happiness of Saints, the crown of glory, the garland of felicity; this is one of the Seven Beatitudes, and the blessing of blessings, and the harvest of happiness.[2]

8 Then shall we be dunned in the teeth no more with scoffing Ishmalites, saying, where is your God?

9. In this vale of tears, many a poor soul hath been hearkening after his God, saying to every one they met (who professed to be teachers of truth), see ye not, my beloved; see ye not where he feedeth his sheep.

10. But then at this day aforesaid, this inquisition will be turned into true fruition, by the Beatifical Vision of God: this is a joy beyond all joy, without which there could be no joy, for the having of God, and the seeing of God, is the Saints all in all.

11. This is the time that the lost are found, and the undone made happy for ever.

CHAP. VI.

1. The Saints increase in Glory. 2. Of the great Love of the Redeemer to the Saints.

1. NOW for a further heightening of our joy, this know, that we shall not have all our glory and joy at our first entrance into heaven, and yet shall we not know that we want any.

Doctrine 1

2. Wherefore as the revelation of faith, will be continually increasing in us with new wisdom, to all eternity, even so will our joys and glories be increasing likewise to all eternity. But more of this hereafter.

---

[1] Rev. 22.
[2] Matt. 5. Isa. 35, 10.

3. In this new heaven and new earth, will come one joy upon the neck of another, as here in mortality one wave come upon the back of another in this vale of tears; even so, as aforesaid, will one joy come rolling upon the back of another. But I will hasten to particulars.

4. The love of God to his glorified Saints will be a sparkling pearl in the crown of glory.

5. For did not God love his Saints dearly when they were in their blood? How much more, then, will he love them, when made like unto himself?

6. Doth he esteem so well of them when they were in their rags? What affection, then, will he have when they are in their royal robes? I shall hasten to show, and pass on.

CHAP. VII.

1. Of the Joys that come in by Faith, or Faith's Nature described. 2. A Touch of the Angel's Nature.

1. AGAIN, we have more strings to play upon, we have more melody and mirth still, we have more joys springing up, and more roses in our garland, and pearls in our crowns.

2. For though the enjoyment of God, is that which doth produce infinite joys, yet will there be many more ravishing glories bestowed upon us, both within us and without us.

3. Within us, as from the revelation of our faith; without us, as by the use of our spiritual senses, upon variety of heavenly objects, for an eternal delight to the same; of both those in order, and first for the first.

4. As it was the good pleasure of God to create Adam in his own image, both in form and nature, therefore that nature being of the divine nature, it became a fountain, overflowing, with variety of new wisdom, in all his offspring, even as their God is according to its measure.

5. And this is a privilege above the Angels, for the Angels' natures being not satisfactory faith, but desiring reason, therefore they must always be supplied by revelation from the spirit of faith, in the person of the Lord Jesus, the Everlasting Father.

Doctrine 1

6. But every son of Adam, according to his degree in glory, will be as a well springing up unto everlasting life, of revelation of new wisdom, from whence flows new joys, and glory within his own

person, like unto his God; only this, each one shall naturally return the glory and praise unto their well-springs fountain, the Lord Jesus Christ, for this their exaltation upon the glorious throne of his own likeness.

Inference 1

7. For their spirits, being the spirit of faith, which is the spirit of God, which is all purity, and power, and therefore hath power naturally to spring up in revelation of new wisdom, &c.

Inference 1

8. Nevertheless, though their glory be of the same nature with God, as aforesaid, yet they cannot otherwise chuse, but must on necessity be ever casting their crowns, at his glorious feet, saying;

9. Worthy is the Lamb to receive power and glory, wisdom and honor, who through his infinite love hath made us such creatures, as to have a well-spring of wisdom and revelation, arising out or flowing continually within us, for our eternal felicity, joy, and glory.

10. Now from what is said, we may see, what a sea of celestial glory we shall have; nay, it will be so unutterable, as that the verge of our spiritual understandings in our glorified bodies, cannot comprehend it, as to set it forth the extent or measure of it, in its height and depth, because of its growing and increasing nature.

11. Wherefore, then, should it be expected, that mortality should set forth the glory of immortality, as to the measure of their glory; nor let none require of me to do that, for my business is only to set forth the nature, and not the measure, of this their heavenly glory.

Inference 1

12. Now by what is said, we see how far our glory goes beyond the Angels; and from hence is the ground that the Angels will have such love to the Saints.— Shall not I from hence demonstrate the cause why? Take it as follows, and follow as you like, and like as you please; I am satisfied in what I write, and I write what I believe, and believe what I write, and receive comfort.

CHAP. VIII.

1. The Cause of the Angels' Love and Affection to the Saints, the Seed of the Lord's Body.

1. I BEING now to speak of the Angels extraordinary love to the Seed of Adam, and inasmuch as their natures are pure reason, it may be queried by some, whether this their love flow out of their rational nature, yea or no?

2. Now in answer to this, we are to know, that though their rational nature, is a noble nature, yet from that nature, as from itself, hath no power of goodness or strength of stability.

Doctrine 1

3. Therefore it is that the overflowings of the divine spirit of faith, in the person of the Creator, into their desiring nature of reason, is that which is the life of their life.

4. So that revelation of faith, entering into their nature of reason, preserves their reason, and keeps it in purity, and from hence comes forth pure love., to that which is the life of its life.

Inference 1

5. And from these overflowing raptures, is love quickened, so that the Angels love is out of faith's fountain.

Inference 2

6. Now the Angels will ever be desiring the society of the Saints; for if their love be so great to them in mortality, how much greater will it be in immortality and glory?

7. When the ministration of Angels was in being, the saints had their guardian angels waiting upon them; therefore, said the Apostle, your angels continually behold your Father's presence, waiting for messages of love.

Inference 3

8. There is four great festival times, or days to the angels, wherein great gifts of wisdom to them is given; the first was in the assuring to them the eternal love of God towards them.

9. The second was at the day of the incarnation of God, as aforesaid, and the third will be at the resurrection and ascension of God; and this was a great day, for all the host of angels came with Moses and Elias, to associate to their God, and to welcome him home;

therefore, it is written, God is gone up with a shout, this shout was from the holy angels; these three days are over, but the fourth is not yet coming, but it will come at the resurrection and ascension of all saints.

Inference 4

10. Then will the angels rejoice again, and sing forth the praises of the Almighty; they will then show forth their love by leading the saints about, and shewing the glory of their father's kingdom, and of the mansions wrought.

11. Have comfort, here you seed of the Son of Man, for love and wisdom is working for you in heaven; seraphims, and cherubins, angels, and archangels, are providing extraordinary things, to be given to such as are fore-known, and that have been eminent in a commission.

Inference 5

12. Then will Peter's angel take Peter by the hand, and Abraham's and David's, and the Virgin-wife Mary's, and Zachariahs' angels, &c. take them by the hands, and will welcome them into their father's kingdom, and will present to them tokens of unexpressable love.

Inference 6

13. And most assuredly, from the highest order of angels, namely the cherubins, love will abundantly flow from them towards the saints, because of the free electing love of this their glorious God, in his sparing of them at the downfall of that their fellow cherub; as also by assuring them of an eternal enjoyment of the favor of God, and their most merciful Creator, blessed forever. Amen.

CHAP. IX.

1. Shewing what Faith is, and of its Substance. 2. And how Revelation is kindled, and Joy produced, both in God and Man. 3. With the Reward of Revelation.

1, NOW shall I treat again of the nature of faith in a glorified body, because it is the inlet to all our joy.

Doctrine 1

2. Faith is of no great bulk in a saint, though so great and wonderful in wisdom, power, strength, and virtue, as to kindle new revelation; it is a little invisible spark, not so big as a mustard seed, that can kindle revelation so wonderfully, as to create new joys, new songs, and new praise, unto its Creator, and gracious Redeemer, the Lord Jesus Christ, blessed for ever.

Amplified

3. The glory of faith, is a miraculous glory; is it not wonderful that such a thing should be in God? and is it not more wonderful that such a quickening, and an ever new creating, growing, and increasing, nature should be in man? and yet it is true, for it is both in God and man, in a spring of a high nature, after man is immortalized and glorified.

4. Well then may all saints propound that question of the Apostle's, saying, what manner of men shall we be? if David could say that these mortal bodies of ours were fearfully and wonderfully made, how much more may it be said, that the Saint's immortal bodies and souls are gloriously and wonderfully made, considering the operation of that invisible spark of faith, that reigneth in the glorified body?

5. For it is that spiritual spark of faith that maketh the body so to shine.

Inference 1

6. Now faith being such a noble nature, let me next show what is the principal wheel of its motion in a glorified saint, or what that fuel is, that doth kindle revelation, or becomes matter of its operation, the knowledge of which is worth the discovery.

Inference 2

7. Therefore you, the seed of the Lord's own body, may know that this fuel proceeds principally from a clear comprehension of a two-fold action, one in God, and the other in man.

8. That which is in God, is this, all those righteous actions and sufferings of Christ in the days of his flesh for the saints, as each action in every saint doth arise in the mind, it becomes a special fuel to kindle this fire, this love-fire in the glorified saint.

Inference 3

9. Therefore whenever it is that a motion of remembrance of Christ's sufferings for him, doth arise in the mind, it presently creates a sea of celestial joys, from its revelation of new wisdom being occasioned by that motion, and then doth the glorified saint abound with thanksgiving, power, honour, and glory, unto the Lord Jesus, the fountain of this its felicity, joy, and glory.

Inference 4

10. And then, again on the other hand, all those righteous actings and sufferings for truth's sake, that were acted and suffered in our former bodies, by the appointment of our God shall be conveyed into our new spiritual bodies, that are like unto our God; with our memory and senses, and so shall be another glorious fire, naturally to kindle revelation of new wisdom, as aforesaid, &c.

Inference 5

11. Now every revelation will beget a reward, or become a reward, for every revelation will beget a new song, and every new song will fill us with joy, and gladness of heart, and every joy and rejoicing of heart will be a spiritual banquet; and so it will do by feeding upon the righteousness of Christ, and the sufferings of him in the days of his flesh, for us, as aforesaid.

CHAP. X.

1. Shewing the Felicity that comes to the Glorified Saints, by their spiritual Memory, and of the largeness thereof. 2. With the Ground of Revelation, and how it is twofold.

Doctrine 1

1. AGAIN, as the revelation of faith in a glorified body doth abound in new wisdom, and soul ravishing delights, continually bubbling up from its own well-spring; even so the course of its current is supplied from its comprehensive memory, being the store-house of heavenly treasure.

Proved

2. For the saints' spiritual memories will be conveyed into their spiritual glorified bodies, and made one with them, and it will be heightened in its glory, as well as the body, or any other divine virtue, or excellence, for there must be a correspondency of each divine property, member, sense, or faculty.

3. Therefore in our glorified bodies there will be no part defective, but as every member, sense, or faculty was answerable to each other in a perfect man, even so they will be in glory, wherefore our memories being made one with our spiritual bodies you know they must needs become wonderfully comprehensive.

4. Our memories here, whilst in mortality, are many times very defective and weak, we are not able to retain what we see and hear, but what goes in at the one ear, goes out at the other, being like unto a sieve, &c.

5. And one cause of its being so weak and uncomprehensible, is, that several guest of contrary natures, seek for lodging there, for naturally man's reason would have quiet harbour; therefore, to reason in itself, that it may reason with the world, for its honour's sake, and that becomes an enemy to spiritual faith, if faith gain not pre-eminence over it, and it is hard to gain so much lordship, but that it will take up a great deal of room still.

6. Again, another thing that proves defective to the spiritual memory here, in a saint, is a burdening it with more than it can bear; a saint thinks sometime he can never hear of spiritual truth too much, nor read too much, therefore he will read with great zeal and delectation of mind, as long as he can see, and not be weary; because, whilst he hears or reads, the sense of the words are upon his mind, or

memory, but no sooner almost he hath done, but all is slipt out again out of his memory, to the disturbance of his spirit, for the not remembering it no better.

Inference 1

7. But it will not be so with thee, O serious saint, and devout soul, (that now mourns under a weak and treacherous memory) in thy glorified state; but what good thing soever passed through thy heart, shall come into thy heart again, and thou shalt never forget it, but only when faith hath, by a blessed banquet, made thy cup run over, it shall lye down in thy memory and give place to other spiritual motions, and in its time, (if I may so say in that place, where is no time) bubble up again in another heavenly joy; as for example;

Inference 2

8. Did thou hear a word from me, or any other that did comfort thy heart, when thou seest him that so hath done? then there is an occasion for that motion to arise, and if thou seeist that saint a thousand years after, that again, (let us suppose this, though there be no number of days or years) there will arise still another motion of perfect remembrance in thee, of what good joy, or delight thou didst receive from thy spiritual brother, either by hearing or reading.

Inference 1

9. Moreover all the good deeds that ever the saints did, all the good words that ever they spake, and all the truth that ever they heard, and all the evil that ever they resisted, will they perfectly remember, as aforesaid, and every remembrance will occasion new joys, and ravishing glories.

10. Thus will every spiritual motion, thought, desire, word, or deed, that the saints enjoyed in their natural bodies, shall by the infinite power of the Lord, be made one with their spiritual bodies in the highest heavens.

Amplified

11. And then will they remember every cross, every stroke of affliction, and persecutions they underwent in the days of their mortal flesh, for truth's sake; and every one of those sufferings will sensibly feed them by the remembrance thereof, with God-like new joys of wisdom, power, and glory, to eternity.

Cleared

12. From what I have said, we may perceive from whence the principal joys and delight of the glorified saints do arise, and that is from within them, although there be many excellencies, glorious, and without number, without the bodies of saints in this kingdom of eternal glory, to delight the spiritual senses of the saints, (as I shall declare hereafter) for our God will have them to have a most perfect glory, both within and without, like unto himself.

13. Yet the principal glory is founded within, and from thence doth our chief happiness spring, insomuch as that it becomes a well-spring of faith in us, flowing out new streams of eternal felicity.

14. Not that I will affirm that it hath no revelation but what ariseth from its own seed, within its own body; but on the contrary, I am persuaded that it receiveth, at certain times, new revelation from the person of the Creator, even from the glorious words of his mouth.

15. For the Creator and glorious Redeemer will have discourse with his Prophets, and chief Saints, and in the manifestation of that discourse, or divine speech, will arise ravishing joys and new soul delights.

16. Yet, nevertheless, this we are to mind, that the saints, in their glorified estate, do not desire revelation from his person, because they know not of any thing they want, and so they are ever satisfied with their own well-spring, and so are without all capacity of desire, contrary to the angels.

17. And thus we see the Saint's glory heightening and growing greater and greater in their new spiritual bodies.

18. But this is not all, greater enlargements are still incoming, therefore give me leave to prosecute this further, whilst the light of heaven shines in my understanding, and the truth of his promise made clear to me, by that his blessed in-shining love of faith engraven in my heart, by that heavenly diamond pen of prophetical report.

CHAP. XI.

Shewing the Nature of that Spiritual Food a Glorified Saint is fed withall.

1. YOU that further desire to know of the food and raiment that glorified bodies shall be fed and arrayed withall in the kingdom of eternal glory, let them mind the discourse following:

Last witness' testimony

2. Wherefore, as a natural body cannot subsist without natural food, even so aspiritural body cannot subsist without spiritual food; now, as a natural body hath no desire after the things that appertain to the celestial kingdom, so glorified bodies are un-capable of any satisfaction from natural food of this terrestial kingdom.

Doctrine 1

3. But on the contrary, their food is produced within them from a never-failing fountain, arising out of their own spirit, for every revelation of wisdom becomes food, to feed them, and look how many revelations arise, so many sorts of food have they for their eternal nourishment.

4. Therefore the glorified saints are not confined to such and such sorts of food, but as their revelation is from a well-spring of endless virtue, so their food is of such variety, as that it is without knowledge or number, as to the several sorts thereof.

5. Yet, nevertheless, each sort is so delectable to the spiritual taste, as that it becomes such a feast of fat things, such a banquet of beautiful balm, that it ever ravisheth the spirit with the sugared scent and sovereign sweetness of the fame.

Inference 1

6. Ah! my friends, do you not here taste a little how sweet the wine is, that is from the spiritual grape of faith? blessed are they, said our Lord, that hunger and thirst after righteousness, for they shall be filled; this shews that the righteousness of faith is a spiritual banquet to the spiritual convert; here in mortality, whose measure can be but small, because mortality can contain no more but a penny earnest, which fills mortality.

Inference 2

7. But then what a feast will the saint have when he hath a spiritual body, and that body filled with faith? and being so it will never want food, but such glorified creatures may ever at their pleasure go down into the cellar of their soul, and drink wine at their will.

8. Thus we see how they will be eternally nourished, it is not the wine of the natural grape that we shall drink, nor it is not the bread of natural grain that we shall eat, but that bread and wine that we shall feed on, shall be in the revelations, new and rare, that shall continually run in the souls, as in a fountain of endless joy.

9. Therefore, when Christ said unto his disciples, that he would drink no more of the fruits of the vine with them, until he drank it new with them in the kingdom of heaven; he did not mean that they should drink wine in heaven, as they drink the wine of the natural grape here on earth.

10. For though it is not denied but that grapes may grow in heaven, upon trees there, yet certain it is, there is not made the same use of them there, as is here, although they may serve for the delighting of the spiritual senses, as many other herbs, flowers, and fruits, may give a sweet scent to the spiritual senses.

Inference 3

11. But the words of Christ is clear, by saying until I drink it new with you; that is, until I drink it with you in a new way, and manner, or in another sort; it is true it is written, wine gladeneth the heart of God and man;[1] and so it doth, for the wine of the natural grape did glad the heart of God, in his anointed body, in mortal state.

Inference 4

12. Moreover, it may be said, until I drink it new with you, in reference to those new soul delights, in these new created bodies, in that new heaven and new earth, where there is continually new wisdom, and new revelation, which may be called new wine, to make glad the heart withall.

Application

13. Now when this glory is effectual, and the time accomplished, then shall there be no such a thing as hunger, or thirst, any more, but welcome fountain fulness, here human life is preserved, by outward food, as spiritual life is by inward, but when our human life is changed into divine, then shall we have no more need of outward food.

14. Therefore when all elemental matter is thrust out of us, and our spirit made of immortal fire, and our bodies thin light and transparent, answerable to the same, then shall there be no more hunger, nor thirst, as aforesaid, but welcome fountain fullness, for thy streams makes glad the city of God.

15. Then will every glorified saints' faith be the stream, and God the fountain of that stream, and as long as the fountain in God will hold, so long the city stream will hold out.

---

[1] Judg. 9, 13.

16. Not that it flows from God, to them, as to the angels, but it was first given to Adam, and from thence it is generated and derived into all his seed, and so is a generated faith in mortality, and when in its immortal state, it will then in itself become a running river of endless joys.

17. And thus hath the glorious God made his Saints of God-like glory, like himself: we shall eat the same meat, and drink the same drink as our God cloth; then shall every Saint take the cup of salvation, after their coronation, and pledge our Lord, out of that ever-running spring that bubbleth up in his own heart.

Use of consolation

18. Let this comfort the hearts of the poor afflicted souls, who hath faith, and by that faith rests on God. Although the outward man be in want, hold out a while—'tis but one night—you shall be feasted in the morning, and shall sit down in the kingdom of God; and then shall you never hunger nor thirst more, but on the contrary, your faith will afford your spiritual bodies with infinite varieties, and that without labour or toil, so that you shall have store in yourselves, like the widow's oil, which will never decrease, but will become a cruse, ever full of the water of life, &c.

CHAP. XII,

Of the Saints' Clothing in Heaven.

Doctrinal Text

1. I HAVING set forth the food of a glorified Saint, now follows the adornment wherewith the Innocent Spirit is clad and invested withal. In the Revelations by John, we read, that John saw Christ after his glorification, clothed with a garment down to the foot; now such a garment as our Lord is clothed withal, such shall we, according to our measures, that are found alive at his coming.

Explained

2. Now what was that garment that Christ, the Everlasting Father, was clothed withal; it was neither woollen nor linen, but it was his glorious body, of flesh and bone, which glittered as the sun in its strength.

Proved

3. Now as Christ's body became a garment to clothe the Invisible Spirit of Faith withal, even so will our bodies, when immortalized, be a garment of eternal glory; and hence it is that Paul compares them to Christ's body, saying, we shall be like him.

Inference 1

4. The body of mortal man, is the mortal soul's tabernacle, yet this body, which is the soul's clothing, must have clothing itself, or it cannot subsist, as also it were full of shame; for our bodies here are stained with sin, and this sin hath begot shame, and this shame hath begot fig leaves to cover it withal.

5. So that there is Jess beauty now in the soul's clothing, than in the body's clothing; that is, there is less glory upon the outward body, than there is in the covering that is put upon the outward body.

6. But after the Saints are once immortalized and glorified, then will each Saint's body become a robe and garment of eternal glory.

Inference 2

7. Then shall the king's daughter be all glorious without,[1] as well as all glorious within; then will the stain be gone, and the body will shine as the stars, and exceed them in brightness, and whiteness, and sweetness.

8. And then will the garment smell of myrrh, and aloes, and casia, out of the ivory palaces, or mansions of glory; then out of this palace will the rose of rarity arise, with sweet fragrant smells: but who can set forth the glory of this garment? Who can unfold the excellence thereof?

Third testament

9. Suppose a natural body were all covered with gold, and the glittering jewels of this world, yet the glory of it would appear but as the light of a candle, to the sun, in comparison of that glorious garment, wherewith the spiritual body is covered.

Applied

10. These things being so, who would not (with. Paul) desire to be dissolved, or at leastways new clothed, with heaven's house upon them.

---

[1] Psa. 45.

In a use of consolation

11. Comfort yourselves, or be comforted, my poor brethren; though you be clothed here but in vile raiment, yet you see the day is a coming when it shall be put off, and you clothed in change of raiment.

12. Wherefore, though many of us are in the devil's prison, yet we shall be brought forth, and honoured as Joseph was; for though many have lain among the pots, yet shall they be as the wings of a dove, covered with silver, and her feathers with yellow gold.

13. Be not, therefore, discouraged at present calamities, for the Saints are the people that the Lord of Heaven will honour, a little while, and the proud Hamans' will be down, and the poor mourning Mordecais' will be exalted to the Crown Royal, they being the people the Lord will honour.

14. But then the joy that there will be when the King of Heaven will say, Come, ye poor despised Mordecais', you that have been mourning in your sack-cloth and ashes, your shame is past, your suffering is over.

15. Come, now, let the Royal Apparel be brought, which myself doth use to wear, and the white horse that myself doth use to ride upon, which is the righteousness of faith, and the Crown Royal, which is of my own divine nature, and let my beloved ones' be arrayed therewith, for they are those I delight to honour.

16. Then shall our glory be great, and our raiment white as snow, glittering as the sun beams, and we as so many stars or suns in that upper region of light,

17. Then shall crowns be on our heads, and palms in our hands, in sign of victory; and we shall reign as kings for ever, and our clothing will never decay, but will always flourish as the flowers in May, and this will be for ever, world without end. Amen.

CHAP. XIII.

1. The Motion of a glorified Saint is as swift as thought. 2. Of the Quickness of the Eye, and of its ravishing Objects.

Doctrine 1

1. THE Saints shall not only be so glorious in body, but they shall be as swift in motion. Then will these Scriptures be fulfilled, Then shall the lame man leap as a hart, and they that wait upon the Lord shall renew their strength; they shall mount up with their spiritual body as with wings, even as eagles; they shall run, and not be weary; and they shall walk, and not be faint.

Proved

2. These sayings allude to our motional swiftness, but comes too short of it; for we shall not only be so swift as the hart on our pace on that spiritual earth, nor as swift as the eagle, in our ascent in heaven, but we shall be as swift as thought.

3. It will not be with us in our glorified state, as it is with us here; for here we are, as it were, fixed to this earth, for a natural body is not in its proper centre, but when it is fixed upon this earth; therefore if this earth or place should give way, then would this earthly body sink downward also, let it fall never so deep.

4. But it will be otherwise in a glorified body; for spiritual bodies, when they are glorified, then its own nature is its own centre; therefore the nature of it is to stand upon nothing, but can with as much ease ascend or descend, and is as swift as thought, to ascend higher and higher, be it never so high.

5. For the new heaven, being non-globell, therefore the saints can have no let or hinderance to their motional swiftness of body.

6. Here the thought is swift, but its body is slow: here we can think of a friend a hundred or five hundred miles off, and our faith doth many times motion forth upon that account, and receives some pleasure thereby.

7. But if it could as soon be there in person, as in thought, O the joy and felicity it would then have; but that would be heaven on earth, but this is reserved for the glorified body in the heavens above.

8. Now this is no mean part of our glory, that our bodies will be so light, so nimble, and of such agility, as that it can move thousands of

miles in a minute, and like lightning shoot forth themselves at their pleasure, as fiery darts in that region of rest, to divert themselves with the whole creation there.

Doctrine 2

9. Also, the Saints will be as quick in their sight, as in their bodily motion. We shall see as far as possibly we can be made capable to see, and hear as far as is possible we shall be made capable to hear.

10. Oh, glorious kingdom, where all are kings. Oh, glorious kings, where all are so light and full of agility, and so quick of sight, in a kingdom that is boundless, in which we may behold thousands of thousands of heavenly objects. But more of this hereafter.

CHAP. XIV.

The Saints shall perfectly know one another in Heaven.

Doctrine 1

1. OUR glory will still increase, for the Saints will perfectly know one another in heaven. This is a rare rose in our garland; for we shall have such God-like wisdom, as that we shall not only know those there that we have known here, but we shall know those as we never saw.

The doctrine opened

2. Yet this we are to understand, that we shall not know every one there as we knew naturally here; for our natural knowledge will be done away, that our spiritual knowledge may take place, and be all in all, for natural acquaintance and society will be forgotten.

3. Therefore we shall not know one another as to natural relations, as to know or say, this was my husband, or this was my wife, or this was father, mother, sister, child, or brother.

4. But our knowledge will be in relation to spiritual acquaintance, so that those that we have had sweet society withal, and fellowship here in the spiritual, those persons will be known by us there.

The extent of knowledge

5. Now, as the Saints meet with one another in this kingdom of eternal glory, that had communion together here in the kingdom of grace, there will their joys abound with sweet embraces, and their remembrance of their former spiritual acquaintance with each other,

will be as cups of new wine, to refresh their divine spirits with new songs of praise unto their Redeemer.

6. Now from hence, you that have a large stock of the grace of love to the brotherhood, and have conversed with, and read, or heard of, and with many eminent Saints, may gather from hence what virtue your new spiritual and glorified bodies will be possessed of.

The benefit of this knowledge

7. For this knowing each one you have conversed with, and your divine love hath thought upon, or that you have had communion withal, will not be one of the least excellences or precious pearls in your crown.

8. Now there is one thing more, my revelation of faith tells me, that we shall sooner meet with some Saints than with others, when our faith hath a motion of a visit.

How the Saints can find each other

9. Those whom they can see, after the quickest capacity, are the Prophets, Apostles, and the Witnesses of the Spirit; yea, all such as have been Ambassadors, Messengers, or Ministers of God, in any age, for each of these is known by name, and they have their several mansions; also their glory is large, and their crowns richer, than others; therefore they are discerned further.

The kingdom opened

10. So that as it is known here where the king keeps his court, so it is known there where they keep their courts; and as the kings of this earth, and lords of the same, do go their progress here, so doth the Prophets, and Prophet of Prophets, go their progress in heaven, when their wisdom moves them to it.

A way in heaven opened

11. Now how one Saint finds out another Saint, is according to my faith thus; as to the general, the glorified Saint doth mind what prophet such a Saint was under, that they have a mind to see, and then among the Saints under that prophet they can repair.

12. And although that prophet should be distant thousands of miles, and that Saint should be one in a number without number, yet in that the Saint is in motion as swift as thought; it can be there in a moment.

13. And then as soon go through that host of heaven, singing a melodious song of its former spiritual acquaintance, by reading or

hearing of such a Saint's faith and suffering, upon which song two lovers meet, and sweetly greet with an—All hail, dear brother.

The fruition of the Saints society in heaven

14. But then when those Saints meet, who have lived together in one age, and have had sweet refreshing drops of the dew of heaven, from each others' mouths, O what joy will there be? what kisses of love, and lovely embraces; then will love appear to be love, when every Saint's love makes a river of love.

15. Did Jacob and Joseph, after their long absence, when they met, fall one upon the neck of the other, in soul-ravishing love? and will they not much more in heaven, when they meet there?

16. Again, hath not the love of the company of Saints been so sweet to some, that they have gone a hundred miles endways, several times, to see the Saints, and to converse with them? This I can speak experimentally.

17. Now, if the society of Saints have been such a felicity here, what then will it be there, in their rich robes of righteousness and glory?

I Cor. 13 Proved. Opened. Cleared

18. Then shall that Scripture be fulfilled, saying, We shall know as we are known; and that Scripture which saith, there shall you suck and be satisfied, with the breasts of her consolation, and milk out, and be delighted with the abundance of her glory; then when we there see one another, our hearts shall rejoice, and our bones shall flourish as an herb, &c.

CHAP, XV.

1. Shewing of what Stature the Saints are of in Heaven. 2. And how distinguishable one from another.

Doctrine 1

1. IF it should be queried in what stature the Saints shall rise, and of what complexion? the answer may be from those words of Paul, that shall come to a perfect man, unto the measure of the fulness of Christ.[1]

2. Therefore look what stature Christ was on; the same stature shall we be on, for we shall be like him.

---

[1] Ephe. 4, 13.

Proved

3. For as Christ, the Son of Adam, was like the first Adam, so shall we be like both these Adams', and the same in stature; for the same stature the first Adam is of, the same is the second, and the same shall we be.

Secondly

4. Therefore it matters not whether we die infants or old men; for we shall all have one stature, though not all the same degree of glory, so that there will neither be dwarfs nor giants, but the middle stature, of some five feet and a half high.

Thirdly

5. Again, this we may mind, that every glorified Saint, though it is both in form, nature, and stature with God, yet will that supernatural nature be of that variety, as to give a distinction whereby to know each from other.

6. For as it is wonderful to see the extent of nature here in this kind, for amongst all the children of men, can hardly be found two that do exactly answer each other in complexion, but there is some difference to be discerned, though thousands be together, yet are they all distinguishable in countenance, though of one form, nature, or stature.

7. Why thus it will be with us in heaven, and the Angels likewise. Our colour, our glory, and countenance will be distinguishable; it will be just according as the variety of divine properties abound; every property gives the complexion, therefore look what complexion a Saint hath in his resurrection and glorification; that complexion shall he retain, and be known by to eternity.

8. For as an earthly nature gives the complexion here, so doth a heavenly nature there.

9. Here wit and beauty flows from fine blood, as the cause thereof; even from blood in a rational fire, as well as a divine.

10. But there their complexions and beauty flows from a spiritual love-fire, not from blood there; for there will be no blood in our new spiritual bodies.

11. Therefore the divine fire gives the colour; then will the face be ruddy, and the cheeks look like the rose of Sharon, and the eyes will be quick and splendent, like sparks of fire.

12. This is the glory of our Father's children: by-and-bye follows the glory of our Father's kingdom.

CHAP. XVI.

1. Of the great Extent of the Kingdom of Heaven. 2. And the Nature of that Spiritual Earth.

Doctrine 1

1. THE kingdom of eternal glory the Saints are to possess, is of that vastness, that the Saint may ascend as high or as low as he will to eternity, without let or hindrance.

Doctrine 2

2. Again, he may likewise stand and walk upon a spiritual earth, and crystal waters, at his pleasure; although the nature of a glorified spirit is to stand upon nothing, because its own nature is its own centre, so that there needs no sitting nor standing for rest, for motional assent hath no painfulness in it.

Doctrine 3

3. Nevertheless, at its pleasure, it can leap and dance there with each other, as the young lambs upon the green hills here; so then that saying will be fulfilled, Then shall the lame man leap as a hart; they shall run, and not be weary; and they shall walk, and not faint: then shall the Virgin rejoice in the dance, &c.

Inference 1

4. This is that new heaven, and new earth, wherein dwelleth righteousness; it is called hew, because the bodies of the elect were never there before.

Inference 2

5. Again, it is called a new heaven, and new earth, because all things in this world waxeth older and older, as a garment, unto an eternal dissolution.

Inference 3

6. When as the person of God, Elect-men, and Angels in that new heaven, and new earth, become newer and newer, younger and younger, in all unspeakable, new, and glorious delights, continually springing up both within and without.

7. Furthermore, though the Saints may ascend as high and as low as they will, yet is that earth of an infinite circumference; there is no

comparison betwixt that earth and this, this earth is but as the prick of a pin, to that.

8. For this we are to know, that the firmament, where the stars move, doth bound this world, and is much more in circumference than this earth is; how much more then is that new heaven and new earth, that is so far beyond it?

Doctrine 4

9. That world, or new earth was first formed, and this after; whatever here was created or made, was to living creatures in his six day's work, or to any tree, herbs, or fruit, was all made as from that creation above, being the platform, or pattern by which all things here were made by.

Heb. 13 Proved

10. Therefore, it is written, by faith we understand that the worlds were formed by the word of God; so that things that are made are not made of things which do appear; and in another place it is written, that Moses was commanded to make the tabernacle according to the pattern he had seen.

Secondly

11. So that it is clear, that things which we see here, are made of things which do not visibly appear, then they must have their pattern from things that do not appear; but are invisible to us, though visible in the other world.

Thirdly

12. Therefore all variety of fruits, flowers, trees, grass, herbs, together with all beasts, birds, fish, and fowl, are all made according to that creation above the stars.

Inference

13. And if there be any hurtful creature now, or poisonous herb, it had no being in the creation, for before the fall of Adam, there was no hurtful thing upon earth, but the tree of knowledge, treated on in my Second and Third Parts, now from that tree came all evil unto mankind, and from mankinds disobedience came all evil, that is in the creature, or all creatures that are evil.

Inference 2

14. From them sprang the thorn, and the thistle, and many a hurtful herb, and all such sensible creatures, that are evil, had its production from this curse, nature purging itself of that depraved life that is in it, hence comes your adders and; snakes, serpents, toads, frogs, vipers, and all manner of venemous creatures.

Inference 3

15. Thus we see that nature is dependant to God and serviceable to man, and works continually for good to the creation; God finished all his works in six days, but nature is to work as long as the whole universe shall stand.

Inference 4

16. Now if it were not for this working of nature, the creation could not. subsist, for that venemous, poisonable, or corrupted matter that is by privation of a natural blessing, would destroy man and beast if it were not for natures quickening it into life, for to purge the earth by feeding upon that poisonable matter, it being its own nature, and so fit food for it.

Inference 5

17. Again, here you may see that nature works like unto God, in that its works is to bring life out of death, for the death of one thing is the life of another; hence it is that nature is looked upon as a God, and by the blind atheists it is looked upon as the only God, because it gives a life by putrefaction.

Inference 6

18. They not seeing how that it is necessary it should work so under God, seeing God hath put a power in it, for by virtue of an equal as well as a powerful proportion of the four elements, it may form the matter not only into a conceiveable life, but also into male and female, and so come to be capable of generation, though in a different way, as some in the ear, some in the mouth, and other parts, according to the operation of nature.

Inference 7

19. By this we may perceive that there is many creatures, that are nature's workmanship in this world, and had not being in the creation, as cats and rats, &c.

20. But all sorts of cattle, fish, and fowl, with infinite other creatures, had their being then, and were all made out of that creation above, as all the trees, flowers, and fruits, as aforesaid.

21. Now the manner of the creation in this world out of that above, my faith tells was in this manner, following;

Inference 8

22. The Creator, in this his creation of every living creature in heaven, took one of each sort and kind, they being all male creatures, and mortallized the same, sending them down, and so out of each took a female, and so from hence came that union of natures by which every one, through an instinct in nature, cleaveth to his own kind.

Inference 9

23. There is some that do hold, that all this whole creation of living creatures, shall at the end of the world ascend to heaven, from whence they were taken, and they ground from that saying of the Apostle, speaking of the creation, being surely arrived with the Saints in heaven, which, according to their kind, groaned long for deliverance.[1]

Inference 10

24. But to speak of the creation above, and let this creation of living creatures alone, to rest in the dust: you are to know that all that creation above, are in sweet union and harmony, each with other, every creature there is full of love, not only to its own kind, but each to other, that is the kingdom where the lion and the lamb lie down together.[2]

CHAP. XVII.

1. A Kingdom of Love. 2. And of Lovely Things.

Doctrine 1.

1 THIS kingdom of eternal glory is a kingdom of love, there, is not one spark of anger there, for there love is without opposition, as this place is a vale of tears, so it is of love and anger, each runs its round, and we cannot help it.

---

[1] Rom. 8, 21. 22.

[2] Isa. 11, 6. & 65, 25.

Illustrated.

2. If we were not angry in sin, but unto sin. It were well; but afflictions are sometimes so pressing, that we are not only unjustly angry, but are ready to justify unjust anger.

3. But, Oh! happy country, where love is all in all, because no sorrow is there, nor anger; here we are pettish and foolish, and ready to fall out with our best friends, and after, we relent, and are troubled at our unbridled anger.

4. Love is now the comfort of our life, but then it will be the crown of our life, and there shall we love and be loved, and loaded with love as the bee is with honey, and God will set his love on us all, and this his love shall rest on us.

Zeph 3, 17 Applied

5. There is a sweet saying by the Prophet Zeph. the Lord, thy God, (said the prophet) shall save, he will rejoice over thee with joy, he will rest in his love, he will joy over thee with singing.

6. Here is love indeed, this makes glad the city of God, for this city rests in the arms of his love, he rejoicing over them with singing; this will ravish the heart of the elect with astonishing joy, not only to hear the songs of your Lord and Saviour, but to hear the songs of the praises and love of you, and how dear you are to him.

7. Will not this now strike the flint of the heart, and make the fire ascend to heaven, in praises here? how much more will it do it there, where the holy love-fire is ever burning?

8. No heart can now conceive, nor tongue can utter what joy and love, and songs of joy and love, will be betwixt the Redeemer and the redeemed.

9. And as the Saints do all join together singing songs of praise unto their good God, even so likewise they, as children of one father, and heirs of one kingdom, do all mutually embrace each other, and kiss each other, with lovely songs, as they meet, they sweetly greet in this wise;

Songs of joy and praise

10. Hale, my dear brother, have I met with thee?
    O welcome into this felicity,
    Where perfect love and concord doth abound,
    No strife or discord in it can be found.

11. Come, let us love, and in love let us greet
    Our blessed God when we with him do meet;
    O sovereign sweetness, our joy, and eke our crown,
    What thou hast given us, at thy feet we cast down.

12. For thou hast redeemed us with thy precious blood,
    Of God-head-life, laid down in thy manhood;
    Our faith, in which was made the seal of heaven,
    And now the glory of it thou hast given.

13. You are my jewels, will our Lord reply,
    And welcome now into your master's joy,
    For I joy in you, as well as you in me,
    And take you for my sweet society.

14. All my delight on earth was amongst you;
    You had my promise, and now you find it true;
    You did believe me, now shall joys abound,
    Possess all joys that in my courts are found, &c.

CHAP. XVIII.

1. Heaven a Kingdom of Everlasting Peace and Rest.

Doctrine 1

1. AGAIN we shall there possess everlasting peace, without any disturbance, then will that Scripture be fulfilled, that saith, that peace shall be extended as a river,[1]

2. Here we have some drops of peace to keep us from despair, it comes dropping as from a limbeck, but there it will run from the spout, or rather as the river itself, being a flood of peace, that is, peace in abundance; this flood of beatitude will sufficiently be-dew all the whole region of heaven, where we shall eternally dwell.

3. How sweet a thing is peace and quietness; here we are willing to be at quiet with man as we are with God, and our own consciences, but cannot; but as our God is the prince of peace, so his kingdom is a quiet and peaceable possession.

Doctrine 2

4. In this kingdom is no sueing for honour or preferment, but all the hearts of the Saints shall will one thing, as if they were one thing, when any one hath a new joy from a new revelation all will joy in it.

---

[1] Isa. 66, 12.

Exhortation

5. Tug hard for this, you Saints, for this is the kingdom of concord, my meaning is, not that you shall strive and labour as reason doth, with praying and preaching, fasting and mourning, thinking to obtain it by that means, but you must tug hard with the world, that they overcome you not, but hold your faith fast, although it should be unto death.

Applied to the first doctrine

6. A little while and this kingdom is yours, and then you need not fear, for there will be neither enemy to assault, nor enticement to carry away, but sovereign and sure security, and secure quietness, and quiet joyfulness, and joyful blessedness.

Doctrine 3. Peace opened

7. Follow peace, for there is no other righteousness available, but that which is sowed in peace and love, this is the seed of heaven, sow it therefore, and reap in heaven, according to the measure of peace, so will be the joy and glory, for what is peace, but a settled joy in a quiet soul.

Doctrine 4

8. Again, this kingdom is a kingdom of rest, as well as peace, behold the extent thereof in the discourse following.

CHAP. XIX.

Shewing a Cessation from all Toil and Trouble, and from all Sorrow and Mourning.

1. THIS kingdom of heaven is not only a kingdom of peace, but rest likewise; for,

Doctrine proved

2. First we shall rest from all our toil and hard labour that our necessity requires us to take, in order to the maintaining of ourselves and families, and this is no small burthen to be freed from, for the generality of the Saints are poor, and have little of this world's goods, or if some have, can scarce hold it and their faith both, but persecution takes it away.

3. Furthermore they can hardly tell how to live, if they have but small, because it cannot oppress nor defraud, cousen or cheat, and dissemble as hypocrites and prophane worldlings can.

4. Therefore is compelled to hard labour, getting his living with the sweat of his brow, lying down with weary bones.

5. But Oh I sweet rest that is reserved for us, thither do we hasten, and when mortality is swallowed up, then will our rest be glorious, and our bones shall flourish as an herb.

Doctrine 2

6. Secondly, we shall rest from all sorrows, for there will be no more sorrow there; here we are continually exposed to sorrows and troubles; man is born to trouble as the spark fly upwards, we are brought forth of the womb in sorrow, and our mother's sorrows are multiplied by our birth, so that we may be called the sons of sorrow.[1]

7. This world is a vale of tears, and an inlet to all sorrows to all Saints, be they Prophets or Apostles, they cannot be exempted, nay they have the greatest share of sorrows, because they have the greatest share of sufferings, because they are appointed for the greatest glory.

8. The reason why the Saints have so much sorrow is, because they must suffer their hell, in the devil's heaven, therefore, said Christ, ye shall weep and lament, but the world shall rejoice, and you shall be sorrowful, but your sorrow shall be turned into joy.[2]

Text applied

9. From hence we see that our God hath disposed of joys and sorrows by turns, we are to mourn while worldlings rejoice, that then when they mourn, we may rejoice.[3]

10. Now you weak Saints, you are too dainty and curious, if besides the joys of heaven laid up for you, you should yet look for a liberal portion of delights and pleasures of this world, you cannot learn Christ but by the cross, nor gain heaven but by contempt of earth, mind Scripture order.[4]

11. But you, my friends, that have and do suffer for your faith,[5] and that are made to weep now, for sorrow of heart, you shall then

---

[1] Isa. 14, 3. & 35, 10.
[2] John 16, 20.
[3] Psa. 38, 17.
[4] Jer. 20, 18. Matt. 10, 38. Luke 14, 32. 1 Cor. 2, 2. Gal. 2, 20 & 6, 14.
[5] Isa. 65,1 4.

sing for joy of heart, then shall that prophecy of David be fulfilled, they that sow in tears, shall reap in joy.[1] So Revel. 21, 4.

12. Then shall that sweet promise of the Lord, by David, be fulfilled, their soul shall be as a watered garden, and they shall not sorrow any more at all,[2] but then shall the virgin rejoice in the dance, and I will turn their mourning into joy; and again, the ransomed of the Lord shall come to Zion, with singing and everlasting joy upon their heads, they shall obtain joy and gladness, and sorrow and sighing shall flee away.[3]

CHAP. XX.

Shewing a Cessation from all Fears and Cares.

Doctrine 1

1. THIRDLY, we shall also rest from all our fears and cares incident to us in this mortality; here we are pestered with very many fears and cares, some necessary, and some unnecessary, which many times makes our lives troublesome to us; our living amongst wicked persecuting men, is one cause of our fear, and it was one cause of Jacob's fear.

2. Therefore Jacob prayed unto God, saying, deliver me I pray thee, from the hand of my brother, for I fear him, lest he will come and smite me, and the mother with the children.[4]

3. The same fear was in Abraham and Isaac, but most vehement it was in Jacob, and his sons; first in his sons when they were roughly or severely examined before Joseph, and charged for spite, and again, when their monies was found in their sacks' mouths.[5]

4. Then began that passion of fear to revive again, and upon their return home, telling their father what evil had befallen them, and how that they had engaged to bring their youngest brother, Benjamin, before the prince of Egypt, then was Jacob's soul surprised with fear, trouble, and anguish of spirit.

5. But upon Jacob's sons' return into Egypt, and being sent for to come before Joseph, then they began to fear they should be made bond-slaves, but most especially when the cup was found in Benjamin's sack, then did fear and horror lay hold on them, and the

---

[1] Psa. 126, 5.
[2] Jer. 31, 12. Verse 13.
[3] Isa. 51, 11.
[4] Gen. 32, 11.
[5] Gen. 43.

fire of affliction went through every part of them, until it found out their iniquity.

6. Therefore, said they unto Joseph, what shall we say unto our Lord, and how shall we clear ourselves, God hath found out our iniquity? as if they should say, we have sinned here too far, and now do we suffer for it, we have not a word to speak, it was found in Benjamin's sack, so that both he and we are thy servants, do with us what thou wilt.[1]

7. And as Jacob's sons passed through much fear and purturbation of their minds in their lives, even so did their posterity in the land of Egypt, being there in servitude two hundred years.

8. But most especially at the time of their flight when the sea hemmed them up on one side, and their enemies on the other, so that all hopes of safety was taken away.

9. Then came fear and horror and forced upon them, which had made them almost as dead men, had not Moses comforted them by these words, saying, fear not, stand still and behold the salvation of the Lord, which he will show to you this day.[2]

Doctrine 2. Proved before, as also hereafter

10. All saints have ever been subject to fear, because they are exposed, and ever lie open to affliction both inward and outward, more than any other people, for though they be the people of God's love yet are they the object of the world's wrath, and must come under the rod of railing Rabshaker.

Doctrine 3

11. And furthermore in that many times sin is made the punishment of sin, and suffering lies upon all sin, therefore the Saints are as much afraid of their internal enemies as external, and so they are afraid of their own evil thoughts, which provokes them to disobedience, and so becomes an inlet to fear.

12. But lest their fears should too much abound, God through his mercy, puts a stop to it, either by a promise of deliverance or by deliverance itself, and so makes joy take place of fear, as it is written, say to them that are of a fearful heart, be strong, fear not, behold your God will come, he will come and save you.[3]

---

[1] Gen. 44, 12.
[2] Exod. 14, 13.
[3] Ezek. 35, 4.

13. Again, it is written, fear not I have redeemed thee, I am with thee, thou shalt not be ashamed, fear not daughter of Zion, fear none of those things that thou shalt suffer, fear not little flock, he that looseth his life shall find it, fear not thou worm, Jacob.[1]

14. By those things the Saint's life is preserved, otherways griefs and fears would be intolerable.

15. But, O! glorious state, when we shall come to rest from all fears, why in heaven there will be no such a thing as fear, for as the Prophet Isaiah saith, it shall come to pass at that day, the Lord shall give thee rest from thy sorrow, and from thy fear, and from thy hard bondage, wherein thou wast made to serve.[2]

16. For in this kingdom of Heaven will be no purturbation of mind, no there will not be that passion of hope, for hope will be swallowed up in the enjoyment of the things hoped for, but there will be perfect fruition, and fear shall never enter into the borders thereof.

Exhortation

17. Therefore you that are of a fearful heart, have strength, get boldness, and, if fear of offending enter your hearts, let the love of obedience dispossess it, and if fear of oppression possess you, let your eye look upon the recompense of reward, which will he vengeance to those that trouble you, but to you, rest with God.[3]

18. By this means, fear will be extinguished, courage augmented, and love fortified and inflamed, to bear you through a tedious pilgrimage until you come at your rest.

---

[1] Isa. 35, 4. & 43, 1., & 54, 4. & chap 41. Luke 12, 32. John 12, 15.
[2] Isa. 14, 3.
[3] 2 Thess. 1.

CHAP. XXI.

1. We shall be freed from all Sufferings. 2. And delivered from all Afflictions and Persecutions. 3. And Triumph over Death, Devil, and Hell. 4. A Sonnet of the Joys of Heaven.

Doctrine 1

1. MOREOVER we shall rest from all manner of disturbances, from all sickness, or sadness, from all troubles, and fears, from all pain and prisons, and also we shall be freed from all persecuting devils. [1]

2. Then you that did loose your lives for Christ, shall find them, and you shall be brought no more before the devil's judgment seat, to deny or defy the faith of Christ the true God.

3. But when our tormenters are tormented, then comes our songs of triumph, for our pains being past we shall feel their strokes no more.

Doctrine 2

4. Then shall each Saint shew to each other, the prints and tokens of the marks of their martyrdom, and it shall be so conspicuous in some, that he that runs may read, a part of the nature of the Saint's suffering, upon the sight of his spiritual body.

5. For where the devil's darts did make entrance, the print of that wound will visibly appear, and yet no deformity in that part when immortalized.

6. For as the print of the wounds that our Lord Christ received in his natural body,[2] remained in his spiritual body after his resurrection, even so it will with the Saints, and that place will shine as a star, or glitter as a jewel when the body is glorified.

Doctrine 3

7. Then blessed Paul, happy art thou, with all the rest of the Apostles, and messengers of God, that suffered martyrdom for their faith and ministry, your stripes and strokes will be turned into golden streams, you that could kiss the cross shall then wear the crown.

8. Then may it be said, what now is become of all your strokes and imprisonments, of your taunts, scoffs, and scorns, that your enemies

---

[1] 2 Thess. 1.
[2] John 20, 27.

cast upon you? what is become now of all your pains, griefs, and groans, for all your hard usage?

9. Where are all the task masters of Egypt, and your grievous burthens that were on your backs, the thorns that were in your flesh, and the swords that were in your sides?

10. Now is Zacharias got from his murderers, and place of his murder, Daniel, Jeremiah, and Joseph, feels no more the pain of imprisonment, hunger, thirst, or nakedness, nor Isaiah the pains of the same; now are the Apostles brought from under their shackles, their prison doors are opened, they are raised from death, and delivered out of the claws of the lion.

11. John that was beheaded, his body and his head are met again, and a massive crown of glory is set upon it; Stephen now feels not the stones, nor Agnes the sword in her side, that she so willingly did embrace, when she saw the executioner coming, with a drawn sword in his hand, she crying out, saying, I will willingly receive into my paps the length of his sword, and into my breast will I draw the force thereof, even unto the hilt, that I may be married to Christ my spouse.

12. Neither doth Italia, the virgin, feel now the pain of the halter, nor of that devil hangman's instruments that pulled her one joint from another, nor the talons of wild beasts scratching her sides, to the hard bones, her pain is past, her joy is come, and she is come to her joy, her Lord Christ, whom she loved unto death; I speak as if it were already done, because faith is sure it will be done, and lives in eternity.

13. Now also is Saint Lawrence, that mirror of patience, got from off the gridiron, he feels not the pain of his frying any more, yet in the midst of his frying fiery trial, he could pour forth these words, saying,

14. This side is roasted enough,
    Now turn up, O! tyrant great,
    And try, whether roasted or raw,
    Thou countest the better meat.

15. Could this blessed martyr express himself so in the time of his tears? how then will he sing in the day of his triumph? methinks I hear him sing, (though that time is not yet come, but my faith living in eternity, looks upon it as; at present being.)

16. O! well, beloved body now,
    My darling and my dear,
    The gridiron and the fiery flame,
    Cannot touch us here.

17. The pain is past, the joy is come,
>   The crown is on our head,
>   Put on us by our soverign Lord,.
>   For whose sake we suffered.

18. And now, O! tyrant, that did scorch
>   Me in the fiery flame,
>   As thou madest me drink of that cup,
>   Now pledge me in the same.

19. And when thy fiery brimstone soul
>   And body, down is tied,
>   After ten thousand years, or more,
>   Turn up the other side.

20. O! blessed be my glorious Lord,
>   That hath rewarded me,
>   And poured down his vengeance great,
>   On such great tyranny.

21. And you blessed Apostles all,
>   How dear are you to me,
>   Which by your doctrine, hath me brought,
>   To this felicity, joy, and glory.

22. So having been long upon this subject, it being the delicate dish my soul delighted to feed upon, shall now conclude the same in these verses, following:—

1. My studious heart meditating,
>   Good matter doth indite,
>   My subject is,
>   Of the Saint's bliss,
>   Of which I mean to write.

2. If I the tongue of Angels had,
>   Yet cannot I declare,
>   The mighty joys,
>   Above the skies,
>   Prepared for us are.

3. Yet this I know, in measure small,
>   That we shall there enjoy,
>   A kingdom's crown,
>   That will weigh down,
>   All earthly majesty.

4. For we that have received faith,
>   From our good God above,
>   Do plainly see,

        And none but we,
        His glory and his love.

5. For this we know, that his person,
        Doth glitter like the sun,
        Yea, is more light,
        And shines more bright,
        Than ever it hath done.

6. Behold, now, shall not the Saint's joys,
        Make them to shout and sing,
        Seeing they be,
        Made strong to see,
        Their Lord and Sovereign King.

7. Also our bodies, they will shine,
        With sparkling beams of light,
        The ruby,
        And the diamond,
        Will not shine half so bright.

8. Our eyes, our ears will be so quick,
        So sparkling, and so clear,
        A thousand mile,
        Without all toil,
        At one time see and hear.

9. Our bodies likewise, they will be,
        As swift as any thought,
        For to ascend,
        Where is no end,
        Or any side found out.

10. For heaven it is non globell,
        Therefore the Saints they may,
        Ascend on high,
        Infinitely,
        Without all stop or stay.

11. Also in the same glorious place,
        Or kingdom without end,
        There likewise,
        Is all rarities,
        Yet nothing to offend.

12. There is all manner of creatures
        In heaven, as here below,
        They differ not,
        In form one jot,

But in glory they do.

13. For they being all immortal,
       All males, and void of ire,
       Their nature's life,
       Is sensative,
       The Angel's pure desire.

14. Adam's nature it is the same
       As God's is, which is faith,
       But Angels all,
       Are rational,
       Even as the Scriptures saith.

15. Yet Saints, Angels, and all creatures,
       Full of glory shall be,
       Sense hath some star,
       Reason much more,
       Yet short of faith's decree.

16. For faith is a well-spring of life,
       Which in the Saints do rise,
       With new increase,
       Of love and peace.
       And of celestial joys.

17. So that the soul is ravished
       With the same joys it hath,
       Considering
       That running spring,
       That doth flow out from faith.

18. Again, I say, a further joy,
       That there we shall embrace,
       Our God shall we
       Most perfectly,
       Behold his blessed face.

19. Also our spiritual senses,
       No sweet objects shall want,
       For every thing
       Is ravishing
       For to delight the Saint.

20. Again, there is a spiritual earth
       For Saints to tread upon,
       Shining most bright
       With radiant light,
       Like to the jasper stone.

21. Also there is all manner of trees,
        Herbs, grass, fruits, as here
        These perishing,
        Those flourishing,
        For ever, and for ever.

18. Also there is all manner of flowers,
        That do there do grow,
        What colours there,
        Doth then appear,
        Will be a glorious show.

19. With chirping birds, on every tree,
        Most sweetly there they sing,
        With notes so high,
        Melodiously,
        That all the place doth ring.

20. But when we Saints do all ascend,
        And on our harps do play,
        Angels us meet,
        And sweetly greet,
        And thus begin to say.

21. All glory, laud, and praise be given
        To Christ Jesus our King,
        Then all Saints they
        Amen do say,
        And then begin to sing.

22. O! glorious Lord and sweet Saviour,
        What joys hast thou us given,
        What tongues of praise,
        With golden keys
        To harp in thy new heaven.

23. Then like young lambs on the green-hills,
        We'll leap and skip for joy,
        And when we please
        Shall at our ease
        As swift as eagles fly.

24. And thus farewell, my true friends all,
        Until we there do meet,
        For then we shall,
        When we meet all,
        Each other sweetly greet.

                        Finis without finis.

The Author having left a blank page, by mistake, in his MMS. inserted the following verses, which occurred in the middle of a chapter, and the subject not being connected with the chapter, it was thought best to insert them at the end of the work.

1. Rejoice my friends, all ye,
    That sensible now be,
    Of redemption,
    By Christ alone,
    From every evil way.

2. For he is our light and life,
    Our freedom from all strife,
    Our only joy,
    The reason why,
    I shall declare in brief.

3. For he saved us from sin,
    Which we had wallowed in,
    By faith in those,
    Whom he had chose,
    Amongst the sons of men.

4. Let now the world delight,
    In darkness and in night,
    But we will sing,
    To Christ our king,
    From his most glorious light.

5. Our sins are washed away,
    No guilt or stain doth stay,
    By the life's blood,
    Of Christ's manhood,
    Which he for us did pay.

6. He being God and Man,
    In one single person,
    Did not deny,
    For us to die,
    Because we were his own.

7. Behold a mystery,
    The Lord of Life did die,
    Both natures pure,
    Did death endure,
    Three days in grave did lie.

8. But death it was too weak,
      The Lord through it did break,
      And conquered death,
      Sin hell and earth,
      For all his elect's sake.

9. So did ascend on high,
      Above the starry sky.
      For to abide,
      Being glorified,
      To all eternity.

10. This is our God alone,
      We have no more than one,
      Christ, God, and Man,
      In one person,
      Clothed with flesh and bone.

11. Who doth this God despise,
      So glorious in our eyes,
      Shall never get,
      No benefit,
      By Christ's own sacrifice.

12. But happy shall they be,
      That understand truly,
      What God hath done,
      In his own Son,
      And knows this mystery.

13. But now I here intend,
      To draw unto an end,
      Farewell to you,
      That this doth view,
      And not it reprehend.

THE END.

Printed by W. SMITH, King Street, Long Acre

A
SYSTEM
of
RELIGION,

TREATING OF THE FOLLOWING HEADS:

I. Of the Nature of GOD, and that Jesus Christ is the Only One and True GOD.

II. Of the Trinity, in a manner wholly differing from either the *Athanasians* or *Arians*, nearer to the plain literal Text of the Scripture, and less liable to philosophical objections.

III. Of the Devil; that he is no where to be found, but incarnate in man.

IV. Of the Soul's dying with the Body until the Resurrection, shewing that the notion of an immaterial Soul distinct from the body, is an inconceivable philosophical absurdity, and against the whole tenor of the Scripture.

V. That there are in man two principles natural to his constitution, a good and a bad, which necessarily determine his actions, and are at enmity with each other; and how to know which is predominant.

VI. Of Predestination.

VII. A philosophical manner of accounting for the Resurrection.

FAITHFULLY COLLECTED FROM A CURIOUS MANUSCRIPT
FOUND AMONG THE PAPERS OF

THOMAS TOMKINSON, Gent.

LONDON:

RE-PRINTED BY T. GOODE, 30 AYLESBURY STREET,

1857.

PRINTED IN THE YEAR 1729.

REVISED AND CORRECTED BY ISAAC FROST, Sen.,

AND RE-PRINTED FOR

ISAAC FROST, WILLIAM CATES and JOSEPH GANDAR

1857.

PREFACE.

It is the great blessing and privilege of Protestant liberty, that the right of interpreting and reasoning upon the Holy Scriptures, is not only preserved in its *natural channel* of private judgment, but *freed* from the *slavery* of implicit faith, and usurped claims of infallible authority; which will plead for any *seeming particularity* in the following treatise. And, as its designs being to reconcile some difficult points of religion, in a manner that appeared the most rational, in order to vindicate religion itself, from the bold and shocking treatment of some modern pretenders to free thinking, so this will be a sufficient defence of the undertaking.

The ensuing treatise, as by the title we are already informed, presents us with a system of religion, having Uniformity in its parts, perfectly consistent with itself, and consonant to the literal tenour of the Scriptures, especially as they are translated into the vulgar tongues. Yet is here no notion of any *immaterial being* at all; but the author proves the *mind,* or *soul of man,* to be material and mortal till the resurrection; that there is no *spirit devil* distinct from *man;* and that there are two Seeds a good and bad, which are originally and by generation, in a man's constitution.

So that, I think, every one who professes himself a Christian, (let his manner of worship be what it will) ought to hold himself highly indebted to him, for this honest attempt to rescue the text of the Scriptures (by giving it a direct, plain, and simple construction) from the darkness in which abundance of atheistical enthusiasts have always, to some degree or other, artfully and assiduously endeavoured to cloud and involve it; and for his asserting, by the virtue of mere faith, the literal meaning of the sacred writings, in opposition to the proud and perplexing spirit of factious Reason, whose assistance he would scorn, though it would make for his purpose.

However this is evident, that he hath accounted for *Scripture-predestination,* by his principle of the two Seeds:—And that by showing, that it is only a part of the wicked Angel himself, produced in the generation of mankind, which is punished, he has, in some measure, made it more reconcileable to justice, than the common predestination: and I do not see, but that he has done this with great force.—And if you admit, with him, that *reason* must not interpose with *Holy Writ,* but that the Scripture is in its own plain sense, an indisputable authority; and allow him only to take the fall of man in an allegorical sense, (which I think he has strongly justified from Ezekiel xxxvii.3 to the end) I say, I cannot see it will be easy to refute him.

The other principle of the Souls sleeping, might have been supported by the same arguments; as also a philosophical turn might have been given to his excluding all immaterial beings out of his system of religion: For some Philosophers teach, by many strong arguments, that man can have no notion of an immaterial substance: And some go so far as to say, it is nonsense, since all our ideas are of what our external senses see, or compounded of what they have seen, which can be nothing but matter.

Now, who could have expected that these principles could be consistent with Christianity, or with any religion at all? Yet, you see here, he hath a complete *system of Christianity,* agreeable to the Soul's sleeping, and that there is no Immaterial Being; and has proved, that the Soul of man lives not, but during the life of the body till the resurrection.

The aforesaid principles are so strongly supported by the plain literal words of several texts of Scripture, that admitting him what no Christian can deny him, with the absolute authority of the Scripture, without the interposition of Human Reason, and there can be no answering him.

There is something in his accounting for the scriptural appearances of the Devil, which seems liable to some small objection; but when we consider the surprising turn he has given to the temptation of Christ, by declaring the tempter to be a subtle ruler of the Jews, one cannot help being amazed to see so unexpected a system made so perfect, and so strongly defended.

The resurrection answers all the purposes of the Christian religion, and therefore makes this scheme perfectly orthodox. And his expecting, that a *new body* will be struck out of some particle of the *old;* containing the spark of life or fire, as a grain of wheat does the vegetative life of its kind, which brings forth a new plant, yet visibly dies itself; this, I say, hath again given a very agreeable and strong turn to the whole. And if he had thought proper to have had recourse to the philosophy of the infinite Divisibility of matter, it would greatly have helped him.

But I have nothing to do to assist him; neither would he give me any thanks for it, was he capable of knowing it: for he had, what he strongly believed, a much greater dictator, and therefore declined all Helps from Reason and Philosophy.

The treatises which have of late been published against all revealed religion; and the scurrilous and profane ridicule, which it has particularly suffered from the madness and buffoonry of a late author, ought to make the publication of this work esteemed the more by every impartial and considerate Reader.

A

SYSTEM

OF

RELIGION,

SINGULAR AND SURPRISING.

Mat. xiii. [1] 37, 38, 39, 40, 41, 42, 43.

He answered, and said unto them, He that soweth the good Seed, is the Son of Man.

The Field is the World: The good seed are the Children of the Kingdom; but the Tares are the Children of the wicked One.

The Enemy that sowed them is the Devil: The Harvest is the End of the World; and the Reapers are the Angels.

As therefore the Tares are gathered, and burnt in the Fire: So shall it be in the End of this World.

The Son of Man shall send forth his Angels, and they shall gather out of his Kingdom all Things that offend, and them that do iniquity:

And shall cast them into a furnace of fire; there shall be wailing and gnashing of teeth.

Then shall the Righteous shine forth as the Sun in the Kingdom of their Father: Who hath ears to hear let him hear.

---

[1] The above general test commences Matthew xiii. 3.

CHAP. I.

The first Doctrine which is taught in this Text, is, *That this Son of Man is the Lord Jesus Christ; who is the only true God*: and though he is called by several titles, as Father, Son and Spirit, yet he is not, nor can he be proved to be, any other, than ONE personal Glory in the Form of a Man; nor was he any other before time, in time, and to all eternity will remain so.

THAT the Son of Man should be the Eternal God is a great mystery to know, and to declare; yet the knowledge thereof is revealed to us so far, that to our understanding it appears, that he who made Man, became Man, and dwelt among us.

He that was the Seedsman became seed himself; therefore called (Gen. iii) the seed of the woman, because he took *Seed* of the Virgin Mary, which was that of Abraham, which was that of Adam, which was the *seed* of God: So that he took upon him his own nature, but changed into the condition of mortality, by dying unto his own nature which was made mortal, and so quickening in that mortal nature, he became the Son of Man as to the human nature; but as to the divine nature he was the very God as well as very Man.

John xvii. 3, it is written, It is Life eternal to know the true God, and Jesus Christ whom he hath sent.

These two distinctions, (viz.) The true God and — he hath sent; doth not divide the titles into two persons any more than those other sayings of Paul: Phil. iv. 20. 1 Thes. i. 3 and iii. 11. [Now unto God] and [our Father be Glory] but it is so expressed, referring to the twofold appearance of God.

Hence the meaning of these words is no more than if it were read thus, "It is eternal life to know that Jesus Christ is the true God." Thus that Scripture is unfolded, and joins and twists itself with this other Scripture, He that hath the Son hath life, 1 John v, 12. Now these two sayings joined together with a third become impregnable. He that hath the Son hath the Father also, 1 John ii. 23.

God was from eternity: That is, He was without all beginning, and before all time; therefore let none ask these questions, What was before God? Or how God came to be God? For nothing can be before or after Eternity; nor is there any knowledge of the beginning of what had no beginning. Therefore a Being that is from eternity cannot know its own beginning. God was himself alone, before any sensible living creature appeared in his sight, and yet did he not want company to associate himself with, because he was a kingdom in himself. For this we are to mind, that our God is a kingdom himself, and a kingdom in himself; therefore in his mortal state He called himself the kingdom.

Luke x. 11. And John calls him after his glorification, the new Jerusalem, and the City of God. Rev. xxi. 2.

And our Lord may most fitly be called a kingdom and city, if we seriously ponder in our minds, the variety of those divine qualifications that are inherent in his blessed person: For these glorious and heavenly properties, operating in the person of God, do make him become a city in himself; for what necessity of much company without, when there is such society within, and in such harmony; and it must needs be, in that it all proceeds from one divine voice.

A taste of this is most livelily felt by many of these children of the kingdom; for as their Lord is, so are they in their measure; for the divine nature in them came from the same fountain. Now those that have these companions within, have many times more variety of pleasures, than if they had an hundred companions without, unless they be such that in wisdom and nature answer to the spiritual companions within; then, if they do, there is a blessed union. Even thus it was with God, he having these divine properties infinitely dwelling in him, must needs possess full satisfaction in himself; and not only so, but, from his heavenly and blessed nature of unutterable infinity, he must, of necessity, abound with continual new joys and new ravishing glories.

Wherefore from his divine revelation of himself to himself, and increase of new wisdom, power and glory, he did see that his unsearchable wisdom lay hid in the infinite power of his word speaking; the knowledge of his mighty power, together with his royal will and pleasure, was the glorious wheel, that moved him to form living creatures to appear in his sight.

Which, upon the counsel of His will, he did most abundantly. *Angels* and *men* were the chief, being made purposely for his spiritual society; and then did the Creator take pleasure in the works of his hands: The word hand is used, because the hand is an emblem of power. But the Creator's work in the creation of everything, was without bodily labour; it lay in the virtue of his word, speaking only.

And now, had the most high God enlarged his kingdom, and got spiritual companions without him, men and angels; but man is the chief, he having the nearest fellowship. 1st John i. 3.

CHAP. II.

I. That there is no Nature without a Form.

II. That the Creator is God of a glorious Form from all Eternity.

III. That God is in the form of a Man.

THERE is an absolute necessity for God to continue and remain in his own divine centre, and so for ever be a distinct glorious Being; that as in time he gave being to every creature, so there should still be, and remain an everlasting distinction between the changeable creature and the unchangeable Creator. For if it were, as some have imagined, that the Creator was an infinite Spirit, that is, of *Infinite Immensity,* without any body or form; and that this formless Spirit infused itself into the whole Creation, then could there be no God at all, unless the creature were God, it all participating of his spirit, in that its life were God's life and spirit, and then there would be as many gods as living creatures, and the ox and ass were more noble than an angel.

We are, nevertheless, not to imagine, that the uncreated majesty, before he became flesh, did consist of elementary matter, but was a bright shining glory of uncompounded purity, of so unutterable a nature, as that it was swifter than thought, clearer than crystal, more pure than the purest gold, and infinitely more glorious than the sun.

Moreover, although the body of the uncreated Majesty was of so pure, thin, soft, light and sweet a nature; yet was it absolutely, from the crown of his glorious head to the sole of his divine feet, like unto the first man Adam; it was not the Visibility of their persons that differed, but the Glory of them only. Behold, and wonder, that this infinite spiritual body should change itself into flesh! Yea, be wrapt up in flesh, and remain now in a body of flesh and bone! But this body being now glorified is as glorious, yea, this his body of flesh and bone is more glorious than it was before, when it was a spiritual body; for a very glimpse of this his now body of flesh and bone glorified, struck Paul blind; and so it would have dazzled John's eyes too, if his eyes had not been strengthened above nature, or the person of Jesus presented unto him with a part of his glory vailed. And though the Creator did in time change his god-head glory into flesh; yet the purity of his nature neither was, nor could be changed, but only his infinity laid down into flesh for a season, that he might, for an everlasting astonishment unto men and angels, clothe his god-head spirit with pure human flesh.

A System of Religion

And although the uncreated Majesty was of so pure, thin, light, soft and sweet a nature when a spiritual body, and in this glorified body of flesh and bone more glorious, yet was it before time, in time, and to all eternity no other than ONE personal glory in the form of a man; for (as is said before) it is absolutely from the crown of his glorious head to the sole of his divine feet, like unto the first man Adam; not the visibility of their persons that differed, but the glory of them only.

For do you not find it written, Phil, ii. 6 and 7, that Christ is not only equal with the Father, but in the very form of God? then must God be in the very form of man, if Christ was in the form of a man.

Again doth not the Scripture abundantly prove this? What is the meaning of Moses, when he said, that God created Man in his own image, and in his own likeness? Had not these words relation to Adam's body as well as his spirit? It is indeed written, Ephes iv. 24, that, *we are created after the image of God in righteousness and holiness*.

Can righteousness and holiness act forth themselves without a body? Or do you ever read, that righteousness and holiness were ever acted forth, in, or by any other form but the form of a man? When God said, *Be ye holy as I am holy;* what! must the Souls run out of the bodies to be like him? If they did they would be nothing. Where would mercy and justice, meekness and humility be found? There could be no such virtues known, or have being, were they not found to centre in a body. It is said, *We are created into Christ Jesus unto good works;* can good works be done by the soul without the body?

The reason of this doctrine's being so resisted by the learned philosophers, is through the narrowness of their understandings, in not being able to conceive, that because they themselves have vile and vicious lusts, that therefore whatsoever is in the form of a man must have all the evils and frailties of themselves.

And though it may be true, that several of the great heathen philosophers, and also the Jews, have opposed this doctrine; and that also many of those who pretend to Christianity, have mixed their own carnal reason with the Scriptures, and thereby corrupted the meanings of the texts, and resisted the truth; yet this doth nothing avail, for antiquity and tradition cannot make error and falsehood Truth, notwithstanding custom and practice may have for a time established them; for there have been wrong principles ever since Cain, therefore in matters of religion there is no pleading of antiquity, custom and tradition; for Antichrist was in Cain before Christ was in Abel.

This is the doctrine and language of Moses, and all the true prophets; that God hath a glorious body, and that body in the form of a man.

Moses's testimony is, that God created man in his own image, similitude and likeness: He also saith, that God *talked* with Adam, and *walked* with Enoch; and Abraham, Isaac and Jacob *talked* with God; and it was God that *wrestled* with Jacob; not that God's spiritual body was changed from its nature, but only vailed with a solid substance. Much as the angels, when they appeared to our forefathers; they then, as it were, divested themselves of their glory, and appeared as mortalized for a season, and so did eat and drink with men as if they had been mortal; when as it is certain, that they remained spiritual, and the meat they eat did not pass through them as it doth with man, but was dissolved or swallowed up in their own nature; for their internal fiery glory did convert it into its own substance, as we find the nature of fire is to diminish a substance and take it into itself.

Thus when the great Jehovah hath appeared unto man, he hath either vailed himself, or vailed the eyes of his servants, that his glory might appear, but as their spirits might be capable to behold it; for no mortal eye is able to behold God in the glory of his essence and person.

Therefore when the glorious God, upon the request of Moses, would manifest unto him his personal presence in his form and glory; yet nevertheless was he constrained to cover the eyes of Moses, whilst his face and fiery flaming eyes were towards him; to the end that Moses might have power in the organ of his external eye, to behold the glory of his backparts. Wherefore the Lord put Moses in the clift of a rock, and laid his hand on Moses's face, until he had passed by, because his face was too glorious for mortal eyes to behold.

Moses saith, that God *looked* down from Heaven; that God *came* down from Heaven; that God *went up* to Heaven; that God *heard*; that God *saw*; that God had *eyes, ears, hands* and *mouth,* whereby he *spake* the ten words of the law; and not only so, but he *wrote* them with his *fingers.*

Moreover, doth not David attribute *hands, ears, mouth* and *tongue* unto God. And in the 94th Psalm he proveth undeniably, that God hath all these parts of a body. In that Psalm David was troubled to see wickedness so much abound, and he shows the cause wherefore it was; that the hearts of wicked men were fully set in them to do evil; and it was because they thought God was some infinite formless spirit, that could neither hear nor understand. But for this their wicked imagination David calls them fools and brutish people;

and convinces them of their ignorance, telling them; that he that made the eye, shall he not see; that he that planted the ear, shall he not hear; and he that teacheth man knowledge, shall he not have a heart of his own to understand?

CHAP. III.

The Father, Son and Spirit are one Essence.

The first doctrine which we have before observed to be taught in this text, is, that the Lord Jesus Christ, who is there called the Son of Man, is the true God: And though he is called by several titles, as Father, Son and Spirit, yet is God but ONE personal glory in the form of a man.

As the *soul, body* and *spirit* of man are united and knit together, making one essence, or individual substance, distinct in itself; so are *father, son* and *spirit* as truly joined together; and this the Scripture, and all true prophets do positively affirm.

For may it not as well be said, that man doth consist of three persons, because Paul prayed the soul, body and spirit might be kept blameless? How can God, who is one in himself, be divided into three persons?

If the Creator was one eternal being, distinct from all other beings, is it not necessary that he should so continue in his own divine centre? Infinity hath power to change its glory into flesh, but not to create other deities out of himself; because that would be against his glory.

And the most wise creator can make nothing against his glory, but for his glory only.

For if he should make out of himself other two gods, as Son and Holy Ghost, and they both being distinct from him, they would on necessity require sovereignty; for God can be no God without sovereignty.

Where would his Prerogative be? There can be but one prerogative, for if there be three, the kingdom is divided and cannot stand, Mark iii. 24.

But this kingdom of one God will stand: because there is but One Sole King, and he hath said, He will not give his glory to another; yet all glory was given unto Christ, because he was the sole God: Men and angels, principalities and powers, yea all things in Heaven and Earth did, and for ever shall bow to him, and to no other.

If by the titles Father, Son and Holy Ghost, were not meant one individual, substantial, personal God; but that instead thereof we were to understand a Son and Holy Ghost distinct from the Father; then what kind of God would the Father be? For if he hath invested the Son with all power in Heaven above, and in the Earth beneath, and hath made the Holy Ghost co-operator with the Son, in order to the sanctification and government of the church, the Son being made head of it, and of all things else; I say, what kind of God do you make of the Father?

Do you make any God of him at all? Do you not make him useless, seeing he hath nothing to do, nothing to govern. Surely you think, that one of your Gods grew weary with governing, as Pharaoh king of Egypt did, who made Joseph sole governor of his kingdom, and he himself did nothing: Or else you think, that he is old, and willing to be at rest; and therefore having made a son out of himself, and an Holy Ghost, that he hath begot out of his son and himself, doth therefore dispose of the government to them wholly and absolutely.

If there be a Son and Holy Ghost distinct from a Father, they can be no more than creatures, because they receive their being and perfection from the Creator and not from themselves.

How can there be any affinity, or essential *Oneness,* betwixt a spirit without a body, and a spirit with a body? Can the Son, that is a corporeal person, and hath a body, be said to be in the Father, if the Father hath no body, shape, or form?

If the Holy Ghost is a person proceeding from the Father and the Son, how can he be co-equal and co-eternal with the Father and the Son? Can that which receives its being from another, be equal with that which hath its being of itself?

Can time be equal with eternity? If the Holy Ghost proceeded from a Father and a Son, then is he but a God of Time, and not a God of Eternity; and such a God may end in time.

Again, if the Son was from *eternity,* how could he be *begotten?* and if the Holy Ghost was from *eternity,* how could he *proceed,* and take his original from Father and Son, if the three persons were each of them eternal, that is, without all beginning; then they could not give being one to another.

If the Son was begotten by the Father from all Eternity, and begotten again, when he was incarnate of the Virgin Mary, in a body of flesh, then it seems he was a *double Son,* and *Twice* begotton, or *Twice* made by the Father, and yet this Son must be said to be *Equal* with the Father, though it is nevertheless confessed he was made *Lower* then the Angels.

From hence it is, that those who hold this Doctrine, worship a Divided God, or Three Distinct Gods: and therefore do they make their Prayers in *Distinct* Forms, and pray to one of their Gods alter one Manner, and another after another Manner; making in reality three Gods, as distinct from one another as three men, John, James and Peter; but this divided God, or God with three heads is a monstrous god, no where to be found but in their own idle dreams, and is not the true God; for there is no such double begetting, nor proceeding as they imagine, for though God is in a sense said to be one in three, and three in one, yet is he not in three persons, he is only *one God* with three titles; *We worship a God in one person with three titles, Father, Son and Spirit*; but it is a self-begotten God, and not a God begotten by another.

Oh, the darkness that lies upon some of the learned! Did they heed the Scriptures, they would see that the Son was but once begotten or made; and that was God's begetting himself into a Son, according as it is written, God *became flesh*, it is not said, that God sent a Son to become flesh, that was begot by him before.

But the meaning of those words are no other, than that God sent forth Himself to be made of a woman, to redeem us from the curse of the law, according as it is written, I lay down my life of myself.

Now where Christ saith, that of himself he can do nothing; and that he bears not witness of himself; and that he came not of himself, and the like; that self he speaks of is but his human nature, and that makes him but man; that is as much as to say, not of myself in my mortal, weak nature.

It is said, that he gave himself for us, is it not wrong then to say, that God sent forth any Son but himself? Again it is said, I have sworn by myself, that unto me every knee shall bow. Now who was this that sware so by himself? Paul saith it was Christ, and he sware by himself, because there was none greater than himself. Heb. vi. 13.

For Christ's nature, which is divine, is that self which can do all things; and which is equal with himself now since his Incarnation with what he was before; and is the very Father, and hath power to do all things, having glorified himself in his new body of flesh, which was conceived of the Virgin by his almighty power, that could live and die, and live again, and now he lives for evermore; being one personal majesty, distinct from Heavens, Earth, Angels, Men, and all things for everlasting.

Now where was there a Father but in that Son? Where was there a Son but in that Father? One God and Father in one person alone, the glorious body, wherewith the divine Godhead (which is the everlasting

Father) is cloathed, in his dearly beloved Son, in whom his spirit eternally delighted.

And this is the faith of the holy seed, and which was long since taught, and believed; viz.:

That God was in the form of a Man, that *Christ Jesus* was that *God,* his Godhead is the *Everlasting* Father, his now glorified Body the Son, and his powerful Spirit the Holy Ghost.

Thus then you have what is to be understood by One in Three, or Three in One; which is no more than that these denominations, Father, Son and Spirit are *three Titles*, according to the different appearances of the One God.

CHAP IV.

That the Man, Jesus Christ *is this only* One *and True God, we shall further prove by the following strong and unanswerable arguments.*

ARGUMENT THE FIRST.

Prop. I.

There is but one God, which was a substantial, sensible life and light in form from all eternity.

Prop. II.

Christ Jesus was a substantial, sensible light and life in form from all eternity.

Concl.

Therefore Christ Jesus is the only true God.

The first proposition, viz. That there is but one God, and he was in form from all eternity, is already proved. The Second is clear from Scripture, as in Isaiah lxiii. 16. *O Lord! Thou art our Father, and Redeemer, thy name is everlasting.* See also Psalm xciii. 2. Here the Prophet expressly makes God the Father and the Redeemer to be the same.

David in the 45th Psalm 6, alluding to Christ, says, *His throne was for ever and ever.* And to this the Author of the Epistle to the Hebrews refers in Heb. i. 8, with this compare Rev. iii. 21.

Moreover in Tim. i. 17. and vi. 15. Paul salutes Jesus Christ by the titles of King eternal, immortal, and only wise God.

Christ himself, in John 8. 58. saith, before Abraham was, *I am*. And in John xvii. 5. In his prayer to his Divinity, he tells us of a Glory, which he *had* before all worlds.

So that we see Christ was God from Eternity; and there can be but one God from Eternity.

THE SECOND ARGUMENT.

Prop. I.

He that is Creator of the World, and all things therein, must be God.

Prop. II.

Christ is the Creator of the World, and all things therein.

Concl.

Therefore Christ is God,

The First needs no proof, nobody denying it. The second is thus proved: In the 43rd. of Isaiah you will find these words, Thus saith the Lord who created thee, O Jacob, and redeemed thee, O Israel; fear not, for I have redeemed thee. So also, chap, xliv. 24. Thus saith the Lord thy Redeemer, and he that formed thee from the womb, I am the Lord that maketh all things by *myself.*

But a most invincible and clear proof, taking off all possibility of objection, is in the begining of St. John's Gospel, where he expressly says, that Christ was the Word, and by *this word* all Things were made that were made; and *this word* was mad*e flesh,* and came down, and dwelt among us, &c. John i.

THE THIRD ARGUMENT.

Prop. 1.

He that hath all power in Heaven and Earth is God.

Prop. 2.

Christ hath all power in Heaven and Earth.

Concl.

Therefore Christ is God.

The first Proposition is universal, and objected against by nobody. The second hath been abundantly proved already; and it would be an unnecessary repetition to do it here. The consequence is natural.

THE FOURTH ARGUMENT.

Prop. I.

He that was the Lord God of the holy Prophets and Apostles, was the true God.

Prop. II.

Christ Jesus was the Lord God of the holy Prophets and Apostles.

Concl.

Therefore Christ Jesus is the true God.

Both these, first and second propositions, are universal, and will admit of no objections; nor is there any objection possible to be made, without destroying the authority of the whole Scripture, and the whole Christian system: Therefore no stronger proof can be required.

THE FIFTH ARGUMENT.

Prop. I.

Divine Worship is due to none but the true God.

Prop. II.

Divine Worship is due to Jesus Christ.

Concl.

Therefore Jesus Christ is the true God.

The first proposition is clear from the whole tenour of the Old Testament, but more expressly in the Ten Words of the law. Thou shalt have none other Gods but me. Thou shalt not bow down to them, nor worship them, See Exodus xx, Mat. iv. 10. and Luke iv. 8. Thou shalt worship the Lord, thy God and him only shalt thou serve. In Isaiah xlii. 8, God saith, He will not give his glory to another. So also in Deut. xi. 13. and 1 Sam. vii. 3. that God only was to be worshiped with all the soul and all the heart.

The second proposition is clear from the whole tenour of the New Testament, viz. That all glory by men and Angels was given to Jesus Christ. See Paul's words, Phil. ii. 10. At the name of Jesus every knee shall bow. See the same doctrine also in Rom. xiv. 9. Paul also in Acts xxiv. 14. tells the Jews, that *in the way which they called Heresy so* worshiped *he the God of his Fathers*; which was the God of Abraham, Isaac and Jacob; for these were Paul's fathers, and Jesus was the God whom he worshiped, and which every thing in heaven and earth did likewise. See Heb. i. 6. See more in Eph. v. 14. Phil. ii. 10. Rev. iv. 10. and 7. 11 and 14. *3*. 4.

THE SIXTH ARGUMENT.

Prop. I.

He that can pardon, and take away Sin by his own power, is the true God.

Prop. II.

Christ Jesus hath the Power in himself to pardon, and take away Sin.[1]

Concl.

Therefore Christ Jesus is the true God.

The first proposition is universally acknowledged, and needs no proof. And the second is disputed by none who call themselves *Christians*; for it was for this reason Christ came into the world, *to seek and to save those which were lost;* and indeed, the whole Christian doctrine of man's Salvation depends on it.

In Mat. i. 21. it is written, And she shall bring forth a Son, and they shall call his name Jesus; and he shall save his people from their sins. And in Mat. ix, 2. to the man sick of the Palsy he said, Go thy way, thy sins are forgiven. And when the Jews murmured, saying, who is this that forgiveth sins? Christ expressly said it was done on purpose to let them see, that He, the Son of Man had power on Earth to forgive sins.

And it was Jesus Christ, who was the Lamb of God, who took away the sins of the world.

---

[1] Note —God was in Christ reconciling the world unto himself, 2 Cor. v. 19.

Now, how God gave himself for us, and how he begat himself into Flesh, is already proved at large, and to prevent needless repetition see pages 18, 19, 20, aforegoing.

We might here bring many more arguments to prove *Christ to be the Only true God*; such as these which follow.

That He is the Only giver of all true saving Faith and Grace.

That He is the Only giver of Eternal Life.

That He knows men's hearts, and did know their secret thoughts while he was on earth.

That all the Miracles which he performed, of healing the diseased, raising the dead, and the like, he did them all by his own power, and in his own name. And that the Apostles did the same in his name only; but these are such well known and indisputable things, and have already been said under other heads in this treatise, that there is no occasion for more arguments, to prove that *Jesus Christ is the Only One and True God.*[1]

---

[1] Note. Acts ii. 36, Therefore let all the house of Israel know assuredly, that God hath made that same Jesus whom ye have crucified, both Lord and Christ.

OF THE

ORIGINAL

OF THE

DEVIL

AND

That He is no where to be found but in Man.

The *Wicked* one, in our text, who sowed the tares, was the serpent who was cast out of Heaven, as it is written in Rev. xii. 12. Woe unto the inhabitants of the earth; for the devil is come down amongst you; and this was that serpent which tempted Eve.

This serpent angel overpowering Eve by his subtilty, caused her to consent unto him (she being left to her own strength) upon whose condescension he entered her womb; for that he was a body, though a spiritual one, and therefore capable so to do, though he was not a gross substance.

Wherefore as soon as he had entered her womb, he became united to her soul and body; his serpentine nature dissolved itself in her, and defiled her throughout, corrupting her pure nature whereby when she conceived naturally, it was a Serpent-Dragon-Devil in a Man-child: this was her first begotten Son, and was called Cain,

From hence it is, that Cain became the Father of all Reprobates; and that the scripture fathereth all wickedness upon him, as Christ himself said to the Scribes who resisted him, Ye are of your Father the Devil, who was a liar and a murderer from the begining. It is also written, Not as Cain, who was of the *wicked one*, and slew his brother, &c. For he was of that wicked one, or rather, he was *the wicked one* himself, the Serpent-Angel by transmutation became seed, and thus transferred, and transmuted himself into Flesh,

Thus was the race of Mankind corrupted, and this corruption was brought more into conjunction, when the Sons of God (that is to say, the sons of Seth) took wives of the daughters of men (that is to say of the daughters of Cain.)

Thus then the seed of the Devil is in man, growing up in his wicked nature and where then shall we look for the true Devil, but in man?

And now, you seed of the wicked one, be not angry with me for showing you the Devil; for the sight of him will not make you afraid,

The Devil is not a spirit in the air, but a lying, lustful spirit in the heart, he comes not flying into a man's mouth as a bird into a nest; it is the conception of Sin is the *entrance* of Satan. See, and compare Psalm xviii. Acts, v. 4. James i. 12. 14. 15.

The Devil springs out of his own seed, which is in Man's heart, as the thorn and thistle, out of their corrupted mother, the earth.

This is taught by Christ, Mark iv 19. The word of Faith is seemingly scattered into corrupted Man's nature, which is called *thorny ground;* but in come several Devils, and repulse it. (Remark now.) What are these Devils? and from whence do they come? These Devils are *cares* of the world, *Riches, Deceit and Lusts*, which produce Ambition, Adultery, Murder, &c.

These are the Devils which enter into a man, and defile him? they do not come from without: It is that which is *within* man, being of his natural constitution, as the Scriptures do abundantly declare.

Which was by the *Serpent-Angel* generating himself into flesh, and it is this Flesh, which is the Poison and Venom, and Dragon-devil, which *streamed* through the loins of Cain, and his offspring, and by conjunction (as. beforesaid) This became *Poison* in the bodies of men and women, in all the sons and daughters of Adam.

It is this fallen Angel's nature in man, which is the Original of all sin and evil.

Pride, Envy, and *Lust* are the fallen Angel's nature in man, when this fallen Angel's nature moves, (that is, when Lust moves) and the motion is nursed by the heart, and puts forth to act, then is sin produced, and the fallen Angel's nature is predominant. Therefore is man said to be tempted by the Devil, when he is enticed and drawn aside by his own *Lust,* which is the Devil's nature *within* him.

For whosoever serves Lust serves the Devil; and when a man is given up to his *own lusts*, he is given up to the Devil; for God gives no one up to any other Devil.

Wherefore Peter speaking of the most wicked people that should be in the latter ages, he gives them the Epithet of *walking after their own Lusts.* 2 Pet. ii. 18, & 3. 3.

It is said, God gave the murmuring Israelites up to their (own) Hearts Lusts; it is not said, that God gave them up to Lust, but their (own) Hearts Lust, to show that sin or evil is from man's own nature, and so Paul preaches.

The original of false worship springs from man's *own* Lusts. 2 Tim. iv. 3. Compare Mark iv. 19. John viii. 44.

This Lust is a grand Devil, or the Father of all evil; for Peter saith, *the corruption of the world came in by it:* Therefore when it is said, that man is tempted to evil, you may know it is meant of his being delivered to *himself,* for every man of himself is a Devil.

Therefore watch for the devil *within,* and look not for him *without;* examine your hearts, and see if Pride, Lust, and other such like spirits be not in you; if they be, down with them with all speed, or they will down with you, and then would you be tormented with them for ever.

For know, that every *reigning sin* is a *raging spirit;* therefore so many sorts or kinds of sin, so many sorts of foul spirits are there; every evil motion and action makes a wicked spirit.

There is the spirit of jealousy; the spirit of treachery, the spirit of whoredom, the spirit of giddiness, the spirit of sorcery, the spirit of fear, the spirit of the world. Acts xvi. 16. Rom. viii. 15. 2 Tim. i. 7. 1 Cor. ii. 12.

Now all these spirits are but man's own spirit, Ezek. xiii. 3. and this spirit is the spirit of the Devil; and when several of these are together in man, then is that man called a *cage of unclean birds*, an *hold of foul spirits*, and an *habitation of devils*.

For this is clear, that if man conceives sin from his own nature, and is enticed from his *own lusts* which are natural to his constitution, then is his own lust the devil who tempts him to evil.

Thus you see that lust is an evil spirit, and a devil which is to be resisted, and all other actions of corrupt nature are evil spirits, and must be fought withal, and mortified by spirits of a contrary nature; which are as follows.

The spirit of Wisdom, Judgment, and Knowledge.[1]

The spirit of praise, the spirit of comfort, the spirit of joy, the spirit of humility.[2]

---

[1] Deut. iv. 9. Eph. i, 17. Isa. xxyiii. 5. 1 Peter iv. 14. Psalm ix, 4.
[2] Is lxi, 1, 2, 3, & 66 2. Mat. v. 3. 1 Cor. iv. 21, Gal. vi. 1. 1 Pet. 3, 4,

The spirit of love, charity, and Holiness, the spirit of truth, or true faith.

This truth, or true faith is the glory of all, because it compriseth all virtue, and so it hath the single name of the good spirit of God; as lust compriseth all vice, and from its original seed and operating nature, bears the name of wicked one, devil, or evil spirit.

Thus you see how the spirit of *truth,* and the spirit of *lust* do branch forth themselves, and what their weapons are on each side. Also you may see what soldiers are raised out of these two men or two natures, who are in arms against each other till one is subdued; therefore, if you will live in peace, gain to yourselves these good spirits, and you will easily overcome all your domestic enemies.

For hope not to have pardon by lessening of sin and saying, "I am sorry for what I have done, and that it was not myself, but the temptation of the devil, who crept into my will and understanding and seduced me."

For it is evident, there is no other Satan, but man's own lust and pride; nor any *invisible* Devil or *formless* spirit that can suggest an evil notion, but man's own spirit-

It was not an invisible devil or Satan distinct from David, Peter and Judas, which caused them to sin; *nor* was it God that either did, or could tempt them to sin.

It was Peter himself, in his proper person, that was called Satan, when his pride had got to that head, to persuade Christ from suffering death.

And David might as well have been called Satan, for *numbering the people;* for it was his own seed of the angel's fallen nature, which was the satan that stood up in his heart, and tempted him. It was this spirit of pride which looked on its own strength, thinking that victory was to be got by numbers, not remembering that God had promised that he would fight for them, and *one man should chase a thousand.*

But after this was done David's heart smote him. Observe well it was *his heart* smote him; by that which he sinned by that was he punished; he doth not charge any Satan or evil spirit with the sin that he had done; no spirit without him, or distinct from him, but he chargeth his own soul with the evil.

And notwithstanding the Scripture saith, that on Judas's taking the sop, the devil entered into him. It is plain, it was not an evil spirit distinct from his own spirit which entered into him, for three reasons: First, Christ called him [the man Judas] a devil. Secondly, Judas himself charged his own sin wholly on himself, and did not excuse himself by saying, An invisible devil without him, seduced him to it,. Thirdly, He had no partner to share his punishment, or bear part of his sorrow.

The Devil that entered into him at the receiving the sop, was a motion of covetousness, treachery, and a resolution to betray his Lord and Master.

This was the Satan that entered into Judas, for the conception of sin is the entrance of Satan.

And why may not the Devil which tempted Christ be a man? A Scribe, or Lawyer of great subtilty, and the end of his temptation was, that he and the rest of the rulers of the Jews, might be Lords of the earth.

For if Christ would have submitted to become a temporal king, the Rulers would have gloried in it; for they saw his power was so great, that if they could have prevailed with him to have submitted (which they called worshiping) they knew they should have been able to conquer the whole world.

And who need to doubt this after they see that Christ told this devil tempter; It is written, *thou shalt* worship *the Lord thy God and him,* only shalt thou serve.[1]

Now where is it written, that invisible bodiless Devils should worship God? but in Deut. iv, you will find that to the people of Israel it was said, Thou shalt worship the Lord thy God, and him only shalt thou serve.

Certain it is, that there ever was a diabolical Power reigning in the world from the days of Cain; but this diabolical Power was never acted forth against God, or his saints, by any invisible spirit, or devil, but by man-devil only.

All the evil in the world proceeds from this *diabolical power*, derived to man from Cain, by the seed of the *fallen angel*. What devils were those that afflicted the Israelites in Moses's time, and persecuted the Christians in the primitive time, were they not men devils? Was not Pharaoh a man? Senacherib a man? Herod a man, though John calls him a red dragon? And were not the Scribes and Pharisees men; though Christ calls them Serpents? Judas a man, though called a devil? And was not Nero a man, though Paul calls him a Lion? These were not invisible spirit-devils.

---

[1] See Mat. iv. 10. & Luke. iv. 8.

What was it that put Pharaoh in action? Was it not his own spirit? As is clear from these words, I have stirred thee up, saith God, (thee up) not another to tempt thee, but *thee* only, thy own Spirit; and to that end, have I hardened thy heart.

Which is as much as to say, "I have with-held good motions from it, and have left him to take counsel of his own wicked heart where the seed of rebellion is present; and from hence it was, that Pharaoh resisted God, saying, What is the Lord, that I should obey his voice?

This was a proud devil in Pharaohs heart, which made him resist all the miracles which Moses wrought; whereas Darius was converted by one miracle, and acknowledged Daniel's God.

Observe, it is no where said, a devil was commanded to enter into him, but his own heart was hardened: The evil is not produced from without them, but from within, being engendered from the seed of whence they come, and the Evil is hid in them, as fire is in a flint, and brought to life by striking upon it.

But God hath power over man's heart, and when man hath displeased him, and he would give him plagues in this life, he can stir him up enemies, as he did to Solomon, not invisible, formless spirits, but men adversaries.

Neither can there be worse devils than wicked men. Are not the haters of God and his workmanship men-devils? Are not murderers of mankind great devils? The cruel barbarous tormentors and murderers of the Saints are greater devils, but the greatest dragon-devils of all were the murderers of Christ the Eternal God, yet these devils were men devils.

The Saints in all ages prayed against no other devils but wicked men without them, and their own corrupt hearts within them.

Therefore let not a wicked man flatter himself; for of himself he is a devil, and without Grace a damned devil too.

A wicked man's own soul runs mad to Sin; there needs no other devil to compel him to evil.

The worst of men are forced to acknowledge that their sin is of themselves; *I have sinned,* says Judas, in betraying innocent blood, Mat. xxvii. 4. I have sinned, says Pharaoh. There was no laying their sins at the doors of any other devils.

This made David cry out against himself, and water his couch with his tears, so did Peter likewise.

A System of Religion

Paul also, exclaimed against himself for his evil actions in persecuting the saints, saying, O! wretched man that I am, &c. I am the chief of sinners. I was mad against the saints.

Thus we see that saints and reprobates do both of them acknowledge, that sin issues from themselves.

God doth not (as appears by Scripture) charge man's sin upon any other creature or devil. Every man must suffer for his own sin.

For, O! man, I tell thee thy sins are begot by thine *own* invention, hatched in thine *own* heart, and acted by thine *own* will; so that thou weavest the web of thine *own* woe, and spinnest the thread of thine *own* thraldom.

Therefore shun naughtiness, and kill the devil by good works; learn to know the Angels and Spirits of the Lord, which we have before showed you, from the Angels and Spirits of Satan; for if you cleave to wicked spirits, you shall be tormented of the spirits whom you serve; but if you acquaint yourselves with the angels and spirits of love, peace, humility, and truth, you shall have comfort.

As the Apostle James saith, God giveth grace unto the humble; submit yourselves therefore unto God! Resist the Devil and he will fly from you; that is to say, there is grace and favour held forth unto you, if you can but condemn yourselves for your sin.

If you can but humble yourselves for your iniquities, and receive the grace of faith and love which is preached unto you, whereby you may gain power to resist the Devil, which is lust, pride, and envy, and then God will not reject you; for he resisteth the proud and envious Devil; but He giveth grace to the humble and penitent soul, that warreth against lust, pride and envy, by beating down those motions when they arise in the heart.

So that when any evil motion is conceived in your heart, then mind the grace which is given you, which will be stirred up by meditations on it, and the good motions arising from this Grace will be a power sufficient to expel the evil before it become a stinging serpent; and then have you not only resisted the devil, but he will fly from you, as a mist doth from the sun, as not being able to bear its heat and light.

Of The
SOUL

When God made Adam, he formed his body of dust, then breathed upon it, and immediately it became a living soul.

Adam's soul was never sensible of its existence, nor was it complete but in a body: it was the breath of the immortal God, and the dust of the earth which became one essence, that is, a living soul, which was the man Adam.

We are nowhere told in Scripture, that the Creator made *souls* without *bodies* neither in Heaven or earth, the soul and body was always an individual essence, One distinct living creature.

The soul is the author and cause of every action; it is that which acts and lives, thinks and perceives: All our motions of walking, talking, eating drinking, sleeping and waking, are from the soul as the first mover; for it is in every part of the body of a sound person: So that a man cannot be pricked by a pin, but the *soul* feels it.

No action is done by the body without the soul, except by some external, superior force; as a virgin may be ravished by violence, and her body defiled, but this is none of her actions, because her soul consented not; therefore it is not her sin.

What the soul wills the body performs, and what the body acts the soul wills.

Therefore it is the soul which sins, because the body cannot sin without the soul, neither can the soul sin without the body.

For a man can say no ill thing, nor do any ill action without a tongue to speak, and the members of the body to act. Hence arises these two conclusions.

1st.

The soul cannot sin without the body.

2nd.

The body cannot sin, nor live without the soul.

Neither can a good man show his goodness without a body. How can it be said such an one is a wise, a just or an holy man, if there were not some action seen of his Wisdom, Justice, and Holiness? And can such an act be done without a body? Or can the body be wise, just, and good without the soul?

If the soul and body were not always one individual essence, but that the soul was infused in the mother's womb, then how could the soul be capable of sin, seeing it came immediately from Heaven? if you say evil comes by imitation, try it, lock up a child from evil company, and see if the corrupt seed of its own evil lust and appetites will not bud forth and produce evil.

A learned *Rabbi* of the Jews being asked when sin entered into man? answered, at the time of formation; therein agreeing with David, who said, *in sin had his Mother conceived him.*

If men did but understand the scriptures, and had faith to believe them, they would find that the body and soul of man is but *one essence*, both living and dying, and proceeds according to the course of nature by generation, and by virtue of the word of the Lord to Adam and Eve; be fruitful, and multiply, and replenish the earth. Now if they had generated only bodies, and not souls, how could the earth have been replenished with men and women?

If they generated, and brought forth nothing that had life and breath in it, it could not be mankind, but stupid, senseless matter in the images only of men and women, unless it had a power and virtue to quicken into life.

If as some learned men say, God infuses the soul, then it will be necessary to ask them some questions; as, whether it is by breathing into this babe (if a mass of flesh may be called so) as he did into Adam's body of dust? Or is one made on purpose for this body at that time? Or is it one that hath been formerly made, and pre-existed, which God now sends down to enliven and animate this body?

Further, it might be requisite for them to tell us, whether it is a *good* soul or a *bad*? If it come from Heaven, and be *good*; or breathed in as Adam's was, how comes it to sin? If they say by Adam's fall, that cannot be.

If Adam did not generate the soul as well as the body, then is there not one *soul* related to Adam; for they came from Heaven as well as Adam; and if they had not of Adam's spirit, then they could not fall in Adam.

But whether these souls are made already, or whether they be then made on purpose, the notions are equally absurd; for this makes God's work not to be finished the sixth day, and that he now enjoys his rest, as the scriptures say; but God at this rate must attend at the begetting every child; nay, he must assist every lascivious person in his unlawful lusts; and after the manner these wretches talk, a bastard cannot be begotten without he joins issue. Is not this to make the Holy God, who is *of purer eyes than to behold iniquity*, co-partner with every wicked man in his worst actions.

This is the consequence of not attending to what the scriptures teach us; there we shall find it written, that Abraham took Sarah his wife, and Lot, his brother's son, and the Souls that he had got in Haran, and went for to go into the land of Canaan.

Again, it is written, that all the Souls which came into Egypt, which came out of his Loins, were in the whole sixty six. Here we see, that Souls came out of their Loins as well

But to this some very learnedly reply, that souls here signify no more than persons. Blind reasoning! Would they have a senseless lump of matter without a soul be a person? what is a person, but a substance of one, it must necessarily follow, what is attributed to the one belongs to the other also; therefore where the body is mentioned in scripture, except it be expressed a dead body, both body and soul is to be understood as in Judges, viii. 30. it is said, Gideon had seventy sons of his body begotten; the whole man of body and soul is here meant; for a dead body cannot get a living body or soul: As John saith.

And this is clear from Mat. xxvii. 52. where it is said, that *many dead bodies arose out of their Graves.* Did therefore their bodies arise without their souls?

Thus have we seen, that the soul of man is by traduction, and not by infusion; that both soul and body are begotten together, and never did exist asunder, nor can they be separated one from another: No, not in death; for the soul must die with the body the *first* death.

The Apostle prays, that the *soul, body and spirit may be kept blameless unto the coining of the Lord.* Observe here two things.

First,

That the soul, body, and spirit are in one essence, and one man; as father, son, and spirit are but one God.

Secondly,

That this one essence of soul, body, and spirit is to remain here on earth until the coming of the Lord: for if the soul could have gone to Heaven without its body, the Apostle had no need to have prayed that it might be kept blameless until the Lord's coming.

Can a soul be faulty after it is immortalized in heaven? There was no need of praying for it after the death of the body.

The Lord, in comforting his Disciples at his departure, tells them, *After* he had prepared thrones for them in heaven, and made all things ready, he would *come again,* and *fetch* them to him.

Observe, Christ doth not tell them that their souls should follow him *presently,* but ordered them to wait for his coming; as if he should have said, "Lie down, and rest till all things are completed in their proper time." As in the parable which is our text, it is said the *tares and wheat must both grow together until they are ripe for the harvest.*

It is said of David, that he slept with his fathers, and was buried in his city; it is not said he went to heaven, but on the contrary, the Apostle said, that David was *not* ascended into heaven. Christ was ascended, but David remained in the grave. Acts ii. 34.

David also was himself well acquainted with this doctrine, therefore he saith, Psalm civ. 33. He would praise God whilst he had a being; for when 1 go down to the pit shall the dust praise thee?—xxx. 9.

In Psalm lxxxix. 48. he saith, What man is he that liveth, and shall not see death? Shall he deliver his soul from the grave?[1]

So king Hezekiah on his recovery saith, I said in the cutting off of my days, I shall go to the gates of the grave; but the Lord hath spoken to me, and done it! O Lord, by these things do men live, and in all these things is the life of my SPIRIT. For thou hast in love to my soul delivered it from death; the grave cannot praise thee; death cannot celebrate thee: They that go down into the pit cannot pray, or hope for thy truth. The living praise thee, as I do this day. All the scriptures are full of the proof of this.

Every soul *that sins shall die.* Sin is the author of death. It is this which gives it strength and predominancy. It is obedience to sin which brings obstruction to life; therefore he, and none but he, who can clear himself from all sin, may free himself from all death. But, who can do this?

It is said, that Adam *was made a living soul*; but Christ *was made a quickning spirit* of that soul. Now this quickning, or quickning of the elect, is used in the scripture in a twofold sense; one more mystical, as when it is meant of the quickning from the death of sin: The other

---

[1] See further Psalm, xlii. 2. & xvii. 15-. & vi. 5.

is meant a quickning into life, from the death of nature, as at the resurrection.

So also by the *second death* is meant in scripture, *the death of sin*; and the future punishment which sin brings on the wicked, is called the *second death.*

These two quicknings are also the two resurrections mentioned in scripture. It is said, *blessed is he who hath part in the* first, *of such the* second *death shall have no power.*

So where the scripture saith, that *every sin is not unto death*, it is meant of this second death.

After this manner is to be understood that scripture, which saith, *he that believeth in me shall never die*; that is, he shall never die the second, or eternal death. It is plain, it hath this mystical meaning from that other place, which saith, *he that eateth of the bread of life shall never die.*

Where the word of God hath given assurance of eternal life, that assurance is looked on as eternal life itself, because they who believe the word know nothing can prevent it: Therefore compare the texts aforegoing with John. xi. where it is said of Lazarus, that *though he were dead, yet should he live;* also that other scripture which speaks of *eternal life abiding in them.*

And the scriptures do for two great reasons, in some places, intimate an *immediate glory after death.*

The first is, The faithful at their death do by their faith see, and live in eternity; and thus link time and eternity together.

The second is, There is no time to the dead; the next thing after death is judgment.

Therefore, though a *soul* should lie in the grave five thousand years, yet at the resurrection it would not be conscious of any time it had lain there.

The scripture-language is not of souls going to Heaven, but when it speaks of men departing this life, it saith, *they die,* or *fall asleep.* It is said; that Abraham, Isaac, and Jacob are dead, and fallen asleep; that Stephen *fell asleep,* that others slept with their fathers; but there is not one word of souls going to Heaven.

When Lazarus died, it is said *he fell asleep*; and that he was dead: Therefore when Christ came to raise him to life, he looked down into the Grave, and with a loud voice said, Lazarus come forth.

Observe, the Lord called him not from Heaven, but from the Grave.

So likewise, when Christ was risen from the dead, some of the Saints which slept in the grave, arose also, and appeared unto many.

It is not said, that souls came from Heaven, but that they arose from the Grave; which was done by virtue of Christ's resurrection, it having an influence upon them, did cause them to rise as a specimen of his mighty power.

Paul, reproving the Thessalonians for their immoderate bewailing the death of their friends, tells them, *that they must not mourn as men without hope*; for, saith he, *these* your friends *that sleep in Jesus will God bring with him when he cometh.*

Now the Apostle doth not comfort them by saying, *Your friends souls are in Heaven*, but he comforts them with the doctrine of the resurrection.

In 1 Cor. Xv. Paul preacheth the Resurrection of Saints to life at the last day, and proves it by the resurrection of Christ from the dead by undeniable evidences; as, by Peter, then of the twelve, by himself with five hundred brethren besides; of whom, saith he, the greater part remain to this present time, but some are fallen asleep. He doth not say they were gone to Heaven, or their Souls were in Heaven, but they *were fallen asleep.*

And it is certain, that Paul knew very well that they were not in Heaven; for observe diligently his words, verse 12. He there reproveth them which deny the resurrection of the dead, saying, And if there be no resurrection of the dead, then Christ is not risen; and if Christ be not risen, then is our preaching vain, and you are yet in your sins; and those which are fallen asleep in Jesus are perished.

Is it not plain, that Paul taught if there was no resurrection their *souls* were perished as well as their *bodies*; for if the souls of these saints had been in Heaven, then could not their faith and the Apostles preaching have been in vain; for what great matter were it, if there bodies did lie and rot in the grave, so that their souls were happy?

Therefore doth he go on in the next verse, saying, If in this life only we have hope, we are of all men most miserable. For the saints through their faith in the resurrection of soul and body do deny themselves temporal pleasures, and willingly suffer the reproach of the world; so that if there should not be a resurrection they are of all men most miserable; and the Atheists have the advantage of the saints; they speak and act boldly as they think, saying, Let us eat, drink, and be merry; for tomorrow we shall die, and there's an end.

Therefore if the Apostle had spoken only of the resurrection of the body, and not of the soul, he needed not to have said, that their Faith, holiness, Worship, Baptism and Suffering had been all in vain, and of no effect; but Paul knew well there could be no happiness without a resurrection.

And this was Daniel's knowledge and faith likewise; therefore says he chap. xii. Many of them who sleep in the dust of the earth shall awake. Their souls were neither in happiness nor misery, but with their bodies in the dust; and at the resurrection the *just shall awake and shine as the stars;* and therefore it was, that he was bid to go his way also into the dust until the end, for till then he should not appear; but at the fulness of time, he with the rest should arise, and stand in his lot with the just, to receive the reward of Eternal Life.

Job is a witness of this, though the authority of the book is questioned by some, yet all admit it to be a true history, that there was such a person, and that he was an holy man, and *one that feared God*, he hath most strongly taught this doctrine.

In Chap, xxi, it is said, The wicked do spend their days in wealth, but they go suddenly down to the grave; one dies in his full strength, another dies in the bitterness of his soul, and never eats in pleasure as the other did; but, saith he, they shall both sleep in the dust, and the worms shall cover them. Mind here, he doth not say, their souls shall go into eternal torment, and their bodies to the grave; but they must sleep in the dust. v. 30. The wicked, (saith he) must be kept till the day of destruction; and they are to be brought forth in the day of wrath; but until then they are to be brought to the grave, and remain in the heap.

Chap. xiv. he saith, Are not man's days determined? Also there is hope of a tree if it be cut down, and the stock thereof remain in the ground, yet by the ascent of water it may bud and bring forth bows again; but man is sick, dieth, and perisheth; and where is he? Man sleepeth and waketh not from his sleep, till the heavens be no more.

Job prayeth, that God would take away his life, and hide him in the grave until his wrath was passed over, and then to bring him out again, a. Here is it not plain, that Job knew nothing of the body's going into the grave by itself, and the soul's going out of it? This would not have evaded God's wrath.

Ver. 14. talking interrogatively, *If a man die shall he live again!* He answereth affirmatively, that *lie shall*, and that *he will wait till his change cometh.* The Lord shall call me, and I shall answer him, though now he numbers my steps, and scourges me for my sins.

His faith was strong in the resurrection, his hope was there, and his love was great to his Redeemer. I know (says he) that my

Redeemer liveth, and though I die, and worms destroy my body, yet I shall see him at the LAST DAY. Chap. xix.

Job doth not expect eternal happiness till the last day, nor to see his Redeemer till the end of the world; but after death the grave must retain him until then. And his trouble makes him wish for death as for hid treasure, because death is insensible of pain, and is to the just as a sweet sleep.

But the notion of the soul's going immediately to heaven, puts men on other means of flying from the miseries of life; they have no need to wait for God's time, and the manner of dying which he hath appointed; for they are taught to believe that death doth not kill, it doth only fetch the soul out of the body, as the stroke of a steel upon a flint fetcheth out the fire; so death at one stroke snatches the soul out of the body, and carries it straight to the Elisian Fields to heaven into Abraham's bosom.

This makes many desperate, and lay violent hands on themselves; and others, through fiery zeal in wrong principles, run headlong to dungeons, to fire and faggot, and bid defiance to death; for *death doth not kill*, say they.

Ambitious men, who aim at supreme power, and to be sole lord's of the world, have been the principal promoters of this doctrine; they preach it themselves to their armies in fine orations, and with rhetorical flourishes to make themselves admired as Gods, and life despised, when it is lost in such an hero's cause. They procure, also, men, who excel in philosophy, and are skilled in logical subtilties, to inculcate a notion so useful to their ambition, and by this means it is propagated in the world; for who will not fight, and kill, or be killed to obtain glory? What signifies a little pain in a plausible cause, where there is no death, nor life cannot be lost; nay, where the soul only escapes, by this means, out of a prison.

For the heathen philosophers, as *Thales, Democritus, Plato,* and others taught, that the body was a prison to the Soul; and that at death the soul slips out of it into another world, either of pleasure or misery; that *pleasure* they called the *Elisian Fields.*

Origen also, as well as Plato and the Chaldean philosophers taught, "That souls were made all together at some one time beforehand, and afterwards sent into bodies as into so many dark lanthorns; and according to the behaviour of these naked spirits before they were embodied, there were suitable mansions prepared for them."

" That a soul who had walked acceptably with God, was put into a finer prison, and was cloathed with a more elegant and amiable body;

and the soul which had displeased God, and provoked his Creator, was put into a darker dungeon, a more obscure and uncomely body."

"The soul only is the man, say they, the body is only the case or cover of it; and that God, as they hold, is a spirit without a *body,* so *souls* must leave their *bodies* entirely before they can be joined with God."

But Job was of another opinion, though it may be, he was no more than a Philosopher too; he did not expect eternal happiness, nor to be with God till the end of the world, any more than Paul did.

It is also further evident, that the soul doth not partake of eternal happiness until the last coming of Christ, for the saints are bid to be in a waiting and watching posture, until the very time of Christ's second coming, as is set forth in the parable of the *Five wise virgins.*

There are two things which the saints in all ages of the world have waited for: The first is *Their God's becoming flesh;* and the second is, *For his coming in glory.* We that live now near the end of the world, and have known of his coming in flesh, and of the virtue thereof, are waiting for his *second coming*; because our happiness in eternal glory comes not until our Lord comes to fetch us, according to his promise and our faith.

We, who are of the true church, do wait with the church, for the personal appearing of the most high and mighty God the Lord Jesus, in Heaven, in order to our felicity, joy, and glory.

Those who expect a God here upon this earth, after any other manner than a personal Jesus, seated on a throne of eternal glory in the Heaven above, will never find him; and whoever looks for a God to come before the end of the world, or a God without a personal form, will find their hopes vain.

Because it is as much out of the way of truth, as the *mosaical Jew,* who is yet gazing for his first coming.

Therefore did the apostle say, that *the Saints waited for the Lord from Heaven.* 1 Thes. i. 10. Phil. iii. 20. And in Heb. x. 36. The Apostle exhorts them to patience, and tells them, that they shall enjoy the promise after they have done the will of God; for, saith he, a little while, and the promise comes; wait a little while, and he that shall come, will come, and will not tarry.

As if he should have said, "Have you not faith? If you have, live by it; and let it cause you to wait, for his promise of coming is sure. Apply it to yourselves then, and by virtue thereof possess your souls with patience, waiting for your Lord; who will come in a little time, and then he will deliver you from all your " troubles, and give you felicity, joy, and glory with himself for ever.

Thus we see, that the scriptures are full of exhortations hereunto; and hence it is, that the very last words in the bible of the second record hath this petition of the Saints put up unto their God, saying, *Come Lord Jesus, come quickly;* because the afflicted Saints knew they could never be avenged on their persecutors, nor attain to a personal happiness until the coming of their God, the Lord Jesus Christ blessed for ever, Amen.

Further evidence of the soul's resting with the body is, that the scripture hath no where attributed to the Saints *Eternal Joy, Felicity*, and *Glory*; but at the Resurrection day, when the Saints bodies are changed from *corruption* to *incorruption;* from mortality to *immortality*; then comes the rejoicing day.

For though the divine part of the man was breathed, by the immortal God, yet it was made one essence with a body taken out of the dust; therefore it must either change to mortality, or change mortality to it; for mortality and immortality cannot dwell together.

The soul cannot rejoice while the body is in the grave; for the scriptures do no where say, that the soul can go to Heaven, and rejoice there, and leave the body behind it to rot, and stink in the grave.

It is not possible to conceive, that the soul can be conscious of its existence, it cannot be sensible of itself if it center not in a body; there is no such thing; but life to one, life to both; death to one, death to both.

Did ever any man read in either Prophet or Apostle, that the soul should have any particular joy at the end of this life under the death of its body, and then a further joy at its resurrection, at the end of the world?

That saying of Christ to the believing thief on the cross, contains nothing against our doctrine; for the paradise in which both Christ and the converted thief was in, was in the peace of their own minds, in the assurance and knowledge of life everlasting by faith.

Nothing is more evident than this, for Christ himself did not ascend from the grave till the third day after, nor into Heaven till forty days after.

The day of conversion is a joyful resurrection day, because it is the seal of the other; but there is no entering into our Lord's *immortal* joy, till the *resurrection* at the end of the world.

Therefore saith Paul, We are your rejoicing, even as you are ours in the day of the Lord Jesus.

In Phil. ii. 16. he encourageth the saints to stand fast to their faith, and that for two causes. First, For that his own labour might not be in vain. And secondly, That he might rejoice in the day of the Lord Jesus. Paul doth not speak here of any joy he should have at the coming of Death, but at the *coming of Jesus.* So also in 1 Thes. ii. 19 & 20., he saith, the Believers will be their (the Apostles) hope, joy, and crown; yet it is but in the Day of the Lord Jesus, and not before.

The saints joy of salutation with one another doth not come in at the coming of death, but at the coming of Jesus: Therefore, saith Peter, rejoice, in as much as you are partakers of Christ's suffering, that when his glory shall be revealed, you may be glad also with exceeding joy.

Thus we see that *joy* and *Jesus* come together. When the saints die, they are said to rest in their graves for a while, there to remain till *the harvest be ripe. Rev. vi. 11.*

So that some saints joys must not be made perfect until all be made perfect. One must not got to heaven this year, and another the next: but all will be happy together.

The day of glory is at the glorious appearance of the great God; and this is the day of goal delivery, the *All Saints day; This is the Holy day which the Lord hath made*, or will make in order to all saints glory.

Paul waited for a *crown*, and said, *there was one laid up for him*; yet did he not expect to wear this crown until the day of the Lord's appearance.

1 Thes. ii. 19. So Peter also says, that when the chief Shepherd should appear, then the believers in him should receive a *Crown of Life*, but not before.

For what reward soever the saints were promised after death, the scripture does not say that any is given till the end of the world.

Therefore it is written Rev. xxii. 12. *Behold I come quickly, and my* Reward *is with me.* Here we see every man will have his reward given him when Christ comes. And this is agreeable to that saying concerning the *Talents given to the Servants,* that after a *long time* the Lord cometh, and reckoneth with them. This *long time* was until the end of the world, and the reckoning day is the resurrection day; then will he reckon with him that had the *one talent* of the law, and with the other that had the *five talents* of

Grace, and will crown his own gifts with a Come ye blessed of my Father, inherit the kingdom prepared for you.

Paul also tells us, that we shall reign in life; for by Jesus, death shall be swallowed up through life, Rom. v. 17. 2 Cor. v. 4. 1 Cor. 15.

He also further says, that Our life is hid with Christ; and When Christ shall appear we shall appear with him.

Our life is hid, saith the Apostle; and this is a comfort to the Saints, that though they are dead in themselves, yet are they alive in Christ's breast, and hid there.

This is the *Book of Life, wherein the Saints names are written*; therefore though they are dead in nature, yet they may be said to be alive; because they are in the memory of Christ, which is the *Book of Life in which their* new names *are written with the white stone;* and this they know in their life-time, and see and live through faith.

Another evidence of this doctrine is, that When Christ comes to Judgment, all that are in the grave shall hear his voice and come forth; those that have done *good* to the resurrection of life, and those who have done *Evil* to the resurrection of condemnation.

Observe, That the souls of men go not to either *sensible* joy or sorrow at their death, but into the *grave*, and in the *grave* Christ finds them, and from the Earth and Sea he raiseth them up.

Rev. xx. The Seas gave up the dead which were in it; and Death and Hell, and the Grave delivered the dead which were in them; and they were judged every man according to his works; and Death and Hell were cast into the Lake of Fire: And this the second death.

See also 1 Cor. xv. 52. And 1 Thes. iv. 16. saith Paul, The trumpet shall sound, the Lord shall descend with a shout, with the voice of the Arch-Angel, and with the trump of God.

This trumpet will be the great voice of God, therefore it is said, The Seas shall cast forth their dead at the command of Jesus.

Where then, or from whence do their souls come, but with their bodies? For, observe, after their resurrection they have their everlasting doom.

The *reward* of works is then given, and not before. See 2 Cor. V. 10. So that it is clear, the *body* and *soul* are raised together, and have their sentence given to them together.

It is contrary to sound reason as well as to scripture, to believe that the wicked should stand twice before God to be judged; once at death, and again at the resurrection.

From henceforth let no sober man oppose this doctrine of the *Soul's sleeping with the body*; seeing the scriptures do so abundantly demonstrate the same; but let them give glory to the Lord God Almighty, who can, and will give every dead soul his life again.

OF THE TWO NATURES Which are in MAN.

That they proceed from a Good and Bad seed: Of their Enmity, and their Original.

EXPERIENCE shows us, that there are in the present constitution of mankind two natures or dispositions, directly opposite to each other; which are discovered by inclinations to good, and inclinations to evil.

And as the scripture saith, James iii. 11. One fountain cannot bring forth a sweet water, and a bitter; so one nature cannot bring forth sin and sanctity; but they must proceed from two several roots or causes.

Know then, that the *tree of knowledge* of *good* and *evil,* which stood in the midst of the garden of Eden, is to be understood in an allegorical and spiritual sense, as is also, the *fruit of that tree,* which the serpent is said to have tempted *Eve* to eat of.

For the eating of an apple could not have contracted an hereditary evil, as is generally said by those who take this in the vulgar manner.

But we are here taught by this allegory to understand, that by the eating of this forbidden fruit is meant Eve's receiving the Serpent, who was the fallen Angel, into her womb; where he transferred himself, and became transmuted into flesh, for she conceived on this, and bare Cain.

And when *she had eaten of this forbidden fruit*, that is, when she had taken his evil nature into her, she gained the knowledge of the good she had lost, and of the evil she had procured for herself, and all her posterity; but after her firstborn son Cain was born, she was willing to conceit he was of her husband's begetting, until she saw his actions as he grew up, and then she perceived he was of the seed of that evil tree.

It is expressly said in 1 John iii.12. that Cain was of the wicked one. Now the scripture calls Adam, the Son of God; therefore Adam was not the wicked one, and Cain consequently was not of his begetting.

The scripture in many places seems to delight in describing men under the similitude of trees; such as the *good* and *wild Olive Tree,* of the *Vine, and many other such like. But in* Ezek. xxxi. we have the very same allusion unto trees, and of trees also in the garden of God, and the garden of Eden, in the following manner.

Ezek. xxxi. 2.

Son of man speak unto Pharaoh, King of Egypt, and to his multitude, whom art thou like in thy greatness?

Ver. 3.

Behold the Assyrian was a Cedar in Lebanon with his branches, and with a shadowing shroud, and of an high stature; and his top was among the thick boughs.

Ver. 4.

The waters made him great, and deep set him on high, with her rivers round about her plants, and sent out her little rivers unto all the trees of the field.

Ver. 5.

Therefore his height was exalted above all the trees of the field, and his boughs were multiplied, and his branches became long, because of the multitude of waters when he shot forth.

Ver. 6.

All the fowls of heaven made their nests in his bough, and under his branches did all the beasts of the field bring forth their young; and under his shadow dwell all great nations. Thus was he fair in his greatness, in the length of his branches, for his root was by the great waters.

Ver. 8.

The Cedars in the Garden of God could not hide him: The Fir Trees were not like his boughs, and the Chesnut Trees were not like his branches, not any tree in the Garden of God was like unto him in his beauty.

Ver. 9.

I have made him fair by the multitude of his branches; so that all the Trees of Eden, that were in the Garden of God, envied him.

Ver. 16. —

And all the Trees of Eden, the choice and best of Lebanon, all that drink water shall be comforted in the nether parts of the earth.

Ver. 18.

To whom art thou thus like in glory, and in greatness among the trees of Eden? yet shalt thou be brought down with]the trees of Eden unto the nether parts of the earth; thou shalt lie in the midst of the uncircumcised, with them that be slain with the sword: This is Pharaoh and all his multitude, saith the Lord.

Is not this just such an allegory as that of Eve's fall, and the Tree of Knowledge of good and evil in the garden of Eden?

But this doctrine is most clearly proved in Gen. iii. 15, where God says, that there shall be *enmity* between the *seed* of the *woman,* and the *seed* of the *serpent.* Now where was the seed of the serpent at that time, but in the womb of Eve in Cain? and this was the cause of the enmity that is between these two natures: For if Adam had begot Cain, and all mankind had proceeded from him, then evil could not have been hereditarily in the world. For Adam came immediately from God, and was pure and perfect before he was corrupted by conjunction with Eve after her fall; but when the impure deceiver had defiled her, then was there a corrupt, baneful and envious seed warring against Adam's pure seed; for Adam could not have conveyed a nature to his posterity, which was not his own nature: Now his own nature tended to nothing but sanctity, love, purity and peace.

The original then of this bad disposition, which experience shows us to be in man, is this wicked nature, this evil seed of the fallen Angel, which is transferred more or less into the whole race from Cain.

The original of the good is from Adam, who was made perfect; and his good seed is transferred into all his race, and Cain's into his.

Now the conjunction of these two seeds in the whole human race, hath been ever since *the Sons of God* (that is to say) the sons of *Seth,* the son of *Adam, took them wives of the daughters* of wicked *men,* which were the sons of *Cain,* Gen. vi. 2. Thus these two seeds came to be mixed in one person.

And these two natures are often mentioned in scripture by the words, *flesh* and *spirit,* and by many names and distinctions; and men are distinguished into good or bad, according as the seed of *Adam,* or the seed of *Cain* is predominant in them.

Christ calls the wicked a generation of vipers, and a wicked generation proceeding from Cain; in our text they are called the *Children of the wicked one*; in another place, the Lord, and his beloved Apostle calls them *children of the Devil*; also *children of this world*: Paul calls them *children of disobedience*, and Peter, *covetous* and *cursed children.* Moses calls them *corrupters of themselves,* saying, their spot and mark is not the mark of the children of God. They are also called *evil seed, children of the devil,* and *sons of Belial.*

The others are distinguished by contrary names, as in my text, they are called the *seed of the son of man.* Isaiah calls them the *holy seed.* Peter and Paul the *seed of the blessed of the Lord.* They are also called the *children of the highest, children of light, children of the resurrection, sons of God, sons of the living God, dear children of God.* And the whole scriptures are full of proofs of the reality of their being two seeds; and of the names and distinctions by which they are called.

OF

PREDESTINATION.

IN my text mention is made of two seeds: Of which one is said to be the *Children of the Kingdom*; the other are *Tares,* which the *Evil one sowed,* and they are to be flung into the fire.

The original of these two seeds we have already seen and proved to be from Adam, who was the son of God; and from Cain, who was the serpent, which is the fallen Angel or true devil.

Now these two had a law of generation; the one originally in a natural and procreative way; the other was capable of dissolving himself into seed, as he did in the woman; and then also in a procreative way into posterity.

And of these two came the whole race of mankind; so that it is no wonder to find the scriptures set forth so often, and so strongly intimate that there are some pre-ordained to Eternal life, and others to Eternal death.

Adam, and all his true posterity, that is, every one in whom Adam's pure seed is predominant, are pre-ordained by God's decrees to Eternal life.

But for the Devil and his Angels eternal torments are prepared, as in Jude vi. This Devil and his Angels are Cain and his offspring; for when the Serpent was cursed, all his seed was cursed with him.

And therefore is that saying of Paul, that God *loved* Jacob, *and hated* Esau, *before they had done either Good or Evil. Rom. ix.*

For the Creator, upon the conception of Esau and Jacob, did discern the roots they both sprang from, as Esau from the predominancy of Cain's seed, and Jacob from that of Adam, which was of God; and from hence it was they became the objects of love and hatred; and here are the grounds of mercy and anger, blessing and cursing, life and death, salvation and damnation.

And none who own the scripture can deny this to be the true meaning of it; for the words are full, clear, and invincible, that the Apostle says, They were loved and hated before they had done Good or Evil.

So also saith Malachy, and in Chap, i. 3 & 4. he calls the children of Esau, *The borders of wickedness, and the People in whom he hath indignation for ever.* And when the scriptures are so express, there is no denying it without denying the authority of the scripture; nor of explaining it after the humour of some men, who say *it was* Jacob's *and* Esau's *good and evil works, which occasioned this love and hatred*; for the Apostle hath so clearly expressed himself, that no such explanation can be justified.

But it is plain, that it was not Esau's works which was the cause of the hatred; for we see that his father Isaac thought that Esau, his eldest son, had been the chosen of God, therefore he intended to have given him the spiritual blessing, had not Rebecca prevented it.

And if it had been to be obtained by man's diligence, or that man had a freedom of will to choose, or refuse this eternal blessing, then Esau had received it; for he had a belief that his father was a prophet, and his carriage was so obliging, that his father was deceived by it, and thought that he had been elected of God; How diligent was he to serve, and obey his father's commands, *He went out forthwith.* How careful also of his father's blessing and how greatly he valued it, is to be seen in the sincere grief of heart which lie expressed, when his father had told him he had *blessed* Jacob, *and he should be blessed.*

Esau cryed out with a great and bitter cry, saying, Bless me, even me also, O my Father! And again, Hast thou not reserved a blessing for me? Even a third time he requested it, saying, Hast thou but one blessing, O my Father! Bless me, even me also; and Esau lift up his voice and wept.

See here now what virtue there was in Esau's good works: Where is the power of free-will? Here is *will,* here is *desire;* but where is the *power*? The heavenly blessing and birth-right are both lost, and will not be gained notwithstanding all this struggle.

And we see by this, that the gift of eternal life depends not on man's will or power, work or wisdom.

There is another turn or explanation, which some please their fancies in giving to these texts of scripture, which is, that it is in relation to God's *Foreknowledge* of Jacob and Esau, and his *Fore-Seeing* them in men's estate, and perceiving their good or evil actions.

Notwithstanding there are no evil actions of *Esau* recorded in scripture; and it is plain his father knew of none that might cause his rejection. And these pleadings for works, and forced explanations are only the humours and fancies of carnal reasonings, which will not attend to the express tenour of the scripture; for the Apostle hath most clearly foreseen and prevented these objections, and closed the argument, by giving the true reason, in Rom. ix. which is, *That the purpose of* God *might stand according to* Election.

Now it is not often known who are elected, and who are rejected; for though it lies in the seed, and we see the outward fruit of that seed, yet we cannot give a final judgment of an eternal state, from some few operations of the seed; for when we see a man wallowing in sin and uncleanness, like the swine in the mire, we may say, that he acts from the seed of the serpent, and so is in the way of the rejected.

But whether he will be damned or no, is not known, he may be a *vessel of honour*, and *called* in time, and the good seed may be stirred up to act in him, and get the pre-eminence; but if his sin grow so high as to despise the truth, or judge things he knows not of, or to forsake the truth as *Demas* did, then he manifests himself to be the seed of the serpent, and appointed for wrath. So also an hypocrite may go far in a seeming purity and outward profession, yet he hath not the holy seed in his heart.

For we have this mark given us to judge by, as appears by *John*, 1 Epi. v. 6. who saith, If any man see his brother sin a sin not unto death, he shall ask, and shall have life *by that means* given unto him. But then it is presupposed that this brother hath the seed of faith; and so the faith of one, and the prayer of the other may produce the effect.

The Apostle tells us what this *sin unto death* is, that we may discover a reprobate by, and that is, *the despising truth*; and for such an one he forbids praying, saying, *there remains no more sacrifice*; but on the contrary to lay the curse.

Good motions are the blossoms of election, and good actions the Fruit; so are also faith, and a belief of the truth. So on the contrary, wickedness proceeds from the wicked and reprobate, the works of darkness and unbelief are inseparable; for infidelity and disobedience are the marks of reprobation.

There are *two daughters* of election, which are faith and holiness, these are *fruits* of election, and belong to it after vocation.

Vocation is the confirmation of election, according to the Apostle Peter's words, 1 Pet. i. 2. Elect according to the foreknowledge of God through sanctification of holiness and belief of the truth. So 2 Thes. ii. 13. Paul saith, God hath from the beginning chosen you to salvation through sanctification of the spirit and belief of the truth. Not that sanctification, &c. is the *cause* of election but the *fruit,* and so becomes the *evidence* of eternal life.

For though our election is sure as to God's eternal purpose and foreknowledge, yet do we not know the benefit of it to ourselves, until it be sealed, and made sure to us evidently in our vocation and obedience of faith: For what comfort can any man have, to believe that

God is sure in his purposes, and that there are a certain number of elect; unless he have an assurance in himself, that he is one of those who are elected, and shall assuredly be saved?

Therefore though election is before vocation, yet can there not be the knowledge of it without vocation. Although Peter, in 2 Ep. i. 10. exhorts the saints to *make their calling and* Election *sure;* let them but make their *Calling* sure, and they need not fear their *Election;* for *Election* is God's gift, and *Vocation* is the *Seal* which makes the inheritance certain.

It is a good sign of election being sure, when a person is entirely resigned to God's dispensation, and with a true humility of heart submits to the eternal purpose of God, before he knows whether he is elected or rejected, is contented to be disposed of as God hath appointed, and resolved never to speak ill of his name, but sincerely to pray, that His will may be done upon Earth as it is in Heaven; who is satisfied, and will not dispute God's sovereignty and power, nor his prerogative will and pleasure, though it be against himself.

And why will man be so proud to contend with God; Hath not the Potter power over the clay, to make one vessel to honour, and another to dishonour? Rom. ix. 21, It is abundantly declared in the scripture, especially by the Apostle Paul, Rom. ix. 18. He will have mercy, on whom he will have mercy, and whom he will he hardeneth.

Is it not as plain as words can express it, that God made all things for his own glory, and the wicked for the day of wrath? Prov. xvi. 4.

And Moses also said to Pharaoh in the name of God, Exod. ix. 16. For this same purpose have I stirred thee up, that I might show my power on thee; and that my name may be declared throughout all the earth.

And is it not also written, Rom. ix. 22 & 23. What if God willing to show his wrath, and to make his power known, endured with much long-suffering the vessels of wrath fitted to destruction? And that he might make known the riches of his glory on the vessels of mercy, which he had afore prepared unto glory.

And who shall call God to account for his doings! If he hath revealed unto us his pleasure, who shall gainsay it? though it were as in Mat. xiii. 15. referring to the prophet Isaiah, Chap, vi. 10. Make the heart of this people fat, their ears heavy, and their eyes blind, lest they should hear with their ears, and see with their eyes, and understand with their hearts, and be converted, and I should heal them.

And this is for the manifestation of God's justice on the evil seed of the Serpent, and his mercy to Adam's which is his own.

And so full and clear is the scripture in this, that it were endless to turn to all the places; besides all do acknowledge this, who acknowledge the absolute authority of the scripture, and who take it for God's revealed will; but there are some, who by narrow, blind philosophical views, mix their own carnal reasoning with it, or set reason up wholly above it, and expound and stretch the scripture, and distinguish upon it to what they would have it, to make it speak their own minds and not God's. Thus some, who are afraid positively to deny the doctrine of election, because the scripture is so full of it, yet they explain it away by talking of a *secret will* and a *revealed will* of God; and by his secret will he rejects some, and by his revealed will he would have all to be saved.

Now what presumption and absurdity is this? What have they to do with God's secret will? for what is not revealed is unknown; but God's will in this case is revealed particularly and clearly by the Apostle *Paul*.

And they might bring it clearer to their own philosophical curiosity too, if they would but regard it; for the scripture is perfect and consistent with itself one place with another, and not contradictory as they imagine, but easy to be understood; and it is their mixing their own reason with scripture which blinds them.

For if they did but know that there are two opposite seeds in mankind, and that the wicked seed is the fallen Angel himself transmuted into flesh, they might see that God's hatred is just and good. For it is only punishing the Angel for his rebellion in heaven, and for his inveterate malice, in endeavouring to corrupt the good seed of Adam, by transferring himself into the woman, and mixing his evil nature in the whole race; these must continue together, as in our text, Mat. xiii. 40. *till the end of the world;* when they shall be separated, and those which the wicked one hath sowed will be thrown into the fire; and the others are the children of God.

Now an Elect Vessel may be filthily polluted, and look like reprobate silver until conversion; therefore it is said in Eph. ii. 3. that the *Elect are the Children of wrath as well as others*. This is not to be understood that the Elect are under the same wrath with the seed of the serpent; but God's wrath is upon the corrupted part of their nature, that is, upon their sin; but if there is the pure seed in the heart, God stretcheth forth his mercy to them, and quickens it, till it grow up to faith; then doth it get predominant, and by an union and sympathy in nature it flies to, and embraceth Christ as its own life; and this is the ground on which Election is founded, *viz.* in *Adam*; for *Adam* was the first object of mercy.

Therefore we are to look no higher than *Adam* for it; for though *Peter* says, 1 Ep. i. 20. *Elect before the foundation of the world.* This is to be understood of God's purpose to make *Adam*, and his race, whom he decreed should inherit Eternal Life; and *Adam* being created the decree was perfected.

Therefore in whatsoever person the true and pure seed of *Adam* is, the Spirit of God will find it, and quicken it into faith, and bring it into eternal life.

But until God works in us to righteousness, we can do nothing of ourselves; for that which should act forth unto holiness is asleep, as if it were dead in us, until divine grace awakens it.

There is nothing of man's work, but God's gracious will, which works out our salvation. Proud man would be his own Saviour if his will had but power; but man is, in his corrupted state, averse to goodness, and his repentance from his own natural motion is of no efficacy; for God is not to be flattered like a Courtier, or to be wrought upon like weak men, who can be diverted from their purposes by pitiful tales and well made speeches.

It is written, Rom. xi. 29. The gift and calling of God is without repentance. Also Isa. lxv. 1. I was found of him that sought me not. Rom. ix. 16. It is not in him that willeth, nor in him that runneth.

For until the Lord hath presented the crown of glory, there can be no walking in God's way, as David says, Psalm cxix. 32. When thou hast enlarged my heart, then will I run the ways of thy commandments. For the Lord cannot truly be known, till his name and nature be found written in the heart; when this is done, then the soul, that was backward to all goodness, is now by virtue of that divine light, made willing to choose the better part, and not before.

Therefore let sin, or seeming sanctity be what they will, it is the *Prerogative, Power, Will* and *Pleasure* of God the Creator, is all, who has fixed the state of all things that are already created, and directed their conditions. And *Condemnation* and *Salvation* so determined are consistent with the manifestation of his infinite power and glory.

OF THE

RESURRECTION.

THE learned in human philosophy do make a jest of the Resurrection; because say they, How can the particles which compose these bodies meet again, and join together, after they have many times changed places, and some of them been in other bodies?

But see how their boasted knowledge deceives them! They frame absurdities themselves, and father them on the scriptures, and then answer them.

We are not told in the scripture, that the very same particles of our bodies which we have here will be gathered together, united, and raised at the last day, but that the seed of the body and soul can never be lost or destroyed; and if we attend to the Apostle Paul, we find that he hath explained it under the similitude of a corn of wheat, which being sowed in the earth, dies of itself; but springs forth in a new one.

The substance of the old grain rots in the earth, but there is an imperceptible life in it, which perishes not, but in its due time is quickened, and springs up into new wheat.

So although the particles, which composed the bulk of this body, are perished and separated; yet is there an invisible principle or seed still remaining, which will spring forth, and have its proper existence in a new body, when it is quickened by the voice of God.

For the spirit of every seed exists always, and at the resurrection the children of God, and of the fallen Angel will each have their own proper bodies without mixture.

And for this cause will the saints bodies be changed, because these old bodies have something of the evil nature in them; but when they are raised again, those vile corrupted parts will be left behind, and they will have bodies, new, pure, and glorious; as the Apostle says, Phil. iii. 21. When our Lord comes, he will change our vile bodies, and make them like unto his glorious body.

And although the spark of fire be hid as in a flint, until it is struck, yet light shall come forth from where there was once light; though it hath been extinct in death, the breath of an Almighty God can rekindle it; this will be done by a word's speaking, for God's all-powerful spirit will make the spirits of the dead take fire, and live again.

The seed of the serpent will also spring up that day in bodies suitable to their evil nature and wicked lives, they will have the mortification of seeing the saints whom they cruelly used, and despised in this life, mount up to heaven in triumph, while themselves will be left behind on this earth to receive their punishment on the spot where they committed their actions, and with their own malignant spirits and awakened consciences, to torment themselves in a place, which will then be deprived of all light and comfort.

But when the Lord Jesus, who is the most high God, hath spoke forth the powerful word of *Come, ye blessed,* the seed of Adam in glorious bodies, such as his own, will enter with him and his Angels into his everlasting kingdom; where every one of their tongues will be as an harp, to sound forth the praise of the Lord God Almighty.

Even as Christ himself teaches us in the parable which we chose for our text, Mat. xiii. 3. *Then shall the righteous shine forth as the Sun in the Kingdom of their Father.*

FINIS.

T. GOODE, PRINTER. 30, AYLESBURY STREET, CLERKENWELL.

THE HARMONY

of the

THREE COMMISSIONS

OR

NONE BUT CHRIST:

Wherein is infallibly declared that all *Prophets* in the Time of the *Law*, or under the *first Commission*, and all *Apostles* and *Ministers* in the Time of the *Gospel*, do each of them unanimously agree in their Doctrine concerning GOD.

And that according to the Doctrine of the *third Commission*, which Doctrine was in the two first *Commissions*, and is more fuller in this, being the *Commissions* of the *Spirit*; namely, that there *is None but* CHRIST, *None but* CHRIST: no other *God* but our *Lord, Jesus Christ*, now in Heaven glorified.

THE FIRST RECORD EVIDENCED.

Unto us a Child *is born: unto us a* Son *is given: He shall be called the mighty God and the everlasting Father. Isa.* ix. 6.

THE SECOND RECORD EVIDENCED.

Great is the Mystery of Godliness; God *manifested in Flesh. There are three that bear Record in Heaven, &c. I. John* v.

THE THIRD RECORD EVIDENCED.

In the Days of the Voice of the seventh Angel, when he shall begin to sound, the Mystery of God shall be finished.

BY THOMAS TOMKINSON.

First written in the Year of our *Lord God* 1692; revised and abridged by the *Author*, and Printed in the Year 1757.

REPRINTED FOR J. MAY, BY T. C. ANNALL, DEAL,

1822.

NONE BUT CHRIST.

CHAP. I.

Shewing how that Moses, his faith and Doctrine was pitched upon God's becoming Flesh and so a Saviour.

SECT. I.

Moses's testimony

NO sooner was man fallen and life lost, but *Moses* tells us of a gracious promise in these words; *the seed of the woman shall break the serpent's head.*[1]

Now, from my faith, who have learned under the commission of the spirit, it is as much as if God the creator should say,[2] "Hath the serpent angel that I cast out of Heaven for his rebellion, undone thee; now my mercy is such, as that it shall occasion thy greater glory through patience in suffering, and belief in my words, for I will become seed; yea very man, that may die for thy ransom; but he that hath undone thee shall be undone, for I will break his head with an eternal blow. Thou shalt die but one death, but he shall die not only a first death, but a second death also: thy death is but the bruising of the heel; therefore have patience for these thy sufferings, and have faith as to thy redemption from the same."[3]

Here now is the true God made manifest by *Moses* to become seed of *Adam's* seed, and flesh of his flesh; so that *Adam* being the seed or nature of God, God would take upon him his own seed of the light of life eternal that he might raise the seed of Adam to a distinct glory like unto himself.[4]

Therefore, from hence I infer, they that will have a God disunited from the seed and nature of *Adam*, will never find a saving God, but the seed of *Adam* as they were first taught by *Moses*, and ever after by true prophets and apostles ever more to worship God as hidden in man, or as becoming man.

---

[1] Gen. iii. 15.
[2] xii. 3. xxii. 18. xviii. 18.
[3] See the confirmation of this doctrine aforesaid by references to other prophets and apostles writings. Rev. xii. 12. Rom. ix. 18. Acts Xiii. 23. Rom. i. 3. Heb. ii. 14, 16. Isa, liii. 8, 9,10. Jude vii. Matt. xxv. 46.
[4] Gen. xii. 3.

Abraham, Isaac and *Jacob*, whom *Moses* makes the father of the faithful, worshipped God as becoming man, and so a *Jesus* or *Saviour*: therefore, when God told *Abraham*: *That in his seed all the nations of the world should be blessed*, gave *Abraham* to understand; that he would become seed.

Therefore said that seed, when he was come, "*Abraham* saw my day and was glad," the covenant that God made to *Abraham* was as a glass,[1] in which he beheld his Redeemer in a body of flesh, every time that God blessed *Abraham*; *Abraham* in that blessing saw *Christ, God, Man* in a body of flesh and bone, of his seed blessed for ever; and beheld him as the one only and alone true God, not minding any God or Father distinct from him.

When *Abraham* was offering up his son, as soon as God bad him stay his hand, he looked and saw a ram in a bush, then did his faith see God ready to suffer when he saw that ram die, and the blood run out; then from that type he saw the antitype, even the blood of that immaculate lamb run out as a river to wash away the sins of all his spiritual seed.

Moreover, where his son *Isaac* was offered intentionally, there was the God of heaven offered really; hence it is that *Abraham* gives that place the name of *Jehovath Iruth*, which signifies, "in the mount of the Lord it shall be seen."

This mount of the Lord was all *Abraham's* spiritual seed; this was the house of that *Jehovah*, or *Jesus*, and it is they only that see what is wrought there upon that hill or mount *Sion*; none others knew the nature of that work of redemption; for in this mount of the Lord is salvation wrought by this *Jehovah* becoming *Jesus*, and no where else.

SECT. II.

Again *Moses* declares *Isaac's* God to be the same with *Abraham's* having the same blessings;[2] it runs all upon this; *in thee and in thy seed shall all the nations* (or elect in all nations) *be saved*; and so also with *Jacob*; in all which was the fountain or life or salvation but by God's becoming flesh.

After *Jacob* had seen the vision and received the blessing, then was he strongly confirmed in the faith of his God's becoming flesh to save him and his seed; *this is the house of God* (saith *Jacob*) *this is the gate of heaven*;[3] here *Jacob* saw that God was to come down from

---

[1] Gen. xxii. 13.
[2] Gen. xxvlііі. 14.
[3] xxviii. 17.

heaven to take seed of him (whose house he and his seed and he saw the ladder reared, and all the three commissions were as three staves to the ladder.[1] In that place did *Jacob* set up a stone that lay under his head for his pillow, and hallowed it, calling it by the name of *Bethel*, the house of God; that stone was the pillar the house stood on; for the stone that was under his head was him that *David* called, the *lifter up of his head, Psal.* iii. 3.

It was not a material stone, though that was made the sign of it; but it was a stone cut out of the mountain of *Bethlem Judath* for *Christ* came of *Judath*, so *Judath* became the praise of God and the head of *Israel*; for the headstone was hewn out there. See and compare *Dan.* ii. 34. *Mica.* v. 2. *Matt* ii. 6.

The stone that was *Jacob's* pillow was *Jacob's* God and *Jacob's* guide and *Israel's* shepherd; Therefore, said *Jacob*, when he blessed *Joseph* upon his death-bed, *that the arms of Joseph were made strong by the hands of the mighty God of Jacob: from which is the shepherd, the stone of Israel.*[2] Who now was this shepherd and stone of *Israel*, but *Jesus Christ* the Lord? and who was this *Christ?* but the mighty God of *Jacob*; none but the true *Israel* knows the voice of this shepherd, nor hath his head lift up by any other stone but by this living stone. See and compare *Matt.* xxi. 42. *Luke* xii. 17. *Psal* xlv. 3. *Esa.* ix. 6. *Psal* iii, 3. I *Pet.* ii. 4, *Zech.* iii. 9.

SECT. III.

Moses, having given us a description of the God of our fathers,[3] goes farther, shewing more abundantly in his other books of God's becoming flesh, or man, to die for man; and therefore he tells us, that God in his commission to him did proclaim himself the God of *Abraham*, the God of *Isaac*, and the God of *Jacob*;[4] and that he called himself to him by the name of *I am*.

Now *Jesus* that was born of a virgin two thousand years after, declared himself to be *that I am*. Now this I am first, and I am last, *Alpha* and *Omega*, excludes all co-partners; for none is to share with the Holy One of *Israel*. See and compare *Isa.* xliv. 6. *John* viii. 58. *Rev.* i. 17. *Isa.* xlii. 8.

Now this I am, was the Lord that *Moses* said should *reign for ever and ever.*[5] See *Duet.* vi. 14. and xviii. 15. *and that he should become a*

---

[1] ver 18.
[2] Gen. xlix. 24.
[3] Exod. iii. 6.
[4] ver. 14.
[5] Moses's testimony. Exod. xv.

prophet himself like unto him. Now *Moses* was a great prophet, but most of his works was in giving forth a fiery law unto the rational nature of that nation of the *Jews,* and an external and visible worship also, which was to serve for the seed of reason.

For there was written the law in the seed and nature of reason, which is the angels nature. Now *Moses* acted as a God in the person of the angel, or tree of knowledge of good and evil, and so his giving forth that outward letter of the law to that seed, was to shew that law more plain that was written within, and to enlighten reason in its way to do as he is done unto,[1] but not as he would be done unto, that only reaches faith's nature. *Matt.* v. 38. 39. and vii. 12.

Now this law of retaliation reason counts just, but then it comes to be pinched in this, in that the law doth condemn reason for not doing that as the letter of the law doth say thou shalt do or not do: now this law working a fear of eternal death, puts reason on to fast and pray, and to offer sacrifice and to work for life.[2] *Isa.* i, 11, and lviii. 3.

Therefore when *Moses* had given reason a law, he gave him an outward visible tabernacle,[3] as also he gave them several outward legal ceremonies which was to signify the true tabernacle itself, and that true spiritual worship that did belong to it, being as a pattern to set forth those spiritual and heavenly things that were to be acted in the commission of *Jesus*; but reason being blind, it could never see into the substance, but rested in the shadow. See *Heb.* viii. 5. *Acts* vii. 53. *Heb.* ix. 5, 9, and x. 1.

Now the elect seed of *Abraham,* they had not this law given unto them;[4] for grace came not by *Moses* but by *Jesus. John* i. 17, yet did they worship in that visible temple; but then they by faith saw the substance which now I am coming to set forth, only this, by the way, that we may see what the substance of the law is, and in what nature it was written, and how by it is kept in awe, which proves beneficial to the innocent seeds of faith, the seeds of the Lord's own body.

---

[1] xxi. 24.
[2] Moses's testimony. Gen. iv. 3.
[3] Exod. xxv. 8. ver. 40.
[4] Deut. xi. 26. vi. 16. Gen. iii. 24. iv. 13.

SECT. IV.

All the ceremonial worship, with the manner and nature of it, did all prefigure the coming of God in flesh, behold some instances when *Israel* passed through the *Red-sea*, the elect *Israel* received a spiritual baptism from the penetrating waters of the clouds. The rock that *Moses* smote[1] was the faith of God's becoming flesh; for *Paul* said after that, that rock was *Christ*, 1 *Cor.* x. 1. Observe, it is said, that that rock followed them; which rock was *Christ*. Now this *Christ* was called by *Moses* the angel of God: now although *Paul's Christ* was called by *Moses* the angel of the Lord,[2] yet is this angel no other but God himself, as you may see *Exodus* iii. where it is thus written, *And the,: angel of the Lord appeared unto Moses in a flame of fire, and the Lord God called unto Moses out of the bush, and said, I am the God of thy fathers,* &c.

Here faith sees clearly, that that angel was Christ, and that Christ was the God of *Abraham*.[3] It is further written, that when *Abraham* stretched out his hand to have slain his son *Isaac, that the angel of the Lord called to him out of heaven.* Now was this angel of the Lord any other but *Christ* himself in his spiritual body? This is he that is the redeeming angel, according as *Israel* said, *the angel that redeemed me bless the lads,*[4] meaning *Ephraim* and *Manasseh.*

Wherefore then, as the angel of the Lord is the Lord himself, even so Christ the son of God is God himself: for why may not the title, *Son of God*, be as truly God, as angel of God is truly God; yet not all angels of God are God, so not all that are called sons of God are God; for there is but one angel of God which is God, and but one son of God which is God, and this angel of God was Christ, and this Christ was the Lord God Almighty, that looked through the clouds upon the *Egyptians*, and became there a man of war, and caused the sea to overwhelm them.[5]

This is *Israel's* God and rock, that *Paul* said they drank of; this was *Moses* and *David's* and *Peter's* rock,[6] in which they drank water of life with honey and oil. All the seed of *Israel* have but one rock, out of which they suck water and oil, and honey which is converted into peace of conscience, joy in the spirit, and assurance of eternal life. The water begets the peace, the oil brings joy, and the honey turns

---

[1] Numb. xx. 11.
[2] Exod. xiv. 19.
[3] Gen. xxii. 11.
[4] Gen. xlviii. 16.
[5] Exod. xlv. 24. and xv. 3.
[6] Duet. xxxii. 13, 4, and xxxiii. 19. Numb. xx. 8.

into the assurance of eternal life. See and compare *Psal.* lxxviii. 35. *John* iv. 14. *Isa.* lxvi. 11. *Psal.* viii. 2.

SECT. V.

The manna that the children of *Israel* were fed withal in the wilderness,[1] did typify another kind of bread, the elect seed did see into the mystery, and were satisfied with a spiritual food; for, from these words which God said, *I will rain bread from heaven for you*, all the true seed looked then for the coming of their Messiah. *Isa.* xxxiii. 16. *Isa.* xlvi. 1.

The ignorant and carnal *Jews* called it manna, which signifies what is this, or what new thing is this, being hidden to them, *Revel* ii. 17. so when the true bread came down from heaven,[2] their posterity said, as their fathers, What is this? Who is this? What new doctrine is this? How can this man give us himself to eat? *John* vi. 11.

This was the consecrated bread, that the true priests did bless,[3] the hallowed and pure shew-bread continually upon the pure table of gold; this is the holy bread, and only offered by a holy priest that hath no imperfection. Take and eat this bread from the high priest of God, being festival and appointed for every sabbath-day, being for such as are entered into their rest.

What was the ground of the priests and holy men of old, at their feasts, to take up a loaf or shiver of bread in his hand, looking up to heaven, and blessing God before they eat,[4] was not there the true bread pointed at, and when Christ came, then the true bread was come, and shewed his disciples it was to be broken for them.

The Scribes and Pharisees, that sat in *Moses's* chair, they observed the outward letter and ceremony in the blessing of the bread, but it wrought no further then, than the bread that perisheth, and every professor now as well as then, if he is for having his righteousness seen when he eats, then straight off with his hat, and his eyes towards heaven, but it is but to bless God for that perishing bread that feeds the body; it is not for the bread he hath eaten to eternal life, for of that bread he hath none, and so is always hungering and thirsting, notwithstanding his eating and drinking.

For he neither looks for, nor lacks no God from heaven, that brake his body for him, or shed his blood for him; for his God cannot die, or

---

[1] Exod. xvi. 15. Deut. viii. 3. Exod. xvi. 4.
[2] xxiv. 6. Exod. xxv. 30.
[3] Numb. iv. 7.
[4] Exod. xxiv. 24.

had any blood to shed, it is the earthly bread, that is Iris blessing by the law and birth-right, which he claims as his right by his obedience to the letter of the law, *Matt.* vi. 5, 16.

But the true *Israel* is the true christian; for to him Christ's body is meat indeed, and his blood that was spilt is drink indeed; and he that hath eaten and drunken once by faith in his person, it is enough, do but once eat and drink (not in an outward sacramental ceremonial ways, but of the thing signified) and it is enough, eat once, drink once, and live for ever. *John* vi. 58.

This converts prayers into praises, and spiritual meats begets spiritual worship of internal praise, which is invisible proceeding from the virtue of this invisible life, quickened by that invisible bread that came down from heaven. *John* vi. 41.

So that all outward worship now it is left to the hypocrite, who loves to make fair shew, and for this their long prayers they have their reward in the fruit of the vine, and in this manna or perishing bread which is given them.

SECT. VI.

Again, the blood that was for the atonement of sin, was the blood of the immaculate lamb; all the blood that was offered by the law,[1] was all as a type or figure of the blood of the Lord God, the promised seed to redeem *Israel.*

This blood was a covenant when *Moses* held it up, and said this is the blood of the new covenant, when the blood was sprinkled upon the people, then were they sanctified in the virtue of that blood, not in that blood of bulls or goats, but the blood of a lamb; not in the blood of that lamb that was to be killed at the door of the tabernacle that was made by *Moses,* but in the blood of that lamb of God, or the lamb which was God, and was the true tabernacle; a tabernacle from which the precious blood did issue out; it came out of that house, out of that heart, and out of that door, that was made by the spear in the side of *Jesus*; there it was that the blood came running out, and it was a door for the faith of his elect to enter in, and be cleansed; to apply that blood to itself, and be saved. This was that cleft of a rock in which they fled for refuge. *Isaiah* iv. 6. *Psal* xciv. 22.

When an atonement was to be made by blood, the offering was to be killed by the side of the altar, and the blood wrung out there by the door of the tabernacle, then was part of that blood sprinkled round about upon the altar, and *Moses* was to take of the blood that was

---

[1] Exod. xxiv. 8.

upon the altar, and to sprinkle it with the anointing oil upon *Aaron*, his sons, and upon their garments, and they should be hallowed.[1]

The sanctification was from the blood as it first came, and was sanctified from the altar, and the oil had its virtue as from the altar; the altar was first sanctified, and then all from the life of it was sanctified, and reconciliation wrought thereby.

Now as to the spiritual sense, Christ was afterwards made plain to be both the offering and the altar; for when he was come, he sanctified himself, that all might be sanctified in him. *Heb.* xiii. 10. *John* xvii. In a word, Christ is the true temple, the altar, the priest, he to whom it was offered, and he that was offered.

The priests of the ceremonies were all for shadows of good things to come: all the offerings they were of no esteem by the Lord, when there was not an eye that could pierce through the ceremony, and see into the substance, and walk by that, and that it was a lamb without spot that was capable to make an atonement for sin, even God himself, by the shedding of his precious blood.

This was the faith of *Abraham*, *Isaac*, and *Jacob*, and it was the faith of *Enoch* first, and of all the twelve patriarchs, as is seen by their blessings to their spiritual children, and it was the faith of *Moses*, the first writer of holy writ, and God's first witness, as abundantly further might be shewed, but this may be enough to satisfy the elect. So that by the testimony of *Moses*,

There is none but Christ, none but Christ, no other God but the man Christ *Jesus* our Lord, now in glory, in a body of flesh and bone blessed for ever. *Amen.*

---

[1] Exod. xxi. 6.

CHAP. II.

Shewing how David's Faith and Doctrine was pitched upon God *as becoming man, and for a Saviour and Redeemer, and so made himself capable to suffer the pains of death for the redemption of him and all his elect seed.*

SECT. I.

David's testimony[1]

IN *Psalm* the first, *David* brings in the man as blest that delight in the law of the Lord, and in *Psalm* cxix. he counteth him an undefiled, or a perfect man that doth so. Now this Lord is Jehovah becoming *Jesus*, and this law was to keep his statutes; which statutes was to believe in him, and trust in him with that affiance that he would become flesh.

So that he that had this law of given him,[2] he would worship the law-giver, which is no other but *Jesus*. See *Isa.* ii. 3: viii. 16. li. 4, 7. *John* i. 17.

Now such a godly man is to have the blessing of being directed, of keeping all the precepts, and to be fruitful in the knowledge and love of his redeeming Lord, and to stand in the judgment, and to be justified in the same.[3]

Therefore it is said, that *the Lord knoweth the way of the righteous*;[4] that is, he approveth of it, and justifieth their faith; but as for the other side, that set themselves against the true God, and his spiritual worshippers, they shall not stand in judgment, but shall be dashed in pieces by him whom they esteemed not to be God. *Isa.* xix. 3. *Luke* xix. 27. *Jer.* xx. 11. *Isa.* viii. 10.

In *Psalm* the second, *David* shews the decree how that God would become man, and humble himself into the name of a son, and this should become a stumbling block to kings and rulers; so that they should take counsel against this son, and so against God saying, the kings of the earth set themselves against the Lord, and against his *Christ*.[5]

---

[1] Psal. ii. 12. and ix. 10. and xix. 8. and cxix. 171.
[2] Psal. xix. 7. and cxix. 1. 18. 97. 142. 174.
[3] Psal. i. 3. 5. Psal. xxiii. 8.
[4] Psal. i. 6.
[5] Psal. ii. ver. 2.

This doth not mean that the Lord and *Christ* are two distinct persons; and though it is said, *Let* [us] *break their bands*, and again, *I will set my king upon my holy hill of Sion*,[1] and again, *thou art my son, ask of me*, &c.

Now these plurality of words, do not make plurality of persons, but of titles only, which is occasioned from the two natures of diety and humanity united in one person; for observe, when it comes to the work., it centres again in one person, as ver. 6. it is said, *then shall* [he] *speak unto them in* [his] *wrath, and vex them in* [his] *sore displeasure.*[2] Now this [*he*] in the single person is no other but *Christ*, that son that should pour out his wrath upon his enemies, as is plain by the last verse, saying, *Kiss the son lest he be angry, and you perish through his anger.*

That is, submit yourself, and worship the son with a divine adoration,[3] for he is God, and will rule over all rebels with a rod of iron. *Isa.* xlix. 7. *Zeph.* ii. 11.

That *Christ* is the one only and alone true God, it is evident by *David* in this place; for first, he is set upon *Sion's* hill, to be *Sion's* king and God, and to govern it by laws spiritual.

Secondly,

He hath attained to have all the elect for his inheritance, and his extent is to the uttermost parts of the earth,[4] where then should there be any other God; for if he have all in possession, then all other Gods are excluded from government.

Thirdly,

This son is said to be of that power, as to dash all his, and his saints enemies to powder, who shall make laws to subject and hinder *Sion* from worshipping their king that is set upon their hill,[5] and therefore, upon pain of damnation, are required to be so wise as to submit to him either feignedly or unfeignedly. *Isa.* xl. 10. *Rev.* xii. 5.

Fourthly,

Who should this son of God be, but God himself, seeing all divine worship is to be performed to him.[6]

---

[1] ver. 6.
[2] Psal. cxiii. 6.
[3] Psal. xlv. 1.
[4] Psal. ii. 6.
[5] Psal. ii. ver. 9. Psal. cx. 2.
[6] Psal. ii. 11.

Lastly,

This *Christ* must needs be father as well as son, seeing that all such are pronounced cursed that reject him for their governor, and all those pronounced blessed that put their trust in him.[1]

All these sayings of waiting, hoping and trusting in God, have all a dependence of the promise of God's becoming flesh, and so a son to redeem, and may be all applied hither.

SECT. II.

David, in the third *Psalm*, finding great opposition betwixt his, and his Lords enemies, because he pitched his faith upon a God in the form of a man, the reviling this God, as in *Psalm* ii. do now set themselves against all that put their trust upon this son of God,[2] and therefore they tell *David*, and all that are of his faith, that their God is a weak God, and there is no help for them in him, and so conclude with a *Selath*, as a note of their great rejoicing.

It is as if they should say, his God is not our God, our God is a paternal fire or spirit, God without any body; that is, so vastly infinite as to be every where at one, and the same time, and is amongst us, and lives in us, but he looks upon his God to be a substance, and in heaven at a distance, and looketh, and expecteth, and waiteth for his coming down to this earth, and to conquer for him here in a body or person like himself, and that he shall suffer death. This is a God like to help him indeed! Let him fly like a bird to this God,[3] and see what he can do for him,[4] but there will be no help for him in this his mortal mortal and dying God : we will not wait for such a God, for such a God cannot help him. Ha, ha! we shall see it, *Selath.*

David, seeing how the enemy reproached him, he the more trusted in his God, saying; *thou O Lord, art a shield for me, my glory and the lifter up of my head.* [5]

As if the prophet should say, still my faith and trust shall support me; for that which they count my shame,[6] I know to be my glory; for this son of God is a son and a shield about me: for first, he is a sun to enlighten me to walk in his way,[7] and secondly, he is a shield to

---

[1] Psal. ii. ver. 12. Psal. xl. 4. 16.
[2] Psal. lxxi. 11.
[3] Psal. xi. 1.
[4] cxliii. 9.
[5] Psal. iii. 3.
[6] Psal. iv. 2.
[7] lxxxiv. 11.

defend my head and to guard my heart,[1] and also he is the lifter up of my head,[2] in that he is the resurrection and the life; for though my enemy should so far prevail, as to send me down to the grave, yet will I not be dismayed; for they will prevail so far against my lord, but in a moment his God-head-spirit shall lift up his head, and then will he have attained to that power as to raise up my head; *and I shall sing praise to his name, for salvation belongeth unto all his people.*[3] *Selath.*

Again, the prophet longed hard for the accomplishment of the promise;[4] and he, seeing it certain by faith, therefore he brings in the faithful to welcome God to judgment. In this *Psalm* is a song to the praise of *Christ*, as the most high God; and the song is continued in the next *Psalm*, and in the second verse his power is described, saying; *that out of the mouths of sucklings he had ordained truth.*[5]

David in the 5th verse, speaketh a little intricately, as thus; first saith he, speaking of *Christ*'s humiliation, *that he was made a little lower than the angels*;[6] but the next words exalts him again, saying, *thou hast crowned him with glory and honour*; which was in these things; first, in that he had the sole dominion over all things; and secondly, in that all things are said to be put under his feet.

Again, *David* brings in *Christ*'s manhood, speaking to his godhead, saying, *thou hast delivered me from the strivings of the people, and thou hast made me the head of the heathen. A people shall serve me, hear me, and obey me, &c.*[7] How full are these words? what God can there then be besides

The twenty-second *Psalm* is a prophecy or a rehearsal of all those great sufferings of *Jesus* in the days of his flesh, and a foretelling of his crying unto God in that time of his passion.

So that when *Jesus* cried; "my God, my God, why hast thou forsaken me;" it was to fulfil this prophecy; for the Creator being become a creature, was to learn obedience; a wonderful example of humility.

---

[1] ix. 13.
[2] iv. 8.
[3] lxviii. 18.
[4] vii.
[5] viii. 2.
[6] ver. 5.
[7] Psalm. ix.

SECT III.

David calls the Lord his shepherd,[1] now *Israel* hath but one shepherd, as I shewed before, now the pasture of these sheep is said to be by the rivers of waters; now there is no living waters or spiritual pastures but in a personal God, Man, *Christ Jesus*; this was that water as *David* so longed for out of the well of *Bethlem*.[2]

This was faith in those days, and the substance of *David's* prayers and praises; was in pursuit of those gifts and graces promised to God's true prophets for the comfort of elect sons and daughters of *Sion*;[3] so that I shall abridge my discourse to the lxxiind *Psalm*, and to to the first verse of the lxxvith *Psalm*, and then draw to a conclusion of this testimony, otherwise my volume will be too large.

In *Psa.* lxxii. there is a desire or prayer, that the *Messiah*, the king of *Israel* may prepare himself for the work of redemption, as verse the first.

Secondly, in the second verse a promise is made to faith, that he shall come and be judge. The nature of his judgment is two-fold: first in righteousness, secondly in judgment. The persons to be judged by him are set down in the fourth verse: first he shall judge the poor of the people, secondly, he shall judge the wicked men and oppressor.

Thirdly, the Nature of the judgment is further described; as thus; first, he shall judge the poor of the people, that is, he shall find faith in them, and so shall justify them, and give them the seal of the assurance of everlasting life.

Secondly, he will also meet with the wicked; and then he shall condemn him and break him in pieces in the peace of his mind as in the second *Psalm*.

Again, the 6th and 7th verses are a description of the fruits and effects of that judgment; first, from this seal of redemption true worship takes place in these words; *they shall fear thee*, that is, *they shall worship thee as long as the sun and moon endures*.

Secondly, this doctrine of salvation coming from heaven, doth so water the earth or heart of man, as that it becomes fruitful in every good work as joy, love, peace, &c.

Thirdly, the extent of this peace is said to be till there be no moon; so long as there is men on this earth and faith in these men, so long there will be peace.

---

[1] Psal. xxiii. 1.
[2] II Sam. xxiii. 15.
[3] Psal. lxxii. ult.

The Harmony of the Three Commissions 513

Peace shall never cease springing up; but, as the influence of the moon causes the fruits of this natural earth to grow and increase, even so will the influence of the son of righteousness make peace to run as a river, making the water of life to run in the vein of faith.

Again, the seventh verse is a donation of all unto *Christ*, declaring him to have dominion from sea to sea, and so lord of the whole creation; it is further said, that all that live in the wilderness shall bow before him, and kings shall bring presents and fall down before him, and that all nations should serve him.

All kings are his vicegerents, for they are in the place of *Christ*, as he is Creator, and so they judge as Gods. Therefore obedience was ever wild to authority; for all kings do either feignedly or unfeignedly worship God by words and laws, though they know him not. But the kings that worship *Christ*, as *Christ* truly, are such as are spiritually anointed by him; for every christian is a king, but every king is not a Christian:

For although all men acknowledged a God, that are truly rational, yet the Prophet saith,[1] that God is only known in *Judah*,[2] and that his name is great no where so much as in *Israel*,[3] now how comes it that God is more known in *Judah* than elsewhere? is it not because it was the way of God from heaven? for the promise of God's becoming flesh is founded there; salvation begins there; it takes root there; even from *Judah*, from *Jess*, and so from *David*; here is the spring of life, and the God of life, and salvation is known here, being a branch from thence. *Isa.* lxv. 9.

Doth not that saying of *David* sound to this sense?[4] and is it not as if he should say,. my dependence is of *Israel*, and so of *Judah*, that out of her the Saviour of the world shall come; for God shall be incarnate, and proceed from princely *Judah*,[5] and shall be a God of substance, and of man's substance he shall partake, and be both God and man in one blessed and single person, not an airy God, void of substance. *I. John* iii. II. *Phil.* ii. 7. *Heb.* i. 3. *Ephesians* ii. 2. as the workers of iniquity affirm; for say they, *we will break their cords asunder*, which are twisted together of God and man; for we will not have any God that comes out of *Judah-Bethlehem*; we will not have a God that hath man's nature in him, we will break those cords and bands of being drawn with a man or a God like a man that is visible,

---

[1] Psal. lxxvi. 1.
[2] lx. 7.
[3] cxiv. 2.
[4] lxviii. 11.
[5] lxxviii. 68. Psal. lxxiii. 25. cxliii. ix.

and may be seen.¹ See and compare *Hos.* xi. 4. *Isa.* vii. 6, 17. viii, 6, ver. 6, 9, 10, 14. Our God springs not out of *Judah*; for out of *Judah* comes a substance; but God is not a substance that can be seen, felt, or understood; this is to make God subscribed to one place at one time, who is omnipresent in all places at once, therefore let the people fly to this their God like a man, and of man's seed, and see whether he can help them.² See *Micah.* vii, *Isa,* vii. 6, and 8. ix. 10, 12;

This was the faith and language of the enemies of *Sion,* and *Sion's* God in the days of old, not only in the heathens that were without the written law of *Moses,* but of all the carnal seed that made an outward profession and pretended obedience to that law. It is confessed that reason the angel's nature fallen can do no less than to acknowledge, there is a God, and that he must be just and holy, and that obedience is due to him; but the highest, and most piercing reason that is, can never be able to know him truly what he is in his form and nature; neither doth the written law of *Moses;* nor the law in nature reveal him any other way, but as their creator and preserver, with a tye of obedience to his revealed law of nature, but not the revealed law of faith, that's not for them.

Therefore it is that the God of truth ever avails his blessed person to reason, and reveals himself to faith;³ because he will save that seed; and his way to save the house of this true *Israel* is to become seed of that seed, and in this seed he is only to be known, and his name is to be great here, after he hath wrought their redemption by his death and resurrection; the prophet *David* saw this, and left it upon Record for a comfort to all the elect seed,⁴ he by faith saw the manner of his triumph over sin, death, hell and the grave, in his glorious ascension; and therefore with admiration cries out, saying; *God is gone up with a shout; sing praises.* This was *Jesus Christ,* and this was *David's* God, that was despised by the world,⁵ but was great in *Judah,* and known only to *Israel.* So that by the testimony of *David,* there is none but *Christ!* none but *Christ!* no other God but the man *Christ Jesus* our Lord, though man and all the seed of the fallen angels should gainsay it.

---

[1] Psal. ii. 3. xxii. 6.
[2] xciv. 9, 10. and lxiv. 5. cxliii. 9. xi. 1. xliii. 3. and cxv. 3.
[3] Psal. xxxvi. 9. & cxic. xcviii. xcix. c. xlvii. ult. xlviii. ult.
[4] xlvii. 1. 6.
[5] Psal. xxii. 6.

CHAP. III.

Shewing how that the prophet Isaiah's faith and doctrine was wholly fixed upon God's becoming flesh; and he had no other worshipped, nor taught, expected, waited, or looked for any other saving God but Christ the Lord only.

SECT. I.

Isaiah's testimony

ALTHOUGH the prophet *Isaiah* lived several hundred of years before the Incarnation of God; yet was all faith fixed upon him in a body of flesh and bone; for the prophet shewed that his birth in a virgin's seed was *Sion's* birth, salvation and assurance; for as soon as he took our nature and Godhead united with manhood, as soon as he had brought himself the first begotten of God, then came man actually to be entered into the salvation : therefore said the prophet, *that out of Sion shall go forth the word, and that word should judge among the nations.*[1] *Micah* iv. 2. *Psal.* cx. 6.

These things will be in their time said the prophet,[2] and he then intimates that the saints oppressors, that made us fly to our rock, they should then fly to their light of reason, which is their rock; but saith he, their rock shall not save them, though their reason which is their rock, tells them that their bow and their shield shall save them, and their strong horses shall save them, which are their formalities in their rationality,[3] *Psal.* xxxiii. 14. *Matt.* vi. 16. but they that fight against *Israel*'s God, shall be tumbled down into the dust by that God-Man that comes out of *Sion*,[4] though they be the great men of the earth, called *tall cedars*, but they be brought into the dust by a first death; yet this our God-Man that is to judge amongst the nations shall raise them again out of their holes, then will the sight of him be terrible, which will make them desire they might go down into their holes again for fear of his majesty, even *Jesus Christ, Sion's* God and king.

It is good to mind what the prophet saith concerning God, because he did set the person of God. Some of the *Jewish* Rabbies say, that *Isaiah* was put to death, because he held that God was corpereal;

---

[1] Isa. xxv. 3, 4, 11, 12 and 13.
[2] xxxi. 1, 2. lviii. 2, 3.
[3] Chap. ii. 19.
[4] ver. 21.

Whether this was so or no, it matters not, but certain it is, that *Isaiah* did behold the similitude of God as well as *Moses*,[1] therefore mind well that prophet's doctrine that hath seen God; he will speak wonderful things of God; that prophet's doctrine will run all of God hidden in man, or becoming man. And now to the prophet's doctrine, he upon the description of the vision of God, cries out, saying, *Woe is me, I am a man undone, I am of unclean lips, and yet mine eyes have seen the king, the Lord of Hosts.*[2]

Now this king and Lord of Host, was no other but the apostle's *Jesus*, whom they worshipped under that title of Son or Saviour. See *Matt.* xiii. 14. *John* xii. 40, 41.

In chap. vii. there is said to be a conspiracy against *Judah*, but said the prophet *Judah* shall stand,[3] and he gives *Ahaz* the king a sign of it, and the sign was the thing signified, saying in this manner, *A virgin shall conceive and bear a son, and call his name Emanuel, or God with us. Matt.* i. This sign is given to a king, and yet a sign that should every where be fought against by kings and rulers. Therefore the prophet, in this chapter and the next, speaking of the enemies of truth that fight against the true God, under the name of *Rezen* king of *Syria*, and *Pekath*, who took evil counsel against *Judah*, refusing the waters of *Shiloh* that go softly, without noise, which waters was the doctrine of the *Messias.*[4]

Therefore, say they, *Let us go up against Judah, and vex her;* and his enemy was king *Rezen* and *Reason*, the king that *Tophet* was prepared for.[5] It is the seed of the fallen angel, and the piercing wisdom of that seed, that do as the prophet saith, band themselves as one man to fight against spiritual *Judah*.

Now, their going up against *Judah*, was to go against the God of *Judah*, but the world was then as it is now, not to worship a God that should take seed of *Judah*, but, said the prophet, though there be a con federacy and consultation against the servants of the true God, yet no counsel against that Lord should stand, though all opinions in religions stand against the faith and worship due to this soil born of a virgin, though he be God with us, yet will he prove to be God against them.[6]

---

[1] Isa. vi. 5.
[2] Isa. xi. 10. 13.
[3] Chap. vii. 14. vi. 12.
[4] Isa. viii. 12. vi.
[5] xxx. 33.
[6] vi. 5, 9. viii. 10, 12. xix. 3, 11. and 30, 1. viii. 14.

Therefore said the prophet, fear them not, for though of your own family, your tribe and kindred conspire against you, because of your faith in the Lord of Hosts coming of *Judah*, yet fear not their power. Let it be in what age it will, but let him be your God, and he will be your sanctuary, and a hiding place for you.

But unto your kindred, the carnal seed in both houses, he shall be a stone of stumbling, and a rock of offence, and so shall all his servants his apostles; for the law is sealed amongst them.[1] *Jer.* xix. 7. *Matt.* xii. 14. and xxvi. 59. I. Pet. ii. 8. ix 1,2,6.

Again, in chap. ix. the birth of *Christ* is described to be wonderful,[2] both in relation to his ministry, person, name, office, and authority. First, he brings him in as a son; but, secondly, he shews, that though he hath but the denomination of a son, yet nevertheless; he should in time be called by the name of mighty God, and everlasting Father. Now this being so, how can there be any other God; for there can be but one Almighty God. The prophet, in another place, speaking of the restitution of the elect *Israel*, saith, that they shall return to the mighty God; who then is he but the Lord *Jesus Christ*.[3]

The prophet hath no comfort for the elect, but by telling them almost at the end of every sentence, that their salvation lay in their God's becoming seed of *Abraham*'s seed.

And the prophet further sheweth, the peaceable effects of *Christ*'s kingdom, insomuch as that he saith, *nothing shall be hurtful in all that holy mountain, but that the wolf shall dwell with the lamb, and the leopard shall lie down with the kid and calf, and the young child shall lead them.*[4]

The wolf, the lion, the calf, the cow and the leopard; all the unruly passions of the spirit of reason, the angel's nature-fallen, shall all be subdued and conquered by belief in the true Saviour, and that little child of faith shall lead them and keep them in awe; also the lion shall eat straw with the ox; that is, that strong spirit of reason which was king and master of the house, shall now submit itself to suffering, or be content with a mean estate, diet, or a dinner of herbs; whatever faith the man child commands, it obeys; and this is the peaceable kingdom of *Christ*, that most high and mighty God. Romans, viii. 13. *Col.* iii. 5.

---

[1] Isa. lxv. 9. viii. 13, 14, 15, to 21.
[2] ix. 1, 2, 6.
[3] Isa. x. 20, 21. xxvi. 3 and 4. l. 10 and xlviii. 2.
[4] xi. 6, 7.

Again, so glorious shall this rest be, as that it shall (saith the prophet) destroy the tongue of the *Egyptian* sea, and all the seven streams thereof shall be smitten.

This shall be accomplished (said the prophet) when the Lord shall set his hand the second time to recover the remnant of his people. [1]

The first time that God shall put his hand to recover his people was at that time as that child was born, and Son given, who is said to be the root of *Jesse*, the promise given was a seal of the performance thereof.

The second time that God shall put his hand to the spiritual recovering of his people, is to be at that time, as this Son is to be called the mighty God, and everlasting Father, and this second time calls the *Jews*, and makes them know, that this *Jesus Christ*, their Lord, is that high and mighty God, and that everlasting Father. *Rom.* xi. 25, 26.

Now at this time, the prophet saith, that the adorers of *Jesus* with weapons spiritual shall fight against the tongue of the *Egyptian* sea, and the seven streams thereof being the seven anti-churches of *Europe*.

For these undoubtedly are the isles in which great London is fixed, being called the ends of the earth, that at this day are afraid of the stroke from his last witness, that this *Jesus Christ* is that high and mighty God, and everlasting Father, to fulfil the prophecy of *Isaiah*,[2] the declaration of which moved the isles, so they drew near and came, but *Israel* chosen out of the isles was assisted to bear witness, and encouraged in this manner.[3]

Fear not I am with thee, thou art my servant, and I am thy God, the first and the last; all that are incensed against thee shall perish, and thou shalt set forth my praise in the islands, now this second time to recover the remnant of my people.[4]

This makes the sinners in *Sion* afraid, who profess the name of the Son, but deny him to be the high and mighty God, and everlasting Father.

---

[1] Ver. 10, 11.
[2] Isa. xi. 9.
[3] ver. 10.
[4] Chap. xiii. 12. xxxiii. 14.

SECT. II.

Again, the prophet saith,[1] that the Lord that proceeds from *Judah* shall have the government in his hand, and shall be a father to the inhabitants of Jerusalem, and to the house of *Judah*, and shall have the key of *David* to open and none shall shut, and shut and none shall open, is not this the Lord *Jesus*, and is not this *Jesus* that Father aforesaid. *Rev.* iii. 7. *Matt*, xvi.27. and xix. 28. *Rev.* v. 5, and xxii. 16.

And though the following verse doth say, they shall hang upon him all the glory of his father's house, yet there must be no Father but him; for if all the Fathers glory be upon him, then is he the Father himself.

Now he may well be the glory of a Father's house;[2] for the prophet brings him in afterwards as a God of such power as to raise the dead, and give reward to all, and that he would swallow up death in victory. See *Matt*, xi. 5, and xvi. 27. I, *Cor.* xv.

All the redeemed shall own this God to be their God. *Isaiah* neither owned nor taught the elect any other God; so that this is the prophet's doctrine, and the language of *Canaan*, the redeemed of the Lord, and all the church's hopes; therefore when he was coming, then was the church in a readiness to receive him, having their faith grounded upon the prophet's spiritual declarations; for then they should cry out in that day, saying, Lo, this is our God, we have waited for him, and he shall save us. This is the Lord, and we have waited for him, we will be glad and rejoice in hi& salvation.[3]

The substance of this prophet *Isaiah*'s doctrine runs all upon this God manifested in flesh. Let us trace him a little in his words, for our consolation in truth's confirmation, and we shall find how the stream of his doctrine runs, which is in this manner.[4]

O ye house of *Judah*, and chosen of God, wait for your Lord, for his promise is sure, and he hath insured me, that he will come, and by revelation I know it, and am to report the same to his redeemed ones, for he will descend from heaven the throne of his glory, into the lowest part of the earth, a virgins womb, and will be incarnate of *Judah*'s seed, and born of a virgin, all power, wisdom, and glory shall be hung upon him:[5] by faith I see these things as already accomplished,

---

[1] xxii, 21, 23 and 24.
[2] Chap. xxiv. 21, 22, 23.
[3] xxvi. 1, 2, 5, 12.
[4] xliii. 4 and lx. 9, and lv. 3.
[5] vii. 14.

because it is sure, I see him by faith to sit upon the throne of *David*, in the spirit of wisdom, judging the work, and with the rod of his mouth slaying the wicked: when he comes; his people shall know that he is their God by his law written in their hearts, and they shall hear him say, Behold, it is I, who was the first and am the last, and besides me there is no Saviour, look upon me and be saved; for my glory I will not give to another; I am your God, ye are my witnesses that I am God.[1]

Again, as this Son or Saviour of *Israel* is the true God, and so received by the elect, yet by faith I see him despised by all others, and rejected,[2] who set themselves against this Lord, as an imperfect God, because of his sufferings; so that there was no beauty nor comeliness in his person, as to please the principality of the world: therefore they shall despise him and reject him, because he will become a man of sorrows, and making his bed with the wicked.

Yet notwithstanding this, this our Lord is our resurrection, a sure stone, a precious corner stone, and we build upon him for eternal life. This our Lord is wonderful in his Appearance, and as it were hideth himself in man's nature, yet shall every knee bow unto him.[3]

Yet though we wait and trust in this Lord; who is the hope of *Israel*, yet who will believe this report, that God shall have his glory wrapt up in flesh, and to have his visage so marr'd, that used to shine as the sun : yet he is our God, though by faith I see him coming from *Edom* with dyed garments, treading the wine-press alone,[4] yet mighty to save, giving life by death, who finding none that could do it, neither in heaven nor earth but himself; therefore it was his own arm that brought salvation. This is the loving kindness of the Lord to ransom us, by laying down his life for us. Lo, this is *Israel*'s God, and in this God we glory.[5]

Thus by the testimony of this evangelical prophet *Isaiah*, it is infallibly proved against all gainsayers under heaven, that

There is none but *Christ*, none but *Christ*, no other God or Saviour but the man *Christ Jesus* in glory.

---

[1] xi. 14. xl. 9. and lxv. 1. xli. 4. xliii. 10, 11. and xliv. 8.
[2] xlix. 7. liii. 7.
[3] xxvi. 19. xxviii. 16. xiv. 15, 23.
[4] lxiii. 5, 7.
[5] liii. 12 and lix. 16. and lxiii. 5.

CHAP. IV.

Shewing how the prophet Jeremiah's doctrine and faith was pitched upon God's becoming flesh, and the just lived by faith in that doctrine.

Jeremiah's testimony

SECT. I.

THE prophet Jeremiah's doctrine is one and the same with the other before, as to the knowledge and worship of the true God; namely, that the Creator of *Israel* is the redeemer of *Israel*, and the way of this redemption is by Gods becoming flesh. All prophets harp on this string, and the apostles play melodiously upon it, and the witnesses of the spirit do finish the mystery. See the references that leads to the mystery,

A great part of this prophets doctrine is about the *Jews* being carried to *Babylon*[1], but the doctrine of their restoration is by him made a type of the deliverance from sin, by the coming of God in a way of a lineal descent, which mysterious sayings puzzled the carnal *Jew*, but the elect saw into the substance, and could distinguish words privative from positive, and temporal from spiritual.

But to come to the matter, the prophet shews, chap. iii. what a great apostacy was amongst the *Jews*, yet saith the prophet a few of them shall be recalled. There is an election, as one of a city, and two of a tribe, that shall be brought to *Sion*.

Now here the prophet contends with the outward *Jew*; and, in his contention, whispers in words of peace and comfort to the elect. So there is an intermixture of judgments and mercies, according to the nature of the seeds it is spoken to. Hence it is worth the minding to know when the spirit of revelation speaks to reason, and when to faith, for instance,

In verse 12th, the prophet hath these words, *Return thou backsliding Israel, and I will not cause mine anger to fall upon you, &c.*[2] These words I conceive were spoken to the seed and nature of reason, the angels nature-fallen, who had the law moral written in the seed, telling them, that all obedience was due to God, and upon this obedience earthly blessings are given as a reward of well-doing.

---

[1] Ch. iii. 6.
[2] Chap. iii. 12.

But in the 14th verse it is said, *Turn backsliding children, for I am married unto you, and will take you one of a city and two of a tribe, &c.* These words are spoken to the seed and nature of faith, which was the seed of God, and was fallen in *Adam.*

And this nature being fallen, God hath *mercy* on it, and turns it, by giving them the knowledge of himself, the other must turn themselves to justice and legal righteousness, but faith turneth, or rather is turned to embrace the true God, saying, if thou return, return unto me.[1] This God is God manifested, or to be manifested in flesh, as the next verse proves.

But to give a further distinction of the original, from whence truth and falsehood doth arise, as in reference to God, and the worship that pleases him, and to *Baal* and the worship that pleases him, behold their play on both sides.[2] First, as to the seed of the fallen angel, it is contrary in its priestly teachings to the seed of fallen *Adam,* after recalled and renewed by the second *Adam*; for the original of their teaching is not from revelation of faith, but from the dictates and imagination of reason, which is a deceit of their own heart; and so they, from their study in reason that is natural, teach a lye, and a false God in the name of the true.

Therefore it errs, and the more it searches into spiritual things the more it errs; for it may search after morality by the candle of the law, and from thence may speak a high language, to the admiration of its own seed that are of a lower capacity, if it be sober and learned; but it but gropes in the dark, if it apply its study to the finding put spiritual secrets, for that is locked up from that seed, therefore they have nothing of substance, but only a form of goodly words.

Now the prophet *Jeremiah* shews the fallacy by their practice, and discovers them clearly to a discerning eye. His words are to this purpose following, both to priest and people.[3]

Behold you trust in lying words, when you come into my temple to worship, saying, no evil shall befal you, if you but make a shew of holiness there, crying the temple of the Lord; whilst you thus boast of the temple (yet that temple is but a den of robbers). What are you else but robbers and thieves? Do you not steal my word every man from his neighbour, who are my prophets, and take from here a little, and there a little, that will serve your turn, and then father it upon God, and say; thus saith the Lord.[4] And then you add your own devices

---

[1] xxxi. 18, 19. vi. 2.
[2] xiv. 15. xxiv. 16. Ver 26. xvii. 9, 10.
[3] Chap. vii. 2, 4.
[4] xxiii. 30. xiv. 10, 14. xxx. 31.

The Harmony of the Three Commissions 523

and formalities to it, the deceit of your own heart; thus like vagabonds you wander from scripture to scripture, and it must speak what your reason doth imagine, See and compare *John* x. 8. *Isa.* xii. 6. *Acts* xix. 13. *Rev.* xxii. 18. *Jude* xlii. 2 *Cor.* ii. 17. *Mal.* ii. 8.

Again, what are you but murderers? you are all unto me as *Sodom*, ever resisting the hope of *Israel*. What shall men call you but reprobate silver? Seeing the Lord hath rejected you, depart therefore from him, and be written in the earth, and not in the writings of the house of the true *Israel*.[1]

O Lord, thou knowest all their councils against me and against thee to slay us, though they boast of their priests office, as that the scriptures belongeth to them;[2] yet do they scoff at thy word of promise. O let me see thy vengeance on them, and let them be confounded that persecute me, thy true prophet, &c.[3] But then as for thy chosen ones and ministers of the true sanctuary, they trust not in themselves, but in the hope of *Israel*. Now observe the doctrine evangelical, to the elect seed.

SECT. II.

The day is come, saith the prophet,[4] that the Lord will raise unto *David* a righteous branch, and he shall build the temple; this is the temple that was to be built without noise or tumult. Again, a king shall reign and prosper; in his days *Judah* shall be saved, and his name is the Lord our righteousness, now *Israel* hath but one king, and that king is *Christ*, and but one saving God, and *Christ* is that God.

All *Israel*'s righteousness of justification, sanctification, wisdom, or what other glorious qualification soever[5] flows or ariseth from that fountain of faith in the person of *Christ*, giving the whole glory of their salvation to him; whether before he became flesh or after, all is one, and all centre in one, for the promise was sure.

Therefore the prophet is absolute in his declarations to the foil power of speaking forth his divine revelations in this wise aforesaid,[6] and as hereafter follows, saying; I who am a prophet ordained and chose by voice of words from the God of truth, had his word put into my mouth, whereby I was impowered to throw down all false Gods

---

[1] iv. 31. and vi. 20. and xvii. 13. xxiii. 14. xxiv. 15.
[2] xvii. 15, 18.
[3] ver. 7.
[4] Chap. xxiii. 5. vii. 4.and xxxiii. 15.
[5] ix. 23. and xxi. 27. and li. 10.
[6] xv. 9, 16, 18. xxiv. 6.

and false worships, and to build and plant the chosen of *Judah* into the faith of that good thing promised the righteous branch of *David*; which is no other thing but the Lord our righteousness, in which I, and all true prophets, pronounce salvation.[1]

So that salvation is not from the great mountains and hills of lofty imaginations from the arms of flesh, but it is in that Lord and God coming of the seed of *David*, who is to be born of a woman. This is the doctrine of righteousness and the evidence of heaven. O you seed and children of the promise, believe, hope, trust, wait for the coming or growing up of this branch of this man of this king, which is your king, and be blessed.[2] *Isa.* ii. 2. *Obadiah* i. 6, 8, 21. In the latter days you shall consider all this, &c.

Again, in Chap. 31, the prophet poureth forth life in these words, saying;[3] the Lord hath created a new thing upon the earth.

A woman shall compass a man: here doth the prophet declare that God would become man; for this man was God the Father, and this woman was the virgin wife, *Mary*. the true seed of *Israel* did in the prophets days believe this was true, and would come to pass in due time, and the true seed of *Israel* at this time, being the latter days in which they were to consider of it; doth certainly now know, and with confidence and boldness, yet with all humility and soberness, do affirm against all gainsayers under heaven, that the man *Christ Jesus*. So exalted through the scriptures of truth, was and is, and is to come, the most high and mighty God and everlasting Father, being, in one sing le body or person of flesh and bone, now in heaven glorified, blessed for ever. *Amen.*

Now the prophet calls this a new thing, but the prophet *Isaiah* saith, that this new thing is a hidden thing: and that it cannot be known by the carnal seed. And therefore saith the prophet Jeremiah, this new thing that is created, doth create a new creature, and in it a new covenant, whereby they shall know that new thing, that new Jerusalem, that came down from heaven to be made that new and living way.

This new created thing created every thing new and old; but none knows him aright but such as have the new creation; therefore said *Habak.* chap. i. 5. *Wonder marvelously; for I will work a work in your days, which you shall not believe though it be told you.*

But it is the elect that do find out the path of God, and do trace the footsteps of the spirit in every commission, whereby they are given

---

[1] xxiii. 5, 6. and xxxii. 14, 15, 16.
[2] xliii. 16. iii. 23. xvii. 15. 1. 6. li. 25. xxxi. 32. lii. 23.
[3] xxxi. 32.

to know variety of new and wonderful things; as now to know that this new-created thing that had uncreated itself, created every thing, and as to his saints he created a new heart, a new covenant, a new name, and a new song of praise in that name to this God-Man, compassed about with a woman.

What then shall we say of a Woman; no ill, for though a woman was the inlet to sin, yet a woman was the outlet of sin, and the inlet of salvation; so that let a woman, but especially this woman, be, by all the elect in all ages, counted blessed, who bore the blessed babe, and God of all life.

And though the first woman compassed a man of death, hell and damnation; yet let not her after-seed by *Adam* speak ill of her: because they and her were blessed by a gracious promise of an after redemption, which was and is by this new created man compassed by a woman.

A woman shall compass a man.

God is a man, and was in the form of a man before he was compassed about with a woman; for man was created in his image both as to form and nature: and *Moses* calls God a man of war, and this new thing, in his state of mortality said, that no man was perfectly good, but one, which was God, and so the first man *Adam* was from the earth, the second man *Adam* was the Lord from heaven.

A woman shall compasss a man.

The true God of *Israel* hath been compassed about five several ways. First, he hath been compassed about by his angels in heaven. Secondly, he hath been compassed about by a woman on earth. Thirdly, he hath been compassed about by our infirmities. Fourthly, he hath been compassed about by bulls of Bashan. And lastly, he hath been compassed about with death, hell and the grave. *Psal.* lxviii. 17. Luke i. 1. Heb. v. 2. *Psalm*, xxii. 12. xviii. 4, 5.

But now in these latter days this God-Man hath enlarged his glory;[1] now shall none hereafter compass him about; but his saints and angels round about his throne, the bulls of *Bashan* shall no more compass him about, nor the red dragon and his bloody priests that caused such mourning in *Rama*, in slaying the young children to slay him.

But as the Lord by his spirit of faith, love, joy, and peace doth compass his saints about; even so do the saints by their new songs of praise compass their redeemer about, giving him thanks for that his

---

[1] Ch. iii. 21.

wonderful work of his vouchsafing to condescend so low, as to become man of the seed of *David*, as aforesaid, to save his elect.

Let this suffice from the prophet *Jeremiah*; and to the elect it is enough; it is clear as the light; it is evident; it is certain; it is sure without doubt, and without scruple to him whose name is written in the book of life, that,

There is none but *Christ*: none but *Christ*: no other God, but the man *Christ Jesus*, now in glory above the stars.

CHAP. V.

Shewing the prophet Ezekiel's *testimony to our Lord Jesus Christ, to be his God, and the God of all the true seed of Israel*

Ezekiel's testimony

THE prophet in his first chapter shews his commission from heaven, as all true prophets are able to do; for it is the ever living word spoken out of the mouth of God that makes a man a commissioner, but *Baal's* priests, cannot pretend to this; for their God is speechless, having no tongue to speak at all; but I pass them by and come to learn of a true prophet.

The most part of the prophecy by *Ezekiel* is a foretelling and threatening the *Jews* of great judgments to be inflicted upon them under their captivity, as a reward for their injustice, oppression, idolatry, and cruelty; and persuading them to repentance, that they might not be destroyed; saying to them in this wise.

Turn you, turn you from your evil ways; for will ye die, ye house of Israel, as I live saith the Lord, I have no pleasure in the death of the wicked, &c.[1]

Now, what death is this that the prophet meaneth? that the Lord hath no pleasure in? In answer hereto, that the ways of the Lord, concerning this it is written.[2] I call heaven and earth to record (saith *Moses*) that I have set before you line and death, blessing and cursing; chuse the one and live; chuse the other and die: now hath not that carnal line their desire? you have a law which, if you keep, you shall live by it, but, if you break it, you shall be destroyed; for if you be willing and obedient, you shall eat the good of the land; but, if you refuse and rebel, you shall die; that is, you shall be destroyed by sword, plague, famine, or the like. See *Deut.* iv. 13, 40. chap, v. 4. 6.

Now, as touching this death, the Lord hath no pleasure; and therefore, that they might not die but live if possible, he caused the law to be daily read, and to exhort them again and again, that they might not forget but might be obedient thereunto. *Deut.* vii. 6, 9. chap. xvii. 19, 20. chap. xxxi. 12, 13. *Josh.* xxxviii. 24, 35.

Now, his saying he had no pleasure in the death of the wicked was no more but this, that the fig-tree should not blossom, neither should fruit be in the vines; the labour of the olive shall fail; and the fields

---

[1] xiv. 6. and xviii. 21, 20. and xxxiii. 11.
[2] xviii/ 25/ and xxxiii. 20.

shall yield no meat; the flocks should be cut off from the field; their goods shall become a booty, and their houses a desolation; this is the death and destruction that *Christ* hath no pleasure in; nor had, when he wept over *Jerusalem. Habakkuk* iii. 17.

All such places threaten an external death, for the law's curse goes no farther than the penetrating down into the grave.[1] *Psalm.* xxxi. 17. *Isa.* xiv. 11.

But the wonderful mystery of God's becoming flesh, and suffering death in that flesh; and, after rising again through Godhead power, brings that rebellious seed into a capacity of a resurrection to a second death, which is a living death and a dying life. *Isa.* ii. 19, 21. and 26, 29. *John* v. 58. *Heb.* ii. 14.

For if God had not come to die, the saints had been no better than the reprobate; for all would have gone to the grave, and the law could not raise them again. 1 *Cor.* xv.

So no more of this subject here, this I thought convenient, to put the free-willers rub out of the way: who would have eternal salvation offered unto all: and that there is but one seed or generation of mankind; and so may all be saved, if they will: but this their principle destroys God's prerogative power, and makes him inferior to the kings of the earth; and besides, it is absolute nonsense; for if all men proceed from one seed or root, then, being all of one nature, they must either all he saved or all damned. *Isa.* xiiii. 13.

But the scriptures are clear to prove two seeds, and that there is an election in *Israel*, and the Lord by his prophets doth mark them out, and call that people who are but a remnant out of a multitude of professors, to the faith and worship of *Christ* in spirit and truth. *Isa.* xix. and xi. 11, 16. These saith the prophet are the chosen, let us set a mark on them.[2]

God will save this little remnant, calling them his flock; and in order thereto, he will, saith the prophet,[3] set up one shepherd over them, and this shepherd is God the Lord *Jesus*, and all the elect *Israel* are his sheep or flock; and as he is called their shepherd, so is he called also their alone king; that only king was to rule that one only nation, and that king that was that nation's God, was to proceed from *David*[4] which is none but *Christ*, and this shepherd, this king, this prince of *Israel*, should bless them with showers of blessings. Here we see that this chosen flock hath but one shepherd over them, one

---

[1] Ch. xxxi. 14, 17. and xxxii. 21, 22, 24. and xxxvii. 4, 12, 13.
[2] Ch. xiv. 22.
[3] ix. 4. xxxiv. 23. Ver. 31.
[4] xxxvii. 22.

prince and king over them, and that prince, king, and shepherd, is no other but *Christ Jesus* their Lord God and Saviour.

This king, prince and shepherd, makes a covenant with his people,[1] and the covenant is, (saith the prophet) that he will be their God, and they shall be his people; and behold those privileges, the graces and gifts are so plentiful, that they are said to overflow as a river, in peace, love, joy, wisdom, and all other graces;[2] and all flows from this shepherd bringing his sheep to such fountains as riseth higher and higher; first to the ankles, then to the knees, then to the loins. Every dispensation or commission rises higher and higher in its wisdom and revelation, in this mystery of its Gods becoming flesh. So that now in these latter days, this refreshing stream is risen up to the loins, and so up to a river to swim and bathe themselves in, to their everlasting consolation. A mystery so deep, that the tongue of men nor angels cannot reach in words to unfold it in its fulness. It is enough that we are made worthy to know that our God did become flesh, and that we know the nature of that wonderful humility and condescension of our God in love. According to our measures in this our state of mortality, it is here, through grace, given us as an earnest penny or seal of What wisdom and glory he will bestow upon all his flock hereafter, each, one according to his faith and wisdom, he had in that commission or prophecy he was under, shall have glory according at the next appearing of this king and shepherd of *Israel*, according to the scriptures of truth.

And, in the mean time, they shall feed in goodly pastures; therefore saith the prophet,[3] they shall feed upon the banks and borders of this sanctuary waters, for there grows trees of meat there, whose leaf will not fade, nor fruit consume, but shall bring forth new fruit that shall be for meat, and the leaf thereof for medicine, (even the doctrine of this *Messiah*) and *Joseph* shall have two portions, a blessed reward to believing *Ephraim*.[4] *Gen.* xlviii. 20.

Thus by the testimony of *Ezekiel*, and abundantly more by him than what is here expressed, it is clear and evident, that

There is none but *Christ*: none but *Christ*: no other God, but the man *Christ Jesus*, his Lord, and ours blessed for ever, Amen.

---

[1] xxxiv.
[2] lxvii. 3, 4, 5.
[3] ver. 12.
[4] ver. 13.

CHAP. VI.

Shewing how Daniel's faith was pitched upon God's becoming flesh, and that eternal happiness depended thereupon.

Daniel's testimony

DANIEL begins to describe *Christ's* kingdom[1] as to his incarnation, from great *Nebuchadnezzar's* dream, that under the fourth monarchy it should take its beginning, and then it should destroy all such as should oppose that kingdom with a seal of eternal death; for till then, sin, death, devil and hell reigned without controul.

But after the entering in of the fourth monarchy, though it was as iron, yet notwithstanding all this, the God of heaven said *Daniel* shall set up his kingdom.[2] Now this God of heaven was the God of *Abraham*, which was no other than *Christ*. For in this king's dream, he saw a stone cut out without hands, and become a great mountain, insomuch that it tilled the whole earth. Now this stone was the stone of *Israel* prophesied of before, as hath been shewed, as *Gen.* xlix. 24 *Psal.* cxviii.22. This stone was seen in the king's dream to become a great mountain. Now this king was a mountain himself, and a very great mountain, but this visional mountain of his put him in great fear, as if his mountain should be smitten down by it, though he could not tell by whom it should be, or what it should be, neither could the astrologers, the philosophers, or any of the wise men in all *Chaldea*, his kingdom, when they were summoned together, tell the king what this stone was, for their knowledge and faith was quite contrary to *Daniel's*. Therefore they tell the king, that none can tell this dream, no not one man upon the earth (say they),[3] except the gods whose dwelling is not in flesh, there was not one among all the seed of the fallen angel that ever did prophecy, or could believe that God would become flesh of *Adam's* flesh, and bone of his bone; they can sooner believe that man's spirit will become God, than God to become man, and it was ever the principle of reason to believe so, when clothed in flesh; for, say they, reason is God's nature, and God is nature without form.

And *Plato*, that great heathen philosopher and ancient, who lived in those days of the prophet *Daniel*, and was one of those wise sages, hath wrote thus, that there is no way to happiness but by the footsteps of reason, calling it the nature of God; also the *Platonists* say

---

[1] Dan. ii. 44.
[2] ver. 20, 23.
[3] Ch. ii. 11.

that the devils are reason, but yet spirits without bodies, as their gods was: so that those wise heathens in *Daniel's* time, did make God's nature, and devil's nature to be all alike reason, and like spirit. But in my treatise of Truth's Triumph, I have shewed, that if God's nature, and the devil's nature be Reason, then nothing could hinder but that the devils might be holy, as well as the gods; and the reason is because nature distributing itself into several beings, makes all these beings correspondent with itself, and in harmony one with another.

Therefore it is evident, that the true God was never known by any but by true prophets of the Lord's own sending, and by such as have faith to understand, and faith to believe their report: and for God to become flesh, was ever too mysterious for any to know, understand, and believe, but the seed of his own body only.

Again, this stone cut of the mountain of *Bethlehem-Judah*, or kingdom, comes of itself; no man had a hand in it, it was God-head power.[1] Therefore let builders and false priests refuse this stone, yet will it become the chief corner-stone, that shall hold up the house, church, and kingdom, against that iron monarchy, with its ten horns, and that one peeping horn that proceeded from the ten horns, with that spiritual whore that sat upon them all, even mystery *Babylon*; the mother of harlots who sits upon all those great mountains. *Daniel* saith, that this stone arising out of *Judah* should be too hard for them all; for let kings and emperors refuse this stone, and raise war against it, although they be of gold, of brass, and of iron, shall they be all broke as clay, as *Isa.* xlv. 9, and xli. 25.

Mind one thing here, that the greatest power is ever attributed unto God, after he hath transmuted his divine God-head into flesh; for then doth he war against man in man, and then is the God of heaven captain over his elect seed, to fight and make war with the devil clothed in flesh, See *Hosea* xiii. 14. I *Cor.* xv. 55, and the ground of this was, because the devil was Lord of hell and death, until that the Lord *Christ* had suffered death, and rose again, by which means he gained power over death, devil, hell, and the grave. *Heb.* ii. 14. *Rev.* i. 18, and so he finished the transgression, and ended sin in the seed of Adam, by making reconciliation for it in the body of his flesh, and so brought in everlasting righteousness according to the prophet *Daniel*.[2]

And by this glorious work of God's clothing his God-head spirit with pure human flesh,[3] he created power in his saints as kings and judges under him to execute his wrath against all those mighty

---

[1] Ch. vii. 14.
[2] xi. 24.
[3] viii. 25. vii. 27. xi. 32. vii. 9.

princes that set themselves against *Michael* their captain, with the seals of eternal death.

The prophet by vision did behold *Christ*, and in his appearance he was like unto the Son of man, and further saith, that he came to the Ancient of Days, and received of him dominion, glory, and a kingdom. Now, who was that which was invested with power, glory, dominion, and an everlasting kingdom, but the Ancient of Days himself; for as the prophet *Isaiah* said, that God would not give his glory to another, and *Daniel* saith here, that this Ancient of Days had given him that was like the Son of man, all people and nations to worship and serve him; what then could this Son of man be, but the Ancient of Days himself, and in that he became man, appeared under a twofold condition, Son of man as from his incarnation, and Ancient of Days as before his assumption of human nature, yet one and the same God, though under a twofold condition; for *Christ* was the *I am* that chose *Moses*, and when he was in the state of mortality, he told the unbelieving *Jews*, that he was before *Abraham*, and that *Abraham* believed in him and was blessed, and all his spiritual seed in that belief of his becoming flesh, was blessed in that blessing from this *Messias*, which was that Ancient of Days; for *Daniel* owned but one God of a single person. So for further proof, *Micah* v. 2.

Daniel beheld wonderful things, as in reference to this mystery of his God's bringing in everlasting righteousness; he was so ravished with the delight thereof, and several others with there running too and fro in those revelations and visions to increase knowledge,[1] and would fain have seen further into it, but what was revealed to *Daniel* was sufficient at that time, both for him and for the select; for further knowledge of it was to be sealed up till the time was accomplished; for this being but under the first commission, or first testament, so this mystery was to be declared but in part, being the first witness or first record; but the following witnesses will finish the mystery of God, according as it is written: at the mouth of two or three witnesses every thing should be established; so upon the coming of the last witness then the revelation of the mystery of God shall be accomplished and finished; and this son of man, that hath all power, glory and dominion put into his hands, and that shall everlastingly reign king over all people and nations according to *Daniel* and all true prophets, then shall he be known to be the mighty God and everlasting Father. Thus by testimony of *Daniel*,

There is none but *Christ*: none but *Christ*: no other God, but the man *Christ Jesus* in glory.

---

[1] xii. 4.

CHAP. VII.

Shewing how that the prophet Hosea's faith and doctrine was pitched upon God's becoming fleshy and all the saints hope and happiness depended thereon.

Hosea's testimony

NOW I come to mid the doctrine of all the twelve small prophets, and they will be found to be the comforters of *Sion*, and all harp upon the same string as the other prophets did before them.

This prophet hath judgments and mercies mixt, according to the operation of the two seeds, but the house of *Judah* were to have the everlasting blessings.[1] The seed of *Reason* had their blessing according to their obedience; but then it was but by their bow and sword there corn, wine and oil.[2] But their casting away, is, saith the prophet, an utter rejection, that rejected the Lord from heaven, and would not have a God clothed in flesh to rule over them.[3]

It is said, I will save the house of *Judah* by the Lord their God, and when *Israel* was a child, then I loved him; now this child was the seed of *Isaac*, and this Lord God of *Judah* proceeded from that child *Israel*, and was prophesied of, to be a child himself, and to be called out of *Egypt* according to this prophet;[4] *out of Egypt have I called my son*; so that *Israel*'s saving God was no other but *Jesus Christ*, born of a virgin, persecuted into *Egypt* by a red dragon devil, honoured and called forth again when that dragon was dead.

Now this prophet whispers inwards into the hearts of the elect,[5] telling them that the Lord is coming to make the Gentiles his people; and he brings in the elect *Jews* also, and orders them to chuse to themselves this seed of *Israel*, this child that was to be called out of *Egypt*, to be that one head or shepherd to rule over them; for he was to come, and then he should be the Lord and king in the latter days.[6]

Again in chap. X. the prophet adviseth the elect to wait for their God, until he come, for his going forth will be in the morning, and shall be as the rain; now it is, as if the prophet should say, wait for him, for he will come, as sure as the morning will come, and when he

---

[1] Ch. i. 7. ii. 8.
[2] Chap. x. 8.
[3] iv. 14.
[4] xi. 1.
[5] i. 10, 11.
[6] Ch. iii. 4.

comes, then comes grace in abundance, which will be to the soul as showers of rain is to the earth.[1]

Therefore seek till he come, he never seeketh in vain, that is first sought of the Lord; for his mercy is such, as that he is found of then& that sought him not, he will call the Gentiles that never sought for him, and he will reject that carnal *Jew* that shall seek him, but shall not find him; but let elect *Israel* seek, and when he appears they shall say, my God, we know thee by virtue of the dew or rain that is fallen upon me.[2]

And as the prophet advised the elect to seek the Lord, so likeways he admonished them to hear how graciously the Lord speaks unto them, and that in this manner.[3]

I am the Lord thy God, and thou shalt know no God but me; for there is no saviour besides me, I am thy help and the king of *Israel*, thy king, all other kings shall xi 4 and utterly be destroyed.[4]

I draw you with the cords of a man becoming a man like you; I give you myself to eat: I will be your king, and be death's death to save you.

The Lord, by his prophet, having thus spoken to the elect,[5] now his chosen ones answer unto him again, saying; we know thee to be our God, and will keep close to thee; *Assur* shall not save us; we will not ride upon their horses; for all is flesh and not spirit. Their prophets are fools, their spiritual men are mad, and have a multitude of iniquities; and one is their great hatred to the watchers of *Ephraim* in the house of God, and will have no king but *Caesar*, or what *Caesar* shall command; but our king is the Lord our God, who will ransom us from the power of the grave, and will be death's death, and the graves destruction.[6]

And now being enlightened by true prophesy, we will say, what have we any more to do with idols,[7] we have heard of him, and we shall see him, and taste of the fruit of the tree of life; yea, and have tasted by faith. Whether then shall we go? We will not leave this Lord, we will not be for another man, but for this man, this God-man, that we have chosen for our king and head.

---

[1] x. 12. xiv. 16.
[2] xiii. 2.
[3] xiii. 4.
[4] ver. 10. xi 4. and xiii. 14.
[5] xxiii. 11. and xiv. 3. and ix. 7, 8. and x. 3.
[6] xiii. 14.
[7] xiv. 8.

Temporal kings are the supreme head of a carnal church, but we have no such head but the Lord our righteousness is our head, and from him we will not go.

Thus by the testimony of the prophet *Hosea*, and the true church in his days, it is evident, that

There is none but *Christ*; none but *Christ*; no other God but the man *Christ Jesus*[3] now in glory.

CHAP. VIII.

Shewing that the prophet Joel's God is the saints Jesus.

Joel's testimony

THE prophet Joel, after he had denounced testimony great judgments to the wicked seed of captivity, famine, and of God's forsaking them, and withholding from them their meat-offerings, and drink-offerings, counting the very prayers of their priests at his altars as the howling of a dog.

After these things he brings in the Lord as gracious and merciful to his own select people, speaking to them in the manner following:[1]

My people that doth wait for me, shall never be ashamed in putting their trust in me; for I will come and be in the midst of *Israel*; for where two or three are gathered together in my name, they are my church, and they shall know me to be their God, and shall not be ashamed, and make haste from me: for it shall come to pass afterwards, that I will pour out my spirit upon the seed of faith that waited for me, and they shall prophecy and preach my name, and I will shew the wonders in heaven and earth; *for the sun shall be turned into darkness, and the moon into blood.*[2]

For the Redeemer of *Israel* shall suffer death : this is; the wonder in heaven.

And the moon shall be turned into blood: this shall be a wonder in earth.

For the law shall be turned into blood; that is, into persecution, because righteousness is denied to be had by it.

But it shall come to pass, that notwithstanding that persecution, that whosoever called upon God, the sun of righteousness and glory,

---

[1] ii. 26, 27.
[2] ver. 28, 30, 31.

that was darkened as their God, shall be saved; for in mount *Sion* is deliverance, and you shall know that I am the Lord your God that dwell there.[1]

But the sun must be turned into darkness, for *Egypt* and *Edom* must be plat withal, for the Lord will be crucified there. Therefore in the valley of *Jehosaphat* they shall be met withal, because they have shed innocent blood there, out of *Judah*, but life shall be regained, and Judah shall abide for ever, and be made glorious by that new Jerusalem that will come from heaven, and shall be blessed and live for ever; for because he lives, his saints shall live also.[2]

This is the doctrine of *Joel*. Who then must this *Judah* be? this *Jerusalem* be? this darkened sun be? this innocent blood of *Judah* be? this king and judge of the world be? this God and Saviour of *Israel* be? but the Lord *Jesus Christ* blessed for ever. Amen.

So that by this testimony of *Joel*, all those true saints in this age of the world, may understand by the gift of the spirit of faith, now stirred up by prophecy, that there is none but *Christ*, none but *Christ*; no other God but the man *Christ Jesus* in glory, though millions of men should gainsay it.

---

[1] iii. 17.
[2] Ver. 15. 2, 19. ver. 20.

CHAP. IX.

Shewing that the prophet Amos's faith and doctrine was in God's becoming flesh.

Amos's testimony

THIS prophet Amos was sent to pronounce judgments against *Syria*, the *Philistines*, *Tyrus*, *Edom*, *Amon*, and *Moab*, for their several transgressions, afterwards the prophet comes to reprove all the twelve tribes of *Israel* for their several transgressions, which was in forsaking his law, and despising his commandments. Now all other nations, they being not in covenant, are not said to break his law, because no outward law was given to them, but the law that was written in their consciences, but *Israel* had an outward law to shew them what was written within, and the prophet finding them guilty of all the great transgressions, and much more greater than the heathen, therefore called by three transgressions, and by four; but the prophet gives a catalogue of many more in number, though all may be comprised in them, as,[1]

First, They are said to walk in lies. 2ndly, They sell the righteous for silver. 3rdly, They covet their neighbour's goods, and pant after the dust of the earth, and commit adultery, &c. 4thly, They drink the wine of the condemned in the house of God, and would not let true prophets prophesy, or once to speak, but stir up violence and robbery, turning judgments to wormwood. 5thly, They resist the just, and rejoice in their persecuting priests, which the prophet calls a thing of nought. Lastly, They long that the sabbath were over, that they may buy the poor for silver; and this is none of the least transgressions.[2]

Wherefore the prophet seeing their great wickedness and apostacy from their law, cries out, saying, *O Lord God, forgive, I beseech thee, by whom shall* Jacob *arise, for he is small*. Now the prophet brings in the Lord as answering to the two seeds saying, that he will repent him, and have mercy and forgiveness of the one seed, hut the other he will judge for their cruelty and wrath, and for their selling the righteoues for silver.

Being as if the Lord should say,[3] shall I forgive this wicked people that offer a sacrifice of thanksgiving with leven, and come to *Bethel* and transgress, I hate and despise your offerings; and though you pretend you look for my appearing, because all my prophets prophesy

---

[1] Ch. ii. 4. ii. 7, 8. iii. 10. v. 7.
[2] ver. 12. vi. 1. 13. viii. 5, 7.
[3] iv. 5.

of it, what good shall my coming do you; for that day will be darkness and not light unto you: for you shall be as blind men, and shall not know me, for the sun shall go down at noon-day.[1] When I am coming, I shall suffer, and the sun shall suffer likewise for a time, but you shall suffer forever, that buy the righteous for silver, and sell him for a pair of shoes; is this to desire my coming, and my day, and then to sell me for silver? I have sworn by the excellency of *Jacob*, surely I will never forget any of their works (now how should such a people be saved) that swore thy God, O *Dan*, liveth.

Now the prophet seeing the wickedness of this seed, and God's just wrath against it, cries out again, the second time, saying, *O Lord God, cease, I beseech thee, by whom shall* Jacob *arise, for he is small*. This *Jacob* that the prophet meant, was the elect *Israel*; for as he saw the destruction of the one seed, so he would see the restoration of the other; for he knew that God had a people, though they were not visible at that time, error and idolatry ruling and bearing sway over all: for the righteous then must not speak a word, but were commanded silence.[2]

But the prophet knowing that the promise was sure, therefore it was answered him by revelation from the Lord, saying, the days come, I will raise up the tabernacle of *David* that is fallen.[3] I will let these wicked *Jews* go, and will bring in a number of the *Gentiles* in their room, to glorify my name; they shall seek after me, and turn to God, and worship in the beauty of holiness; for the mountains shall drop sweet wine in this new raised tabernacle of *David*, which shall refresh the heart with peace and joy, and assurance of everlasting life. This is the sweet wine of that glorious tabernacle that shall dwell with men, in which the saints shall perform true worship. Thus by the testimony of Amos.

There is none but *Christ;* none but *Christ;* no other God or Saviour but the man *Christ Jesus* in glory.

---

[1] v. 18. viii. 9.
[2] v. 10, 13.
[3] ver. 4.

CHAP. X.

Shewing that the prophet Obadiah's *faith, and doctrine was pitched upon God's becoming flesh.*

Obadiah's testimony

THE prophet having denounced judgments upon *Edom* for their pride and wickedness against *Jacob*, shewing the manner and nature of the actions of *Esau's* posterity against *Judah*, their wickedness, hatred and pride, running in its cursed line, God's judgments pursuing it from generation to generation. Now after the former part of his prophesy against *Edom*, and his lofty wisdom, which was his mount, he turneth the residue of his prophesy to *Jacob* and *Judah*, the seed of *Abraham* according to the promise, and his declarations are short but sweet, saying in this wise.

Upon mount *Sion* shall be deliverance, for saviours shall come up there to judge the mount of *Esau*,[1] and there shall be holiness there, because the holy Lord God, that rules in *Sion* shall be born there. Destruction shall come upon *Edom*, a fire out of *Jacob* shall devour her, and burn her mighty men, and destroy her wise; for by fire and by the sword (not a sword of steel, but the sword of the spirit) will the Lord plead with her, and *Sion* shall possess *Esau's* possessions in the sale of his birthright: so that the spiritual *Canaan* belongs to *Jacob* and his spiritual seed; that is, the land of uprightness, and the holy land. *Isa*, xxvi, 10, and lxii. 12. *Gen.* xxv. 32, and xxii 17. *Psal.* cxliii. 10.

It is not the earth we tread on the upright land, that *Israel* is to possess, if it were, then where must the called *Gentiles* be; but it is the regenerated or new heart in the faith, knowledge, and belief of your God's coming; that is, the land of *Israel* that flows with milk and honey, and this is the land to be tilled and sown, and the fruits of that ground shall be blessed, and the seed shall prosper and be peaceable. See and compare *Isa.* lxvi. 11, 16, and lv. 1. *Ezek.* xxxvii. 14, 22. *Hos.* x. 12.

And this is the land the Lord inherits, and is their portion, and they are his, which makes *Esau* very angry in the loss of this birthright, and so much the more, by how much the more the people of *Jacob* shall prevail against them; for they have power and authority from that God which *Esau* rejected, to judge the mount and very pinnacle of the temple of *Esau*; for they shall trample upon the world's

---

[1] Ch. i. 17, 18.

wisdom, power, and glory, and break the head of aspiring, reason, the proud cherub's nature, and the kingdom shall be the Lord *Christ*'s.

Thus by the testimony of *Obadiah's*, there is none but *Christ*; none but *Christ*; no other God but the man *Christ Jesus* in glory, whom we adore and worship.

CHAP XI.

Sheweth that the prophet Jonah's faith and doctrine was in God's becoming flesh.

Jonah's testimony

THE prophet *Jonah* being sent to *Nineveh*,[1] to denounce the sentence of destruction upon it for its wickedness, he disobeyed the Lord, and fled from his presence, being unwilling to be a messenger of such sad tidings, and I am apt to believe that all true prophets are unwilling at first hand (as *Jonah* was) to go forth upon messages of the Lord, because life and death is delivered into their hands. This made one prophet cry out, saying, (at the time of his being chosen), *Woe is me, I am a man undone, another to say, I am of uncircumcised lips, send by whom thou wilt send.*

But false prophets, upon the least appearance from a mere dream or vision Within or without, or from the hopes of gaining riches or honour, are ever forward to run into the ministry, and the ground of all is this; namely, the spirit of faith is ever willing to sit still and be quiet under his vine, and under his fig-tree, but the spirit of reason would ever be in church or state, and so heaves himself on for preferment, and for a name, who loves to be called master, and to sit with princes. But *Jonah's* disobedience brought but a temporal curse upon him, as being cast into the whale's belly.[2] Now *Jonah* being cast into the whale's belly was made a type of *Christ*, the eternal God, being in the grave; for as *Jonah* was three days and three nights in the whale's belly, so was the God of *Jonah* three days and three nights in the heart of the earth. Matt. xii. 40.

And when the prophet prayed there saying, I will sacrifice unto thee with the voice of thanksgiving, I will pay that which I have promised, salvation belongeth unto the Lord; then did the prophet see redemption by *Jesus*, which was his God, becoming flesh, or man to die for man, and to lie in the grave for a moment.

Again, where he saith, I will pay that which I have vowed; those words relate likewise to God himself, as well as the prophet; for he by faith beheld God making a vow to himself to purchase redemption by death.

Again, When the prophet said, thou hast brought my soul from corruption, then did he intimate and preach to the discerning seed,

---

[1] Chap. i.
[2] ver. 15.

that his Redeemer's soul should not be left in hell or the grave, *Acts* ii. 27.

Jonah preached *Christ* more in the whale's belly, and saw more than when he was forth; when he was in the greatest darkness as to the outward man, then was he in the greatest light as to the inner man; for the internal eye could look towards the holy temple of God, not to the temple made with hands, as of wood and stone, but to a temple of flesh and bone, even to the body of *Christ*, which was to be, and was in faith's account voluntarily offered up. *Heb*. x. 10. This was the sacrifice, the living sacrifice, that caused thanksgiving. So that by the testimony of the prophet *Jonah*,

There is none but *Christ*: none but *Christ*: no other God, but the man *Christ Jesus* in glory.

CHAP. XII.

Sheweth that the prophet Micah's faith, life, and doctrine was pitched wholly upon God's becoming man to save man.

Micah's testimony

THE prophet *Micah* sheweth the wrath of God upon the wicked seed of the house of *Jacob*, and contends with their rulers for their oppression and pride, and with their priests and prophets that preached for hire, and walk in lies, and tells them that God was coming to punish them, and to trample upon their high places of worship, and their high priests too.[1]

The Lord by the prophet further told them, that their worship and offering were all contemptible; for all that the Lord required was but these three things; First, *To do justice*; Secondly, *To love mercy*; and, Thirdly, *To walk humbly with God.*[2]

But these two latter things are proper for the elect, for to show mercy and to walk humbly, is also to do justice; that is, doing the two first, then to walk humbly, that is to hold themselves to the prerogative power of God, to do with them he pleases.

Now to these that could receive no mercy from their oppressors, to these the Lord promiseth mercy, by becoming flesh to redeem them; for, said the prophet,[3] they are so merciless, that the best of them is but as a brier, and the most upright among them is sharper than a thorn hedge; for they will give no conscience liberty.

But to leave that seed to their law, and the wrath of God in that law for them to struggle withal, and come to the prophet's spiritual declarations to the seed of faith, whom he is minded to honour.

The prophet, when he had said that the Lord will come down from heaven,[4] afterwards altereth the word a little, saying, I will bring an heir unto thee, and this heir that he was to bring, is called the glory of *Israel*. This is *Isaac*'s heir, and the heir of heirs, even God himself.

And when the heir of heirs shall come, then, saith the prophet,[5] the wicked shall lay siege against him, and when they see him, they

---

[1] Ch. i. ii. iii.
[2] Ch. ii. iii.
[3] ii. 2, 3, and 30, and vii. 4.
[4] i. 3, 15.
[5] v. 4.

will say, not knowing what they say, *This is the heir, come let us hill him, that the inheritance may be ours by law.*

But this heir conquering by death, will say, *those mine enemies that would not have me to rule over them,* when I come in my great power, they shall move out of their holes like worms; they shall be afraid of me, the Lord God whom they scoffed at, saying, where is the Lord God, behold now shall they be trodden down, *bring them before me that may slay them.*[1]

But as for them that received me in *Bethlehem,* I will have compassion; for who is a God like thee, saith the prophet.[2]

As if the prophet should say,[3] is there any God like unto our God, that will become a child, be born, and made heir of earth as well as heaven, and also will make us all heirs with him of that purchased kingdom of heaven. In a short time after he comes, his power will be known and felt to all people, good and bad; for who is a God like him that comes out of *Sion,* as to his birth, and after out of *Egypt* as to his conquest. These ways of his coining forth are marvellous things; his works wonderful, and his counsels admirable.

As to the wicked, when he comes, he will blind their eyes, they shall not know him, but shall have him in derision, and though he is the judge of *Israel,* yet they shall smite him with a rod upon the cheek, and when they have put him to death, they will then say, now where is your God, but they shall afterwards see to their shame, and be confounded, when our God ariseth to make his power known, then shall they be afraid of this child, of theis heir, of this judge, of this man, of this king, that came down from heaven, and by the way of *Sion,* and is *Sion*'s God, Lord, and *Christ.* Therefore wait for him about Bethlehem, though a place of small account amongst the thousands of a blinded *Israel;* yet from thence look for him, for from thence he shall come forth, that is to be the ruler of *Israel,* whose goings forth have (been as well) from of old, from everlasting as in time. This is the Lord our God, and *Sion* will behold it in the latter days.

And then will *Sion* make her return of thankfulness, joy, and praise, in this manner following,[4] Come and let us unto the mountain of the Lord, he will teach us his way; he hath called us unto him, and we will walk in his paths, which are paths of peace, and a law of love : our kingdom is a kingdom of concord, therefore we shall beat our swords into ploughshares, and not learn war any more, as with a

---

[1] vii. 17. ver. 40.
[2] v. 2.
[3] iv. 3, 8. vii. 15, 17. iv. 12.
[4] iv. 2.

sword of steel, but with the sword of the spirit only, and with that we shall thresh, beat, and cut in pieces many people, and we shall sit every one under his vine, none shall make us afraid; for who is a God like our God, who will gather us as sheafs into his floor.[1]

Thus by the clear testimony of the prophet *Micah*.

There is none but *Christ*; none but *Christ* i no other God but the man *Christ Jesus* in glory only.

---

[1] iv. 4, 12.

CHAP. XIII.

Shewing that the prophet Nahum's faith and doctrine was pitched wholly upon God's becoming flesh.

Nahum's testimony

THE prophet *Nahum* had a Vision of the judgment of *Nineveh*,[1] wherein all wicked people are included, therefore said the prophet, woe to the bloody city; this city is every where where wickedness is; this city is called a well favoured harlot, and the outward beauty, or outward pomp, whether as to religion or state policy, doth bewitch the nations; for the subtility of reason is a witch, and the highest reason captivates the lowest, and becomes a mistress. These are the women; this is the whore, this is the harlot, whether *Nineveh* or *Babylon* that selleth nations.

But after the prophet had delivered his vision of judgments upon the wicked city,[2] he turns himself to the holy city, the seed of faith; the true church, to comfort her, saying in this wise, the Lord is good, a strong hold in the day of trouble, and he knoweth, and owneth them that trust in him.

This strong hold is manifested in flesh, and faith in this God is a stronger hold than the well-favoured harlot hath or can have, though their reasons and outward shews their bulwarks, and their formless God their strong hold.

But this will not save them in the day of trouble, but the Lord that comes of *Judah* will be *Judah*'s hold and sanctuary, when persecution comes from reasons mount in this seeming beautiful city.

Now the prophet shews, that all the elect were waiting for his coming, and in chap, i. he presents him to them in a note of admiration, saying, Behold upon the mountains the feet of him that bringeth good tidings, and publisheth peace, as if the prophet should further say,

Behold by faith I see him that is the saver of *Israel* coming, leaping and skipping upon the mountains,[3] skipping first from heaven to earth; 2dly, From the earth to the cradle; 3dly, From the cradle to the cross; and lastly, From the cross to the crown again. This will make

---

[1] Chap. iv. iii. 1, 4, 14.
[2] i, 7.
[3] i. 15.

Judah keep the solemn feasts, seeing she is to be freed and delivered from the wicked city.

Thus by the testimony of this prophet *Nahum.*

There is none but *Christ*; none but *Christ*; no other God at all but the man *Christ Jesus* only.

CHAP. XIV.

Shewing the prophet Habakkuk's faith and doctrine was founded on Gods becoming flesh, or man.

Habakkuk's testimony

THE prophet in his spiritual declarations[1] to the elect, begins his prophesy, saying, how long shall I cry, O Lord, and thou wilt not hear: for he saw that almost all were grown incredulous, not looking after the accomplishment of the promise, or believing there ever would be such a thing, and hence at the very time, when the Lord from heaven should come by his commission of blood, the prophet did see by faith, that most men would look upon him, wonder, and perish through their rejecting of him.[2]

But saith the prophet,[3] I will stand upon my watch, I will wait that I may be answered by vision, and the vision was that the Lord God would come; for said he, it is certain, and the just shall live by faith in the person of him, who was their Lord, and would become man; therefore saith the prophet,[4] wait for him, wait with me, for the vision is for an appointed time, but at the end it shall speak, and not lie; wait for it, for it will assuredly come : for it is by faith that the just do live, and faith gives assurance that the Lord, the promise, the king of *Israel*, the Holy One,[5] the mighty God, the Rock, the Lord of Host, the glorious Lord, and Lord in his holy temple, that was from everlasting, and made the mountains to tremble. I say, wait for this God, for he will come and bring forth salvation for his people.

Let the heathen, and all that will not believe this, wonder and perish;[6] for behold it will be such a work, that the multitude can in no

---

[1] Ch. i. 2.
[2] iii. 14. xvi. 17.
[3] ii. 1.
[4] i. 12. ii. 13, 14, 20.
[5] iii. 13, 18.
[6] i. 5.

wise believe, no not those that seem the most devout, and most zealous, and the most honourable. These shall all wonder at the work, and perish through unbelief; for it is the just that live (not by reason) but by faith. Therefore let such as have faith wait with me, and if I can see but little of this faith in any, yet I will not be dismayed, though the fig-tree do not blossom, &c.[1] yet I know he will come; therefore will I rejoice, by this my faith, in the God of my salvation; for this vision gives wisdom in the knowledge hereof, as the waters cover the sea.[2]

Thus by the testimony of the prophet *Habakkuk*.

There is none but *Christ*: none but *Christ*: no other but our God-man, *Christ Jesus*, blessed for ever.

---

[1] iii. 17, 18.
[2] ii. 14.

CHAP. XV.

Shewing how that the prophet Zephaniah's doctrine was founded on God's becoming flesh.

Zephaniah's testimony

THE prophet (as all other prophets) having to do with two sorts of people in his doctrine to the elect, brings in God to them as preparing a sacrifice, yet upon the declaration thereof, there is a short interruption, saying, Hold thy peace, as if he should say, I see into the mystery of our God's incarnation; but to the end that those may remain blind, that enquire not after the Lord, nor have not sought the Lord, but sware by *Milchom*, putting God and *Belial* together, I am to hold my peace from being too plain as let them understand.

But as for the elect, my poor afflicted people, they may perceive who it is that prepares the sacrifice, and bid the guests,[1] for the Lord God of heaven will come, and make a feast, and *Judah* shall feed there, and be at rest. But such must have the garment of the house, the king's livery, made up of the righteousness of faith in the person of a redeemer who is to come; wait for him in that garment of belief. But such as come to the sacrifice shall be punished that are clothed with strange apparel. *Matt.* xxii. 11.

Our God is coming, prepare for joy, and when he comes, he shall famish *Milchom*, *Belial*, and all the gods of the earth, who refuse our Lord and Saviour; they shall have no satisfaction or comfort, but shall suffer hunger in the midst of plenty; for they shall have a famine of peace.

But all those that faith hath meekened, he will give them not only a new robe, but a new language also; this will teach them to call upon the name of the Lord in truth; when this language speaks, all other languages are but babble.

Now this Lord that gives this lip and language,[2] is no other but *Christ*, and though these be his poor afflicted ones, yet they are required by the prophet to sing and rejoice tor the coming of *Christ*, their king, as thus,

Sing, O daughter of *Sion*, shout O *Israel*, be glad and rejoice, O *Jerusalem*, the king of *Israel*, even the Lord is in the midst of thee; he

---

[1] ii. 7. i. 7. iii. 17, 18.
[2] iii, 9, 13.

will save, he will rejoice over thee with joy, as over the lost sheep of the house of *Israel*.

Now doth not the prophet here exclude all other Gods; therefore by the testimony of this prophet Zephaniah, it is clear, it is plain, it is to us certain and sure, that

There is none but *Christ*; none but *Christ*; no other God but the man *Christ Jesus* in glory.

CHAP. XVI.

Shewing how that the prophet Haggai's faith was founded on God's becoming flesh.

Haggai's testimony

THIS prophet gives the same evidence with the rest of the prophets, when he comes to preach to the select seed of *Adam*,[1] and under the type of the first temple he brings in the second, making it more glorious than the first, and *Zerubabel* was the figure of him that was to come to build the house, and to lay peace in the foundation in that his second temple, and then would he shake the heaven of men's hearts, that for sought justification by the law in the worship of the first temple, as if the prophet should say, those that look for *Christ*, the kingdom of God, they cannot be shaken, because their faith and confidence is fixed upon him that will stand fast for ever; for that kingdom cannot be moved.[2]

The heart of him that is strong in believing in him, shall be filled with joy, love and peace, and this is the silver and the gold most precious.[3]

Be strong, O *Zerubabel*, and *Joshua*, and all the people of the land, that you may make this temple glorious for a while, to please the zealots of the law, who love a glittering outward shew: but this temple shall not stand for ever, though now new, yet a newer will come, that is not made with hands, it shall stand for ever, and be filled with glory, and when you lay the head corner stone, then shout for joy, all you people that see the signification of it, and cry grace, grace, it is grace to the first house, but grace, grace, to the second. The first house, whilst building, holds a sword of steel in one hand to resist the enemy with, but the second house holds the sword of the spirit, and this is the sword that shall cut through all flesh, and shake both the heavens and earth, as aforesaid.

Thus by this prophet it is as clear as the light, that

There is none but Christ; none but Christ; no other God but the man Christ Jesus our Lord.

---

[1] Ch. ii. ix.
[2] i. 7.
[3] ver. 8.

CHAP. XVII.

Shewing how that the prophet Zechariah's faith and doctrine was pitched wholly upon God's becoming flesh.

Zechariah's testimony

THE prophet Zachariah living at the same time as the prophet Haggai, was sent with the like message concerning the restoration of Jerusalem; the substance of it, as to the elect, is as follows.[1]

Be silent before all flesh (saith the prophet) before the Lord, for he is risen up out of his holy temple, being now to be sent (or to come of his own free good will) unto thee, O Jerusalem. Here the prophet by faith, seeing him coming, preacheth him out in the manner following.

Behold the Lord, even the man whose name is the branch, and he shall build the temple. Therefore shew forth your joy, you virgin daughter of *Sion*, to whom knowledge and belief is given, and peace is planted;[2] for he will dwell among you, and be with you; he will build the temple, and is the head-stone of it, and the stone with seven eyes upon it. Seven several portions, divers gifts and graced all flows from this stone, *Rev.* xiv. 31, from this rock, from this Lord that is a coming to save his people, and he shall bear the glory, and sit and rule upon his throne; for there is no co-partner with him, and his dominion shall be from sea to sea, tor that there is none that shareth with him.[3]

Sing therefore, and rejoice, for the thing is done, and the headstone is brought forth with shouting, crying, grace, grace, to it, *John* i. 17. Rejoice, therefore, you that are not yet his people by covenant. I. Pet. i. 2, 3, 4, when he comes he shall call the *Gentiles*, and speak peace unto them, being a priest upon his throne.[4]

Rejoice, therefore greatly, O daughter of *Sion*, for behold thou hast but one king, and he cometh, he cometh from amongst thee as a man to save man. *Luke* xix. 38, he is just, having salvation, lowly, and riding upon an ass. *Matt.* xi. 28, be you humble and receive him, and hold to him, for he is the covenant of life, the fountain, set open, and the Lord your God.

---

[1] Chap. ii. 13.
[2] iv. 12. ii. 10.
[3] iii. 9. iv. 7. v. 13.
[4] iv. 7. ix. 9, 10. viii. 22.

This is he that saves the house of *Joseph*,[1] and loves *Ephraim*, because *Ephraim* has no other God, and so makes his heart to rejoice, and will cause their children to see and know, that this king that comes riding in such great humility to *Jerusalem*, is that Lord God from heaven, that is coming to build up *Jerusalem*.

Behold him, behold him, O *Sion*, for he comes unto thee with redeeming grace; hearken, and you may hear him speak to you in this wise, saying,

I will come, and save my people, and will make myself known to them, and will rejoice over them, and love them freely; for my love is such, as that I will lay down my life for them; for by the blood of the covenant I have sent forth the prisoners, even the prisoners of hope that waited for me.[2]

They hoped for me, and my promise was to redeem them; they beheld my promise, and now I have sealed the covenant with my blood, and they are redeemed thereby.

I am valued by the wicked but at a low rate, I bade them, if they think good, give me my price, and if not forbear; so they weighed for my price thirty pieces of silver, a goodly price was I praised at.[3] *Matt.* xxvii. 9.

But I being the shepherd of *Israel*, they shall smite me, and the sheep shall be scattered; they shall look upon me whom they have pierced,[4] and shall quake and tremble, lament and howl, when after all this they see me come with power and glory to give reward, when I stand on mount *Olivet*,[5] *Matt.* xxvi. 30. There will they apprehend me, and there will I shew myself unto them at the last day, with all my saints and angels about me. From thence shall I ascend, and to that place shall I descend, then will I smite all people that fight against *Jerusalem*.[6] And the elect seed for whom I shall die, they shall look upon me also, at that day, whom their sins have pierced, and shall mourn for me.

At that time will there be silence in heaven for half an hour, *Rev.* viii. 1. namely, for three days and a half, nothing will rejoice but sin and satan, the grave and hell; but though the sheep then be scattered, and the elect families do mourn, yet as soon as the king of *Israel* is revived, they shall revive.

---

[1] x. 6.
[2] ix. 11.
[3] xi. 12.
[4] xii. 10.
[5] xiv. 4.
[6] xiv. 12.

Thus the prophet's doctrine is clear, that there is no other God but he that came from heaven, and took our nature upon him and so laid down his whole life for our ransom; so that there is to be no more kings, but this one Lord, and whosoever, saith the prophet, worshippeth any other God, shall be destroyed.

Also, saith the prophet, all the elect in all nations, and families shall come, and worship this king as the Lord of host, and keep the feast of tabernacles yearly, and it shall rain righteousness upon all that come, and they shall be separated from others;[1] for no cursed *Canaanites* shall be amongst them, all idol shepherds shall be cut off that own not the shepherd, the stone of *Israel*, to be the true God, and there is no other.

This is the substance of the doctrine of the kingdom of God, the king of *Israel*, by this evangelical prophet : so that it is as clear as the sun at noon-day, to any that have but the least measure of true faith, that by the testimony of the prophet *Zachariah* that

There is none but *Christ*; none but *Christ*; no other God but the Lord *Jesus Christ*, now in glory.

CHAP. XVIII

Sheweth that the prophet Malachi's faith and doctrine to the elect, was wholly fixed upon God's becoming flesh, and so a Saviour.

Malachi's testimony

THE prophet Malachi, the beginning of his prophesy grounds upon two seeds, with rejection to the one, and election to the other, most of his two first chapters treats upon *Esau's* nature, though in carnal *Israel's* seed, and shews that that nature, whether in Gentile or *Jew*, will never please God, let it act forth itself in religion, or any other way.

But the prophet in the other two chapters directs his speech to the elect seed:[2] for that seed being under the blessing (though in captivity, darkness, and ignorance, of the mind) it must have words to quicken that seed as lay dead, that so it might be capable of its blessings, which are spiritual and eternal.

And the other seed of *Israel*, according to its obedience or disobedience, it is met withal by the prophet; for in its obeying the

---

[1] xiv. 17.
[2] Ch. iii.

law, it will have the blessing of the law, and if disobey the law it will have the curse.[1]

Wherefore then doth not the prophet speak unto both seeds in the manner following; you that boast of your worship, your offerings and sacrifices signify nothing, your oblations are nothing; if you behold hot me coming down from heaven, all your building which you have set up, shall be thrown down by me.[2]

You have no offering that answers my offering; you offer the blind and the lame, I offer myself pure, and in all perfection. See the laws of purification. *Levit.* xxi. 17,18.

But to return to my own people with a spiritual covenant; for that is with you, even you of the spiritual *Levi*, and my word and command is there, which makes them to give glory to my name;[3] for my covenant is life and peace. I am he, and will send my messenger before me to prepare my way; he shall be the messenger of my covenant, which is myself;[4] you are seeking for me, wait for I shall suddenly come. I have hearkened and heard, how that you my persecuted flock, have privately met together to meditate upon my name, and now when I come, I will remember you: for you are in my book of remembrance, and are the jewels of me the Son of righteousness, who is coming with healing in his wings. Behold my messenger is at hand, and he shall bear the name of *Elias*; this *Elias* must come to prepare the way, not in person, but in spirit, in the spirit and power of *Elias*. I shall come before him, and yet I shall send him by *Elias*; then shall those that receive him turn to me their Lord, and be blessed for evermore. *Amen.*

This is the substance of the prophet *Malachi's* doctrine of the one only true God.

Thus we see that all the prophets of the first commission do unanimously agree together in their doctrine of one personal God; so that by the evidence of them all as a perfect witness, it is as clear as the light to all that are appointed to eternal life by *Jesus Christ* our Lord, that

There is none but *Christ*: none but *Christ*: no other God before or besides, or distinct from the Lord *Jesus Christ*, though millions of men should gainsay it.

---

[1] iii. 10. ii. 2, 9.
[2] i. 4, 8. i. 11, 13.
[3] ii. 3. ii. 5.
[4] ver. 6.

NONE BUT CHRIST.

PART II.

CHAP. I.

Shewing that all the apostles of the Lord Jesus Christ do give evidence, that the foundation of all happiness, according to the prophets, lay in God's becoming flesh, and that their Lord Jesus Christ was that God now becoming flesh.

Matthew's testimony

THE four Evangelists writings is that spiritual sepulchre of *Jesus*[1] wherein lieth buried that incomprehensible mystery of God's cloathing himself with flesh and bone, that he might make himself capable to suffer death, knowing within himself that he had power to quicken again into life.

But to come to their evidence, let us begin with *Matthew*, and see whether he doth own any other God, but the Lord *Jesus* only.

In his first chapter he laying down the genealogy and birth of *Jesus*, brings it to this, that *Mary* the virgin was found with child of the Holy Ghost. And *Luke* saith, that the virgin wife *Mary* was Over shadowed by the Holy Ghost, which Holy Ghost was the Holy God, and from hence *Matthew* gives him his name from the angel, answerable to his nature, *Jesus* a Saviour of his people; so that this child *Jesus* had a people of his own, of whom he was their Saviour, and lest it should be thought from that his mean appearance, that he was not of capacity sufficiently to save, therefore, said the apostle, he is God as well as man, and his name shall be called *Immanuel,* which by interpretation is, *God with us.*[2]

Now seeing it is so, that *Christ Jesus* is God with us, and not only so, but God with us, his own people, then we need not fear, neither need his saints seek help from any other God.

Neither did the apostles believe, worship, or serve any other God or Lord at all, notwithstanding those several titles of Father, Son, or Holy Ghost.

---

[1] Matt. xvi. 21.

[2] Ver. 23.

The Harmony of the Three Commissions 557

But then it may be demanded how we are to understand those sayings of Matthew, of Gods forewarning the wise men in a dream,[1] and of the Father of *Christ* so often mentioned by the apostles, as if it should imply another God, or Father besides *Christ*. Now the answer to this may serve for all other places of the like nature, therefore take it as follows.

Before that God became man, he perfectly foresaw all things that should be done.

Therefore he spake the decree, and left the virtue of his word in the hands of trustees in the heavens above, the virtue of which word may be called God, for there is spirit and life in the word of God.[2] *John* vi. 63.

And because that God-head power cannot be acted but in a personal being,[3] therefore did the Lord of heaven make *Moses* and *Elias* his representatives, through his committing unto them his everliving word before spoken unto them; which everliving word before spoken was the God that warned the wise men as abovesaid, and raised from the dead.[4]

And that *Moses* and *Elias* had this power and authority given them, is evident,[5] and the apostle proves it from his Lord's own words, chapter xxi. In that parable *Christ* saith, that the Son of Man (meaning himself) is as a man taking a far journey, who, left his house, and gave authority to his servants. See for one of them, *Rev*, xix. 10.

Now this Son of Man was no other but God himself, who came into this far country, and gave authority to his servants *Moses* and *Elias*, to watch over their Lord, and all other things (they being taken up to heaven for that end and purpose) until such time as their Lord was asended again.

This opens all those places of mention being made of the Father; for all such places do either relate to the God-head spirit of *Christ* within his blessed body, or to his own representative power, committed into the hands of his deputies *Moses* and Elias.[6]

Observe, for further proof, when *Christ* was transfigured on the mount, was not *Moses* and *Elias* the instruments thereof, again, was

---

[1] ii. 12.
[2] xxiv. 35.
[3] iv. 6. compared with Psalm xci. 11.
[4] ii. 12.
[5] xvi. 33.
[6] xi. 25. xxv. 34. and xxvi. 39.

it not one of them that comforted him in his passion when he was to drink that dreadful cup.[1]

Again *Elias* and *Moses* were them two angels that attended *Christ's* sepulchre, and rolled away the stone from thence, and were instrumental to his resurrection.[2]

Had there been any other God would he not have appeared, did God appear to *Abraham*, to *Isaac*, to *Jacob*, to *Moses*, and the prophets, and would he neglect his son; O no, O no! for this Son, was himself, and that voice that came out of the clouds, saying, *This is my beloved Son*, proceeded either from *Moses* or *Elias*.— This fulfils that scripture, *He shall call me Father, and I will say he is my Son*, Psal, lxxxix. 26.

Moreover, where it is prophesied of that *Elias* should come, *Christ* declares by his apostle, that *John Baptist* was that *Elias*, and the faith of the scripture is, that *John* had his commission from *Elias*, and so came in the spirit and power of *Elias*.[3] *Mal.* iv. 5.

Furthermore, *Moses* and *Elias*, were the watchers of *Israel*, they watched over *Christ* in his birth, in his transfiguration, in his passion, in his grave, in his resurrection, and in his ascension, saying to the spectators that saw him ascend, this same *Jesus* that you see to ascend, you shall in like manner see him descend. *Acts* i. 11.

Much more might be said, but it is sufficient to the seed of faith, Now to go on observe the doctrine of *Jesus Christ*, God blessed for ever.

Come unto me, all ye that are heavy laden with your sins,[4] and under the bands of a legal administration, *and I will ease you, and give you rest*. The yoke I shall lay upon you, is but to believe in me, which belief is the true baptism; that is, to receive me as the Lord and Saviour; for to that end I came, even to seek and to save the lost sheep of the house of *Israel*, whose righteousness is not in the law, but in belief of me.

Therefore, whoever doth so far believe me, as to forsake all for my sake, and cleave to me as their Lord and Saviour, he shall have everlasting life; for I came to give my life a ransom for my elect. I am the king of *Israel*, and now the kingdom of God is amongst you. I am the stone that was prophesied of to be rejected, but shall bruise them to pieces that do reject me.

---

[1] xvii. 2, 3. xxvii. 39.
[2] xxviii. 2.
[3] xi. 14. xvii. 12.
[4] viii. 2. 13. xi. 28.

The Harmony of the Three Commissions 559

But he that receives me is blessed, and he that suffers for me is blessed, and he that hungers and thirsts after my righteousness is blessed; I am he in whom the Gentiles are to trust.[1]

The Scribes and Pharisees glory in their temple: I am greater than their temple, for I am the Lord of the temple, nor their sabbath is not so great as me, for I am Lord of the sabbath also; yea, I am the Lord of Hosts, for all the angels of heaven are mine, and are to do my will when I come in a Father's glory, which I had from all eternity: then it will be known who I am, and that the scriptures did bear witness of me, and that I am he in whom the *Gentiles* trust.

But before this day of my exaltation I. shall be betrayed into the hands of sinners, and shall be condemned to death, but shall rise again to a Father's glory, and shall manifest the same, by becoming the judge of quick and dead, and to give reward to small and great; by this you may know who I am.[2]

And you my disciples shall bear witness to me, and my name shall be preached through the world, and false prophets, and false preachers shall arise, and shall preach ray name, but it shall be but for lucre's sake, and honour;[3] for my name shall be common, but my nature and person shall not be known amongst them. But when I come to put an end to this wicked world, then will I plead with them, and bid them, *Depart from me as workers of iniquity*; and to the sheep that are at my right-hand, they shall hear me say, *Come ye blessed of my Father* (of my God-head spirit, which is the everlasting Father) *inherit the kingdom prepared for you before the foundation of the world.*

---

[1] v. 10, 6 and 13, 26. xvi, 27. xiii. 41. xxiv. 31. xxv. 31. xxvi. 54. xii. 21.
[2] xx. 18. and xxvi. 45. xxvii. 63. xxiv. 14, 11.
[3] xvii. 16, 22.

CHAP. II.

Shewing that the gospel by Mark, is the same with Matthew; namely, that Christ Jesus is the one only and alone true God.

Mark's testimony

THE apostle begins his history with these words, The beginning of the gospel of *Jesus Christ, the Son of God.*[1]

Now this Son of God was no other but God himself becoming a Son, and the apostle cites *Malachi* the prophet to prove it, saying, *Behold I send my messenger to prepare thy way.* Now whose way was it that *John* was sent to prepare, but the Lord God of heaven himself, and therefore the apostle brings in *John,* saying, *Prepare the way of the Lord,* who is become flesh, and so a Son, and in that Son an actual Redeemer, and so may be called the beginning of the gospel of *Jesus Christ,* or as *John* calls it, the beginning of the word, which word was made flesh, and was God, and the christians never had more than one God, not a divided God into several persons, but one personal *Jesus* only.

And here the gospel centres, and to know *Jesus* is to know the gospel, and the coming of him in the flesh is the beginning of the gospel; the knowledge and belief of which, is eternal salvation: and there is no knowing of God savingly, but in *Jesus Christ*; for peace and salvation is spoke to us only in the name of *Jesus.*

The apostle in his history of his gospel, brings in his messenger, *John Baptist,* preparing the way of the Lord, and he makes his doctrine with the other apostles to this effect following.

Now is coming the day of salvation,[2] the kingdom of God (which is *Christ*) is at hand, which is the coming in of life and salvation, being glad tidings of gospel love, I come before to give notice hereof, and to prepare the way of the Lord God.

I baptize you with a preparative baptism of water. I have but the shadow, he hath the substance, even the water of the life eternal, which gives peace; this is his baptism that cleanseth from sin, and giveth life. *John* i. 29.

You are all hasty to come to my baptism, if that would serve you, you would be all saved; if you will be saved, then shew your fruits of faith, and go to him and be cleansed, for my baptism doth but prepare

---

[1] Mark. i. 1.
[2] Chap. i. 7.

for this; for after I have delivered my message, mine must decrease, but his spiritual baptism must increase. My baptism is but to shew you where life and salvation is to be had; *therefore behold the lamb of God which taketh away the sins of the world.* This none can do, but this lamb of God, which is God. *Matt.* iii. 2.

I am not so great as you take me to be, being the least in the kingdom of God, being the concluder of the. law, and the forerunner of the gospel, even the. Lord, who is mighty, and then I, whose shoe lachet I am not worthy to unloose, for he was before me; therefore all that will not yield to him, and receive him as their Lord and Saviour, shall be cut down as with a hatchet, and to suffer a fiery vengeance of an eternal wrath.

Again, this evangelist doth prove from all the mighty miracles done by *Christ*, and the manner of the doing of them, that he was God as well as man, and not only so, but *Mark*, and the other apostles do clearly demonstrate, that he did it solely from his own God-head power, as also what miracles soever were wrought by them, was all done by his name and power.[1]

Observe the power of *Christ*; for by three sentences he cures three persons of their several diseases; as thus, 1st. *Be thou clean.* 2nd, *Be thou opened.* 3rd, *I say unto thee, Damsel arise.* Now the word being spoken, the work was done. The curse of the fig-tree was in these words, never, *no man eat fruit of thee hereafter*, and the fig-tree immediately withered — *Christ* by one word speaking, rebuked the wind and the sea, by saying, *Be still.*[2]

All this is evident proof that *Christ* is not only God, but that there is none distinct from him; for he calls to no God or Father without him; but his own word is his own work.

And the miracles that were wrought by the apostles were all wrought in his name;[3] therefore, said *Christ*, *In my name you shall cast out devils, &c.* and *John* saith, that life is in his name, chap. xx. 31, and *Christ* said, that they were to ask life in his name: what was that, but to ask life of God in that name and person of *Jesus*? *Jesus Christ* being that God that is the giver of life and salvation; and therefore said *Peter*, there is no other name under heaven whereby salvation can be had, but in the name, power, and merit of *Jesus*, These three words comprise all, and make good that prayer of *Christ*, saying, Father, glorify thy name, *John* xii. 28, which how that is, *Christ* himself shews in his other prayer, *John* xvii. 5. *Glorify me* (saith

---

[1] ii. 5, 11. ix. 25. viii. 19, 34, 41. iv. 39.
[2] vii. 30. v. 41. xi. 14.
[3] xvi. 17.

he) *with thine own self with the same glory I had with thee before the world was.*

So that it is clear and evident, that *Christ* was God himself, only his God-head was eclipsed in Manhood for a moment; but this Godhead and Manhood in that single person of *Christ*, was that name that was to possess a father's glory, and was that name the apostle said was above every name, and to that name *Jesus* or *Christ*, *every knee shall bow, as well in heaven as in earth. Phil.* ii. 9, 10, and it is written upon that body of flesh and bone, the name of King of kings and Lord of lords. *Rev.* xix. 16.

But further, mind how this apostle *Mark* brings in his Lord and Master, as *Matthew* did, speaking in this wise, saying,

The kingdom of God is at hand, the gospel is come unto you, which bringeth life and salvation; I am he which am come to preach life and salvation. I am the way, the truth, and the life, and that one good God that will give my life for a ransom.[1]

All that do believe in me are blessed, for their faith in me shall make them whole and whoever shall lose his life for my sake, shall find it again, and whoever gives any thing for my sake, shall not lose his reward; for life and salvation is mine to give. Therefore believe in me, and you have faith in God; for I will lay down my life for you, for I am to be killed, but shall rise again in three days;[2] for I am that stone which the builders and teachers of the law reject, but have you faith in me, and it will remove mountains.[3] He therefore, that is baptized through belief of me, shall be saved: for belief is the baptism of the holy Spirit.

But he that believeth not shall be damned, none can deliver out of my hand, when at the right-hand of all power, because all power will be mine.[4] *Heb.* viii. 1. and xiii. and xii. 2.

Salvation and damnation are both in my power.

This is now the substance of the gospel by *St. Mark*, who bears witness.

That there is none but *Christ*; none but *Christ*; no other God but our Lord *Jesus Christ*, now in glory.

---

[1] i. 1. x. 18, 45.
[2] xi. 22.
[3] x. 18. xi. 28.
[4] xvi. 16, 19.

CHAP. III.

Shewing that the gospel by St. Luke is the same with Matthew and Mark, proving the Lord Jesus (Christ to be the one only and alone true God.

Luke's testimony

ST. LUKE in his first chapter,[1] treating of the birth, of *Jesus*, brings in the angel *Gabriel*, giving testimony, that that child *Jesus*, was God manifested in flesh, therefore calls him the just, and the holy thing, and that his kingdom should be an everlasting kingdom, nevertheless he should be called the Son of God.[2]

Had the angel said he should be called God, the word could not have born it, although *Isaiah* said he should be called the mighty God, but that was not to be till this last age, as that the mystery of God should be finished.

Again, *Luke* tell us,[3] that *Elizabeth* by revelation did declare, that the babe that then was in the womb of the virgin *Mary*, was no other but God, saying in her salutation, *Blessed art thou amongst women, and blessed is the fruit of thy womb, and whence is this to me, that the mother of my Lord should come to me.*

Again, *Luke* did declare,[4] that the virgin, through revelation, at that instant did know, that that holy thing that had entered her womb, was God; for she gave God-head glory to that babe within her, saying, *My soul doth magnify the Lord, and my spirit rejoiceth in God my Saviour.*

At this blessed conception of the virgin, *Zacharias* being filled with the gift of the Holy Ghost, gave all the glory to that child *Jesus*, saying, *Blessed be the Lord God of Israel, for he hath visited and redeemed his people*, which is as much as if he should say.

Now is the promise made good, the Lord God is come from heaven to visit us,[5] and being the horn of salvation will redeem us, being the light sprung from heaven to give light of salvation; and thou, child of mine, which is now born unto me, shalt be called prophet of the highest, who is not yet born, but in the womb of a woman, springing up from a virgin of the seed of *David*, thou art to prepare the way

---

[1] Ch. i. 35.
[2] i. 33.
[3] i. 42.
[4] ver. 28, 46, 47.
[5] i. 69, 74, 75.

before the face of the highest, even that babe which is the high and mighty God.

No sooner was this blessed babe born, but an infinite number of angels came down to celebrate the Lord's nativity with songs of joy, to set forth their inexpressible love to the seed of *Adam*.[1]

When old *Simeon* took the child *Jesus* in his arms, and blessed him, then did he bless God that had blessed him; for he saw, by faith, that the child *Jesus* was God, otherwise he could not be the light of the Gentiles, nor the glory of his people *Israel*.[2]

Now *Israel* was forbid to glory in any but God, because God would retain his glory to himself, but this blessed babe was that blessed God that *Israel* was to glory in.[3]— *Isa.* xlii. 8.

Luke saith further, that the grace of God was upon *Jesus*, and that he increased in wisdom and stature, and in favour with God and man.

Now *Jesus* must needs have the grace of God upon him, seeing he was God, and so he had the gifts and graces of God above measure. *John* iii. 34. *Christ* may well be said to increase in the favour of God; is it any other, but that he increased in strength and God-head, power, grace, and virtue, &c.

Now behold the doctrine of *Jesus* testified of by Luke to be in the manner following.

John Baptists disciples came to *Jesus*, saying, *Art thou he that shall come, or shall we look for another?*

Jesus said unto them, (having cured several diseases at that time) *Go and tell John what you have seen and heard.*[4]

1. Tell *John* that the blind do see. *Isa.* xxxv. 6, therefore I am he.

2. Tell *John* the lame walk, therefore I am he. *Matt.* xv, 30.

3. Tell *John* the lepers are cleansed, the deaf hear, and the dead are raised, therefore I am he.

4. Tell *John* the poor have the gospel preached, and that they are blessed that are not offended with me.

5. I am he that *Isaiah* speaks of, and the prophets speak of: tell *John* I am he, the first and last: I am he.

---

[1] ii. 13.
[2] ii. 28.
[3] ver. 32. xxiv. 26.
[4] vii. 20.

6. I am come, and done such works as never man could do, therefore I am he, and tell *John* I am he, and he knows I am he, and witnesses to it.

Jesus, having preached thus to *John's* disciples and the multitude,[1] turns his discourse to his own disciples, sending forth seventy of them, speaking to this effect:

Pray you that the lord of the harvest would send forth labourers into his harvest. Now I am he that am the Lord of the harvest, and I send you. Go your ways, 'tis I that send you. I am your Lord, set forth my name; he that despiseth you despiseth me, and him that despiseth me, despiseth my Father or God-head spirit, and so sins against the Holy Ghost, being the spirit of true prophesy, and so shall be damned to all eternity

Therefore tread on these serpents that blaspheme,[2] and in that you find my words to be true, and the devils are subject to you through my name, yet rejoice not so much in that, as in that your names are written in heaven, and that the mystery of the gospel is revealed to you.

Therefore I am thankful to the God-head spirit, who at this instant springeth up, and maketh me to rejoice, seeing he hath hid these things from the learned, and revealed them to babes.

Wherefore he that learns from me the mystery of the gospel will have cause to rejoice, and will know the Father, but there can be no knowing of me but by the Holy Ghost.

I cannot declare to you so much now as when I am in the glory of the Father, then will I send the Holy Ghost.[3] Therefore, you my apostles, wait till then, and tarry at *Jerusalem*, until you be indued with power from on high; for when I am ascended and glorified, it shall be done, and all things needful to be known shall come into your remembrance, then shall my blessing take effect upon you, and you shall worship me as your Lord and God. *Amen.* So it shall be.

This is the substance of the gospel by *St. Luke*, who bears witness that according to the doctrine now stated,

That there is none but *Christ*; none but *Christ*; no other God but our Lord *Jesus Christ*, now in glory.

---

[1] x. 1, 2, 3, 16.
[2] x. 19. xx. 21.
[3] xiii. 12. xxiv. 49, 51, 53.

CHAP. IV.

Shewing that the gospel by John, his three Epistles, and his Revelations wrote in Patmos, is the same with Matthew, Mark, and Luke, proving clearly, and much more abundantly the divinity of Christ, and that he is the one only and alone true God, in a body of flesh and bone, now in heaven glorified.

SECT. I.

John's testimony

JESUS *Christ* is most clearly proved to be the only true God in these six doctrines following.[1]

First, *Jesus Christ* is said to come from heaven, and that he is above all, and that his glory was wrapt up in mortal flesh, nevertheless, the apostle saith, he is above all, now being ascended; coming down only to give life unto the elect world.[2]

Now *Christ* being above all, and his name above every name in heaven and earth, where then must there be a God above him.[3]

Secondly, The apostle saith, that this God became man, by taking flesh upon him. God was made flesh (saith he) and we beheld his glory as a son from a father.[4]

Now, if there never was but one God, then it must needs be that God made or begot himself into a son; so that God is *Christ* come in the flesh, and he that so believes, is of God; but, saith *John*, there are deceivers gone out, that deny this doctrine of God coming in the flesh, they are of Anti-christ.[5]

As if he should say, in the latter times false prophets shall go out of the true doctrine delivered by us, and shall seduce many; they shall hold forth another *Christ*, for they will have a *Christ* without flesh or a body, or person of his own, and a Father-God that hath no body.[6]

But you that have the unction, will own that *Christ* came in the flesh, and then you have God in that flesh, and the Father in that

---

[1] iii. 13.
[2] Ch. i. 14. vi. 51. and viii. 23.
[3] xiv. 14. and xvi. 24. and xx. 31.
[4] i. 14.
[5] I. John. iv. 2, 3.
[6] I. John. ii. 18. II. John vii.

Son; and so he is God become flesh and bone, in a real body of his own, in which his whole name is written, and is read by the spirit.[1]

Thirdly, *Christ* by his becoming flesh and suffering death in that flesh, became the author of eternal life to those that believe him, and of damnation to those that reject him: therefore, said *John*, he that believeth on the Son is not condemned, but he that believeth not, is condemned already.[2]

And the Lord that is this Son, saith thus, in the authority of a God, he that believeth in me hath everlasting life, and if he were dead, yet will I raise him at the last day; for I am the resurrection and the life; but such as will not receive me, shall die in their sins, and be raised again by me to be damned. You seed of the serpent, you ask who I am, when you have lift up the Son of Man, then you shall know to your sorrow who I am, and that I was before *Abraham*, and the *I am* that spake to *Moses*.[3]

By this it is clear that there is no God but *Christ*, who hath both life and death in his hands, and the keys of *David*, and sword with two edges, and is judge of quick and dead, as now follows.[4]

Fourthly, All power is *Christ*'s being judge of quick and dead. Do you murmur, said *Christ*, because I make myself equal with God? know further, that as the Father raiseth the dead, and quickeneth them, even so the Son quickeneth whom he will.[5]

Here now is Father-hood and Son-ship in an equal power, who must we cleave to as Lord over us? must it not be the Son, yea, for the next words makes the Son sole Lord and whole judge; whereby it is clear, that the Son in his deity doth ever comprise the Father, and, therefore, said *Christ*, the Father judgeth no man, but hath committed all judgment to the Son to the end that all men may honour the Son with the same honour as was due to the Father.[6]

Here it is clear, that Father and Son are one personal being, who then after the sight hereof, will be so bold as to say they are two persons distinct from each other.

When *Jesus Christ*, the Son, is upon his throne, as judge of all, when then sits the Father, certainly it is so, that one throne serves one personal God-man *Christ Jesus*, now in heaven glorified, and one

---

[1] I. John ii. 20, 24, 27, 28, and iii. 24.
[2] Rev. xix. 16. i. 13, 14. John iii. 18. xxxvi. 13. vi. 6, 8.
[3] xi. 26. x. 10. John. v. 30. viii. 28, 58. Rev. i, 18. \nxd xx. 1.
[4] iii. 7. and ii. 16.
[5] v. 42. vi. 63.
[6] John. v. 22. Rev. xix. 16.

faith hath but that one Lord of a single person, as its object to pitch upon.

Fifthly, *Christ Jesus* is said by *John* to be Creator as well as Redeemer In the beginning was the word, which was *Jesus Christ* and by *Jesus Christ* was every thing made that was made, so *Paul* declares the same.[1] *Eph.* ii, 10. *Heb.* i. 2. *Eph.* iii. 9, *Phil.* iii. 21. *Col.* i. 16.

It is further said, that he made the world, though the world knew him not;[2] where then is there a Creator distinct from the Redeemer, and where is there a Father now but in that Son.

Sixthly, and lastly, The apostle, though he speaks much of the Father, yet his positive sayings centres in the Son, and proves that whosoever hath the Son, hath the Father. Therefore, said *Christ*, I and the Father are one, not two persons, but one personal glory; and when Philip desired *Christ* to shew them the Father, he told him that they that saw him saw the Father, and that the Father was in him, all power was his, and all in his hand.

Again, the apostle in his epistle, though he speaks of the Father's sending the Son yet nevertheless this Son is owned by him. to be the Father himself therefore called the eternal life which was with the Father; what is that, but that he is the Father of eternal life himself? for, saith he, Abide in him, that was from the beginning, what was this abiding in him, but their believing him to be God; for, saith *John*, he that abides in the doctrine of *Christ*, hath both the Father and the Son.[3]

Again, saith *John*, Abide in him[4] (not in them;) now this him was *Jesus*, as the next words shew, saying, that when he shall appear, we may have confidence. Again, saith *John*, Behold what manner of love the Father hath bestowed upon us, that we should be called the sons of God.

Now this Father and God is all comprised in the person of *Christ*, as the next verse shews, saving, and now are we the sons of God, and we know that when he shall appear, (namely *Christ*, that God) we shall be like him, for we shall see him as he is (not as he is in reason's account, but as he is in faith's account) one personal God, and under the title of *Christ* or Son shall be very God and eternal life; all other God's are idols.[5]

---

[1] John i. 1, 3. v. 12, 13, 14. Rev. iv. 11.
[2] i. 10.
[3] I. John i. 2. I. John ii. 20, 27, 28. II. John 9.
[4] I. John ii. 27.
[5] I. John iii. 2. John v. 21.

Therefore abide in *Christ*, stick close to that name, for the Father is there, salvation and eternal life is there. He that brings not this doctrine, receive him not, nor bid him God-speed, for he is an antichrist that denieth *Christ* to be God become flesh, and Father to become a Son; so that to have that Son is to have the Father, and there is the God-speed and blessing.

SECT. II.

I must still follow the evangelist, because he follows none but the Lamb, nor owns no God but he, if we but see into the spirit and life of his words, and to my faith and light, he speaks in this manner following.

Hearken to our message which we have received from him that was from the beginning, which is, which was, and which is to come; the Almighty, even *Jesus Christ*. Our fellowship is with the Father, and with the Son, (not with them as two, but with him) with him that is both Father and Son; if you own this Son to be your God, you want not the Father.[1]

We know that the Son of God is come, and this is he that is now come by blood, who came before by water, and we bear witness to this blood, and that he is God under the title of Son, and the spirit that not only assisteth us, but cometh after as a witness itself, and is truth, doth and will bear record unto the truth of *Christ*, being God, and are to finish this mystery of God, and in the days of the voice of the seventh angel, when he shall begin to sound, then shall the third witness or record come forth to finish the mystery of God, which when it comes it will declare its message as we have declared ours.[2]

But in the sounding of all these counterfeit angels, truth will be trode under foot, for the letter of our declarations will be given unto the Gentiles, and they shall make merchandize of it, after they have put us true ministers to death, and they will get riches and honour by their ministry of the letter, and they will teach a false god, a false devils a false heaven, and a false hell, and no true faith will appear.

But when the third record comes in, then will the spirit of life from God enter into the letter of our declarations (which will be as a dead body) and make it for to stand upon its feet by a lively interpretation thereof, and the true believers under that witness, will be the dead men that shall not live again, until the thousand years be finished and more, and then shall truth appear again upon the earth to complete true prophesy, in a full witness to that record in heaven, of Father,

---

[1] i. 1, 8. ii. 27 and iii. 2.
[2] Rev. x. 1, 7. and xi. 2, 11.

Son, and Holy Ghost, being one Lord *Jesus Christ* All other gods are idols. *Amen.*[1]

Let the sober peruse the scriptures in the margin and see whether the apostle speaks not in this sense abovesaid.

This apostle *John* sets forth the glory of his Lord with great splendor.[2] No greater titles of honour and dignity, name and renown, was ever by the prophets attributed to Jehovah in the law, than *John* doth to *Jesus* in the gospel, calling him the true God, the great God, the very God, the almighty God, the Alpha and Omega, the first and the last, the King of Kings, and Lord of Lords, and Creator of the Worlds, and that he hath the keys of *David*, and the sword with two edges, and had the seven stars in his right hand, and that he searcheth the hearts and reins of all men and sitteth upon his throne alone, whose eyes are as a flame of fire, and feet like burning brass, and his voice as the sounding of many waters, and his countenance as the sun; for the kingdom of heaven hath no need of the sun, for the Lord God, which is the Lamb is the light thereof, and that shining body from that spark of fiery faith, illuminates all things; for I saw his person, and witness to him.[3]

Thus we see that this beloved apostle, who leaned upon *Jesus*'s breast, and sucked revelation there, being more conversant in divine secrets than any other apostle, did own no other God but *Jesus Christ* his Lord.

Therefore by the testimony of *John*, with *Matthew*, *Mark*, and *Luke*, it is as clear as the light, that according as the doctrine is stated now in this last stage, and under this record prophesied of by *St. John*, to the finishing of that mystery that hath been hid from age,

That there is none but *Christ*; none but *Christ*; no other God or Father, but our Lord *Jesus Christ*, now in glory.

---

[1] Rev. xx. 5. I. John v. 20, 21.
[2] John xvii. 3. Rev. xix. 6, 17, and i. 8. and xxi. 6, 16, i. John i. 1. Rev. i. 5. John v. 20. Rev. ii.
[3] xxi. 23.

CHAP. V.

Shewing that Pauls doctrine is the same with the rest of the apostles, proving clearly to all that have faith in his doctrine, and the knowledge of discerning given, that the Lord Jesus Christ is the God become flesh, and is the one only and alone true God, and everlasting Father.

Paul's testimony

ALTHOUGH *Paul* doth in several places make mention of the father of our Lord *Jesus Christ*,[1] as the rest of the apostles do, because their commission was but the commission of blood, and so must render *Christ* as a son, yet nevertheless *Paul* owned no other God or Father, but what lived and reigned essentially in *Jesus*, as will appear in the following discourse.

Paul doth declare in each of his epistles, that he is the apostle of *Jesus Christ*, and that he had not his commission from man, or by man, but by the Lord *Jesus Christ* himself, then in heaven glorified;[2] for no God ever appeared or spoke to *Paul* but *Jesus* only; and although *Paul* doth say, that he is an apostle of *Jesus Christ*, and of God the Father, yet this God the Father was no other but that powerful voice out of the blessed mouth of that glorious *Jesus*, which said, *Saul, Saul, why persecuted thou me*. I have made him a chosen vessel to declare my name. In these words was the God and Father manifested.

So that *Paul*'s commission from God the Father, was through the mouth of *Jesus Christ*, and the life and virtue of those words in *Paul*, was the Holy Ghost, or the gift of the Holy Ghost, which impowered him to be an able minister, to set forth, and preach the name of *Jesus Christ*, as Lord and Saviour.[3]

Again, if *Paul* saith in some places,[4] that God sent his Son, and gave his Son in other places, he saith that *Christ* gave himself: so let this last word stand as positive for the only God, to those that now look for salvation by *Christ*; and it is but as to say as the prophet *Isaiah* had said, being no intercessor I became the intercessor myself, and so said this Lord God, when he was come, *I lay down my life of*

---

[1] Rom. i. 1. I. Cor. i. 1. II. Cor. i. 1. and Gal. i. 1, 12, 15.
[2] Acts ix. 17. xv. 4. compared with Acts xxii. 14.
[3] II. Cor. iii. 6.
[4] Rom. viii. 3. Gal. iv. 4. and i. 4. Eph. v. 2, 25. Rom. viii. 24. Titus. ii. 14. Heb. i. 3.

myself; I have power to lay it down of myself and have power to take it up of myself. See *Isa.* lix. 16, and lxiii. 5.

For this is *Paul's* doctrine,[1] God became man, and so an advocate, which could not be, unless the Godhead was in him; for man without God, could not be an advocate, because no man is pure, but each defiled; but that which can be without spot is capable to be an intercessor.

Therefore it was that the apostle said,[2] that God was in *Christ*, reconciling the elect world unto himself, and lest it should be thought, that God should be in *Christ* but in part, or by an influential light, as in others, therefore, said *Paul*, the whole God-head lived in *Christ* bodily,[3] or personally, then it will follow, that God lives wholly in *Christ*, and from hence these two doctrines are clear.

First, That God is not bodiless, but hath a body to live in, and that body is the body of *Christ*, which body was, and now is, the eternal Son of God.[4]

Secondly, Where *Christ* is, there God is; for if the God-head be wholly in him, then is *Christ* whole God, and then there will be no Father to send a Son, but that Son which is himself, his divine God-head spirit being the everlasting Father.

Again, if *Christ* had not been the alone true God, *Paul* could not have said that he purchased the church with his blood;[5] and further, the apostle said, that he purchased it to himself, who then are they to worship but *Christ*? Surely it is God in *Christ*, and not God without *Christ* that the saints do worship.

Did *Paul* ever preach any other God but *Christ*, witness that to the goaler,[6] yet this faith was judged heresy; but said *Paul*, that which you call heresy, so worship I the God of my fathers; which God was no other but *Christ*. Therefore, said *Paul*, speaking of election and the promise, meaning *Christ*, *of whose ate the fathers, and of whom concerning the flesh* (that is bodily flesh) Christ came, who is God blessed forever. Amen.

Here *Paul* shews that *Christ* was God over all, and puts an *Amen* to it; what can be more plain? Nay, so great was his love to *Jesus*, that he mentions his name a matter of seven times in one chapter.

---

[1] Heb. vii. 46. and ix. 14. Gal. iii. 20.
[2] II. Cor. v. 15.
[3] Col. ii. 9.
[4] Phil. ii. 1. Heb. x. 5.
[5] Acts xx. 28.
[6] Acts xvi. 31.

The Harmony of the Three Commissions 573

And doth not his doctrine arise to that pitch, as to bless all such as believe in, and love the Lord *Jesus*,[1] and to curse all such as love not the Lord *Jesus* in sincerity and truth, and is not his faith and doctrine according as hereafter follows.[2]

Walk so as you have us for an example, for I must tell you, that I live by faith of him who loved me, and gave himself for me, being God over all.

Now would I be found in his righteousness : before I knew him I was for my own righteousness, as if I could perform the law, but now it is the Lord Jesus *Christ* that I fix upon for eternal life, and count every thing but dung and dog's-meat that I may win *Christ*. Nothing relishes but *Christ*, nothing pleases but *Christ*, nor satisfies but *Christ*; for he is righteousness, justification, wisdom, and sanctification; yea, all in all to me.[3]

So that the only knowledge I press after, is to know *Christ* in his mighty power, as to live and die, and to live again; for he being risen and ascended to the right-hand of all power, which is a Father's glory.[4]

Therefore I now look for him, according to his promise,[5] from heaven, to raise the dead, that died in the faith of him; for if he had not died and rose again, the dead would never have been raised, then had it been well for the wicked, but miserable for us that suffer for righteousness of believing in him. But behold our Lord is risen, and so is the first fruits of those that sleep in him; and as surely as he is risen, so as surely he will raise all his saints that did believe in him, to receive with him the glory prepared. Therefore look for this Lord *Jesus Christ* from heaven, and look for him only, and for no other God.[6]

But you must wait with patience a while; for before this be, there will be a falling away from this faith, which we preach to you, and they will teach another gospel:[7] leaving the simplicity of *Christ*, they will make a shew of faith, and of *Christ*, but it shall be but in contention and strife. Therefore seeing they will depart from the faith of *Jesus* (seated on his throne in the highest heavens by his person, and in the lowest hearts by faith) he will depart from them, and will

---

[1] I. Cor. vii. 3. and xvi. 22. Eph. vi.
[2] ver. 3. 22. Phil. iii. 17. Rom. ix. 5. Phil. iii. 6, 8. Gal. ii. Rom xiv.
[3] I. Cor. i. 30.
[4] I Cor. ii. 2.
[5] I Cor. xv. 17, 18, 20. I. Thefs. iv. 14.
[6] Col. iii. 3, 4. I. Thess. i. 10. Phil. iii. 9. Heb. ix. 28.
[7] II. Thess. ii. 3. II. Cor. xi. 3, 4, 14. II. Tim. iii. 5, 6, 7. and iv. 3. Philip. i. 15, 16.

according to the desire of their corrupt minds, will send them strong delusions.

Then shall iniquity abound,[1] and false teachers in a mystery, and all great wisdom, and fleshly learning must handle the matter, to delude the simple, and presently after, the man of sin, or last great antichrist, shall be revealed; but in those days there shall be a call again, for the *Jews* shall be called to the knowledge of our Lord *Jesus*, and revelation, faith and knowledge in the mystery of godliness shall arise,[2] and fight again with the mystery of iniquity, and shall strike at the man of sin with the breath of God in that revelation aforesaid.

Therefore look not for the coming of the Lord till those things be fulfilled, yet keep your watch, and stand you fast, that we may rejoice with you at that day, and then shall they have the revelation of his wrath, that had not the revelation of faith in his person, in that their day.[3]

But as for you, that admitted the faith of the oppression of God[4], when becomes in his glory, he shall be admired by you; for you will admire at the glory and sun-shiny brightness of his blessed person; and you shall admire at his love and joy in iu.21, you, as to make your persons like unto his own glorious person; for he hath a person of his own, equal with God, without robbery.[5]

Again, *Paul* writing to *Timothy*, having in his epistle to him, set forth all grace, mercy, and peace, from *Jesus Christ* his Lord, afterwards ascribes all glory and honour unto *Jesus Christ*, calling him king eternal, immortal, invisible, and the only wise God;[6] and concludes it, that all honour may be done to him, saying, *To him be honour and glory, for ever and ever, Amen.* Here *Paul* instructeth *Timothy* where and who the Father is: even in the person of *Jesus*, is God and Father, lord and king, grace, mercy, and peace, life, and glory, and that for everlasting.

Paul lays *Timothy* a foundation, and would have *Timothy* to build thereon, being the pillar and ground of truth, the mystery of godliness; no God but what is in *Jesus*, no God but the Lord *Jesus*, and no Father to ascribe glory to, that is distinct from the Son.[7]

---

[1] 2. Thess. ii.7. Phil. iii. 19. Col. ii. 8, 16. 1 Tim. vi. 5. 2. Tim. iii. 9.
[2] Rom.xi.25, 26.
[3] 2 Thess. ii. 3. and iii. 2, 3. and 2 Th. i. 7, 8. 2 Thess. ii. 10.
[4] 2 Thes. i. 10.
[5] Phil. iii. 21. and ii. 6. 1 Cor. viii. 6.
[6] 1 Tim. i. 15.
[7] 1 Tim. iii. 15, 16. and i. 2.

Wherefore then, the substance of *Paul's* foundation doctrine to *Timothy* runs thus:

Unto Timothy, my own son in the faith: I greet thee well, as an apostle of Jesus Christ, and by his commandment which is my hope, my trust, and my lord, The good thing, by me given thee, make use of, even faith, which is wrought in thee and given thee by the laying on of hands, as I am ordained a preacher in verity and truth, as it is in Jesus; so have I ordained thee: I charge thee therefore, before Jesus Christ my lord, that thou observe my commandment. Be strong in the grace that is in Jesus, and hold fast the form of sound words, which lies all in Jesus Christ, from which many shall swerve, and are already gone.[1]

But the true faith, life, and doctrine, I have declared to thee; therefore let thy prophesying appear, and be not ashamed of the truth.

For in this Jesus have I believed and taught to be lord and saviour; and let none trouble me henceforward; for I know in whom I have believed; I am the apostle of Jesus Christ; this is my authority, my answer to all that oppose me is, I know in whom I have believed, even in Jesus Christ. Let this stand as a bulwark or foundation.

Therefore, O Timothy, observe my doctrine, and build upon these twelve articles of my faith, which I will here lay before thee.

1. I believe that Jesus Christ is God manifested in flesh.[2]

2. I believe that Jesus hath abolished death, and brought eternal life.[3]

3. I believe that Jesus Christ is our God and Saviour, hope and trust.[4]

4. I believe that Jesus Christ is the blessed Lord God.[5]

5. I believe that Jesus Christ is the most wise God.[6]

6. I believe that Jesus Christ is the immortal and eternal Lord God. Tim. i. 17.[1]

---

[1] 1 Tim. i. 2. xii. 17. 2 Tim. i. 14. 1 Tim. iv. 14. 2 Tim. vi. 20. 1 Tim ii. 7, and 6, 11, 14. 1 Tim. v. 31. 2 Tim. iv. 21, and 1, 1, 6. 1 Tim. iv. 8, 15. 2 Tim. i. 8, 12.
[2] 1 Tim. ii. 3.
[3] 2 Tim. i. 10.
[4] I. Tim. ii. 15.
[5] 1 Tim. ii. 3.
[6] Tim. i. 17.

7. I believe that Jesus is the only potentate. [2]

8. I believe that Jesus Christ is God of all power, honour, and glory. [3]

9. I believe that Jesus Christ is the blessed and everliving God. [4]

10. I believe that Jesus Christ is King of kings, and Lord of lords. [5]

11. I believe that Jesus Christ is the Saviour of men that are saved. [6]

12. I believe that Jesus Christ is judge, both of quick and dead. [7]

This is Paul's faith and doctrine to Timothy, and when he writes to Philemon, once doth he mention God as Father,[8] but be mentions him eight times as Jesus, as thus

NONE BUT CHRIST

1. I am a prisoner for the testimony; of Jesus.

2. I am Paul the aged, a prisoner of Jesus.

3. Grace and peace to you from Jesus.

4. I rejoice at thy faith in Jesus.

5. All the good things you enjoy are in Jesus.

6. Still refresh thou my bowels in Jesus.

7. Salute Epapaus my fellow-prisoner in Jesus.

8. The grace of our Lord Jesus be with you. Amen.

Thus we see now of whom the ends of the world are come, that Paul owned worshipped, believed, loved, served, or taught, no other God but Jesus Christ, their Lord and ours.

Observe Paul's positive proofs of Jesus Christ being sole God. Not one of those sayings of his, but they will stand as a God against all other sayings, and make all other scriptures bow to them; for positive can stand of itself, when privative cannot, as God can stand of himself; so that by this, you that have faith may see that Christ can

---

[1] vi. 16.
[2] vi. 16.
[3] vi. 16.
[4] iii. 15.
[5] i. 15.
[6] ii. 4.
[7] 2 Tim. iv.
[8] Phil. ver. 1.

stand of himself. Behold Paul's positive saying is summed up into those heads above, and in these which follow.

1. There is no truth but what is in Jesus, then no God but Jesus.[1]

2. Believe only in Jesus justifies; so no God but Jesus Christ.[2]

3. Every knee is commanded to bow to Jesus; so no God but Christ Jesus.[3]

4. Whoever calls on Jesus as Lord, shall be saved; so none but Christ.[4]

5. Christ is the image of the invisible God; so none but Christ.[5]

6. Jesus Christ had the God-head bodily in him; so none but Christ.[6]

7. God was in Christ, reconciling the world unto himself; so no God but Christ.[7]

8. Jesus Christ gave himself for us; so none but Christ.[8]

9. All riches, wisdom, and grace are in Christ, Eph. iii. 11. so none but Christ.[9]

10. The world was created by Christ, Col. i. 16. so none but Christ.[10]

11. Christ upholds all things by his power; so none but Christ.[11]

12. In Christ is hid all treasures of wisdom, &c. so none but Christ.[12]

13. One God as one faith, even Jesus who is above all: so none but Christ.[13]

14. Jesus Christ, the high and mighty God; so none but Christ.[1]

---

[1] Eph. iv. 21.
[2] Rom. v. 9.
[3] Psal. ii. 10.
[4] Rom. x.
[5] Heb. i. 3.
[6] Col. ii. 9.
[7] 2 *Cor.* ix. 15.
[8] Gal. i. 4.
[9] Col. ii. 3.
[10] Eph. iii. 9.
[11] Heb. i. 3.
[12] Col. ii. 3.
[13] Eph. iv. 5, 6.

15. Jesus Christ is God over all blessed for ever. Amen. So none but Christ.

Thus by the testimony of Paul, that learned doctor in the spirit, who had been wrapt up into heaven, and saw things unutterable; yet hath he uttered enough to shew,

That there is none but Christ; none but Christ; no other God but our Lord Jesus Christ, though millions of men should gainsay it.

CHAP. VI.

Shewing that Peter, the apostle of Jesus, taught nor preached no other God but our Lord Jesus Christ only.

Peter's testimony

PETER, although he had his doubts and failings rather more than the other apostles after his call, before the Holy Ghost was given (to shew that without Jesus we can do nothing that is good) yet was made chief of the apostles, being so rewarded for his testimony, upon his answer to Christ, saying thus: I believe thou art Christ, the Son of the living God.

Now when Peter had laid down his foundation, he builded upon it,[2] and miracles were wrought for a confirmation thereof, and all the glory of the miracles given to Christ; therefore when Peter healed the lame man, by saying, In the name Jesus Christ of Nazareth, rise up and walk.

Now his faith in *Peter's* words raised him, and he went with them into the temple praising God; which God was no other but *Jesus* that had made him whole; for as no other name was called on to heal him; so no other God had that worship of praise given him but *Jesus* that healed him, and therefore, said *Peter*, it is the faith in the name of *Jesus* that hath made him whole.

And now doth *Peter* begin to make the name of *Jesus* glorious,[3] ascribing all power and glory, life and salvation unto *Jesus*. Therefore, he told the *Jews* that they slew the Lord of all life, and though it be said in the same verse,[4] that God raised him from the dead, yet *Peter* doth not mean that there was a God above him, as distinct from him, but he means his God-head spirit within his blessed body, that quickened in a moment, and he knowing the virtue thereof there ore said that it was impossible that he should be kept under death.

---

[1] Heb.vii.26.
[2] Acts iii. 8 and iv. 12.
[3] iii. 15.
[4] ii. 24.

The Harmony of the Three Commissions

Peter begins his first epistle thus,[1] saying, *Blessed be the God, and Father of our Lord Jesus Christ, which according to his mercy hath begotten us again unto a lively hope, by the resurrection of Jesus Christ.*

Doth *Peter* here bless any God distinct from *Christ*?[2] no; for this God and Father is no other but the life, soul, and spirit of *Christ*, and it was faith in the word of *Christ* that begat them to a lively hope; for that word of *Christ* was God and the Father: for *Christ* had told them before that his word was spirit and life. *John* vi. 63, 68, and that spirit and life was that Father that raised him from death.

Again, saith *Peter*,[3] this word brings salvation. This salvation did the prophets of old serch after, and the spirit of *Christ* was in them: who then was this *Christ* that gave that spirit, but God the Father then cloathed in his spiritual body of uncompounded purity, which was his eternal Son? and what God was that which raised *Christ*, but that spirit of *Christ* which was in the prophets of old in the seed of faith, searching and inquiring for the time of his becoming flesh to save them.

For if God had not become flesh, and died, and risen again, there could never been any salvation for those that died and roted in the grave: for if God would have saved any, he must have taken them up as he did *Moses, Elias*, and *Enoch*, and as he did *Lazarus* before he saw corruption. I. *Cor.* xv. 15, 16, 18.

But to come to the substance; of *Peter's* doctrine,[4] as in reference to faith's object, which is *Jesus Christ*, and you will find it to run in this line following.

Who by *Christ* you do believe in God, do believe him to be God, who by that uncorruptible seed, doth make you to believe in *Christ*, who is God.[5] If your faith be there, it will be precious, when you groundly believe the virtue of his blood that redeemed you, and have tasted the graciousness of *Jesus* by that your new birth, it will be found to your praise at his appearing, who then will give a crown of life. Come to him as a living stone, you are the house and church of the living God.[6] If your faith be strong in him; if you make this *Christ* your rock, your God, your Lord and Saviour, grow in grace, and in the knowledge of *Christ*, the more knowledge, the more love, the more

---

[1] I. Pet. i. 3. iii. 21, 22.
[2] iii. 18. i. 23.
[3] i. 9. ver. 10.
[4] i. 24. ver. 11, 23.
[5] I. Pet. i. 8. ii. 3. and i. 23. and iv. 14. v. 4. ii. 4, 5.
[6] iv. 11. 2 Pet. iii. 18. 1 Pet. iv. 8. ii. 1.

love, the more charity; let faith have its perfect work. There was false prophets, and there will arise false teachers, that will pretend to *Christ*, but it will be but to gain riches and honour. Those will be against all dominion, but such as upholds them, and the will as *Balaam*, bless and curse for wealth, and presume to speak evil of things they know not. [1]

And though they will prophesy in words,[2] that *Christ* is their Saviour, and purchased their redemption by his death, yet they will not give him his honour, power, glory, and dominion, but do you that are his saints, do you give him all glory, who hath really bought and purchased you by his precious blood. He hath not bought false teachers by the shedding of his blood as to purchase them, but he hath bought them so, as to have power to damn damnable hereticks with eternal torments, and all unrighteousness likewise that oppose his blessed person, and will have a God besides him.[3]

Our beloved brother *Paul* hath wrote of those things aforesaid,[4] according to the wisdom given him, and some of his sayings are hard to be understood, which unlearned men in the spirit wrest as they do other scriptures unto their own destruction; for it will appear evident that such things are done;[5] for,

1st, Observe that they that divide *Christ* from God, do wrest the scriptures to their own destruction.[6] *Eph.* iv. 5, 9, 10. *Col.* ii. 6.

2ndly, And they that seek to be redeemed by corruptible things, do wrest the scriptures to their own destruction.[7] *Rom.* xiii. 3. *Heb.* ix. 12, 14, and x. 19, 29. *Col.* ii. 20, 22.

3rdly, And they that teach and preach for money, do wrest the scriptures to their own destruction.[8] I. *Tim.* vi. 5, 9. *Jude* xi.

4thly, And they that deny the Lord that bought them, to be the alone true God, do wrest the scriptures to their own destruction. *Jude* iv.

5thly, And they that argue from God's long suffering, that there will be no end of the world, nor day of judgment, do wrest the scriptures to their own destruction.[1] I. *Cor.* xv. 32. *Rom.* ii. 4.

---

[1] iii. 10, 15, 13, 19.
[2] iv. 11. 2 Pet. iii. 18. 1 Pet. i. 18, 19.
[3] 2 Pet. ii.
[4] 2 Pet. iii. 16. ver. 9.
[5] 2 Pet. ii. 1.
[6] I. Pet. ii. 4. i. 18.
[7] 2 Pet. ii. 3, 15.
[8] ii. 1.

6thly, And they that glory in a God or *Christ* within them, and deny his person without them, do wrest the scriptures to their own destruction.[2] *Rom.* x. 6, 7, 8. *Eph.* iii. 11. *Col.* iii. 3.

7thly, And they that hold forth a God of several persons, or a God of an infinite formless spirit, without any person, do likewise wrest the scriptures to their own destruction.[3] I. *Cor.* viii. 6. *Heb.* i. 3.

8thly, And they that think to be saved by a bare profession of faith, without a lively operation thereof, do like wise wrest the scriptures to their own destruction.[4] — *Rom.* ii. 20. 2 *Tim.* iii. 5.

9thly, And they that hold free will, and that a man hath power in himself to be saved, do wrest the scriptures to their own destruction.[5] *Eph.* ii. 8.

10th, And they that give not the Lord *Jesus* full prerogative, power of life and death, salvation and damnation, do likewise wrest the scriptures to their own destruction.[6] *Rom.* ix. 20.

But you, my brethren, seeing you know these things before, and have that grace of wisdom, beware that you be not led away into these heresies, and fall from your own stedfastness, but grow in grace, in the true knowledge of *Jesus Christ*, give glory unto him as your Lord and Saviour for ever and ever. *Amen.*[7]

Thus it is evident by the testimony of holy *Peter*, that great apostle of *Jesus*, that was witness of his death, resurrection, and ascension, that according to the doctrine stated, which is the true Christian doctrine now in this age, that

There is nor never was, none but *Christ*, none but *Christ*; no other God but our Lord *Jesus Christ*, now in heaven glorified in a body of flesh and bone, brighter than the sun, clearer than crystal, swifter than thought, and sweeter than roses, to whom be glory tor ever and ever. *Amen.*

---

[1] iii. 4.
[2] iii. 10, 17.
[3] ii. 16.
[4] i. 9.
[5] I. Pet. i. 18, 18, 19, 20, 23, 24.
[6] I. Pet. ii. 8.
[7] 2 Pet. iii. 17, 18.

CHAP. VII.

Shewing that the apostle James, his doctrine and faith, was pitched upon Jesus Christ, as the one only and alone true God.

James's testimony

THE first verse of *James's* salutation[1] declares that he owned no other God *James* but the Lord *Jesus*; for, saith he, I am the servant of God and the Lord *Jesus Christ*. *James* did not serve two masters, for God and *Christ* are one, and that particle and, doth not divide betwixt God and *Christ*, but shews the union of the two natures; for, if and should make a person, then the national church might make four persons in the God-head, from that saying of *Paul*, in his exhortation to the saints, to get a full understanding, and then make their acknowledgment of the mystery of God, and of the Father, and of *Christ*, then add the Holy Ghost to God and Father, and *Christ*, and there is four.

Again *James* saith,[2] that every good gift is from the Father of lights: this is *Christ*, and no other; for he had told *James* before that he was the light of the world, and here *James* preacheth him so, for all grace comes from him. Light is glory, and *James* calls *Christ* not only Lord, or his Lord, but Lord of glory,[3] which shews that all glory and dominion is his.

If *Christ* be God of all power and glory, what room is there for any other Father or God. This *Jesus* is he that *James* bids the persecuted saints to wait for from heaven. He did not tell them of any other God that to come from there, even *Christ* that died for them rose again, and ascended; this was their God they were to wait for.

Now the apostle speaking of their waiting for *Jesus*, doth not only intend them at that time in his days, but all saints in all ages following; for those that died then may be said to wait yet, and those that live now, were exhorted to wait then; for the time from then till now is but as one day in faith's account.

For there is no sensibleness of time in death: so that those that died in the apostles days, are but as a day before us, and the end of the world will be but as a day after us.

---

[1] James i.
[2] i. 17.
[3] ii. 1.

So that eternal life is not yet attained to any otherwise, than in the soul of assurance, First, the Lord of life must come,[1] and all saints whilst in life are to be in a waiting posture, even unto the death of the soul, which is a sweet sleep in *Jesus*, and when he doth appear, then shall they appear in glory; for he is the resurrection and the life. I. *Thess.* i. 10. II. *Thess.* iii. 10. *Col.* iii. 4.

Thus we see that *James* grounded the twelve tribes in faith and obedience to *Jesus Christ* only: for, saith he,

NONE BUT CHRIST

1. *Jesus Christ* was the Father of lights.[2]
2. *Jesus Christ* was him that begot them.[3]
3. *Jesus Christ* was the saints law-giver.[4]
4. *Jesus Christ* was the Lord of all glory.[5]
5. *Jesus Christ* was the judge at the door.[6]
6. *Jesus Christ* was the God looked for from heaven.[7]
7. *Jesus Christ* was the God of the *Gentiles*.[8]
8. *Jesus Christ* is Lord and God, and giver of grace and wisdom.[9]

Thus by the testimony of *James*, the apostle of our Lord, it is made clear and evident enough to the wise, that

There is none but *Christ*; none but *Christ*; no other God but our Lord *Jesus Christ*, now in glory.

---

[1] v. 9.
[2] ii. 17.
[3] 18.
[4] iv. 13.
[5] ii. 1.
[6] v. 9.
[7] v. 8.
[8] v. 4.
[9] iv. 6. and i. 8.

CHAP. VIII.

Shewing that the apostle Jude, the brother of James, that his doctrine is agreeing with the rest, proving Jesus Christ to be the one only and alone true God.

Jude's testimony

IN verse the first, he, as all the rest, does read his commission, and his commission was from *Jesus Christ*; this shews his authority.

Now if a man pretend to be a messenger of God, and cannot produce a commission from God by voice of words, or from him that is so chosen, he manifests himself to be a deceiver and a counterfeit.

But to the matter in hand, *Jude*, as a true apostle directs his epistle to the most holy in faith, being by him described to be such, who were sanctified by God the Father and preseved in *Jesus Christ*, and called.

Now though the sanctification is ascribed to God the Father, yet this God and Father is but Lord and *Christ*, for he is it that sanctifies as well as he preserves and calls, and thereupon he had said in his prayer to his God-head spirit when earth, for their sakes I sanctify myself,[1] that they might be sanctified through faith in me, who am the the truth, and thus writes *Paul*, saying, *Christ* sanctified his church by his word, and again, *Christ* sanctified his people with his own blood; that is, by faith in his blood. *Heb.* xiii. 12. *Eph.* v. 26.

All prophets and apostles have given forth, that God would, and did become man, and would shed his blood for the redemption of his elect. This being done and preached forth, the elect, through this report, laid hold of it, and believed it, according to the report, and so came to be sanctified, and made a holy faith.

So that God the father is no other but *Christ* himself, even the word of his power, What is it that is given or done to the saints, but it flows from *Christ*? Doth not *Jude* here ascribe all gifts, grace, and power, to *Christ*. Observe these six in particular, as

1. It is *Christ* that shews his mercy to you.[2] *Heb.* ii. 17.

2. It is *Christ* that preserveth you, and hath called you to the faith.[3] II. *Timothy* iv. 18.

---

[1] ver. 24.
[2] ver. 21.
[3] 24.

3. It is *Christ Jesus* that gives to you eternal life.[1] *John* vi. 68, and x. 38, compared.

4. It is *Christ* that gives you peace, and multiplies your grace.[2] *John* xiv. 27, and i. 17.

5. It is *Christ* that keeps you from falling into error.[3] *Rev.* iii. 10.

6. And it is *Christ*, that at the last day will present you faultless before the presence of his glory, which is himself.[4] *Col.* i. 28.

So that it is clear by *Jude*, that *Christ* is Father as well as Son; so that according to *Paul*, the whole God-head centres here, and the faith in its being so, doth wholly sanctify, as *Paul* likewise said, as 1 *Thess.* v. 23, for all true faith pitcheth here, even before the presence of the glory of *Christ*, as *Jude* saith.

This Jude calls the great mercy answering that divine faith,[5] that the saints shall be admitted into the presence of the glory of *Christ*, when as all such as denied his power of God-head glory, and live in wickedness, shall with Cain, their Father, depart from the presence of the glory of *Christ*, and fall before him.[6]

Therefore the apostle exhorts the saints to mind his doctrine, and keep close to their faith in *Jesus*; and seeing there did rise up many opposers of his doctrine, and further would do, put them forward for growth of faith, that they might be able to resist seducers, that would shake their faith in *Christ*, and yet would come to their feasts of charity as devils transformed into a shew of Christianity,[7] pretending to belief in *Jesus* as a Saviour of them, but not as their Lord, And so were for the turning the grace of God into wantonness, and not only so, but would deny that the Lord *Jesus* was the one only Lord God.

But observe the apostles words well, and it will appear in substance as hereafter follow:

Beloved, you had need of further exhortation, and an increase of grace to withstand these seducers, being reprobates, and appointed for wrath. We have delivered to you the church's faith, which all the elect must have, and so may be called a common salvation faith.[8] Mind, therefore, the doctrine which you have been taught by us; for

---

[1] 21.
[2] 24.
[3] 24.
[4] 24, 25.
[5] 24.
[6] 11.
[7] 2,12,4,18.
[8] ver. 4.

deceivers will arise with false doctrines, and would take you off from your most holy faith, but you may know them by these works, and there small esteem of *Jesus*, although they profess him in words, for they will deny his power and glory. Therefore, if you live in what age you will, and find that men teach *Jesus Christ*, contrary to the common faith delivered you by us apostles, reject them, and try their spirits by our words,[1] and let the conclusion of my epistle be the touch-stone, and the preservation of you for future times, which is thus written.[2] *Now unto him which is able to keep you from falling, and and to present you faultless before the presence of his glory with exceeding joy, To this only wise God our Saviour, be glory and majesty, dominion and power, now. and evermore.* Amen.

So that whoever shall hereafter pretend to preach *Christ*, and shall diminish this his power, and dominion of being Lord and God, he is to be rejected by all that have the holy faith that was once delivered to the saints in exercise, and they may be further known by their pride, coveteousness, and persecution; for,

1st, They will ascribe honour unto themselves, and will apply themselves to the humours of such as are able to prefer them, and if they can set forth articles that may be received by the great and honourable of the world, then will they sacrifice to it.[3]

2nd, This pusheth them on to covetousness, for they are for getting riches, and are hunger bit; they run after reward, and will teach any thing for money, being greedy dogs.[4]

Also, they are such trencher chaplains, and flattering parasites, that they will praise and applaud their patrons or benefactors, let them be never so wicked, telling them that if they do but observe such a principle or method of worship as they prescribe, and accept of them for their minister to pray for them, they shall be saved, for God is merciful. Thus they have their persons in admiration because of advantage.[5]

3rd. That nothing shall hinder their honour and glory, therefore they seek to surpass the harmless innocent souls, scoffing at them, and laugh them to scorn, and complain against the faithful with hard speeches, blaspheming against those things of the spirit which they

---

[1] 3.
[2] 24, 25.
[3] ver. 16.
[4] 11.
[5] 16.

do not know, and against dominion, and so they bring in persecution.[1]

This is the evidence, that they are of those that were of old ordained to this condemnation, even as *Korah, Dathan,* and *Abiram* would have wrested *Moses* priesthood out of his hand, and so are reserved for judgment.

But at the coming of *Jesus Christ,* then woe unto them that go after them, *Balaam* and *Korah*; woe unto those wandering stars that wander from scripture to scripture, and father to father, and then cry, thus saith the Lord, and then speak evil of things they knew not, that are truly the Lords. In fine, woe unto those seducers, that when they cannot subvert the harmless saints with fear, and smooth speeches, that then seek by great swelling words to frighten them to their obedience.[2]

But you obedient children, who are sanctified, preserved, and called by *Jesus Christ,* stand up, quit you like men, and contend for the faith against these men, or wandering stars, that are creeping into a profession of *Jesus,* but not in truth.

So I shall take leave of you, and leave you to him, namely, *Jesus Christ,* who is able too keep you, and preserve you from such an apostacy.[3] When he comes in glory, he only will receive you, who is the only wise God our Saviour, to whom be glory and dominion for ever. *Amen.* Hold to this, and be blessed, though it is the dominion spoke against.

Thus the apostle, seeing the dangerousness of the times ensuing, and of these cokels so springing up amongst the wheat, arms the believers of the twelve tribes, whether then, or thereafter, with arguments of power against them, giving them good proof of the doctrine of the true God, the Lord *Jesus Christ,* as may clearly be seen by this paraphrase upon his epistle. Read it deliberately, and see whether it be not harmonious. So that to my faith it is clear, that by the testimony of *Jude* the apostle,

There is none but *Christ*; none but *Christ*; no other God but our Lord *Jesus Christ,* now seated upon his throne glory.

---

[1] 10, 9.
[2] 13.
[3] verse last.

CHAP. IX.

Shewing that Thomas the apostle of Jesus acknowledged no God but Jesus.

Thomas's testimony

THERE is never an epistle of *Thomas* that is extant, there is they say that goes by his name, but not own in the primitive times, nor spoke of, as ever I could hear; but it is probable there were writings of his, but it matters not much, for the confession of his faith in *Jesus*, after his resurrection, was sufficient; for had he wrote never so much on *Jesus*, his Lord, he could have gone no higher in his doctrine of *Jesus Christ*, than he did, as his fellow apostle affirms of him.

For his doubting the truth of *Christ*'s resurrection was the occasion of strengthening the saints, both then and for future times more abundantly in their faith and assured confidence, that he was their Lord and God.

Therefore when *Christ* bid *Thomas* come near unto him,[1] and feel the print of the nails in his hands, that had been nailed to the cross, and to put his hand into his side that was pierced with the sword, and saying to *Thomas, Be not faithless, but believing,*

Here *Thomas* doing as *Jesus Christ* bid him, was thereupon fully convinced, that it was his Lord and master, and from the spring of his faith (in the virtue of *Christ*'s word) *Be not faithless, but believing*, cried out saying, *My Lord, and my God.*[2]

Jesus Christ hearing this confession of faith in him, owned his confession, and as his Lord and God blessed him, saying, *Thomas, because thou hast seen me, thou hast believed me to be thy Lord and God; thou art blessed in this belief.*

But blessed shall all them be, though they have not seen, as thou hast, and yet have; or shall believe me to be their Lord and God, as thou hast done.

Here hath *Thomas* given an approved demonstration of his faith; and as his faith was great, so was his blessing; and as *Thomas* was the first that set to his seal upon his Lord's resurrection, that he was his Lord and his God.

---

[1] John. xx.
[2] ver. 28.

Even so, *Thomas* was the first that the Lord *Jesus Christ* sealed with the seal of eternal life for that his confession aforesaid.[1]

Now was the promise come, and the covenant sealed between *Thomas* and his Lord, and the other apostles, and their Lord, and all believers with them, I will be your God, and you shall be my people. Herein lies every true believer's happiness to pitch his faith wholly upon *Jesus Christ*. Therefore let *Thomas*'s confession be the patron of our faith, and then will his blessing be the evidence of ours.

Therefore let every one prove their blessing from the proof of their faith, setting to this seal, *My Lord and my God.*

All the prophets in the time of the law, and the believers of their doctrine, had this proof of faith of God hidden in man, or to become man, longing and waiting for the accomplishment thereof, as I have abundantly shewed, and in this they were blessed.

So here, *Thomas*, and all the apostles in the time of the gospel, with their ordained ministers and saints, had this proof of faith in *Jesus*, their Lord and God, and in this were blessed.

So the witness or last record prophesied of by *John*, that beloved apostle, and the believers of truth, have this proof of faith, none but *Christ*, and in this we know that we are blessed.

Thus by the testimony of all the prophets, apostles, and witnesses of *Christ Jesus*, and of *Christ Jesus* himself, the true and faithful witness, and the *Amen*, that,

There is none but *Christ*; none but *Christ*: no other God but the man *Christ Jesus* our Lord, though men or angels should gainsay it.

And from faith we say and affirm, that crowns of immortal glory are prepared for all those that receive this doctrine in the love of it, when the Lord *Jesus Christ*, that high and mighty God shall visibly appear, then shall all saints have the reward of their faith and love, and shall behold his blessed person face to face, with astonishing new joys for everlasting, according to truth of holy writ. *Amen.*

---

[1] ver. 29.

A

LETTER

from the same

AUTHOR.

My beloved Friends, in and about London:

I FIND there is great strife and division among you, and am grieved that the only true church should not only suffer affliction from the common enemies, but also from her intended friends. That such as call themselves sons of the church, should rebel against the church; that they should cry Hosanna to the church, and yet crucify the church. Take care you struggle not beyond the bounds of love, but hold the unity of the spirit in the bond of peace. There must needs be unity in the seed of *Adam*, because they are the seed of God. Let all saints take care they retain the life of love: if they fall into wrangling and discord, they are in danger of the pure life's withdrawing, and in a moment may be deprived of what they seemed to have. We are all one man's children; we have God to our Father, and the church to our Mother. We being brethren, let there be no strife betwixt us, and then the God of peace and love will be with us. This love is the anointing oil, it makes prophets, priests, and kings unto God. There is no light of truth were there is not love. We are all fed with one food, and are all at one table, where we eat the bread of life, and drink the water of life; how then can there be any strife, where there is the soul satisfying bread. We eat the hidden manna, and drink out of the rock of ages. Have but the wedding garment of love and obedience here, and we shall have the robe of glory hereafter. Strange! that any that profess the faith should have a schismatical retragradation to union and concord. Beware to sow division least you reap damnation. They are not all *Israelites* that are of *Israel*. If any be contentious, let him question his own heart, for he is under cither desertion of the spirit of faith, or a delusion of the spirit of reason. The saints do not straggle as lost sheep, but keep together, as a shepherd keepeth his sheep; for a stranger they will not follow.

THOMAS TOMKINSON

FINIS.

ANNALL., PRINTER, DEAL

A

PRACTICAL

DISCOURSE

UPON

𝕿𝖍𝖊 𝕰𝖕𝖎𝖘𝖙𝖑𝖊,

BY JUDE.

𝕺𝖗𝖎𝖌𝖎𝖓𝖆𝖑𝖑𝖞 𝖂𝖗𝖎𝖙𝖙𝖊𝖓

BY

THOMAS TOMKINSON, Gent.

BEING A COPY OF A MANUSCRIPT LEFT WITH

THOMAS TOMKINSON, JUN.

HIS GRANDSON.

DEAL:

PRINTED FOR JAMES MAY, & JOSEPH GANDAR,

BY J. B. UNDERDOWN.

1823.

THE

EPISTLE DEDICATORY

TO all true believers of this third and last Spiritual Commission in Derbyshire and Staffordshire, my own native country, present I this Epistle, wishing all your healths and happiness with increase of grace and love, wisdom and understanding in the doctrine and faith of this Commission of the Spirit you are under.

For faith under every Commission of God is of a growing nature, and the witness of the spirit as well as the witnesses of water and blood have said, that Revelation will grow and increase so long as the world doth last.

Now in that, one of you have wrote to me, to give you my faith and experience upon the Epistle by Jude, and his letter was thus

"SIR,

"I have with very much care perused the Epistle of the Apostle Jude, and find in it many profound mysteries, and hard to be understood in general from the 4th verse to the end; and since the death of the two last witnesses of the spirit, I know no man that hath so great understanding to unfold those hidden mysteries and obscure places of scriptures, comparatively to yourself

"I therefore desire you would for my satisfaction, and for the understanding of future ages, make known the meaning of Jude in his Epistle, and in so doing you will very much oblige me, who am, and will be ready to serve you in what I can.

WILLIAM HALL."

Now from hence I have answered my friends request according to my ability, and this let me say to you; that in regard I have been educated in the Commission of the Spirit above these forty years, besides the many letters which I have received from the Witnesses of the Spirit myself. As also the various disputes between one of them and others, with the variety of queries proposed to him by myself and others, and have been answered by them, likewise having seen many of their letters to others that are not in Print.

By all which I have been edified and made capable to answer the request. And now have I done it according to my abilities for the satisfaction of them and several others, that desire it also, and may be beneficial to others that are inquiring after truth.

A Practical Discourse Upon Jude

And whereas the doctrine of the Commissioned Messengers of God is ever made the ground of true faith, and therefore it is, that the Apostles do many times allude to the writings of Moses and the Prophets for confirmation of their doctrine; because some of those mysteries were fore-prophesied of, by them. But they were not instructed in those things by virtue of their prophetical letter; but by the inspiration of, and from the Holy Spirit

Now it hath been the practice of most men to quote the scriptures of the Old and New Testament for the confirmation of their doctrine, though few rightly understand the spiritual meaning thereof. They have only two Records to prove by. But in this treatise I have produced the doctrine of three Records, for confirmation of what I write. As in the margin I have alluded to the former Commissions for confirmation of the third.

And in many places in Jude, have brought the third Record to interpret the other two, or to confirm them. As upon verse 12th and 20th, where I made use of the Prophet's words which he wrote to me, which I have found for an interpretation of those two material points of doctrine, and so in other verses I have cited their writings for proof of the doctrine. And so in other places I have also cited the books and the writings of the National Ministry, in order to their connection.

Now in that I have not only alluded to the two former commissions, for proof of the doctrine, but living in the time that the third commission was on the stage to finish the mystery of God, have thereupon touched upon it, as upon a third string or instrument of music; which sounds harmoniously, and sweetly in the ears of every spiritual Christian. That Father, Son, and Spirit in the Lord Jesus Christ, one personal God for ever blessed. To whom, saith Jude, "Be all glory, honour, majesty, wisdom and power for ever. *Amen* and *Amen.*

In which faith I salute you,

Thomas Tomkinson.

THE CONTENTS

OF THE

GENERAL EPISTLE,

BY JUDE.

1st Verse to the 4th, he exhorteth them to be constant in the profession of their faith.

4th Verse to the 20th, False teachers are crept in, to seduce them, for whose damnable doctrine and manners, horrible punishments are prepared,

20th Verse. Whereas the Godly by the assistance of the Holy Spirit, and prayers to God, may persevere, and grow in grace, keep themselves, and recover others, out of the snares of those Deceivers.

THE

GENERAL EPISTLE BY JUDE.

1. Jude, the Servant of Jesus Christ, and Brother to them that are sanctified by God the Father, and preserved in Christ Jesus, and called

2. Beloved, when I gave all diligence to write unto you of the common Salvation, it was needful for me to write onto you, and exhort you that ye should earnestly contend for the faith which was once delivered unto the saints.

3. Mercy and peace unto you and love be multiplied.

4. For there are certain men crept in unawares who were before of old ordained for this condemnation. Ungodly men, turning the grace of God into lasciviousness, and denying the only Lord God, and our Lord Jesus Christ.

5. I will therefore put you in remembrance, though ye once knew this, how that the Lord, having saved; the people out of the land of Egypt, afterward destroyed them that believed not.

6. And the angels which kept not their first estate, but left their own habitations, he hath reserved in everlasting; chains under darkness, unto the judgment of the great day.

7. Even as Sodom and Gomorrah, and the cities about them in like manner, giving themselves over to fornication, and going after strange flesh, are set forth for an example; suffering the vengeance of eternal fire.

8. Likewise also these filthy dreamers defile the flesh, despise dominion, and speak evil of dignities.

9. Yet Michael the archangel, when contending with the Devil he disputed about the body of Moses, durst not bring against him a railing accusation, but said, the Lord rebuke thee.

10. But these speak evil of those things which they know not: but what they know naturally, as brute beasts, in those things they corrupt themselves.

11. Woe unto them! for they have gone in the way of Cain, and ran greedily after the error of Balaam for reward, and perished in the gainsaying of Core.

12. These are spots in your feasts of charity, when they feast with feeding themselves without fear: clouds they are without water, carried about of winds; trees whose fruit withereth, without fruit, twice dead, plucked up by the roots.

13. Raging waves of the sea, foaming out their own shame; wandering stars, to whom is reserved the blackness of darkness for ever.

14. And Enoch also, the seventh from Adam, prophesied of these, saying, Behold, the Lord, cometh with ten thousand of his saints.

15. To execute judgment upon all and to convince all that are ungodly anions them of all their ungodly deed which they have ungodly committed, and of all their hard speeches which ungodly sinners have spoken against him.

16. There are murmurers, complainers, walking after their own lusts; and their mouth speaketh great swelling words, having men's person's in admiration, because of advantage.

17. But beloved, remember ye the words which were spoken before, of the Apostles of our Lord Jesus Christ.

18. How that they told you there should be mockers in the last time, who

should walk after their own ungodly lusts.
19.   These be they who separate themselves, sensual, having not the spirit.
20.   But ye, beloved, building up yourselves on your most holy faith, praying in the Holy Ghost.
21.   Keep yourselves in the love of God, looking for the mercy of our Lord Jeans Christ unto eternal life.
22.   And of some have compassion, making a difference.
23.   And others save with fear, pulling them out of the fire; hating even the garments spotted by the flesh.
24.   Now unto him that is able to keep you from falling, and to present you faultless before the presence of his glory with exceeding joy.
25.   To the only wise God our Saviour, be glory and majesty, dominion and power, both now and ever.—
Amen

A Practical Discourse Upon Jude 597

CONTENTS

How we are made the servants of God, &c.	A	604
Who are made so by Creation	B	—
Why Cain's Offering was not, so acceptable as Abel's	C	605
How God manifested himself in the flesh	D	—
What the two Laws signify	E	—
By which Laws we are to examine ourselves	F	—
And especially Ministers		—
Pastors, how they ought to prove their Commission	G	—
Or their danger in assuming to Breach		—
To whom preservation and vocation are attributed	H	606
To whom sin is not imputed	I	—
What is perfect faith and true faith and charity	J	—
What makes a true Christian	K	—
The Divine Qualifications, what they are	L	—
What Divine Love is, and its nature and efficacy	L	—
What may be called Hell	M	—
How envy is to be killed	N	608
No salvation for those that despise true Prophecy	N	608
No salvation to be had, but by faith in Christ only	O	609
The 19th verse of the 44th Chap, of Eze. explained	P	610
Who are the Roman Gentiles	P	611
What is the nature of Faith in God, his saints, &c.	Q	—
What is the Sword, that keeps the tree of Life	R	612
How Faith was first Generated or grounded	S	—
Old Faith may be renewed, but no new faith given	T	613
Difference between Ministers of God, and of Men	U	—
Non-commissioned Ministers compared to Thieves	V	—
Who are Devils incarnate	V	614
What are the two great Attributes of God	W	—
Tophet of old, what ordained for	A	—
What is meant by the Breath of the Lord	B	615
The Difference of the two Seed	C	—
Election and Rejection opposed, by whom	D	—
The difference and nature of Angels	E	615

And with what food they are supplied,	F	616
None but the Seed of the Serpent Reprobated	G	—
The seed of Adam, God's own seed	H	—
Upon what the Doctrine of Freewill is grounded	I	—
Upon what the Catholic Faith was grounded	K	—
And how it came to be called Catholic		—
The Evil consequences of false Teachers	L	617
How the Holy City is trodden under foot	M	618
Lasciviousness how described	N	—
The Romish Church, what it is	O	—
The Pope, how called	P	—
Peter was never at Rome, and why	Q	—
The carnal liberty the Pope allows himself	R	619
Also the Cardinals, Abbots, and Priests in general	S	—
Phillips's Observations thereon	T	—
Priests forbidden marriage, under what pretence	V	—
Popes and Popish saints, keep whores	U	—
Pope John killed by an Italian, for adultery	W	—
Pope Sextus gives liberty for sodomy	X	—
Pope Alexander and son, knew their daughters carnally	Y	—
Athanasius, of heinous crimes, by whom	Z	620
The wickedness of those people, if he was innocent	A	—
Christ's death sufficient for our salvation	B	—
In what manner the Romans acknowledged Christ	C	621
As also the Catholics		—
The Arians Opinion concerning Christ	D	—
Of Faith and Reason, the satisfaction of the one	E	—
And condemnation of the other		—
That the murmuring Israelites were seed of the	F	622
Serpents, as many as fell in the Wilderness, and		—
Why they may be said to be		—
What is meant by the Manna in the Wilderness	G	—
What is signified by the Water	G	—
Eternal salvation by Faith, and how	H	623
Christ's meaning of those, that did eat Manna, &c.	I	—
And are dead, it was an eternal Death, having the	I	—

A Practical Discourse Upon Jude

Fear and seal of eternal death abiding in them		—
Eternal Life and Death is made manifest	K	—
By this commission of the Spirit		—
The Prophet's Opinion of Literal Professors	L	624
The common opinion of the war in Heaven, between	M	—
Michael and his angels, the Dragon and his angels		—
The Prophet's interpretation thereof, & the Dragon	N	—
What is meant by the tree of knowledge, &c.	O	—
The Devil explained	P	625
What are the weapons of Christ in true believers	Q	—
What are the weapons of persecuting believers	R	—
And what they themselves are		—
The explanation of the Red Dragon and the Woman	S	—
What was the Earth that helped the woman	T	—
What the wisdom of Reason is, how called	T	—
And of what nature they are	V	—
Of the several orders of Angels and their Office	W	—
And for what they were in part created for		—
Of the Angel that was cast down, and the Prophet's observations thereon	X	—
The Angels that kept not their first estate, compared to Sodomites	Y	626
No act or deed can be done by spirits without bodies	Z	—
No punishment for the Devil and his Angels before the day of judgment	A	—
None could be guilty of original sin, if the soul was not traditionally given	B	
And St. Augustin owned it before the Plageans	B	—
Observations on the same	C	—
Sodomites and false Teachers from one Root	D	627
That sin and the devil, are man's own nature	E	628
Faith and Reason what they are, and the difference explained	F	—
How sin is conceived, and inferences drawn	G	—
Queries concerning the tree of knowledge of good and evil, which Adam and Eve was not to eat of	H	629
What were the Horns of that Beast that was to make the Whore desolate	I	630
The aspiring- nature of Priests, &c. exerting themselves to be Judges over Temporal as well as Spiritual laws; set forth in divers examples	K	631
Tyranny of Theobald, Archbishop of Canterbury, and murders committed in his successors reign	L	—
Whether a Believer of this commission may take any Public Office	M	—

Nature of Oaths, sufficient reasons for not swearing	N	—
Who Michael the Archangel is found to be, both in the Type and Antitype	O	632
Who that Devil was that tempted Christ	P	—
Who were the angels that ministered to Christ after His dispute with the devil about the body of Moses	Q	633
What is translation, and why Enoch was capable to be translated	R	—
Reason cannot believe that there are any bodies in Heaven, though Moses and Elias were seen in bodily shapes by Peter, James, and John, at Christ's transfiguration, and known by them	S	—
What is the Devil's seed and nature	T	—
The infallible mark of a reprobate	V	634
Learned men of reason, forbid to despise Revelation	V	—
Why no creature hath reason, but angels and men	W	—
The Qualifications of Reason	X	635
The Moral Law written in Reason's Nature, and	Y	—
The Nature of the Moral Law		—
Under a simile of Hagar and Ishmael		—
Reason hath the Lordship of this World	Z	—
Kiss the Son lest he be angry, what is meant by it	A	636
Which is the doctrine of Reprobation	A	—
Dr. Dodwell's pleasing doctrine, that none shall be	B	—
Damned for temporal sins, his citations thereon	B	637
Such Ecclesiastics as may or may not be saved	C	—
Reasons why Cain murdered his Brother Abel	D	—
None more guilty of lies or murder, than Baal's Priests, and their persecuting spirits	E	—
Heresy, a capital crime amongst the Roman Baalists	F	638
The blood thirsty Emperor Theodisius, &c.	G	—
Maxentius the Roman Emperor	H	—
A Bill found against St Austin for murder	I	—
Oaths imposed in all Countries	K	639
Two Popes elected, horrid wickedness & mischiefs	L	—
King Henry's request to Pope Gregory thereon	M	—
Bloodshed and cruelties of Leo and his Cardinal	N	—
The Rise of the Protestant Church	O	640
Ceremonies at the Consecration of a Bishop	P	—
Observations on the Romish and Protestant Church	Q	641

A Practical Discourse Upon Jude

The bloodshed that ensued thereon, between the Romans and Protestants, the Romans defeated by Zisco, the Protestant General	R	642
Protestants burnt by Papists, Jewel's word, &c.	S	—
Contemplations of Baal's divines, riches, honor, &c.	T	—
Wages of the call of that Ministry	T	—
How Baalists were esteemed by Prophets, &c.	V	643
Which of the 7 churches are most countenanced, have the largest endowments, &c.	W	—
Extensive bounds, Lands, &c. held under the Pope	X	—
See, in Italy & England, in Henry the 8th's reign, number of Monks and Friars in Italy, France, and Germany, number of Bishop and Archbishops in Spain, and riches in plate in Naples	Y	—
Observations upon those Riches	Z	644
Who those are, that perish in the gainsaying of Core	A	—
What is meant by spots in the feasts of Charity	B	645
Who are called empty Clouds and Trees, &c.	C	646
Troubled Waters, Wandering Stars		—
And reserved for Punishment		—
The Lambs of God have and are to suffer by Priests	D	—
What Paul calls these voluptuous Priests	E	—
How the elect of God are taught	F	647
And how preserved in their innocency		—
The invisible motions of the spirit	G	—
Obedience and Charity are sufficient for salvation	G	—
Without external worship		—
Two Queries worthy observation, answered	H	—
The comfort of such as believe and are taught by the Spirit	I	—
What the Reprobate seed in the fallen angels	K	648
Well of water is in them		—
What the well of water in a true Believer	L	—
What false Teachers, sure compared to	M	—
Who are said to be twice dead and pluck up by the	N	649
Roots, and why called wandering Stars, &c.	N	649
What is typified by the seven Sons of Scava, Isaiah xi 19, To what competed	O	650
The tongue of the Egyptian sea what it signifies	P	—
The state of the damned	Q	651
Enoch's Prophecies explained		98

The Reprobate seed's displeasure and unbelief, &c.	S	652
Enoch's Prophecies traditionally delivered	T	—
The Prophecies of Enoch concerning the coming of God in the Flesh, for the salvation, &c.	V	653
The Testimonies of the Sons of Jacob	W	—
That God would become flesh not unknown even to Adam, as also the resurrection, &c.	X	654
False Ministers called Murmurers, complainers, &c.	Y	—
No beast so subtil as the serpent, and no devil, &c.	Z	655
Further remarks upon Priestcraft	A	—
What infects and poisons the great men of the age	B	—
False Priests, Mockers, and makers of the Sects	D	656
Division these mockers make amongst themselves	E	657
How and when the mystery of God was finished	F	—
What are the seven Churches of Europe	G	—
From whence Presbytery had its first rise	H	—
Their Power in their Parishes	I	—
Calvin's stark doctrine, Remarks upon, &c	K	—
The Author's appeal and answer thereto	L	658
Only one seed is understood by the Calvinists	M	—
Two seeds made clear by seed of Faith	N	—
One of which died, and how	O	—
How the Presbytery are to examine themselves	P	—
The Independent Church, why so called	Q	—
The Ranter why so called, and their Principles, &c.	R	659
The Baptists Religion, and Profession	R	—
The Commission of the Spirit came forth into this unbelieving world, upon what account	S	660
The seventh and last anti-church, remarks thereon	T	—
How the Quaker got his name	V	—
Quakers deny the Person of God without them	W	—
Their Blasphemy	X	661
The last Witnesses opinion of their Faith	Y	—
No pleading antiquity for the proof of a true church	Z	—
St. Peter is the Rock, on which our Saviour built his church, that the gates of hell should not prevail against it. Explained	A	662
And also that the gates of Hell shall not prevail against the faith which the commission of the spirit is built upon	B	—

What is meant by striking the Rock &c.	C	—
No Prayer acceptable to God, but what proceeds from the Spirit of Divine Faith	D	—
Faith must be given to a Saint before it can be asked, and why	E	—
In what manner did our blessed Saviour's Apostles make use of the form of Prayer, he gave them	F	—
The danger of saying that Prayer, &c.	G	—
True Prayer consists not in words	H	—
The excellency of Mercy is above all sacrifice	H	—
An Elect Vessel may be liable to sin &c.	I	663
The plucking our Brethren out of purgatory	K	664
We are to mortify the old man, and the seed, &c.	L	—
The Elect of God may fall, but not totally	M	—
How the Elect of God are preserved, &c.	N	—
The Prayer of St. Jude	O	—
What is preservation and Vocation	P	665
Nothing too hard for Christ when the Spirit moves	Q	—
There is no other God, but Christ Jesus only	R	—

A

PRACTICAL DISCOURSE,

UPON

THE EPISTLE BY JUDE.

CHAP. I.

Jude, the Servant of Jesus Christ, and Brother of James, which are sanctified and preserved in Jesus Christ, and called.—ver. 1.

FIRST, Jude calls himself the servant of Jesus Christ, as by commission from heaven; and this his commission with the rest of his fellow-apostles, was from no other but Jesus Christ their God and Saviour.

And when he was in mortal state he chose them to be his disciples, witnesses and messengers to declare his mind, concerning eternal life and death, through the whole world.[1] And that they should call no man master but himself. And promised them the assurance of eternal life, and the assistance of his holy spirit,[2] to empower them to set life and death before men, and that after his death, resurrection, and ascension; he would send them down from heaven the Holy Ghost.[3] And that they were to stay at Jerusalem, to wait there for a promise of the same, which he did; and it was made good upon them, as may be read, Acts 2nd, and then were they endued with power, by that gift of the Holy Ghost,[4] to preach the everlasting gospel to every creature, as a stumbling block, and a saver of death unto death, to one seed or people, and a precious stone, and saver of life unto life to another seed or people. And yet all people may be said to be the servants of God,[5] but none are the servants of God as to eternal life but by redemption.[6] Others are, as by creation. For the word creation or creature shews a creator, and a command of obedience to be due to

---

[1] Mat. xxiii. 10.
[2] John xv. 23.
[3] Acts i. 4.
[4] John xx. 23. Peter i. 1. II. Cor. ii. 26.
[5] A
[6] B

him, for no nature could acknowledge any obedience to be due unto God, unless he were guided thereto by a light or law from him which formed him.[1] And from thence it was, that Cain had as much wisdom to offer sacrifice to God as Abel, but not so acceptable, because it was not offered in faith, but in reason, which is the Angel's fallen nature.[2] For those that are spiritual may undoubtedly know, that it was impossible for men or angels to be void of all law in their creation. (Because this last Witness saith), the Creator himself became subject to his own law, when his divine Godhead was transmuted into pure Manhood.[3] 'Tis truth, the uncreated eternal God was above all law, and so incapable of any kind of law, before he descended from his infinite glory, into the womb of a woman; but that he might be capable of a condescension of a servant for the manifestation of his infinite wisdom, power, and glory in a body of flesh, unto elect men and angels.[4] Therefore he did transmute his unchangeable Godhead into the likeness of sinful mortals, for a season, that he might become the heavenly pattern of perfect obedience to his own law, in the visible sight of elect men and angels. For Christ is God manifest in the flesh. This being so, then it is certain, that the uncreated Godhead itself is unto created Beings of men or angels, either a law of perfect faith and pure burning love in them, towards God and man unto life eternal, or else the fiery law of unbelieving, burning envy in them against God, elect men and angels unto death eternal.[5]

Thus, therefore, let men examine themselves of which law they are under, and whose servants they are, and of their obedience, and more especially those men who pretend to be the ministers and messengers of God to preach his name.[6]

Let such prove their commission[7] from heaven by voice of words, words, or from him that was so chosen, otherwise they may reckon themselves to be of the number of those preachers, who pleaded their ministry with Christ, and Mat vii. were answered with an, I know you not, depart from me ye workers of iniquity.[8]

Again, Jude calls himself the brother of James to distinguish him as (conceived) from Judas Iscariot, who betrayed his Lord and Master. This Jude and James are called the sons of Joseph by a

---

[1] C
[2] Divine Looking Glass.
[3] D
[4] Heb. v. 8, 9.
[5] E
[6] F
[7] G
[8] Mat. vii. 23.

former wife, and were brought up in husbandry and tilling of the land; but whether so or not, it is not material, for a human testimony, serves for a human testimony. But what we have recorded in scripture is of divine authority, as is infallibly true, and so may resolve our faith in the spiritual sense of the words, which if a true and commissioned Prophet or Apostle of God hath interpreted, then it becomes a foundation for faith to build upon; but to proceed. Jude directs his Epistle to the elect of God, who had received the faith of Jesus Christ by their ministry, naming them to be such as are, first, sanctified by God the Father, and secondly, preserved in Jesus Christ, and called.[1] Here we see their sanctification is attributed to God the Father, and preservation and vocation to Jesus Christ, as two distinct persons, which cannot be; for then there must be two Gods; but as preservation and vocation are here attributed to Jesus Christ, even so is sanctification in several scriptures attributed to Christ Jesus only,[2] and to the spirit of divine faith, and faith in his blood, for it is Christ Jesus that sanctifies his church that is subject to him, believing in his name and in the virtue of his blood as beforesaid; all which doth produce eternal life, which is the only sanctification.[3] Then, whither else shall we go, as the Apostle said, when there is no eternal life to be had but by faith in him only;[4] and it is he that is the author and giver of our faith, which faith is the only righteousness and holiness of his church, and where faith is wrought, sin is never imputed, for that righteousness justifies and gives power. Now, to believe that Christ sanctifies his own church with his own blood that vas offered up by the eternal spirit, and that the eternal spirit passed through death, this is true faith so to believe.[5]

That the body of Christ was the body of God,[6] this I say is perfect faith to believe,[7] and to believe that the blood of Christ was the the blood of God,[8] is perfect charity, and this faith and love makes a true christian; having the true baptism of the spirit,[9] now, under the commission of the spirit, which whosoever denies, he rejects Christianity as the scriptures verify.

---

[1] H
[2] Heb. xiii. 12. Eph. v. 24, 26. Acts. xx. 28. Cor. xii. 30. Acts. xxvi. 18. Rom xv. 16.
[3] Rom. v. 8, 9, 17.
[4] I
[5] John vi. 53.
[6] J
[7] II. Thes. v. 13. Mat. iii. 11.
[8] K
[9] Eph. iv. 4, 5, 6.

Again, the elect seed or sanctified people of God, are said to be preserved in Jesus Christ, and called;[1] some translations render it thus preserved or reserved from heretics, which is a good preservation; and in that translation the words (are called) are left out, which occasions no doubt in me, because the first words include it; being called to preach the gospel, all the saints are called in that call to believe their report, for how can they hear without a preacher, or how can they preach unless they be sent;[2] neither could those divine qualifications of mercy, love, and peace be known or begot, but by that ministry which follows in the next verse.

CHAP. II.

Mercy unto you, and peace and love be multiplied. — ver. 2.

WHAT are those graces but a seal of life begot by a true ministry. First, mercy as it is new born, is tender of compassion to all men, according to the doctrine of the two first records of the law and the Prophets;[3] Christ and his Apostles, and the third record gives evidence to the same, saying, that a merciful man instead of taking advantage of the civil law, for the imprisoning or cutting off the most wicked man, if it be possible, he will overcome him with love. Secondly, the grace of the law is the same nature under every commission. For saith the third commission, love is such a divine balsam that it cureth a wounded spirit, and rejoiceth a broken heart,[4] reviveth a dying soul, relieveth wounds made by envy's weapon; it clothed the naked, feedeth the hungry, and visiteth the sick. And thirdly, (as to the other grace) of peace, it is of that extent as is said by an Apostle, it passeth all understanding of reason,[5] but is ever comprehended by the wisdom of faith, because it is a fruit of it, and flows from it as from a river. Dives, the rich man in the parable wanted this peace, and desired but one drop of it, but could not have it. Now, if one drop is so desirable, in order to cool the heat of sin in an accusing conscience,[6] (which may be called hell) what then is a river worth, that is continually flowing in the hearts of the saints, which is the garden of God, and city of Sion.[7]

---

[1] Rom. x. 14, 15.
[2] L
[3] Divine Looking Glass.
[4] L
[5] Phil. iv. 7.
[6] M
[7] Isa. lvii. 20, 21.

Oh! how sweet was the promise of God by the Prophet Isaiah to this city,[1] saying, I will extend peace unto her like a river, and the glory of the Gentiles like flowing streams. And Jude, the Apostle, was one of the conduit pipes in this doctrine of free grace.—

Wherefore, then it follows, that where this mercy, love, and peace is, that there is the true church of God, and no where else; as the graces are invisible, so is the church invisible, but it sees itself, and its God sees it likewise. Now, in this church there is no discord, but a perfect quietness of mind, for it is the borders of Jerusalem, and there is the peaceable kingdom, where neither strife nor war is found, being a peaceable habitation.[2]

For the gospel or second record witnesseth,[3] and this of the spirit with it, that love must lie down at envy's feet, and kill envy by its patience and suffering. When the Jews were building their second Jerusalem Temple,[4] to worship in, they held the sword of steel in one hand, and wrought with the other; but the wall and that worship was to be pulled down, and that sword sheathed, and never to be drawn again; but were ordered, that if they were drawn, they should be for no other use, but to be made into plough-shares; and the gospel worshippers in the spirit of mercy, love, and peace should never learn war any more with any sword, but that of the spirit, which kills envy by its patience; and these spiritual words of truth reacheth the consciences of gainsaying and blaspheming devils, with the seal of the second death;[5] and this power belongs to all living, loving saints, for love and mercy extends not so far as to the eternal salvation of that seed,[6] that shall ever blaspheme against the Holy Ghost, and are despisers of prophecy.[7]

By what is said concerning these three daughters of faith, all such as are under the teachings of the spirit, may rejoice in their operations in virtue and goodness,[8] but much more, when they consider that they are of a growing nature, and so are said to be multiplied. Now, we may know thus much, that as these heavenly graces are in God,[9] they they are infinite and beyond measure; but as they are in his saints, though they are beams from the same sun, yet they are but finite, and

---

[1] Isa. lxvi. 12. Joh. iv. 24.
[2] Mal. iii. 16, 17. Eph. iv. 3. Isa. xxxii. 17. Mat. xii. 19.
[3] N
[4] Neh. iv. 17.
[5] Rev. ii. 29.
[6] N
[7] I. Cor. vi. 7. Psa. cxlix. John v. 26.
[8] ver. 3.
[9] Job. iii. 34. Rom. xii. 3.

in measure, but being rightly rooted, and well watered, it brings forth in some thirty, many sixty, and in others, a hundred-fold.[1] For grace is of a growing nature. You shall grow up, said the Prophet, like calves in the stall;[2] and what are those things they grow up in? but in the revelation of the mind of God in the scriptures,[3] which revelation is always increasing, especially in the time of a commission, when a true Prophet or Minister, or Apostle, is to be spoken with, or their writings to repair to,[4] and the Apostles exhorted the saints to grow in the knowledge and grace of our Lord Jesus Christ. And the third witness saith, that the saints are God's lights in this world,[5] being such as are are for his judges over all his enemies that despise Revelation.

CHAP. III.

AGAIN, the Apostle Jude in his 3rd verse, salutes the saints in a most loving manner, calling them his beloved, because they are beloved of God. And Paul and Peter, and the rest of the Apostles have done the like, and it can be no other in a true ministry;[6] for such such never lord it over God's heritage, to whom they are sent, but are examples to the flock, and seek their salvation, in giving them the seal and assurance thereof; where they find faith is, and what they do require of them for it, nothing but the return of that love to Jesus Christ, which their ministry begot in them, even the love of Jesus Christ, for his redeeming love, (as in verse 21st) and to establish and build up themselves in that holy faith preached unto them; that by this faith and love, they may be able to withstand all gainsayers.[7] And And three times upon this, he calls them his beloved. So Jude sought not for their wealth, but welfare. For as every commissioned Prophet or Apostle of Christ, hath Christ for his altar,[8] there to feed with revelation, and revelation doth feed the saints with that spiritual food, which none can eat of who serve an outward tabernacle, and feed at an outward carnal altar, as all the national Priests do, crying to their hearers, pay your tythes, and bring in your offerings. But more of that hereafter. Secondly, the Apostle exhorts the saints, that they earnestly contend for the faith, which he calls the common salvation. Now, the doctrine of Christ's death, resurrection, and ascension, may be called the common salvation, because there is no way to salvation, but by

---

[1] Mat. xiii. 23.
[2] Mal. iv. 2. II Peter iii. 18.
[3] Thes. i. 3.
[4] Isa. xxix. 19. Col. iii. 11.
[5] Mat. xiii. 52
[6] Rom. xi. 7, 16, 18. Col. iii. 12.
[7] II. Thes. 2. 13. Rev. xx. 9. Rom. viii. 35, 39. Eph. xiii. 14, 15.
[8] Heb. xiii. 10.

faith in Christ Jesus as Lord and Saviour only,[1] and that he is to judge both the quick and the dead. And Paul called Titus his own son according to the common faith in Christ, and makes all the saints to be called one common wealth of Israel.[2] And the Apostles were made Governors unto this commonwealth, and gave forth their Master's law unto it,[3] *and as* there is a spiritual commonwealth, *so there is* a temporal commonwealth in all nations *and* kingdoms, being governed by the wisdom *of* reason, as the other *is* by faith.[4] *And hence* it was, was, that in my remembrance *we had* as great a change in government in this nation; insomuch that our monies were coined with this inscription on the one side, "The Commonwealth of England" and on the other side, "God with us," and truly God was with us then in a spiritual manner;[5] for not only the persecuting Bishops were expelled out of all Government, both as to Church and State, being first voted out of Parliament House.

Then the Witnesses of the Spirit came forth who had time to spread truth into the world, which hath enlightened thousands, being a still and quiet people, and obedient to all civil law.

Thirdly, as there is one commonwealth or law as to the state of government in nations, so there is one common faith preached in it; which is not the apostles salvation faith, but it is a traditional faith, which is not a saving faith.[6][7] We read that when the sacrifices and ordinances were in force at Jerusalem, then was the inward Temple and outward Court joined to the Temple, which Court was a common place for all people to meet in;[8] but none were to enter the inner Temple but the high Priest in the time of their worship, and Kings, those that were confessors of the true God, and approved of by the teachers of the law.[9] Now the Apostle John in Revelations saith, that this outward court was not to be measured, but was to be cast out, which outward court did signify the visible scriptures, as saith the last witnesses, and was given unto the Gentiles, and this court or scriptures,[10] which is made common to all men, and that which is

---

[1] O
[2] John vi. 69. Acts x. 42. Titus i. 4. Eph.ii. 12.
[3] Rom. xiii. 7.
[4] Isa. viii. 9, 10. Which is now fulfilled in the blessed Immanual our God: or God with us.
[5] Mat. i. 21.
[6] Eze. xl. 19.
[7] P.
[8] ch. xlii. 14, 20.
[9] c. xliv. 17. I. Kings. xiv. 3.
[10] Divine book p.98.

unmeasured and cast out, did signify all the outward unbelieving Jews and Gentiles, and the inner Temple of the spirit of the scriptures, did signify all the elect Jews that believed, and Gentiles also in that glorious altar, being the body or tabernacle of the eternal spirit, unto which altar or godhead person, the true worshippers virtually unite.[1]

Now, the court of the Temple was an outward ornament or witness unto the glory or beauty within the Temple; so likewise, the court of the visible scriptures is an ornament or testimony unto that eternal spirit of all truth within, and the temple, body, or tabernacle of the everliving God; and virtually, in a great measure, living in the temples or bodies of his elect; that enables them to give a true distinction between the things of eternal life, and eternal death. Now those Roman Gentiles through the conquest of the Jews, did possess the literal records of the two commissions,[2] and not only worship it instead of the eternal spirit, but also by cruel persecutions (for 1300 years) were to tyrannize over the City of the spiritual gentiles, that could not bow down to their inventions. And those Gentiles are they which the apostles foresaw, as also did Peter and John see their approach, and power, and practice; and therefore exhorts the Elect, that with all earnestness, they should contend for the Faith; and as John said, to hold it fast, and let none take their Crown.

And though all true Prophets, Apostles, and Saints are the most peaceful men in the world, yet cannot abide strife and contention in this case.

This, a Prophet of old cried out saying, "Woe is me, my Mother, that thou hast born me a man of strife,"[3] and Christ and his apostles have foretold and shewed the cause of it, and that it was necessary, that Heresy should be, for to prove the righteousness, and make them keep faster hold upon Jesus Christ their Lord to whom their are virtually united, and their faith pitched upon; and in order hereunto they are to put the Armour of proof, and having done all to stand.[4]

But before I treat of this Heresy, it will be requisite to declare according to my understanding. First, what the nature of faith is in God.[5] Secondly, what it is in his saints. Thirdly, when and how it was first given. These are glorious things to know, if I can unfold them, or rather being unfolded unto me, by this last witness, take what I have learned in the blessing thereof, for each others consolation. First, this

---

[1] Rev. xxi. 3.
[2] P.
[3] Jer. xv. 10, 18, 19. Isa. xii. 15, 16.
[4] I. Cor. xi. 7.
[5] Q.

faith as it is in God, is a sacred and invisible life; for as men consists of form and nature, so God that made all things, hath form and nature also, and not an infinite spirit without form, as blind reason imagines; but our God is a glorious body of uncompounded purity, full of power from his Godhead spirit and divine nature,[1] which is all faith, being light, heat, and motion, and is omnipotent in all righteous actings, according to his Royal Will; being full satisfaction in itself, having no desire in him, for desire is a want, and want is a dissatisfaction, which cannot be inherent in God. Now all this power of light and life is from one fiery spark, according as Christ said to his Apostles, that if they had but as much faith as a grain of mustard seed, they might say to that mountain, be thou removed into the sea, and it should obey them but none are capable of such a quantity of faith, but the per son of the everliving God only, as saith the last witness.[2]

Secondly, now this faith must be believed by faith in all the elect seed of God, created in his own image both in form and nature;[3] for after his body was formed, he breathed into his nostrils the breath of life, which life,[4] as St. Peter saith, was of divine nature; so that faith in the elect is in the same nature as it is in God, only differing in measure, and so in all divine properties;[5] otherways, it had not been proper to have required the saints to be merciful, perfect, and holy, as God is holy, perfect, and merciful, meaning in its nature, but not in measure;[6] for in God it is infinitely infinite beyond measure, as hath been said before. But then, on the contrary, there is a faith in the fallen angel's seed, but it is without power, for no man can live in the world without either a true faith or a false faith, and the devils are said to have faith and do believe and tremble,[7] which devils are wicked men and women, and not spirits without bodies as men do vainly imagine, for spirits without bodies cannot tremble. Reason, which is sober, doth ever own there is a God,[8] and why? because the moral law is written in reason's nature, and so motions forth the obedience due to God, and that it will be hanged or damned, if it obey it not. And this is the flaming sword, that keeps the way of the tree of life,[9] and so deters that seed from much wickedness, otherways the

---

[1] Jer. xxxii. 27.
[2] Divine
[3] Luke vi. 36.
[4] Mat. v. 48.
[5] I. Pet. i. 15.
[6] Heb. i. 9.
[7] James ii.
[8] R.
[9] Genesis.

elect of God could not live.¹ Again, the world's faith is grounded or founded upon tradition, as aforesaid, and on custom also; For be they Jews, Turks, or literal professors, each people live according to their accustomed religion, and will all draw swords for their commonwealth. One fighting for the alcoran, the other for the letter of the bible, one for a God of three persons, and another for a God of no person, but a spirit; and this spirit God subscribed to no place, but to all places at one and the same time, and all their worship is false worship, and their faith is a false faith, and lies in wickedness, as John declares.² Again, as God created Adam and Eve, male and female, so he gave faith but once, and ever since men have generated this faith, by which man became a living soul; which did not all die in Adam, but left its seed in generation till it came to behold that personal faith,³ from whence it first had its being. So that there is no new faith given, but the old one awakened or renewed; and so acts forth from the same principles of light and life; and from that power under a commission, it attains to that satisfaction, as to have the assurance of eternal life. This is that faith which the saints are to contend for.

CHAP. IV.

For there are certain men crept in unawares, who were before ordained unto this condemnation, ungodly men, turning the grace of God into lasciviousness, and denying the only Lord God and our Lord Jesus Christ.

THE Apostle Peter, speaking of the same men, saith,⁴ that they came in privily, being then unknown to the saints, for it is a true ministry that maketh saints; yet they came as if they had been true ministers, and so of power to head the church, and to rule the same by ecclesiastical laws.⁵

But these certain men were crept in,⁶ though not called to the ministry by true ordained or apostolical men, as Timothy and Titus were, but went of themselves, and ordained themselves, and one another;⁷ so entered in, but not by the door, because neither Christ,

---

[1] S.
[2] John 1. 5. Gen. i. 15. Rom. ix. 29.
[3] T
[4] Pet. ii. 2.
[5] Mat. xxiv. 24.
[6] U.
[7] John x. 1. Mat. vii. 23. Rev. xx. 15.

his Apostles, or true ministers chosen by them, owned them,[1] and that because they were never book in God's commission book; their names never being written there,[2] and therefore, though they may be owned by man, yet Christ calls them but thieves and robbers, and deceivers of the people, like priests, like people, that both may fall into the ditch.[3] For what is it that provokes them to seek pre-eminence in church and state, but silver and honour amongst princes; for it is evident, that whosoever preaches by commission of earthly powers, preaches for gain; which gain is their godliness, and their belly, (as St. Paul said) is their God.[4] For all such as mind earthly things have the title of ungodly men, so that as the ministers of God are godly men, so the ministers of satan which are ministers of men, and made by men, are ungodly men; so there is a strife betwixt men and men; Godlike men and ungodlike men. Those like God are saints, but those unlike God are. devils; not only like devils, but are devils incarnate, bringing in damnable heresies, and from hence are said to be ordained to condemnation.[5][6]

Here now is judgment given against reprobate preachers, being not commissioned of God by the testimony of the Apostles (to wit) Jude and Peter. From these two words, old and ordained; the word old hath relation to the time of the fate of the reprobate angel, as in verse sixth will shew; the word ordained stands upon God's decree, and his decree as to mankind stands upon God's great attributes of justice and mercy; for, if God had not made a people for his wrath, his attributes of justice and mercy could never have been known,[7] and also had he not made a people for his mercy,[8] his other good attributes of mercy could not have been known, and then, how could the saints and elect angels ever have praised his mercy, had they not known of his justice. The Prophet Isaiah saith,[9] that Tophet is ordained of old,[10] and the spirit of reason (which is the king) is that which must abide in Tophet, it being both king and governor of this world. It is reason that hath a law given to it, and it is reason, the

---

[1] V.
[2] See what book they are recorded in, in the Prophets letter to G. Fox.
[3] Joh. xxi. 9.
[4] Isa. lvi. 11. I. Tim. vi. 5. Phil. ii. 21. & iii. 10.
[5] V.
[6] II. Pet. ii. 1.
[7] W.
[8] Rom. ix. 22.
[9] Isa. xxx. 33.
[10] A.

king, that doth break laws; for it was reason that slew Abel, the Prophets, and Christ himself.[1]

Again, this fire is the motion of sin, which proceedeth from the seed of reason; and the wait action of sin is that pile of wood, which is acted forth by the wisdom of reason; and as for the breath of the Lord, it is meant the law of Moses, or moral law;[2] for the law may be called the breath of the Lord, because the law is as a pair of bellows, which doth blow up motions and actions of sin to a flame; where the worm never dies, nor the fire never goes out. Thus the prerogative power of Clod over his creatures, both of faith and reason, which are two distinct seeds, sons, or generations of mankind, which is plainly seen and known to the one seed, but is blinded from the other, insomuch that the prerogative power of God in election reprobation,[3] or rejection, is opposed by almost all sects and opinions in the world, as well Heathens as Literal Accutants,[4] who use all their serpentine reason to evade that doctrine. One of the new light of the age, amongst others his brethren, says, in one of his books against this commission most blasphemely,[5] (to wit) that the principles of election and rejection, is not only inconsistent to reason; (which he makes his God) but that it is accursed by scripture; and further saith, that if God should do so, he would be worse and more cruel, than either men or devils. Oh! monstrum horrendum.

Wherefore, then, this principle of election and rejection stand good as my faith assures me, and as the scriptures affirm, (see Margin) Which way then will that seed that oppose it be able to deliver themselves, or reverse that decree or make it void; let them try their power, or try their will by which they teach: that all men may be saved if they will. If thine heart rebel, says he, use violence with it, by rational persuasion out of the law; if it be too weak, call for the spirit of God to enforce thy reason, that thy reason may enforce thy will.[6] Let thy reason say unto God, Lord thou hast given me reason to command my thoughts, and my soul to love and worship thee. Why then, seeing freewill and choice are the means appointed by God to the attainment of faith, shall not I use the means, for now it is thy own power and choice whether thou wilt be saved or not. These words were thundered from a Pulpit. But this doctrine is contrary to Jude or

---

[1] L. M. on the xi. of Revelation Page 105. Matt. 21. 25.
[2] B.
[3] C.
[4] D.
[5] W. Pen the Quaker c.v. of his Book.
[6] L. M. answer to W. Pen c. 5. Isa. xlii. 1. Mat. xxiv. 21, 24. Mark xiii. 10. Luke xviii. 7. Rom. ix. to v. 16. See Baxter's saints for his opinion of free will.

his doctrine, as also to all the Prophets and Apostles; for by this doctrine, man is his own saviour, and reason the serpent-angers nature is that man, that would be saved by, his own strength.[1] For though the angel's nature is pure reason, yet this we must know, that reason fallen is impure;[2] neither could the purity of the angels nature continue, if it were not continually supplied by revelation from the person of their Creator, into their desiring natures, and that their nature's are desire, is clear, by that of Peter, the first Epistle verse the 12th. Now, if so, that the angels are of a desiring nature after the wisdom of the Creator, in his wonderful work of redemption; then that inflowing wisdom in their desiring natures, becomes that spiritual manna or heavenly food by which they live.

This then being so, how shall reason fallen from its purity in the downfall of that serpent-angel in all impurity, and so reprobated to eternity in its seed, that live so long as to be capable of the breach of the law.[3] I say, how can it ever attain to heaven from whence it was cast out; seeing God did not take upon him the nature of angels, but the seed of Abraham, which was the seed of Adam, which was his own seed.[4] Now must this damned reason command faith to help and serve it, and tell God he *shall* do for them, and *ought* to do for them, insomuch, that if he will not mind their wills, and will not save them, to tell him he is worse than either men or devils. But are not these devils charging God with unrighteousness, for their devilish belief will have no other effect, but to harbour fear and trembling where their reason is so presumptuous and censorious.[5] Thus we see that the doctrine of universal and sufficient grace and freewill, is grounded upon reason or rational wisdom, power, and glory;[6] and this is that which constituted the first Anti-church of Europe, by the name of universal or Catholic faith; and as the father began the children followed, so every succeeding church or sect of people count themselves as universal, and as Catholic as their fathers or grandfather's were; but the foundation of their building lies all upon reason, which will prove a sandy foundation.[7]

From hence it is, that the scriptures must be interpreted by them, by the rule of that wisdom or reason, and yet know nothing of heavenly things, but earthly things only; nevertheless, nothing is to be approved of but the dictates of reason, and yet knows nothing of

---

[1] E.
[2] Divine Book. F.
[3] G.
[4] Heb. ii. 16. H.
[5] I.
[6] K.
[7] I. Cor. ii. 4.

heavenly but earthly things only, the dictates of reason and its private will and desire.[1] And it is that which the Apostle calls the will of man, when as on the contrary he saith, true prophecy is by the moving of the Holy Ghost or spirit of divine faith, being the seed and nature of God, and so not from the will of man.[2] The private spirit of impure reason it may be called private, because iniquity is a mystery, and hath deceit in it, being the devil transformed into an angel of light.[3] But to come now to their further devilish doctrine.

But wherefore is it, that such presumptuous words are spoken, and why election and rejection is so much abhorred. Is it not saith the last Witnesses, because they do not know themselves elected, nor their own salvation, for if they did, they would never have abhorred their own election.[4] For reason in man is subject to abhor or scorn, that another should be made better than itself, or in a better condition.

CHAP. V.

Turning the grace of God into lasciviousness. ver. 4.

NOW, let us inquire who these persons are who preach this damnable doctrine, as Peter calls it; and well it may be called so, seeing that the grace of God which had appeared and taught them to deny all ungodliness and worldly lusts;[5] not that they were established in the Apostle's time, but since, by these established teachers, who have turned them into all ungodliness and worldly lusts, as Jude. John, Peter, and Paul foresaw by the spirit of prophecy, and some of them attempted it in their days, for saith John,[6] they are all gone out from us, because they were not of us. And And I find it written in Church History, that some crept privately into the seven churches of Asia, and did teach that fornication was no sin, and John speaks of it likewise, by which said one (Clement), the gate of righteousness was shut up, which gate, he called Christ.

Now from hence it come to pass, that according to the prophecy of John,[7] the candle stick, which had the true light in it was removed;[8] what with these teachers and false preachers, and what with

---

[1] II. Pet. i. 21.
[2] Gal. ii. 4.
[3] II. Cor. xi. 14.
[4] L. M. answer to Pens book.
[5] Tit. ii. 11, 12.
[6] John. i.
[7] Rev. ii. 5.
[8] L.

persecution, that in process of time, error got a head, and preaching carnal things to carnal ears, came to be established by false Priestcraft and worldly authority. Since which time to this, the studies of the devil has been turned into religion and will-worship, and so no true faith, but a traditional one as beforesaid. Since which time the elect of God have been kept in darkness and ignorance, many of them believing that the learned Men and Priests of this world had power successively to set up gospel ordinances, or visible worship to please God.[1] And thus have the Gentiles, the Roman Catholics, the Papists, trod the holy city underfoot, since the unmeasured court was cast out; and the same fell into their hands, of which they have made great merchandize of, it has made them rich, and puffed them up with such pride, that they stile themselves by the name of Holy Mother, the Church. But to consider their doctrine and practice, the fruits of which will prove it a most unholy church, with a witness, as by this their turning the grace of God into lasciviousness and wantonness.

Now what this lasciviousness was,[2] may be understood by Paul's words, who in one place[3] joins lasciviousness and fornication together, and in the second place he joins both with adultery, and in a third place saith, that they who do such things, cannot inherit the kingdom of Heaven or God;[4] and it is so much more notoriously wicked, when it is countenanced by a teacher.[5] Again, this National Romish and Monarchial Church has maintained this doctrine, and their ministry doth both by law and custom ratify it; notwithstanding the spirit being got into the church of Ephesus, yet both Christ and his saints utterly abhorred it.[6] But the head of this Anti-church of Rome, (the Bishop) is called Papa, Pope, or Father, calling himself Apostolical, and Peter's successor;[7] but Peter condemned it, and called it a devilish doctrine; neither can it be proved that Peter ever was at Rome, unless we take their lying legends for proof, for the scripture proves it not;[8] but if we seriously consider Pauls Epistles written from Rome, as in the Galatians, Philipians, Ephesians, Colosians, and the second of Timothy, with his rehearsals and salutations of friends, from thence we may be satisfied that Peter never was there;[9] although their history saith, they were both martyred in Rome

---

[1] M.
[2] N.
[3] II Cor. xii. 21. Gal. v. 19. I. Cor. vi. 10.
[4] Rom. i. 31. c. ii. 21, 22.
[5] O.
[6] Rev. ii. 6.
[7] P.
[8] II. Pet. ii. 1. Tim. iv. 1.
[9] Q.

in one year. Their history differs about the succession after Peter. But to the matter aforesaid. The Pope doth not only allow himself a concubine, but gives liberty to his Bishops and Priests to do the same, those that are in holy orders as they call it; but their committing adultery, theft, or minder, whether in Priest or People, they can have pardon over and over again for money.[1] Whereas the true Apostolical Church granted one repentance for one sin after conversion, and no more. But their church granteth hundreds,[2] and have their confessions and absolutions accordingly, so makes sin and sanctity rule by turns, as a saint to-day and a devil to-morrow; then confession and absolution follows, and so a saint again the next day, and the day following a devil again.[3] As one Phillips, a preacher, in his prayer said, said, "Lord, we sin, then we pray, and then to our sins again, as if we should ask thee leave to offend," so they go their rounds like a horse in a mill.[4] Here may be brought in that laying of Moses, namely, that he washed himself after touching a dead body,"[5] but if he toucheth it again, what availeth his washing. But to the matter aforesaid, keeping concubines is by that church reckoned no sin, and for others that are not under the Pope also, yet if the ministers of them have occasion to act in that nature, having no wife, become Popes also in this case, and if they think it is a sin, yet can they as Pope's absolve themselves.[6]

Now, the Priests of the Romish Church are forbid marriage under the pretence of purity, saying, they are married to Christ, and so cannot give themselves to another.[7]— In the first Council of Nice, they they would have established that law, (against Priest's marriage) had not one man withstood them with reasons which overpowered them. One argument against it might be quoted from the Apostle Paul's words, how that to forbid marriage was the doctrine of the devil. But this devilish doctrine took place afterwards, and their great doctors allowed of concubines as much as their great St. Augustin, as they called him, who lived in the 4th century, and kept his concubine. Pope John the 12th, he was accused of downright adultery, and Pope John the 23rd, was deposed by the Council of Constantine, it being proved against him.[8] First, that he had hired a person to destroy Alexander, his predecessor; secondly, that he was a heretic and held with the mortality of the soul; and thirdly, that he was an adulterer and

---

[1] R.
[2] S.
[3] T.
[4] Num. xix. 11, 12.
[5] Eccle. xxxiv. 25.
[6] V.
[7] U. Fox's Book of Martyrs.
[8] Sang's History of the Roman Empire.

sodomite. There was at this Council, 346 Archbishops, 564 Abbots, and 450 Common Whores. Pope John the 14th, in the year 965, was killed by an Italian, who found him in bed with his wife.[1] And Pope Sextus gave liberty to the Cardinal of Luey, to use sodomy. Likewise, it is said, that Pope Alexander the 6th, knew his own daughter, and Valence did the like. I might mentioned many more, but shall conclude with mentioning one more of this bastard church, which I know will be thought incredible; but having it from an eminent Author of the Church of England, I shall here relate the same.[2] In the year of our Lord 335, a Council was held at Tyre, with a command that Athanasius should appear, and he appearing, was forced to plead.[3] He He was accused by the Arian Bishops with many great crimes, as first, he was accused of having ravished a woman, and one who had before vowed virginity. Secondly, he was accused of cruelty and murder. Thirdly, of profanation and impiety, though this was contradicted by the Catholic Bishops, yet their evidence was disproved. But another Council was held, when the Emperor drew his sword, and accused Athanasius himself, saying, his testimony was sufficient, and thereupon the Catholic Bishops as well as the Arians, condemned him. There were 300 Bishops in that Synod.

This is that Athanasius who drew up the Nicean Creed so exalted by Papists and Episcopal Father and Son, whether the testimony against him was true or not, still the trial was a matter of fact;[4] for. if Athanasius was innocent of the charge laid against him, then all those Catholic Bishops were wicked, with a witness, who had before acquitted him, but now for fear of their Lord and Emperor, whose creatures they were, turned cat in pan, and condemned Athanasius. Oh! horrid wickedness, who sees it not.

CHAP. VI.

And denying the only Lord God, and our Lord Jesus Christ. —ver. 4.

THIS is not to be understood partly of God the Father, and partly of Jesus Christ, but altogether of Jesus Christ; because it runs parallel with Peter of denying the Lord that bought them.[5] So that by Peter's words it doth appear, that they had acknowledged Christ so far, as that he had bought and purchased their salvation with his blood. But then, they became so very licentious as to teach

---

[1] W, X, Y.
[2] Dr. Sherlock, Dean of St. Paul's.
[3] Z.
[4] A.
[5] II. Pet. ii. 1.

that frailties of nature, were not inconsistent with Christianity. For Christ having fulfilled the law for us, by his death and resurrection;[1] which was sufficient for our salvation. From hence, then it is evident that they owned Christ for their Saviour, but not their Lord; and so would have him to save them in their sins, but not from their sins, which was the end of his coming.[2]—

And it is written, thou shalt call his name Jesus, who shall save his people from their sins. But these men must have liberty and sin, and yet so as not to stand off; but come to confession and absolution as aforesaid, twice or thrice a year, and so quit with God for Christ's sake, that they might begin to sin again upon a new score. Neither could they believe or own that Godhead and Manhood made one Person in Christ, and so one only and alone Lord God.

But Jesus Christ must either be inferior to the only Lord God, (as the Arians held) or if he be God, yet must be a second Person, and so distinct from the only Lord God the Father, as the Catholics teach, which was contrary to the Apostles doctrine of Christ, calling him the only Lord God, the true God, and the only wise God, as in the last verse of Jude; ascribing to him all glory, majesty, dominion and power for ever.[3]

Now these titles of only Lord God, &c. excludes all co-partnership, it is not that particle (and) which makes Persons, but shews the union of natures, divine and human, which is God and Man in one single Person, and is most proper if it be read thus: denying the only Lord God our Lord Jesus Christ, its but the same in that other scripture, where John calls Christ the true God and eternal life; all other Gods are but idols.[4]

These are all positive scriptures, and as God commands all other scriptures to bow to them, so that there is enough said to satisfy the seed of faith, but the seed of reason will never be satisfied, so I wrote not this for their satisfaction, but conviction, knowing they are not appointed to believe unto salvation, but on the contrary were of old ordained to condemnation, as aforesaid, and as hereafter follows.[5]

---

[1] B.
[2] C. Mat. i. 21.
[3] D.
[4] John xi. 3. v. 20.
[5] E.

CHAP. VII.

I will therefore put you in remembrance, though ye once knew this; that the Lord having saved his People out of the Land of Egypt, destroyed them that believed not.[1]

HERE, the Apostle Jude brings in an example of vengeance against the infidelity, and the unbelief of those carnal murmuring Jews which came out of Egypt by the Red Sea, by the conduct of Moses and Joshua. And though they were the children of Abraham, Isaac, and Jacob, and might boast themselves of that descent and parentage, yet though they passed through their loins, yet were they the very seed of the serpent; and all those miracles which they saw wrought availeth them nothing.[2] Though the elect might read of their distinction in the Record of Moses, yet by this of Jude, they might further know that their destruction was not only temporal, but an eternal death lay in it. These being the same Jews that Christ spake of, that did eat Manna in the Wilderness, and were dead; and those unbelieving Jews which then opposed Christ, were of the same seed as those that rebelled against God in the Wilderness.

Now we are given to understand, that the manna which Moses fed the children of Israel with, was only a type or shadow of the heavenly bread which was the body of Christ;[3] but the seed of reason in those murmuring Jews, could see nothing of a spiritual nature in it, and therefore the people spake against Moses, saying, "why have you brought us out of Egypt to die in the Wilderness, for we have nothing to eat but this manna, neither have we any thing to drink but this water which cometh out of the rock;" the manna was only to signify the true bread of life, which was the flesh of Christ, and the water did signify his blood, which was poured out of his blessed Body, which was the Rock.[4] Therefore the meaning of Christ to those of the Jews in the 6th Chapter of John, (as now saith the last Witnesses) is this; Your Fathers did eat Manna in the Wilderness and are dead, which meaning is, that those Fathers of yours, who tempted God, in that they tempted Moses, they were overthrown by natural Plagues in the Wilderness, that is, they were damned to Eternity; for all those that fell in the Wilderness through unbelief, and murmured against God, were all damned to Eternity. Else would it have been to no purpose for Christ to say, your Fathers did eat Manna in the Wilderness and are

---

[1] Num. xi. Num. xvi. 13, 78. Num. xxxi. 14.
[2] F.
[3] G.
[4] G.

dead, but whosoever shall eat of this bread which I shall give him, shall live for ever.

Now there were a great many of the seed of faith in that nation of the Jews, which did see the substance of those types and shadows, which the manna and the water did signify; as also divers of other things; yet they all died a natural death, and those that did eat of the true bread when it was come, as the Apostles and Believers in Christ's time, they all died a natural death, as well as those that died in the Wilderness, or was overthrown there and slain through unbelief; but the words of Christ hath this meaning;[1] that whosoever believes that my flesh is the flesh of God, (which is that bread of life) and that my blood is the blood of God, or the water of life, which that manna and water Moses gave you did signify, shall never die; that is, he that believes this, hath passed from death to life; that is, he is passed from the fear of eternal death, to have the assurance of eternal life, which doth abide in him; so that he who believes shall not see death, but falleth asleep in the full assurance of eternal life, and faith which God hath promised; who hath power and is able to perform, and give them the end of their faith, which is life eternal.

But on the contrary, those that did eat manna and were dead, it was spoken in reference to eternal death or the second death abiding in them;[2] which fear and seal in spiritual things, is many times taken for the things themselves; so that by what is here said, it may be clear to all such as have faith in the scriptures, being in its true spiritual sense, that the destruction of those unbelieving Israelites in the wilderness was not only a temporal, but an eternal death lay in their unbelief, whatever can or shall be said against it by the Trencher Chaplains, and Silver-souled Merchants of this perishing world. For this I shall say, that although the first commission of Moses and the Prophets speaks little of eternal death, but as only a penetrating down into the grave, and there leaves them, because God was not then come in the flesh, nor suffered, nor risen, nor ascended, with his triumph over death, hell, the devil, and the grave, but by these two last commissions, eternal life and death is made manifest, and immortality brought to light.[3]

Yet in the first commission, when Ezekiel summoned all the great Potentates of the earth to the grave,[4] where they should lay their swords under their heads; yet he tells them their iniquity should lay upon their bones, which shewed or rather hinted of the resurrection of

---

[1] H.
[2] I.
[3] K.
[4] Ex. xxxii.

those bones, as well as the bones of all Israel, c. 37. Daniel also, and the other Prophets, yea Enoch taught it, as appears by Jude in the 14th and 15th verses, which will hereafter bespoken of. But the great men of the earth being made lords thereof; have, and do make it their only heaven, not expecting any iniquity could lay upon their bones; neither can I expect how literal Professors can expect any thing upon their bones, whilst they expect and believe that their souls can go to heaven without their bodies.[1]

CHAP. VIII.

And the angels which kept not their first estate, he hath reserved in everlasting chains under darkness, unto the judgment of the great day. Even as Sodom and Gomorrah and the cities about them in like manner, giving themselves over to fornication, and going after strange flesh, are set forth for an example; suffering the vengeance of eternal fire.

THIS scripture by Jude and Peter, puzzles all the learned men in the world, they know not what to make of it. But the common opinion established by the National Church or Ministry is, that there was a rebellion broke out in Heaven, and a war ensued,[2] angel against angel, in which war, God the Creator sided with one part, and threw the other down upon this earth, being millions of them, who all became devils which are said to be in chains, but what those chains are. they know not; and yet they say these devils can go to and fro and tempt men to sin, and all the evil that is done, is by the instigation of these spirit or hags being all without bodies, and these bodiless devils bear all the blame, and so would have them bear all the punishment too.

That there ever was a war in Heaven, we do utterly deny.[3] We do know that a war was said to be in Heaven between Michael and his Angels, and the Dragon and his Angels, but it was upon this earth. For as there was one angel and but one angel, that was puffed up with pride, after God had withheld from him the overflowing of divine revelation, into his desiring nature of reason; upon which the Creator dethroned him, and threw him down upon this earth; where his desired kingdom of godlike glory was prepared for him in a lineal way;[4] and therefore, it is said by John, Revelations 12th chapter, Woe

---

[1] L.
[2] M.
[3] N.
[4] O.

to the inhabitants of the earth, for the devil, (not devils)[1] is come down amongst you, and this is that serpent angel which tempted Eve, called the tree of knowledge of good and evil; and Cain was that devil transmuted into flesh, being the first born of Eve, so the first born child of the devil;[2] and so he became (and none but he alone) the first born child of the devil or Belzebub that Prince of Devils, and the only father of all those angels of darkness (spoken of here by the Apostle Jude) that are kept or reserved under chains of darkness of unbelief, unto the great day of judgment. The war that is said to be in Heaven is on this earth; so that Michael is the spirit of the Lord Jesus in his angelical believers;[3] whose weapons are faith, love, and patience; and the Dragon is the spirit of cursed Cain in his persecuting believers, whose weapons are swords, guns, and so forth; and this Dragon and his angels are the spirit of Cain, who was the spirit of the serpent angel aforesaid.[4]

Again, that great Red Dragon and his men of war, that is said to stand before the woman (the Virgin Mary) to devour the child Jesus.[5] This Dragon was Herod, and the earth that helped the woman, was those children that Herod slew, which was that earth that swallowed up that flood of persecution,[6] Yet this Herod and his sons who were called beasts, are said to have their original from Heaven;[7] because they were the seed of the serpent angel that was cast down from Heaven; but it came lineally from Cain; so that all those angels or no other men, and such as have a share of the wisdom of reason, (the fallen angel's nature) are fit to be Governors, and may, and are called Princes, Angels, yea Gods; and are said to be from Heaven or Paradise, as a state of glory; and at last centres his principality in the cherub or one of the cherubims. For there are several orders of angels in Heaven, as cherubims seraphims, &c. as chief.[8] As for that order of of ministering spirits, I am persuaded in my mind, they were created to be serviceable to the elect seed of Adam, who by commission from Heaven, have often appeared to some of the Prophets, Apostles, or chosen ones, for their consolation, or with certain messages. And that angel which the Lord cast out or down from Heaven, for his pride, I am persuaded, was also one of those Cherubims.[9] It is also wonderful

---

[1] Commission Book.
[2] P.
[3] Divine Book.
[4] Q, R.
[5] S.
[6] T.
[7] V.
[8] W.
[9] X.

to consider of that mighty wisdom and prerogative power in the most High and Glorious Creator, that one of the most glorious Angels in Heaven, should become one of the greatest Devils in the flesh, and that one of the greatest devils in nature, should become one of the most glorious saints in Heaven.[1] Cain and Mary Magdalen in due time time may clear this, as saith the last Witness. Again, these angels that kept not their first estate, must needs be men, because the sodomites and they, acted both alike;[2] the sodomites are said to be cast down, as as well as the Angels, and were part of those runagate angels, therefore it is said in like manner that they were cast down to hell, which could not be said in like manner, if they were not men and women. But saith the apostle, even in like manner Sodom and Gomorrah, giving themselves over to fornication and defilement of the flesh, are the angels spoken of, who if they were spirit devils without bodies, they could not commit fornication with women;[3] so that these two apostles Jude and Peter, together with John, makes a third witness; this being a threefold cord will not be easily broken.

Again, it is further said, that those angels are kept in chains unto the judgment of the great day. From hence, then it is plain, that there is no punishment for the devil and his angels until that judgment day.[4] Whereas Jude saith, that Sodom suffered vengeance of eternal fire; it was no other but that eternal fire is included in their temporal overthrow as hath been before shown by those who felt in the wilderness, For there is no time to the dead, but the next thing after, is judgment and execution. The soul dies with the body in all mankind, both in saints and serpents, only these three, Enoch, Moses, and Elias; yea, Christ himself made his bed with the wicked for three days, and if Christ's soul did die ours must; for as the soul and body receives life together, lives together, and dies together, so they must both rise together.[5]

For all sober reason doth hold, that the soul is extraduce as they call it from the Father to the Son for several reasons; as first, they say if the soul was not by tradition, none could be guilty of original sin.[6] This argument so puzzled St. Augustin (as they call him, who was then Bishop of Hyppo), that he was forced to own it, or he could not tell how to deal with the Plageans who denied original sin.[7] Secondly, from that place, Exodus c. i. v. 5, and Gen. c. xlvi. v. 26, 27. Thirdly,

---

[1] J. Reeve's Epistles.
[2] Y.
[3] Z.
[4] A.
[5] Gen. xvii. 14.
[6] B.
[7] C.

then they say, that man were worse than a beast, that gets both matter and form.— Fourthly, that every like begets its like.— Fifthly, Gods command would be useless to increase and multiply. Sixthly, if not so, God would infuse a soul to be punished both here and hereafter for another's sin. Seventhly, God would seem to connive at fornication and adultery. Eightly, if the soul be infused what is begotten? nothing. For a body cannot generate without a soul.

CHAP. IX.

Likewise also those filthy dreamers defile the flesh, despise dominion, and speak evil of dignities. —ver. 8.

NOW, the apostle returns from his setting forth those examples of God's wrath and vengeance against those angels and sodomites, charging the like transgressions upon those false teachers, calling them filthy dreamers,[1] showing their practice to be like those of the angels and sodomites, being all from one root; for the wickedness of these satanical angels are ranked into three heads, or three wicked spirits or principles; as first, they defile the flesh; secondly, they despise dominion; thirdly, they speak evil of dignities; fourthly, they speak evil (as in the second verse) of things they know not. I shall treat of each of these in order; but first of their being called dreamers.

First, these men are not only called dreamers, but filthy dreamers, now they must be filthy because they defile the flesh: now in the time of the law dreaming of marvellous things, that were of great concernment, not only because the Lord himself did often appear in dreams and visions of the night; but likewise, because some of his servants had the gift of true interpretation of them in their time; but dreams now are of no value to us, because we know that instead of dreams,— God himself is the alone teacher of his elect, by the immediate inspiration of his most holy spirit. Secondly, but these men are called dreamers because of their wisdom as to spiritual matters, which proceedeth from no other foundation but from the imagination of impure reason; so that all visions are but imaginary dreams. For whatever flows not from the revelation of faith, must of necessity arise from the imagination of reason, and the false priests and national preachers of the law, vaunting themselves of their dreams, using the words of the prophets, but perverting the sense, not knowing the meaning thereof;[2] therefore all are visions and imaginary notions, and so four hundred of Baal's Priests were but the deceit of their own

---

[1] D.
[2] Jer. xxiii. 25. c. xxvi. 28, 32. c. xxix. 8, 9.

hearts. For this we may know, that there are waking dreams as well as sleeping dreams.[1] For imagination is a familiar spirit, and is begot out of the womb of reason, which is the mother, and the imagination of the heart is the father that begets this familiar spirit, and this familiar spirit is the son of imagination, which is reason's wisdom, and this son begets a God without a body, and a devil that flies in the air without a body, and cries I have seen, I have seen, but what can be seen? an invisible nothing, nothing but a perishing dream and a nonsensical fancy, for any one to imagine the devil to be in hell-fire, and out of the fire, in chains, and yet at liberty to tempt man, and all at the same time. These are the fruits of these filthy dreamers, and the next is the devil in the flesh. The sodomites and the angels are charged with fornication and going after strange flesh, and verse 10th they are said to corrupt themselves; verse 18th, these are said to walk after their own lusts; verse 19th, sensuality, and verse 25th, are said to be spotted by the flesh.[2] Now I am of this mind, that all these sayings bear but one sense, viz. that sin and the devil are man's own seed proceeding from men's lusts, or in other places called the lust of the flesh.[3] Reason is called the flesh as faith is called the spirit, for the scriptures take no notice of the outward bodily flesh; but as the two seeds operate in them, either to the purifying of the mind or the defilement of it, which purity and defilement doth arise from the two seeds. So that which is born of the flesh is flesh, and that which is born of the spirit is spirit, and it is these seeds which bring forth two motions and two voices, as speaking in man as also in two wisdoms, and so each seed brings forth its own body.[4] For as faith was but once given as aforesaid, so reason and sense was but once given likewise, and it continues its kind by generation.[5] But reason fallen is impure, so from that impurity comes polution and defilement, for who can bring a clean thing out of an unclean.[6] Again, we are to understand thus much, that by the place of conception of sin is in the heart, and if conception do not die before it quickens into life; that is into action, then it brings forth death which is the punishment due for such sins that are alive in men's actions, for whether it be murder, adultery, or theft as it is committed, it is first conceived in the heart by the motions of the flesh.

---

[1] Last Witness upon the Witch of Endor.
[2] E, F.
[3] Last Witness upon the 11 c. of Revelation. 11, 12. John iii. 5, 6. Gal. iv. 28. v. 17, 19.
[4] Jam. iii. 15.
[5] G.
[6] Mat. xxv. 35. xv. 19.

In Exodus it is written, thou shalt, saith the law of Moses, "take all the fat that covereth the inwards, and the caul that covereth the liver, and the two kidnies, and the fat that is upon them, and burn them upon the altar."[1] First, this was an offering under the law to atone for sin, signifying the conception that covers man's heart; such as carnal reason, unbelief, evil thoughts, and wicked imaginations; and these must be mortified, for though your piercing wisdom of reason be ever so high and lofty, you must submit or die.[2] Secondly, the kidnies and reins which are the instruments of generation, in the scripture sense are meant the inmost affections and desires, and are joined to the heart, which must also be mortified, for this desire and affection of lust and pleasure is inherent in the fallen nature of reason, so that it is man's own seed that sins, and for this comes the wrath of God; but upon whom! why, upon men and women who are called the children of disobedience.[3]

Thirdly, moreover it is the kidnies that are the seats of lust and not the brains, for that is the seat of reason and argument; though the motions of the mind pass through the whole soul, and if they be evil, then they are the only tempters of man.[4] Fourthly, therefore let not any man lay his brats at other men's doors, but let every man charge his own soul with the evil he commits.[5] For this is to be minded, that there is no creature that sinneth but man, who had a law given him to walk by, which law saith, "thou man, thou shalt not tempt the Lord thy God to commit murder, adultery, or steal," &c. &c.[6]

Fifthly, the scriptures were given forth to men and women, to saint and serpent, and the law was given to man devil, and the gospel to man saint, and each hath his law written in his own heart.

Sixthly, there is no kind of living creature that is defiled while it is alive, but man only, no, nor any tree or herb but what was good in its creation.[7]

What tree was that in the garden of Eden, called the Tree of Knowledge of Good and Evil, of which Adam and Eve were not to eat of?[8] Was it of this creation? or was that serpent a natural beast?[9] It is is a beastly imagination to think so, and much more are they in

---

[1] Exo. xxix. 13.
[2] Rom. viii. 13. Col. iii. 5. I. Cor. ii. 5, 6, 7.
[3] Epe. ii. 2.
[4] Jam. i. 14.
[5] Exo. xx. 14. Deu. vi. 16.
[6] Jam. i. 17.
[7] Gen. i. 25.
[8] Gen. xvi. 17.
[9] H.

chains of darkness who so imagines it, or so teaches it, and in the snares of the devil that defile the flesh, which devil is their own lust, as aforesaid.[1]

CHAP. X.

The next charge to these filthy dreamers is, that they despise dominion.

DOMINION has a twofold meaning, one a temporal and the other spiritual; the temporal lies in kings and magistrates of kingdoms, both of which will be further treated of hereafter.

For all men, without respect of persons, do owe obedience to the king or supreme power which they are under; for God hath placed them in that power to rule and judge the people. And whether a magistrate be just or unjust, yet they are obliged to obey him,[2] and he he must be obeyed in all things relating to the civil law; for a magistrate represents the person of God, who can do nothing but equal justice to all men; if magistrates should act any unjust thing in their places, yet it is no less than rebellion to resist them in their places, but men are obliged to suffer patiently leaving all things to God; for God who sets up Governors, (and sometimes in his wrath too), can pull them down when he pleases as he did Nebuchadnezzar, and at his pleasure suffer one wicked man to destroy another, according to the Apostle John, who saith,[3] that the ten horns of the beast should hate the whore, and make her desolate. Now these ten horns were several kings or princes under the beast or emperor, who were to execute his will in persecuting the saints; but after that it is said, they had power given them to hate the whore and make her desolate.[4]

Now, it was not the beast nor the emperor which gave them this power, but it was God himself; for said John, God put it in the hearts of wicked men to hate the whore that must be made desolate; and the last whore, was the first that succeeded the ten persecutions, and she hath sat almost upon all nations; and these kings, princes, and people that God hath made the instruments thereof, are wicked men; for all that fight with swords and guns or any other carnal weapons are wicked men, and though the kings and princes have of late fought against the whore, yet notwithstanding this whore despised their dominion. Now it may seem strange that the national priests should

---

[1] Gen. iii. 14.
[2] Rom. xiii. 1. Jer. xxix. 7. Mat. xvii. 22. c. xxii. 21.
[3] The whole Book of Revelation. Jer. xxix. 7.
[4] I.

ever despise that dominion, which upheld them in the church authority, so far as to be judges in all spiritual matters. Yet, when they had attained to this authority, (so far as to be judges) they were not satisfied, but through pride and ambition they have at several times exalted themselves, so as they would not only be judges in spiritual matters but in temporal also;[1] and so from their angelical pride would not allow any temporal judges to meddle with matters of the clergy; but would be concerned in both courts and both laws themselves, and so would be lords not only over all inferior people, but also over kings and princes too. As Bishop Certius of Alexandria,[2] challenged himself the government of, and over all temporal matters, and Pope Boniface the VIIIth declared himself lord of all the world, and that emperors, kings, and

The history of England saith, that Theobald, Archbishop of Canterbury, troubled all England (his power was so great) with the sword and bloody wars;[3] and Becket that succeeded him was not much better, being both a soldier and a courtier, and it was told the King by the Lord Chief Justice, that the clergy had committed above a hundred murders since his reign, and the cause of it was that the Commons had ordained that such priests as were found guilty of grievous crimes should be degraded, and there was thousands of such in the land. This is that temporal power and dominion which these National Priests depise, when they cannot have their own ends, which is to be above all; likewise their father the fallen angel, who would not only have been over all the other angels, but above God himself.

Again, these men spoken of by Jude do not only despise the temporal dominion aforesaid, but they also despise the evangelical and spiritual dominion. For these whores and harlots would never have Christ reign over them, and yet none babble more of a Christ and a crucifix than they who will reign over his seed by penal laws of their own making. But now we are speaking of dominion aforesaid, if it should be asked whether a believer of this Commission of the Spirit may take upon him any temporal office, such as Justice of the Peace, Constable, and the like;[4] my answer is, they ought not, neither can he do it if he minds the peace of his own conscience more than money or worldly honors, because Christ's kingdom is not of this world;[5] and besides there are no offices without imposing oaths, which are snares, and are to be avoided.[6] Now of oaths, there are two sorts, an assertory

---

[1] K.
[2] Who lived in the 4th Century.
[3] L.
[4] M.
[5] Luk. xxii. 25. Joh. xviii. 36.
[6] N

assertory and a promissary oath, which promissary oath is, when one or more affix God's name that they will do so or not do what they promise, this oath is unlawful. It is well said of one, who being required to swear or take such and such an oath, answered, " how shall I swear to defend such a man when I cannot defend myself; for man is but a creature, and has not so much power over himself as even to think a good thought, and much more to do a good thing.[1] But an assertory oath is, what a man knows to be certainly true, and what the immediate sense of seeing and hearing assures him, and this to inform a judge or jury to the end, that justice may be administered or determined by it, and this is the oath that Paul makes the end of all strife. Yet Michael, the Archangel, contending with the devil about the body of Moses, durst not bring against him a railing accusation, but said, the Lord rebuke thee. All the anti-churches in Europe are at a loss in this scripture, and know not what to make of it, or who this Michael the archangel should be; but the spirit of God in this Commission have traced the paths, and hath found out that this Michael here spoken of by Jude the apostle,[2] was John the high Priest in the type, and Jesus Christ in the anti-type, who is the high and heavenly priest of our salvation.[3] And the Prophet Zachariah saw in a vision, the redemption of the seed of faith by Christ, under the type of Joshua the high Priest, standing before the Lord at his right hand to resist him.[4] This high priest, saith the last witness was Christ clothed with filthy garments when he became flesh, being so mean in his apparel that he was not like the High Priest's in former times, as not having a breast plate and ephod, with a bell and pomegranates all of pure gold, with all sorts of precious stones; as also purple, scarlet, and fine linen, as may be read in the law of Moses.[5] This was an external glory which prefigured the internal, and reason was wonderfully pleased with it.[6] Yet this high priest Jesus, though so plain in his apparel, called himself the Son of God, and this Satan that stood at the right hand,[7] was the spirit of unclean reason in that scribe or pharisee that tempted Christ, from his subtle reason of that pinnacle of the temple, his own head, and not the pinnacle of a material steeple, for that devil could not carry Christ in the air as airy spirits believe. But this satan or devil being man, spoke on the height and head of his reason, saying, cast thyself down, for it is written, he shall give his angels charge over thee, that thou dash not thy foot

---

[1] N
[2] O.
[3] Zac. vi. 12.
[4] Isa. l. ii.
[5] Exo. xxix. 5, 30.
[6] Psl. xlv. 2, 3.
[7] P. Mat. iv. 5.

against a stone,¹ that is, (saith this witness) submit yourself to us, and be our king and governor; then shall we overcome all nations and all people in the world; for thy angels will keep thee, and thou shalt not be overcome by any attempt whatsoever. Now the Prophet saith, this dispute was about the body of Moses, and after the dispute was over; it is said, the angels came and administered unto him, which angels were Moses and Elias;² but whether there was any dispute about the body of Moses by Joshua and the devil, the scriptures are silent as to that. Yet without doubt, this satan or devil denied that Moses had any body, or took any with him to heaven, but in all likelihood disputed against it; or, that it was buried, and might bring a scripture proof for it too.³ For that seed not understanding translating, may call it a burial, but reason cannot understand that God translated him as he did Enoch, by having those elements of earth and water taken from him, by that mortal fire, which mortal fire became immortal by the power of God. But this doctrine is too sublime to be comprehended by natural reason, for that nature cannot believe that there are any bodies in heaven, though the scriptures mention that Moses and Elias appeared to Jesus from that blessed place, which is attested by Peter, James, and John who all saw them, and knew them, and named them.⁴ But for all the opposition this devil made against Christ, yet Christ did not bring against him any railing accusation, for that is the devil's seed and nature, and not God's;⁵ therefore Christ having learned obedience in his mortal state, did not so much as bring an accusation against him that sought his life, but said, I accuse you not to the Father, but there is one who accuseth you, even Moses in whom ye trust.⁶ For his messengers do never accuse any man of sin, but gives judgment upon them for their sin, and that follows in these words of Christ, saying, the Lord rebuke thee.⁷

Now Christ was that Lord himself, and this rebuke took place in his conscience, and he being conquered went away according as Christ said, the prince of this world cometh so. and hath nothing in me.⁸

---

¹ Psal. xi. 6.
² Q.
³ Deut. xxiv. 5, 6. Heb. xi. 5. R.
⁴ S. Mar. ix. 4, 5.
⁵ I. Tim. vi. 6, 4. T.
⁶ John. v. 45.
⁷ Mat. xvii. 18.
⁸ Mat. iv. 11. John. xiv. 30.

CHAP. XI.

But these speak evil of those things which they know not; but what they know naturally, as brute beasts, in those things they corrupt themselves. —ver. 10.

THOSE things, these non-commissioned preachers and their hearers speak evil of, are the principles and doctrines of faith, which always surmount their reason when it is at the best, but much more when it is besotted with sensuality and is drowned in voluptiousness, and so becomes brutish. But let their reason be what it will, if it once rise so high as to become so censorious as to judge of things that are of a spiritual nature which they know not, it becomes an infallible mark of a reprobate, and bring such a plague with it as hath in it the certain seal of damnation.[1] It is said by Paul, the Apostle, that the carnal man knows not the things that are of God; and why so? because they are to be spiritually discerned; now if he knows them not, yet doth not despise them, he is to be pitied, and may hereafter come to believe to the saving of his soul; but if he once takes upon him to judge of divine things which he knows nothing of, and being convinced he knows them not; he then becomes his own judge and condemns himself, and so hath the plague of a tormenting conscience.

Now divine revelation is one of the chief things in which many unlearned men in their spirit of faith, and most of the learned men in reason are forbid to judge and despise;[2] because they have it not in themselves, but what they know naturally of themselves as brute beasts, or as Peter saith, but those as natural brute beasts made to be taken and destroyed; they speak evil of things they know not, and shall utterly perish in their own corruption.[3] In some translations it is is rendered thus, as brute beast without reason, that is, they know nothing but what they know by the very guidance of nature, as only having the senses of seeing, touching, and tasting, but want the use of sober reason, of angels and men.

There is another seed and nature, called faith, and that makes a man which is called a new man; the other is the old man or elder brother;[4] because Cain was before either Abel or Seth and had this world given him, and reason is the governor thereof, and fit to govern;

---

[1] V. I. Cor. i.

[2] Jer. xviii. 18. I. Kings xxii. 24.

[3] V. II. Pet. ii.

[4] W. Rom. vii. 22. I. Cor. ii. 11, 19. Ephe. iv. 22, 24. II. Thes. ii. 3. I. Pet. iii. 4. Mat. iv. Gen.

for it is reason that learns all arts, sciences, and trades, raises cities and kingdoms, and makes laws as well as breaks them.

Now this reason is wisdom, for it discerns between good and evil, though it hath not power to chuse good or refuse evil;[1] yet it comprehends all words or languages, whether they are spoken proper or improper, and to be mighty in disputes (from a strong memory) about the glorious things of eternity, having read much of the eternal records of the Prophets or Apostles; but for the real understanding of them, whether there is any such eternal things or not, it hath no certain knowledge at all of that, but of thoughts only, as that it may be true or not, and all for want of an infallibility, which is the testimony of the spirit of faith, Which is truth itself; but as aforesaid, all great wisdom is in the eternal visible things of this world, and so is only a judge of things felt, heard, or seen within its own orb. But although it is a wisdom fit for the government of this world, yet the greatest thing is to know how it is to be governed, for it is but a creature and must have a rule to govern and be governed by. Now this rule which it is to be governed by is the moral law, and this moral law hath God written in reason's nature, which is to keep reason in obedience, being in its own nature rash and violent, yea earthly, sensual, and devilish.[2] This moral law being not only a candle to enlighten it in its paths, but to curb it when it is unruly, so becomes serviceable and makes it sober; but more especially when faith is by this sober reason submitted to, so far as to be handmaid to her mistress of divine faith; for if Hagar shall wait on her mistress Sarah, she may become serviceable so far as to make use of arguments to illustrate truth in the balance of its own reason, for the confounding of the serpentine subtility of rash and disobedient reason; but when Hagar will not be serviceable and become submissive, then turn her out of doors; if Ishmael mock the son of the free woman, then turn him out also, with his mother-in-law.[3]

Again, seeing reason hath the lordship of this world,[4] it is to exercise himself in piercing reason in order thereunto, and therefore, he that hath the greatest share of this perishing reason or angelical wisdom, should have the greatest share of government, and to such the scriptures exhorts, saying, Be ye wise, O kings, and be you learned, Oh! ye judges of the earth; but then it follows, Kiss the son, lest he be angry. Now what are they to be instructed or learned in, is it in any other books but the moral and civil law. This then were excellent, and it hath a double excellency if they have but so much

---

[1] X
[2] Y.
[3] Gen. xxi. Gal. i. v. 30.
[4] Z.

faith as to kiss the son, that is, to submit to the son;[1] so far as not to usurp a spiritual authority or prerogative power over the scripture, faith; or conscience, but to keep themselves to their own throne, and let God rule his throne; then they may become nursing fathers and queens, nursing mothers to the harmless saints, this, is a good kingly government. But these false priests and people here spoken of, are not under such government, but they have their reason stupified and drowned in voluptuousness and sensuality in their gormandizing feasts, and so overcharge nature with surfeiting lusts and wantonness, much more than brute beasts. But as this verse sets forth their earthly pleasures and sensualities to the corrupting of themselves, so the next verse sets forth their descent and devilish practices, to be their utter overthrow. But before I treat of that, a few words of Peter's, where he saith, that they were made to be taken and destroyed; here is the doctrine of reprobation, which is inculcated by the apostle. Can this seed deliver itself? when as it is said to be made on purpose for destruction, and this destruction will prove an eternal one, as in the 4th, 5th, 6th, and 7th verses of Jude doth witness, and Peter witnesseth it likewise, and so doth Jude again, verses the 11th and 12th, besides an abundant more places in scripture. Tint all these false prophets, I mean priests of Baal, do hope and teach otherwise, and some of them teach that none will be damned for a temporal sin.

One Doctor Dodwell, a learned Doctor in Cambridge, preached a very pleasing doctrine, and saith, that those scriptures that speak of God's stirring up, haying for an example, and making the wicked for the day of wrath,[2] saith, it is all but temporal punishments, and he further says, that the New Testament represents these punishments as not to be prepared for man, but for the devil and his angels, and he cites the following scriptures, Ephesians, v. 6,—Collosions, iii. 6.—Romans ix. 22. This punishment, says he, can be no other but the wrath designed for the devils, which men are no ways entitled to, and then he adds, saying, that Presbytery and others that refuse to be governed by Bishops are to be treated in no other way than as enemies and fellow-rebels with the devil; and upon the 19th of Jude, he saith, the Catholics did believe that the soul of man was mortal. Again, he saith, there was no breach of the law till Moses who made the first law, and that all that died between Adam and Moses will lay in the dust eternally, and so have no immortality; and would seem to prove it from Romans c. iv. 15.; when the law was given, it was not so absolute regal, (saith he) because it was in the power of each freewill to exempt itself from the power of the law; and also he makes Sodom

---

[1] A.
[2] B.

and Gomorrah's punishment a temporal one, and so are never to rise again.[1]

What wicked man is there that will not like this doctrine. But I'll pass him by as a man of great learning in Greek, but none in grace.

CHAP. XII.

Woe unto them! for they are gone in the way of Cain, and ran greedily after the error of Balaam for reward, and perished in the gainsaying of Core.

HERE is a sad judgment pronounced against ecclesiastics, which is a national church ministery; if that church which they govern be like their teachers, then its like church like people, being both blind, they must fall into the ditch. But few of those will be saved unless they lay down their ministry before they die, yet several of their hearers may, as will appear in the next verse.[2]

But these being no other than Baal's priests, having their commission from man, being descended from their grandfather Cain, and go in his way, but run, and that greedily after their father Balaam; so much the more, and by how much the more they apprehend great advantage by it, such as riches, honour, and pleasure; this is their delight and the wages they run for. For even the church lands and livings which Balak gives, as well as lordships, they will not lose one penny of it, because it is sacred; so the church rights being in zeal to the good old causes, yet it is said to be in the way of Cain.

Now the way of Cain is no other than murder and lies, for Cain murdered his brother Abel that he might have the lordship of the world in his hands, and when God asked Cain where his brother was, he answered the Lord with a lie, saying he knew not, and in a taunting imperious manner said, Am I my brother's keeper.[3]

Now are there any people in the world that have been more guilty of lies and murder, than these Baalists and National Priests,[4] especially of the Turkish Christian and the Roman Clergy, as all history doth abundantly relate.

For as soon as this new set-up-church (called the catholic church) was established by Imperial Authority, it was laying the foundation of their religion in blood; inasmuch, that if any man should any way

---

[1] B.
[2] C.
[3] D.
[4] E.

gainsay or oppose their outside form of worship, or if they refused to drink of the wine of her fornication, (though out of a golden cup, which is their fair outside show) they must be compelled, not only to drink the wine of her fornication, but her wrath too.

For if they will not drink it freely and willingly[1], then the whore will pot poison into the cup, and her wrath into the wine, (as the last witness saith) and make them drink both together, else excommunication or confiscation of their goods, or death itself.

The first bloody law enacted by this first anti-church, as I have read of, was in the time of Emperor Theodosius and Maxentius[2].

The Council being called in the year 381, in this Council, by the instigation of two Bishops, several Dissenting Christian Professors were given over to the Secular Power, and put to death by Maxentius[3] who was cousin-german to the Emperor Constantine. So that heresy was made a capital crime, and one of these heresies is said to be, that they held no trinity in persons in the godhead, but that Jesus Christ was both Father, Son, and Holy Ghost, if this was so, then the holy city was trod under foot indeed.

And although St. Martin (as the Pope has made him, being Bishop of Towers) was present at that council, and was against that bloody law; yet Maxentius[4] compelled him to give that bloody sentence; but he was afterwards wounded in his conscience for it; and he having a hand in the death of these poor innocents, proved himself more wicked than the rest, in that he gave judgment against them, even against his own conscience.

This was about eight years after the death of their great Bishop Athanasius, who drew up the articles of the church faith. Although their church was so young, being as it were in its infancy, yet it began to look dreadful. See Etchard's history of the Roman Emperors, Vol. III. page 137.

2ndly. And as they began so that bloody church went on. For in the fourth century, Bishop Nestorius sounding his trumpet in a sermon before the Emperor, crying aloud, and saying, "Give a land, O! Emperor! cleansed from heretics, and I will give thee heaven. Help me against the Arians, and I will help thee to subdue the Persians, who are thy enemies.

3rdly, And in the fifth century, Austin, their English Apostle and Bishop of Canterbury, was of the same stamp; he having preferred a bill against them in Parliament,[5] and this Austin not having the fear of God before his eyes, did maliciously and feloniously plot and contrive

---

[1] Rev. xvii. 4, 13. 16, 17.
[2] F
[3] G
[4] H
[5] I

the death of 1200 monks of Bangor, and four substantial witnesses made oath that he moved the Papan King to do it.

And now Rome having got itself the mother church, and the Pope supreme head of it; then the clergy in all countries took this oath.[1]

The Oath

"I, such a one, sware to be true to Saint Peter and the Holy Father of Rome, and to the Pope the Holy Father, and to defend it against all men, and all heretics and schismatics to our Holy Father, I will persecute to the utmost of my power. So help me God, and the Holy Evangelists;" which is as much as to say; if I do not so, let me be damned. Oh! horrible wickedness!

But to proceed a little farther, in process of time it came to pass, that two Popes were chosen at onetime by several parties; namely, Pope Clement and Pope Urbin; the violence and fury of these two holy Popes against each other occasioned a desperate war between them, and damnable curses against each other, wherein many thousands were killed.[2]

And in the days of King Henry the IVth, there were two other Popes in their church at that time, whereof King Henry wrote to Pope Gregory, and tells him of 200,000 that were slain upon the account of him;[3] and to the other Anti-Pope fighting in camp for the title of the Bishopric, telling him he ought to be grieved for the same, and desiring him rather to decline the honour of the Apostolic See, than suffer such horrible bloodshed.

But one story more brings us down to the time of God's putting it into the hearts of Princes to hate this scarlet whore, whose bloodshed and cruelties were so great in the year 1500.

Pope Leo the Xth, and his Cardinal fell out,[4] which occasioned another bloody war between them, when tire Pope raised 40,000 men, most of them under his own pay, and these Priests, Bishops, and Clergy heading that army, they joined in battle, and there has not been seen in all Italy a battle more furious and dreadful; for it is said, that on both sides were slain 25,000 souls. This battle made mightily for the second anti-church, the Protestant one of Europe; the angels thereof then sounding the trumpets of their ministry, as Luther, Swinglers, and others of great power.

---

[1] K
[2] L.
[3] M.
[4] N.

CHAP. XIII.

The Rise of the Protestant Church.

THIS Episcopal or Protestant Church, so called from their protesting against the Popish Superstition, as to the substance of their religion, they are all one and the same;[1] so that if one is true, the other is true, and if one is false, the other is false likewise; for the essentials of their faith are one and the same, so that most of the differences between them lay in circumstances and ceremonies.

Now these new priests to establish themselves against the old priests their fathers, would gratify the magistrates for assisting them with that glorious title of making them the supreme head of the church, instead of their father, the Pope; thinking themselves fitter to rule than he, he being as they thought blind with age.

Now the younger brethren or children making the magistrate the supreme head of the church, the prince upon this, having been so priest-ridden, before they could shake him off, was resolved to make the younger brother the better man, and Martin must now be preferred before Peter, and will install himself in Peters place; so their bishops shall be as great as the Popish bishops, and appoint them the Fame consecration and ordination. For here, in England, all the Bishops are subject to the Archbishop of Canterbury, he being the Pope of England, and all other Bishops take the oath of canonical obedience to him, and he is as his father the Papist was, made the first Peer of the Realm, next to the Royal Family; and he, with York, hath the title of Grace, and as the other Bishops are stiled the Right Reverend, the Archbishops are stiled the Most Reverend, and the inferior Clergy Reverend.

Again, after a Protestant Bishop is consecrated,[2] he is brought into the King's or Queen's presence to do homage for his temporality or barony, and he compounds for his first year's profit or wages for his ministry; and though this is the very same wages as the Papists, yet the Papists call them the Bishops of another world; and are very angry with them, and there is some reason for it too. That the Protestant who is the younger son, should be so vicious and unjust, as not only to usurp authority over their father's estate, but to depose their elder brother and seize his estate, both house and land; and yet be so impudent as to say, God hath given it them.

Did not that brother run greedily to get that estate, and is not this brother as greedy in striving to get it again. Is not this robbing Peter to

---

[1] O.
[2] P.

pay Paul, or clothe Martin, one brother, and rob another; being both of them brethren in iniquity, and no iniquity is like the clergy's, and no craft is like priestcraft. Be angry with me on both sides if you can, for all the world have reason to be any with you, who have robbed them and cheated them of a great part of their estates, as will be shewn hereafter.

But behold the actions of this new church, in order to the raising of itself.

CHAP. XIV.

IT hath been first shown, that the foundation of the Romish Church was laid in blood, and if we mind the actions of the Protestant Church, we shall find that it was founded in blood likewise; for when this church extricated itself from Rome, and shook off its ceremonies, it did not shake off the sword of steel, but took that sword with them that had been bathed in the blood of many, but having sheathed it for a while; but when they saw that they had got power, then they put on their armour and drew these swords, and would sheath them in the blood of their brethren that opposed them.

Now we are to mind, that that religion which puts on armour and fights with the sword of steel, never acknowledges God by his testament or titles, nor knows nothing of angelical divine love, or gospel patience.

But this carnal or Protestant Church in Germany, having got the King of Bohemia, on their side, and some other Princes, took up arms as aforesaid, and the time being come to fulfil the scriptures, of God's putting it in their hearts to do his will, in hating the whore and making her desolate, the time of her wickedness being at the full.[1] These Princes raised an army which was commanded by one Zisco, and having obtained certain churches of kings, wherein they might freely preach, they told the people that the Pope was an anti-christ, and that John Huss and Jeremiah Prague were the two last witnesses. This doctrine so exasperated the people as to fight valiantly, and suppressed many monasteries, and drew away the Popish priests and monks out of them.

And Zisco having got a great number of men of war took several garrisons, and the Emperor, by the Pope's persuasions, sent an army against them of 15,000; but the Protestants overcame them, and took the city of Campton by force, and burnt all the Popish Priests there.

---

[1] Q.

And Zisco fought a third battle and got the victory, and slew 9000 Papists. He again fought a fourth a battle, and slew 3000, and put the rest to flight.

In time, he fought nine battles, and overcame in all;[1] then Zisco died, and they chosed another General; then the Pope and the Emperor came with a second supply of 80,000 men, but the Protestants overcame them also, after which they came to a treaty of peace; but the Turks coming against the Emperor, besieged Vienna with an army of 200,000, the Protestants joining with the Papists they obtained a great victory, where 80,000 of the Turks was slain. Then the Protestants in a few years after came to have their worship established by kings and queens; and the magistrates and ministers joined together in that church, to be judges of heresy as the papists did; as Bishop Jewel, in Queen Elizabeth's reign said, we do persecute all heretics us our forefathers did in former times; 27 papists were taken in a meeting and imprisoned and bore to the faggots at Paul's Cross.

At another time one man and ten women were condemned and eight banished, and command was given out for their burning in Smithfield,[2] In the 23rd year of her reign, it was enacted treason to draw any one from the faith and worship then established.

But it is not proper to bring this history of their cruelty lower down or too near the present time, least following truth too near the heels, a man may have his teeth knocked out, as saith Sir Walter Raleigh, in his epistle to the History of the World.

CHAP. XV.

Run, and that greedily, after the error of Balaam for reward.

THERE are many great errors in a false ministry, but these are counted neither errors nor novelty,[3] for every man loves gain, and gain is accounted godliness, and the national ministry were never more godly than gainful; for there is but a wish and a would upon godliness; as Balaam for a righteous death, and all the Baalists are the same. But there is a must upon riches by that generation, as I would be godly, but I must be rich; I must be honorable, I must take my pleasure, I must and I will if I can be a companion for princes, and will honour them, and sew pillows under their elbows; I will give them ease and respect, and will have their persons in admiration because of advantage. I must and will have my dues, the church hath given it

---

[1] R.
[2] S.
[3] T.

me, it is my right, and I must and I will have that right and maintain it; that my successor is not wronged; not that I care so much for my successor, but it is my own interest which I principally aim at.

Here lies the spirit, the life, the religion of Baal's priests, and honour is the high price of the call of man unto this ministry.

These are the men that the prophets and apostles and witnesses of the spirit call greedy dogs, that can never have enough.[1] These snarle at a man that will stand in his way, (when he is upon his run) to hinder him from a large living, for his ninny nonnies.

But these preachers are rarely provided for, whether they are Romish, Episcopal, or Presbytery, for these three are the only countenanced churches in Europe.[2]

But of these three, the Papists have the most plentiful endowments and rewards, where they have power of government,[3] insomuch that the History of England mentions, that the Friars, Abbots, and Monks had got in their hands, in the reign of King Henry the VIIIth, a third part of their lands.

The Popes church in Italy is now of that extent, that it reaches from sea to sea, being one hundred miles in breadth, and three hundred miles long.[4] There are reckoned to be of Monks and Friars in Italy, France, Germany, and Spain, no less than 1,000,000, all of which depends upon the Pope's authority.[5] Every convent or monastery being a garrison to defend the Pope, which is so rich and of such power, as that he is able to raise twenty thousand foot, and two thousand horse in less than a month.

These are the waters that the whore sits on, and as to the other clergy, their tythes and references are reckoned in France, to be twelve hundred thousand pounds, and that they possess seven parts in twelve, besides all their standing rents, of offerings, burials, and dirges.[6] There being in that kingdom alone, 13 Archbishops, 104 Bishops, 1450 Abbots, 550 Arch priors, 567 Nunneries, 700 Convents of Friars, and the Popish Priests are 130,000 taking in all inferior orders, and though the parishes are but 27,400, yet there are reckoned 15,000,000 of people in France, whereof the clergy do make 3,000,000, which is a fifth part of the whole.

---

[1] V.
[2] W.
[3] W.
[4] Dr. Heylin's Book of Cosmography p. 114.
[5] X.
[6] Y.

In Spain, are eleven Archbishops and 52 Bishops.[1] Dr. Burnet, bishop of Salisbury saith, that the Hospitals of Naples amounts to one hundred thousand pounds, and that the plate of the churches in Naples amounts to two millions of pounds, and that there are several pieces of plate said to be worth two thousand five hundred pounds, which is all dead and useless, saith the Doctor.[2]

Now all these riches, honour, and glory, hath been got by this race of running, and there will never want race-men so long as the wages will be given.

Now these three churches of Papists, Episcopal, and Presbytery, must share it amongst them, unless the magistracy will cast off all their ministry and make use of it themselves, which can hardly be done because the magistracy will have one ministry or other, as long as the world doth last; and there is a necessity there should be a public ministry, as well as a public magistracy.

CHAP. XVI.

And perish in the gainsaying of Core,

THIS Core and Moses were brother's children, Core was of the tribe of Levi, who of course were to officiate in the Priest's office, for which they had the tenth of the people's goods allowed them.[3]

Now his employment was not to come near the altar, for that did belong to the high Priest, but they were to attend in the sanctuary, in praying and offering sacrifice. These called in Dathan and Abiram to oppose Moses, and would have supplanted him in his Priesthood, and have assumed to themselves both civil and ecclesiastic government, which was peculiar to Moses and Aaron; just like the Presbytery by the Episcopacy, hating to be inferior to them. For pride and ambition runs in a line, and acts according as Core did, and so falls with them, for presuming to take upon them the office of a minister of the gospel without a commission from heaven; so through pride would be the companions of princes, and men of consequence and renown, as Corah, Dathan, and Abiram were, being men renowned for wealth and wisdom, and men of great presence. Core, being a Levite, and so apt to teach, the other two were statesmen, which made the conspiracy greater;[4] therefore, said one, Woe to the wicked, (meaning Coran), and and Woe to his neighbours, as Dathan and Abiram; these came to

---

[1] Y.

[2] Z.

[3] A.

[4] A.

spiritual wickedness together; and would be offering strange fire to the Lord: such are all national ministry's, whether public or private. What is all their worship and offerings but strange fire, for not one of them are of God, but all are fighters against the true ministry, and against such as cannot fall down and worship in their vain-glorious synagogues, all these are included with Corah, Dathan, and Abiram, as they committed spiritual wickedness together.

CHAP. XVII.

These are spots in your feasts of charity, when they feast with you, feeding themselves without fear: clouds they are without water, carried about of winds; trees whose fruit withereth, without fruit, twice dead, plucked up by the roots, verse 12. Raging waves of the sea, foaming out their shame; wandering stars, to whom is reserved the blackness of darkness for ever.—verse 13.

THOSE who run so greedily after the error of Balaam for reward, are the persons that are here called spots in their feasts of charity.[1] They are the ministers and teachers of the people, though spotted and spurious, yet they are not spotted alone, but the people walking in the same ungodly way, are included with their teachers.[2] The spots and corruptions of these teachers are such, as by their actions and fruit may be easily discerned by a judicious eye, that they are not the ministers of God, but quite contrary. For in their first exercise of sacred things, they are said to be fed without fear, even at such a time as they are feasting with the elect of God.

Secondly, they are called empty clouds, and have no refreshing drops of water to comfort God's elect, who are starved under them.[3]

Thirdly, they are not only called trees, which are not only dead, but twice dead and plucked up by the roots.[4]

Fourthly, they are not as troubled waters only casting up mire and dirt; but as raging waves of the sea, foaming out their own hatred, envy, and malice, when crost, which is their shame.

Fifthly, they are not only stars, but wandering stars from place to place, from duty to duty; but they give so dark a light that neither

---

[1] B.
[2] verse. 23.
[3] C.
[4] C.

themselves nor others can see which way to walk. But of each of these in their place and order.

Sixthly, they are reserved to punishment.[1]

First, the Apostle Jude intimates very plainly to us, that the elect seed were to be captivated under a false ministry; for the administrators and the administrations were to cease together, when they had finished their testimony, and done what was appointed them; having the outward court of the scriptures, and the external worship given them by stealth, took possession of them, and the elect of God were elected to be captivated under them, and to submit to their worship, believing that the learned men of the world, (the Priests) have power successively to set up gospel ordinances or visible ordinances to please God. But for such whose consciences were very tender and could not submit, being (by the grace of God) more enlightened, such were to be trodden under foot, persecuted, and put to death.[2] But for the others who were kept in blindness and darkness, so as to believe that these men had the power of wisdom to interpret scriptures, and to teach them how to worship God; also these Priests told them, that God had a visible church and ever would have, which was a national ministry, set up in imitation of the Apostles doctrine and practice.

For these feasts of charity was a formal worship, and was annexed to the Lord's Supper, and these established ministers practised it, and liked such love feasts for voluptuousness sake, being as Paul said, "belly Gods."[3] But these Priests instead of feeding their sheep, they were fed by *them*, under the law spoken of by Ezekiel, saying,[4] Woe to the shepherds who feed themselves instead of their sheep, and clothe themselves with their wool; and the sheep became meat to all the beasts of the field, and were scattered because there was no shepherd; it became a dark day, and my sheep must eat that which my shepherds have fouled and spoiled with their feet, but I will judge between cattle and cattle, and between the sheep and the goats.

Thus, it was by these Priests, and under them in the time of the law, there not being Prophets under every age to instruct the elect; and it was so after the Apostles time, after the false Priests had got in the chair.— Then the sheep or lambs of Christ were forced to eat that which they had trampled with their feet, and took their own imaginations for revelations; yet these innocent lambs being charitable, were free to believe them who little deserved it; in that they

---

[1] C.
[2] D.
[3] I. Cor. xi. 21. Phil. iii. 19. E.
[4] Ezek. c. xxxiv.

fed so greedily, as the carnal Israelites did on the manna; never fearing the wrath of God, from the consequences of their rioting, though they were to be taken and destroyed, flattering themselves that God would not damn man for momentary pleasures which they could not avoid. But some may say here, Are the elect taught who are under a false ministry? and of what use is that ministry to them?

Answer.[1] God teaches the elect by the inspiration of his most holy spirit, where his commissioned messengers are not, by which they are preserved from the breach of the law, and preserved in innoceney of life; though they may know no other but that Jesus Christ is the son of God.[2] But love, charity, and obedience, (so far as they know by the invisible motions of the spirit), are sufficient for their salvation, without a necessity of submission to an external worship.

But then, if it be queried, saying, must we have no public ministry? if so, are we not worse than the Turks or Heathens?[3]

To this I answer. That we are better than Turks or Heathens in a non-commissioned ministry of God, why?[4] Because they hold forth to the people, the letter of the scriptures, and the necessity of obedience to the moral and civil laws; and this is of great use and necessity to the seed of reason.

Secondly. It is also of great use to the elect of God who are congregated amongst them, and becomes a means sometimes to be delivered from them; as when the elect vessel hearing a national preacher read and recite the scriptures, he is convinced of the truth of them.[5] Now what doth he is such a case? Why truly, he justifies the ministry of the Prophets and Apostles, (as saith the last witness) and sits down in peace of his own mind, and he becomes wiser than his teacher, by seeing him dark in spiritual things, so hears him no more, but pityeth him.[6] Such is the condition of all that are taught by the spirit.

Again, it may be doubted by some, whether all the elect living in these days, are appointed to believe in this commission of the spirit; or shall not their innocency of life save them now, as well as when there was no true ministry. Answer,—there is none of the seed of faith now living, if they hear the report of the doctrine of this last

---

[1] F.
[2] G.
[3] H.
[4] H.
[5] J. R. to Mr. Sedgwick, a Minister.
[6] I.

commission of the spirit, but they will believe the same;[1] although the other seed, which is the seed of reason cannot believe it. But for such as have not heard of it, but die in the innocency thereof, their innocency of life will save them; but they cannot be so happy; because, they want the assurance of life eternal, which a true commission gives them.

CHAP. XVIII.

Secondly, these Preachers are called clouds without waters, being carried about with winds.

CLOUDS without water are they, which are without the water of life running in the veins of faith, the cloud being a confused cloud, a bare opinion, empty of all spiritual refreshment. Peter calls them wells without water; yet these wells or clouds have waters in them, but not the waters of life; as the last witness in a letter to me writes,[2] saying, the reprobate seed in the fallen-angel, hath a well of water in them, and this well of water is dug in them by false teachers or preachers, and out of this well doth waters arise, which are the waters of death, which is unbelief, a troubled mind, a wounded conscience, and the fear of eternal death.[3]

But on the contrary, there is a well of living water in every true believer, and God's messengers did dig this well.[4] In that faith comes by hearing the word of God preached, but how can he preach except he is sent. This water is always springing up with revelation of heavenly wisdom, peace of conscience, and joy in the Holy Ghost, with the assurance of eternal life. It is a great benefit and blessing living under a true ministry chosen and sent of God.[5] Thirdly, Jude calls them false teachers without fruit, that is, without good fruit. The tree of knowledge since it brought forth evil, it has lost good and remains evil continually. For a corrupt tree will bring forth corrupt fruit, though it may flourish outwardly, and appear beautifully green, and adorned with leaves, yet bears no fruit, as the fig tree which was cursed by our blessed saviour, and these trees spoken of by Jude and Peter were cursed likewise, and their leaves of goodly words, and fruits of legal righteousness were withered and decayed; not being like the leaves of the tree of life.

---

[1] J.
[2] Dated July 29th, 1679.
[3] K.
[4] L.
[5] M.

For those were medicinal and healed nations, being the doctrine of faith and love in a form of sound words, having spirit and life in them, delivered by the twelve apostles, who were those twelve manner of fruits, proceeding from the tree of life.[1]

But the doctrine of these false teachers did yield no fruit of godliness. But the Curse having taken hold of them, they withered and died; and were not only dead, but twice dead; plucked up by the roots.[2] They were first dead in trespasses and sins, though afterwards they pretended redemption from those sins, by Christ shedding of his blood for them; but their turning the grace of God into lasciviousness and denying the Lord Jesus Christ to be the only Lord God, they brought upon themselves another death sealed up in it; and it could be no otherwise, in that the ground of their hearts brought no other fruit, but pricking thorns and briars; so were to be plucked up by the roots as fuel for eternal burning, under a second death or dying life, always dying but never dead.

CHAP. XIX.

FOURTHLY, they are not only as troubled waters casting up mire and dirt, but as raging waves of the seas, foaming out their shame of hatred, malice, and envy; having own no bounds to their passions; so that a man may as soon stop the raging waves of the seas, as to divert their wrath when it is once kindled, this I know by experience; but I shall pass it by, and treat of their denomination, called, wandering stars.

Now these ministers are called stars, being not fixed in that heavenly orb of divine faith, which should stand still in the mind, and behold the salvation of God in themselves, from whence revelation doth arise and flow.[3]

But the ministers of all the seven churches of Asia, what are they?[4] but wandering stars and false vapours, (like will-with-a-wisp) or a going fire, leading men out of the way of all true knowledge, and so they wander from duty to duty, from scripture to scripture, from father to fathers, as Eusebius, Socrates, Athanasius, Augustin, St. Jerome, St. Hierom, and St. Chrysostom, with abundance of more made saints; from all these they seek straw and stubble to make full tale of bricks to build with. Likewise the Heathen Philosophers must put in their helping hands, and no right ministers or light stars,

---

[1] L. M. of Rev. c. xi. page 51.
[2] N.
[3] Exo. xiv. 13. I. Cor. xvi. 13.
[4] N.

without they have read Aristotle, Plato, Tully, Homer, Plutarch, Pliny, Pythagoras, and Senica, with many more. Then from all these their work is framed, and a text from scripture is taken and divided into several parts or heads, and several doctrines raised with reasons and uses, so many, as that every made saint, philosopher or heathen writer must contribute to the building or making up of this babble; and the greatest scholars that have Aristotle, Cicero, and Plato in their heads are *very* sots; and a church that must be conducted by such shall always be learning, but *never* come to the knowledge of the truth. So that all these wandering stars are no less than spiritual vagabonds, adjuring by Jesus whom Paul preached; as if they were Paul and Peter themselves, yet understood not what the apostles Jesus is or was, no more than those vagabond sons of Scava did, who were the chief Priests.

These seven sons of Scava are a type of the stars or angels of the seven churches of Europe,[1] and that prophecy of Isaiah, chapter xi. verse 15th, of destroying the tongue of the Egyptian sea in all its seven streams, as my faith hath extended itself to those times, called the second time, (verse 11th) which hand that recovers the remnant of his people is no other but Israel's Redeemer, even Christ Jesus, who was in chapter 9th and 6th verse, called the everlasting Father, and Almighty God, (that is) he should be so called by this third and last commission of the spirit, which will destroy the tongue of the Egyptian sea; as my faith is in these words.[2]

Sixthly, these wandering stars are said to be reserved to the blackness of darkness for ever.[3] This will be the state of these wandering stars and to all their adherents, when this black day comes they will wander no more, which will be at the end of the world, when God doth raise the dead, and the elect are ascended; then will a flood of fire be poured down to burn up all the glory and beauty of this world to ashes and sand; but will not be so favorable as to burn the wicked reprobate; when all is burned, then will the sun, moon, and stars, which are the natural lights of heaven, go out like the snuff of a candle, never to give their lights any more.

Then as the commission of the spirit says,[4] will their bodies which they so pampered, news from and made their kingdom of heaven, then become their kingdom of hell, and those proud spirits their devil shut up close prisoners, souls and bodies without motioning the least comfort, to give them any ease at all in this place of darkness, of

---

[1] O.
[2] P.
[3] P.
[4] Reeves's Joyful news from Heaven.

which, the three days and three nights darkness in Egypt was a type;[1] in which darkness they shall hear one another's doleful cries, and cursed blasphemies, but shall never see one another's dreadful faces; neither can they stir from the place of their resurrection; having bodies as heavy as lead and as black as pitch. But no more of this here, for the world cannot bear to hear the report of it, although they must bear the punishment. For this is the testimony of all the three commissions.

CHAP. XX.

And Enoch also the seventh from Adam, prophesied of these, saying, Behold, the Lord cometh with ten thousand of his saints, to execute judgment upon all, and to convince all that are ungodly among them, of all their ungodly deeds, which they have ungodly committed, and of all their hard speeches which ungodly sinners have spoken against him. —ver 14 and 15.

THESE are murmurers and complainers,[2] walking after their own lusts; and their mouths speaketh great swelling words, having men's persons in admiration, because of advantage.

1st Observation

Mind here, and observe,[3] how the Apostle brings in Enoch as a witness to this; and of the judgment and condemnation of the reprobate seed, of which, these wandering stars are part of; the whole of which prophecies of Enoch gave to our forefathers of Adam's seed and nature, some knowledge of a day of judgment and condemnation of ungodly men, and that delivered down traditionally from Enoch to Noah, and from thence to Abraham, Isaac, and Jacob, and so down to Moses. So that God hath not left himself without a witness, of the sin and judgment of that seed, which at the end of the world, will be inflicted upon them, as also to encourage the elect with faith and patience to wait their time of their own deliverance.

---

[1] Q. Exo. xi. 22. Rev. xv. 20. Joel ii. 6. Rev. xvi. 21.
[2] verse 16.
[3] R.

2nd observation

But part of this reprobate unbelieving seed are angry, and greatly displeased at this epistle by Jude,[1] and say, it was never written by him, but count it Apocrypha, saying, we have no scripture of Enoch's writing, neither say they, have we any account of that dispute between Michael and the devil about the body of Moses, which Jude here speaks of.

And why are they so much against this Epistle by Jude? why because Gods prerogative power in his condemnation of the reprobate seed; and that Christ Jesus is that God, and the only and alone saviour of all that shall be saved; and that there should be two seeds, the one elected to eternal life, the other reprobated to eternal death.

3rd observation

Again, mind and observe thus much,[2] that though we have not Enochs prophecies on record, yet it is certain that there were such prophecies on record, but whether they were in books or in parchments it is not certain; but they might be brought down traditionally from father to son. For Enoch being the seventh from Adam, all the heads of these six families were alive in the days of his prophecies; for Enoch was born about the 622nd year of the world, and Adam living 930 years, so that Adam lived till the 308th year of Enoch's life; so that Adam received great benefit and comfort, (so did all the spiritual seed) by Enoch's prophecies, as being the priest of God; and all were taught by him. For all the generations following Enoch, they taught it to their children traditionally, and this was as effectual as if they had been in books. For Methusalem was Enoch's son, and he lived through many generations, even within one year of the flood, which came down successively to Noah, which was 1600 years from thence to Abraham, Isaac, and Jacobs and so until Moses; then came forth a written law, and Moses wrote of Enoch; otherwise, how could he have known that Enoch walked with God, and how God took him up to heaven, the residence of his glory.

In a word, Methusalem, Enoch's son, lived many hundred years with Adam and Shem, and Noah's son lived long with Methusalem, and Isaac lived fifty years with Shem; so that those three men, from the beginning of the world until Moses's fiftieth year, was longer than the birth of Christ to these our days.

Moreover, the prophecies of Enoch concerning the coming of God in the flesh for the salvation of the elect seed of Adam, and the day of

---

[1] S.
[2] T.

judgment and condemnation of the seed of the serpent, called the sons and daughters of Belial; were very well known to the twelve Patriarchs, who were the sons of Jacob, as doth appear in their last Will and Testament to their children, which prophecies were from Enoch; as was said by them in several places, and of several of their testimonies, I shall only recite these following,[1]

First, God shall himself raise unto you my children, the light of the righteous, saith Zebulon; he shall redeem the seed of Adam from bondage of Belial, and you shall see God in the shape of man.[2]

Second., Simeon, God shall take a body upon him, eating and drinking with man, shall save man.

Third, God hath chosen Judah to be a king of all people; therefore worship you his seed said Reuben, for he shall die for you, and reign with you, world without end.

Fourth, I saw, that out of Judah was born a virgin, having a white silken robe, and out of her came forth the Immaculate Lamb, in him joined the angels and men, said Joseph to his children.

Fifth, the Holy One of Israel shall reign over you my children, (said Dan) in holiness and poverty, and he that believeth in him, shall certainly reign with him in heaven.

Sixth, by faith shall help and welfare spring up unto Israel, (said Nepthalim) and in him shall Jacob be blessed.

Seventh, God shall appear amongst men upon the earth to save the flock of Israel, said Isachar.

Eighth, you my children (said Asher) shall be dispersed and despised by reason of your sin, until the Highest doth visit the earth, eating and drinking as man with man, and breaking the serpent's head in pieces, without noise; he shall save Israel by water, being God hidden in man, shall the Saviour come.

Ninth, my son, understand that the Lord shall execute judgment upon the children of men because of their unbelief; even when the stones shall cleave asunder; the sun shall be darkened; and all creatures troubled at the invisible spirit and spoiling of hell, in the passion of the Highest, said Levi.

Tenth, the Lord shall take the kingdom upon him, and as many as believe in him at the latter time, shall rise again to glory, and the others to shame.

---

[1] V.
[2] W.

CHAP. XXI

THESE are the testimonies of Jacob's sons,[1] and so it was with Jacob their father, and so down to Enoch, and so to Adam, and so all the fathers and their children from Enoch, were educated in the faith of God, and his becoming flesh, and of a resurrection, and of a day of judgment to the two seeds, the one saw, the other executed. Now as to their execution, I need not treat of it here, having spoken of the nature and punishment of the reprobate's torments in the last chapter.

Now, in the 15th verse, the Apostle pointing his discourse and doctrine of this false ministry, making further discovery of their wicked actions; as first, calling them murmurers and complainers; secondly, walking after their own lusts; thirdly, they speak great swelling words; fourthly, they are full of hypocrisy and dissimulation, gaining to themselves honor and riches.

First, as to their murmering and complaining, it is against such as stand in the way of their preferment, or to such as reprove them for their lustful practices; to which their nature's are prone.[2]

Secondly, their great swelling words of blasphemy and reproach against any that they think hinders them in any way from promotion, or shall gainsay their doctrine, calling them heretics, and their words and principles of the devil; then comes their great swelling words of hatred, wrath, malice, and envy; so that these four spirits of envy, wrath, hatred, and malice, are the spawn of the devil.

These are the same spirits which John calls evil birds, caged up in the own bellies, and there sealed to eternal torments. For their worms will never die, and the fire which is blown up by the law, will never go out in a blasphemer of the Holy Ghost.

Thirdly, their own lusts are their own heavens; this is the third time that the Apostle hath charged all sin and evil upon man's own lust.[3] What is that then, but the devil? therefore, if a man will but resist lust, he then doth resist the devil;[4] as one of Jacob's sons said, Kill the devil by your good works, and by your shutting of evil. Again, their wrath and malice is against all that oppose their doctrine, or that otherways make a stand against their honour and preferment. So on the other hand, by their subtilty they insinuate themselves into the

---

[1] X.

[2] Y.

[3] Jam. i. 11. Hos. xiii. 9. Joh. ii.15. Psa. lxxxi. 13. Rom. i. 24. Eze. iii. 21.

[4] Acts xiv. 10. Epe. xxiii.

company of great men; such as rule and govern the church and state, in order to get promotion; and therefore, says Jude, they have men's persons in admiration, because of advantage.

No beast is so subtile as the serpent.[1] No man so cunning and deceitful as the devil. And no devil, since the prince of devils became flesh, shall, or can out do priestcraft.

Remark

The old translation renders it thus, having them in reverence; who are more reverenced than the rich and honorable, especially such as sit in the stern of government.

Remark.

So this is a national ministry, and the chief governors of the church and state is their own devotee.[2] And what is all this for? is it not for honor and riches, and to be the companions of princes, to sit at their tables, to swell and to tell old fables. Now to these they crouch and cringe, they bow and bend as if they were God Almighty; giving them flattering titles, as patrons of piety, with a God bless his worship, his honor, or his lordship, &c. &c.

The divines, said Burton, in his book of melancholy, who reckoned himself a divine also, if he is a rich man he is only a devotee, and if he is rich no matter how he got it. Oh! he is an honest man. Oh! his child is a golden child, let him be ever so ordinary.

And if at a feast he drinks healths, says, I have not drank up my cup, yea, says this Priest, you have drank like a Prince, as if Princes were the only drinkers; but it is flattery and priestcraft which poisons most great men of this world.[3] Now how false and contrary are these false Apostles, compared to the true and blessed Apostles; for Paul said to the saints, that they never used flattering words as a cloak of covetousness, neither did they seek glory from man.

But these time serving men will be angry at such as take Paul's side against them; so I will pass on, to make observations on the next three verses, and then I have done with them, and so hath the Apostle Jude likewise.

---

[1] Z.
[2] A.
[3] B. Thes. ii. 5.

CHAP. XXII.

Beloved, remember ye the words which were before spoken of the Apostles of our Lord Jesus Christ; How that they told you, that there should be mockers in the last times, who should walk after their own ungodly lusts. —These be they who separate themselves, sensual, not having the spirit. —ver. 17,18, and 19.

THE Apostle being now come to a conclusion in his large description of this false ministry, turns his discourse to the elect, the beloved of God, exhorting them to call to mind the doctrine of his fellow-apostles, as well as his; as Peter, Paul, and John who had also foretold the coming of these false priests in the latter times, whom they call mockers and makers of sects, as the old translation hath it; and now these last times reacheth up to these days, and the elect of God in these days are part of that beloved seed, that are now to mind the words of the Apostles of our Lord Jesus Christ, it being written for your understandings; on whom the ends of the world is coming, and the spirit is coming with it, as John, Jude, Peter, and Paul hath declared, which doth discover and make appear who these mockers and makers of sects or churches are.

For we know that there hath been mockers in all ages and times, who were ever ready to ridicule the godly, as Ishmael mocked his brother Isaac, it is probable, he called him the son of promise, in scorn, as the Scribes and Pharisees mocked our blessed Saviour, in scorn of his word and doctrine.[1]

But this mocking that was to be in the last days was higher; for though they did not only pretend to be christians, but teachers of christians as ministers of Christ, and yet did mock at Christianity itself in its prophecied innocency, and not only so, but the ungodly lusts of some of these sects, led them to believe that there would be no resurrection or day of judgment. But more of this hereafter.

The Apostle saith, that they separate themselves; it is true, the elect were required to separate themselves from idolatry and false worship; but not from their company, for then they must have gone out of the world, for they were every where.

But these sects or separates here spoken of, do make a division amongst themselves; for though they have all one God, yet they worship him several ways, according to their imaginary sensual spirit, they not having the spirit of truth, through which they divide

---

[1] D.

themselves into several churches, and cry, Lo! here is Christ, and there is Christ.[1]

But the elect are forewarned of them, for they are found to be but anti-churches, though in imitation of the seven true churches of Asia, and these anti-angels were foreseen of John, when he said, that in the days of the voice of the seventh angel, when he should begin to sound, the mystery of God should be finished; but the seven true angels of the churches of Asia, sounded forth the trumpet of their ministry 1300 years before, and the mystery of God was not then finished.[2]

And these seven anti-angels of Europe have all sounded, and are now sounding the seventh and last anti-angel, for the commission of the spirit is come forth, and the mystery of God is finished; and the mystery of iniquity is discovered.[3]

The seven anti-angels of Europe are as follows: 1st, Papist; 2nd, Episcopal; 3rd, Presbytery; 4th, The Independent; 5th, The Baptist; 6th, The Ranter, and 7th, The Quaker, which is the last.

The two first anti-churches of Papist and Episcopal have been spoken of already, and the Presbytery in part, but I shall say something more of the Presbytery, in shewing the difference from the other two, as well as the difference of the other four anti-churches.

The third anti-church is of Presbytery this church is fathered upon John Calvin,[4] and differs little from Episcopal doctrine, for they are Episcopally diluted, that is, they make no difference between a Bishop and a Presbyter; saying, there are but two orders in the church, vix. Presbyter and Deacon, and that the Apostles were to have no successors. So that, though the Presbyterians disown Bishops, yet they make themselves as much and as great as they; appropriating to themselves as much power in their parishes, as they, the Bishops have in their Diocess; so that they are Pope's in their parishes, as well as Bishop's are in their great Cathedral's and Diocess.[5]

And Calvin who heads this people, is as dark in his doctrine, as either Popery or Episcopacy;[6] for, though he holds with Predestination, yet upon very weak grounds; for, says he, the ground and cause of man's election sprung through the election of Christ; for, says he, God chose Christ and gave him honour, that afterwards he might make some other's partakers of his gifts. Now, says he, in the

---

[1] E.
[2] F.
[3] G.
[4] H.
[5] I.
[6] K.

whole seed of Adam, God saw nothing worthy of election; therefore, he turned his eyes to Christ, to choose as it were, members put of his body.

Here, I appeal to sober reason, whether this doctrine flows from an angel of light or an angel of darkness; for, it is certain that God took upon the seed of Adam, and Adam's seed was faith, and that seed of faith was the seed of God.[1] So God took upon himself his own seed of the light of life eternal. Then surely there must be something worthy of love in Adam's seed, or God would never have taken it upon him.

Moreover, doth not the trumpeter ground his election of man on two Gods; God must look upon Christ, and Christ must look upon the one part of the seed of Adam, taking and chusing one, and rejecting the other; and yet children of the one and the same father.[2] So that this angelical preacher understands no more than one scripture seed, and that the seed of Adam; then it must follow that that seed will be either all saved or all damned.

But the scripture is clear to us, that all that die in Adam, will be made alive by Christ.[3][4]

But there is another seed that never died in Adam,[5] but in the serpent angel, so will never be made alive by Christ, but must surely perish eternally, as hath been before-mentioned.

Therefore, you Presbytery examine yourselves, whether you are of the seed of the serpent or the seed of Adam, and though you are a great people, and mightily multiplied in a few years, yet look about you and trust not to your Gods, for they will deceive you.[6]

The next church is the Independent, so called, because it seems to have no dependance on outward ordinances and ceremonies, and yet these use baptism, but baptize no children except those of believing parents.[7]

And as to their doctrine or articles of faith, it is the same as the Presbytery, only more moderate in judgment, and are safer from persecution; only they differ from them in the point of their ministry; for the lay people chuse their own ministers out of themselves, and

---

[1] L.
[2] M.
[3] N. I. Cor. xv. 22.
[4] O.
[5] Luke xix. 9 and 10.
[6] P.
[7] Q.

divests them again at their own will and pleasure, and so are but ministers of men.

These four churches have their commissions from men, and are chosen by the magistrates power and authority, therefore the magistrates appoints them a maintenance.

The Baptists are the next church, and sets up their ministry from the letter of scripture; so they act from the dead letter, having no commission from God or man; they baptize no children, but what profess faith and repentance before they are baptized; and so have their name from that; yet, with the repetition of the letter of the scripture.[1] Their doctrine of free-will, and of Christ dying for all men; they thunder in a pulpit of their unknown God; in their Trinity of Persons; reaching no higher in this, than the other four churches before them, and the fifth monarchy men are only a branch of them, as the Antinomian is of the Independent.

The next church or sect is the Ranter who broke out in this last age, in the time of the civil wars in England;[2] from these came forth all manner of wickedness, which gave them the name of Ranter; but before they fell into that high Rant, their first principle was this, (to wit) that God was a spirit and lived and reigned and ruled in all things; so that all things were God, or came out of God, and would turn into God again.

For they held one Almighty Power,[3] and that power was God, and how that God, heaven, and hell were all one in the root; and therefore, writes of them, saying, Who knows but as God who is an infinite spirit, was in unity with itself from eternity; so all those things which appear now in a contrariety of names and titles, of God, Devil, Heaven, and Hell; may hereafter come to agree in one sweet harmony and union together; as all waters run into one sea, and yet no fuller, even so saith he, will all things run into God, who will be all in all. But this Man afterwards turns Quaker, but still holds to his former doctrine of God being a spirit without a body.

From such principled men as these are, came those mockers and scoffers, which Paul, Jude, and Peter prophecied of, who scoff at a day of judgment; saying, where is the promise of such a day?[4] do not all things continue alike as they were from the beginning? So their doctrine was the most tempting principle to sin of any that ever appeared,

---

[1] R.
[2] R.
[3] Isaac Pennington, Esq.
[4] II. Pet. iii. 3.

From these came forth all new invented blasphemy, bitter imprecations, and horrid oaths.[1]

But God blessed for evermore, hath sent a commission into the world, to seal up such persons to the wrath to come, and all such as desire the same, and mock at true prophecy, and the true believers thereof, and at a day of judgment of ungodly men.[2]

The 7th and last anti-church of Europe is the Quakers, many of whom proceed from the Ranters; who being smitten in conscience for their wickedness, thought to heal themselves of their deadly wounds of soul condemning thoughts, by a more precise life of seeming purity. They are called Quakers from their witchcraft fits of foaming at the mouth, when they were moved to speak in a trembling condition. One John Robbins was the head of this sect, called Quakers, as John Tanee was the head of the Ranters or mystery Babylon.[3] So Robbins was the head of all false prophets, and false Christ's, being the last great antichrist prophecied of in the second of Thessalonians. When his wickedness was at the full, the Lord sent his messenger to denounce his judgment upon the prince of this prince of devils, and the heads of several of this last church, for robbing Christ of his glory, for they have got their God and Christ all within them; but their witchcraft fits are now gone.[4] Observe, how they deny the person of God without them, and are now but as other people, only making a bawling of their God and Christ within them, which light is discovered to be nothing else, but the light of the moral law accusing or else excusing according to their actions, as it doth the heathen.[5]

Therefore, said one of them,[6] let us but soberly consider what Christ is, and we shall the better know, whether moral men are to be reckoned christians; for what is Christ but meekness, justice, and mercy; can we then deny a meek man to be a christian.

Thus meekness and justice is their Christ; yet their Christ hath no body;[7] but their bodies must be his body, and that legal or natural light, must be their light and Christ. They also believe that Christ is not distinct from the saints;[8] and that the soul say they, is not a creature, but infinite in itself, and without beginning or ending;

---

[1] S.
[2] T.
[3] Thes. ii.
[4] W.
[5] Romans.
[6] William Penn's address to the Protestants.
[7] Fox's Mystery page 20. 246.
[8] Hogwell's Book, p. 29, 90 & 222.

another of them says, that they have the spirit of God, and are equal with God.[1]

These, their principles, are taken from the Ranters. They are all God's in their own esteem, and they make no more of the blood of Christ, than the blood of another man.

Doth thou look for Christ at he was the son of Mary to appear outwardly in a bodily shape to save thee, (said George Whitehead, the Quaker)[2] thou mayest look until thine eyes drop out, before thou wilt see such an appearance.[3]

Now such men as own no other spiritual God, but what is within them, are in the deepest darkness of all mankind, concerning (rod and his worship, or they who worship the literal word light, instead of Jesus Christ the eternal word, as saith this last witness.

And so much as to the seven churches of Europe, who are guided by the spirit of antichrist; and ever since Cain, anti-christ hath been in this world, but Christ came into this world when Abel was born.[4] So that antichrist was before Christ. So that for these sects, there is no pleading antiquity, for the proof of a true church.

CHAP. XXIII.

But ye, beloved building up yourselves on your most holy faith, praying in the Holy Ghost, keep yourselves in the love of God, looking for the mercy of our Lord Jesus Christ unto eternal life. And of some have compassion, making a difference. And others save with fear, pulling them out of the fire; hating even the garments spotted by the flesh—ver. 20, 21, 22, and 23.

FIRST, here is nothing of difficulty in these exhortations, but may be well understood by such as have true faith in the doctrine of the true commissioned messengers of God.

As it is faith that builds the house, so the house stands by faith, if a holy faith, then a holy house, for the church of God is God's House, and the faith which the Apostles preached was that rock on which the church was built.

---

[1] X.
[2] Whitehead's nature of Christianity.
[3] Y.
[4] Z.

For when Peter had made a confession of his faith unto his Lord,[1] he made answer saying, that upon that rock he would build his church, that is as this last witness interprets it,[2] upon this faith thou art of Peter, will I build my church; so that the gates of hell shall not prevail against it; and so it is by every commissioned prophet, for his faith and commission is the rock for all the seed of faith to build upon.

Again, the last witness hath further said,[3] that every commission, whether of Moses and the Prophets, or of Christ and his Apostles, or of the Witnesses of the Spirit, is a rock for all the seed of faith to build upon; neither will the gates of hell prevail against the faith, which is built upon this Commission of the Spirit, no more than it did in Peter and the other Apostles, but it shall be as a rock in this last age.

And when a commission doth smite the rock,[4] that is, by giving a true interpretation of the scriptures, there will waters of life flow from thence; for there is no balm of Gilead to be had, but in one personal God, even Christ Jesus only.[5]

This faith keeps this church in the love of God, which is no other as Jude saith in the next verse, but Jesus Christ, and on him alone they wait for his mercy, and his coming, to give them the reward of their faith, which is eternal life, and to crown his own gifts of faith and prayer.[6] As thus, saith Jude, praying in the Holy Ghost; from which we may observe, that no prayer is acceptable to God, but what flows from the Holy Ghost, that is, from the spirit of divine faith.

Now, in this we may know, that this faith must be first given to a saint before it can be asked, and therefore it must be quickened in the seed, before it can cry Abba Father; for no sacrifice is acceptable with God, but what is offered up in faith.[7] For without faith it is impossible impossible to please God, as saith the scriptures; so that it is not from books of other men's work or form.[8] And though our Lord gives a pattern of Prayer to his disciples before they had their commission, yet we do not find that they ever made use of that form of words, but only in virtue and spirit of them. For a vain-glorious worshipper or a literalist, when he prays in these words of, forgiving his trespasses, as he forgives such as trespass against him; if he has not mercy in his soul to his brethren, he curseth himself

---

[1] A.
[2] Letter to E. S. Dated July, 14, 1744.
[3] B.
[4] C.
[5] In a Letter to T. T. March 14, 1744.
[6] D.
[7] E.
[8] F.

Again, all such as pray to be seen of men, the scripture brands as hypocrites.

But as this third and last commission of the spirit saith,[1] that where the light is spiritual, they that hear of immortal glory, sounds a trumpet no more in their prayers, than their alms; and that the excellency of mercy is above all sacrifice; and also it is that true prayer consists not in words, but in the inward speaking of the spirit in all stillness of soul, which is the only prayer of all those that are under the teachings of the spirit.

But glittering words, flowing from natural parts only, in merciless men, are an abomination to God.

CHAP. XIV.

Jude exhorteth the saints to keep themselves in the love of God, and to wait for the mercy of Jesus Christ.

ALL that is acted and done by faith in building up that spiritual house, (as hath been shewed in verse 22), he lets them understand that some of the elect seed were deluded by them so far, as to take a liberty in voluptuousness and the works of the flesh.

Now, in the 22nd verse, the Apostle exhorts them to a purity of life, giving them to understand, that if grace is not prevalent, sin will be committed, having its several stains and spots; and advises them to beware, and to have that wisdom as to distinguish between offender and offenders, and therefore, saith he, of some have compassion making a difference.

Now in this word compassion doth consist the tender love of the saints in the time of a commission or true ministry, each one according to his light, endeavouring to reclaim such as are brought into error, either as to judgment or practice; and there is a difference to be put between offender and offenders, because some offend through ignorance, and some in obstinacy, causing division, as also of evil conversation.

These under the Apostle's commission were, cut off by church censure,[2] as the man who committed fornication, whom Paul ordered to excommunicated,[3] which was done by the church, to let him see that he was left to satan, which was his own fleshly lusts, whereby he

---

[1] I.
[2] I.
[3] I. Cor. v. 5.

might know how that in that state he could not be saved: yet this man proved an elect vessel; and he was three days under this excommunication, suffering for his sin, in all which time he was under the terror of the law, and an accusing conscience which were his judges, and this made that little spark of faith cry out for mercy, which when Paul did write his 2nd Epistle to Corinth, he hearing by Titus of his repentance, exhorted believers to forgive him, and comfort him, telling him that his repentance was sufficient, and a repentance not to be repented of.[1]

Thus Paul became to the saints, as well as Jude, examples of pity and compassion, and exhorting the believers that in meekness they should instruct those that oppose themselves; if God, with a peradventure, would give them a repentance.

Verse 23rd, others save with fear.

Now to save them with fear according to my faith is, to let them know the danger of their condition, that if such and such sins be not repented of before they die, they cannot be saved, as it was by the man aforesaid.[2]

This was the fire they were plucked out of, and the whole purgatory, for the motion of sin is a fire, and the moral law being written in that sinning nature, keeps it burning and in torment to all such as are not saved by this fear, or delivered from this spotted garment; being the old man and the seed of the fallen-angel, which must be mortified by a law of perfect faith; then is sin cast out and the law which blew up that flame, is quiet in that soul.[3]

The elect of God though they may fall, yet not totally; but if they do fall, so as to break the moral law in act and deed, it is in the time of a true ministry, which hath that quickening power of giving faith and pardon of sin.[4]

But the elect of God that live between a commission, or in such a time as there is no true ministry; the elective love of God preserves them from committing sin by act as aforesaid, which is plain by the Apostle Jude in his last verse, saying thus;

Now unto him that is able to keep you from falling, before the presence of his glory with exceeding joy, to the only wise God our

---

[1] II. Cor. ii. v. 6, 7, 8, 9.
[2] K.
[3] L.
[4] M.

Saviour be glory, majesty, dominion and power, both now and for ever. Amen.[1]

Now here doth the Apostle bring his Epistle to a conclusion, and leaves the saints to the safe keeping of the same Lord,[2] which he commanded them to for preservation and vocation, which was no other than the Lord Jesus Christ, as in verse 1st saying, preserved in Jesus Christ, and tells them that he is able to keep them from falling, and to preserve them from heresies.[3]

And Paul tells the Phillippians that Christ is able to subdue all things unto himself. And in another place, that he is able to succour them that are tempted.[4] So that nothing is too hard for Christ to do, when his Godhead spirit moves him to it; he had power of himself to lay down his life, and he had power of himself to take it up again; and how could this be, if he were not God; neither could he be judge of the quick and the dead, if he were not God.

Neither could the Saints with all the Prophets and Apostles be raised from death, and brought into the presence of his glory, with bodies like unto his own glorious body, (which occasions that great and exceeding joy of theirs) if he was not the only Lord and Saviour; neither would the Apostles have offered up that praise and glory to him, had there been any other God distinct from him; neither would they have ascribed to him all glory, majesty, dominion and power, if he was not the very Alpha and Omega.

Therefore, without all controversy, according to the doctrine of this Apostle, Christ is the only and alone true God; so shall I conclude this Epistle, with the doctrine of this last Commission, who finishes this last Mystery of God, saying, there is none but Christ; there is none but Christ; and no other God but the man Jesus Christ, though men or angels should gainsay it.[5] And blessed are all those that are not offended with this great Truth.—Amen.

---

[1] O.
[2] P.
[3] Phil. iii. 21.
[4] Q.
[5] R.

DICTIONARY OF NATIONAL BIOGRAPHY

SADDINGTON, JOHN (1634?-1679), Muggletonian, was born at Arnesby, Leicestershire, about 1634, and was engaged in London in the sugar trade. He was among the earliest adherents to the system of John Reeve (1608-1658) [q. v.] and Lodowicke Muggleton [q. v.], and hence was known as the 'eldest son' of their movement. He was a tall, handsome man, and an intelligent writer; his strenuous support in 1671 was of essential service to Muggleton's cause. He died in London on 11 Sept, 1679. Two only of his pieces have been printed: 1. 'A Prospective Glass for Saints and Sinners' 1673, 4to; reprinted, Deal, 1823, 8vo. 2. 'The Articles of True Faith,' written in 1675, but not printed till 1830, 8vo. Of his unprinted pieces in the Muggletonian archives, the most important is 'The Wormes Conquest,' a poem of 1677, on the trial of Muggleton, who is the 'worme.'

[Saddington's printed and manuscript writings; Muggleton's Acts and Letters; Ancient and Modern Muggletonians (Transactions of Liverpool Lit. and Phil. Soc. 4 April 1870); Smith's Bibliotheca Anti-Quakeriana, 1873, pp. 321 sq.]   A. G.

A
PROSPECTIVE-GLASS
FOR
SAINTS & SINNERS:

Whereby may appear and be seen,

1. The Author's Life expressed in the first Epistle.

2. That there is no true Peace of mind in those that account themselves Believers, so long as they lead a corrupt life.

3. What great Enemies the Riches of this World, and Poverty are to Truth.

4. What that truth and true knowledge is which giveth satisfaction to the mind of Man in this life.

And several other things necessary to salvation.

BY JOHN SADDINGTON,

A true Believer of the Witnesses of the Spirit, sent forth
by the immediate voice of God Almighty,
in the Year, 1651.

PRINTED IN THE YEAR 1673, AND REPRINTED FOR J. MAY,
BY J. B. UNDERDOWN, DEAL

1823

AN
EPISTLE IN GENERAL

Courteous Reader,

IT is to be hoped upon thy perusal of this little Book, called a Prospective-Glass, thou wilt see and discern therein a rule to walk by.

2. It directeth to no other work but to keep that peace which every true believer maketh with God, whenever he or she doth receive truth in the love thereof, and to keep themselves unspotted in this world.

3. To use moderation in all things, to the glory of God, and peace of their own minds; whereby others will be encouraged by their peaceable spirits, to come to the knowledge of the truth.

4. It was neither the lives nor conversation of the saints that are now called believers; nor the fewness or small number of them that believed; nor the multitude of despisers that caused me to believe.

5. But as soon as the declaration of the witnesses of the spirit sounded in my ears, the scales fell from my eyes, and immediately I did see that it was truth.

6. And blessed be the most high God, by believing of his last messengers, I have had the assurance of salvation these seventeen years and upwards.

7. By experience do I write what manner of lives the saints ought to live. And because I assuredly know thereby, that there can be no true peace in any believer so long as there is any manner of evil acted by him, therefore have I prepared this Glass, wherein he may see his own folly, and learn to resist every thing that is known to break the peace of the mind.

8. Every thing that breaketh the peace of the mind is an enemy to truth, and every one that is a despiser of truth is an enemy to God, and to their own souls. And there is no spiritual truth, or true knowledge of the true God Christ Jesus, but what is declared by the witnesses of the spirit, as will appear in my following discourse.

9, Did I not know myself armed: with moderation, and that I had overcome those enemies that formerly were disturbing, my peace, I durst not have published this to the world.

10. By publishing hereof I shall become a mark for every one to shoot at: Blessed be God, there is none that can fling dirt in my face for any evil actions practised by me formerly.

11. Now some will shoot their arrows at me in love, others in hatred, but blessed be my God, I am able to withstand them, and there is no envious arrow able to hurt me.

12. Though this small treatise of mine is not beautified with the excellency of man's speech (which is gained by human learning, and therefore called Man's Wisdom, which is at enmity with God) but it is declared in plainness of speech, and in sincerity and truth by that faith in me; which is at peace with God.

13. Yet I know I shall be judged by those that the world calleth godly, wise and learned, to be incapable to know the mind of God in the scriptures, because I have not been brought up and educated in human learning.

14. But though I am not so strongly furnished with man's strength, which is the several languages taught by men: Yet blessed be my Redeemer, I am so well taught by that ancient school-master, the nature of faith in me, whereby I am able to declare the truth.

15. Therefore let none be so conceited of learned men, as if the word of God came only to them, and from them; for we know that most part of the holy scriptures were written-by such men as were not educated in human learning.

16. The Pharisaical Jews and Sadduces who were most learned, could not find out the time when Christ should come, by all their learning; And so still, all those who by the world are accounted weak and foolish, are made wise and valiant in the service of Christ,

17. If a man could read all the languages in the world, he could not by that find out, know, or believe what the true God is in his form and nature. Yet to him that knoweth what the true God is, human learning is a good help and hand-maid to enable him to illustrate and set forth the glorious things of eternity, whereby the seed of reason might the more admire them.

18, For my part, when I was but a child, I delighted so much in learning, that I was never well contented but when I was at school learning to read and write; and I did take more delight in reading the bible and other good books (as the Practice of Piety, Prayer Books, and the like) than could be expected from one of my age, this was the first degree of knowledge I had.

19. And I am confident had my parents then been able and willing to have kept me at school, I should have attained to as much human learning as could have been taught me by man.

20. The next thing that I took delight in, was learning such Catechisms as were set out by learned men, and hearing of sermons, keeping close to the church. The Presbyterians being then in power, and very powerful they were in their way.

21. Then according to my knowledge, I thought that was the true church, and that the ministers thereof were the only ministers of God. This was the second degree of knowledge I had, and there I staid,

thinking that all those who opposed them were those false teachers that should come in sheep's cloathing, and daub with untempered mortar.

22. Whilst I thought myself secure there, being still but young; for, about the year 1652 I was not above 18 years of age, I saw a book intituled, sword doubled, or The Terror of Tythes, Written by a Minister; that all those that were ministers of the gospel (or otherwise called themselves so), he himself being one of them.

23. I say, he proved all of them that took tythes to be murderers, oppressors of the poor, and robbers of God, for which he said he was so tormented in his mind, that he was forced to rise out of his bed in the night, and to go into a secret place to repent of that wickedness.

24. And to that purpose did he write several sheets of paper. When I had viewed that book, then was I lost in myself, because those Ministers in whom then I put my trust, were such as took tythes.

25. Then I knew not which way to go to find out truth, yet still I went to hear the Presbyterians, and sometimes the Independents and Baptists. And I was very zealous in praying and repeating of sermons. I could have sat from morning to evening to have heard those that were counted able men preach.

26. I could never find any difference in the foundation between the Presbyterians, Independents and the Baptists; for though they differ something in point of worship, yet they all own one God, and one Devil.

27. They all hold forth that the soul of man is immortal, and such like. They all teach pleasing things to the ear, yet I could find no more satisfaction by hearing one than I did by hearing the other in point of salvation. None of them could give me any assurance of that; and the assurance of my salvation was all that I looked after.

28. Had the Quakers come forth plentifully a little sooner they would have catched me with their snares; for when that trumpet first sounded in mine ears, they came forth with such a seeming pure language and life, which I from my childhood was a lover of.

29. But blessed be my God, I was settled in the knowledge of truth before I came to be acquainted with that Antichristian spirit in the Quakers, who deny, or will not acknowledge the resurrection of the body of Christ.

30. About the latter end of the year 1654, I heard of The witnesses of the Spirit, which I had heard of in 1653, by the name of two prophets, then prisoners in old Bridewell, London, for declaring their commission which they had received from the Throne of Glory, which gave them power to be the chief judges of all spiritual matters in this world.

31. But when I heard of them by a fellow-prentice of mine, that was in Bridewell at the same time, and in the same room with them; he telling me there was two prophets there. I having read that many false prophets should come in the last times, I thought they might

be two of them, Also the second time I heard of them, I was not satisfied.

32. Again, I was informed of them by a friend of mine, of whom I borrowed a book of theirs, intituled A Transcendent Spiritual Treatise; upon the reading whereof I found such excellent truths declared, that I was not able to resist or oppose any thing that was written therein, but immediately became obedient unto it.

33. As soon the voice of the true shepherd had sounded in mine ears, the light of truth shined so bright into my soul, that I could see my salvation purchased with the blood of Christ, the only and alone true God.

34. Though there is no outward miracles done by the Witnesses of the Spirit, yet that glorious language and heavenly matter which is written by them, (which is the work of the spirit) maketh it appear that they are what they declare themselves to be.

35. Prophesying serveth for believers, and signs and wonders are to convince unbelievers, but not to convert them.

There is enough written by the Witnesses of the Spirit to convince the whole world, if they would take the pains to read it.

36. Therefore I desire all that read this little book, and desire to be further satisfied of the matters therein contained, that they will have recourse to the writings of the witnesses themselves

37. There, they who have discerning eyes, being of the seed of the woman, or faith, will be fully satisfied concerning all things of eternity.

JOHN SADDINGTON.

AN

EPISTLE

WRITTEN

TO THE BELIEVERS OF THE WITNESSES OF THE SPIRIT.

MY clearly beloved Spiritual Friends in London, the several Counties of Middlesex, Leicester, Nottingham, Stafford, Derby, Cambridge, Essex, Kent, and all other places in England; I salute you in the spirit of truth.

2. Not forgetting those in Ireland, Spain, the Indies, or in any other remote place in the world, who are all my beloved Friends and brethren in the knowledge of truth.

3. If there be any among you that is given to lasciviousness, drunkenness, idleness, passion, breaking of promises, or any other vice whatsoever, let it all be forsaken for the truth's sake.

4. Every evil action that is committed by a believer doth disturb the well-spring of faith in him; whereby it cannot run so clear as his doth in him that is cleansed from evil, as in this Glass you may see.

5. I was moved by the seed of faith in me, long ago, to write a book to the same purpose that I have written this, but when I well considered what I was to undertake, I had several stops put to it.

6. Sometimes I thought there was no occasion for me to write, so long as there was a prophet alive. Also I thought myself insufficient to write that which should be printed, because I was not a latin scholar.

7. But the chief thing that kept me from writing a book of, or for the life and conversation of the saints was, because I could not do it without reflecting upon myself.

8. So I did forbear publishing any thing, until such time as that I had cast the beam out of mine own eye first, that I might see clearly to east the mote out of my brother's eye.

9. Therefore I desire you all, not to think that I have written this book to charge any of you with sin; but to be the means of restraining you from running wilfully into that which is evil, and a dishonor to truth.

10. I have been for several years together moved by that seed of faith in me, to write against those things, which by experience I know breaketh the peace of the mind; and that well-spring of faith which sprung up so plentifully in me, and caused me to write this small treatise; I hope it will, and do heartily wish, and desire it may prove beneficial to other believers, as it hath done to me, and cause them to

cease from all manner of evil, and wholly follow after that which is righteous in the sight of God and men, as I now do, blessed be my God for it; and for no other end have I published this to the world.

11. Thus desiring that the said well-spring of faith in every one of you may run so clear, that every one who heareth of it, may desire to have some of the same to refresh their spirits, and to allay their thirsts, which is best done by the increasing in purity, piety, and practice: and so conclude this Epistle.

JOHN SADDINGTON.

CHAP I.

What manner of lives the Saints ought to live in this World.

IT was the saying of the Prophet Isaiah, chap. viii. ver. 20. To the Law and to the Testimony, if they speak not according to this word, it is because there is no light in them.

2. Though I am no prophet, nor the son of a prophet, yet by that light of faith in me, which I have received by believing the report of the Lord's last prophets do I bear witness, that the whole law and testimony of the scriptures are true.

3. There are three testimonies, laws, or records which agree in one on this earth, as it is written. The first, Moses and the other prophets, signified the water. The second, was Christ and his apostles, which signified the blood. The third, the last messengers, or prophets herein mentioned, which signifieth the spirit; and all these agree in one.

4. They that bear not witness to the testimonies of these three; it is, because there is no light in them. And let the testimony of a good conscience also bear witness in all true believers.

5. They who are true believers of the third and last testament of God, sent forth and declared to the world in this last age, are also true believers of the two former, and do walk in the true light.

6. Let all those that have received, or shall receive the true light, so walk, that their temporal actions may not dim the light of their spiritual knowledge.

7. Let those take as much delight in walking uprightly before God, and in the sight of men, as they do in declaring that knowledge which they have of God unto men.

8. Then their light will shew itself to be that true and gracious light, by which all true believers may see their way to eternal life.

9. Let no saint break his own peace by any unseemly action; but let them walk in all respects as becometh saints; for the fruits of the spirit of life is all goodness, righteousness, and truth.

10. They that are believers of the witnesses of the spirit, and walk contrary to the spirit of truth, do not only break their own peace, but they do also lay a stumbling stone tot others to fall at, which causeth truth to be evil spoken of.

11. It hath pleased our God to send his last messengers into the world in these our days, to declare unto us, secret and sacred things, that were hid from all former ages and generations of men.

12. We do assuredly know what, and where our God is; that his eternal spirit is clothed with that blessed body of Christ Jesus glorified, our blessed Redeemer, whom the heaven of glory will retain until the end of time.

13. At his next corning time will be swallowed up into eternity.

14. Christ will come no more to reign upon this earth with his saints, as it is imagined by many, but they are not taught by the spirit of truth.

15. Let not us who have the true knowledge of God and our own nature, walk as if we were ignorant of what we profess to know.

16. But let us make use of our spiritual wisdom in such sort, as that the world may stand in admiration, and may have cause to say of us, verily, and of a truth, the nature of God is in them, they are the chosen people of God.

14. Our light ought to shine clear in this world. It is written, A candle is not lighted to be put under a bushel, but on a candlestick, So every one that hath his knowledge enlightened in the truth, with the light of life eternal, he must let that light shine in the world.

18. He that hath true faith (the nature whereof is to purify both heart and life), if he walk otherwise, contrary to what knowledge he professeth he hath received, (especially before the faces of unbelievers) it doth darken his faith so much, that the light of it cannot be seen no more than the light of a candle that is under a bushel.

19. Therefore let not, us that have a pure and clear light, walk as if we were in darkness, or were men of no understanding.

20. It is a shame for one that is a true believer, and a saint of God, to carry himself so disorderly as to be checked by devils for his disorderly carriage.

21. I desire, and exhort every one that is a true believer of the Lord's last-messengers, to walk circumspectly in their lives and conversation.

22. And as the apostle exhorted his in his time, Let no evil communication come out your mouths, but rather that which is edifying unto others, lest we grieve the holy spirit of God in us, and make ourselves a reproach.

23. The world is ignorant of what we are made to know, even the way to salvation.

24. None in the world can have assurance of their salvation in this life, but those that are believers of the spiritual commission given by the Lord to his last messengers, as aforesaid.

25. I do not plead for righteous acting, thinking thereby to merit heaven, for we have gained the assurance of that by believing the report of the Lord's true ministers, Which are the Witnesses of the Spirit.

26. Our blessed Saviour himself said, John, vi. 29. the whole work of the Lord was to believe in him whom he had sent; therefore it is by faith, and not by any other works that we are saved.

27. Yet where there is true faith, let not the righteousness of the law be wanting.—Righteous actions are very good ornaments for to set forth and illustrate faith.

28. He that breaketh the law, or worketh any manner of evil, breaketh his own peace; and if a man be not at peace in himself, how can he be at peace with God. You know it is written, If our consciences accuse us, God is greater than our consciences.

29. Therefore, this I would have all believers do, to walk uprightly before God, and to keep themselves blameless and unspotted in this world, and to walk with a pure language and life as becometh saints.

30. I do not desire that a greater burthen should be laid upon the saints than they are able to bear; for I have learned to forgive my brother, if he sinneth against me or against his own soul.

31. Nevertheless, I would not have any saint to abuse himself in any thing that is accounted evil, for, as St. Paul saith, Those things that are lawful for us to do, are not convenient to be done.

32. Let is follow after those things which bringeth peace to ourselves and edifieth others, as meekness, love, and chastity, with all righteousness which is acceptable with our God Christ Jesus glorified, and approved of by men, whereby the truth may not be evil spoken of

33. Neither let us give occasion to devils, (devilish men and women) by our bad walking to speak evil of those glorious truths, which they are not worthy to know.

34. But let us walk humbly before our God, that our innocent lives may be a pattern to the world, that have no other hopes of glory but by their moral righteousness, which is of no value in comparison to true faith.

35. Though moral righteousness is a very good and decent ornament to set forth faith, yet he that is ever so moral, or endued with the righteousness or the law, if he be a despiser of truth, by not having faith to believe the messengers of God, and their declarations, all his righteousness will stand him in no stead in the day of the Lord's account.

36. As for us, who have true faith to believe the report of the Lord's last true prophets and Witnesses of the Spirit. Let us be clothed with righteousness as with a garment.

37. Because we are found worthy to be of the family of God, and none in the world but the believers above-mentioned, are chosen to be of his household; therefore, there is no garment but that of righteousness suitable for a saint to wear in this world.

38. Wherefore, we must be sure to walk sincerely in all things, that we may honor our Father, our King, our Lord and Master, even the Lord Jesus Christ.

39. He alone is Lord both of heaven and earth, and he hath clothed us with rich and costly robes, the garment of salvation, and by this we know he love thus, because these robes which he hath freely given us, cost him so dear a rate as his Godhead life, and his most precious blood.

40. What care therefore ought we to take, least at any time we should defile these garments, which could not have been bought with

any other price, but with the blood of the eternal God, which was shed by the unbelieving Jews, according to his eternal decree.

41. That he might raise all, both Jew and Gentile, that do truly believe and own him to be their God and Saviour to a glorious and everliving life, in that Kingdom of Glory where they shall behold the fiery glorious face of God to all eternity.

42. And he will likewise raise all unbelieving Jews and Gentiles, to a shameful and painful ever-dying death.

43. When they are in possession of that misery which they were foretold of, then will they cry and howl, but all in vain; and the knowledge of their abiding in that torment to eternity, will make them blaspheme the name of our God continually.

44. And the remembrance of their despising of the Declaration and Messengers of that glorious God Christ, when they where in mortality, will be as fresh fuel laid upon a fire, for it will make their tormented souls and bodies burn more fiercely.

45. The Creator hath decreed that punishment for all unbelievers, that their souls shall bring forth spiritual dark bodies at the resurrection, which souls and bodies will burn together hotter than natural fire and brimstone.

46. So on the contrary, when they that are the elect of God, shall be in possession of that kingdom, of glory, where that blessed body of God is, and where Moses, Elias, and the holy angels are resident.

47. Then shall we be full of joy unspeakable, where we shall sing hallelujahs and praises unto our God, our king, and our redeemer, the Lord Jesus Christ.

48. And the remembrance of those good actions which we acted for Christ in the time of our mortality will cause new joys to arise, in us. And then shall we sing aloud unto our God, which, sitteth upon the throne of glory to eternity.

49. Now we knowing how that the remembrance of good things acted by us in this life, will advance our glory in the life to come; let us be sure, therefore, to do all, things that will be to the glory of God, and honor to his commission given forth in these our days, of which we are partakers in that we have faith to believe the report of his last prophets.

50. Again, it is good for us, to leave off frothy discourse and, simple actions, for such things when afterwards considered, do often disturb the peace of a saint.

51. because when such things are acted by believers, they make words of truth seem as idle stories to the people of the world, who understand not the power and liberty of believers in the time of a commission.

52. But nevertheless, I would have all believers learn to be wise, sober, and moderate in all things; because when words of truth are spoken by a sober, wise man, whose life and conversation is suitable

to what he doth declare, his words make a great impression upon the hearts of them that hear him.

53. They who love moral righteousness, though they are ignorant of truth, yet they are very zealous in worshipping of their unknown God, and allow not of any wickedness.

54. I say when these sort of ignorant men hear truth spoken, and declared by those that they look upon to be as righteous as themselves in all things, (except worshipping of God in outward ordinances as they do) then are they smitten to the heart.

55. When they hear those that know truth, and what the true God is, declare that the worshipping of God in outward ordinances, to be seen of men is of no value, and that all the righteousness of the law is of no effect, to those that despise the Witnesses of the spirit, and the doctrine declared by them.

56. Then do those, and such like words take possession of the mind of those righteous men, which hear them spoken by wise sober men, and they cannot dispossess them any more

57. When words of truth have once taken place in the mind of man, either that faith in him doth feed so plentifully on them, that the nourishment it receiveth from them, causeth it to grow up to the assurance of eternal life.

58. Or else the reason in man is enraged, because it cannot remove those words of truth which, have taken possession in the mind.

59. So that truth doth torment the minds of those in this who cannot receive it to the saving of their Souls.

60. These things hundreds can witness the truth of by Experience, some to their eternal joy, and others to their everlasting sorrow.

61. Thus do we see what power and strength the ministry of the spirit hath upon all persons to whom it hath been clearly demonstrated.

62. The righteousness of the law (as I have said) is a good ornament to set forth that truth declared by the Witnesses of the Spirit.

63. Wherefore my earnest desire is that all true believers may be dressed therewith, that the unbelievers may have no just cause to speak evil of those men that have faith in the true God.

CHAP II.

How hard a matter it is to please the Devil; and what those are to believe that expect comfort by believing; and what saints are to strive about.

I KNOW there are a sort of people that will find fault with the soberest men living. For if a man be of a melancholy disposition, and not of a cheerful spirit, when such a man declareth truth, then its probable it will be said his melancholy spirit hath made him mad, and they will not mind his words; because they think those things declared by him, are but some whimseys which arise out of his melancholy mind.

2. Secondly, if a man be of a merry disposition and given to civil jesting, then those that are ignorant of truth, will be ready to say, this man cannot have that knowledge he professeth to have of God, for if he had, he would not be so merry.

3. For say they, truth is solid and civil; and though they see no incivility in their mirth, yet they will be finding fault with it, so that it is a very hard matter to please the devil; I mean the devilish natures of men and women.

4. There are many who are of the seed of the serpent, that are more zealous in the way of their worshipping the unknown God, and more precise in their words, than many saints are.

5. Therefore, it is no marvel to us to hear and know, that the devil or his ministers are transformed as into angels of light; for we know who the devil is, and who are his ministers.

6. We also know, that their Pharisaical way of ceremonial worshipping of their unknown God, seemeth far more pure to the eye of reason, than the saints more plain way of worshipping of that glorified man Christ Jesus in spirit and truth.

7. Him they are, or ought to know to be the only and alone true God; and truly to know Jesus Christ to be the only true God, is life eternal.

8. Therefore, by our knowing and true believing that Christ was not only the son of God, and saviour of the world; but that he alone was the eternal Father and Creator of both worlds, angels and men, we have eternal life abiding in us.

9. And by our knowing the decree of God from the creation of the world, in his disposing of the two seeds, the seed of the woman and the seed of the serpent; and knowing the natures of them, and what they are, is the substance whereby we know the assurance of our salvation in this life.

10. Again, I know many will ask me, How they shall come to that knowledge, whereby they may be assured of their salvation?

11. To this I answer. There no other way for any man to be assured of his salvation in this life, but by believing that Christ, the true God, did speak to John Reeve, to the hearing of the ear, and that he did give John Reeve and Lodowick Muggleton, commission to declare his mind unto this bloody and unbelieving world, as is declared by them, and it is sufficient to believe their doctrine only.

12. For some will say, they believe there is no God but Christ; others will say, they believe the soul dieth with the body; and some will say, there is no devil but men and women.

13. But I say, that only to believe these things is of no value; for except a man can believe the doctors to be true, there can be no benefit by their doctrines declared by them.

14. Therefore, whosoever expects peace and satisfaction of mind by the doctrine declared by the Witnesses of the Spirit; they must first set to their seals, that they were truly sent forth by the true God, to make his mind known in this our age.

15. What man can find any peace or comfort by reading the Scriptures, and believing that Moses did punish the Egyptians with several plagues.

16 And to believe that the apostles did care many diseases, and suffer many punishments to be inflicted upon them for Christ's sake.

17. Or to believe that Christ did cast out many devils, and raise the dead; I say to believe these things, and many more that are spoken of in scripture, and yet cannot believe that Moses was a true Prophet, and that Peter and Paul and the rest were true Apostles, or that Jesus was a true Christ?

18. I say, they that cannot believe these things can have no true peace or comfort, nor any benefit by believing any part of the Scriptures.

19. Nay, if it were possible for a man to believe all that is declared by the prophets of old, and the apostles, and by Christ himself, and yet cannot believe that these men that declared such things were true ministers; then all their faith is vain, and will stand them in no stead in the day of the Lord.

20. So on the contrary, though there may be many temporal failings among the saints; yet by their true believing in God and his messengers, all their sins will be forgiven them, and their faith will make them whole.

21. But I would not have any true believer take hold of these words of mine, whereby to Five in sin, or to lead a corrupt life; for that evil committed by the saints can no ways be justified, but their sins will be pardoned, because it was for the sins of believers for which Christ died, and his death was so effectual, that none that truly believe in him shall perish, though their sins be ever so great.

22. But if there be any believers that do lead a corrupt life, they can have no peace in their minds, because the corruptness of their natures doth drown that peace, which would flow from their faith.

23. But all these believers that lead a just and holy life, have the fountain of peace in them, which is past the knowledge of man to express the comfort of.

24, Now let every believer strive to excel each other in virtue, that their faith may pour forth like rivers of living water, that every one which heareth of the truth may desire to receive it.

CHAP. III.

What an enemy the riches of this world is to truth. And how all things are possible for God to do, which his glory moveth him to do, And how the world's riches is of the nature of a loadstone.

AGAIN, all those that are willing to yield obedience to faith, whereby they may live in perfect peace in this life; they must be sure to withstand the grand enemies of truth, which are riches and poverty. Therefore, doth St. Paul desire, that he may be fed with food convenient for him, neither with riches, lest he should boast, nor with poverty, lest he should steal.

2. First, let no saint strive for honor in this world, for that is a cord which draweth many to destruction, both in this life and that which is to come.

3. We see how hard a thing it is for any man to join with truth, that is rich and in honor in this world; because he knoweth that he cannot keep his honor among the great ones of this world, if he worship God only in spirit and truth.

4. Therefore it is in vain for any that received the truth in the love thereof, for to think to keep his spiritual peace in this and yet strive to climb up to the top of mountains in worldly honor; no, that cannot possibly be, for before he getteth half way to that estate he aimeth at, he will pluck such stones upon his own head that will break his peace, and make him wish that he had been content to walk upon plain ground, where he might have been in safety with peace in his mind.

5. Whereas now he findeth nothing but distraction and trouble, with all those incumbrances wherewith he hath entangled himself to gain the honor and riches in this world, which is not to be regarded by a spiritual wise man.

6. Because they break the peace of the mind and vex the pure peaceable spirit of truth that envieth no man, nor coveteth after riches, but having wherewith to supply its wants, is therewith content.

7. Therefore let no man that is a believer, make himself a servant to iniquity, which is vanity, when he is the Lord's freeman, and may live in purity.

8. Secondly, he that setteth his mind so much on this world, that he cannot. see himself happy without riches and honor in this world; though he knows there is a crown of glory prepared for him hereafter in another world, its a wonder if he be not taken prisoner by those snares which his reason hath lead him into.

9. And if he be once taken captive by the riches and honor of this world, which belongeth chiefly to the seed of the serpent; then it will stop that current of faith, and break his peace with God, so great enemies are the riches and honor of this world to the spirit of truth.

10. And I do believe there are very few but can witness this to be true, that so long as a man is pressing forward to get riches in this world, or so long as he delighteth to be in worldly honor; his mind cannot be at such perfect liberty to mind the things of eternity, as those are, who desire no more than as much as will keep them from want, and from being a burthen to others.

11. By experience we have seen and known multitudes of sorrows have fallen upon many that have striven to be great in the world.

12. And daily may see the many outward afflictions that fall upon them, because it appeareth public to us; but what inward grief and trouble there is for the loss of their honor or riches, when they are taken from them, we know not.

13. Therefore let every believer strive to keep his peace with God, for to keep his peace with God, is the greatest riches and honor that a saint can have.

14. And to lose that peace which is of more value than a thousand worlds, how shall he be able to purchase that peace again, when the breaking of it hath wounded his spirit, and a wounded spirit who can bear.

15. Thirdly, do we not see by experience, that most of those that are rich and live in honor in this world, that they are in a miserable state in this world upon a spiritual account; for they are kept in so much slavery by their riches and honor, that they must yield obedience thereunto.

16. Therefore when truth is declared to them, and they are convinced in themselves, that it is truth, yet they will not embrace it in love, for fear they should be converted by it, and so lose their honor in this world.

17. So that we may clearly see what great power, the riches and honor of this world have over them, that have tasted so much sweetness by them.

18. The riches of this world are so sweet, and the perishing honor which belongeth to it so delightful, to enjoy it longer, they will refuse that spiritual wisdom, which will lead all those that enjoy it, to everlasting life and glory undeclarable.

19. When all those who despise truth shall have their reward, which is an ever-dying-death, which will never have an end.

20. Because, then the fire of God's wrath will be kindled in them, which will burn more fierce than any fire and brimstone in this world, for it will never be cooled or quenched to eternity.

21. But if they did but know the worth of true wisdom in this life, they would not despise it; and there is no true spiritual wisdom now in this world, but what is declared by the Witnesses of the Spirit.

22. Therefore all of the seed of faith, or of the woman, are hereby exhorted, and desired to keep their own peace, because they are acquainted with as pure truths as ever was declared by, and, unto

men; and many have sucked therefrom so much sweetness, as hath given them assurance of their salvation.

23. Let us all far more esteem of that glory and honor, which we shall enjoy with our God, his prophets and apostles, the holy angels, and our fellow saints in the heaven of glory to eternity; (having thus in our eye, the recompence of reward) than to any dignity or honor that can be presented to us in this world.

24. And let us slight the preferment of this World, because we know if we do enjoy it; it will endanger (for the reasons aforesaid) or break the peace we have with God, which is of far more value than a thousand worlds.

25. Again, shall the seed of the serpent be willing to lose all the enjoyment of the glory to come on the other side of death, to enjoy their pleasure, or their good things (as they are called) in this life? because they are not certain, or believe not any resurrection.

26. And shall not we be willing to be without the pleasures of this world, (which for the most part, are but the pleasures of sin far a season), because we are hilly satisfied, that there are crowns of glory prepared for us, to wear in the kingdom of glory.

27. Where we shall be in the presence of our glorious God Christ Jesus, who purchased those crowns of glory for us, with the death of his most precious soul; as it is written, He poured out his soul unto death.

28. Again, it is written, The second Adam was a quickening spirit; and therein did Christ Make it plainly appear, that he was that quickening spirit; because he did quicken his most precious soul out of death to life again, by his own power, as he had often said, That he had power to lay down his life, and power to take it up again.

29. And as sure as his words were spirit and life, so sure did he rise again by his own power, without any additional power from any: other God; for there was no God besides himself.

30. But I know these will be counted hard sayings to the seed of reason, who are the seed of the serpent.

31. Although they will professingly say, all things are possible with God, yet they cannot believe that it was possible for God to die; but it was possible for God to die; because it was for his glory, and there is nothing impossible with God that his glorious wisdom moveth him to do.

32. I am sure they whose God could not die, they will never be redeemed from sin; for there was nothing but the blood of God himself, that could wash away the sins of his elect.

33. Therefore, they only that do feed on Christ, by their true believing that he did lay down his Godhead life for them, will be saved, when he cometh to judge the world.

34. And for a man to know in this life, that his sins are forgiven, and that he shall dwell with Christ to eternity, is riches indeed.

35. But for the riches of this world, we see by experience, that they are not only vanity, but they are also the greatest ensnarements that are to deprive men of eternal happiness.

36. And they have so much, as it were, of the nature of the loadstone in them; that if the heart of man be but once touched affectionately with them, it is drawn away with them, and by the strength of them, it is held so fast that it seldom parteth with them, until death by force taketh it away.

37. Therefore let none that knows the nature and danger hereof, suffer themselves to be taken prisoners by those powers from which seldom any are released. And you all know that Christ himself said, It was easier for a camel to go through the eye of a needle, than for a rich man to enter into the kingdom of heaven.

38. Again, I know that as people in Christ's time said, But which of the rulers have believed in him; so do people now cry, what noble or learned men do believe in the Witnesses qf the Spirit; when they themselves are not ignorant of what is written, That few of those that are called wise, noble, or learned are chosen.

39. But if any of the rulers of this city of London, or any one that is in any other place of great authority, should have a desire to be acquainted with the Witnesses of the Spirit, or with some of the believers of them, it must be done secretly.

40. Or else they must come by night as Nicodemus did to Christ. For those that are in power and authority, dare not be seen to have any love for that doctrine which is not allowed by the supreme power of the three nations, for fear they should be brought in question for their faith, and so should be put out of their places of honor in this world.

41. I doubt there are many that are rulers in these kingdoms, that knows no more what the true God is, than Nicodemus did know how he should be born again, though he was a master in Israel.

42. And it is now, as it was in former ages; if the truth be not declared to be truth by the rulers and chief magistrates; then the generality of the people will not suffer it to be spoken before them, without calling it blasphemy, heresy, delusion, or a lie, or such like expressions, wherewith they corrupt themselves; Because they speak evil of those things which they know not, as it is written by St. Jude.

CHAP. IV.

How careful people ought to be, in preserving that which they labour for, because poverty is a great enemy to truth, and breaketh the peace of the mind.

THOUGH we are not to suffer ourselves to be taken captive by the riches of this world, yet we must provide against the other enemy, which is poverty. Poverty will be creeping in, to take possession, if it be not resisted. And though poverty be of such a contrary nature to riches, whereby no man loveth it, because it is not delightful, yet where it takes possession, it is not easily flung out again.

2. Therefore, let no believer give himself too much liberty, lest poverty fall upon him, but when he hath him under him, let him keep him down.

3. And poverty, is easily kept down by industry, by him who is willing to labour, and mindful to preserve that which he hath taken great pains for.

4. Again, it is not the earning of a great deal of money in a day, or in a week, that causeth a man and his family to live comfortably, but the well managing what he getteth, this I know by experience.

5. I have known several men, though not believers, that could by their trades earn, 20, 30, or 40 shillings a week, and some more Money, yet by their immoderate living, being given to extreme wastefulness;

6. Or else being given to idleness, trusting to what they could earn in a day or two in a week, so that their families have lacked both food and raiment, which was convenient for them:

7. When those who could not earn half so much, have by their carefulness lived comfortably, and lacked for nothing that was necessary.

8. Therefore, let every man observe that old Proverb, To cut his Coat according to his Cloth, that is that he spendeth or layeth out no more than what is agreeable to his comings in, and then there will he no want.

9. Again, I know several whose earnings are but small, which will not amount to above six, eight, or ten shillings a week at the most, if they work all the week; and yet these will spend so much of their time idly; and so much of their little earnings wastefully, that they can hardly spare their families money to buy them bread, in time of health and strength.

10. But what will become of them in the time of sickness, lameness, or old age? Surely nothing but sorrow and calamity.

11. Poverty doth make people run into many dangers; many will rather venture their lives by breaking the law, than to want those things that are necessary in this life.

12. Most commonly this want is procured, either by men's extravagance in spending their yearly revenue, or what they have hard laboured for, or else by mispending their time in idleness.

13. I am sure, whosoever is guilty of any of these things, cannot be at peace in his mind upon a spiritual account, and therefore poverty and wastefulness is an enemy to truth.

14. Furthermore, will not the words of a child cut more sharp than a two-edged sword, when he shall ask for bread, and his father or mother hath none to give him, nor money to buy food to satisfy their hungry babes with; this must lie very heavy upon those who have brought themselves into such a condition by their own wilful extravagance or idleness.

15. But it may be, some will say, they have no children, the cry of a child cannot trouble them; but if it be the cry of a wife, or of his own poor soul, being through sickness, lameness, or old age, brought to want food or raiment, and all for want of a providential care in the time of his health, to keep something to help him at such a time when comfort is required; these things must needs break the peace of his mind; therefore poverty is an enemy to truth.

16. Though we are commanded to love our enemies, yet we are not to love such enemies as will break our peace with God, which these enemies before-mentioned will do, if we make a league with them; and it is written, He that provideth not for himself and his family, is worse than an infidel.

17. I hope no believer will be guilty of that sin; neither are we to take hold of those words, Take no care for to-morrow, but let the day bring forth for itself; for those words were chiefly spoken to the apostles, and those whom they ordained to be fellow-labourers with them in the gospel of Christ.

18. They, indeed, were not to take scrip, nor staff, nor two coats a-piece; signifying that they were not to take care in this life for any thing, but to feed the church with the gospel of truth, and temporal necessaries should be added; as it is written, They that preach the Gospel, shall live by the Gospel.

19. Nevertheless, St. Paul saith, that his hands ministered to his necessities, rather than he would be a burthen to the church.

20. Therefore let all believers take such care, that by their labour or lawful industry, they may be able to minister to their own necessities, without being a burthen to the church; which are the household of faithful people. And that they may have something to spare, because it is a greater blessing to give than to receive.

21. I write these things to encourage believers, and all other civil people to be careful and industrious in the time of their health and

strength; and when they have store of employment, to lay by something to help them when either their health, strength, or employment faileth them.

22. Then is the time of their necessity, and in time of necessity and want of bread, the peace of a man's mind is broken; and he hath no more liberty and freedom in his mind, to mind the glorious things of eternity; than he hath whose mind is entangled with the riches and honor of this world; therefore poverty is an enemy to truth.

23. When poverty is come, then doth the thriftless man begin to employ his mind, altogether on worldly things and matters, how he shall escape that great danger he hath brought himself into.

24. To steal he is afraid, to beg he is ashamed, his credit is so bad no body will trust him, and in this condition there can be no peace.

25. Neither can the effects thereof prove good, for he must be forced either to beg, or to take some evil course at last, except some friend or friends take pity on him, and relieve him.

26. Then, if he be brought by that means to see all his former folly, and to repent of it, then the taste of want hath proved good to him.

27. But for my part, I cannot understand what pleasure or delight any man can take in spending and consuming that money in waste which they labour for; when they are sensible what a sad condition many people have brought themselves into, by the like extravagances.

28. Let these things therefore be an example to all believers, lest they should be taken in the same snares with the wicked, and so should undergo that punishment due to them; which is to want all temporal comforts; besides that horror which will be upon the mind for the dishonoring that truth, of which they are partakers.

29. Though it is written, Those that are poor in this world, and rich in faith, are heirs of the kingdom of heaven; yet that was not written to encourage any believer to live in idleness, or to spend his money or time wastefully, whereby to keep himself poor; for poverty (as aforesaid) is an enemy to truth, and to the peace of the mind.

30. Also, he that is rich in faith, hath those riches of temporal wisdom in him, to use the uttermost of his endeavours to keep himself and family, from wanting temporal comforts in this life.

31. If there be any believer that hath been industrious in his calling, and careful to maintain himself and family to the uttermost of his power, not wasteing his time or money idly; I say, if such a one should be brought very low and poor; by either losses, sickness, greatness of charge, having many children, old age, persecution, or such like causes; I have not written any thing hereto hinder those from being relieved.

32. It doth make my soul to mourn, when I hear of a believer who want food or raiment which is convenient for them; and I have always been willing to help such poor believers, and ever shall be, if I have it to give.

33. And I would have all believers according to their ability, to be willing to help such poor believers, whose poverty comes not by their own wilful extravagance.

CHAP. V.

How people ought to be moderate in all things. The comfort of moderation, and the discomfort of immoderation, excess, and extravagance.

MOREOVER, I would have all believers learn to be moderate and temperate in all things; for immoderation and intemperateness destroyeth many a Man, both body and estate.

2. For we see by experience, that those who are extremely given to drinking, that it doth not only waste their estate, but it doth also destroy their health, and disorder their bodies so much; that no wise man will become a slave unto it.

3. All sorts of strong drink doth disturb the head, the stomach, and the minds of men, if they drink to excess. Wherefore then should any man take delight in it? Especially those that know truth? They should abhor the vanity of that vice, which maketh men incapable to know themselves.

4. Secondly, it is not good for any man to do greater work than his strength is able to bear; for though at the present not felt, yet after the prime of his years are past; then he begins to feel the want of that natural strength which he had destroyed.

5. And care herein is to be had not to overlift; or carry over-heavy burthens, or to overheat ourselves in any manner of labour whatsoever, in the time of health and strength whereby to earn extraordinary wages.

6. Then when sickness or lameness cometh by this over-hard working, that money is quickly spent; and besides that, if he recover, he is hardly able to work at all, when he groweth a little more in years.

7. We may observe, that moderation in all things is good in work, as well as in other things; for he that worketh moderately, and worketh six days in a week, shall bring home more money to his family, and keep his health and strength better than he that worketh extremely hard for three or four days in a week, and then playeth the rest, and spendeth what he hath hard laboured for in idle company.

8. Therefore, I desire every believer to take good observation of all these things, and consider well of them; and then that which he findeth to be most to the glory of God, and the peace of his own mind, let him so practice.

9. Again, let all believers strive to be Moderate and temperate in their spirits, not suffering passion to oversway them; for many times oaths are apt to break out of the mouths of men in their passion.

10. However, if not oaths, unseemly words are spoken at such a time, and it is that which cometh out of the mouth that defileth the

man: And what is that which cometh out of the mouth to defile a man? Nothing but vain words and blaspheming.

11. And I would not have any saint to be guilty of blasphemy, or vain words to defile himself.

12. Not but that I know every true believer hath so much faith as will keep from blaspheming against God; but there may be some that may be apt to speak evil of men, undeservedly or unadvisedly.

13. And whosoever doth speak evil of a man blasphemeth against him, by bringing a reproach upon his name; and whoever doth evil to any man sinneth against him.

14. Such are those sins and blasphemies against man which will be forgiven, but they will defile the mind abundantly, and break its peace exceedingly, therefore let no such corruption dwell with believers.

15. Thirdly, let all believers take special care that they do not give themselves to lasciviousness; fornication and adultery are trying sins; there is no temporal sin can lie heavier upon the conscience; except murder; therefore let all believers be sure to keep themselves from all actual sins.

16. Again, let all believers be sure to keep their word of promise upon a temporal account; for, it is the credit and reputation of a man in this life, to keep his word and promise,

17. For when once a man's word will not be taken, because it is usual with him to break his promise; then his reputation sinketh, and no man will trust him with any thing of value.

18. Lastly, above all things, let all believers be sure that they keep close to the truth, so that they do not go a whoring after strange Gods, nor suffer themselves to be defiled with worshipping of idols.

19. The sin of idolatry is as bad as the sin of witchcraft, and the committing of fornication with idols, is worse than any temporal fornication or whoredom, for the one defileth the body, and the other defileth the spirit.

20. No man can say his heart is perfect to the Lord God; when he cannot refrain from going to worship among those that know not God, and bowing himself to idols.

CHAP. VI.

Every true believer is heir to the kingdom of heaven, because he is free-born, and free by redemption.

WHOEVER they are that are believers, yet by that corrupted reason in them, have been overcome to commit evil in any sort whatsoever, they can witness the torment belonging to it in themselves, and thereby they learn to do righteously ever after, having by experience found the difference between doing good and evil.

2. In the apostles time there were some believers, that through the occasion of sin, had such operations in them, knowing by experience the difference between doing good and evil, that they were able to declare unto other believers, what afflictions they had undergone within themselves, for doing those things that were contrary to the spirit of truth.

3. They having by faith overcome those operations, were made the more able to withstand them afterwards; yet nevertheless, lest any believers should through temptation fall wilfully into sin, thinking thereby to be made stronger in faith, St. Paul said, Shall we sin that Grace may abound? God forbid.

4. Therefore it is a greater comfort for all men, especially believers, to live innocently all the days of their lives; than for them to fall once into sin; though, by the forgiveness thereof, they are made more able to withstand temptations afterwards.

5. It is the best for all believers to learn to be temperate and wise, and well to consider the effects that will follow their actions; whereby there may be no cause of repentance afterwards, then shall we keep our peace with God and man.

6. If we do not keep our peace, then are we in bondage, and why should we suffer ourselves to be carried into bondage by iniquity, when our faith and knowledge leadeth us to live in purity.

7. We who are believers are both-free-born, and free by redemption. First, We are free-born, because we are of the seed of faith, called the seed of God's own body, which seed is heir to the kingdom of heaven by birth.

8. Secondly, We are free by redemption, because our God paid a great ransom for it to redeem us from sin and iniquity.

9. Our sins, that is the sins of the elect, were so great, that no other price could satisfy that debt, but the death of the Godhead only.

10. That God who created the world, so loved the world, that is the world of the elect; or the elect in the world, that for their sakes alone did he lay down his Godhead-life for a moment in shame.

11. That is, he suffered that shameful death upon the cross, between two thieves, whereby he was numbered among transgressors,

and all that was, that he might gain to himself power to raise all those to eternal life and glory with himself, that had had faith to believe.

12. That according to his promise he would send his son, or become a child himself in mortality, and all those that had faith to believe that he was the Messiah and Saviour of the world when he was come.

13. And all those that now can truly believe, that he is Father, Son, and Holy Spirit, in one single person glorified, he laid down his Godhead-life for.

14. And also by laying down his life, and rising again, he purchased for himself a double crown of glory and honor.

15. Before eternity became time, and time became eternity again, that is, before God became a pure mortal man, and afterwards immortalized himself again, which is a riddle too hard for the seed of the serpent to understand.

16. I say, before that blessed time, God had the glory and honor of a creator only; but by his death and rising again, he hath now the glory and honor of the redeemer and saviour of the world; therefore, according to his own promise, as it is written in Isaiah, His glory is not given to another.

17. And as he purchased a double glory to himself, so likewise hath he purchased eternal life and glory for us, who do truly believe him to be, the only and alone wise God.

18. And also by his death and resurrection be hath purchased for the unbelieving reprobates. everlasting torments that will never end.

19. What manner of lives therefore ought we to live, because we are sensible for what end and purpose the creator of heaven and earth laid, down his life.

20. Therefore let us strive always to do those things. which we know to be well pleasing to our God; because we only, are the true believers of the Witnesses of the Spirit, which is the Lord's third and last commission or testament; and so are a peculiar people in this generation; knowing more of the mind of God, than any believers did in times past.

21. Wherefore let us not darken this great and marvellous light by any unseemly carriage; but let us abstain from all manner of evil that may any way break our peace, or beget a civil war within us.

22. Which war will not be ended until we lay down those weapons, wherewith we fight against that truth, by which we have received the assurance of our salvation.

23. And by repentance make our peace again, and cease from all manner of evil, then by well doing we shall not only keep our peace with God; but we shall also put to silence all those that shall speak evil of truth.

24. They being ignorant of the power of faith which we have, by believing commissioned men; that had their commission and power given them from Christ himself.

CHAP. VII.

When any evil is committed by a believer, it stoppeth the current of his faith; yet it is the heart that God mindeth, and not the outward appearance. That every believer should weed his own garden.

WE, who are believers of the commission and testament before expressed; knowing that we have our hearts purified by obeying the truth, and having unfeigned love to the prophets of the Lord for the truth's sake: Let us love all purity, for that belongeth to truth. Blessed are the pure in heart, for they shall see God.

2. This also may every believer witness by experience, that whenever he committeth any manner of evil, that evil committed by him as it hath, so it will hinder and stop the current of the well-spring of faith in him, and make it seem as if it were dried up, until it beginneth to spring forth again by repentance.

3. I witness this by experience in myself, and I know there are very few believers (if any at all) but they will witness the same; having had at one time other a taste of it, or will do it, whenever they take a particular account of their folly.

4. Therefore, I would have all believers to muster up all their follies, and the forces of them together, and disband them; and have no more service for those soldiers of vanity who fight against truth.

5. Yet for all this, I know it is the heart God mindeth, and not the outward appearance: for by the outward appearance men are apt to judge either good or evil; but it is only they who see by the eye of faith, and that know the nature of the two seeds (of the serpent, and of the woman) that can give true judgment upon the eternal condition of men.

6. Let men's outward appearances be what they will, by their words they shall be either justified or condemned: for as there are many that make a great profession of righteousness, and in all their dealings are very just, so that none can accuse them for any evil; yet by their despising of truth; we know them to be reprobates.

7. So on the contrary, there may be some of the seed of faith, that by their lives and conversation, are not by the world discerned to have any thing of true knowledge in them, by the outward appearance, because they are full of folly, as being given to jesting, fuddling, breaking their promises, or such like.

8. Which things are not at all justified, and in being, and doing so, they break their own peace, as aforesaid; and to the zealous sort of the seed of reason, it is so ridiculous, that they think there can be no true faith, where there is not a pharisaical holiness to be seen of men.

9. Yet these believers, which by the world are accounted sinners, shall at the day of the Lord appear all glorious, and be crowned with

honor, because they had true faith, and did truly believe that Christ was the only and alone wise God, and that his messengers were true prophets, and that the doctrine declared by them, was true also; therefore it is by faith, and not by outward appearance that men are justified by, in the sight of God.

10. Now even here upon, let all true believers learn to be wise and moderate in all things, upon a temporal account, that they give not offence to others.

11. Neither let believers who walk in the light, lay stumbling-blocks for others to fall at, who walk in darkness; but rather labour to remove all stumbling-stones out of the way, by a pure and holy life.

12. That we, by our upright living, may be the means to draw others from their corrupt lives, to a pure and holy conversation.

13. And sure I am, that there is none of the seed of faith, who have in any sort led a corrupt life; but they are made sensible of their folly, by those afflictions which have fallen upon their minds; by not keeping themselves unspotted to the world.

14. That inward punishment is so uneasy, nay sharp to bear, that it will cause all who have true faith, to weed their gardens so clean from all manner of evil weeds, that the pure flower of faith may spread itself forth.

15. Then will the truth gloriously shine forth in all those believers, who have dispersed the clouds of vanity, and cast out the weeds of folly.

CHAP. VIII.

He is not accounted a wise man that will wilfully wound himself. How we may know when our sins are forgiving

NONE will account that man wise, who will take a sword or knife in his hand and wound himself wilfully, when he knoweth it will put him to a great deal of pain as soon as it is done; besides the lamentable misery he must endure in the curing of it again.

2. Every time his wound is dressed or touched, it pains him more than the making of the wound, which he made in his hasty humour; also, there will be a blemish in the skin a great while after, if ever it do grow up at all.

3. And so it is upon a spiritual account None will take that man to be a spiritual wise man, that will wilfully break and wound his own peace, by breaking the law, or walking any way disorderly, contrary to the law of faith.

4. He that is faithful knoweth, that he shall endure greater affliction upon his mind, after he hath committed evil; then at the time he had the pleasure in the committing of it.

5. As a wound that is deep in the flesh, is more grievous and terrible to the patient, than it was pleasant at the time of wounding; so likewise is every sin or evil in the guilt of it, more terrible to a man that hath true faith when afterwards he considereth what he hath done; than the delight he had in the time of the acting thereof; though he may say, It was but indeed the pleasure of sin for a season.

6. Every time the remembrance of it cometh into his mind, it striketh him to the heart, and woundeth his spirit; and a wounded spirit, who is able to bear.

7. The reflection of evil upon a man's mind, is much like the dressing of a deep wound in the flesh. And as a wound in the flesh, must be often drest; so must he that is faithful, and yet committeth evil expect to hear often of it. Therefore let all believers learn to be wise, and keep themselves unspotted to the world.

8, Again, the blemish and reproach that will be upon a believer's name, for being accounted a sinner, will remain a long time before it be forgotten, if ever it wears out of memory.

9. Therefore let us that know the truth, be an example to others in all things that are just and honest; both in our words, and in the purity of our lives and conversations; that all those who are in the truth, and they who shall come to the knowledge of the truth after us, may rejoice in the publishing of our names, and not to be ashamed to make mention of us.

10. To him that knoweth how to do well, and doeth it not, to him it is sin. Therefore let all true believers learn to do that which is justifiable, both before God and man.

11. There are but two things which a saint hath to mind, that is to keep peace with God, and himself unspotted in the world, and then he may appear with boldness before the throne of grace.

12. Therefore let all believers be sure to wash their hearts clean, with the spirit of truth; for, if there be any evil hid in the heart, that the, world knoweth not of, whereby, to accuse them; yet that watchman which God hath set in the hearts of all men, to watch their actions, will accuse them; if there be any evil lodged in the heart ever so secretly.

13. And this watchman is the law written in our nature; if that can accuse us, then may we be assured to appear before the judge of heaven and earth, because we have broken that peace which we had with him.

14. But if we have broken that peace, that we must be sure to make our peace again by repentance, and hereby, we may know whether our peace be made with God again, or no.

15. First, if we do acknowledge in ourselves that we have broken his law, or done contrary to the light of faith, which is God's divine nature, which as the apostle speaks, the saints or believers are partakers of.

Secondly, if we do find in ourselves a hearty sorrowfulness, whereby we do truly repent that we have offended our God, in sinning against so great a light.

16. Also thirdly, if after this repentance we do forsake all those evil ways which broke our peace, and keep close to the truth in well doing.

17. Then may we be assured that all our transgressions are forgiven; and with boldness appear before the throne of grace, because our sins are blotted out, and will no more be brought into remembrance.

CHAP. IX.

How eternity became time; and the Eternal Father became a Son, born of a Virgin. Now is the prophecy of Isaiah fulfilled.

LET us set our affections wholly on things above, which we know giveth the most, and only satisfaction to the soul and mind of man; so that we may appear to be the elect of God, to whom God hath by his last true prophets revealed, and made known the riches of his glory.

2. Whereby we know how, that it was the pleasure of the glorious God in heaven above, the stars for a time to leave his glorious throne, and to descend into the lower parts of the earth.

3. That earth which God descended into, was the virgins womb, therefore, it is written, He descended into the lower parts of the earth; and I am assured that it cannot be proved by faith, reason, or scriptures, that God did otherwise descend into any other part of the earth on which we tread.

4 And the most high and holy God; the wise creator of all things, was pleased to descend from his immortal throne of glory, into the womb of a virgin, who was but an earthly creature; because she was generated from the first Adam, who was made of the dust of the earth.

5. Yet she was a virgin, and her seed was pure and undefiled; and in her womb did the immortal God, mortalize and dissolve himself into seed; and then did eternity become time; and there did the wise creator cloath his god-head-spirit with flesh and bone, as with a garment,

6. The virgin-wife Mary brought forth her first-born, the son of God, and the eternal father and creator himself. Therefore, it is written, He was in the world, and the world was made by him, but the world knew him not, when he was manifested in the flesh: Also it is written, In him, (that is, in Christ) dwelleth all the fulness of the Godhead bodily.

7. Again, it is written, Isaiah 43, 3, I am the Lord thy God, the Holy One of Israel, thy Saviour. Ver. 11, I, even I, am the Lord, and besides me there is no Saviour. Chap. 44. ver. 6. I, am the first, and I am the last, and besides me there is no God. Chap. 42. ver 8. I am the Lord, that is my name, and my glory I will not give to another. And in the 9th Chap. ver. 6. For unto us a child is born, unto us a Son is given, and the government shall be upon his shoulders, and his name shall be called, the wonderful counsellor; the mighty God; the everlasting Father; the prince of peace. These things were spoken by the prophets long before Christ was born; whereby the eye of faith can clearly see, that there is no Other God but that Christ, which was God manifested in the flesh; seen of angels; preached unto the gentiles; believed on in the world, received up into glory,

8. And therefore, time is become eternity again, and mortality is immortalized; and that God Christ is glorified with the same glory, that he had before he became a child,

9. And since he was glorified he hath said, I am Alpha and Omega, the beginning and the ending, saith the Lord, which is, and which was, and which is to come, the Almighty. And again, saith he, I am the first and the last, I am he that was dead, and am alive, and behold, I live for evermore.

10. Thus, it is plain to all that have true faith, that immortality became mortal, and that mortality is become immortal again: for, had not God become mortal, he could not have suffered that death upon the cross; and were not mortality raised up to immortality, he could not live for evermore.

11. Thus doth faith see how eternity became time, and how time is become eternity again, and that Christ was the creator as well as the redeemer. Many more places of scripture there are to prove the same, which I shall not name here.

12. I am sure it is life eternal to know the true God, and there is no other true God but Christ; and for this our faith do we suffer reproach; because we do trust in the living God, who is a God of a glorious form and substance.

13. But blessed and happy are all those that suffer reproach only, for having faith to believe in the true God. Now, is that prophecy of Isaiah fulfilled, in that he said, That child and son who was born, and given to us, should be called the mighty God, the everlasting Father, the Prince of Peace.

14. For now have the Witnesses of the Spirit declared, that Christ is both Father, Son, and Holy Spirit, in one single person glorified, and there is no salvation to be had without believing their report.

15. From hence, I desire, and earnestly exhort all the seed of faith, who are already come, or shall hereafter come to the knowledge of this blessed truth, to be very careful and sure to keep their peace with God; by keeping close to the truth, and keeping themselves unspotted to the world.

16. Because it hath been the good will and pleasure of our God, to reveal unto us by the mouth and pen of his last true prophets, many things which were not revealed to any age before; therefore, we may justly say, we do know more of the mind of God, than any believers did in any age before us.

17. We know what was declared by the true prophets of old, and the believers in their time could know no more than what was then declared to them; as truly to believe what was declared, was sufficient for them.

18. And the believers in the apostles time knew what was declared by the prophets, and what was declared Ivy the apostles also; so that they had a twofold knowledge whereby they knew more of the mind of God, than those believers did who live in the former prophets time.

19. The apostles doctrine was not the same, that the prophets before. them was, yet it agreed with the same; for as the prophets had declared that the Messiah, or Son of God, and Saviour of the world, should be born of a virgin; and that he should have those titles due to him, which was to be called, The Mighty God, and the Everlasting Father.

20. So likewise did the apostles declare that he was come, and that Jesus, the supposed son of Joseph, was the son of God and saviour of the world; and that the Jews had put to death the Lord of life; and that that was the blood of God which was shed upon the cross; thus the apostles doctrine did agree with the doctrine, which the prophets of old had declared.

CHAP. X.

How the believers of the Witnesses of the Spirit have a threefold knowledge; and the Witnesses of the Spirit, are the third and last witnesses that God will send on this earth, to declare his mind unto the world.

AND we who are believers of the Witnesses of the Spirit, know what was declared by the holy prophets of old; and also what was declared by apostles, and we do firmly believe that their declarations were true.

2. And we do also know, and believe, what is declared by the Witnesses of the Spirit to be true; whereby we have a threefold knowledge; though the declaration or doctrine of the Witnesses of the Spirit is not the same as the prophets and apostles were, yet it doth agree with them.

3. For as the true prophets of old did declare that the God of Israel was the true God, and that besides him there was no Saviour, and that God would not give his glory to another,

4. And as the apostles do declare, That the word was God, and that word was made flesh, and dwelt among them, and that he was manifested in the flesh, and that in him was all fulness, and that the fulness of the Godhead dwelt bodily in Christ.

5. So likewise in confirmation of the true prophets prophecy, and of the apostles declaration, do the Witnesses of the Spirit positively affirm, and declare against men and angels that shall deny it; that there is no other God but that Jehovah, who is called the mighty God of Jacob, and holy one of Israel; who afterwards, according to the report of the prophet Isaiah, was born of a virgin; and that there was no other God but that Jesus, which was crucified by the unbelieving Jews, and he was the true God, whom to know is life eternal; but the world knew him not because they had not faith to believe his words, for had they known him, they would not have put to death the Lord of Life.

6. The everlasting father and creator of all things was in the world, as is testified by St. John, chap. 1. ver. 10. He was in the world, and the world was made by him, and the world knew him not. ver. 14. the apostles themselves beheld his glory, but as the glory of the only begotten of the Father, full of grace and truth, because he was then in mortality.

7. After his death and resurrection, Thomas put his fingers into his side, and called him his Lord, and his God. And he was all the apostles God; and therefore, they call him the only wise God, their Saviour, the Lord of Lords, and King of Kings.

8. Because there was none above him, therefore he did rise from the dead by his own power, and after his resurrection he did ascend

into heaven, as is declared by the apostles; and he is now in heaven glorified with the same glory, he had before he became flesh; therefore his glory is not given to another.

9. The glorified man Christ Jesus, was all the former true prophets God before he became flesh; and he was all the apostles God after he became flesh; so likewise he is the witnesses of the Spirit's God, now he is flesh and bone in heaven glorified; thus it may be clearly discerned by the seed of faith, as they clearly prove him to be father, son, and holy spirit in one single person glorified; and as all honor, praise, and glory doth belong to Christ now he is a spiritual body of flesh and bone in heaven; the witnesses of the Spirit do give no honor, praise, or glory to any other God but to Christ.

He was creator of this world as he was the father; the redeemer of his elect in the world as he was the son; and sanctifier of all his people as he is the holy spirit; and here is the trinity in unity, and the unity in the trinity, yet but one person.

10. Thus it is, and will appear plain to all the seed of faith, that the Witnesses of the Spirit are the third and last prophets or witnesses, that ever God will send on this earth, to declare his mind unto the world.

11. It is written in the first epistle of St. John, chap. 5, ver. 7, 8. There are three that bear record in heaven, the Father, the Son, and the Holy Ghost, (from these words do most people conclude that they are three distinct persons; and yet two of them have neither form or substance) and these three are one. So that it is plain to the seed of faith, (by that text) they are all one in essence, in form, and in substance; which is that glorious bodily substance of Christ:

12. For in him dwelleth the fulness of the Godhead bodily.

13. It is written also, And there are three that bear witness on earth, the spirit, the water, and the blood, and these three agree in one; that is, in their doctrine or declaration they do agree in one, whereby we see the difference between three being one, and three agreeing in one.

14. Though these three which bear witness on earth, agree in their declarations, yet they are several dispensations, and appeared on the earth in several ages.

15. The first witness on earth was Moses, and the rest of the true prophets, which signified the water in the ceremonies of the law; and they did all witness that God would either send a saviour, or become a child in mortality himself, to redeem his people from their sins, as Isaiah prophesied.

16. The second witness was Christ and his apostles, and Christ did witness that he was come to suffer all those things, that the prophets had declared concerning him; so that Christ himself was that witness of the blood; his blood was shed to wash away the sins of the elect;

and the apostles did declare, That they were eye-witnesses both of his death, resurrection, and ascension.

17. So that the second witness, which was Christ and his apostles, did agree with the first witness, which was Moses and the other prophets. For as the first declared how a saviour should be born; so, the second declared that he was born; and what he was to suffer, and did suffer, with his death and resurrection, as aforesaid.

18. And the third and last witness appeared on the earth in the year 1651, who are the Witnesses of the Spirit; and they do positively affirm and declare against men and angels, that shall oppose or deny it; That there, neither is, was, or ever shall be any other God or Saviour, but that God-man Christ Jesus, who laid down his life for the sins of his people, without the gates of Jerusalem; and the third day did rise again, and with the same body that he died and rose again in, was he seen to ascend up into glory in, when the heavens opened to receive him, according as is testified in the scriptures.

19. Therefore, it is plain to all that are not quite blind with ignorance, (even those, of whom it said, They have eyes and see not, ears and hear not, nor hearts to understand) that Father, Son, and Holy Ghost make but one complete person; even the said Lord Jesus Christ, that God man blessed for ever.

20. And therefore is all glory that belongeth to the Father; Son, and Holy Ghost given to Christ by all his chosen people, both prophets, apostles, and saints, as is declared by the Witnesses of the Spirit.

21. Whereby it obligeth all who have faith to believe Christ is God, to believe that John Reeve and Lodowick Muggleton were sent forth by an express command from God, as is testified and declared by them, to declare the mind of God, to a bloody and unbelieving world; because they do unanimously agree with the two former witnesses; namely, the water and the blood, who did declare Christ to be the only wise God and creator of all things.

22. The first is become last, and the last first; the commission of the spirit is last declared unto the world; yet the spirit was before all things, and the two former witnesses, both the prophets and apostles received their commission from that spirit, which was a glorious body in form like a man from all eternity.

CHAP. XI.

Where truth and true knowledge, place, and satisfaction is to be had. And how it keepeth us from going a whoring after strange Gods.

TRUTH, and true knowledge are the things which only can, and do give satisfaction to the mind of man. Truth doth always satisfy those that receive it in the love thereof.

2. There is no truth, nor true faith or knowledge in the world, but what is in the commission of the spirit; therefore no true peace or satisfaction to be had for those who despise it We, who are believers thereof, do know and understand all the things before said.

3. Let it not seem strange to the world, when they shall hear any of us (who are true believers of the Lord's last messengers) say, that we know more of the mind. of God concerning glorious things of eternity, than all the people of the world besides. There are none that know the true God, the right devil, the nature and form of angels, that the soul and body of man dieth together, and that they shall be raised again, and what heaven and hell is, and where they are; but only they who are believers of the commission or Witnesses of the Spirit.

4. Therefore let no believer be ashamed of his faith, but declare it with boldness, if it be required of him in love; and at all times when there is a convenient season, among civil and moderate men, but not among those whom we know to be blasphemers.

5. Christ forbiddeth to give that which is holy unto dogs, and they who despise truth, are, those dogs Christ speaks of, and that which is not to be given them is the bread of life, which is holy; therefore, we are not to declare the eternal truth unto them, because we are children, lest they should bite us.

6. Neither are we to cast these precious pearls of truth before swine, lest they trample them under foot, and turn again and rend us. These swine are such persecuting devils, as will not only despise the truth (as dung) when they hear of it; but they will also seek to destroy him that declareth it, for the truth's sake.

7. But truth doth fully satisfy all those that do receive it with joy, and continue stedfast in it, and it doth become both bread and water of life in them. Truth is the bread of life, because all those that do feed thereon, will hunger no more after the forgiveness of their sins; and their faith will be made so strong, by feeding all their days here on truth, which is Christ, that they will be able hereafter to live with him in glory to eternity.

8. And this glorious truth is also the water of life, in believers of this commission; because it hath purged and cleansed their hearts from all manner of idolatrous worship, or worshipping of idols, or unknown Gods; and it keepeth them from going a whoring after strange Gods; because they are well acquainted with that truth which

declareth them, the true God Christ Jesus, who only, they worship in spirit and truth.

9. And we, who are believers of this last and spiritual commission, are to declare this truth plentifully to all those we find weary, and heavy laden with ignorance; who are yet hungering and thirsting after true knowledge; whereby they might have the assurance of their salvation perfected in this life. To such we are to declare our faith, with soundness of speech that cannot be dented, that those who are against it. may be ashamed.

CHAP. XII.

How all sober men are to labour to know what they believe, that they, may lay hold on the good word of prophesy; and not be fed up with fancies to believe in that, which no man can describe what it is, or where it is

FURTHERMORE, let all sober people labour and strive to know what they do believe; that they may be able to give a substantial answer to all wise men, that shall enquire of them what their faith is; for, it is not sufficient to say as the ignorant do, I believe in God, or I believe that Christ died for all sinners, and I hope to have the same benefit by his death, as others have.

2. Such like words a child may be taught before he knoweth either good or evil, and most religious people's children are educated up in such language; yet their parents know not what, nor where that God is, they teach their children to say they believe in.

3. For all those that are not come to the knowledge of that truth, which will teach them to know what the true God is, though they are accounted wise and prudent by the world; yet they know not what the object of their faith is, because that infinite spirit, as they call it, which they say they believe in; hath neither body, form, or substance, and therefore, neither to be seen, felt, nor understood.

4. These things are accounted wisdom by the world, but to us that know the true God, it is foolishness. And there are none that can come to know what the true God is, and what that true worship is that doth belong to him; but those that have faith to believe, and lay hold of the good word prophesy; and this cannot be learned by children, until they grow up to maturity of years, for they must have good understanding, before they are capable to know what the good word of prophesy meaneth, which is the glad tidings of salvation.

5. There can be no true comfort in uncertain things. What benefit or satisfaction can any man have, by hearing that he hath an estate of great value in another country, but it is neither to be seen nor felt; neither can any man describe what substance it doth contain, nor where it is.

6. Yet hundreds will be justifying that there is such an estate that doth belong to him; but I do say again, what benefit can a man expect from such an estate, if it be valued at 10,000 lib. a year, because it is a shadow, and not a substance.

7. Who would not account him a mad man, or a fool, that would be fed up with such fancies of men, to believe that at one time or other, he should enjoy great happiness and comfort by that estate, which folks talk so much of; though the wisest of them that talk so much in the praise of it, are not able to declare unto him the substance of it, nor in what country it is situated in.

8. Thus it is with such men, that do believe the report of those men who call themselves ministers of the gospel of Christ, when they declare unto the people, and speak much of the glory of God, and of that glory which they shall enjoy with him that walk uprightly before him; and yet they tell the people, that their God hath neither body, form, nor substance; now, if he be a spiritual substance, then he must have a body and form suitable to it.

9. Neither can, or do they tell their ignorant disciples or believers, where that God is, with whom they enjoy their glory; for they say he is every where, and if he be every where, then there is no more glory to be received with God, then we already enjoy.

10. Then it is in vain for saints to believe and expect glory with their God in another world, if God be in all things and places, as most people are taught to believe.

11. Let all wise, sober wise men consider with themselves, what little satisfaction they have found in believing in that unknown God. And what satisfaction can any man have in believing that his body shall be raised again like unto the glorious body of God, and yet believe that God hath no body to enjoy his own glory in again; What satisfaction or felicity, joy, or comfort can any man expect to enjoy in, or with that God in another world, who hath neither body nor form for them to behold.

12. Again, why are the eyes of the people so darkened? or why are they so ignorant to think or believe that God hath neither body nor form? Why? Because it is now, as it was in the former true prophets time, in the days of Isaiah. Isaiah ix. 16. The Teachers cause the people to err, and they that are taught by them are destroyed.

13. And do not all that are now leaders of the people, or teachers of congregations teach the people to believe that God is every where, at one and the same time, without either body or form; as I heard Dr. Jacomb, when he taught (at that place, called St. Martin's Ludgate) his congregation, that they should not think nor believe that God had either head, face, arms or shoulders as a man hath.

14. And the same time his text was, God made man in his own Image; but said he, God created man in righteousness and holiness, like unto himself; so that Mr. Jacomb would have holiness and righteousness to be quite out of form, neither hath his God ever a body for his holiness and righteousness to dwell in, but what he is beholden to his creatures for, because he wanteth a spiritual body of his own.

14. Oh! it is a most gross error, to teach the people to believe that the glorious creator of heaven and earth, hath neither head nor face. Those people so taught, and so believing, by that means despise the true God, who hath, a spiritual body, with all parts like a man in heaven glorified.

16. I say, these people will be destroyed to eternity; for he that teacheth the people to believe that God hath neither head nor face,

had as good teach them to believe that God hath neither eyes to see, nor ears to hear, nor a mouth to speak, and teach them to believe that God is blind, deaf and dumb, and so bid them fall to the idolatrous worshipping of stocks and stones again, as people did in former times before the gospel was preached.

17. But where the gospel is preached, and the truth spread abroad, and where the true God is made known, the worshipping and believing in such a God, that hath neither body nor form, is worse, and more idolatrous than their worshipping of graven images was in former times, before the true God was declared and make known unto us. But now he is declared unto all who have eyes to see, and ears to hear, and none but those that have true faith to believe in him shall be saved.

CHAP. XIII.

In Christ is comprehended the whole Trinity; no man on this earth can prove three Persons in the Trinity,

THAT God who will save all them that believe in him, is the Lord Jesus Christ (before-mentioned) who is both Father, Son, and Holy Ghost in one single person glorified: And that personal God is, a spiritual body in form like a man, and in that blessed body of Christ is comprehended the whole trinity.

2. The life of that blessed body is the eternal Father and mighty God, who clothed himself with flesh and bone in the womb of the virgin, and that flesh and bone is the Son of God. And those powerful words which were spirit and life, that proceeded from the Father within, through the mouth of the Son, was the Holy Ghost. So it is plain there is but one person, though three titles in the trinity; and I am sure there is not a man in the world who is able to prove that the Father, the Son, and the Holy Ghost are three distinct persons.

3. All that teach the people to believe in three persons, may say as Mr. Watton, who was minister of Naptot, in Leicestershire, said unto me in Shasby, If I could not believe that there were three persons and but one God, he could not prove it; and in that he told me the truth.

4. All people that understand what a person is, knoweth that that word person doth signify a body, and all bodies, both spiritual bodies, and temporal bodies, are distinct one from another, except they be monsters. Therefore, if Father, Son, and Holy Ghost be three distinct persons, and every one of them have the title of a God, then there are three Gods.

5. Again, how can any man go about to prove three persons in the trinity, when all those that declare that doctrine deny the Father to be a spiritual body; for say they, God is an Incomprehensible spirit in all things, and in all places at one and the same time.

6. Secondly, they deny the Holy Ghost to be a body; but say they, the Holy Ghost is a sanctifying spirit which proceedeth both from Father and Son; so there they lose the third person.

7. But when they come to the Son, then they say, Christ was born of the Virgin with flesh and bone; so that all religious persons, but the Quakers, will own Christ to have a body now in heaven glorified.

S. And the wisest man living cannot find any other person of God but Christ. For in him dwells all the fulness of the God-head bodily; and he is the first and the last, and it is he that was dead and is alive, and behold he liveth for evermore.

9. Again, it is plain by scripture that God is but in one place at once; for, he came into the garden in the cool of the day to look for Adam; so that God was not in that garden before the cool of the day; for it is said, then he came into the garden, and said, Where art

thou, Adam? and Adam could not have had a thought to hide himself from God, but that he had seen God, with his eyes, and knew he was a spiritual body in form like himself, and that he could be but in one place at once; for Adam did see God face to face when he was in his innocency.

10. Furthermore, had God been a spirit without a body, as people ignorantly imagine him to be, and in every place at one and the same time, then he would have been with Adam at all times, and in all places; so that there would have been no occasion for God to have said, Where art thou, Adam? nor for Adam to have said, I heard thy voice in the garden, and I hid myself

Which words do imply, that God was not always in the garden with Adam; yet sometimes he was there, but when he was there, he was not all over the garden at once, much less then, is he in all places, and in all things in the world at all times.

12. Secondly, it is written, God put Moses into a cleft of the rock, whilst he passed by; therefore, if he God had been in all places, he would have been in the cleft of the rock; also then, he could not have passed by that place, if he had been in it, neither can he be said to pass by that place, which he is never out of, neither was he in that place at that time he passed by it.

13. Again, when God appeared to Moses, in the bush, then was God in no other place in this world at that time, for had he been in all things, all things would have burned as the bush did, and where ever God is, he purifieth that place, and maketh it holy; therefore, the ground on which Moses stood was made holy ground, and. Moses was not suffered to keep his shoes on his feet.

14. Always where God is, that place is holy; surely, no man dare say to the contrary, and then, without all controversy; if God be every where, and in all things in this world, then all things and all places must be holy, or else the immortal God dwelleth with uncleanness.

15. Furthermore, as sure as God is all life and light, so where that glorious God is resident, there is neither death nor darkness. And seeing both death and darkness reigned in this world, why should people be so ignorant to believe that God is always in this world, when by that, it is evident that he is not here at all.

16. Object. But then some may say unto me, You declare that Christ was the eternal Father and mighty God, as well as the Son; why then was there any darkness or death in this world, When Christ was upon the earth?

17. Answ. To that I answer, Though the Creator and eternal Father was in this world, yet his glory could not be seen, because he had clothed himself with pure mortality, wherewith his glory was clouded, which was the cause darkness took its course. And because the immortal God was at that time become pure mortality himself, and

eternity become time; therefore did he suffer death, to seize on all as formerly.

18. There would have been no need of any created light, if God had decreed to have lived in this world in his glory. But as the glorious wisdom of God moved him to create this world; so likewise did his wisdom move him to create such glorious bodies, as sun, moon, and stars, to give light to such creatures as afterwards should be created by him.

19. God did decree within himself to live in that spiritual kingdom of untreated glory, above or beyond the stars, which place of spiritual glory is only fit for such a spiritual glorious Majesty to live in. Again, when Moses was in the mount, then God was there, and no where else, therefore the mount smoked like a furnace and quaked, because the presence of the Almighty God was descended Upon it. And all, both man and beast that did go within the bounds that Moses had set to touch the mount, or to gaze upon it, whilst the presence of God was there, was to be put to death.

20. And Moses was to sanctify the people, and they were to wash their clothes, and not to come at their wives, but to be ready in all holiness when God was to come down upon the mount. And the priests who were to come near the Lord, were to sanctify themselves, yet not to touch the mount whereon God was descended.

21. But now-a-days, they who have gathered congregations, and are teachers of them, they teach the people to believe that God dwelleth always with them, though they are filthy and unclean, and so they make God the author of all wickedness, because they believe God is always present with them.

22. I know what is written in the 139th Psalm, Whither shall I go from thy spirit, or whither shall I fly from thy presence; if I ascend up into heaven, thou art there; if I make my bed in hell, behold thou art there; if I take the wings of the morning, and dwell in the uttermost parts of the sea, there shall thy hands lead me. This is one of the chiefest places, people have to uphold them in that belief, that God is every where at once; but that text hath no such signification in it.

23. Those words of David doth set forth to all the seed of faith, that God by his power can find us out wheresoever we are, and he hath set his watchman to watch us where ever we go; and God's watchman is the law written in our hearts and natures which will accuse us whereever we go to hide ourselves from God.

24. For if we go down into the deep waters, or be buried in the bottom of the Earth, the power of God is there, God can command the Sea, Hell, or the Grave to give up those they keep prisoners there: And in that respect God is in all places by his power, because he hath. power to command all places to deliver up man unto him. There is no resisting of the power of God, for by him all things were created, when his glory will move him to give forth the word of command to destroy all things.

25. Then this fair fabric of the world will become desolate of all its beauty, and become a chaos of confusion, and then if God were in all things, he would destroy part of himself

26. So that it is plain to the seed of faith, that he is no spiritual wise man who believeth, or teacheth others to believe, that God is in all things, and in all places, and hath not a spiritual body of his own to enjoy his glory in.

27. Again, when God wrestled with Jacob, he was in the stature and form of a man.—Here, I know some will say, that it was an angel, and not God that wrestled with Jacob; if it be so granted that it was an angel, then it must be granted that angels have bodies like men.

28. The body of the Almighty God is a spiritual body, in form like the holy angels; and as God is called a spirit, so are the angels called ministering. spirits; but neither God nor the holy angels are bodiless spirits; for both God and the holy angels have spiritual bodies to ascend or descend in at their pleasure.

29. And as sure as those two angels that came to Lot had bodies, so sure have all the angels in heaven bodies; they do not assume to themselves bodies at certain times, as some people vainly imagine, for they were created with spiritual bodies of their own.

30. And God created man in his own image and form, and indeed, it is to be acknowledged, he was created in holiness and righteousness; yet, it is undeniably known, that holiness and righteousness signifies nothing, without bodies to act them in.

31. Ever since the creation of the world, God hath been declared to be in the form of man by all his prophets and apostles. In all appearances hath God appeared unto man in the form of man. And God when he was manifested in flesh, and dwelt among men, said, he was like unto man in all things, sin excepted.

32. It is written, Gen. xxxii. 24. That Jacob was left alone, and there wrestled a man with him until break of the day. ver. 30, And he said, I have seen God face to face, and my life is preserved. Now how could Jacob have seen the face of God, if God had not a face to be seen, (as Mr. Jacomb taught his congregation be had not.)

33. Also it is written, God snake to Moses, mouth to mouth, as a man speaketh to his friend. Could God have a mouth without head or face? Surely no, only blind and unclean reason doth imagine that God is a formless spirit.

34. True it is, that reason's God is without form, for that God which hath neither head nor face, nor any other parts, is a formless thing indeed. But our God is a God in form, he was a spiritual person in the form of a man from all eternity.

35. After he became a child of flesh, blood, and bone, in the womb, of the virgin-wife, Mary, and was born and brought forth into this world, be grew up in stature to be a pure man in mortality; then could

both saints and devils behold his blessed face and live, because he was then in the state of mortality, yet without sin.

36. But when God was upon this earth, that all might see him and his wonderful works; yet we read in the scripture how few believed in him; none but the seed of faith; the seed of God in the generation of Adam; there were none else that could believe that Jesus was the Son of God.

37. The seed of reason, that is, the seed of the serpent in the generation of cursed Cain, did despise him, and call him blasphemer, and at last they put him to death.

38. Therefore, let us not wonder there are so few that can believe, that that Jesus is now both Father, Son, and Holy Ghost, in one single Person in heaven glorified.

89. Again, when the three children were preserved in the fiery furnace, one like the Son of Man was seen to walk there. So, John the divine, in a vision, saw one like the Son of Man to lay his hand on him. So it is clear to all the seed of faith, that God and his angels always appeared like men, whether it was in vision, dream, revelation, or to the sight of the natural eye,

40. Therefore, why should men be so ignorant to think or believe that God hath no parts at all? But the reason why all people cannot believe the truth is, because there is two seeds and generations from the beginning of the world; that is, the seed of the woman, and the seed of the serpent.

41. These two seeds have brought forth two generations; the seed of the woman is the generation of Adam, of which, was the blessed Seth, who called upon the name of the Lord; and Seth was given to Adam in the room of righteous Abel, whom Cain slew; and the offspring or generation of Seth are they that believe, understand, know, and see by the eye of faith in this world, that the glorious body of God is in the form of man in heaven, where they will behold him face to face in glory, after they have passed from death to eternal life.

42. And the seed of the serpent are the generation of cursed Cain; for the serpent was that unclean angel who was cast out of heaven, and it was he that was the Tree of Knowledge of Good and Evil; and it was of that tree which Eve did eat, and her eating was believing his godlike words, wherewith he persuaded her, that they should be as Gods, knowing good and evil, if she would but adhere to him, and yield to his desire, which she did.

43. Thus came sin into the world, and death by sin (which the apostle hints at), Eve yielding unto the temptations of the said fallen angel, for none knew good or evil but he; she not knowing what the issue of it would be, immediately he pierced into, or through her secret parts into her womb, dissolved himself into seed and nature, which seed quickened again into mortal life in the womb of Eve.

44. So the devil clothed himself in the womb of Eve, and she brought forth her firstborn son of the devil, though she said, She had

gotten him from the Lord; and he was the very devil himself, and his name was called Cain, according to his nature, cursed. And this Cain begat sons and daughters, of whose generation are the greatest part of the people in the world.

45. And as their father, the devil, (who was a deceiver, liar, and a murderer from the beginning) did lose his glory by rebelling against his creator, when he was in heaven; so likewise he lost the knowledge of himself by dissolving himself into seed in the womb of Eve, as aforesaid.

46. After he was born into this world, he could never attain to the knowledge of God or himself any more; nor is there any of his seed that shall ever come to the knowledge of the true God, or their own natures, only they may call, Lord, Lord, and say as the generations of the same seed before them have done, Have not we Abraham to our Father, &c.

47 This seed and generation of men will never behold the face of that glorious God, who they have denied to have a face of his own; neither (as I said before) can they attain to the knowledge to know what themselves are, so long as they live in this world.

48. But as for the children who are of the serpent's seed, and yet die in their infancy, they will be raised up to the same state of glory, as that Serpent-Tree of Knowledge of Good and Evil was in, before his fall, for God is just, and he will not punish any child with everlasting punishment for the sins of the parents.

49. All those that are appointed to everlasting destruction, are likewise appointed to live to the years of maturity in this life, that they may fight against God, by opposing his truth declared by his messengers; that they may be damned for their own wickedness and unbelief.

50. Though it is written, Jacob have I loved, and Esau have I hated, before they had done either good or evil; yet we are to mind that they were appointed to live to the years of maturity to fulfil the decree of God; and they could not die in their infancy, because God had likewise said, in Rebecca's womb were two nations; therefore, they were to live to be men, that there might come two great nations out of their loins, to fulfil God's decree in those words.

CHAP. XIV.

God is not in this world at all; but at such times as his glory moveth him to come down for a time; neither doth God dwell in this world any other way, but in the hearts of his saints by faith. There is no salvation for those that refuse Christ to be their God.

IT is written, Gen. c. 35, v. 1, Jacob was commanded to make an altar unto that God who appeared to him, when he parted from his Brother Esau, ver. 9. God appeared to Jacob again, ver. 11. God told Jacob plainly, that he was God Almighty, and bid him be fruitful and multiply. ver 13, God went from the place where he talked with him. So that it plainly appears by scripture, that it was God that appeared to Jacob, and God was then in a body, and distinct from all things.

2. After this, God went up into glory again, his wisdom having moved him to leave that place for a time, until he was pleased to come down again to talk with Jacob, as he did to several other men, whom he loved.

3. That Melchisedeck, king of Salem, who met Abram in the way, and brought bread and wine unto him, was God himself, and then he was in the person of a man.

4. Again, God talked with Abram in the ninetieth year of his age, and said to him, (as he did to Jacob) I am God Almighty; then Abram fell on his face before God; and then God changed Abram's name to Abraham, as you may read. Gen. 17.

5. Also it is said, there came three angels unto Abraham, and Abraham caused them to come to him under a tree, and washed their feet, and gave them meat; one of them was God and that was he whom Abraham treated so much with for Sodom; and the two angels went to Sodom, and they were in the forms of men, and taken for men.

6. In several other places in Holy Writ, God is said to come down from heaven; and in some places, God is said to look down from heaven; so that all who have any faith in the scriptures, or are not blind with ignorance, may know that God is not in the world at all, but at such time as his glorious wisdom moveth him to leave his throne for a moment, or small space of time, to come down and talk with his creatures.

7. As he did to Abraham, Jacob, Moses, and such like men, and then to ascend to his throne of glory again; therefore, how can any wise sober man imagine or think, that God is always in this world, and in all things, when by the holy scriptures, it is proved to the contrary.

8. Object. But I know many people will object, and say, How can this be true, that so many men have seen the face of God, when it is written, that no man can see the face of God and live.

9. Answ. When the glorious wisdom of God moved him to leave his heavenly throne, and come down into this world, and speak to his creatures on this earth; then God did leave his bright burning glory behind him, or else cover it with a veil, whereby man might be able to behold his face and live,

10. When God said, no man could see his face and live, then was he in his kingdom of glory; and true it is, that no man in mortality, can behold the bright burning glorious. face of God in his glory, and live; for, if the eye of man be not able to look upon the created sun, when it shineth in its strength; much less is he able to look upon the Creator, when he sitteth on the throne of heaven, where his face shineth ten times brighter than the created sun in its strength; and this, I think, that there is no man who doth own there is a God, dareth to deny.

11. Then how can they believe that God is at all times in this world, seeing that when the created sun is gone down, there is present darkness all over this part of the world; but where the Creator is, there is no need of the Created sun to give light.

12. The light of that sun is no more to the light of God himself; than the light of a Candle is to the sun; therefore, it is plain, God dwelleth in this world, no otherwise than in the hearts of his saints by faith.

13. Furthermore, I would not have any of the seed of faith to be so ignorant, as to think or believe, that God is so large in person, as to sit upon his throne in heaven, and at the same time to touch this earth with his foot, though it is written, Heaven is my throne, and the earth is my footstool.

14. For there is spiritual earth in the kingdom of glory; for our blessed God to set his divine feet upon; yet this earth is counted with. God to be as his footstool in this respect; because the kingdom in heaven above, doth so much exceed this world in glory, that this earth or world, with all its beauty, wherein there is so many thrones for kings and emperors to sit on, yet all their thrones, and the glory belonging to them, are but as a footstool, in comparison to that glorious throne whereon our blessed God Christ Jesus sitteth in another world, above or beyond the stars.

15. But I know, when these sayings of mine are spread abroad in the world, most people will be filled with envy against them, and contradict them with blasphemy, as the Jews did the preaching of St. Paul and Barnabas, Acts, 13, 45.

16. For now-a-days, the generality of people can no more endure to hear Christ declared to be, the Almighty God, and Everlasting Father, according to the prophecy of Isaiah, ix. 6, than the Jews could endure

to hear Jesus to be declared to be the Son of God and Saviour of the world.

17. Therefore, as sure as there was no salvation for those that did despise Jesus, and refuse him to be their God and Saviour, when he was upon this earth, according as he was declared to be by his apostle; so sure it is now, there is no salvation or them, that do despise the blessed body of Christ Jesus in heaven glorified, refusing him to be their God, who hath a spiritual body, to enjoy his glory in, or chose themselves a bodiless God without form or substance to rule over them, contrary to the declaration of the last true prophets or messengers of God.

18. Therefore, there is none who hath either heard their declaration, or read their writings that can plead ignorance, and say, they never heard plainly what the true God was, or is; but there are many thousands who may plead that they wanted faith to believe in that God, which is but in one place at once, and I am sure, all those that want faith to believe in that God in this world, will want glory in heaven hereafter.

CHAP. XV.

The soul of man is generated with its body therefore it liveth and dieth with the body, and is never parted from it.

IT is generally believed, that the cause of a man's dying is, because the soul departeth from the body, but that is only imagination, for the soul of man can live no longer without his body, than the body can without the soul.

2. For the soul of a man cometh out of the loins of a man as well as the body, as is it written—out of Jacob's loins, came threescore and sixteen souls; and the soul doth lie secretly hid in the seed, like a spark of invisible tire, and that is the life of the seed.

3. God hath placed seed in man to cause it to spring forth of his loins, therefore did he bid them, Adam and Eve, increase and multiply, which was to replenish the earth; ever since, hath every seed brought forth its own body, according as God had decreed they should, without any immediate help from him.

4. For God did decree before he made a woman, that that the seed of man being sown in the womb of a woman, should there die, and quicken again, by the power of his creative word, when he bid them increase and multiply.

5. As God said, Let there be light, and let there be a firmament, and it was so; and let the waters be gathered into one place, and they were so; and do so continue by the power of that word, which commanded them so to appear.

6. So doth every seed bring forth its own body, whether it be man or beast, according to the time of life which God appointed at the first, without any more additional help from him.

7. Let it not be thought by any, that God doth infuse a soul into a child, after the man hath given his seed to the woman; (this would make him a partaker with the adulterers) but the soul, which is the life of the seed, (as aforesaid) dieth in the womb, and quickeneth again in the womb of the woman, as the wheat-corn or other grain dieth, and quickeneth in the womb of the earth.

8. At the first, when God created Adam, he did breath into his nostrils, the breath of life; and that breath of life became living soul in Adam; and that living soul brought forth seed, and that seed, according to the prerogative power of God hath brought forth its own likeness ever since.

9. And as the soul is granted by most people to be the life of the body, when it is born into this world; so, of necessity, it must be the life of the seed, or else the seed of man could not bring forth a body, for want of life; any more then the wheat-corn can bring forth a body, if the flower, which is the soul or life of the corn be taken out, and the husk only flung into the earth.

10. Therefore, it is plain, that the soul is the life of the seed, and that it is conceived in the womb by generation with the body, and it is born into the world with the body, so it lives and dies with it, and must lie in the earth with the body, and both rise together.

11. Then shall they enter either into everlasting joy or torment; for as the body and soul had their beginning together in times and lived together and sinned together, so shall they begin their eternal joy or torment together, these have God joined together, and will never put them asunder; it is impossible for the soul and body to part, because God hath decreed it to the contrary.

12. The believers of the said commissioners of the spirit, their declaration or testimony, they being the afore-mentioned messengers or witnesses of the most high God, the Lord Jesus Christ, concerning the eternal condition of all men; they do yield to the death of their souls with their bodies, and do believe with the full assurance of faith, that they shall both be raised again together at the last day, and in the mean time their lives are hid with Christ in God.

CHAP. XVI.

There are several degrees of knowledge, but no degree able to give true rest to the mind, until a man can believe the true messengers of God.

IT is generally seen and known, that there are several degrees of knowledge in temporal things, as in all arts and sciences, they that are ingenious do well mind those that are accounted good workmen, or cunning artificers, whereby they grow up from one degree of knowledge to another, until such time that they have attained to that degree of knowledge which they aimed at, and which they had so long laboured to finish, and then they are at rest.

2. But if they can never find out, or attain to that mystery, they did so long seek after; then are they always dissatisfied, and die in ignorance of what they desired to know.

3. And as there are several degrees of knowledge in temporal things, so are there several degrees of knowledge in spiritual things; therefore do all men that are naturally given to seek after God, especially those of the Jewish nature, they take great notice of the preaching of men, which way they teach men to worship God.

4. Then they enter into church-fellowship with some of them, and stay there awhile, and see nothing but vanity there, then they enter into another, where they see a little more light, and there they stay awhile.

5. As their knowledge increaseth, so still they get out of one church-fellowship into another, and so from one degree of knowledge to another, and still into the greater light, thinking to find peace and comfort there, but can find none.

6. Thus have many run through all, or most of the church-fellowships in England, and at last could find no true peace; because in all this, their travel, they could not attain to the thing they aimed at, which is the assurance of their salvation.

7. The reason, why, in all this, their seeking and travelling up and down from one church to another, they could not attain to the assurance of their salvation is, because there is no assurance to be had in any spiritual appearance, where the minister thereof, is not sent of God, therefore it is written, That many shall say, Lord, Lord, have we not prayed and preached in thy name, and cast out devils in thy name, and such like; yet God will charge it upon them as a work of iniquity.

8. There is not now a minister in the world, that dare to own himself to be immediately sent of God, to declare his mind unto the world; but the Witnesses of the Spirit only:

9. All they who can truly own them and their doctrine to be true, will quickly see and be satisfied with the assurance of their salvation

perfected; then they will be at rest when they know what, and where their God is; and there is no other way to come to the knowledge of God, but by believing the report of the Lord's last witnesses or prophets, which are his only ministers now in this world.

10. Therefore, as soon as a man can set to his seal, that the Witnesses Of the Spirit were. truly sent forth of God, and that their doctrine is true also, then can he clearly see that his whole work of looking after God is finished.

11. Then will he say, that he hath found that God to his comfort, who in, and by believing his true prophets hath given him peace of mind, and the full assurance of faith, that after death he will raise him up to everlasting life, where he shall never lose him more.

12. This I can witness in myself, and so can many more besides me, blessed for ever be the name of Christ Jesus, the only and alone wise God for revealing himself, and his mind so clearly unto us, by his last messengers.

CHAP. XVII.

Truth is a pearl of great price, therefore a man must part with all to purchase it. And those only that hold out in their faith to their lives end, shall be saved; but for those that fall back, and withdraw their love from it, for them there is no redemption.

THE doctrine or declaration of the Witnesses of the Spirit, is a pearl of such great price, (this by experience I also know) that no man can purchase it without he parteth with all he hath, that is, without he parteth with all his former righteousness wherewith he used to worship his unknown God in outward ordinances; lifting up his eyes and his hands in long prayers, Pharisee-like, to be seen of men.

2. I say, all these (which were complained of in the times both of the prophets and apostles, and by Christ himself) were beggarly elements, and must be parted from, though they are esteemed of great value by the world.

3. They that will embrace truth must be stripped, and left naked and bare; for God will not accept of any man so long as he clotheth himself with ceremonies, which are as filthy rags in the sight of God, for so doth the world ignorantly worship their unknown bodiless God.

4. They who are willing to worship the true God, who was, and ever will be a spiritual body in heaven glorified, they are to worship him in spirit and truth.

5. The Lord now, is not to be seen with mortal eyes; all men must now venture their eternal happiness, or else they will never be at peace, because there is no other way to please God, but wholly to rely upon the words of his said prophets.

6. Therefore, woe unto all those that have already, or hereafter, shall taste of the good word of God delivered by them, and afterwards fall back from it.

7. It is now, as it was when Christ was upon the earth; then, said he, Except you can believe that I am he, you shall die in your sins John viii. 24, in which words he told them, that he was the Saviour of the world, but they understood him not.

8. The generality of people did rather chuse, (which was a most sad choice) to die in their sins, than to believe that Jesus, the supposed son of Joseph, was the Son of God; although they saw him and heard his words, and of such wonderful works and miracles as he did and wrought amongst them; whereby it appears plainly, that signs and wonders are for unbelievers.

9. Notwithstanding what was said by our blessed Saviour when he was on earth, That a wicked and adulterous Generation looketh after signs; yet, in these our days, people cry out for signs and miracles; but as Christ said to them, John, xv. 22, If he had not come and

spoken to them, they had not had sin, but now they have no cloak for their sin.

10. So likewise now, in this our age, the Witnesses of the Spirit have appeared, of whom, one of them is living in this present year, 1673; and they have plainly told the people, that they were sent forth by the command of God, to declare his mind unto the world, whereby they might believe in the true God, and be saved, therefore they are left without excuse.

11. Yet the generality of people (as the generations before them) do rather chuse to die in their sins, than believe that John Reeve and Lodowick Muggleton should be the teachers of the whole world. Here it is to be minded, that they who never heard of them nor their doctrine, are free from rebellion.

12. But all they who have talked with them, or have read their writings, or have discoursed with any of the believers of them, about the truths by them delivered, they have no cloak for their sin; if they do rebel against that truth declared by and from them.

13. Therefore let every one who hath tasted the sweetness, comfort, and satisfaction of mind in the receiving and believing of these precious truths, take heed unto themselves, that they slide not back; for they only who keep their confidence in obedience to the truth, and hold out to the end of their lives, shall be saved.

14. For all those that sin wilfully after they have received the truth, in the knowledge and love thereof, there remaineth no more sacrifice for that sin, Heb. x. 26. You may read at large, in that chapter, what manner of sin that was, for which there was to be no sacrifice.

15. It will be found to be the sin of falling away from that truth, which they once received and rejoiced in, for saith the apostle, If they who despised Moses's law were to die without mercy, how much more or sorer punishment, suppose ye, shall be thought worthy for those that account the blood of the covenant, wherewith they were sanctified, an unholy thing.

16. It is the same thing now in the time of the commission of the spirit, (how lightly so-ever people make of it) whoever they be, that do enter themselves as believers, and doth rejoice therein for a time, and confesseth that he seeth his salvation perfected by believing the said prophet's report, and yet for all this, fall back, and withdraw their love from it, as some lately have done, great will be their punishment.

17. And the days we now live in, may be compared to the days wherein David lived, for hath not the Lord shewed us strange things, and made us drink the wine of astonishment.

18. In that God hath been pleased to declare himself unto us, by the mouths of his last true messengers, and some who received their message and declarations with much seeming comfort and satisfaction; and thereby procured great acquaintance with the prophet now alive, and had words (as David expresseth it), as smooth

as butter, and softer than, oil, yet have they magnified themselves with reproaches for his love in declaring the mind of God to them.

19. Had he known that there had been war in their hearts, he would have hid it from them; notwithstanding the discovery they have made of their own natures, it is, in vain for them to fight with him who is too powerful for them. If they shall continue to shoot their arrows (bitter words) against him, they will return to their own destruction.

20. And again, by the prophets affirming some assertions to be true, wherein were some sayings hard to be borne from pride and passion, he hath been called by some, a devil to his face, and disowning him to be any longer their teacher.

21. Thus have they exalted themselves above him, imagining in themselves that they were wiser and knew more then he did, from whom they had received all their knowledge; and thus did their aspiring thoughts exalt themselves above their teacher, just as the serpent-angel, of whose seed they are, did exalt himself above his Creator.

22. And as the creator of all things that were created flung that Angel down from heaven for his pride and presumptions and took his power from him, so that he can never ascend up again.

23. So likewise hath the Lord's messengers flung those men out of heaven, and taken away their power, that is, he hath flung them out of all heavenly peace. He that is at peace with God in this life, may he said to be in heaven, though upon earth,

24. Besides, he hath taken the power from them, for now they have no power to bring any one into the knowledge of the truth, nor to defend their own faith.

25. Whatsoever believers do upon this account, they must do it by virtue of that power which they believe the commissioner hath; but one of them said, that he valued the prophets power no more than a child's of a day old; in so saying, they condemn their own faith, by rebelling against their own knowledge and belief

26. Because formerly, they did declare to believe that he had received his commission from God, and that he was a true prophet, messenger, or minister of God, and that he had power given him in his commission to set life and death before men.

27. Which is no other, but to pronounce men blessed or cursed to eternity; according as they do either believe or despise them, and their declarations.

28. So long as they did continue stedfast in that belief, they were in perfect peace; because they were sanctified by his ministry; but now they have changed their belief, from believing him to a true prophet, or minister of God, and instead thereof; call him a devil, and disown his power.

29. Herein do they judge themselves unworthy to have any benefit by the commission of the spirit, for as at first they did look upon him

to have such power, as to give them a blessing, and therefore did crave it of him.

30. So long as they continued subject to him, they found the benefit of it, by that peace and comfort they received by it; but since they have resisted his power and rebelled against him, they have lost the benefit of his blessing.

31. So that saying is made good, The dog is returned to his vomit, and the sow that was washed, into her wallowing in the mire.

32. Now they despise the power of God in his messenger, and account his revelation an unholy thing, chusing rather to perish, than submit themselves unto him, whom they once owned to be a true prophet and messenger of God.

33. Therefore hath the only minister of God in this world, withdrawn his love from them, by which means they will become filthy and unclean; because they are fallen back from the truth, so far that they cannot be renewed by repentance.

34. Because the falling back from the truth after they have received it, is that sin unto death, for which there is no repentance nor sacrifice.

35. Therefore hath the prophet's wrath taken place in them, because they will never be settled in true peace more.

36. Let these things therefore be an example to all that have faith in the commission of the spirit, that they may hold fast the truth unto the end of their lives, and not rebel against the prophet of the Lord, least they come to be cast out of the favour of God, as those men are, to their eternal sorrow.

37. Two things I have to add, before I conclude this chapter, first, to exhort all not to startle or be troubled, much less to scoff or upbraid that the breaches are thus come; for it is no otherwise then hath fallen out, and is expressed in holy writ in the two former commissions.

38. Secondly, although there did arise dissension, discord, and rebellion before-mentioned; yet even thereby, there hath been opened more secret and heavenly truths, then otherwise would have been, as the time when they shall be made public will demonstrate, to the satisfaction of all the true believers, the seed of faith. It was said, by our Lord, when he was on earth, That in the world there would be offence, but woe is on them by whom they come.

CHAP. XVIII.

How all the seed of faith may be made able to say with me, and all true believers; that they can read that new name written in themselves, and what the hidden manna is.

NOW I have in plainness of speech declared that my faith is fully grounded upon the doctrine declared by the Witnesses of the Spirit. Also I have declared what, and where that God is, who is the true object of my faith.

2. And I do heartily desire, that all the seed of faith may come to the true knowledge of my God, who is Christ Jesus glorified, and by the true knowing of him, and truly believing in him, he made able to say with me, and all true believers, that they can read that new name written in themselves, which is given to all that overcometh and forsaketh the idolatrous worshipping of idols, and unknown Gods, and cleave close to the true God, by worshipping him only in spirit and truth.

3. The new name is the assurance of salvation, and the white stone, wherein it is written, is the heart, that is made clean by believing the truth.

4. The assurance of salvation is so secretly hid in the heart, that no man can know it, except he that receiveth it, for it is only written in the heart of every true believer; therefore, no man can read it in another, but he that is settled in the practice, and knowledge of truth, can know it in himself.

5. This is the hidden manna which all true believers feed upon; and it is called hidden manna, because it is hidden in the heart, where no unbeliever or despiser of truth can see, or find it out, to be refreshed by it.

6. Blessed for evermore be the name of our God, for revealing his will and mind to us, declared in the sacred scriptures, penned by the true prophets and apostles of old; but now made manifest by the mouth and pen of his last messengers, which giveth to all that can truly believe them, peace of mind (in this life), and the assurance of everlasting life in the world to come.

7. Even so, come Lord Jesus, come quickly, and put an end to all time, that we who are thine elect, may be crowned with that glory which thou hast prepared for us, and all those that love thee, to wear in the presence of thy most glorious Majesty, with the true prophets, and apostles, to all eternity. Amen, Amen.

UNDERDOWN, PRINTER, DEAL.

THE ARTICLES OF TRUE FAITH,

DEPENDING UPON THE

COMMISSION OF THE SPIRIT.

DRAWN UP INTO

FORTY-EIGHT HEADS,

BY

JOHN SADDINGTON,
AN ANCIENT BELIEVER,

FOR THE

BENEFIT OF OTHER BELIEVERS,

That now are, or hereafter shall come to believe;

AND TO CONFOUND AND DISPROVE ALL DESPISERS, THAT SAY,

"WE KNOW NOT WHAT WE BELIEVE."

ANNO M.DC.LXXV.

PRINTED 1830.

REPRINTED SEPTEMBER, 1880,
FOR
ISAAC FROST, SON of ISAAC FROST, St. John's Square, Clerkenwell;
AND
MRS. HUNTLEY, DAUGHTER of JOSEPH FROST,   "   "   "

H. DONGRAY, Printer, Walthamstow.

HERE, I HAVE WRITTEN THE

ARTICLES OF MY FAITH,

WHICH I WILL WITNESS TO BE TRUE,

WITH THE

DEATH OF MY SOUL,

IF IT BE REQUIRED OF ME;

Therefore let not the words of any Canaanitish Devil, prophane Esau, scoffing Ishmael, or railing Rabshakeh, be credited, when they vilify and belie

THE BELIEVERS OF THE

WITNESSES OF THE SPIRIT,

IN SAYING,

'THAT THEY DO OWN NEITHER GOD NOR DEVIL,'

Or when they cast any other scandalous reproaches contrary to Truth upon us that truly know GOD.

JOHN SADDINGTON.

THE ARTICLES OF TRUE FAITH.

ARTICLE I.

I do firmly believe that there is a God, full of all spiritual glory, above or beyond the stars.

II.

I do believe that God is a God of substance, and that that most glorious, most wise, and almighty God, that is so often spoken of in Holy Scripture, was a spiritual glorious body, in form like a man, from all eternity.

III.

I do believe that the most wise God did create the holy angels of that dust above the stars with glorious spiritual bodies, in form like Himself.

IV.

I do believe that God did withhold the spiritual food of inspiration from one of those glorious angels which He had created; and then, for want of that spiritual food, which kept his nature in obedience to his Creator, he immediately began to imagine within himself high and lofty thoughts against God his Creator.

V.

I do believe that that angel did think himself more fit to rule over his fellow-creatures than God his Creator, for which pride and presumption that angel became accursed in himself, and for his rebellion did God afterwards fling him down into this world, and called him a devil, a serpent, &c.

VI.

I do believe that earth and water were from eternity, but without form until such time as the most wise God did create them into formable bodies.

VII.

I do believe that God created the man Adam of the dust of this earth and breathed into him the breath of life, which became a living soul in Adam, and then was Adam in the form of God, his Creator, though not so glorious.

VIII.

I do believe that Adam was created so pure that death could not have seized on him had he continued in his created purity.

IX.

I do believe that as soon as Adam had sinned then did death enter into this world and arrest Adam, with such a great action of debt that neither soul nor body could escape out of his hand; for as both had sinned so both were carried to the prison of the grave.

X.

I do believe that when God said to Adam, "Encrease and multiply," and when He said "Let every seed bring forth its own body," then did the wise Creator give power to all seed, both in man and beast, in herbs and trees, to bring forth their own bodies, without any more additional help from Him.

XI.

I do believe that God created the sun, moon, and stars, and placed them in the firmament of heaven, for signs and for seasons, and appointed every one of them his office; and as God commanded them at first, so still do they supply this world with all manner of weather, as heat, cold, rain, snow, &c., without troubling the Creator in the least.

XII.

I do believe that the souls of all men since Adam were generated and came forth of the loins of their father, with their bodies, therefore are as mortal as their bodies, and must die with them, and lie in the earth with their bodies until the resurrection day.

XIII.

I do believe that the Tree of Life and the Tree of Knowledge of good and evil, which Moses spake and wrote of were no wooden trees growing out of the ground.

XIV.

I do believe that tree Tree of Life, which Moses wrote of, was the same God that created the world.

XV.

I do believe that the Tree of Knowledge of good and evil was that serpent angel which God cast out of heaven down to this earth for his rebellion.

XVI.

I do believe that that outcast angel was the serpent which tempted Eve, and that he was at that same time a spiritual body in the form of Adam.

XVII.

I do believe that that outcast angel or serpent-tree of knowledge of good and evil did enter into the womb of Eve, and dissolve his spiritual body into seed, which seed died and quickened again in the womb of Eve.

XVIII.

I do believe that Eve brought forth her first born the son of the devil, and very devil himself.

XIX.

I do believe that there is no other devil but man and woman; since the first devil, that serpent angel devil, became seed in the womb of Eve, and clothed himself with flesh and bone.

XX.

I do believe that Cain was not the son of Adam, though he was the son of Eve,

XXI.

I do believe that the seed of the woman and the seed of the serpent are two distinct generations of men and women in this world.

XXII.

I do believe that the seed of the woman is the generation of faithful people, which proceed from the loins of blessed Seth, who was the son of Adam, who was the son of God.

XXIII.

I do believe the seed of the serpent is the generation of unbelievers or reprobate men and women, which proceed from the loins of cursed Cain, the son of the devil, and the first lying and murdering devil that ever was.

XXIV.

I do believe that those men and women that blaspheme against God and despise his messengers are those angels which are said to be cast out of heaven with the devil their father.

XXV.

I do believe that that difference and opposition which ariseth between believers and unbelievers concerning their faith in God is that enmity which God said He would put between the serpent and the woman and between his seed and her seed.

XXVI.

I do believe that Moses, David, Isaiah, Jeremiah, and several others were true prophets, and penmen of holy writ.

XXVII.

I do believe that God took up Moses and Elias bodily into heaven and there glorified them, to represent his glorious person while he went that sore journey in the flesh.

XXVIII.

I do believe that God gave Moses and Elias full power to govern heaven and earth for that time He was in this world.

XXIX.

I do believe that Moses and Elias were those two angels that were to watch over Christ when He was in mortality, lest at any time He should dash His foot against a stone.

XXX.

I do believe that the most glorious and wise Creator left His throne of glory for a time and come down into this world, and entered into the virgin's womb and there died, or laid down his immortality by dissolving into seed, and immediately quickened again into pure mortality.

XXXI.

I do believe that that child Jesus, which was born of the Virgin-wife, Mary, was both the Son of God, the everlasting Father, and Creator of all things that were created.

XXXII.

I do believe that the flesh of Christ was the flesh of God, and that the blood of Christ was the blood of God.

XXXIII.

I do believe that Christ laid down His God-head life for a moment, when the vail of the temple was rent in twain, and that the graves gave up their dead at His resurrection.

XXXIV.

I do believe that no other blood but the blood of the eternal God could wash away the sins of the elect.

XXXV.

I do believe that Christ's death was so effectual that all those for whom He died will be raised again to eternal life and glory.

XXXVI.

I do believe that Christ was a quickening spirit, and that He did quicken out of death to life by His own power.

XXXVII.

I do believe that that ever blessed Soul or Spirit, which in holy writ is called the Godhead, did quicken in that body of flesh and bone of Christ, which was laid in the sepulchre, and raised it again from death to everlasting life.

XXXVIII.

I do believe that blessed body of flesh and bone of Christ neither did nor could see corruption, or be left in the grave, because it was a pure mortal body, without sin, spot or blemish, before His death.

XXXIX.

I do believe that Christ was visibly seen by the apostles and by private believers after His resurrection.

XL.

I do believe that Christ did and was visibly seen to ascend into heaven with that same body in which He suffered death and arose again.

XLI.

I do believe that the apostles' doctrine and declaration of Christ is true.

XLII.

I do believe that that Spiritual Godhead, or Godhead Spirit, which was before anything was created, and which created all this that were created, is now in heaven, clothed with that blessed body of Christ Jesus glorified.

XLIII.

I do believe that God will raise the souls and bodies of all men out of their graves, some to an ever-living glorious live, and other some to an ever-dying painful death which will never end.

XLIV.

I do believe that God spake to JOHN REEVE to the hearing of the ear, and that God chose JOHN REEVE to be his last messenger to this unbelieving world, and that God gave him LODOWICKE MUGGLETON to be his mouth to declare the mind of GOD to us in this, our age.

XLV.

I do believe, the doctrine and declaration of JOHN REEVE and LODOWICKE MUGGLETON, to be as true as the doctrine declared by Moses, the Prophets, and Apostles of old.

XLVI.

I do believe there will be no salvation at the day of the Lord, for those that were in the time of Moses and the other prophets, who did not lay hold on God's promises made unto them by his prophets, when they prophesied, that God would send a Son, a Saviour, or become a child himself to redeem his people.

VLVII.

I do believe, there will be no salvation for those that were in Christ's time who heard of him, but could not believe him to be the Son of God, and Saviour of the world.

XLVIII.

I do believe, there will be no salvation for those that are in these our days, who have heard of the witnesses of the Spirit, and have seen or heard their declaration; and yet cannot believe that Jesus Christ is the only wise God; Father, Son, and Holy Spirit, in one single person glorified; and that it is life eternal, truly to know him so to be.

www.ingramcontent.com/pod-product-compliance
Lightning Source LLC
Chambersburg PA
CBHW071212290426
44108CB00013B/1169